D1252684

FEAC™ Certified Enterprise Architect CEA Study Guide

FEAC™ Certified Enterprise Architect CEA Study Guide

FEAC™ Institute Press by
Prakash C. Rao, Ann Reedy, Ph.D.,
and Beryl Bellman, Ph.D.

New York Chicago San Francisco Lisbon London Madrid
Mexico City Milan New Delhi San Juan Seoul Singapore Sydney Toronto

The McGraw·Hill Companies

Cataloging-in-Publication Data is on file with the Library of Congress

McGraw-Hill books are available at special quantity discounts to use as premiums and sales promotions, or for use in corporate training programs. To contact a representative, please e-mail us at bulksales@mcgraw-hill.com.

FEAC™ Certified Enterprise Architect CEA Study Guide

1 2 3 4 5 6 7 8 9 0   DOC DOC   1 0 9 8 7 6 5 4 3 2 1

ISBN: Book p/n 978-0-07-175611-2 and CD p/n 978-0-07-175610-5
of set 978-0-07-175613-6

MHID: Book p/n 0-07-175611-6 and CD p/n 0-07-175610-8
of set 0-07-175613-2

Sponsoring Editor Wendy Rinaldi	**Copy Editor** Andy Saff	**Composition** Cenveo Publisher Services
Editorial Supervisor Jody McKenzie	**Proofreader** Claire Splan	**Illustration** Cenveo Publisher Services
Project Manager Vastavikta Sharma, Cenveo Publisher Services	**Indexer** Jack Lewis	**Art Director, Cover** Jeff Weeks
Acquisitions Coordinator Joya Anthony	**Production Supervisor** Jim Kussow	

We want to thank our editors at McGraw Hill, Wendy Rinaldi, Joya Anthony and Jody McKenzie, and the invaluable editorial assistance of Andy Saff and Vastavikta Sharma. Without their patience, cooperation, and suggestions this work would not have been possible.

Isaac Newton famously said, "I reach further because I stand on the shoulders of giants!" This book is humbly dedicated to all the giants of enterprise architecture—sung and unsung—on whose shoulders we stand. We hope that this book will also be the basis for you to reach further.

ABOUT THE AUTHORS

Prakash Rao is a Certified Enterprise Architect with a graduate degree in computer science from the University of Minnesota and an undergraduate degree in electronics and telecommunications engineering. Starting as a Research Scientist in the Corporate Computer Science Center at Honeywell, Inc., in the early 1980s, he has been active as a researcher, Program Manager, and Line Manager and also in systems business development at Honeywell. He was the cofounder of InfoSpan Corporation, one of the industry's first open standard repositories.

He has been teaching enterprise architecture (EA) at the Federated Enterprise Architecture Certification (FEAC) Institute in the capacity of a faculty member for many years and has also co-trained over a thousand staff from the United States Air Force (USAF) at various USAF locations worldwide. Prakash is also a practicing enterprise architect with over 15 years of experience in EA, including participating in one of the earliest EA implementations at USAF Air Mobility Command with EA pioneers John Zachman and Dr. Steven Spewak in the mid-1990s. He has been active as an invited speaker, facilitator, trainer, consultant, and architecture subject matter expert in several engagements over the last 15 years. He is currently the Chief Architect at Metadata Management Corporation (MMC) in Fairfax, Virginia. For 15 years, MMC has provided architecture consulting, architecture repository, and architecture data management services to various federal agencies and defense organizations.

As a cofounder of a venture-funded startup, Prakash has seen firsthand the applicability and usefulness of enterprise architecture techniques to the organizing, management, evolution, and governance of startup as well as ongoing enterprises. As a practitioner for more than 15 years, he brings a real-world experience to his teaching and training methods.

Dr. Ann Reedy has a Ph.D. in computer science with a specialty in formal languages. She has over 30 years experience in both academia and the contracting community. She taught both graduate and undergraduate classes in computer science at the University of Iowa and the University of Nebraska, Lincoln. Her initial work in the contracting community involved development of analyst support systems with complex databases. This work evolved into a project involving the development and use of a Software Engineering Environment. Dr. Reedy published articles on software engineering environments and was active in the Association for Computing Machinery Special Interest Group on Ada.

When Dr. Reedy joined the MITRE Corporation, she worked on contributing to and editing the C4ISR Architecture Framework as it developed and evolved into DoDAF 1.0. She adapted the DoDAF for various U.S. government departments or agencies such as the Treasury Department and worked on the evolution of the early Federal Enterprise Architecture Framework. She has worked on enterprise architectures for Treasury Headquarters, Customs, IRS, DoD, DHS, FAA, and other agencies. This work has involved development of EA views, technical standards, EA governance, enterprise transition, and scenario-based architectures. She has contributed to research work and publications on the inter-relationships of security and enterprise architecture and on security design and requirements patterns. She continues to be interested in the issues including security-related data in DoDAF-based enterprise architectures. She currently teaches DoDAF classes for the FEAC Institute and continues to work part -time for MITRE.

Dr. Beryl Bellman is cofounder and Academic Director of the FEAC Institute and is also a tenured full professor of Communication at California State University, Los Angeles.

He has been involved in teaching, research, publishing, consulting, and project management in the fields of enterprise architecture, knowledge management, and organizational communications/behavior for over 42 years and has an excellent reputation in both academia and professional consulting. He held faculty and research positions at the University of California San Diego, State University of New York (SUNY) Stonybrook, City University of New York (CUNY) Graduate Center, and California Institute of the Arts, and was Research Director of the Western Behavioral Sciences Institute prior to his current university position.

In addition to holding academic positions, he has some 25 years' concurrent consulting experience in both government and the private sectors, and has been a Principal Consultant and Project Manager with three major enterprise architecture consulting companies. Bellman has consulted in enterprise architecture–related programs in the public sector for the Department of Defense (DoD), Department of Agriculture, the Forest Service, Department of Energy, the Department of Justice, the Immigration and Naturalization Service (INS), and the White House for the Executive Office of the President and was a contract consultant for NCR, AT&T, ASK, RAND, and Digital Equipment Corporation, working for their internal and external customers. This included doing EA in the aerospace, financial, banking, pharmaceutical, entertainment, and manufacturing sectors.

He has published several books and numerous articles in journals and edited books, and is a frequent presenter at national and international professional and academic conferences. He also is certified with The Open Group Architecture Framework (TOGAF) 8 and 9 and instructs TOGAF 9 courses at FEAC as well as courses in both the Federated Enterprise Architecture Framework (FEAF) and Department of Defense Architecture Framework (DoDAF) certification programs.

CONTENTS AT A GLANCE

CONTENTS

Part I
Foundation Concepts

Part II
Architecture Development and Use

Part V
Resources

FOREWORD

The idea of enterprise architecture has been around for a *lot* of years. I have written 58 articles and a book on the subject myself. The first article I wrote was in 1982, when I discovered my framework graphic appearing in a copyrighted company document and it dawned on me that I needed to write something that I could copyright to preserve my own ability to work on my own framework. That article was written in 1982, published internally at IBM in 1984, and then in the *IBM Systems Journal* in 1987.

In fact, I might have coined the term "enterprise architecture" myself because when I would try to explain the idea in the early days, it was such a foreign concept that people just couldn't get it! I would say, "well, it is kind of like a framework for information systems architecture," and then people would say, "oh, yeah, I kind of get the idea."

I have lived to regret using the words "information systems" in conjunction with "architecture" ever since. I don't know how many articles I have written arguing the case that enterprise architecture has everything to do with engineering and manufacturing *enterprises* and nothing to do with building and running systems.

I believe that it was Fred Brooks who said, "Programming is manufacturing, not engineering." That would explain the observation that for the last 75 years or so that those of us from the information community (that is, electronic data processing [EDP], automatic data processing [ADP], data processing [DP], information systems [IS], management information systems [MIS], information technology [IT], information management [IM], IM/IT, or whatever—we have changed the name on the door a bunch of times, but we have never changed what goes on behind the door, which is basically data processing) have been *manufacturing* the enterprise before it was ever *engineered*. No wonder we end up with a "legacy" regardless of the technology, the newness of the operating system, or the cleverness of the programming; we end up with *systems*, not a coherent, optimal, lean and mean, dynamic, interoperable, flexible, and aligned *enterprise*.

All along, our intent has been to build systems—not to engineer enterprises. What do you suppose we invariably end up with? Systems! And, in the words of Albert Einstein, "keeping on doing the same thing and expecting different results is one definition of insanity."

For all the years that the idea of enterprise architecture has been around—
40 years that I personally know about myself—it has never acquired traction in the
general marketplace. The stress levels in the general management community are so
high that they haven't had time to consider anything like enterprise architecture.
Enterprise architecture is not even on its radar. The information community (and
general management as well) seems to have this unquenchable penchant for "silver
bullets," searching for the Holy Grail: it is the next technological innovation that
will have the answer!

No. The enterprise problem is not a technical problem; it is an *engineering* problem.

Jay Forrester of the Massachusetts Institute of Technology (MIT), the author of
Industrial Dynamics, in a speech at Seville University on December 15, 1998, said:
"Organizations built by committee and intuition perform no better than an airplane
built by the same methods. … As in bad airplane design, which no pilot can fly
successfully, such badly designed corporations lie beyond the ability of real-life
managers. … A fundamental difference exists between an enterprise operator and an
enterprise designer. A manager runs an organization just as a pilot runs an airplane.
Success of a pilot depends on an aircraft designer who created a successful airplane
… who designed the corporation that a manager runs?"

Typically, I entitle my seminar material "Enterprise Physics 101" because physics
is "the study of the natural or material world and phenomena" (American Heritage
College Dictionary) and engineering principles are based on natural laws. And, I
would suggest that until we understand the natural laws relative to any subject or
discipline, typically embodied in an ontology, nothing is repeatable and nothing
is predictable. There is no discipline. That is, until we understand the natural
laws, everything is based on experience, heuristics, and "best practices" … *not*
engineering.

By the way, I never said, "stop the music for 15 or 20 years and build all these
models, and then you can build some more systems." I *did* say, between now and
some later day, you'd better accumulate an inventory of these enterprise engineering
artifacts, iteratively and incrementally, ensuring that they are reused in every
implementation until that day when you will have a "critical mass" of engineered
artifacts that can be used to assemble dynamically the enterprise to order, that is, to
employ the concepts of "mass-customization" to engineering and manufacture the
enterprise.

In 1999, I wrote an article, "Enterprise Architecture: The Issue of the Century,"
in which I argued that the enterprise that can accommodate the issues of enterprise
architecture will have the opportunity to stay in the game, but that the enterprise
that cannot accommodate the issues of enterprise architecture is *not* going to be

in the game. I think that we are presently beginning to see the realization of that prophecy, and yet I still don't think that many people have an understanding of the profound significance of this issue.

However, after all of these years since the introduction of computers into the commercial marketplace, I think that there is substantial evidence that the world is at the enterprise architecture "tipping point"!

The world is beginning to penetrate the Information Age and massive changes are being manifest in the global community. We have not likely seen a magnitude of such changes since the Industrial Revolution several hundred years ago.

Somehow or other, I stumbled across the pattern of descriptive representations (architecture) of complex objects such as buildings, airplanes, automobiles, computers, and so on, and identified the enterprise equivalents. I wish I could tell you that I was so smart that I intended all along to discover the ontology of architecture; however, only in retrospect I can see that it happened to fall on my desk one day. If this is the case (and every day I am more confident that it is), it may well be the foundation that will make enterprise architecture a discipline, repeatable and predictable.

The Federated Enterprise Architecture Certification (FEAC) Program was the first academically based enterprise architecture certification program and has operated for more than nine years. The program continues only to increase in visibility and acceptance in the public as well as private domains.

Last week, I met with 20 Ph.D. students in the enterprise architecture Ph.D. program at the Meraka Institute in Johannesburg, South Africa, a research institute supporting several of the major universities in South Africa.

In the last 60 days, I have been in Dallas twice, Washington, Johannesburg, Cape Town, Dubai, Hong Kong, Shanghai, Singapore, Kuala Lumpur, London, Frankfurt, Munich, Zurich, and Paris and have talked to well over 500 people intensely interested in enterprise architecture. The audiences in Australia and India tend to exceed these numbers substantially. I would observe that this is a pretty good sampling across the globe, and that the intensity of interest only increases each day that goes by.

Two years ago, one of the major tool vendors, Sybase PowerDesigner, asked my permission to map its metamodel against my framework ontology and prove that it could make the tool behave like an engineering tool instead of a manufacturing tool. At the London Enterprise Architecture Conference, Sybase PowerDesigner demonstrated what it has achieved and I was very impressed. Then in Frankfurt last month, I was asked the same permission by a representative of System Architect with particular interest in the small and medium-sized enterprise market. Although these are only two data points, I think they constitute a trend. I would suggest that there is an awakening in the tool community and I hope that every tool supplier will ultimately do the same.

The time has come for this book, *FEAC™ Certified Enterprise Architect CEA Study Guide*. I know the authors and I know their industry experience; I know their academic experience; I know their tooling experience; and I have taught in the FEAC program for the past eight years as a distinguished lecturer.

I am confident that enterprise architecture *is* the issue of the century. Now is the time to find out everything you can about this subject and aggressively practice it. Every day that goes by that you are not accumulating some architectural constructs and adding them to inventory is a day that you have lost. At some point, the enterprise must have a critical mass of enterprise architecture artifacts from which the enterprise can be dynamically changed to accommodate the extreme complexities and rates of change characteristic of the Information Age. If you don't have them when you need them, it is going to be too late.

Last week in Johannesburg, the young man who was introducing me used an interesting metaphor. He said, "If you wear your tires bald, drive in the rain, and hit a puddle, you are in the ditch … it is too late. Therefore, either fix your tires … or don't drive when it rains, and it could rain at any time!"

There is a message here: *Sooner or later it is going to rain. Start fixing your tires.*

Read this book! Start *doing* enterprise architecture. *FEAC™ Certified Enterprise Architect CEA Study Guide* is a good place to start. Actually engineering the enterprise will not only serve the enterprise by enabling extreme complexity and extreme change, but it will also serve to improve the ability and quality of building and running systems in response to accommodating short-term demand.

John A. Zachman
Zachman International
Glendale, California
June 2011

ACKNOWLEDGMENTS

Prakash Rao: I wish to acknowledge my debt of gratitude first and foremost to my immediate family—my wife Malathi and our children—for their support during the intense effort involved in producing a work of this size and scope. I also wish to thank my friend and well-wisher Paula Pahos for the many years of interesting debates, discussions, and arguments on aspects of enterprise architecting and for collaborating on many ingenious workarounds to ensure constant progress. I wish to dedicate this book to my father, C. S. S. Rao, who passed away this year and did not live to see the completed work. As an ex–Chief Executive Officer of a large telecommunications corporation, he would have loved to have participated in the debate. And for all the people who have touched me in so many ways, thank you—you know who you are!

In a vast and evolving field such as enterprise architecture, a book like this is best supplemented with readings and references from the body of knowledge and practice. Modeling techniques have been around for more than two decades and are as much a specialty skill as an art. The new The Open Group Architecture Framework (TOGAF) is increasingly rich in process definition and a program/project-oriented approach to enterprise architecting. The Department of Defense Architecture Framework (DoDAF) continues to evolve and the Office of Management and Budget (OMB) continues to change its primary emphasis as new management challenges face the nation. As practitioners, we will have a front seat in viewing these changes. As actors, we also hope to influence these changes in a planned and deliberate manner that reduces risk and adverse impacts and furthers the mission of the enterprise.

Ann Reedy: I wish to express my thanks to my husband Dr. Christopher L. Reedy for his patience and support during the development of this book and to my coauthors for their continuing encouragement and support. I would like to thank the other FEAC instructors and staff for their insights and support as well as the FEAC DoDAF students, from whom I have learned perhaps more than they have learned from me. Finally, I would like to thank my colleagues, past and present, especially Kathie Sowell, at the MITRE Corporation, with whom I have enjoyed stimulating conversations about architecture and related issues over the years. As always, any opinions expressed in this book are mine and do not represent positions of the MITRE Corporation.

Beryl Bellman: I want to express my deep gratitude to my wonderful wife, Dr. Suzanne Regan, who provides support and encouragement in all of my work and teaching. I also thank my son Che for taking after his father and in his interest and dedication to advancing enterprise architecture. I also thank my daughter Sarah, who is now in the midst of her university studies and who makes her dad so very proud. I also thank my business partners and cofounders of FEAC, Felix Rausch and Barbara Charuhas Rausch, for their support. I also thank the outstanding FEAC faculty, who contribute to our discipline and from whom I continually learn. And, I also am most grateful to my colleagues in the EA and related professional associations with whom I am affiliated and in many of which I have been honored by being given a leadership role. I must also thank my colleagues at California State University–Los Angeles and in my department, as well as those at California State University–East Bay and National University for their support of our programs.

PREFACE

Since early 2002, the Federated Enterprise Architecture Certification (FEAC™) Institute has been teaching enterprise architecture (EA), providing university academic credit, and certifying practitioners who have acquired the knowledge to actually apply the discipline of enterprise architecture to complex, real-world problems. As early pioneers, we have seen how the EA discipline has evolved and taken hold and how it has helped in the success of many organizations, programs, and projects, both in the government and the private sector. This is a book that is born out of eight-plus years of providing hands-on instruction and EA certification to hundreds of students who initially implemented real EA projects in three months time during their study at the FEAC Institute and saw how the projects progressed further at their workplace after they formally became Certified Enterprise Architects (CEAs).

The book is the culmination of the experience of developing EA as both a practitioner-based and academic discipline by the FEAC faculty and instructors, producing 1,200 graduates from 2002 through 2010. We consider ourselves privileged to have been a vital force in shaping this powerful new discipline. We see EA as holistic, as it involves the entire enterprise: uniting business with the technological infrastructure that supports it, and bringing education, rigorous planning, consistency and accountability to business and solution architectures. We consider the content of our program to be important to every form of EA discipline instruction, so this book is relevant not only to our students but to everyone seeking professional EA knowledge and certification.

What makes this such a timely book is that it is based on nine years of successfully educating practitioners in the EA discipline while upholding the highest standard for certification in the overall discipline of enterprise architecture, not just for one specific framework, methodology, tool, or approach by itself. Our slogan is as follows: The enterprise architecture discipline is the 21st century way of getting our arms around complexity. The FEAC Institute is tool neutral and framework agnostic. This discipline was born out of the fact that changes in industry today are blindingly fast, relentless, multifaceted, and unforgiving. What is not rational at this time is to keep looking for silver bullets, magic, and shrink-wrapped prices when it comes to better planning for such changing complexities. In today's complex organizations, with so many complex, dynamic information flows, to decipher the information in a meaningful and contextual way, one must learn to use this new and "disruptive" discipline.

Most importantly the FEAC Institute, from its inception, was associated with a public state university, the California State University East Bay, which officially accredited all of our courses in its catalogue as either academic or continuing education courses.

We have steadfastly held to our initial principles to be EA tool–neutral and always formulating the inclusion of all the latest frameworks and methodologies.

In addition, the certification process practicum produced some 350 projects by teams, most of which were projects that tackled real objectives for their organizations, often kick-starting organizationwide efforts. These practicum included, but are not limited to, data center consolidation, National Aeronautics and Space Administration (NASA) mission planning, Enterprise Resource Planning (ERP) systems consolidation within large companies, data architecting, security architecting, alignment of information technology (IT) with business processes, data center consolidation, ID management plans, service-oriented architecture (SOA) and cloud designs, sophisticated business strategies and governance, plus many other large and complex projects across the private sector and government.

The achievements by our students are the difference we are making in the real world and are the reason that most of our instructors and faculty have continued to work with us over the years and reap the deeply rewarding satisfaction that comes with our students' successes.

We want to thank all of the CEA graduates, instructors, and faculty for their support and continued input to help us continually improve the curriculum and experience to be gained by the graduates.

I want to especially thank my partner and cofounder of FEAC, Dr. Beryl Bellman, for carrying the academic management load of FEAC, Dr. Ann Reedy for being an all-purpose hitter and innovation force, and Prakash Rao for his incredible energy and vision about enterprise architecture and how we can optimize its implementation, as well as for his vision for this book.

We also want to mention several people without whom we would not be here today because of their dedication and assistance early on to help make FEAC a success. We thank Mike Tiemann, who was a fellow architect and entrepreneur in government and is one of the leading FEA experts in the United States, for his continued insights and being an ombudsman for us and the American Council for Technology/ Industry Advisory Council (ACT/IAC); Robert Moore, whose encouragement and help and dedication in getting it all started in 2002 was irreplaceable along with his teaching and contributions to the curriculum; and Rob Thomas II, who in 2001 encouraged us to go ahead and take the plunge to start FEAC Institute and is now a member of our faculty. Special thanks go to John Zachman, who has been a special lecturer since 2002 and an ongoing inspiration to both our faculty and students. We also want to recognize our other esteemed faculty, who continually make our EA programs so successful: Dr. Dan Spar, Patrick Bolton, Cortland Coghill, and Dick Burk. We also thank the more than 25 additional instructors who teach case studies and special topics within the program. We also wish to thank our wonderful alumni, who promote FEAC as the EA discipline, and whose advice has enabled us to continually improve the quality of what we teach.

This book is the first in a series of books on the discipline of enterprise architecture by the FEAC Press in collaboration with McGraw-Hill. Together we plan to publish a set of books that address different sectors in the private sector and government.

Felix A. A. Rausch
Cofounder
FEAC Institute
Alexandria, Virginia

INTRODUCTION

Enterprise architecture is a vast subject that has come to incorporate elements from a variety of established practices—from systems engineering to project management, from strategic planning to operations and maintenance. The focus of enterprise architecture has always been holistically on the enterprise. The usefulness of architecture is in breaking down the complex animal we call the enterprise into components and putting them back together in context.

Boiling the ocean can be a frustrating exercise. This book takes a divide-and-conquer approach to the challenge of understanding enterprise architecting.

Part I establishes some of the core concepts needed by the practitioner. The Federated Enterprise Architecture Certification (FEAC) teaching curriculum is based on understanding these concepts as well as the relationships between them.

Part II is all about doing. It describes a step-by-step method for implementing enterprise architectures. The various frameworks for enterprise architecture, such as the federal, Defense Department and the Open Group frameworks have tended to be viewed as religions by their adherents. This book has taken a more general approach based on the Department of Defense Architecture Framework (DoDAF) Six Step process, which incorporates the steps in each of these frameworks. The reader is referred to The Open Group Architecture Framework (TOGAF) for a more in-depth treatment of the architecting process.

Part III is an instruction on modeling techniques that are applicable to enterprise architecture. The DoDAF-described models are used as illustrations, but the important thing for the practitioner to follow is modeling based on "fit for purpose"—building the models that supply the data needed for the analysis to be performed—to show the way to the implementation roadmap for enterprise transformation.

Part IV is a reference section that provides definitions and pointers to further readings. In an evolving field, these definitions are constantly changing as new discoveries are made and new patterns emerge based on observation and practice.

Part V describes a hypothetical airport as a case study to provide the full context for the examples described in the book. The case study attempts to bring out the real issues faced by enterprises within a narrower scope required for the limited size of a book.

Part V also provides reference material for the enterprise architect such as a discussion of tools and repositories, a term glossary, and a index.

The book uses a common, fictitious example throughout: Richard M. Nixon International Airport, which is undergoing a transformation from a sleepy municipal airport to a viable alternative to Los Angeles International. Our belief is that this example provides a rich canvas for several case studies to support various aspects of business that are based on the use of enterprise architecture—from capability-based planning, to systems formulation (system of systems, family of systems, and integrated solutions), to operational analysis, human resources, resource planning, capital planning, and strategic planning—leading to five-year roadmaps for systems and technology implementation and so on. The benefit of using an airport as an example is that the subject is likely familiar to most students.

About the Digital Content

The CD-ROM accompanying this book contains the major documentation for both the Federal Enterprise Architecture Framework (FEAF) and Department of Defense Architecture Framework (DoDAF) programs in the FEAC Institute. This documentation is included in several folders organized into two parts.

Folder 1 concerns the FEAF. The first subfolder is for the Federal Enterprise Architecture (FEA), containing the major documents about creating FEA and its Reference Models. The second subfolder contains documents pertaining to assessing enterprise architecture (EA) and improving EA management. The third subfolder contains government policy documents concerning the use of EA. The fourth subfolder contains documents pertaining to the Federal Segment Architecture Methodology (FSAM).

Folder 2 contains folders pertaining to the Department of Defense Architecture Framework. The first subfolder contains DoDAF version 1.5 and the second subfolder contains the main books used in DoDAF version 2.0. The third subfolder contains the *DoDAF Journal*, which includes a number of documents concerning the implementation of DoDAF and related topics. The final subfolder contains other information relevant to DoDAF 2.0. In addition, sample certification examinations for both the FEAF and DoDAF programs and a list of relevant study questions are provided in Folder 3. Folder 4 contains the electronic version of this book.

Part 1

Foundation Concepts

1.1

Why EA and Why This Book

The information technology (IT) company Gartner Inc. (Fenn & Raskino, 2008) has discovered a pattern of hope and disappointment that has plagued almost every highly touted innovation and its adoption by otherwise highly capable and successful enterprises. Gartner coined the term "hype cycle" for this phenomenon. This cycle begins with initial enthusiasm and inflated expectations; results in disappointment when expectations are not met; and ultimately leads to the realization that value can still be realized, albeit more gradually and over a sustained period of time (see Figure 1.1-1). Nowhere was the existence of the hype cycle more evident than in the area of information technology.

Some of the innovations that drove this high sense of inflated expectation and are still fueling the hype cycle are

- Increases in processing speeds and decreases in cost
- Increases in memory size and decreases in cost
- Ubiquitous use of computing through small, fast, cheap processing
- The emergence of the computer as a personal appliance
- Increases in communications speeds and decreases in cost
- Increases in processing capability and improvements in processing algorithms
- Cheap, ubiquitous computer devices
- Technology miniaturization and portability advance

FIGURE 1.1-1

Gartner's
Hype Cycle of
Innovation

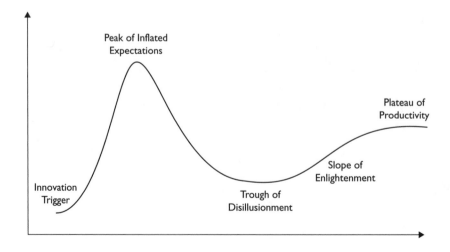

- Rapid improvements in absorption of technology among the nontechnical population
- Fusion of business and consumer use of IT

The phenomenon of enterprise spending in this explosion of technology innovation was that of a child in a candy store with a full wallet. Enterprises blithely purchased technology products—sometimes at the individual level, often at the department level, and very rarely at the enterprise level.

Out of the realization that enterprises were spending out of fascination with technology without a clear cost/benefit equation, industry took the first step: appoint a single person and organization to account for and manage centrally the burgeoning IT budget that was being spent in many places within the organization. This function, called the Chief Information Officer (CIO), became the person responsible for approving IT purchases and also the person accountable for the alignment of IT investments to the business of the enterprise. Just as other enterprise costs were measured and expected to be in line with the scale and operations of the enterprise, IT spending was being held to the same standard.

The innovative trigger for the enterprise architecture (EA) hype cycle was the clear emergence that EA was the tool of choice for matching IT investments to the business that they supported. EA allowed the traceability of IT investments to enterprise factors in terms of the activities, locations, organizations, products and services, lines of business, business areas, strategic goals and objectives, and the transformation processes of the enterprise. A seminal work in this area was the methodology for "Enterprise Architecture Planning" by Steven Spewak in the early 1990s, which was quickly adopted by many. Enterprise Architecture Planning (EAP) and other frameworks are discussed in Chapter 1.2.

Emergence of EA

This section presents a few examples of events that have shaped the evolution of enterprise architecture over the years.

Early 1990s: Emergence of the CIO as an Executive Role and a Seat for IT at the Table

During the same early 1990s period, the new role of the Chief Information Officer was also taking shape as enterprises realized the strategic advantage of the information that they collected in the course of running their businesses. Many industry studies during this period that outlined the top ten challenges for a CIO consistently spoke about two persistent problems: (1) the growing application backlog as the IT shop struggled with rolling out applications fast enough to keep pace with changes in the business and the environment and (2) the need for alignment of IT expenditure to the business. The CIO was in the same executive meetings with the Chief Executive Officer (CEO), the Chief Operating Officer (COO), and the Chief Financial Officer (CFO), and the questions that came from such meetings were not technology-related but rather on how technology created opportunity and how a business case for a technology expense is to be made.

1994: Federal IT Expenditure Was on the GAO's Radar

The need to establish alignment came from the realization that IT had become a significant expense, but IT projects were mushrooming from sheer demand and it was not possible to corral the various categories under which IT money was being spent. In 1994, the Government Accounting Office (GAO), later renamed the Government Accountability Office, surveyed best practices in commercial companies that were able to account for their IT spending and justify the spending by explicitly showing the connection between the IT and the business or alignment. The GAO recommended that the federal government—which was also spending large amounts of money on IT—embark upon measures that would address the issue of IT alignment to the business as well as measures to help architecture solve the problems with stovepipe projects that duplicated effort, created redundant capabilities and data, and required a huge cost in post-implementation interoperability measures such as data exchange interfaces to stitch the output of stovepipe projects together. The GAO also recommended that a formal position of CIO be established within agencies to provide accountability for IT expenses and that all IT expenses be visible to the CIO from a vantage point so that agencies could aggregate the costs of IT and report costs more accurately.

It is important to note that the interest of the GAO, from its very charter and composition, was primarily on the financial aspects and governance of IT, not so much on the burgeoning complexity, the increasing backlog, and the plethora of expensive interfaces that were bandaging systems together haphazardly and delicately.

The corresponding movement within the commercial world to govern financial investments was being developed by the International Council on System Engineering (INCOSE). Control Objectives for Information Technology (COBIT) was one of the best practices and standards that emerged as a result of applying investment and governance measures to IT in a manner similar to other business functions.

1996: Clinger-Cohen Act: The ITMRA Compliance Threat

Congress took to heart the GAO's recommendations and passed the Information Technology Management Reform Act (ITMRA) in 1996 (see Figure 1.1-2). This is also more famously known as the Clinger-Cohen Act (CCA) after its sponsors.

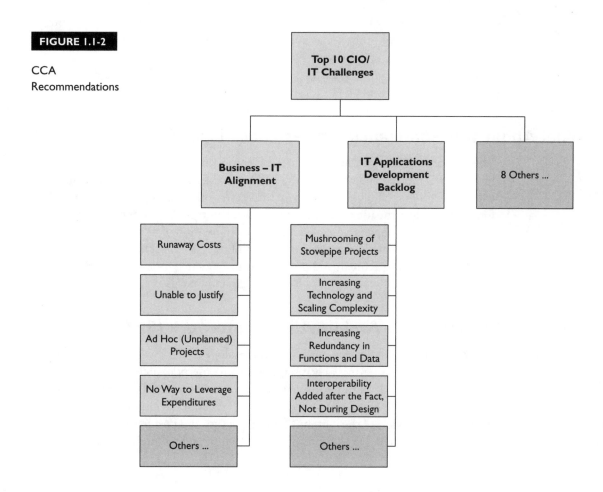

FIGURE 1.1-2

CCA
Recommendations

The CCA mandated the following, under penalties of law:

- Every agency must publish an enterprise architecture that details the business structures of the agency.
- Every agency must appoint a formal position of Chief Information Officer responsible for all IT operations and accountable for all IT expenditures.
- The CIO is responsible for the production of the agency enterprise architecture.
- All agency IT investments must be tied to the enterprise architecture. Business cases must be produced for major investments. No money would be available for initiatives that were not supported by a business case.
- The Office of Management and Budget (OMB) is responsible for governing the provisions of the CCA and maintaining the overall Federal Enterprise Architecture.
- The OMB will monitor and govern IT investments.

What About the Nonfinancial Issues That Plagued the CIO?

The task of dealing with the nonfinancial IT problems that were addressed neither by the GAO recommendations nor the CCA was the subject of much discussion within the Federal CIO Council. An architecture working group (AWG) was formed to explore the use of architecture techniques to ameliorate the issues of interoperability, complexity management, the elimination of redundancies, the expediting of IT to market, and the reduction of the backlog. The framework first articulated by John Zachman and the EAP techniques first articulated by Steven Spewak were the early foundations for the discipline we call enterprise architecture.

1999: Federal Enterprise Architecture Framework (FEAF)

The National Institute of Standards and Technology (NIST) was responsible for developing standards for this new discipline called enterprise architecture by the publishing of the Federal Enterprise Architecture Framework (FEAF) in 1999. The primary basis for the FEAF was the Spewak EAP. Spewak's technique was based on defining an as-is view of the current IT infrastructure and postulating a vision of the future or "to-be" state. He also recommended that the representation of the as-is view be performed by recording the current inventory of systems and the current structure of business operations. The representation of the as-is view is analyzed to distill the enterprise architecture which is a combination of the data architecture, the applications architecture, and the technology architectures respectively.

1999–2000: The Y2K Threat

At the end of 1999, enterprises were mortally afraid of the change in millennium. They feared that the data they had collected over the decades would become unusable because the year was stored in two digits (with an implied prefix of "19" for the 20th century) and that the calculations that computed differences and added years to a baseline would need to factor in the leading two digits as well. There was a flurry of "remediation" activity where enterprises compiled a list of all applications, short-listed the ones that contained two-digit date fields for remediation, and then established and executed plans to change the code and test the applications with haste.

At the end of 1999 and into the year 2000, few cases appeared, if any, of catastrophic consequences from a bad choice in date storage format. But the benefit of the inventorying exercise is that enterprises now had authoritative lists of IT applications that they could point to, price out, and establish transformation and modernization roadmaps for.

2001: The Disaster Recovery Threat

When the terrorist-flown planes hit the two World Trade Center towers, many enterprises that were doing business at that location were affected. And destroyed along with the towers were computer records, processing equipment, people, networks, and facilities. Recovery in many cases was arduous and, in one case, disastrous. The firm of Cantor Fitzgerald, located in the North Tower, never recovered from the devastation of its facilities. Continuity of operations (COOP) planning is an important enterprise process that requires a holistic view of systems, people, facilities, information, and other items—the architecture elements that are typically part of an enterprise architecture representation. And the disaster of 9/11 brought home the importance of baselining the enterprise architecture—to resume or transfer operations smoothly in the event of disaster.

Today: Current Enterprise Challenges

In today's environment, as enterprises become more and more dependent on information to fuel their enterprises and information technology to propel their enterprises, large and small, they face a number of challenges that affect their planning environment; their ability to make decisions; their ability to assess, evaluate, and prioritize the many alternatives; and their ability to face new pressures from regulation, globalization, intense competition, and dramatic changes in their environments. Many enterprises have not been able to address these challenges successfully, as the evidence of a long list of failed multimillion-dollar IT initiatives seems to convey. The complexity and scale of some of these projects in the domain of information technology, though comparable to large civil engineering works or the building of airframes, do not appear to have benefited from a holistic, structured planning approach combined with an integrated, well-managed implementation approach that leverages planned risks to choose good design trade-offs. In short, the use of architecture for the planning phases is required to deal with the complexity and scale of the implementation phase. A systematic application of architecture is therefore the subject of this textbook.

Figure 1.1-3 shows how the Clinger-Cohen Act forces the responsibility of developing an enterprise architecture down to each federal agency, holding the Agency head responsible for the submission and instructing the Chief Information Officer to develop the enterprise architecture for each agency while holding the Office of Management and Budget accountable for the governance of the capital spending based on the enterprise architecture for the entire federal enterprise.

FIGURE 1.1-3

One of the Top Ten Challenges for the CIO: Alignment of IT and Business

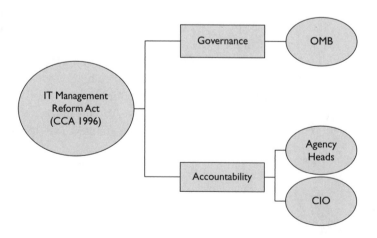

The following are a few of the many challenges that enterprises face today:

- Unacceptable numbers of failed large IT projects.
- The need for a faster tempo of operations, resulting in the need to detect and eliminate latencies and reduce the length of the connection to the customer. In the cases of military operations, the need to reduce latency of intelligence, imagery, and other situation assessment and operating picture elements to provide better operational planning and execution capabilities.
- Mergers and divestitures where new parts of the IT environments are acquired from merged enterprises, bringing in diversity in standards, information representations, architectures, cultures, and equipment.
- Globalization where parts of the workforce are located in different regions of the world, with their own cultures and local constraints on power, equipment, languages, and other factors.
- A changing workforce with new ways of interaction and collaboration; different expectations of their work environment; and increased exposure to computers, applications, information, and networking.
- Increasing expenses in information technology as a whole despite dramatic decreases in per-unit cost of processing and memory because of labor, the need to control obsolescence, the evolution of standards, and the need to provide constantly faster and faster processing and increasing memory.
- Increases in the complexity and scale of IT projects both in terms of scope and reach. Consequent needs for orchestrating work outputs of large numbers of professionals located all over the globe to complete projects successfully. Inability to fully assess the impact of complexity and scale at the planning or implementation level.
- Rampant adoption of technology based on competitors' use of technology, vendor push, as well as the pressure to align with contemporary standards.
- Rampant outsourcing, based on financial analyses, competitive price pressures, as well as the current enterprise focus on the core mission and the decision to outsource all noncritical supporting services.
- Dramatic opportunities posed by evolving architecture styles such as service-oriented architectures and cloud computing that change the way systems have been built in the past and introduce new planning challenges of migrating ponderous current systems infrastructures to a different type of architectural future.

The Case for Enterprise Architecture

The famous Finnish architect Eero Saarinen recommends, as a design principle: "Always design a thing by considering it in its next larger context—a chair in a room, a room in a house, a house in an environment, an environment in a city plan".

A business process—a collection of activities directed toward achieving a business objective—does not stand simply as a list of tasks. It also involves outputs of those tasks, some of which are inputs to tasks belonging to other business processes. The tasks involve performers who are also performers of tasks for other business processes. The performance of tasks requires the existence of organizational relationships that are part of the organization chart for the enterprise.

Although we will formally define and elaborate on enterprises and enterprise architecture, we define *enterprise* loosely as a shared endeavor at any level directed toward a common objective. This definition allows us to cover any level of abstraction—from the executive branch of the U.S. government as one of the three branches of government to the Department of Homeland Security as a cabinet-level organization to the Customs and Immigration Services Agency (CIS) to a regional office located in Philadelphia, Pennsylvania, to a software development effort for a $41 million software system. An *architecture*, loosely defined, is the structure of components and their relationships. When architecture is applied to enterprise, we get *enterprise architecture*: the structure of components of an enterprise and their relationships.

Communication

Enterprise architecture deals with a *uniform* way to represent the larger context and to *communicate* that context to everyone in the enterprise who is an interested party in some enterprise process. That larger context may embrace elements inside and outside the enterprise and frequently does so.

Notice the emphasis on *uniformity* and *communication*.

In the day-to-day world, communication is accomplished by spoken and written language. There is an assumption that the speaker and the listener are able to understand the same vocabulary and the same sentence structures and grammar, and are able to comprehend the meaning (semantics) of the content of the conversation. Enterprise architecture establishes the common vocabulary for an enterprise, the grammar and the semantics for various stakeholders to communicate understanding of architecture elements, and the relationships among architecture elements. As we will see in other chapters of the book, this entails the following topics.

Unifying Architecture Frameworks

An architecture framework establishes a set of terms that describe the various types of architecture elements. For example, the Department of Defense (DoD) Architecture Framework defines architecture elements such as Activity, Performer, Location, and Information. It further specifies Activity as performed by humans or as performed by an automated system; Performer as a human, organizational, or notional performer or as a system, a business service, or a software service. The adoption of a single common framework throughout an enterprise ensures that all architecture-related terms are couched using the same underlying terminology. If two collaborating enterprises were to adopt different frameworks, they run the risk of speaking past each other and may need translation to understand each other.

A Rich Set of Models

Once a set of common vocabulary terms is defined, the next challenge is that of developing common grammars or sentence structures that can be commonly understood by diverse groups of people. In architecture work, as in any other area, a picture is worth a thousand words. But a picture is simply a cartoon without a blueprinting discipline that standardizes what the elements in the picture represent. The picture must make consistent use of the same symbols for items of the same type. Similarly, the picture must describe what the connections among symbols mean. Randomly drawn pictures are therefore not the answer to providing a uniform and consistent way to communicate. Over time, many methodologies have evolved that have standardized the blueprinting of models that support the various activities of the enterprise. In Chapter 5.1 of this book, we will discuss some of these methodologies. But for the concern of this chapter, enterprise architecture involves representing architecture elements and their relationships using commonly understood and consistently applied models. This consistency can be achieved more easily by using a common set of automated or nonautomated template-based tools throughput the enterprise rather than relying on individual modelers to conform to common standards.

It is limiting to think of models as simply the artifacts of IT specification, analysis, design, and construction when the scope of modeling is not restricted to software development, but rather the enterprise as a whole.

True, the evolution of modeling technologies such as the Unified Modeling Language (UML) and Structured Analysis and Design Technique (SADT) are directly derived from the software development domain. IT personnel first had to wrestle with the problem of modeling business processes, states, and electronic information to be able to represent the requirements that they were asked to implement within an automated system. In fact, the computer-aided manufacturing program that produced the information definition (IDEF) series of modeling techniques directly piggybacked and evolved the techniques of progressive refinement and decomposition that are part of structured analysis.

The use of models in EA is not restricted to the ones that are used for software or business process modeling. For example, because a stakeholder has a financial interest in a software development as an investment, we need to view the models that are submitted for capital planning and investment control decision making also as legitimate EA models, in the manner we consider data models, functional decompositions, or object class models as representative of the types of models required for enterprise architecture representation. In the U.S. government, in fact, a federal agency is required to submit business case justification in financial terms to the Office of Management and Budget in support of a request to pursue an initiative. Commercial enterprises also frequently have investment review boards that review proposals to start or continue new projects.

Models convey knowledge of a certain aspect of the enterprise to a specific audience who can use them for analysis and to make decisions.

For example, in the U.S. federal government, submission of the A-300 business case justification models to a Capital Planning and Investment Council allows the council to make a decision on which investments to approve and which investments to curtail because of budget constraints or perceived irrelevance to the mission of the enterprise.

Another example, in the U.S. Department of Defense, an information support plan might be developed that describes the burden that a proposed system places on shared infrastructure such as network bandwidth or transactions on a shared database server. Infrastructure planners might use such a plan either to curtail the initiative or to develop the common infrastructure to incorporate the needs of the initiatives.

Transformation

Enterprises are constantly transforming—sometimes proactively as part of a planned improvement or reactively struggling and kicking as a response to changes in environment or competition. In either case, any successful transformation is predicated on the following:

- A clear understanding of the *current state*—what we will call the baseline or as-is state. The as-is state of the enterprise may be represented in many dimensions: current motivation, current set of products and services, current business processes, current organizational structures, current event responses, current operating locations, and so on.

- A clear understanding of the *objective* or *target state*—what we will call the to-be or target state. The to-be state of the enterprise must also be represented in the same dimensions as the as-is state. From this representation comes an understanding of what remains the same, what cannot change easily and must stay, and what must change.

- A clear *transformation plan* or *roadmap* that will transform the enterprise from the as-is state to the to-be state. This plan has to have a timeline that is acceptable within the window of change; otherwise, we risk a transformation that is too late—usually calling for enterprise triage measures. The roadmap generally consists of a number of concurrent initiatives or projects that must all support one another and join to provide the net transformation effect that the enterprise desires.

The representation of the as-is state of the enterprise, the to-be state of the enterprise, and the planning of the transformation roadmap (family of solutions) are all part of the enterprise architecting effort.

Addressing a Family of Problems and Solutions Simultaneously

Enterprise architecture provides a common context for a large family of problems and solutions. Today, the disciplines of systems engineering, software development, and project management amongst others have evolved into detailed bodies of knowledge and practice that have become powerful tools for solving individual problems. But enterprise architecture is the discipline that provides a context for solving, not the individual problem, but a family of problems without the risk of solving one problem only to aggravate or cause another because of ignorance of the overall context in which the problem is being solved.

Systems Engineering

The area of systems engineering has progressed tremendously and developed several successful methods of planning, designing, implementing, testing, simulating, and deploying complex systems. Formal methods are available for capturing systems requirements, analyzing systems requirements, and building various types of analytical models for representing various dimensions of a system. Systems engineering also deals with design constraints and trade-offs involved in designing for competing constraints. For systems that are built in isolation of each other, these techniques have been more than adequate. The techniques of systems engineering can span the abstraction of analysis to the detail of design and implementation. As the scale of systems has increased as well as the number of design variables, ill-understood coupling of system variables has resulted in unintended design consequences. Systems engineering practice is trying to evolve to meet the need of complex, large-scale systems.

Software Development

The software lifecycle has also been well studied and documented. Most enterprises with a mature software development culture have documented software development lifecycles (SDLCs) with standards, methods, tools, and workflow as well as gates or review points for each phase of the lifecycle to manage cost, schedule, and quality for a software development project. The SDLC that started as a progression of water-tight development phases that delivered results only after a couple of years to a problem that disappeared a year ago has yielded to rapid application development, spiral methods for delivery, and agile development and Scrum techniques—always trying to shorten the gap between the specification of requirements and the delivery of working software.

Project Management

The discipline of project management has also evolved to its current level of rigor and quality with the establishment of commonly understood project management techniques; risk management processes; project reporting techniques; and techniques for managing cost, schedule, and quality. With the emergence of earned value management (EVM) as a measure to assess the health of projects, enterprises are looking at effective project management as a silver bullet. Unfortunately, the root cause of project failure is seldom the failure of project management—it goes deeper to the limited understanding of the complexity of the problem, or the lack of depth during the planning, scoping phase, and many times to the law of unintended consequences.

Arguably, at the head of all of these—which is the point at which an enterprise plans a specific systems development, software development, or project—there are few alternatives for analyzing the portfolio of systems, software development projects, or initiative projects. This is where enterprise architecture comes in. Enterprise architecture provides a representation means for the planner to analyze a family of projects or initiatives, a family of systems, or a family of services. This analysis is very important because each of the ingredients of such portfolios makes a demand on capital and working capital funds, development resources, management attention, and has different, often disruptive effects on the enterprise while it is under way.

Leveraging Patterns

Patterns are repeatable configurations of elements. In enterprise architecture work, patterns are complex combinations of architecture elements that provide a repeatable design. An example of an enterprise architecture pattern is a fast food franchise that makes burgers. The architectural pattern for the process of making the burger is the combination of the activities involved in making a burger, the skill sets of the personnel involved, training on the operations involved, the specific equipment that is involved in the making of burgers, and any other items required to specify completely all the factors that go into repeatedly making burgers that are consistently the same. Along with the specification of the "hard items" is also a recipe for temperatures, times, ingredients, and preparation instructions. The success of the franchise in turning out repeatedly consistent product is predicated on standardizing all of these elements and not allowing variation. This is frequently a condition that the franchisor places on a franchisee.

Enterprises can leverage patterns for expanding their operations in a reliable and repeatable manner. At the same time, they can exploit regional and local differences to customize patterns for better fit in areas where such diversity is important.

For example, developing an enterprise architecture enables an enterprise to identify and use patterns in supporting standardization efforts, improving business processes, or scaling up operations.

Decision Support

All enterprise operations and transformations involve decision making. Decision making involves looking at information. Decision making also involves looking at candidate alternatives and determining a course of action based on selecting the best of these alternatives. Decisions are often made with limited information and the assumption of calculated risks. Decision making at the planning level often can have a significantly larger impact on cost, schedule, and quality than decisions made lower down in the implementation phases.

Enterprise architecture is a knowledge base for the executive decision maker at the planning level. By providing the right information along with the assessment of impacts, the enterprise architecture can provide a basis for informed decision making that increases the probability of plans that will successfully turn into implementation reality.

As executives and decision makers start using the enterprise architecture information in their decision making, they will find (a) needs for additional information that the enterprise architecture representation has not captured, (b) new uses of enterprise architecture information, (c) shortfalls of critical information that is required but is not available, or (d) inaccurate and out-of-date information that is not fit for use in the planning without introducing new risks from inaccurate data.

As we will see in Chapter 2.2, scoping and planning the purpose of an EA effort are critical to managing the success of the EA efforts and the usefulness of the information delivered to decision makers.

Enterprise Architecture Certification

The haphazard and often unpredictable rate of progress of enterprise architecture thus far has been directly attributable to individual efforts and specific efforts rather than a more general widespread awareness and competency base that can produce repeatable and workman-like results.

Development as a Practitioner-Driven Discipline

We presented the hype cycle in the introductory section of this chapter. EA has had its own hype cycle. The triggering event was the passing of the Clinger-Cohen Act and the consequent gold rush to the enterprise architecture field to satisfy the sudden demand for enterprise architects.

Enterprise architecture developed as a practitioner-based discipline rather than being grounded in any specific academic discipline. It began with the need for an integrated IT architecture that encompasses multiple views of the enterprise to reduce redundancy and gaps in investments and assist IT strategic planning. It soon became apparent that to accomplish this goal, EA required a holistic enterprise view that not only includes business perspectives and requirements but needs to be driven by them. EA emerged as a way for an enterprise to be fully integrated and in communication with itself and its business partners to enable all enterprise stakeholders both to manage complexity and to understand and handle the impact of any proposed change in business strategies, information, and technology at every level.

This shift from an IT to an enterprise-wide program raises serious issues regarding what needs to be incorporated in an EA education and what skills and knowledge must be tested to ensure that someone is a fully trained and proficient enterprise architect. The education of an enterprise architect involves being competent in multiple disciplines. An architect must be a systems thinker with an understanding of organizational development, business processes, strategic planning, governance, program management, and related topics relevant to the views of the business planner and owner. At the same time, the architect must have expertise with the wide range of methods relevant to building information, data, application, and technical models.

The Need for Multidisciplinary Skills

The education of an enterprise architect involves being competent in multiple disciplines. These comprise, on the one hand, the contributions to a wide range of fields contributing to the study of organizational theory. These include social and business sciences, such as anthropology, business administration, communications, linguistics, public administration, and political science. These disciplines introduce to EA such areas of involvement as the study of values, ethics, complexity science, organizational behavior, organizational structure, organizational development, communication and social networks, communities and networks of practice, leadership, management theory, organizational culture and climate, industrial psychology, policy analysis, semantics and structures of meaning, and belief systems.

Relationships to Other Bodies of Knowledge

Concomitantly, the discipline of EA is connected to general systems theory and systems engineering. This introduces systems engineering, engineering management, technology management, computer sciences, information sciences, and operations research as input fields. These contribute to process analysis, technology assessment, requirements analysis, cost engineering, quality control, project management, environment scanning, business reengineering, enterprise engineering, and Six Sigma.

With inputs from the organizational and systems sciences, a number of emerging fields have developed within EA that are relevant to understanding the influence it has on enterprises of every size. These include information resources management, information assurance, security management, and records and data management, enterprise resource planning (ERP), service-oriented architecture (SOA), and cloud computing. In turn, EA contributes to a range of new, emergent concepts including solutions lifecycle development, portfolio management, capital planning and investment control, knowledge management, e-government and e-commerce, business transformation, ubiquitous computing, as well as DoD-relevant concepts such as the global information grid and the Joint Capabilities Integration and Development System (JCIDS) (discussed later in this book).

As we shall see, EA has both a hard side and a soft side. As Marc Lankhorst noted next to its architecture, "which could be viewed as the 'hard part of the company,' the soft part, its culture, is formed by its people and leadership and is of equal if not higher importance in achieving (organization) goals" (Lankhorst et al., 2009: 9). Yet organizational behavior, culture, and other aspects of the soft side of a company can be modeled and incorporated into EA. This will be discussed later. The point now is that EA draws from a wide body of knowledge of which an enterprise architect should be aware.

EA Knowledge and Expertise

By examining government and industry initiatives and the growing appearance of EA within university departments, we can address what constitutes a viable EA body of knowledge and the particular skills in systems thinking, program management, enterprise modeling, and organizational development that are involved.

In this context, we must consider how these competencies can be realistically tested to certify architects to ensure that they possess both knowledge about EA and knowledge of how to create enterprise architecture. This is one of the major goals of this text.

In a recent report the Gartner Group warned of a danger that due to the recent proliferation of training and certification programs, the viability of the certification process could be questioned. A related problem is in how enterprise architecture has been treated in academia. Over the past few years, EA education has found its way into various curricula but as a part of a degree program rather than as a stand-alone degree program. EA is now moving from being taught as a module in a particular course to being a course on its own to being several courses in a program allowing students to major or minor in it. This advance, however, contains a risk of EA being subsumed under a single technical IT discipline, thus leading to a lack of acknowledgment of the range of competencies recognized by practicing EA practitioners. This portends a possible retreat from the advances that have been made in moving EA from being IT-centric to a true enterprise-level concern.

In this chapter, we consider the knowledge, skills, and competencies required of architects and what type of processes are needed to test their acquisition for certification effectively. The recognition of the broad body of knowledge that this entails is behind several current initiatives to define competency framework for certification of architects by such bodies as the DoD Office of the CIO, the Academic Coalition of the Industry Advisory Council, the Open Group, and Center for Advancement of Enterprise Architecture as a Profession (CAEAP). After examining these government and industry initiatives and the discussions within university departments as EA programs are being developed, we then address what constitutes a viable EA body of knowledge and the particular skills in systems thinking, program management, enterprise modeling, organizational theory, and organizational development that are involved. In this context, we consider how these competencies can be realistically tested to certify architects to ensure that they possess both knowledge about and knowledge of how to create enterprise architecture.

What It Means to Be Certified

Certification in most areas refers to a formal procedure to recognize the knowledge, skills, and experience of members of a profession. This is most often done in part by asking candidates to demonstrate their knowledge through some form of examination procedure. In most but not all instances, certification is done through some external body or organization that is recognized as a credible body to assess capabilities. In many disciplines, such as medicine, education, and law, this certification is under the authority of major professional organizations and/or governmental entities. There are also a number of technical certifications that are promoted by industrial organizations that test for competencies with a defined body of knowledge and skill sets. These range from certifications in specific products such as those offered by Microsoft, CISCO, and Oracle to the mastery of a set of approaches that are often incorporated into the curricula of various university departments. These include such fields as program management, Six Sigma, information assurance, and the like.

As the discipline of EA emerged in the late 1980s and became mandated by governments—such as when the Clinger-Cohen Act of 1996 required all United States federal agencies and the Department of Defense to use architectural principles to manage their information technology resources—a critical need emerged to ensure that those responsible for doing EA had mastery of the body of knowledge and skills involved. It was with this challenge in mind that in 2001 Felix Rausch and Beryl Bellman founded the FEAC Institute as the first organization to offer formal EA education and certification in the Federal Enterprise Architecture (FEA) and the Department of Defense Architecture Framework (DoDAF). FEAC originally was an acronym for Federal Enterprise Architecture Certification, and later expanded its definition to Federated Enterprise Architecture Certification, to include, in addition to EA in the federal sector, the knowledge, lessons learned, models, and capabilities of other types of enterprises.

The need for education and certification in EA is exemplified in a true, albeit humorous, story about one of our FEAC students early in the Department of Defense Architecture Framework (DoDAF) program. The major FEAC programs in FEA and DoDAF both entail 200 contact hours of mixed mode or blended education combining face-to-face with online learning given within five graduate-level courses affiliated with FEAC's university partners. Students in the program receive continuing education units or, upon payment of tuition fees, receive from FEAC's partners graduate engineering units that are applicable to a number of graduate programs. The program is delivered by having students attend the first 40 hours in a weeklong face-to-face instructional setting. The students then participate for three to four weeks in the FEAC Virtual University, where they take part in online discussions, submit individual and team-based assignments, and take examinations on the topics involved in the first part of the program. Students then return for a second face-to-face, 40-hour, weeklong session, after which they once again take part in the Virtual University. During the course of the entire program, students undertake an actual enterprise architecture project where they build a set of relevant EA models (artifacts or products) that comprise part of a real EA project or practicum.[1] At the end of the program, students take a formal written certification exam (composed of essay and diagrammatic answers) and then formally present and defend their practicum before a faculty panel and their fellow students.[2] They also write up their practicum projects as theses or narrative reports that are targeted to their internal or external EA customer.

In the case of the previously mentioned DoDAF example, the student told several of our faculty at the end of the first face-to-face session that he was especially concerned that at that point he had little knowledge of EA but was assigned to a major initiative in his branch of the military. The faculty assured him we would work closely and mentor him throughout the process to ensure the quality of his practicum and that he obtained the requisite knowledge and skills. When the student returned for the second face-to-face session a month later, he expressed his excitement and gratitude for the attention the faculty provided him, but said he

---

[1] These models are presented in Chapter 1.3.
[2] Sample tests are included on the CD.

was now especially concerned because during the intervening period, he had been appointed Chief Architect and now had to do really well.

This is more than an entertaining anecdote, as it seriously reflects what many architects experienced particularly in the earlier part of the decade. EA was not a subject taught within an academic discipline and was at most a topic mentioned only in the context of some other course. Architects had to learn on the job and quickly master the frameworks, views, models, artifacts, and deliverables that were specified in a number of mostly government-published documents. The FEAC Institute was founded upon and is organized to provide this education and certification. FEAC offers both education and testing of EA competencies and is the only certification that requires individuals to build actual enterprise architectures as part of the process.

Other EA certifications are on the market, and former FEAC faculty members established several of them. Although these programs offer training in EA, they do not require students to demonstrate how to actually create EA models and artifacts and be evaluated in their competencies for doing so. These programs attest at different levels that the student has attended training and can discuss what is involved in developing enterprise architecture. What distinguishes FEAC is ability to both "talk the talk" as well as "walk the walk."

In this book, we prepare readers to meet the requirements for FEAC certification. As a textbook for FEAC courses, the book includes content for the five FEAC courses in its programs. These range from EA framework basics, planning for architecture development and use, EA implementation, and EA integration. In this context, we present the essential components and uses of enterprise architecture and describe the large set of models or products that are used to build them. These include the views and all of the models and products comprising the current Department of Defense Architecture Framework (DoDAF 2.0), which we have found relevant to every architecture framework. We also discuss a range of reference models relevant to enterprise architecture, beginning with a focus on those mandated by the United States Office of Management and Budget, and then relate them to reference models being developed for the DoDAF as well as those used in other frameworks such as The Open Group Architecture Framework (TOGAF).

We also discuss how to engage in EA analysis. This includes the types of queries and reports that can be generated from enterprise architecture, especially facilitated by the use of one of the viable EA tools. We also discuss how to integrate EA with a number of other critical processes, such as portfolio management, capital planning and investment control (CPIC), information assurance and security, and the relevance and use of Federal Segment Architecture Methodology (FSAM), as well as Rapid Segment Architecture Methodology (RSAM), developed by Health and Human Services, which tailors FSAM for shorter timeframes and projects. Although several of these approaches have been developed for the United States federal agency context, they are also relevant to both other governmental (state and local as well as other international initiatives) and commercial contexts.

The Relevance of This Text to Other EA Certifications

In 1984, John Zachman, while at IBM, developed the first IT architecture framework, which he continued to develop into the most recognized enterprise architecture framework, the Zachman Framework (Zachman, 1987). The Zachman Framework provides five different views (planner, owner, designer, builder, and subcontractor), each addressing the set of Aristotelian interrogatives (what, who, when, how, where, and why) to create a set of 36 cells or primitives that contain different possible types of models. The set of possible models within a cell constitutes composites that are integrated sets of products for each view. As discussed in more detail shortly, the Zachman Framework is a schema or what he also analogizes to a periodic table of elements for an enterprise. It is not a methodology, but rather a guide for locating work done in various architectures, and serves as a benchmark for comparative frameworks.

For a number of years, Zachman resisted various attempts by various organizations to purchase his framework as their intellectual property. When one of the authors of this book first met Zachman while the former was a contract consultant to NCR, the company wanted to negotiate such a relationship. Zachman instead maintained the integrity of his concept, wanting it to serve as a general basis for all architectural work. NCR developed its own version, the Global IT Planning Methodology (GITP), which, like all other frameworks, is comparable to the Zachman Framework. In this sense, the Zachman Framework is a kind of meta-framework.

Because the Zachman Framework is ubiquitous, it did not require or specify a particular body of knowledge relevant for a certification process. The importance of Zachman's work cannot be understated, as it is foundational in the development and evolution of EA. For this reason, it is discussed in some detail in this book with an orientation toward how other frameworks can be mapped to it and enable cross-framework comparisons.

Zachman Institute Certification

Although virtually all EA certifications recognize the Zachman Framework, in 2005 Zachman, in collaboration with some colleagues, developed a certification program that entails attendance at a weeklong workshop and also added a classification schema based on years of experience and recommendations by other architects to achieve different levels of certification status. Again, this text covers the essential concepts relevant to those workshops and addresses the body of knowledge that Zachman and his associates consider relevant to being Zachman-certified.

The Open Group Certification

During the 1990s, The Open Group (TOG) began developing The Open Group Architecture Framework (TOGAF). This led to a number of versions of their architecture beginning with a proof of need in 1994. The "proof of concept" for the framework in 1995 resulted in the first version. This was followed by continued developments of the parts of TOGAF to be discussed later in this book, which included the Architecture Development Methodology (ADM), the Architecture and Solution Continuum, Reference Models (RMs), and so on. This resulted in the first major rollout in 2001 of TOGAF 7, which was based on the DoD C4ISR (command, control, communications, computers, intelligence, surveillance and reconnaissance) and the DoD models from the Command and Control System Target Architecture (C2STA).

In 2001, the same year FEAC was founded and established its unique and rigorous certification programs, TOG initiated its certification training courses for version 7. Students obtained certification by attending a weeklong workshop. As TOGAF developed over the next several years with TOGAF 8 and TOGAF 8.1, the certification process was roughly the same. Then, in February 2009, TOG introduced TOGAF 9 and for the first time required that students pass two levels of certification examinations, administered by Prometrics, to achieve certification. The exams are multiple-choice questions. Again, this text provides an overview to help readers who want to take the level 1 and level 2 exams.

Certification Process and Certificates

An important distinction needs to be made at this point between certification and certificates. Many of the "certification programs" on the market are in reality "certificate programs," where one is given a document attesting to the completion of a workshop or even some course of training. By "certification," we mean in contrast that after students undertake the requisite training and education in a field, they are examined according to their competencies and ability within it. This is what distinguishes FEAC certification from other programs currently on the market.

FEAC Certification Process

FEAC certifies and ensures that students have demonstrated the knowledge, skills, and capabilities of an architect by creating an actual EA in a practicum thesis project for their work program. This includes creating the full set of artifacts (models) comprising enterprise architecture—with a focus on all of the DoDAF 2.0's 52 models and views. As discussed later, FEAC uses the DoDAF 2.0 as a comprehensive set of views and models that are also found in whole or in part in the other major architecture frameworks. Besides ensuring that students know how to build effectively the range of models or artifacts involved, FEAC attests that students are able to select the appropriate views and models for an EA that satisfactorily fit their project's purpose. In this way, FEAC ensures that its graduates both can "talk the EA talk" as well as "walk the EA walk."

Learning Objectives for This Book

It is the goal of this book to prepare the reader for FEAC certification by covering the major EA concepts and helping the reader to demonstrate competencies in the following areas:

- Be able to select and build appropriate artifacts and models for fit-for-purpose architectures
- Be able to develop EA principles
- Understand and be able to use Reference Models, including the FEA RM
- Be able to create segment architectures using FSAM and RSAM
- Be able to employ TOGAF ADM, Spewak, and DoDAF Six Step methodologies
- Be able to engage in EA analysis and build actual customer deliverables
- Be able to utilize EA for Capital Planning and Investment Control (CPIC) in FEA, Joint Capabilities Integration and Development System (JCIDS) in DoDAF, and Portfolio Management

- Integrate Enterprise Security Architecture into EA
- Be able to utilize EA for SOA and cloud computing
- Be able to conduct EA analysis and queries
- Use EA for organizational transformation

Scope of the FEAC Certification Syllabus

The FEAC certification process is based on the following foundation.

Formal Coursework

Five core courses are taken over a period of about three months that cover the material presented in this book:

- Framework Basics
- Core Models of a Integrated Architecture
- EA Planning
- EA Implementation
- EA Integration

Additional special topics cover contemporary subjects allied to enterprise architecture, such as the DoD JCIDS, Portfolio Management, and SOA.

Formally graded assignments and examinations in each of the individual subjects test the candidate's knowledge of and familiarity with the subject.

Practicum Project

To obtain FEAC certification, students are required to create a portion of an enterprise architecture, which can be part of a larger EA effort for a governmental agency, military organization, or company. Because FEAC works in conjunction with our accredited university partners, this work is done within the timeframe of an academic term of three months. Consequently, it is beyond the scope of our programs for any student to create most organizational architectures. What is important to FEAC is that students are able to demonstrate their understanding of EA and be able to construct real EA models that can be used as actual deliverables in a larger EA program. However, in some instances, a full EA is possible; these are smaller projects that can be managed within the academic term.

We care that students be able to define clearly an architectural problem that can be addressed using enterprise architecture. Students must be able to select a set of models from those available and with that set build architectural building blocks and artifacts that have real purpose. Consequently, time and project management are critical to the process. Some examples of delimited practicum that our students have developed include the following:

- Global Disaster Response Planning (GDRP) enterprise architecture as the DoD's approach to construct timely and agile crisis action plans that fulfill national security objectives. This practicum modeled the as-is GDRP enterprise architecture effort, including descriptions of the architecture artifacts.

- A Tornado Notification Enterprise Architecture for the National Weather Service (NWS). The practicum provided models detailing the NWS tornado notification process.

- Reference architecture relevant to identity management implementations within the federal enterprise such that it can be continuously aligned and integrated to realize both the citizen-centric performance objectives of the federal government and the simplification of the Federal Enterprise Architecture.

- Communications and data restoration architecture that integrates into and complements the present National Aeronautics and Space Administration (NASA) Enterprise Architecture. The practicum defines a complementary architecture that facilitates the use of NASA Marshal Space Flight Center communication and data restoration services at any NASA facility during a disaster (natural or otherwise).

Questions

1. Discuss what motivates (or hinders) EA development in your organization. What are the key drivers for EA in your enterprise? What are the key de-motivators?

2. How does the Gartner Group's hype cycle relate to your organization's adoption of EA? Where is your enterprise in the continuum of expectations

related to EA? What has been the history of your organization with respect to other new technologies, such as SOA, cloud computing, and semantic web technology?

3. What were the early reasons for the emergence of EA? Are those reasons still valid? Are there new reasons driving the need for EA? What are they?

4. What are the provisions of the Clinger-Cohen Act, in brief? What was the driver for the Clinger-Cohen Act? Are the factors that led to the Clinger-Cohen Act pre-1996 still valid today?

5. What is the relationship between enterprise architecture and enterprise transformation? What are the dimensions of enterprise transformation?

6. What is the relationship between enterprise architecture and systems engineering? How are they different?

7. What is the role of project management as a discipline in enterprise architecture? Think of two roles: projects that are related to the development of the EA itself and projects that represent transformation initiatives or investments.

8. What is the relationship between enterprise architecture and the SDLC? What is the role of EA in defining requirements for software development?

9. What are patterns? How are patterns useful in codifying knowledge representations? How are patterns used to replicate entire enterprise structures? Discuss the applicability of EA patterns in constructing, for example, fast food franchises.

10. Why is EA certification beneficial to enterprises? What are the elements of EA certification? How is EA certification as described in this book different from or similar to other certification processes such as product certifications from, for example, Microsoft or professional certifications such as the Project Management Institute?

11. Should EA be restricted to use in information technology planning or is it applicable to all aspects of the enterprise such as the value-added business processes, inbound logistics, outbound logistics, and sales and marketing, for instance? Discuss why, or why not, and present examples of how EA can be used in the IT realm as well as in the business realm.

Reference List

Fenn, Jackie, and Raskino, Mark. (2008). *Mastering the hype cycle: how to choose the right innovation at the right time.* Cambridge, Massachusetts: Gartner Inc., Harvard Business Press.

Lankhorst, Marc. 2009. *Enterprise architecture at work: modeling, communication and analysis.* Springer.

Zachman, John. 1987. *A framework for information systems architecture.* IBM Publication G321-5298.

1.2

Enterprise
Architecture
Concepts

T his section of the book introduces fundamental concepts related to enterprise architecture. The purpose of this chapter is to lay the groundwork of terminology that is used throughout the book and to provide a grasp of the fundamentals of enterprise architecture.

Enterprise

An enterprise, informally, is a group of people engaged in purposeful activities with a common motive. This broad definition includes large corporations such as IBM and AT&T as well as small businesses, the executive branch of the United States government, and a small municipal agency. The enterprise test is that the motivation be common and that the activities be collaborative in support of the common purpose.

Why is an enterprise concept important? The enterprise concept raises the collaboration aspect and the common motivation that people tend to forget in their preoccupation with daily activities. An enterprise exists for a larger purpose than the output of daily activities. Threads link the activity and output of one person or organization with the activity and output of others. Understanding these linkages is a very important aspect of streamlining the collection of activities that together fulfill the purpose of the enterprise.

Enterprises can be defined at any level of abstraction. General Motors as an enterprise supplies automotive products and solutions to the world. But a manufacturer of transmission assemblies, supplying General Motors with transmission assemblies for automobile manufacture, is also an enterprise. The hardware parts supplier supplying parts to the transmission manufacturer is likewise an enterprise. Therefore, before proceeding to develop an enterprise architecture, the first order of business is to describe carefully the scope or extent of the enterprise.

It is important to understand the relationships between the component enterprises of a larger enterprise as well as relationships between partner enterprises. These relationships may be dictatorial as in the case of reporting organizations or may be diplomatic for organizations that do not have formal reporting relationships. Some of the issues related to culture are discussed in Chapter 2.1 as well as styles of influencing that may be brought to bear in managing these inter-enterprise relationships.

How does one break up complexity of enterprises into smaller units? In the commercial world, a large complex enterprise is broken down into smaller business units, each responsible for some area of business or "product lines." In the government, often, this breakdown of the enterprise is in the form of functional organizations responsible for various business functions. In holding companies, each part of the business that forms a conglomerate is a smaller enterprise that has a financial (profit and loss) relationship with the parent enterprise.

Segments

In any case, governing a large enterprise involves partitioning the large enterprise into smaller enterprises called *enterprise segments*, or *segments* for short. At each stage, of the partitioning, one or more criteria may be used to determine the scope of the segments:

- **Partitioning along business areas**   Widely differing business areas are partitioned into widely different sub-enterprises. An area of business may therefore be an enterprise segment. If the business areas are large and complex, a further partitioning may be required.
- **Partitioning along product lines or service areas**   In product- or service-based enterprises, each product line or service area may have differing characteristics and therefore different "enterprise patterns" for fulfillment. An area of business, line of business, product line, or service area may be a legitimate segment of an enterprise architecture. If the product line is broad or complex to produce, further partitioning into smaller segments may be required.
- **Partitioning along functional lines**   Areas such as marketing, sales, engineering, and manufacturing may all be segments of the larger enterprise architecture. Functional architectures, without the integrating mechanism that unifies the functions and cross-threads processes that are performed by individual functions, results in stovepipe processes that may be optimized by the function but not for the enterprise. If the portion producing hubcaps efficiently produces 200 hubcaps a minute for an assembly line assembling 1 car per minute, which consumes only 4 of the hubcaps, producing more hubcaps faster will not improve the overall throughput of cars coming off the assembly line.

Why is segmenting the complexity of enterprise architecture into manageable portions useful?

Decomposition is a common technique to address the analysis of complex concepts. Decomposing a large enterprise into segments helps make the architecture development and the analysis easier. Also, the large, complex enterprise is an abstract concept for most stakeholders involved in the day-to-day operations of the enterprise. Decomposing an enterprise into something smaller also brings closeness of the issues and architecture elements to such stakeholders. Arguably, the stakeholder pyramid has a small but very influential group at the top, for which the enterprise vantage point is both important and useful. But there is a larger group of stakeholders in the middle and at the bottom of the stakeholder pyramid who have a stake in the daily operations of the enterprise. Without bringing the detail down to their level of abstraction, the enterprise architecture simply becomes an academic exercise for upper management.

Segments also provide direct visibility of operations that can be tied to specific projects and initiatives. This direct tie-in allows portfolio managers who are balancing the investments in projects and initiatives to make a more accurate impact assessment of the project/initiative on the specific operational activities undertaken within an enterprise segment.

Initiatives and Solutions

What is a solution? A solution is a system that provides automated or nonautomated support for business processes. We use the word *system* in the general sense as a set of components that together provide the functionality support and desired outputs for a business process. A system may be comprised of smaller systems or cooperate and collaborate with other systems. We use the terms *family of systems* and *system of systems* to designate these relationships.

An initiative or a project is responsible for delivering a single solution or a family of solutions or for contributing to some aspect of a solution. An initiative is a collection or resources aimed at achieving an explicit purpose or outcome. A project is a schedule of activities that will implement an initiative and expend the resources allocated to that initiative. Together, initiatives and projects are used to transform an enterprise to a desired end state. Enterprise architecture provides the knowledge base for planning this transformation in an orderly manner, recognizing dependencies, risks, and issues before actual transformation projects are undertaken.

Architecture

What is an architecture? Very simply, an architecture—or more correctly, an architecture description—is a representation of the elements and the relationships between those elements as well as the rules that guide the behavior of those elements.

Formally, an architecture is defined by ANSI/IEEE Standard 1471-2000 as "The fundamental organization of a system, embodied in its components, their relationships to each other and the environment, and the principles governing its design and evolution."

An architecture has notions of the following:

- Components that form a whole
- Relationships among the components
- Principles that govern the design of the components
- Principles that govern the evolution of the components as well as their relationships in the context of the system they comprise

Architectural Description

An architectural description is an electronic or paper representation of all aspects of an architecture. We will use the term *architecture description* synonymously with the word *architecture* throughout this book.

An architectural description is a strategic information asset that describes the current and/or desired relationships among an organization's business, mission, and management processes and the supporting infrastructure (Department of Defense Architecture Framework 2.0, 2009).

An architectural description is a formal description of an information system, organized in a way that supports reasoning about the structural properties of the system. It defines the components or building blocks that make up the overall information system and provides a plan from which products can be procured, and systems developed, that will work together to implement the overall system. It thus enables you to manage your overall IT investment in a way that meets the needs of your business (The Open Group Architecture Framework Version 9, 2009).

Architectural descriptions define a strategy for managing change, along with transitional processes needed to develop the state of a business or mission into one that is more efficient, effective, current, and capable of providing those actions needed to fulfill its goals and objectives.

Architectural descriptions may illustrate an organization, or a part of it, as it presently exists; any changes desired (whether operational or technology-driven); and the strategies and projects employed to achieve the desired transformation.

An architectural description also defines principles and goals and sets direction on issues, such as the promotion of interoperability, intra- and interagency information sharing, and improved processes that facilitate key DoD program decisions.

Implicit and Explicit Architectural Descriptions

Architecture (or some planned thinking, planned arrangement, and planned layout) exists in everything we see around us. Architecture exists in the way the runways and taxiways were laid out at Richard M. Nixon Airport. Architecture exists in the way the information systems were first conceived and planned for back office operations. Architecture exists in the terminal buildings, their floor plans, the concourses, and the layout of the various airport facilities. Architecture existed in the building of the ancient pyramids in Egypt, architecture existed for the design of the rule-changing IBM 370 mainframe computer, and architecture exists in every video game played by teenagers today.

Architectures are often implicit to the world at large or manifest themselves through published "blueprints" that are used by various stakeholders for various purposes (see Figures 1.2-1 and 1.2-2). When the author was working for a large

FIGURE 1.2-1 Implicit Architecture

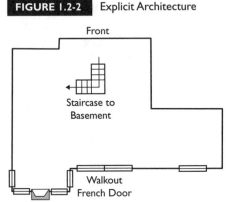

FIGURE 1.2-2 Explicit Architecture

Front

Staircase to
Basement

Walkout
French Door

commercial building heating, ventilation, and air conditioning (HVAC) control supplier, the joke was that the Empire State Building was being held up by all the copper wiring inside! Each succeeding contractor ran its own wires because it did not have the wiring plans and simply cut off the end points of the old wire and left the wire in the building. Implicit architectures are not very useful to people who have to remodel a system, an enterprise segment, or an entire enterprise. Making architectures explicit is therefore the first step in understanding the present state of an enterprise, a segment, or a solution.

As-Is and To-Be Enterprise States

Sometimes it is said that every act of construction must begin with an act of deconstruction. This is because it is only through deconstruction we often divine original intent. We can make a determination if future intent is different from the original intent and make architectural changes accordingly. Deconstruction of current operations, systems, and technology infrastructure results in a baseline or as-is architecture. The enterprise vision or transformation objective results in a target or desired end-state for the enterprise. Figures 1.2-3 and 1.2-4 represent the as-is and the target states respectively.

Considerable debate has occurred within the architecture community over the value of baselining enterprise states. The argument is that, in a constantly

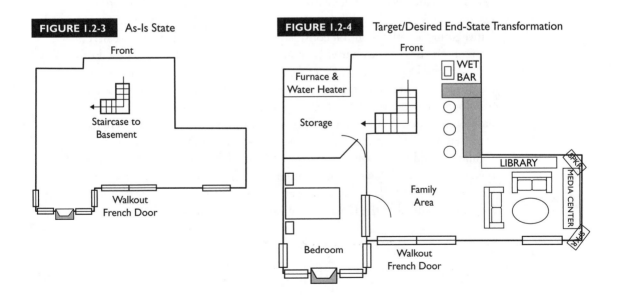

FIGURE 1.2-3 As-Is State

Front

Staircase to Basement

Walkout French Door

FIGURE 1.2-4 Target/Desired End-State Transformation

Front

Furnace & Water Heater

Storage

WET BAR

Family Area

LIBRARY

SPKR MEDIA CENTER SPKR

Bedroom

Walkout French Door

changing world, the architecting enterprise gains more benefit from modeling and moving the enterprise to the target state rather than from spending large amounts of architecting resources looking back at the current state of operations. In areas such as civil engineering projects, any remodeling effort has to ride on the back of an understanding of the current construction. Any act of demolition requires an understanding of what to demolish and to limit the impact of the demolition.

The fact of the matter is that many transformational initiatives in very large organizations such as the Department of Defense have failed to take into account the traumatic changes that are imposed upon the enterprise and often the resulting (often unwitting) sabotage of those initiatives by human beings unwilling to change. A transformation plan is required that reflects understanding of the current state and the cultural factors of the enterprise and sets realistic transformational initiatives that are phased according to the enterprise's ability to absorb change.

The time needed to develop a baseline architecture is often perceived as a luxury in the commercial world, where the pace of change is often forced by competition and alternatives that are outside the control of the architecting enterprise. In this world, in situations where new products and services are offered, entire new enterprises are created by founding, merger, or acquisition. These new enterprises exhibit complex behaviors that must be factored into the transformation plan. Often, these new enterprises behave like startups—an area where traditional enterprise architecture study has not generally focused. They are driven by extreme financial goals under extreme time constraints, often with extreme resource constraints—and the common motivation of individual profit and reward outweighing all other cultural considerations—for a period of a few years.

In enterprises whose charter is enduring, such as federal agencies established by law or the Department of Defense, where doctrine, policy, organization, and force structures and training determine the enterprise's characteristics, the development of an as-is state, the formulation of a to-be or target state, and an orderly transformational plan comprised of initiatives and projects comprise a very viable strategy. Sometimes for enterprises that are founded and based on laws, regulation, and policy, we talk about an idealized "should-be" state that is predicated on compliance with laws, regulations, and policies. Such an enterprise is arguably what is benchmarked during investigations by third-party investigators such as the Inspector General or the Government Accounting Office (GAO).

Benefits of an Explicit Architecture

Why is an architecture concept important? An architecture is an explicit representation of the elements of an enterprise, solution, or segment and their relationships. Without this explicit representation, the enterprise is unable to accomplish the following, for example:

- Prioritize resource allocations between the various competing demands for resources
- Determine the viability of transformation in terms of the impact, the need for resources and change, and the ability to achieve the desired end states
- Govern the expending of current resources to determine whether they are being correctly applied in achieving the enterprise's mission
- Boil down transformational objectives crisply into initiatives (and projects that follow) that focus on aspects of the enterprise for change
- Develop roadmaps for modernization
- Develop roadmaps for orderly replacement of obsolete technology and infrastructure
- Develop roadmaps for acquiring skills and specialties in the workforce required to operate the enterprise into the future

Architecture Viewpoints

The difficulty in representing architecture descriptions in a universal format stems from the fact that different stakeholders of the enterprise have different viewpoints and interests. The person who is looking at the architecture for shared data management has a different view of information than the person building a specific application system for supporting a set of specific business processes.

The need to support multiple viewpoints is therefore fundamental for architecture. During the inception of an architecture development, the architect must determine which viewpoints will be supported by architecture representations. This section describes some examples of architecture viewpoints.

Governance Viewpoint

An example of this viewpoint is from the Office of Management and Budget, which is interested in the prioritization and allocation of funds, issues of capitalization versus working capital, and management of government resources. Architecture models that support governance relate to justification, return on investment, relevance to mission, and capital investment models.

Project Viewpoint

This viewpoint is from stakeholders responsible for programs and projects that are transformational in nature. Architecture models that support a project viewpoint depict project phases and timelines, project relationships and dependencies, and portfolio views of multiple projects.

Capability Viewpoint

In organizations such as the military (including the Coast Guard), first responders such as fire fighters, and emergency services that cannot define specific missions but must remain ready for a family of missions, the act of planning is based on acquiring capabilities that define a state of readiness. The viewpoint of a capability portfolio involves prioritizing investments for acquiring specific capabilities while ignoring other less important ones as well as determining capability dependencies and incorporating the capability dependencies introduced by acquisitions. Architecture models that support the capability viewpoint are capability taxonomies, capability dependencies, relationships among capabilities to the projects, and organizations developing the capabilities.

Operational Viewpoint

In functioning enterprises, the business processes, mission activities, and support activities constitute continuing operations. In the baselining of an enterprise, an understanding of these operations is essential. In the military, a military operation must orchestrate multiple activities from multiple people and ensure information, capabilities, systems, systems functions, and activity handoffs are all represented to ensure completeness and ensure predictable outcomes.

There are many other viewpoints that one can potentially define. One of the functions of an architecture framework is to codify the viewpoints to enable multiple enterprises to align their architectures. For example, the DoD Architecture Framework describes eight common viewpoints:

- All Viewpoint
- Capability Viewpoint (CV)
- Project Viewpoint (PV)
- Operational Viewpoint (OV)
- Systems Viewpoint (SV)
- Services Viewpoint (SvcV)
- Standards Viewpoint (StdV)
- Data and Information Viewpoint (DIV)

The Open Group Architecture Framework (TOGAF) and the Federal Enterprise Architecture Framework (FEAF) also describe common viewpoints, such as the business, data, and application systems.

Architecture Models

Architecture models are electronic or paper representations of some aspect of an architecture for some specific audience. Models are comprised of model elements that are also architecture elements. Model elements have relationships based on some defined semantics—that is, they are not haphazard assemblies of architecture elements but follow constraints described by a methodology or accepted set of practices. These semantics may be driven by the laws of nature, existential relationships, human creations, or abstractions. Architecture models are therefore pictorial or other representations that have structure and meaning to specific audiences.

Models are also blueprints for audiences who understand what they are trying to communicate. Just as a floor plan conveys the layout of various parts of a building to a number of audiences—from the homeowner to the architect to the city inspector—a carefully constructed model that is compliant with conventions and well laid out conveys a wealth of meaning to the right people.

Enterprise Architecture

Informally, an enterprise architecture is the concept of "architecture," presented earlier, applied to the concept of "enterprise," also presented earlier. There are many competing formal definitions for enterprise architecture depending on the interest and viewpoint of the defining organizations:

- An EA provides a clear and comprehensive picture of the structure of an entity, whether it is an organization or a functional or mission area. It is an essential tool for effectively and efficiently engineering business processes and for implementing and evolving supporting systems (Government Accounting Office, 2003). The interest of GAO is accountability.

- Simply stated, enterprise architectures are "blueprints" for systematically and completely defining an organization's current (baseline) or desired (target) environment. Enterprise architectures are essential for evolving information systems, developing new systems, and inserting emerging technologies that optimize their mission value (Federal Chief Information Officer Council, 2001). The interest of the CIO is IT and information systems.

- Enterprise architecture is a management practice to maximize the contribution of an agency's resources, IT investments, and system development activities to achieve the agency's performance goals. Architecture describes clear relationships from strategic goals and objectives through investments to measurable performance improvements for the entire enterprise or a portion (or segment) of the enterprise (Federal Enterprise Architecture Program Office, Office of Management and Budget, 2007). The interest of the OMB is management and financial governance.

- Enterprise architecture is the principle structural mechanism for establishing a basis for assimilating high rates of change, advancing the state of the art in enterprise design, managing the knowledge base of the enterprise, and integrating the technology into the fabric of the enterprise. Enterprise architecture is cross-disciplinary, requiring diverse skills, methods, and tools within and beyond the technology community (Federal Chief Information Officer Council, 1999). The interest of the CIO council in this area is the need for a common architecture framework.

- Enterprise architecture is the organizing logic for business processes and IT infrastructure reflecting the integration and standardization requirements of the firm's operating model (Ross, Jeanne W, Weill, Peter, and Robertson, David, 2001).

■ The National Association of State Chief Information Officers (NASCIO) defines enterprise architecture as follows: "Enterprise architecture is a management engineering discipline that presents a holistic, comprehensive view of the enterprise including strategic planning, organization, relationships, business process, information, and operations. The organization must be viewed as fluid—changing over time as necessary based on the environment and management's response to that environment" (National Association of State Chief Information Officers (NASCIO), 2004). NASCIO's definition is broader than simply the IT perspective and encompasses a more holistic view of the enterprise and starts with the strategic plan.

Architecture Framework

Because architecture development can be performed using a variety of tools and techniques and methodologies, it becomes difficult to compare, contrast, or merge the architectures from two different organizations. Each of these methodologies uses different terminology to represent architecture elements.

Note the following examples:

■ Enterprise 1 is representing the view of data using the Unified Modeling Language (UML) and a class model. The architecture elements in the model representation will include classes, class properties, class operations, and class relationships such as aggregation, association, generalization, and instantiation.

■ Enterprise 2 uses Integrated Definition Language 1X (IDEF1X) as the data modeling technique. This enterprise represents its models using architecture elements such as entity, attribute, relationship, identifying relationship, nonidentifying relationship, and subcategory relationship.

■ Enterprise 1 and Enterprise 2 are sub-enterprises of a larger Enterprise 3. This enterprise wants to compare these models to determine overlapped entities and contradictions in attributes and relationships. Doing so involves familiarity with the two modeling techniques and the ability to transform a model built using one methodology to the other.

■ With a little bit of difficulty, the transformation may be effected. But if the two enterprises did not know that they were trying to rationalize similar types of models (such as in the case when there was a process model with data elements from Enterprise 1 and a data model modeling process items as data objects in Enterprise 2), the problem of transformation may well be unsolvable.

Put simply, an architecture framework rationalizes the vocabulary of architecting and provides a conceptual framework that allows comparison, aggregation, and merging of models from multiple architectures. The DoD Architecture Framework is one such framework that is primarily concerned with standardizing architecture vocabulary.

On the other hand, other frameworks such as the Federal Enterprise Architecture Framework are concerned with categorizing varieties of objects in a standard manner.

We will examine the formal definitions of architecture framework for these various types:

■ An architecture framework provides guidance and rules for structuring, classifying, and organizing architectures (Department of Defense, 2007).

■ The Federal Enterprise Architecture Framework provides an organized structure and a collection of common terms by which federal segments can integrate their respective architectures into the Federal Enterprise Architecture (Federal Chief Information Officer Council, 1999).

■ The Framework for Enterprise Architecture (introduced in the previous chapter as the Zachman Framework) is a classification scheme for descriptive representations—descriptive representations of anything. (I learned about it from looking at descriptive representations of airplanes, buildings, locomotives, battleships, and so on.) I applied the same logical schema to enterprises. The framework has nothing to do with information systems unless the enterprise has some stored programming devices and electronic media installed, in which case those technologies will be described in Row 4 (not Row 1, nor Row 2, nor Row 3). The Rows 1, 2, and 3 models are descriptive of the enterprise independent of any implementation technologies (Zachman, 1987).

Benefits of Architecture Frameworks

The DoD Architecture Framework, for example, promotes the following benefits:

- An architecture framework provides guidance and rules for structuring, classifying, and organizing multiple architecture descriptions.

- A common architecture framework provides the guidance and rules for developing, representing, and understanding multiple architectures based on a common denominator across internal and external organizational boundaries.

- An architecture framework is intended to ensure that architecture descriptions can be compared and related across programs, mission areas, and, ultimately, the enterprise, thus establishing the foundation for analyses that support decision-making processes throughout the enterprise.

- Architecture frameworks first and foremost provide a common organizational structure for multiple diverse architectures. For example, the DoDAF 1.5 organizes architecture views into four types: Operational, Systems and Services, Standards, and All-View (DoDAF 2.0 extends these to eight types). All DoDAF-compliant architectures, when representing operational activities, for example, will use the Operational View. Similarly, the types of models that support these common types of views and their purposes are spelled out in the DoDAF using the same code and name—for example, OV-5 Activity Model. All architecture descriptions that are DoDAF-compliant and provide activity models will use the structure for an OV-5 Activity Model. Using the same framework across multiple enterprises is essential to support comparison of architectures as well as the ability to depict activities, performer relationships and dependencies, and resource exchanges and to define rules of engagement that cross enterprise boundaries.

- Architecture frameworks also provide a common architecture terminology. For example, DoDAF 2.0 defines architectural terms such as performers, activities, system functions, systems, and services. When architectures are compliant to the same framework, they use the same architectural terms. Architectural frameworks are mechanisms designed to prevent architecture description dissonance. By reducing the terminology dissonance, it is possible to increase the ability to compare like terms across architectures and to start developing enterprise taxonomies of architecture term instances that are well arranged and standardized, thus enhancing further abilities to integrate architectures.

The Federal CIO Council promotes the Federal Enterprise Architecture Framework based on the following benefits:

"A federal-wide collaboration tool is needed to collect common architecture information and build a repository for storing this information. A Federal Enterprise Architecture Framework is such a tool and repository.

The framework allows the federal government to accomplish the following:

- Organize federal information on a federal-wide scale
- Promote information sharing among federal organizations
- Help federal organizations develop their architectures
- Help federal organizations quickly develop their IT investment processes
- Serve customer needs better, faster, and cost effectively

Example Architecture Frameworks

The references contain detailed information about the various frameworks mentioned in the subsections that follow. This book presents a short description of some well-known frameworks. Not all of the frameworks discussed may assist in comparison, integration, or aggregation of diverse architectures, but all of them universally help develop a consistent and uniform architecture element terminology and/or taxonomy.

Zachman Framework

First articulated in the 1980s, since then refined moderately, the most durable conceptual framework for architecture work is the Zachman Framework (see Figure 1.2-5). John Zachman observed from philosophy and journalism the six interrogatives (what, how, where, who, when, and why) that were mutually exclusive but collectively complete for describing a situation or set of situations. He noted that these interrogatives were equally applicable to describing a collection of systems that support a business as well as the business operations that the system automates or assists. When he used the six interrogatives as a classification scheme for items in the business and IT world, he found that there were overlapping terms with the same name and different meanings across viewpoints. Zachman then went on to discover that the taxonomy had to be a two-dimensional classification: six interrogatives and six perspectives or viewpoints to resolve classification issues. In essence, each viewpoint introduced its own terminology, and traveling between

FIGURE 1.2-5 Zachman Framework

ENTERPRISE ARCHITECTURE: A FRAMEWORK™

	WHAT Data	HOW Function	WHERE Network	WHO People	WHEN Time	WHY Motivation
SCOPE {contextual}	List of Things Important to the Business Entity = Class of Business Thing	List of Processes the Business Performs Process = Class of Business Process	List of Locations in Which the Business Operates Location = Major Business Location	List of Organizations Important to the Business People = Major Organizational Unit	List of Events/Cycles Significant to the Business Time = Major Business Event/Cycle	Lists of Business Goals/Strategies Ends, Means = Major Business Goal/Strategy
BUSINESS MODEL {conceptual}	E.g. Semantic Model Entity = Business Entity Relationship = Business Relationship	E.g. Business Resource Model Process = Business Process I/O = Business Resources	E.g. Business Logistic System Node = Business Location Link = Business Linkage	E.g. Work Flow Model People = Organizational Unit Work = Work Product	E.g. Master Schedule Time = Business Event Cycle = Business Cycle	E.g. Business Plan End = Business Objective Means = Business Strategy
SYSTEM MODEL {logical}	E.g. Logical Data Model Entity = Data Entity Relationship = Data Relationship	E.g. Application Architecture Process = Application Process I/O = User Views	E.g. Distributed System Architecture Node = D/S Function (Processors, Storage, Etc) Link = Use Characteristics	E.g. Human Interface Architecture People = Role Work = Deliverable	E.g. Processing Structure Event = System Event Cycle = Processing Cycle	E.g. Business Rule Model End = Structural Assertions Means = Action Assertions
TECHNOLOGY MODEL {physical}	E.g. Physical Data Model Entity = Segment/Table/Etc Relationship = Pointer/Key/Etc	E.g. System Design Process = Computer Function I/O = Data Elements/Sets	E.g. Technology Architecture Node = Hardware/System Software Link = Line Specifications	E.g. Presentation Architecture People = User Work = Screen Format	E.g. Control Structure Time = Execute Cycle = Component Cycle	E.g. Rule Design End = Condition Means = Action
DETAILED REPRESENTATIONS {out-of-context}	E.g. Data Definition Entity = Field Relationship = Address	E.g. Program Process = Language Statement I/O = Control Block	E.g. Network Architecture Node = Address Link = Protocol	E.g. Security Architecture People = Identity Work = Job	E.g. Timing Definition Time = Interrupt Cycle = Machine Cycle	E.g. Data Specification End = Sub-condition Means = Step
FUNCTIONING ENTERPRISE	E.g. DATA	E.g. FUNCTION	E.g. NETWORK	E.g. ORGANIZATION	E.g. SCHEDULE	E.g. STRATEGY

viewpoints was not a one-to-many decomposition but more appropriately a many-to-many transformation.

The Zachman Framework provides a formal and highly structured way of defining an enterprise. It is based on a two-dimensional classification model and displayed as a matrix, which utilizes six basic communication interrogatives (what, how, where, who, when, and why) and six distinct, intersecting model types that relate to stakeholder groups (strategists, executive leaders, architects, engineers, technicians, and workers) to give a holistic view of the enterprise. Decomposition of the matrix allows for several diagrams of the same data sets to be developed for the same architecture, where each diagram shows an increasing level of detail.

Federal Enterprise Architecture Framework (FEAF)

In September 1999, the Federal CIO Council published the Federal Enterprise Architecture Framework Version 1.1 for developing an EA within any federal agency or for a system that transcends multiple interagency boundaries. It builds on common business practices and designs that cross organizational boundaries. The FEAF provides an enduring standard for developing and documenting architecture descriptions of high-priority areas. It provides guidance in describing architectures for multi-organizational functional segments of the federal government.

The FEAF partitions a given architecture into business, data, applications, and technology architectures (see Figure 1.2-6). The FEAF currently includes the first three columns of the Zachman framework and the Spewak EA planning methodology.

The FEAF is graphically represented as a 3 × 5 matrix with architecture types (Data, Application, and Technology) on one axis of the matrix, and perspectives (Planner, Owner, Designer, Builder, and Subcontractor) on the other (see Table 1.2-1). The corresponding EA products are listed within the cells of the matrix.

FIGURE 1.2-6

Federal
Enterprise
Architecture
Framework

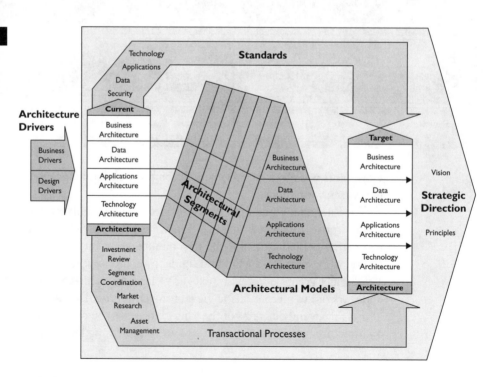

TABLE I.2-I	Mapping FEAF to Zachman Framework Rows		
	Data Architecture	**Application Architecture**	**Technology Architecture**
Planner Perspective	List of Business Objects	List of Business Processes	List of Business Locations
Owner Perspective	Semantic Model	Business Process Model	Business Logistics System
Designer Perspective	Logical Data Model	Application Architecture	System Geographic Deployment Architecture
Builder Perspective	Physical Data Model	Systems Design	Technology Architecture
Subcontractor Perspective	Data Dictionary	Programs	Network Architecture

Department of Defense Architecture Framework (DoDAF) Version 2.0

DoDAF 2.0 was published in May 2009 and incorporates the lessons learned over a decade of DoD architecting using a common framework. DoDAF 2.0 is a first attempt at defining a framework that is more centrally focused on architecture data uniformity and consistency to support federation and integration needs while ensuring that architecture views and products are built "fit for purpose" —that is, they are not simply used to fulfill an obligatory role in some DoD process but are useful internally to the developing enterprises for their own operational, systems, and planning needs.

DoDAF V2.0 is a marked change from earlier versions of the Command, Control, Communications, Computers, Intelligence, Surveillance, and Reconnaissance Architecture Framework (C4ISRAF) or DoDAF, in that architects now have the freedom to create enterprise architectures to meet the demands of their customer requirements. The central core of DoDAF 2.0 is a data-centric approach where the creation of architectures to support decision making is secondary to the collection, storage, and maintenance of data needed for efficient and effective decisions. The architect and stakeholders select views to ensure that architectures will explain current and future states of the process or activity under review. Selecting architectural views carefully ensures that the views adequately explain the requirement and proposed solution in ways that will enhance the audience's understanding.

DoDAF 2.0 also provides, but does not require, a particular methodology in architecture development. The DoD Architecture Framework 2.0 Volume 1 contains numerous examples of how to utilize the DoDAF methodology either

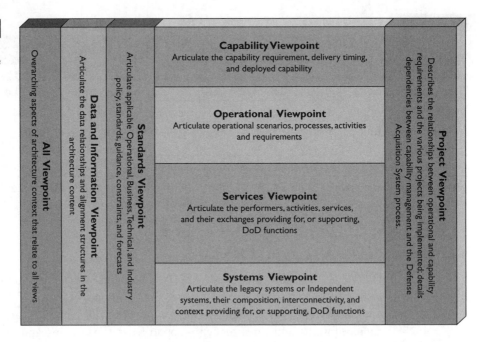

FIGURE 1.2-7

DoD Architecture
Framework
Viewpoints

alone or in conjunction with other methods. This volume provides guidance and suggestions on how to ensure that other proposed methods can be adapted as needed to meet the DoD requirements for data collection and storage.

Similarly, the views presented in DoDAF are examples, intended to serve as a possible visualization of a particular view (see Figure 1.2-7). DoDAF 2.0 also continues to provide support for views (that is, products developed with previous versions of the framework). These views do not require any particular graphical design by toolset vendors.

The Open Group Architecture Framework (TOGAF)

In the commercial EA world, The Open Group developed its own architecture framework that initially was based on a Department of Defense IT model, which has gone through several iterations to its current version, TOGAF 9. This version of the TOGAF is a comprehensive guide that provides a systems development lifecycle approach to developing an EA for organizations, known as the Architecture Development Methodology (ADM) (see Figure 1.2-8). The TOGAF also contains a number of metamodels and reference models, which provide guidance especially at

FIGURE 1.2-8

TOGAF
Architecture
Development
Methodology

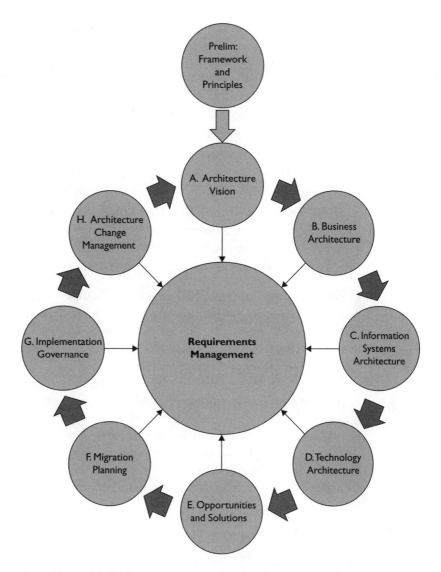

the IT level. The TOGAF recommends a program/project-based process approach that has well-defined tasks and deliverables in the form of artifacts or models not unlike the DoD Architecture Framework.

The TOGAF provides the methods and tools for assisting in the acceptance, production, use, and maintenance of enterprise architecture. It is based on an iterative process model supported by best practices and a reusable set of existing architecture assets. There are four types of architecture commonly accepted as subsets of an overall enterprise architecture, all of which TOGAF is designed to support:

- **Business (or Business Process) Architecture** This defines the business strategy, governance, organization, and key business processes.
- **Data Architecture** This describes the structure of an organization's logical and physical data assets and data management resources.
- **Applications Architecture** This kind of architecture provides a blueprint for the individual application systems to be deployed, their interactions, and their relationships to the core business processes of the organization.
- **Technology Architecture** This describes the logical software and hardware capabilities that are required to support the deployment of business, data, and application services. This includes IT infrastructure, middleware, networks, communications, processing, standards, and so on.

With these architecture types in mind, the TOGAF recognizes that there are two key elements of any enterprise architecture framework: the definition of the deliverables that the architecting activity should produce and a description of the method by which this activity should be done. Although most EA frameworks focus on a specific set of deliverables, few emphasize methods. Because TOGAF is considered a generic framework and is intended to be used in a wide variety of environments, it does not prescribe a specific set of deliverables; rather, it talks in general terms about the types of deliverable that need to be produced and focuses instead on the methods by which these should be developed. Consequently, TOGAF may be used either in its own right, with the generic deliverables that it describes, or these deliverables may be replaced by a more specific set, defined in any other framework (such as products or models described in Chapter 1.1).

Other Frameworks

This book will present other efforts, although not all of them may be deemed as frameworks. Some of them, such as the Enterprise Architecture Planning methodology from the late Dr. Steven Spewak, a pioneer in the area of enterprise architectures, represent a systematic and consistent method (process framework) to develop enterprise architecture and use it for developing and implementing transformation roadmaps. Arguably, EAP was one of the earliest to introduce the terms *business architecture*, *data architecture*, *applications architecture*, and *technology architecture* to the field, though these concepts may be traced back earlier to IBM's Business Systems Planning (BSP).

Enterprise Architecture Planning (EAP)

One of the earliest efforts at defining a framework for enterprise architecture was Spewak's Enterprise Architecture Planning (EAP) method (Spewak, 1992) (see Figure 1.2-9). Both a framework and a step-by-step method for developing and using enterprise architecture, EAP first formalized the needs for an architecture to represent shared items such as application function, shared technology platforms, and data. Formulated in the early 1990s to support the primary transformation of IT systems from the age of mainframes to the age of client-server processing technology, EAP was one of the early attempts to define an enterprisewide business architecture, data architecture, applications architecture, and technical infrastructure architecture, respectively. EAP formed the basis for the Federal Enterprise Architecture Framework established in 1999. The FEAF uses the four elemental architectures of the EAP and defines two transformational states—current baseline or as-is state—and the desired target state or to-be state. Transformation of an enterprise's state involves transforming all four types of architectures.

Although the utility of a unified view of data seems obvious today, in the early 1990s few enterprises perceived the need to unify the view of data. Applications tended to gather and manage their own data. Thus it was that customer information, product information, location information, and other data were sprinkled among many systems, causing update inconsistencies and selective invisibility as enterprises relied more and more on information systems to provide visibility into their businesses.

The vision in those days was a giant database of shared data that could be maintained using consistent business rules and data quality enforcement techniques with a number of lightweight, small-footprint applications accessing and updating the data.

FIGURE 1.2-9

Enterprise
Architecture
Planning

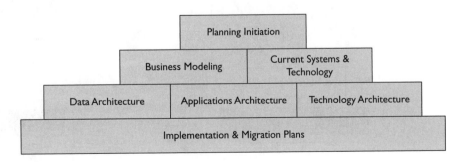

EAP established the first efforts at standardizing architecture elements across the enterprise and wresting control from individual systems and programs to treat the information assets as enterprise resources that need to be planned, managed, and controlled because they touch and affect many stakeholders. Arguably, EAP was the forerunner that inspired many enterprise data models and the current trend toward service-oriented architectures (SOAs).

C4ISR Architecture Framework

One of the earliest Department of Defense–wide architectural frameworks that treated the interplay among operational, systems, and technology elements was the Command, Control, Communications, Computers, Intelligence, Surveillance, and Reconnaissance (C4ISR) Framework (see Figure 1.2-10). The C4ISR Framework was one of the DoD's initial attempts to provide a means for architects to describe architecture in common terms and to build a set of integrated models, called architecture products, that share the same common architecture elements. Over the years, the C4ISR Framework has undergone several evolutions, ultimately generalized into the DoD Architecture Framework, which goes beyond C4ISR interests, and has now been replaced by the DoD Architecture Framework Version 2.0.

FIGURE 1.2-10

C4ISR 2.0 Framework Views and Relationships

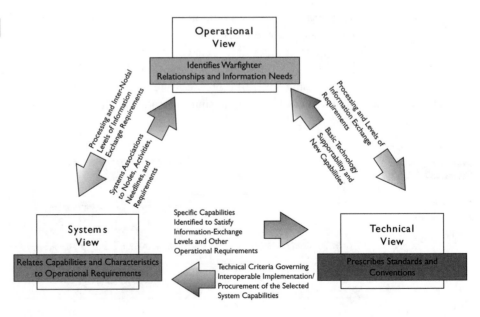

According to the DoD:

> The C4ISR Framework provides the rules, guidance, and product descriptions for developing and presenting architecture descriptions that ensure a common denominator for understanding, comparing, and integrating architectures. The application of the Framework will enable architectures to contribute most effectively to building interoperable and cost-effective military systems.

> The purpose of C4ISR architectures is to improve capabilities by enabling the quick synthesis of "go-to-war" requirements with sound investments leading to the rapid employment of improved operational capabilities, and enabling the efficient engineering of warrior systems. The ability to compare, analyze, and integrate architectures developed by the geographical and functional, unified Commands, Military Services, and Defense Agencies (hereinafter also referred to as Commands, Services, and Agencies, or C/S/As) from a cross-organizational perspective is critical to achieving these objectives.

> The *C4ISR Architecture Framework* is intended to ensure that the architecture descriptions developed by the Commands, Services, and Agencies are inter-relatable between and among each organization's operational, systems, and technical architecture views, and are comparable and integratable across Joint and combined organizational boundaries (C4ISR Architecture Framework Version 2.0 1997).

As implied by the title, the framework is currently directed at C4ISR architectures with the focus on C4ISR support to the warfighter. The objective was to develop a common unifying approach for the commands, military services, and defense agencies to follow in developing their various architectures. Although the specific focus has been C4ISR, the approach defined in the framework is readily extendible to other DoD functional areas, such as personnel management, systems acquisition, and finance.

The framework provides direction on how to *describe* architectures; it does not provide guidance in how to *design or implement* a specific architecture or how to *develop and acquire* systems of systems. The distinction between architecture description and architecture implementation is important to understand.

Although the framework provides a "product-focused" method for standardizing architecture descriptions, the products are intended to represent consistent architectural information. The goal is eventually to reach an "information-focused" method for consistent and integratable architectures. The C4ISR Core Architecture Data Model (CADM) was first articulated in the C4ISR Framework as a universal architecture data model, which is intended as a starting point for organizing and portraying the structure of common architecture information. For Version 2.0 of the framework, standardizing on architecture products is the only practical approach.

Federal Enterprise Architecture (FEA)

The FEA is not an architecture framework; it is the instance of the U.S. federal government's enterprise architecture. The FEA consists of a set of five blueprints that characterizes the operations of the entire federal government. Its taxonomical components—the five reference models—provide a vocabulary for categorizing the architecture elements of U.S. federal agencies. The FEA also formalizes notions of architecture segments and categorizes the various types of segments.

The FEA consists of a set of interrelated reference models designed to facilitate cross-agency analysis and the identification of duplicative investments, gaps, and opportunities for collaboration within and across agencies (see Figure 1.2-11). Collectively, the reference models comprise a framework for describing important elements of the FEA in a common and consistent way.

The five reference models are explained here.

Performance Reference Model (PRM)   The PRM is a framework for performance measurement, providing common output measurements throughout the federal government. It allows agencies to better manage the business of government at a strategic level by providing a means for using an agency's EA to measure the success of IT investments and their impact on strategic outcomes.

FIGURE 1.2-11

Federal
Enterprise
Architecture
Reference Models

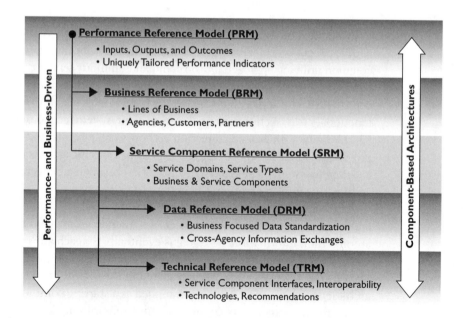

The PRM accomplishes these goals by establishing a common language by which agency EAs can describe the outputs and measures used to achieve program and business objectives. The model articulates the linkage between internal business components and the achievement of business and customer-centric outputs. Most importantly, it facilitates resource-allocation decisions based on comparative determinations of which programs and organizations are more efficient and effective. The taxonomy structure of the PRM is shown in Figure 1.2-12.

Business Reference Model (BRM)   The BRM provides a framework facilitating a functional (rather than organizational) view of the federal government's lines of business (LOBs), including its internal operations and its services for citizens, independent of the agencies, bureaus, and offices performing them. The BRM describes the federal government around common business areas instead of through a stovepiped, agency-by-agency view. It thus promotes agency collaboration and serves as the underlying foundation for the FEA and e-government strategies. The taxonomy structure of the BRM is shown in Figure 1.2-13.

Service Component Reference Model (SRM)   The SRM is a business-driven, functional framework classifying service components according to how they support business and performance objectives. It serves to identify and classify horizontal and vertical service components supporting federal agencies and their IT investments and assets. The model aids in recommending service capabilities to support the reuse of business components and services across the federal government. IT investments

FIGURE 1.2-12

Performance
Reference Model
Elements

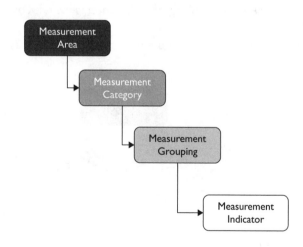

FIGURE 1.2-13

FEA Business
Reference Model
Elements

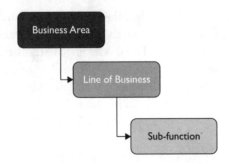

can be service providers or consumers. Service providers allow consumers to reuse
their business and technical capabilities.

The SRM is organized across horizontal service areas, independent of the business
functions, providing a leveragable foundation for reuse of applications, application
capabilities, components, and business services. The taxonomy structure of the SRM
is shown in Figure 1.2-14.

Technical Reference Model (TRM)   The TRM is a component-driven,
technical framework categorizing the standards and technologies to support and
enable the delivery of service components and capabilities. It also unifies existing
agency TRMs and e-government guidance by providing a foundation to advance
the reuse and standardization of technology and service components from a
governmentwide perspective.

Aligning agency capital investments to the TRM leverages a common,
standardized vocabulary, allowing interagency discovery, collaboration, and
interoperability. Agencies and the federal government will benefit from economies
of scale by identifying and reusing the best solutions and technologies to support

FIGURE 1.2-14

FEA Service
Reference Model
Elements

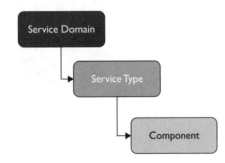

FES Technical
Reference Model
Elements

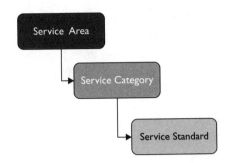

their business functions, mission, and target architecture. The taxonomy structure of the TRM is shown in Figure 1.2-15.

Data Reference Model (DRM)   The DRM is a flexible and standards-based framework to enable information sharing and reuse across the federal government via the standard description and discovery of common data and the promotion of uniform data management practices. The DRM provides a standard means by which data can be described, categorized, and shared. Figure 1.2-16 shows the taxonomy structure of the DRM.

The following are reflected within each of the DRM's three standardization areas:

- **Data Description**   Provides a means to describe data uniformly, thereby supporting its discovery and sharing.
- **Data Context**   Facilitates discovery of data through an approach to the categorization of data according to taxonomies. Additionally, it enables the definition of authoritative data assets within a common community of interest.

FEA Data
Reference Model
Elements

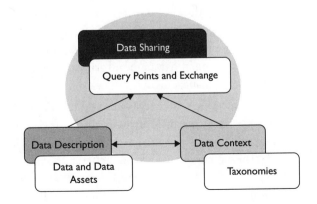

■ **Data Sharing**   Supports the access and exchange of data where access consists of ad hoc requests (such as a query of a data asset), and exchange consists of fixed, reoccurring transactions between parties. It is enabled by capabilities provided by both the Data Context and Data Description standardization areas.

Unlike the other reference models, the DRM is not a taxonomical reference model that displays a standard hierarchy of categories. Rather, it is a framework that agencies can commonly use to express structured, unstructured, and semistructured data in a common way.

Federal Segment Architecture Methodology (FSAM)

Not strictly an architecture framework, the FSAM is more a process framework that defines the processes and deliverables for architecting federal agency segments as registered at the Office of Management and Budget (OMB).

According to the OMB Federal Enterprise Architecture (FEA) Practice Guidance, segment architecture is a "detailed results-oriented architecture (baseline and target) and a transition strategy for a portion or segment of the enterprise." The FSAM supports all three segment types as defined in the OMB FEA Practice Guidance: core mission area, business service, and enterprise service segments. According to the OMB FEA Practice Guidance:

■ A *core mission area segment* represents a unique service area defining the mission or purpose of the agency. Core mission areas are defined by the agency business model (for example, tactical defense, air transportation, energy supply, pollution prevention and control, and emergency response).

■ A *business service segment* includes common or shared business services supporting the core mission areas. Business services are defined by the agency business model and include the foundational mechanisms and back office services used to achieve the purpose of the agency (for example, inspections and auditing, program monitoring, human resource management, and financial management).

■ An *enterprise service segment* includes common or shared IT services supporting core mission areas and business services. Enterprise services are defined by the agency service model and include the applications and service components used to achieve the purpose of the agency (for example, knowledge management, records management, mapping/geographic information system (GIS), business intelligence, and reporting).

The FSAM consists of process steps for developing a core mission area segment architecture (see Figure 1.2-17). The FSAM also includes guidance for tailoring the approach to develop business service and enterprise service segment architectures.

The FSAM is based on the principle that segment architecture development should be driven by segment leadership. The methodology is a scalable and repeatable process designed to help architects engage segment leaders to deliver value-added plans for improved mission delivery. Specifically, FSAM includes guidance to help architects establish clear relationships among strategic goals, detailed business and information management requirements, and measurable performance improvements within the segment. The FSAM helps architects ensure that a well-constructed and defensible plan of action is developed in partnership with segment leaders.

Although the FSAM is prescriptive, it has been designed to allow organization- and segment-specific adaptations. For example, although templates are included in the FSAM, these templates can be modified or tailored to the specific needs of the organization or segment using the FSAM guidance. As a further benefit

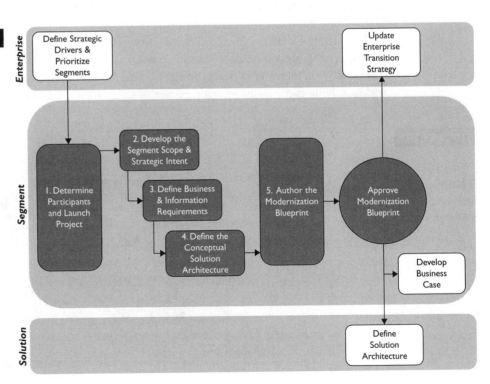

FIGURE 1.2-17

Federal Segment
Architecture
Methodology

to architects, the FSAM provides suggested analytical techniques designed to conform to segment reporting requirements as identified by the OMB FEA Program Management Office (PMO).

NATO Architecture Framework

The North Atlantic Treaty Organization Architecture Framework (NAF) provides the rules, guidance, and product descriptions for developing, presenting, and communicating architectures across NATO and other national boundaries. Earlier versions of NAF were tightly coupled to the DoDAF. NAF's new features include a capability, service-oriented, and program view. DoDAF Version 2.0 has adopted the capability and program views as defined by NAF.

United Kingdom Ministry of Defense Architecture Framework (MODAF)

MODAF is based on the DoDAF Version 1.0 baseline, which it represents through the MODAF Meta Model (M3) (see Figure 1.2-18). MODAF retains compatibility with United States modeling initiatives, but is specifically designed to support architecture modeling for the UK Ministry of Defense (MOD). MODAF uses aspects of the existing DoDAF with additional viewpoints (acquisition and capability) that are required to support MOD processes, procedures, and organizational structures. The additional viewpoints provide a rigorous method for understanding, analyzing, and specifying capabilities, systems, system of systems (SoS), business processes, and

FIGURE 1.2-18

UK Ministry
of Defense
Architecture
Framework

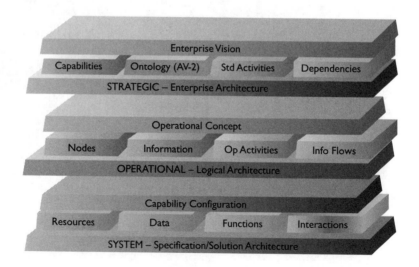

organizational structures. DoDAF Version 2.0 incorporates the data elements from MODAF required to support acquisition and capability views.

Treasury Enterprise Architecture Framework (FEA Practical Guide)

The Treasury Enterprise Architecture Framework (TEAF) is one of the older frameworks that provided more specificity to the FEAF. As a forerunner to the Federal Enterprise Framework, the principles embodied in the TEAF have made their way into more contemporary architecture frameworks. The TEAF draws upon the principles of James Martin's Information Engineering (IE), Spewak's EAP methodology, and the CIO Council's FEAF respectively.

In July 2000, the Department of the Treasury published the Treasury Enterprise Architecture Framework. The TEAF provides (1) guidance to Treasury bureaus concerning the development and evolution of information systems architecture; (2) a unifying concept, common principles, technologies, and standards for information systems; and (3) a template for the development of the EA.

The TEAF describes an architectural framework that supports Treasury's business processes in terms of products (see Figure 1.2-19). This framework guides the development and redesign of the business processes for various bureaus in order to meet the requirements of recent legislation in a rapidly changing technology environment. The TEAF prescribes architectural views and delineates a set of notional products to portray these views.

The TEAF's functional, information, and organizational architecture views collectively model the organization's processes, procedures, and business operations.

FIGURE 1.2-19

Treasury
Enterprise
Architecture
Framework

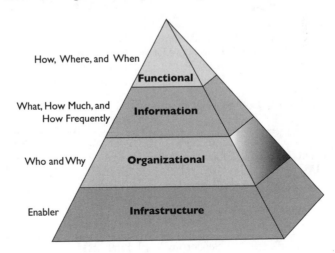

By grounding the architecture in the business of the organization, the TEAF defines the core business procedures and enterprise processes. Through its explicit models, a TEAF-based architecture enables the identification and reasoning of enterprise- and system-level concerns and investment decisions.

The TEAF provides a unifying concept, common terminology and principles, common standards and formats, a normalized context for strategic planning and budget formulation, and a universal approach for resolving policy and management issues. It describes the enterprise information systems architecture and its components, including the architecture's purpose, benefits, characteristics, and structure. The TEAF introduces various architectural views and delineates several modeling techniques. Each view is supported with graphics, data repositories, matrices, or reports (that is, architectural products).

Table 1.2-2 shows a matrix with four views and four perspectives. Essential models are shown across the top two rows of the matrix. It is notable that the TEAF

TABLE 1.2-2	TEAF Mapping to Zachman Framework Rows			
	Functional View	**Information View**	**Organizational View**	**Infrastructure View**
Planner Perspective	Mission and Vision Statements	Information Dictionary	Organization Charts	Technical Reference Model Standards Profile	EA Repository Listings
Owner Perspective	Activity Model Info Assurance Trust Model	Information Exchange Matrix (Conceptual)	Node Connectivity Description (Conceptual)	Info Assurance Risk Assessment System Interface Description (Level 1)	High-Level Modeling
Designer Perspective	Business Process/ System Function Matrix Event Trace Diagrams State Charts	Information Exchange Matrix (Logical) Logical Data Model Data CRUD Matrices	Node Connectivity Description (Logical)	System Interface Description (Level 2 and 3)	Logical Modeling
Builder Perspective	System Functionality Description	Information Exchange Matrix (Physical) Physical Data Model	Node Connectivity Description (Physical)	System Interface Description (Level 4) System Performance Parameters Matrix	Physical Modeling

(▨ - Essential Work Products;   ☐ - Supporting Work Products)

includes an Information Assurance Trust Model, the Technical Reference Model, and Standards Profiles as essential work products. These are not often addressed as critical framework components.

Questions

1. What is an enterprise? What are the fundamental characteristics of an enterprise?
2. What are some methods to reduce the complexity of analyzing a large and complex enterprise?
3. What is enterprise transformation? What are initiatives and projects in the context of enterprise transformation? What is an enterprise transformation roadmap? Why is it useful in guiding the transformation process?
4. What is the definition of architecture? Discuss, using your definition, various characteristics of architecture.
5. What is an architecture description? Discuss the existence of implicit and explicit architecture representations inside your specific enterprise. What is the usefulness of having explicit architecture descriptions? How can architecture descriptions be kept up to date? Discuss the differences in frequency of change of different types of architecture descriptions.
6. What is the purpose of building or representing the as-is state of an enterprise? How would you justify the building of an as-is architecture description for your own enterprise? What information would you need to build the as-is architecture representation of your enterprise?
7. What is the purpose of building a target or to-be state of an enterprise? How would you go about building a to-be state of your enterprise? (Where would you start and what information would you need?)

Reference List

1471-2000 - IEEE Recommended Practice for Architectural Description for Software-Intensive Systems. (2000). Sponsored by the IEEE Computer Society. http://standards.ieee.org/findstds/standard/1471-2000.html

C4ISR Architecture Working Group (AWH). (1997). *C4ISR Architecture Framework Version 2.0*. Volumes I-III. Department of Defense.

Department of Defense. (2007). *Department of Defense Architecture Framework Version 1.5*. Volumes I–III. Department of Defense.

Federal Enterprise Architecture Consolidated Reference Model Document Version 2.3. (2007). Federal Enterprise Architecture Program Office, Office of Management and Budget.

Federal Enterprise Architecture Program. (2005). *The Federal Enterprise Architecture Program Data Reference Model Version 2.0*. Federal Enterprise Architecture Program Office, Office of Management and Budget.

Federal Enterprise Architecture Program Office, Office of Management and Budget. (2007). *FEA Practice Guidance*. Office of Management and Budget.

Federal Chief Information Officer Council. (1999). *Federal Enterprise Architecture Framework Version 1.1*. http://www.cio.gov/Documents/fedarch1.pdf.

Federal Chief Information Officer Council. (2001). *A Practical Guide To Federal Enterprise Architecture*. (Federal) Chief Information Officers' Council.

Federal Segment Architecture Methodology (FSAM). (2008). http://www.fsam.gov.

Government Accounting Office. (2003). *GAO executive guide: information technology: a framework for assessing and improving enterprise architecture management (Version 1.1)*.

Government Accounting Office. National Association of State Chief Information Officers (NASCIO). (2007). *Building better government through enterprise architecture*. http://www.nascio.org.

The Open Group. (2007). *TOGAF Version 8.1.1 Enterprise Edition Study Guide*. Van Haren Publishing. https://www2.opengroup.org/ogsys/jsp/publications/PublicationDetails.jsp?publicationid=12125

Ross, Jeanne W., Weill, Peter, and Robertson, David. (2001). *Enterprise Architecture as Strategy: Creating a Foundation for Business Execution*. Harvard Business School Press.

Spewak, Steven. (1992). *Enterprise Architecture Planning: Developing a Blueprint for Data, Applications and Technology*. John Wiley and Sons.

1.3

Enterprise Architecting

This chapter introduces the basic elements needed for enterprise architecting: the scope of the enterprise, the high-level architecting process, and the types of data involved and their relationships. The scope of the enterprise being architected can range from very large, multimission enterprises such as a federal department to single-business-process, solution-oriented enterprises. The size or scope of the enterprise will affect the content of the architecture as we will see in Chapter 2.2. The high-level architecting process (the Six Step process) sets the context for a detailed architecture development process and focuses on identifying the key goals and outputs of that process. One of the key outputs of the architecture development process is an integrated set of architecture data. The relationships among the data are critical because the goal of EA is to highlight the traceability from business/mission needs to the supporting IT and infrastructure.

Scope of the Enterprise Architecture

There are three basic levels of enterprise architecture: (1) enterprise level; (2) segment level; and (3) solution level. These levels are illustrated in Figure 1.3-1. Enterprise-level architectures are used to support strategic decision making for the enterprise. Segment-level architectures are used to manage coherent sets of related capabilities or business services to ensure coordination and interoperability of related business processes, systems, and data. Solution-level architectures are used to support and manage business process and related system development and acquisition efforts. The solution level includes the concepts of system of systems (SoS) and family of systems (FoS). We will examine each of these levels in this section. We will also examine the concept of federated architecture.

FIGURE 1.3-1

Levels of
Enterprise
Architectures

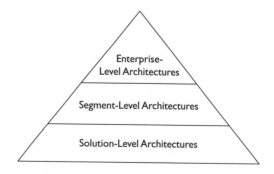

Enterprise Level

The enterprise level includes architectures of enterprises with top-level strategic plans, goals, and objectives as well as multiple projects and a portfolio of IT investments to manage. Here management includes investment or project selection, control, and evaluation (as described in Chapter 2.7).

Here are some example questions or issues that an enterprise-level EA might address:

- How do the business functions or capabilities relate to enterprise strategy and goals?
- Are there dependencies among the capabilities or business functions?
- How will business functions or capability performance be measured?
- When will the capabilities or business functions be implemented and what projects will provide them?
- What organizations will use the capabilities or business functions?
- What organizations are in charge of which projects?
- What are the timelines for the projects and what are the dependencies among them?

An example of an enterprise-level architecture is outlined for the Richard M. Nixon (RMN) Airport Case Study in Chapter 2.2.

When an enterprise is so large that a single architecture is impractical, a federated architecture approach may be used. A federated architecture for an enterprise is made up of an integratable set of independently developed, lower-level architectures. The set of lower-level architectures may be a set of segment-level architectures together with corresponding solution-level architectures, discussed later in this section, or a set of domain architectures, each oriented toward an architectural domain such as business, data, application, and technology. The enterprise has to provide sufficient guidance, such as enterprise-level Reference Models (described in Chapter 1.2), to ensure that the lower-level architectures use consistent terminology and can be integrated.

Segment Level

One way of decomposing an enterprise-level architecture into integratable component architectures is to use segment-level architectures. Each segment-level architecture addresses a core mission area of the enterprise or a common or shared service that supports core mission areas. The common or shared services may be either business services, such as human resources management or financial management, or enterprise services (that is, IT services), such as knowledge management or communications.

The core mission areas associated with segment-level architectures may have strategic plans, goals, and objectives that are consistent with the strategic plans, goals, and objectives of the top-level enterprise. These core mission areas may also manage a subset of the top-level enterprise's projects and a subset of the IT investment portfolio. Thus segment-level architectures may address the same types of questions as an enterprise-level architecture.

For the Department of Defense, examples of segment-level architectures are joint capability areas. Segment-level architectures for other federal agencies are frequently aligned with an agency's lines of business (LOB). For example, some Health and Human Services (HHS) Department segments are Health Care Administration (a core mission area segment) and IT Management (a business service segment) (United States Department of Health and Human Services, 2006). Segment-level architectures may also be used for cross-agency missions such as international trade.

Solution Level

Solution-level architectures are focused on a specific business/mission process solution involving a system or service or set of systems or services. These EAs provide guidance for system/service development projects and are the most closely related to systems architectures. They are frequently used as a way of comparing proposed solutions during an acquisition process. The system development project guidance includes concept of operations, required support for business processes, system interface and interoperability requirements, and technical standards. Solution-level architectures may address systems of systems (SoS) or family of systems (FoS).

An SoS is a set of systems that are the components of a more complex system that shows emergent properties. That is, the capabilities of the whole exceed the capabilities of the component systems. Typically, the component systems are distributed and independently operated and managed. For example, the Global Earth Observation System of Systems (GEOSS) will be a global and flexible network of content providers offering information to decision makers for the benefit of society. GEOSS will link together existing and planned observing systems around the world, using common technical standards so that data from thousands of different instruments can be combined into coherent data sets (www.earthobservations.org/geoss.shtml).

An FoS is a set of separate systems that can be integrated in different ways to provide a variety of mission-related capabilities. For example, consider a set of systems that support search and rescue efforts. These systems would include basic command and control systems and communications systems together with specialty support systems, including mountain search and rescue, sea search and rescue, and desert search and rescue. These systems could be combined as needed for specific search and rescue missions.

Here are some of the basic questions or issues that solution-level architectures address:

- What are the key elements of the operational concept?
- How are the business/mission operations performed?
- Who performs the business/mission operations and what resources are exchanged?
- What are the systems/services and what are their interfaces (both internal and external)?
- How do the systems/services support operations?
- What are the technical standards for the systems/services?

Examples of solution-level architectures include architectures for specific business processes or business services. In the Richard M. Nixon Airport case study example, the solution-level architecture for passenger identification is a specific example of a business service architecture. In the Department of Defense, architectures for specific weapons systems are solution-level architectures.

The Six Step Process

The Six Step process is the high-level or meta-process for architecting. It does not provide a specific, detailed process for developing architecture artifacts, products, or data, but rather sets the context for this more detailed architecture development process. This approach lets the development organization select and use its own detailed architecture development process.

The Six Step process is based on the metaprocess provided by the DoD Architecture Framework (DoDAF) (Department of Defense, 2009) and the *Practical Guide to Federal Enterprise Architecture* (Federal Chief Information Officer Council, 2001). This process is illustrated in Figure 1.3-2. The steps are followed in numerical order, but step 1, "Determine the intended use of the architecture," is placed on top with

FIGURE 1.3-2

The Six Step
Process

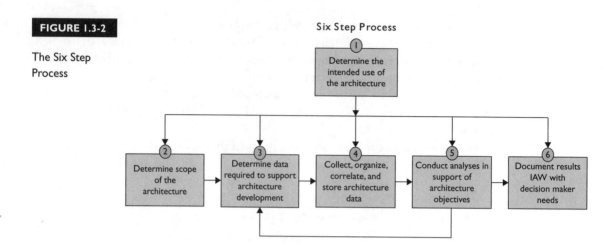

arrows to all the other steps since this step is the critical, and too often skipped, step
that drives all the others. Although only one iteration arrow is included in the figure
(from step 5 to step 3), the process tends to be highly iterative. The architecture team
gains more insight into the architecture domain with each step of the process, and
each new insight may cause the team to return to an earlier step to refine previously
developed material or add new material. Each step of the Six Step process will be briefly
covered in this chapter and then revisited in more detail in following chapters such as
Chapter 2.2.

Step 1: Determine the Intended Use of the Architecture

Step 1 focuses on identifying why the architecture is being built: what problem or
problems the architecture should address, including who the architecture stakeholders
(that is, the users of the architecture) are and what decisions they will use the
architecture to support. Each stakeholder will have a set of specific questions that the
architecture will need to provide the answers to or analyses that the architecture will
need to support. The architecture stakeholders considered here go above and beyond
the usual set of stakeholders considered in system development because a wide range
of decision makers in addition to system or even business process sponsors, owners, or
users may use the architecture information in decision-making processes. For example,
for all federal departments and agencies, the Office of Management and Budget
(OMB) uses architecture information to decide which proposed projects get funding
or which continuing projects get additional funding. In the Department of Defense,
the Battle Integration Laboratories use architecture information to support integration
testing across multiple, independently developed systems.

For example, the purpose of the RMN Airport enterprise-level architecture is to support the transformation of RMN Airport from a civil aviation airport to a viable alternative to Los Angeles International (LAX). Stakeholders in the enterprise-level architecture (that is, users of this architecture) include the appropriate Port Authority, the RMN Airport Management, and, potentially, the local governments of the communities surrounding the airport and the local citizens. The Port Authority and RMN Airport management need the architecture to identify and document the additional capabilities or business services that RMN needs and to support the transition planning and projects for implementing these additional capabilities. The local governments and citizens will use the enterprise-level architecture to analyze and understand how and when the airport changes will impact their communities in terms of noise, additional traffic, and expanded airport space and facilities.

Step 1 is critical because architecture is a decision-making tool, so it is vital to understand the decisions the architecture will be used to support. Many organizations jump immediately to step 4 and start collecting data and building models without careful consideration of what data is actually needed and how the data will be used. As a result, these organizations, after having expended large amounts of money, have found themselves with extensive models and mountains of data but with no real idea of how any of this data will support any of their key decision-making processes.

The material developed in step 1 will drive the selection of data and artifacts for the architecture, the level of detail needed, and completion criteria for the architecture.

Step 2: Determine the Scope of the Architecture

Step 2 focuses on identifying the boundaries of the architecture—what is internal to the architecture and what is outside the scope of the architecture. Scope includes the level of the architecture (that is, enterprise, segment, or solution), mission or organizational boundaries, technology and timeframe constraints, or other scoping issues.

In the RMN Airport case study, the example segment-level architecture is limited to business processes and organizations at RMN Airport that are involved with passenger management, that is, to passenger-related business services. For example, some of these passenger-related business processes could be supplying information to RMN airport financial systems so that the airport can bill an airline for services based on the number of passengers who enter or leave the airport on that airline's flights. However, the financial business processes and systems would be considered outside the scope of the passenger management segment architecture, even though interfaces to these financial business processes and systems would be needed.

Step 3: Determine the Data Needed to Support Architecture Development

Step 3 focuses on identifying the types of data needed to answer the problems and issues identified in step 1, within the scope limitations set out in step 2. Each of the architecture stakeholder questions from step 1 should lead to a set of data types that will be involved in answering the question. For example, if one of the questions is, "What changes will the new systems bring to our business processes?" then the architecture must include the current (as-is) and new (to-be) business process data for the business processes within the mission or organizational and timeframe scope provided by step 2. The types of data involved in the business process architecture and IT and infrastructure architecture are reviewed later in this chapter.

Step 4: Collect, Organize, Correlate, and Store Architecture Data

In step 4, the set of architecture models is selected and developed. The models are selected to cover the data identified in step 3. Mathematical modeling techniques are used to ensure that the data collected is consistent, complete, and correctly correlated. The development organization's specific architecture development process guides the modeling techniques to use and the order in which the models are built. The specific architecture development process also guides the tools and data storage approach used.

Step 5: Conduct Analysis in Support of Architecture Objectives

In step 5, the data resulting from the various modeling efforts in step 4 is analyzed. Two types of analysis may be employed in this step. One type is the analysis needed to address issues involved in the development of the architecture, such as which of several operational process or system support options is most effective, based on the overall performance measures associated with the architecture. Another type is analysis that directly addresses the decision-making processes that the architecture is designed to support. This type of analysis often involves both architectural and, potentially, other types of data such as financial data. Examples of this second type of analysis include business case analysis, return on investment analysis, and various types of performance and sensitivity analysis based on executable architecture modeling.

In all cases, the analysis processes may uncover the need for additional types of data that were not originally identified in step 3. Thus Figure 1.3-2 shows an iteration arrow going from step 5 to step 3. The need for additional types of data also causes iteration on step 4 so that this additional data can be collected, correlated, and integrated with the current architecture data set and stored so that it can be used for further analysis and sharing and future use and reuse.

Step 6: Document Results in Accordance with Decision-Maker Needs

In step 6, the data developed in step 4 and refined through step 5 is used to develop artifacts and products, also called fit-for-purpose views, that are used to communicate the results of the architecture process to the stakeholders and provide direct support to their decision-making processes. For some stakeholders and questions, the results can be documented using the same models the architecture development team developed in step 4. For other stakeholders, the results must be provided in other formats that are more easily understood by nonarchitects, such as bar or pie charts, dashboards, or combinations of simple graphics and text. The fit-for-purpose views or nonmathematical models are based on the consistent, correlated data stored during step 4. For example, to support the local government and citizen stakeholders, the data developed during steps 4 and 5 for the RMN Airport enterprise-level architecture might be used to generate a fit-for-purpose view that consists of a bar chart showing the planned increase in air traffic for the airport by year. This relationship of mathematically based models or architect's views to the consistent, integrated, architectural knowledge base and to the stakeholder-oriented fit-for-purpose views is illustrated in Figure 1.3-3.

For communicating the architecture contents to other architecture teams that are working on related architectures, a standard set of artifacts may be used. For example, the DoDAF provides a standard set of viewpoints and views for communicating architecture results within the DoD architecting community. From the implementation perspective, the knowledge base, built on a common data model, can be shared, and tools can be used to generate the standard views. With standard views, the architects do not have to learn all possible modeling techniques but only those involved with the standard views.

FIGURE 1.3-3

Relationship of
Data and Views in
Architecture

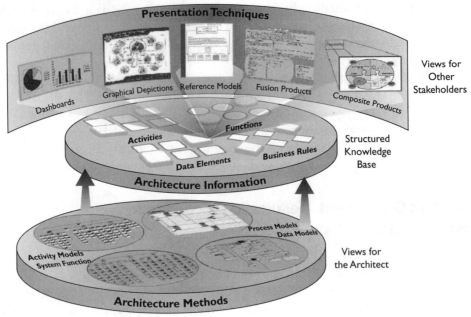

Architecting the Business Domain

The business domain deals with concepts and terms that address operations and business value. This domain focuses on what gets done and how it is managed rather than on IT and automation details. We first present the basic concepts of interest to an enterprise-level architecture and then the basic concepts for solution-level architectures. Segment-level architectures may contain a combination of these concepts.

Enterprise-level architectures tie together enterprise vision, strategy, goals, and objectives to the capabilities that support them, the projects that deliver the capabilities, and the organizations that own the projects or use the capabilities. Both objectives and capabilities may have performance measures associated with them. These concepts and their relationships allow enterprise-level stakeholders to see how proposed or existing projects align with business objectives. The performance measures provide criteria for evaluating whether capabilities being delivered by existing projects are meeting expectations. This information allows the enterprise to manage its investments and coordinate its projects. Figure 1.3-4 shows basic enterprise-level concepts and their relationships. The concepts are the items

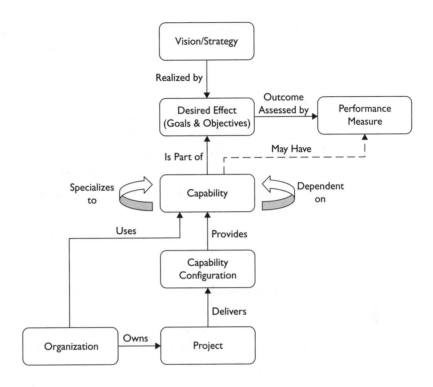

FIGURE 1.3-4

Enterprise-Level
Business Domain
Concepts and
Relationships

in the rounded rectangles and the relationships are indicated by the arrows of any style. For example, a Capability Is Part of a Desired Effect. Dashed arrows represent optional relationships. The remainder of this section discusses the concepts and their relationships.

Most enterprises have a *vision* statement that summarizes its mission and view of current or future business objectives. The enterprise has a *strategy* for achieving its future vision that can be realized by achieving stated *goals* and measurable *objectives*. Thus, business objectives are achieved if they meet their *performance measures*. Another term for these goals and objectives is *desired effects*. A *capability* is the ability to perform a desired business function that creates business value and is part of a desired effect. That is, the capability is necessary to achieving the desired effect of the strategy. Capabilities may be organized in a specialization hierarchy (from most general to most specialized), and one capability may be dependent on other capabilities. Capabilities may also have associated performance measures.

Here are some enterprise-level business domain concept examples from the RMN Airport case study. These concepts are relevant to the midphase to-be architecture that applies to years 5 to 10 of the transition period.

- Vision: RMN Airport becomes a viable alternative to LAX.
- Desired effect (goal/objective) that realizes the vision: Within five years, RMN will have passenger flights to Mexico.
- Performance measure for the objective: the number of flights to and from Mexico per time period. Here are the performance goals for this measure:
  - At year five of the transformation, RMN will have at least one weekly passenger flight to and from Mexico.
  - At year seven of the transformation, RMN will have daily flights to and from destinations in Mexico.
  - At year nine of the transformation, RMN will have daily flights to and from all major Mexican airports and tourist locations (at least five flights daily).
- Capability that is part of the desired effect: RMN will be able to handle passenger management processes for international flights (such as customs and immigration).
- Performance measure (for the capability): The number of passengers who can be handled by customs and immigration per time period on average. Here are the performance goals for this measure:
  - At year five of the transformation, RMN will handle customs and immigration for one incoming international flight (~ 200 passengers) per week at an average.
  - At year seven of the transformation, RMN will handle customs and immigration for one incoming international flight (~ 200 passengers) per day at an average.
  - At year nine of the transformation, RMN will handle customs and immigration for five incoming international flights (~1,000 passengers) per day at an average.

Capabilities are provided by a *capability configuration* of personnel, systems, and software that are developed, delivered, and maintained by projects. Organizations within the enterprise use capabilities in their business processes to create business value. Organizations also own—that is, manage and control—projects.

The organizations that use capabilities may not own the projects that deliver the corresponding capability configurations. Both organizations and projects may be decomposed into subordinate organizations and subprojects, respectively, although these decompositions are not indicated in Figure 1.3-4.

In the business domain, solution-level architectures are focused on the business processes, the roles and organizational structures that perform the processes, and the resources managed and exchanged during the execution of the business processes. These concepts and their relationships allow the enterprise to evaluate current operations, select the best solution alternatives for increasing efficiency or providing new capabilities, and manage the transition for business process improvement. Figure 1.3-5 shows some basic solution-level concepts and their relationships. This figure uses the same notation as Figure 1.3-4. The remainder of this section discusses the concepts and their relationships along with some additional concepts that are not represented in the figure.

Performers are those who perform the activities of a business process. A performer may be a role or an organization, or, in the case of activities that are fully automated, such as a sensor or agent software, a performer may be IT. An *activity* may be an entire business process or a task within a business process. Activities may be

FIGURE 1.3-5

Solution-Level
Business Domain
Concepts and
Relationships

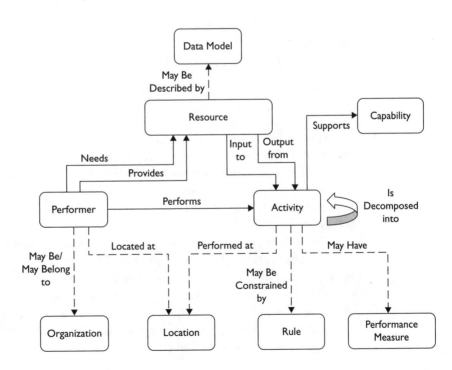

decomposed down to the needed level of detail. An activity or business process may have associated performance measures that provide the criteria for judging the effectiveness of the activity. Activities support capabilities and may be constrained by business *rules* based on policy, operational standards and guidelines, or corporate culture. Performers perform activities at *locations*. Each activity may be performed at one or more locations. Locations may be abstract or logical, such as "Regional Office," if all regional offices are sufficiently alike for the purposes of the architecture, or concrete, such as the St. Louis, Missouri, regional office. Locations are increasingly mobile. Examples of mobile locations are the Combat Information Center aboard an aircraft carrier and the more abstract "personal office" carried by a traveling salesperson in his or her briefcase or car.

To perform their operations, performers may need to exchange *resources* with other performers. These resources may be data, information, personnel types, or materiel (that is, nonpersonnel physical resources). If the resources are data or information that is sufficiently complex in terms of structure or relationships, they may be modeled in a conceptual or logical *data model*.

Here are some solution-level business domain concept examples from the RMN Airport case study:

- Performer: check-in agent
- Performer: passenger
- Organization: airline
- Activity: check in passenger
- Resource: identity documents

The check-in agent (the performer) employed by the airline (the organization) checks in the passenger (the activity). The check-in agent needs the identity document (the resource) from the passenger (performer) to check in the passenger.

There are some additional solution-level concepts that relate to the dynamic behavior of the architecture and that are not covered in Figure 1.3-5. These concepts are the *state* behavior and the *scenario* behavior.

State behavior is typically a characteristic of data entities or information elements, although it may apply to other elements of the architecture. The state of a data entity or information element changes in response to events caused by the execution of business processes. Typically, a data entity or information elements will transition through a sequence of states from some initial state to some terminal state during the course of normal business operations. For example, in the RMN Airport case study, the passenger has state or status that changes as the passenger is processed through the airport and onto the airplane. This state or status is included in the passenger record and is queried and updated by various passenger management processes. Some example statuses for a passenger include checked-in, screened, and boarded.

Not all information or data entities will have interesting state behavior, so this type of behavior is modeled in an architecture only in the case where understanding state behavior is important to understanding the enterprise's business.

An operational scenario shows business behavior in terms of interactions among the performers in response to the specific sequence of events contained in the scenario. The scenario highlights the resource exchanges among performers in response to a specific sequence of events generated by the execution of one or more business processes. The scenarios chosen for an architecture usually relate to key operational concepts or performance or sequences that are critical to security.

Architecting the IT and Infrastructure Domain

The IT and infrastructure domain deals with concepts and terms that address systems, services, standards, and communications and how they support the business domain. This domain focuses on the details of systems or services and infrastructure functions, interfaces, performance, and resource exchanges, and how all these items support business process needs. Here, systems and services are usually provided by automation, but as automation continues to become more sophisticated and the infrastructure more capable and pervasive, systems may be viewed in the traditional systems engineering way as including in organizational structures and personnel. The inclusion of the relationships between systems or services and the business domain is critical. Without this connection, a basic purpose of EA, to ensure that IT supports business needs and goals, cannot be achieved. Because of the need to show this connection, it is hazardous to develop business domain and IT domain architectures independently. There needs to be a strong coordination between the developments of these two domain architectures to achieve an integrated, useful EA.

The IT and infrastructure details are usually of more concern for solution-level architectures, although enterprise-level architectures are concerned with the overall IT and infrastructure interoperability and integration issues, including technical standards and delivery and retirement dates for capability configurations. The IT and infrastructure domain can be viewed using either a system-oriented or a service-oriented approach. We will first present the basic concepts for a system-oriented viewpoint and then the basic concepts for a service-oriented viewpoint. Last, we will discuss some basic concepts for communications infrastructure.

System Viewpoint

A system viewpoint looks at the IT and infrastructure domain as a set of systems with interfaces, where each system performs a set of system functions, exchanges resources (usually data), and has performance measures. Figure 1.3-6 shows some basic IT and infrastructure domain system viewpoint concepts and their relationships, which are discussed in this section along with some additional concepts that are not shown in the figure.

A *system* can be decomposed into component systems (in cases of SoS or FoS), subsystems, or system components. A system (or decomposed system) has *interfaces* to other systems. Each interface carries *data* between (out of and into) systems. Both systems and interfaces may have *standards* that apply to them—that is, systems and their interfaces may implement standards. Each system is located at one or more *locations*. A location may be logical or physical, and it may be mobile.

A system performs a set of *functions*, each of which can be decomposed into sub-functions. Each function has one or more logical *data flows* that carry data to or from that function. Each system can be mapped to the business activities it supports either directly or indirectly through the functions that the system performs. Further, a system is used by performers while the performers are performing a supported activity. (The relationship between performers and activities is not shown in the figure.) Both systems and functions may have performance measures associated with them.

FIGURE 1.3-6

IT and
Infrastructure
Domain System
Viewpoint
Concepts and
Relationships

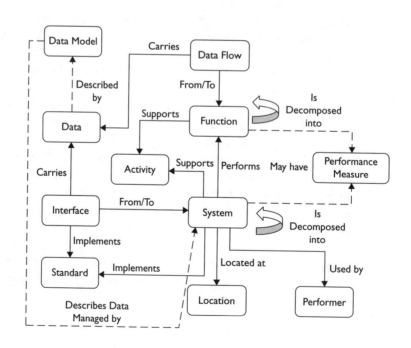

Data models can be used to describe the data managed by a system. For example, a data model can be used to describe the logical or physical schema of a shared database managed by a system. A data model can also be used to describe the data that flows between functions or between systems on interfaces if the data is sufficiently complex.

Here are some solution-level IT and infrastructure concept examples from the RMN Airport case study:

- **System**   Airline reservation and ticketing system (ARTS) client and server
- **Function**   Verify passenger identity
- **Location**   Check-in counter
- **System**   Passenger identification system (PAXIS)
- **Location**   RMN Operations Center
- **Interface**   ARTS to PAXIS
- **Activity**   Check in passenger

The ARTS client (a system), located at the Check-in counter (a location), supports check-in passenger (an activity) by performing verify passenger identity (a function), among other functions. The ARTS server has an interface to PAXIS.

Additional concepts associated with the system viewpoint include system and standard availability, update, and retirement dates and behavior concepts. Like the business domain, a system viewpoint may include system rules that constrain system structure, interfaces, and function. Systems may have internal state. In fact, this is usual for control and similar systems. Unlike with business objects, system behavior is frequently continuous. Systems start in an initial state, transition to a state based on external system inputs, and cycle back to an initial state, ready to begin performing the set of functions again.

A common example of a control system that has a state is the control system for a vending machine. In this case, in its initial state, the machine is ready to accept money. After sufficient money is inserted, the machine transitions to a state where input from the item selection buttons can be accepted. After a legitimate product code (whose cost is equal to or less than the amount previously inserted) is selected and the selected item is dispensed, the machine transitions to a state where change may be calculated and, if necessary, dispensed. Then the machine returns to its initial state.

System *scenarios* are also important for modeling system behavior. A system scenario shows the interactions of systems (or system components) in terms of data exchanges in response to a specific sequence of system events or external inputs, such as sensor inputs. The scenarios selected for an architecture usually relate to key performance or sequences that are critical to security.

Service Viewpoint

A service viewpoint looks at the IT and infrastructure domain as a set of services, usually Web-accessible, that can be quickly configured to create new or updated applications. In the service viewpoint, much of what is considered a "system," including the platform and operating system, becomes infrastructure for the services. Each service is defined with a standard interface. Ideally, multiple implementations of this service may be available, either from multiple vendors or for multiple platforms. Each implementation has a service-level agreement (SLA) that spells out such items as the performance characteristics promised by the service provider. Figure 1.3-7 shows some basic IT and infrastructure domain service viewpoint concepts and their relationships, which are discussed throughout this section along with some additional concepts that are not shown in the figure. In cases where the enterprise relies on outside parties to perform the services, these are not just IT services but business services. For example, a government agency or corporation may

FIGURE 1.3-7

IT and
Infrastructure
Domain Service
Viewpoint
Concepts and
Relationships

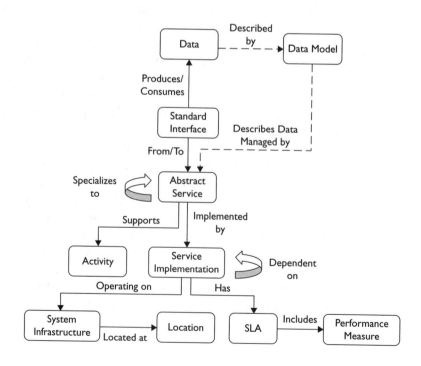

decide to outsource payroll services. The discussion that follows relates primarily to IT services.

Each abstract service may specialize in more specific abstract services. For example, in the case of search and rescue services (which are business services), there may be specialized water search and rescue and mountain search and rescue services. Each abstract service has a *standard interface* as part of its service definition. The standard interface describes the data consumed by the service (that is, the data required as input) and the data produced by the service (that is, the data produced as output). A data model may be used either to describe the data produced and consumed by services if this data is complex, or to describe the data managed by a service if the service is managing a shared database.

Each abstract service has one or more *service implementations*. Implementations may differ in terms of their development and maintenance organizations (that is, implementation may have different vendors), in terms of the platforms they run on, or in terms of their performance characteristics. Each implementation typically has an SLA that includes the performance characteristics that are guaranteed for the service implementation. Each service implementation may also depend on—that is, call upon—other service implementations. For example, a payment-handling service may call on a credit card service and a check handling service. Different implementations of the same service may have different dependencies. Like systems, service implementations run at one or more locations. For services, the concept of location also includes the concept of platform, or system infrastructure, that is supporting the service. The location of the platform may be abstract, physical, or mobile. Unlike with most systems, the number and location of implementations for a given service may change dynamically. That is, if a service implementation at a specific location becomes overloaded with service requests, then additional implementations of that service may be brought up at that location or other locations to maintain response performance. If a service implementation at a specific location becomes inaccessible due to communications problems, additional implementations of that service may be started up in locations that remain accessible.

Like systems, services need to be mapped to the business activities they support. Each service will support one or more business activities.

Additional concepts associated with the service viewpoint include service implementation availability, updates, and retirement dates and behavior concepts. A service or service implementation may have associated rules. For example, a service implementation may have criteria (that is, rules) for deciding when that implementation is becoming overloaded with requests. The related abstract service may have rules for deciding where additional implementations should be instantiated if an implementation becomes overloaded. Like systems, services may have internal state. Service scenarios are also important for modeling the behavior of sets of services.

A service scenario shows the interactions of services in terms of data exchanges (that is, service requests and responses) in response to a specific sequence of events or external inputs caused by the execution of an application that uses the set of services. The service scenarios included in an architecture may be selected to demonstrate the effectiveness of the set of services in supporting critical applications, or they may be selected based on key performance or critical security issues.

Communications Infrastructure

The communications infrastructure consists of the network and communication systems, such as satellite relays, radio repeaters, routers, and gateways, whose purpose is to move data rather than to process it for operational purposes. The communications infrastructure implements the system interfaces shown in Figure 1.3-6 and the communication aspects of service standard interfaces shown in Figure 1.3-7. The communication infrastructure concepts and relationships are shown in Figure 1.3-8 from a system viewpoint perspective. Communications infrastructure information is of interest to stakeholders who focus on reliability and availability of data and security issues.

A system sends data to external systems through one or more *system ports*. Each system port implements a *standard protocol* that is used to send the data via sequence of communications links and communications systems that use the protocol to reach the system port on the receiving system. Frequently, there are multiple possible paths in communications networks that realize system interfaces, especially when the Internet is used.

FIGURE 1.3-8

Communications
Infrastructure
Concepts and
Relationships

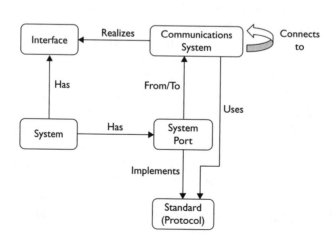

Questions

1. How are the three levels of architecture (enterprise level, segment level, and solution level) related to each other?
2. What types of stakeholders would use enterprise-level architectures?
3. What types of stakeholders would use segment-level architectures?
4. What types of stakeholders would use the solution-level architectures?
5. What is the relationship between an organization's specific architecture development process and the Six Step process?
6. Why should the Six Step process be considered as an iterative process?
7. What architecture concepts are common between the solution-level business domain and the IT and infrastructure domain system viewpoint? What do these common concepts imply about the relationships between the business domain and the IT and infrastructure domain?
8. What architecture concepts are common between the enterprise-level business domain and the solution-level business domain?
9. What are the different architecture concepts that can have performance measures associated with them?
10. What are the different concepts that can be related to data models?

Reference List

Department of Defense. (2009). *Department of Defense Architecture Framework Version 2.0.* www.cio-nil.defense.gov/sites/dodaf20.

Federal Chief Information Officer Council. (2001). *A Practical Guide to Federal Enterprise Architecture Version 1.0.* www.enterprise-architecture.infor/images/Documents/Federal%20Enterprise%20Architecture%20Guide%20v1a.pdf.

Federal Enterprise Architecture Practice Guidance. http://www.egov.gov.

Federal Segment Architecture Methodology (FSAM). http://www.fsam.gov.

Group on Earth Observations. www.earthobservations.org/geoss.shtml.

HHS Enterprise Architecture Segments. (2007). *Department of Defense Architecture Framework Version 2.0.* Volume 1. Practical Guide to Federal Enterprise Architecture.

The Open Group Architecture Framework (Introduction). http://opengroup.org.

United States Department of Health and Human Services Enterprise Architecture Program Management Office. (2006). *HHS Enterprise Architecture Segments Version 1.0.* www.hhs.gov/ocio/ea/easegements.pdf.

Part II

Architecture Development and Use

2.1

The Importance
of Culture

I t is a common assertion that while all humans have culture, it is something learned and, in the case of national and ethnic cultures, passed down from generations. At the same time, many social scientists argue that it is culture that makes us unique, and all human behavior is cultural. Culture is like language (and expressed within it) in that every human society has language and its possession as a symbolic mode of representation is one of the distinguishing features of being human. As with language, the structure of culture functions at an underlying level, and is, as organizational culture theorist Geert Hofstede subtitled one of his books, "software of the mind" (Hofstrede, 2004).

As Hofstede explains, culture involves unwritten rules of a social game, and "is the collective programming of the mind that distinguishes the members of one group or category of people from another." This "collective programming" obtains at every level of culture. One way of understanding culture is as a system; science recognizes that all systems exist within systems—and we must identify in our analysis the boundaries of the system that interests us. If we understand a system as composed of two or more subsystems oriented toward a common purpose we can situate cultures within cultures within cultures. In this manner, we can argue that there is an organizational culture to continuous larger groupings; the largest of which would be human culture. Understanding the underlying systems constituting human culture or human nature was a primary motivation of structuralists such as Claude Levi-Strauss, who deconstructed cross-cultural symbol systems of myth, ritual, art, and other processes looking for underlying and universal patterns (Levi-Strauss, 1983).[1]

We can distinguish between those whose interests are to peal back the layers of culture to locate invariant properties and those who focus on what distinguishes groups from each other. This does not entail a particular disagreement, as the former seek invariance from the study of structural variance. For our purposes, we are concerned with cultural differences and how they affect organizational behavior.

While we recognize differences in organizational culture, they are most often attributed to negative experiences, such as encounters with "not invented here" attitudes—turf battles between and among functional stovepipe organizations in which seeing initiatives such as enterprise architecture are challenged as unwelcome

---

[1] Following the observation of philosopher and anthropologist Levi-Strauss, we can argue that even the Japanese meal of sashimi is not "raw." The eating of raw fish is what bears do—reaching in a pond of water, pulling out a fish, and eating it. However, sashimi is integrally prepared and culturally mediated food. It is in a sense "cooked," in the contrast that Levi-Strauss makes in *The Raw and the Cooked* (1983) or in French, *Le Cru et le cui*. Here *cui* means done or prepared, that is, culturally transformed.

intrusions from management to put another bureaucratic obstacle in the way of those who do the real work.

Culture from this view is seen as an impediment and something that has to be managed, dealt with, and changed. As Hofstede observed, "Culture is more often a source of conflict than of synergy. Cultural differences are a nuisance at best and often a disaster." (Hofstede, www.geert-hofstede.com)

Yet culture, like language, is neutral. It is not defined in terms of content; rather, it exists at the underlying deep structural level that gives rise to surface behavior. Consider the parallels of language and culture. Every language has an underlying structure of an essentially finite number of rules that give rise to a virtually infinite number of possible expressions in the language. The underlying system is often referred to as "deep structure" and the way they appear in discourse as "surface structure." These underlying systems are not always apparent to speakers and need to be discovered in linguistic analysis. For example, the most elementary unit in speech is the phoneme, defined "as the smallest segmental unit of sound employed to form meaningful contrasts between utterances." These structures differ between languages. Take, for instance, the differences between the two kinds of *b* in the lexeme "baseball." To English speakers, it is difficult to recognize they differ in amount of aspiration and we do not distinguish meaning between them. They are considered allophones of the phoneme [b]. In the Kpelle language of Liberia and Guinea, these represent separate phonemes as represented by the existence of minimal pairs of lexemes with different meanings. The unaspirated *b* (or 6) is contrasted to the aspirated *b* such that the term *bala* means a hard mat and the unaspirated *6ala* means a goat. These structures continue throughout the higher-level structures of language. So, for instance, at the morpheme level—or the minimal unit of sound differentiation in language—we can contrast differences in the plural morpheme; for instance, such differences can be noted in the use of the different English allomorphs /s/, /es/, and /z/. Most people after some reflection will recognize the rule for using /s/ and /es/, where the former appears after stops (for example, *cut*, *cuts*) and the latter after sibilants (*bus*, *buses*). However, they often have difficulty with the use of /z/, which appears after the phoneme [y], as in *boyz* or *toyz*. These differences in language rules likewise obtain at the syntactic and semantic levels. These rule differences are not universal; rather, they are language-specific and for the most part are not directly available to consciousness (see Bellman, 1973).[2]

---

[2] Beryl Bellman conducted a sixteen-year study of the Kpelle language as an anthropologist before the onset of the Liberian civil war. He began his research and consulting as an enterprise architect after that period.

•Unlimited number of understandable sentences	•Unlimited number of understandable social situations
•Requires combinational rule system in mind of language user	•Requires combinational rule system in mind of social participant
•Rule system not available to consciousness	•Rule system only partly available to consciousness
•Rule system acquired with only imperfect evidence in environment— virtually no teaching	•Rule system acquired with only imperfect evidence, only partially taught
•Learning requires inner unlearned resources, perhaps partly specific to language	•Learning requires inner unlearned resources, perhaps partly specific to social cognition
•Inner resources determined by genome interacting with process of biological development	•Inner resources determined by genome interacting with process of biological development

Parallels Between Language and Social Cognition
(Ray Jackendoff—Language, Consciousness, Culture)

Every language has its own underlying "deep structure" or rule structures that generate a virtually infinite number of sentences. There is no language superior to another in being able to express information. In this manner, languages represent metaphoric parallel universes. Culture likewise can be understood according to an underlying system of rule-like structures. One way of considering culture is to characterize it as a form of social cognition.[3]

Ray Jackendoff provides an important comparison between language and social cognition, showing how both are comprised of underlying rule patterns that are not directly available to consciousness. In his book *Language, Consciousness, Culture*, he provides the chart shown in Figure 2.1-1 to show these relationships (Jackendoff, 2009).

Both language and culture (characterized as a type of social cognition) have finite underlying structures or combinational rule systems that generate a virtually infinite number of displays—sentences and understandable social situations that are at the surface or surface structures. Although these underlying systematic structures generate meaning, social situations are independent of them. One can communicate any number and kinds of messages with language, as one can perform any number

---

[3] This is the speech act theory as developed from Austin to Searle.

and kinds of culturally relevant behavior. In this manner, we reserve judgment on cultural performance in the same way as we do regarding what might be said.

Using language, one can complement or insult, make promises, offers, or threats, utilizing the similar language principles. As the anthropologist Dell Hymes showed culture is as a system of ideas that underlies and gives meaning to behavior in society, and what is distinctively cultural is a question of capabilities acquired or elicited in social life rather than the behavior or things that are shared (Hymes, 1974). This allows for the same underlying system of rules to elicit outcomes that are oppositional and in conflict with one another. This was the basis for Edgar Schein's observation regarding the culture at the Digital Equipment Corporation, which entailed both "a positive innovative culture that could at the same time grind out 'fabulous new products' and develop such strong internal animosities that groups would accuse one another of lying, cheating and misuse of resources" (Schein, 2004). According to Schein, the underlying cultural grammar at Digital was both responsible for its meteoric rise to success and its eventual downfall.[4]

Although we characterize deep structure as a finite set rule that generates a virtually infinite variety of surface structure (sentences in language and social situations in culture), these rules are highly complex, as described in Chapter 2.2. They are self-adaptive, nonlinear, and complex. The study of these underlying systems is the basis for both linguistic and social science disciplines. We cannot of course predict what will be said in any given conversation, but we can locate devices used at every level of language to produce meaning. This includes understanding what conversational analysts refer to as the simplest systematic of such systems as turn taking, repair work in conversation, and the sequencing of interaction. That is, there is a systematic, as described earlier, at every level from the phonemic, morphemic, syntactic, semantic, and conversational/discourse practices. Some of these structures are invariant to culture, role, motive, situation, and setting, while others are highly context-sensitive. Likewise, for culture there are invariant structures contained in its universal presence in all human societies, and variant structures that allow us to classify cultures according to various values and other dimensions.[5]

The comparison and measuring of differences in value orientation is a significant advance in the study of intercultural communications. Hofstede (2004) developed

---

[4]See discussion in this chapter on Schein.

[5]Conversational analysis began with the work of Harvey Sacks in the 1960s and his colleagues Emmanuel Schegloff and Gail Jefferson. See Silverman (1998). This work has grown into a major field in sociology, communications, anthropology, educational research, and psychology.

a framework for this in his comparative study of IBM in different countries to locate what dimensions differ in behavior by observing and interviewing persons at the same level in the corporate hierarchy around the world. He developed comparisons of value dimensions: power distance, uncertainty avoidance, individualism/collectivism, and masculinity/femininity.

His Power Distance Index (PDI) focuses on the degree of equality, or inequality, among people in society. High-power distance indicates that inequalities of power and wealth exist and are tolerated within the society. Such societies often have caste systems that do not allow upward mobility. In low-power distance societies, there is a deemphasis on structural differentiation, and equality along with opportunity for everyone is emphasized. Hofstede measured power distance according to how those he interviewed responded to such questions as, "how frequently does the following occur: employees being afraid to express disagreement with managers" (Hofstrede, 2004), and subordinates' perception and preference for a boss's decision-making style, choosing among autocratic, paternalistic, or consultative.

Hofstede's distinction between individualism and collectivism focuses on how much a society emphasizes individual versus collective achievement and interpersonal relationships. High individualism stresses individuality and individual rights, and individuals tend toward looser relationships. Low individualism societies emphasize collectivist natures and closer ties between individuals. Such cultures emphasize extended families and everyone assumes responsibility for fellow group members. Hofstede contrasts locus of control and evaluation between these types. If the locus is external, as is found in more collectivistic societies, there is a greater emphasis on fatalism and lack of individual responsibility, whereas an internal focus places greater emphasis on a rejection of submission to authority.

In his interviews, he determined the contrast of individualism versus collectivism according to how his respondents answered questions such as, "try to think of those factors which would be important to you in an ideal job, disregard how they are in your present job: how important is it to you to have…" personal time, freedom to adopt to your own approach to a job, and challenging work to indicate an orientation to individualistic (Hofstrede, 2004). On the other hand, those who emphasized more a desire for training, physical conditions, and use of one's skills tended toward the collectivistic orientation.

Hofstede's Masculinity (MAS) ranking focused on how much a society reinforces traditional masculine work role models of achievement, control, and power. High MAS indicates the culture experiences greater gender differentiation, where males maintain a hegemonic role in the power structure. In low masculinity cultures, there is less discrimination between genders and women are treated with greater equality.

Hofstede contrasted masculine versus feminine cultures according to respondents who ranked a series of preferences regarding work environments. Masculine cultures emphasized earnings, recognition, advancement, and work challenges; whereas at the feminine pole, the stress was on having good working relationships with managers, cooperation with coworkers, the desirability of the area in which they live, and employment security.

His next area of contrast was the level of uncertainty avoidance (UAI). This focuses on the amount of tolerance for ambiguity and uncertainty or unstructured situations. High uncertainty avoidance rankings show a low tolerance for uncertainty and ambiguity, which creates a rule-oriented society that stresses laws, rules, regulations, and controls to reduce the amount of uncertainty. A low ranking indicates less concern about ambiguity and more tolerance for differences of opinion. Low uncertainty avoidance (LUA) societies are less rule-oriented, more accepting of change, and more ready to take risks.[6]

Hofstede's final contrast involves time orientation; high long-term (LTO) versus low. This stresses the amount of focus on traditional versus forward thinking values. High LTO shows a commitment and respect for tradition with a strong work ethic where long-term rewards are anticipated for today's work. In such societies, business often takes longer to develop for outsiders.

One of the authors found a curious example of this several years ago when he learned about a benefit that Canon Business Machines wanted to make to its American managers at a facility in the United States. The company offered to pay for the tuition of all of their managers' children in college so that the cost of education would not be a barrier to entry into any university. Interestingly, the American managers almost universally rebelled against the offer, saying they would prefer receiving the compensation now and would take care of their own children's education. This offer was made during the period when Japanese industry expected workers to remain loyal to their company for their career. This contrasted with American business experience, where advancing in one's career more often involved lateral moves to other companies, and lifelong loyalty to an organization was rare.

Hofstede and those making similar contrasts between cultures proposed the ability to predict types of interactive styles between those expressing such value orientation differences, such as those exemplified in the case of Canon Business Machines just cited. Where Hofstede emphasized intercultural distinctions between national

---

[6]For example, Edward Hall distinguished between high- and low-context cultures, or the amount of information implicit in communications. Also see Talcott Parson's concept of pattern variables in his structures of social action, which was a set of contrasts proposed by Gudykunst and Kim (2002) in their work on intercultural communication differences.

TABLE 2.1-1

Douglas' Ground
Versus Grid
Matrix

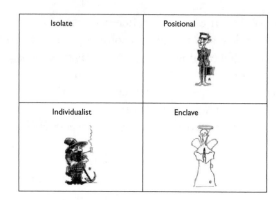

Isolate	Positional
Individualist	Enclave

cultures, different organizations and professions also differ in their expression of these differences. For instance, one might contrast the academic profession along with government careers that provide tenure and more job security with the uncertainty, short-term project orientation, and individual advancement stressed in contract-based consulting professions and in highly competitive industries. Consider how Dan Bricklin and Bob Frankston, the inventors of the first killer application, VisiCalc, as university professors published the source code, as is standard practice for the academic profession. Their reward was tenure and a well-deserved reputation, but they did not become computer billionaires like Bill Gates, Steve Jobs, or Larry Ellison.

Such contrasts of macronational cultural differences with micro-organizational distinctions are also strongly exemplified in anthropologist Mary Douglas' distinction between grid and group. Douglas first discussed this contrast in her *Natural Symbols* (Douglas, 1970), based on research in Central Africa. Douglas was concerned with how people ordered their universe and postulated a system of classification for how they went about doing so. She developed a typology to account for the distribution of values within society and proposed a connection between kinds of social organization and the values that maintain them.

Douglas developed a schema based on two dimensions: ground (referring to a general boundary around a community) that forms the basis of a horizontal axis; and grid (or regulation) on the vertical axis. Members of a society[7] move across the matrix according to choice or circumstances.

Table 2.1-1 shows Douglas' grid/group diagram.

---

[7] Douglas later expanded her theory into the analysis of organizational behavior.

The group dimension is a measure of how much people are controlled by their social group. To be affiliated with a group, individuals need to accept constraints. Groups, on the other hand, require collective pressures to demonstrate loyalty. Douglas points out that this obviously varies with strength. She gives the example of how at one end of the spectrum, one might belong to a religious group and only attend services on holidays, while at the other end one might join a convent or monastery.

The other variable on the grid consists of differences in the amount of control or structure that members of a group accept. On the one hand there are those who live free of group pressures and structural constraints where everything "has to be negotiated ad hoc," while on the other there are those who live in highly structured hierarchical environments. The grid creates four opposed and incompatible types of social control, with various mixtures between the extremes.

Douglas provides characterizations of three ideal types of persona associated with the grid (see Table 2.1-1). She describes these as, "The smug pioneer with his pickaxe, the stern bureaucrat with his briefcase, the holy man with his halo," each exemplifying Max Weber's types of rationality: "bureaucracy, market, and religious charisma" (Douglas, 2006, p. 3). These reflect the three grid-group cultures of the positional, individualist, and sectarian enclave.

Douglas describes how the isolate at the top-right is strong on grid and group. This reflects societies and concomitantly organizations in which all roles are ascribed and behavior is governed by positional rules. The cultural biases are tradition and order. In culture, the roles are ascribed by birth, gender, or family and ranked according to tradition. She refers to this as "positional" as a form of society that uses "extensive classification and programming for solving problems of co-ordination" (Douglas, 2006, p. 4). In the organizational domain, this might be the family-owned and -controlled business where employees can expect to achieve only a certain level within the enterprise.

At the bottom-right are strongly bounded groups with little or no ranking or grading rules for the relations between its members. Douglas considers this to be descriptive of a community of dissidents or sects. This might also pertain to lattice design organizations (Papa, 2008), where there are no bosses. New members are not assigned to departments but find teams that they volunteer to join. The lattice organization encourages direct communication with few intermediaries and little approval seeking. Instead of working through a defined authority structure, team members commit to objectives to make them happen. Lattice organizations have sponsors rather than bosses. According to Papa (2008), such organizations involve heterarchy. These are "self-organizing non-hierarchical systems that are characterized by lateral accountability and by organizational heterogeneity" (Papa, 2008, p. 59). This involves distributed intelligence and diversity. They "encompass multiple communities of knowledge and practice that subscribe to diverse evaluative and performance criteria and answer to different constituencies and principles of accountability" (Papa, 2008, p 59).

At the bottom-left is extreme individualism. This is defined both in terms of weak group and grid controls. The primary form of control is competition. Dominant positions are open to merit. Douglas sees this is as analogous to Weber's commercial society, where individual is concerned only with private benefit. Examples of extreme individualism may be seen in *Wall Street*'s Gordon Gekko's "greed is good" credo and the extremism that led to the near-collapse of banking in 2008. The fourth quadrant is the world of the total isolate and populated by those who withdraw from society. However, an organizational form of this might be the independent researcher and entrepreneur. Douglas later described the grid as the basis for understanding how organizations think. This reflected alternative views of corporate culture.

In such schema, we may be tempted toward a Goethe type of prediction regarding interactions between quadrants in these systems. However, rather than being predictive, we may instead consider these to be elements of cultural grammars that can yield any number of types of surface structures.[8]

Thus, as Douglas argued, culture is not a thing, it is not static but instead is "something which everyone is constantly creating, affirming, and expressing" (Douglas, 1985). From this perspective, culture is not imposed but rather emerges. As Richard Seel maintains, organizational culture "is the emergent result of the continuing negotiations about values, meanings, and proprieties between the members of that organization and with its environment" (Seel, 2000). Culture is the consequence of interactions and negotiations among members of organizations. He argues that to change culture requires one to change the nature of those conversations. This is something nontrivial.

As Harold Garfinkel (1967, p 186) argued for health clinical records, there are "good organizational reasons" for bad organizational behavior. That is, at the macro level, we can easily see "organizational problems," but as we move to what he refers to as the shop floor, we tend to "lose the phenomenon" (Garfinkel, lecture notes) Thus when we try to investigate some macro-organizational problem, we often find good rationales for what is being done at the local level—for example, asking, "Why do you do things in that way?" yields responses that make good sense in the situation and setting where the work actually gets done.

---

[8] Goethe predicated that by understanding personalities of couples, one could predict their future interactions and recombination. He referred to this as elective affinities (*Die Wahlverwandtschaften*), based on a scientific term used during his time to describe the tendency of chemical species to combine.

The Relevance of Culture to Enterprise Architecture

Organizational psychologist Karl Weick describes how every organization, including the most effective ones, are essentially "garrulous, clumsy, superstitious, hypocritical, monstrous, octopoid, wandering and grouchy" (Weick, 1977, p 146). This is because organizations organically emerge out of the communication patterns that develop in the course of doing business and in response to the host of environmental variables in dynamically changing business landscapes. Enterprises are instances of complex adaptive systems having many interacting subcomponents whose interactions yield complex behaviors. Complexity involves a "duality of interactive complex systems," in which "duality" refers to the idea that every action produces a ripple effect, on interdependent actors—the "structure." This ripple effect, in turn, shapes actions.

Enterprises are by their very nature disorganized. Russ Ackoff argued that all organizations are in a mess. It is our job to transform the organization by rolling up our sleeves and beginning to clean that mess. Ackoff described the nature of the problem of messes that faces us. He wrote: "In a real sense, problems do not exist. They are distractions from real situations. The real situations from which they are abstracted are messes. A mess is a system of interrelated problems. We should be concerned with messes, not problems. The solution to a mess is not equal to the sum of the solution to its parts. The solution to its parts should be derived from the solution of the whole; not vice versa. Science has provided powerful methods, techniques and tools for solving problems, but it has provided little that can help in solving messes. The lack of mess-solving capability is the most important challenge facing us" (Ackoff, 1999, p 113).

He advocates that there are five steps involved: the formulation of the mess, ends planning, means planning, resource planning, and the design of implementation and control systems. In one manner or another, most business process renewal or reengineering efforts involve some version of this approach.

The first step is to formulate that mess: "... a corporation's mess is the future implied by its and its environment's current behavior. Every system contains the seeds of its own deterioration and destruction. Therefore the purpose of formulating the mess is to identify the nature of these often concealed threats and to suggest changes that can increase the corporation's ability to survive and thrive" (Ackoff, 1999). Figuring out that mess involves three types of work. The first is an analysis of the state of the organization (or corporation) and how it interacts with the environment. Next is an "obstruction analysis" to identify the obstructions to development. Then we are to prepare reference projections engaging in the four stages leading to the transformation.

This is often easier stated than done. Consider most instances when we decide to clean up some mess, such as spring cleaning or cleaning up our offices after the conclusion of some major project. When I do so, I normally get a number of big, black garbage or lawn bags with the intent to toss away what I no longer need. However, by the end of the day, I am always taken back by the small amount of trash I actually have. It seems that with each file or paper I pick up, there are "strange connections" to other files and projects that are ongoing or I can see the file or paper's potential value toward helping with my next few projects. So, I end up throwing away perhaps copies of documents and a few other nonrelevant materials, but for the most part, I just refile or sort what I already have.

This suggests how the "mess" follows what we have recently learned about the nature of chaotic systems. In spite of perceived disorganized chaos, there seems to be what John Holland calls a "hidden order" to things (Holland, 1996). Rather than systems being totally random and chaotic, they are better understood as highly complex and self-adapting. In such systems, components become associated with each other by what complexity theorists call "strange attractors," which lead to new patterns entailing the emergence of new organizational forms.

As we discussed earlier, there is a distinction between complication and emergence. In the latter, we may understand what components comprise some situation or event. However, in such systems there are often interconnections among components that are almost impossible to take into account. Take, for instance, the phenomenon of weather. Although understanding the dynamics of weather and the range of variables involved, we are, in spite of the literally billions spent on predictive technologies, unable to fully predict conditions. This led to the concept of what has become known as the "butterfly effect," which was originally conceived by Massachusetts Institute of Technology (MIT) meteorologist Edward Lorenz, who created a mathematical model of the weather. He suggested how minute changes, as minimal as the flap of the wing of a butterfly, could have impacts on other molecules that are forming together to create weather patterns. That is, the wing flap gets associated with other molecules through strange attraction and leads to unexpected events. Lorenz's model led him to realize that long-term forecasting was doomed to failure. The butterfly effect suggests that a butterfly flapping its wings can affect the world's weather, and upon the suggestion of another colleague, Lorenz titled a paper he presented to the American Association for the Advancement of Science (AAAS) in 1972, "Does the Flap of a Butterfly's Wings in Brazil Set Off a Tornado in Texas?" that emphasized such interaction (Lorenz, 1972).

We are, however, not condemned to being unable to comprehend complexity. We can, after all, make approximate predictions of weather along with a wide range of natural, cultural, and organizational behavior. We may not be precise, but we can approximate a "for-all-practical-purposes" mode of description. In a very real sense, that is what we intend in modeling the complexity of an enterprise. We can establish relationships among operational systems and technical nodes in highly complex organizations that allow us to better plan for organizational transformation. Such modeling is far superior to no planning at all. This again brings up Ackoff's point about "plan or be planned for." It is important to be proactive and enact the organizations we want to be rather than be reactive to events as they chaotically unfurl.

Enacting Organizations

Karl Weick's portrayal of organizations as wandering and octopoid characterizes how we encounter them. In spite of such ubiquitous chaos, we seem to find order. However, order is something we do to organizations rather than being an inherent property of them. We create order through our beliefs about organizations. These beliefs constitute "cause maps" that we impose on the world and, once imposed, they characterize our view of organizations.

This is also known as the process of structuration (Giddens, 1986). Repeated interactions are the foundation of social structure. Interacting individuals whose activities are constrained by that perceived constructed structure in turn produce structure. Giddens (1986) calls this the duality of structure. This duality describes how social structures constrain choices and at the same time how social structures are created by the activities they constrain.

Structure does not exist in its own right. Rather, it is through enactments that we produce organization as ongoing accomplishments and reify their structure. "The kind of sense that an organization makes of its thoughts and of itself has an effect on its ability to deal with change. An organization that continually sees itself in novel images, images that are permeated with diverse skills and sensitivities, is equipped to deal with altered surroundings when they appear" (Weick, 1989). Weick argues that organizational transformation continually involves enactment. It is a form of social construction in social networks.

Connectedness in organizations characterizes the social networks within them. The study of social networks has led to a field within organizational and communications known as social network theory, which analyzes social relationships according to nodes and types of nodes that define them. There are three types of nodes: (1) operational, (2) systems, and (3) technical. Operational nodes connect the individual actors in networks who have ties that characterize how they are linked. Systems nodes are connections among the structures or systems that individuals create in their communication, and technical nodes are the technical components of those systems. In the DoDAF, each of these types of nodes represents different views whose models are different ways of representing the types of ties and information flows that obtain among them.

The study of social networks in organizations or organizational network analysis offers an approach to understand the internal workings of an organization. One social network consultant, Valdis Krebs, points out how "organization charts prescribe that work and information flow in a hierarchy, but network mapping reveals [they] actually flow through a vast web of informal channels" (Krebs, http://www.orgnet.com/about.html). These informal channels point to significant differences between the formal organizational structural view and what is actually occurring in the daily life of the enterprise. These differences have important impacts on how work gets done and allow analysis of bottlenecks, inefficiencies, and gaps in business processes. They also have critical implications in EA for determining how the information, data, and technical architectures relate to the business.

An important discovery in the study of social networks is the importance of applying graph theory to understand the complexity involved. This goes back to Leonhard Euler (1707–1783) and his solution to the puzzle of the Konigsberg Bridge. The river Pregel divides the town of Konigsberg into four separate land masses: A, B, C, and D (see Figure 2.1-2). Seven bridges connected the various parts of town, and some of the town's curious citizens wondered whether it were possible to take a journey across all seven bridges without having to cross any bridge more than once.

Euler showed why such a journey was impossible with the Konigsberg bridges, and questioned whether such a journey was possible for any network of bridges

FIGURE 2.1-2

The Bridges of
Konigsberg

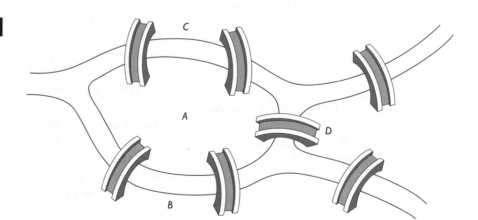

anywhere. He reasoned that for such a journey to be possible, each land mass would have to have an even number of bridges connected to it; or, if the journey were to begin at one land mass and end at another, then exactly those two land masses could have an odd number of connecting bridges while all other land masses must have an even number of connecting bridges. Euler recognized that in order to succeed, a traveler in the middle of the journey would have to enter a land mass by one bridge and leave by another; thus that land mass must have an even number of connecting bridges.

By visibly connecting nodes and defining the types of relationships among them, Euler showed how the displays of network graphs have hidden properties that limit or enhance the ability to do things with them. In so doing, Euler has been attributed with being among the first to show that the construction and structure of graphs or networks are the key to understanding complexity of the world. Graph theory is the substance of contemporary network analysis and, as we shall see, formulates the basis for the range of network type diagrams utilized in different enterprise architectural products. Social network theorist Rob Cross describes organizational network analysis (ONA) as "a powerful means of making invisible patterns of information flow and collaboration in strategically important groups visible" (Cross, 2005). Cross and colleagues interview members of organizations to uncover the types of links that exist between them and graph them out, connecting them as nodes. This often leads to some quite surprising results. In every social network, different people play different roles, ranging from central to peripheral to boundary spanner to isolates.

There is no single network structure or role positioning that is best for all organizations. For instance, in some organizations, a few individuals may be in a highly interactive role connecting different subgroups together. In a close examination of what is occurring, sometimes we find these individuals function more as bottlenecks than enablers. Once their functions within the organization are shared with other positions, information and work flow are made more efficient. However, in some instances, such boundary-spanning positions are relevant, allowing close management of projects.

What is important in network analysis is to uncover whether the structure is intentional and functional or whether they are emergent structures that impede the work and communication flows within the enterprise. Cross, Liedtka, and Weiss (2005) characterized three types of organizational networks, each representing a different value proposition that affects the patterns of collaboration that occur. The authors propose that managers should not force collaboration onto all employees and must take into account the appropriate proposition and organizational mission.

First are customized response networks. These exist in organizational contexts where there is ambiguity in both problems and solutions. Instances might include new product-development companies, high-end investment financial institutions, early-stage drug development teams, and strategy consulting firms. Customized response networks must rapidly define problems and coordinate expertise in response. The quick framing and solving of problems in innovative manner derive value. Second are modular response networks. These exist in contexts where parts of a problem and solution are known but the sequencing of those components is unknown. Cross and his colleagues give as examples surgical teams, business-to-business sales, and midstage drug development teams.

These types of organizations have networks to identify problem elements and be able to deal with them using modularized expertise. Value comes from delivering a unique response based on types of expertise required by particular problems such as a lawsuit or surgical procedure.

Third are routine response networks that are found in standardized work contexts. Here problems and solutions are well defined and predictable. These include call centers, claims processing, and late-stage drug development. Value is derived by efficient and consistent response to established problems.

Each of these network types requires different types of communication flows. In highly innovative and creative contexts, it is important for those directly involved to be in close, frequent communication where expertise is redundant, as well as having boundary-spanning access to other networks dealing with related issues.

However, it is also important, for example, that scientists be able to have independence and not always be closely managed such that their creativity is impeded. In modular response networks, there is more interchangeability of roles and a more structured approach to boundary spanning. In routine response networks, there are defined and structured boundaries with clear lines of authority and role relationships. Figure 2.1-3 shows the parameters for each network type.

As we have discussed, some see culture as very inclusive and define it in ways in which it is hard to conceive of what might be outside of its boundaries: "Culture is the deposit of knowledge, experiences, beliefs, values, attitudes, meanings, hierarchies, religion, timing, roles, spatial relations, concepts of the universe (world view), and material objects and possessions acquired by a group of people in the course of generations through individual and group striving" (Samovar et al., 1981, p 24–25). Anthropological and sociological ethnographers spend years doing ethnographic fieldwork to write up their studies of culture. As enterprise architects, we surely cannot undertake such an effort.[9]

---

[9] For his early work on this, see Romney and D'Andrade (1964).

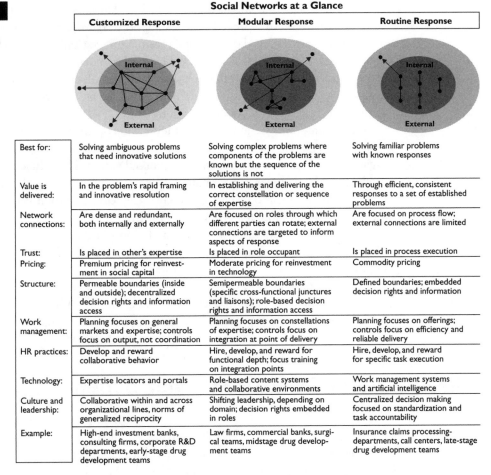

FIGURE 2.1-3

Social Networks (Cross et al., 2006)

Social Networks at a Glance

	Customized Response	Modular Response	Routine Response
Best for:	Solving ambiguous problems that need innovative solutions	Solving complex problems where components of the problems are known but the sequence of the solutions is not	Solving familiar problems with known responses
Value is delivered:	In the problem's rapid framing and innovative resolution	In establishing and delivering the correct constellation or sequence of expertise	Through efficient, consistent responses to a set of established problems
Network connections:	Are dense and redundant, both internally and externally	Are focused on roles through which different parties can rotate; external connections are targeted to inform aspects of response	Are focused on process flow; external connections are limited
Trust:	Is placed in other's expertise	Is placed in role occupant	Is placed in process execution
Pricing:	Premium pricing for reinvestment in social capital	Moderate pricing for reinvestment in technology	Commodity pricing
Structure:	Permeable boundaries (inside and outside); decentralized decision rights and information access	Semipermeable boundaries (specific cross-functional junctures and liaisons); role-based decision rights and information access	Defined boundaries; embedded decision rights and information
Work management:	Planning focuses on general markets and expertise; controls focus on output, not coordination	Planning focuses on constellations of expertise; controls focus on integration at point of delivery	Planning focuses on offerings; controls focus on efficiency and reliable delivery
HR practices:	Develop and reward collaborative behavior	Hire, develop, and reward for functional depth; focus training on integration points	Hire, develop, and reward for specific task execution
Technology:	Expertise locators and portals	Role-based content systems and collaborative environments	Work management systems and artificial intelligence
Culture and leadership:	Collaborative within and across organizational lines, norms of generalized reciprocity	Shifting leadership, depending on domain; decision rights embedded in roles	Centralized decision making focused on standardization and task accountability
Example:	High-end investment banks, consulting firms, corporate R&D departments, early-stage drug development teams	Law firms, commercial banks, surgical teams, midstage drug development teams	Insurance claims processing-departments, call centers, late-stage drug development teams

That is the bad news. A full ethnographic account of culture can take a significant investment of time and effort. The good news is that a full, comprehensive analysis of culture is not required to understand the cultural features that we require in enterprise architecture. Edgar Schein (2010) suggests a "clinical" ethnographic approach. Rather than being concerned with researching the complexity of organizational culture, a clinical perspective entails an action research perspective. Here the goal is to undertake cultural analysis to uncover the basic systemic cultural assumptions that give rise to particular problems, issues, and concerns within an organization. Schein used this approach in, for example, analyzing the Digital Equipment Corporation (DEC) culture, locating those cultural principles or assumptions that led both to its meteoric success and also its eventual decline. He argues we need to understand culture as the "pattern of shared basic assumptions that the group learned as it solved its problems of external adaptation and internal integration, that has worked well enough to be considered valid and ... to be taught to new members as the correct way to perceive, think and feel in relation to those problems" (Schein, 2004). These assumptions are not lists; rather, they are interconnected, networked, and systemic, forming the underlying bases for behavior.

Such assumptions are at the deepest level and constitute what might be considered a grammar of cultural principles that gives rise to two higher levels in organizational culture: its artifacts and espoused values. The artifacts are the visible products of the group or, for our purposes, the primitives we model in EA. The espoused values "focus on what people say is the reason for their behavior, what they ideally would like those reasons to be and ... their rationalizations for behavior" (Schein, 2004)—including the mission and vision, strategies, values, goals, and objectives that are conscious guides. Basic assumptions are the underlying theories of practice in use that actually (rather than assertively) guide behavior and inform group members about how to perceive, think about, and feel about things. Unless we dig down to the level of basic assumptions we cannot decipher artifacts, norms, and values. These assumptions are located only through an analysis of anomalies between observed visible artifacts and espoused beliefs and values.

Three Levels of Culture (Edgar Schein)

Schein (2003) posited three levels of culture: artifacts, espoused values, and tacit assumptions (see Figure 2.1-4). He analyzed five tacit assumptions forming a systemic pattern in DEC's internal relationships (see Figure 2.1-5).

Each of these assumptions was originally advocated by DEC founder Ken Olsen, and then was eventually incorporated into that assumption system. At the center was the assumption that work is fun and that Digital was a culture of innovation. Related to this were four basic assumptions. At the upper-left in Figure 2.1-5's diagram is an entrepreneurial spirit or "rugged individualism," where every member of the organization is in a sense an internal entrepreneur coming up with new ideas. When a new idea is proposed, there is the assumption of personal responsibility where, in the words of Olsen and as often quoted by DEC's senior management, "he who proposes does," and that everyone can be trusted to "do the right thing."

These concepts were also linked to the assumption of being highly volatile and even combative for one's ideas—the assumption of truth through conflict.

FIGURE 2.1-4

The Three Levels
of Culture
(Schein)

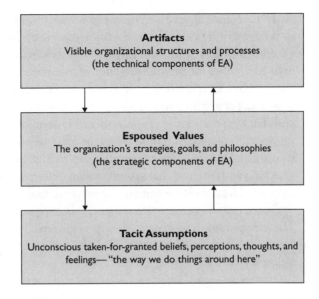

Artifacts
Visible organizational structures and processes
(the technical components of EA)

Espoused Values
The organization's strategies, goals, and philosophies
(the strategic components of EA)

Tacit Assumptions
Unconscious taken-for-granted beliefs, perceptions, thoughts, and
feelings— "the way we do things around here"

FIGURE 2.1-5

Five Tacit
Assumptions of
DEC's Internal
Culture

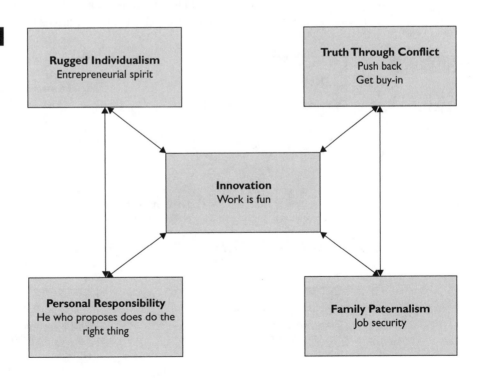

Rugged Individualism
Entrepreneurial spirit

Truth Through Conflict
Push back
Get buy-in

Innovation
Work is fun

Personal Responsibility
He who proposes does do the
right thing

Family Paternalism
Job security

At DEC, engineers received financial rewards when their project was chosen, and so there was a tremendous competition among each other to promote their ideas. Olsen established offsite meetings or "woods meetings" where engineers would fight each other for their ideas. The volatile nature of these meetings was the first reason that Olsen hired Schein as his consultant. However, once a concept was accepted, participants whose ideas were not selected would buy into the winners and push back on their ideas. This argument system for obtaining buy-in on ideas was supported by a kind of tenure system at DEC where once an employee was hired, job security and a strong sense of family paternalism were assumed.

Along with the internal system was an external assumption system for how DEC interacted with its environment for survival, as shown in Figure 2.1-6.

At the center of external assumptions is arrogance—here, engineering arrogance. The idea behind this arrogance is that engineers, scientists, and academics (myself being one) "know what is best." With this are four associated assumptions. One is indigenous to DEC management: that there is central control and the operations committee manages budgets for all projects. That being said, the three other major assumptions address how through "arrogance" problems can be solved. There is the concept of organizational idealism that reasonable people of good will can solve any problem. Engineers can resolve anything. This is strongly linked to a commitment

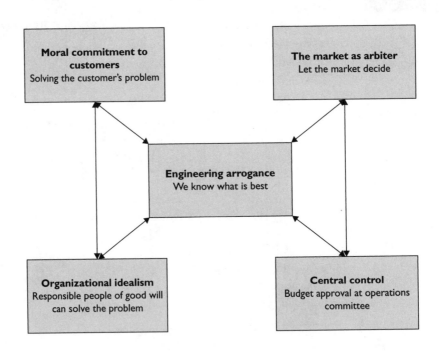

FIGURE 2.1-6

Five Assumptions of the External Environment

to customers and a dedication to solving customer's problems. At DEC, this was expressed in yearly conferences such as the Digital Equipment Company Users' Society (DECUS), a customer membership organization where customers presented both problems and ideas for DEC engineers to take on. Finally, there was the assumption about markets as arbiter. This involved the belief that if good products were made, they would demonstrate their value without having to be strongly promoted.

The latter involved a basic assumption of engineering culture that "good work speaks for itself" and that an engineer "should not have to sell himself." Olsen directly expressed this in his attitude about sales and marketing: "public relations and image building are forms of 'lying' and are to be avoided." This idealism of engineering and dominance over sales resulted in what Schein (2004) described as a lack of "the money gene" in the cultural DNA of DEC and countered DEC's ability to adapt to growth and changes in the business and technological landscapes. Consequently, the same assumptions that resulted in the meteoric success of Digital also underlay its eventual demise.

Schein also provides an analysis of the pharmaceutical company Novartis that stands in interesting contrast to Digital. Whereas DEC emphasized informality and rank and status were based on the actual job being performed by individuals, Novartis instead had a system of managerial ranks based on length of service, overall performance, and personal background of the individual. Thus rank and status had a more permanent quality at Novartis than at DEC, where one's fortunes could rise and fall based on a project. The value set at DEC versus Novartis was seen in the contrast in how meetings were perceived. At DEC, they were places were work gets done, whereas at Novartis they were necessary evils where announcements were made. Both corporations placed high value on individual contribution, but at Novartis one never went outside the chain of command or did things out of line with what one's boss suggested. As we discussed earlier, the tension between organizational artifacts and espoused values provides an avenue to discover the underlying assumptions of culture. In the case of Novartis, as Schein worked under the mandate of helping the corporation become more innovative, the artifact of central importance was a problem in the distribution of his suggestions. His suggestions were sent only after they were requested rather than being distributed by the managers as Schein had asked them to do. The rationale for this is that when a manager is given a job, it becomes the private domain of the individual. Hence there was a strong sense of turf or ownership and the assumption was made that each owner of a piece of the organization would be in charge and on top of his or her area. Only if information was requested was it acceptable to offer an idea. This led Schein to model the assumption system of Novartis as shown in Figure 2.1-7.

FIGURE 2.1-7

Novartis Cultural
Paradigm

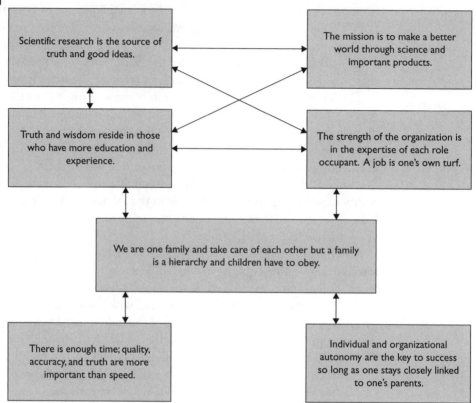

The important point here is how Schein was able to locate an underlying systematic that constitutes what Jackendoff (2009) described as an underlying set of grammatical rules for social cognition, or what we consider here to be culture. Also significant is that these rule sets can be modeled, and they are consistent with a particular set of products in EA: operational or business rules (or OV-6A in the DoDAF).

A business rule is guidance that there is an obligation concerning conduct, action, practice, or procedure within a particular activity or sphere (from the business rules group [BRG]). In DoDAF (and MoDAF), the Operational Rules Model (OV-6a) specifies operational or business rules that are constraints on the way that business is done in the enterprise. At lower levels, OV-6a describes the rules under which the architecture or its nodes behave under specified conditions. Such rules can be expressed in a textual form, as in, "If (these conditions) exist, and (this event) occurs, then (perform these actions)."

Locating Culture as Business Rules

Some rules are located in policy and business process documentation. Although many rules are expressed as formal rules of the business, many others are hidden from view and to be uncovered. Both types constrain activity and provide schema for culturally appropriate organizational behavior. This also is relevant to the work of psychologist David Rumelhart on parallel distributed processing as microstructures of cognition (Rumelhart, 1987). He developed the concept of "story grammars" as cognitive microstructures that constitute formal grammars to capture the structure of stories. A formal grammar is an abstract structure composed of a set of (rewrite) sequencing rules that comprise schema. A schema is an abstract representation of a generic concept for an object, event, or situation. Rumelhart showed that schema consist of a network of interrelationships among the major constituents of the situation represented by the schema. In this way, we can consider a business rule as an instance of this concept, which as I argued can be formally modeled.

This relation of business rule to cultural schema is consistent with linguistic theories of generative grammars and transformational linguistics. This approach, first proposed by Noam Chomsky (1957) asserts there are transformational operations that are defined for any linguistic string (sentence) that modifies (transforms) it; for instance, an assertion may be transformed to a question and then to a request. These are also called "rewrite rules." Anthropologists adapted this idea to develop "rewrite" rules for various cultural concepts or terminological systems, such as kinship. In this way, we can consider a business rule as an instance of this concept, which as I argued can be formally modeled.

In enterprise architecture, the first step in the modeling of business or operational rules is to model them in activity models—the OV5 set of models. That is, business or operational rules can be modeled relevant to each activity and cultural rules can thus be expressed within activities. Such activities can be decomposed into sets of constitutive activities with inheritance, as with an activity tree hierarchy diagram model. These then can be either diagrammatically modeled as an activity model following IDEF0 or Business Process Modeling Notation (BPMN) notation. In the DODAF, there is no single format for OV-6A, as they can also be given as statements, as was discussed previously.[10]

---

[10] IDEF0 involves showing inputs, outputs, controls, and mechanisms, whereas Business Process Modeling Notation (BPMN) shows process flows and connections to resource nodes in swim lanes.

FIGURE 2.1-8

Context Diagram
for Becoming a
Project Manager

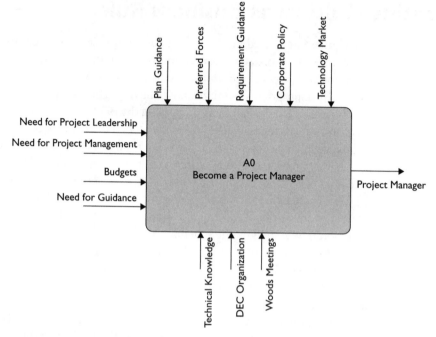

Returning to Schein's example of DEC culture, we might model the activity of becoming a project manager as shown in Figure 2.1-8.

Figure 2.1-8 is a "context diagram" with inputs, outputs, controls, and mechanisms for the highest-level activity in an activity hierarchy, which can be represented as shown in Figure 2.1-9.

Each of these decomposed activities can be modeled using IDEF0 or BPMN in an OV-5b diagram to the most relevant level of descriptive depth, as shown in Figure 2.1-10.

An example of such modeling can be made from an observation from DEC culture as described by Schein. In the 1980s, one of the authors, Beryl Bellman, was the research director at Behavioral Sciences Institute (WBSI) in La Jolla, California, which focused on computer communications and included the formation of the School of Management and Strategic Studies (SMSS).[11] The school was a program

---

[11] The WBSI was founded by Carl Rodgers and Richard Farson and was a research think tank to study small group behavior. Many major researchers were part of the Institute, including Abraham Maslow, who wrote his major work on the hierarchy of needs while at the WBSI. In the 1980s, Farson and his colleagues redefined the mission to focus on computer-mediated communities, which included founding the School of Management and Strategic Studies.

FIGURE 2.1-9

Decomposition
Diagram

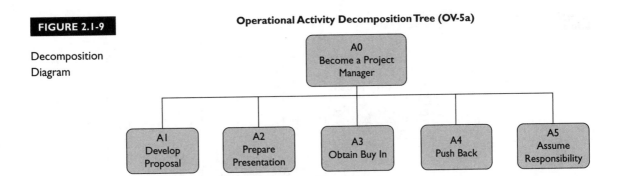

Operational Activity Decomposition Tree (OV-5a)

for senior executives from the public and private sectors, who attended biannual weeklong workshops and then continued their discussions online using computer conferencing and messaging.[12]

An interesting perk of being on the WBSI staff was often being invited to lunch with several of the management teams from the participating organizations. After a short time, Bellman noticed an interesting pattern where at lunch, when the check was presented, a number of executives got up and went to the restroom. He interviewed several of his DEC associates and learned that there was a "cultural" business rule that the highest-ranking person attending such an event was responsible to pay the bill. In this case, there often were several members of DEC with equal rank within the corporation (often at the vice-presidential level) attending the sessions, which potentially created a dilemma or competition for paying the check. This was resolvable by an associated business rule that seniority is established by project rather than rank. That is, the highest-ranking person at the table was the individual of high rank who had been attending the WBSI program for the longest period of time. Thus, those at the table contextually evaluated their relative rank to others in attendance. If others were of higher rank, they remained at the table. However, if others at the table were of equal rank within the company, the person to pay the bill was the person who had been attending the SMSS program the longest. In this case, those of equivalent rank often left the table when the bill was presented, allowing the most senior among them to take out his or her credit card. This cultural business rule structure could be modeled as shown in Figure 2.1-11.

This business rule corresponds to the assumption system structural schema that Schein described for internal integration in the interaction between the two cultural assumptions of family paternalism and truth through conflict. On the one hand,

---

[12] This included all members of the U.S. Army General Staff as well as CEO and upper management from major corporations, including DEC, IBM, Polaroid, and others.

FIGURE 2.1-10

Activity Model

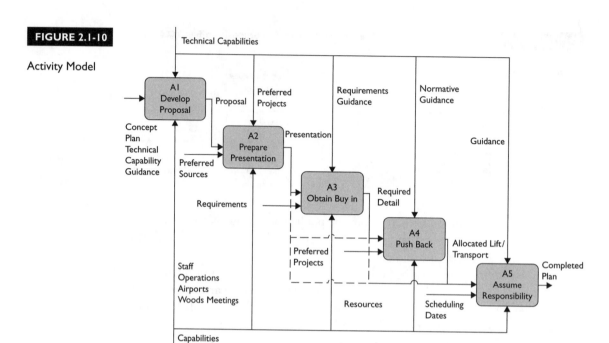

there is the strong integrative function expressed in the assumption about the DEC family, but on the other hand, the "truth through conflict" assumption comes into play when decisions are made. In this case, there is a pushing back and buying in rather than an open negotiation of status in the presence of non–family members.

FIGURE 2.1-11

Cultural Business
Rule

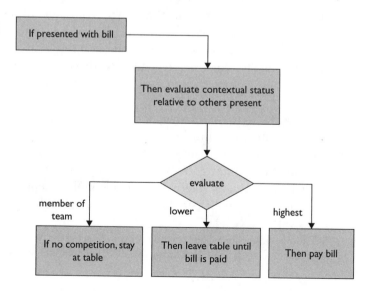

The Emergence of Culture

An enterprise arises from local interaction of often-independent units that exist within a common environment. Each unit or entity interacts with its immediate environment according to a set of low-order rules. The combined effects of these lower order interactions within an environment give rise to higher-order organizational phenomenon or organizational culture. Culture emerges from localized interactions. As culture is grounded at the local level, culture is highly resistant to change.

Organizational culture is an emergent phenomenon. It resembles the process of *stigmergy*, which is a kind of indirect communication and learning by the environment found in social insects. It is a well-known example of self-organization, providing vital clues for understanding how components can interact to produce a complex pattern. Stigmergy is a form of coordination through changes in an environment. Following an example by Deneubourg and his colleagues (1990), if one were to take a bucket of dead ants and scatter them about in a room and then throw in a bucket of live ants afterward and seal off the room, in a few days when we look inside we would find all the ants in a single pile. Deneubourg and his associates (2003) conjectured a probabilistic explanation of this behavior as follows: Faced with a dead ant, a live ant picked it up with probability inversely proportionate to the number of other dead ants in the vicinity. While carrying a dead ant, an ant put it down with probability directly proportional to the density of dead ants in the vicinity. Thus the coordinated behavior of piling dead ants in a single pile resulted from a simple local rule controlling the behavior of a single ant. The piling behavior is accounted for without postulating communication among the ants. Beckers, Holland, and Deneubourg (1994) developed an experiment using robotic ants programmed with a swarm instruction based on the living ants and produced similar results.

An enterprise arises from local interaction of often-independent units that exist within a common environment. Each unit or entity interacts with its immediate environment according to a set of low-order rules. The combined effects of these lower-order interactions within an environment give rise to a higher-order organizational phenomenon or organizational culture. Culture emerges from the sites and surfaces of localized interactions. As culture is grounded at the local level, culture is highly resistant to change. Changing culture entails respecifying local-level rules rather than simply imposing change from the top. Creating enterprise architecture proffers a mechanism to initiate positive change. These underlying local-level rules giving rise to an emergent organizational culture can be modeled to help us understand the implications they have on enterprise architecture at every level.

We have discussed how agent modeling can be described as sets of cultural business rules. These sets comprise different types of strategic interaction games, as exemplified in the classic example of the prisoner's dilemma. However, in game theory the focus has been on one game at a time. Using evolving automata, cognitive behavior is modeled across multiple games, or what Bedner refers to as ensembles of games. This points to a game-theoretic model of culture, as participants simultaneously play out a series of games constituting ensembles that impact the strategy for any particular game.

In this context, Axelrod (1997) characterized cultures as vectors with agent attributes. A shared culture of common attributes emerges when these agents become more like those with whom they interact and also interact with those who share similar attributes. This recommends a new type of explanation for social and cultural phenomenon. As Epstein and Axtell (1996) argue, we should reinterpret the question of explanation by asking "can we grow it?" They maintain that such modeling "allows us to 'grow' social structures ... demonstrating that certain sets of *micro-specifications* are sufficient to generate the *macro-phenomena* of interest." They argue, with this in mind, that social scientists "are presented with 'already emerged' collective phenomena and ... seek *micro-rules* that can generate them." Our point here is that by locating the underlying business rule schema that underlie social contextualized behaviors, we can in a sense run computational models that allow the traceability we suggested earlier between business process proposals and cultural assumptions that are entailed. Such assumptions inform and can be incorporated into enterprise architecture.

Perspectives on Culture

A full understanding of any organizational or enterprise culture requires that one views it from multiple perspectives. Organizational theorist Joanne Martin (2001) argues for a three-perspective view of culture. First is the integration view, where every member of the organization shares culture in an enterprisewide consensus. Where there is lack of consensus, remedial actions are taken or suggestions are made that those who do not agree leave the organization. This view is expressed in solidarity and *esprit de corps*. Next, there is the differentiation or subcultural view. This involves a focus on inconsistent interpretations based on subculture and stakeholder perspectives and entails a loose coupling between representations of the culture as expressed to outsiders versus representations given to insiders. Then there is the fragmentation perspective that focuses on ways in which organizational cultures are inconsistent, ambiguous, and multiplicitous and in a state of flux. This addresses the multiplicities of interpretation that do not coalesce into a collectivitywide consensus of an integration view nor create subcultural consensus of the differentiation perspective.

Each view entails different sets of assumptions, and while each is simultaneously present in every culture at any given time, one of the perspectives can have prominence over others. So when presenting itself to the outside, the integration view shows *esprit de corps* and allows members to see themselves as part of a common culture in spite of the differences that obtain within. In the differentiation view, there are organizational stovepipes and internal competition. There is always a danger of subcultures becoming hostile to each other, turning themselves into contra cultures.

In the RMN Airport example discussed throughout this book, we need to keep in mind these perspectives and that each entails a different level of emergence through interlocking sets of game ensembles. There are the integrated, emergent properties of the coherent culture of RMN as an entity; the divergent subcultures emerging in the context of the various functional organizations of the airport (management, flight control, concessions, the Transportation Security Administration [TSA], and so on); and the emergence of fragmented cultures at the shop floor, with the local-level politics and reliance on "how we go about doing things around here." There is a concatenation of these at any given time, yet they can be modeled and the effects of culture be better understood as they impact the EA of RMN.

Questions

1. Describe the organizational or corporate culture that you must deal with to obtain information relevant to your enterprise architecture.

2. Describe which cultural constraints—social, political, interpersonal, value systems—impact your ability to obtain information and how you plan to deal with them.

3. Using the grid/group model for measuring culture, how would you place the organizational culture of your enterprise?

4. How is culture represented in the different architecture viewpoints?

5. What is the relationship between communication networks and organizational culture?

6. Which column of Zachman Framework is relevant to culture?

7. We discussed how culture assumption systems could be modeled as a special instance of business rules. Such rules can be expressed in a textual form—for example, "If (these conditions) exist, and (this event) occurs, then (perform these actions)"—or shown graphically using a flow diagram. Identify a cultural assumption relationship within your or a client's organization and provide a rule schema for some cultural activity scenario using either textual or a graphical representation.

8. What steps would you engage in to diagnose organizational culture problems and how would you begin to change them?

End Note

Morphemes are either bounded or unbounded. Examples of the latter correspond to lexemes (the spoken equivalent of words, which are written), and the former are those that must be associated with another bounded or unbounded morpheme, such as the plural morpheme we discuss here.

Reference List

Ackoff, Russ. (1981). *Creating the corporate future: plan or be planned for*. Wiley.

Ackoff, Russell, L., with Addison, Herbert J., & Carey, Andrew. (2010). *Systems thinking for curious managers: with 40 new management f-LAWS*. Trinity Press.

Bendor, Jonathon, and Swistak, Piotr. (2001). *The evolution of norms*. American Journal of Sociology, 106 (6), p. 1493–1545.

Chomsky, Noam. (2002). *Syntatic structures* (reprint). Mouton.

Cross, Rob, Laseter, Tim, Parker, Andrew, & Velasquez, Guillermo. (2006). *The basis for creating network links*. Harvard Business Review (November).

Cross, R., Liedtka, J. & Weiss, L. (2005). *A practical guide to social networks*. Harvard Business Review 83(3), p. 124–132.

Depickère S., Fresneau, D., & Deneubourg, J. L. (2004). *A basis for spatial and social patterns in ant species: dynamics and mechanisms of aggregation*. Journal of Insect Behavior, 17(1), p. 81–97.

Douglas, Mary. (1970). *Natural symbols*. Routledge.

Edward N. Lorenz. (1963). *Deterministic nonperiodic flow.* Journal of the Atmospheric Sciences, Vol. 20: 130.

Epstein, Joshua M. and Axtell, Robert L. (1996). *Growing artificial societies: social science from the bottom up.* MIT Press.

Garfinkel, H. (1967). *Good organizational reasons for bad clinical records.* In *Studies in ethnomethodology.* Prentice Hall.

Giddens, A. (1986). *Constitution of society: outline of the theory of structuration.* University of California Press.

Goethe, Johann Wolfgang. (2006 reprint). *Theory of colors.* Dover.

Gudykunst, William & Kim, Young Yum. (2002). *Communicating with strangers.* McGraw Hill.

Hall, Edward. (1990). *The hidden dimension.* Anchor.

Hofstede, Geert. (1996). *Cultures and organizations, software of the mind: intercultural cooperation and its importance for survival.* McGraw Hill.

Hofstede, Geert. (2010). *Cultures and organizations: software for the mind.* McGraw Hill.

Holland, John. (1996). *Hidden order: how adaptation builds complexity.* Basic.

Hymes, Del. (1974). *Foundations of sociolinguistics: an ethnographic approach.* University of Pennsylvania Press.

Hymes, Del. (1974). *The ethnography of speaking.* In Gladwin, T. & Sturtevant, W.C. (eds), *Anthropology and Human Behavior,* The Anthropology Society of Washington, (Washington), 1962.

International Phonetic Association. (1999). *Phonetic description and the IPA chart: handbook of the International Phonetic Association: a guide to the use of the international phonetic alphabet.* Cambridge University Press.

Jackendoff, Ray. (2009). *Language, consciousness, culture.* MIT Press.

Krebs, Valdis. http://www.orgnet.com/VKbio.html.

Levi-Strauss, Claude. (1983). *The raw and the cooked.* University of Chicago Press.

Lorenz, Edward. (1972). *Does the flap of a butterfly's wings in Brazil set off a tornado in Texas?* Paper presented at AAAS.

Martin, Joanne. (2001). *Cultures in organizations: three perspectives.* Oxford University Press.

Martin, Joanne. (2001). *Organizational culture: mapping the terrain.* Sage Press.

McCelland, James and Rumelhart, David. (1987). *Parallel distributed processing: explorations in the microstructure of cognition, vol. 1: foundations.* MIT Press.

Papa, M. J., Daniels, T. D., & Spiker, B. K. (2010). *Organizational communication: perspectives and trends,* 5th edition. Sage.

Parsons, Talcott. (1970). *Social system.* Routeldge, Kegan Paul.

Romney, Kimball, & D'Andrade, Roy. (1964). *Cognitive aspects of English kin terms.* American Anthropologist, 66(3), p. 146–170.

Schein, Edgar. (2003). *Organizational culture and leadership,* 1st edition. Jossey-Bass.

Schein, Edger. (2010). *Organizational culture and leadership,* 4th edition. Jossey-Bass.

Schein, Edger. (2004). *DEC is dead, long live DEC.* Berrett-Koehler.

Seel, Richard. (2000). *Culture and complexity.* Organizations & People, 7(2), p. 2–9.

Silverman, David. (1998). *Harvey Sacks: social science and conversation analysis.* Oxford.

Weick, Karl. (1977). *On re-punctuating the problem in new perspectives on organizational effectiveness.* In Paul Goodman (ed) *New Perspectives on Organizational Effectiveness;* Jossey Bass 1977.

Weick, Kurt. (1995). *Sensemaking in organizations.* Sage.

2.2

Planning the EA

Planning is something no one likes to do, but it is absolutely critical for achieving a useful EA. EA is a decision support tool, not an end unto itself, so a good understanding of the decisions the EA will support and the data needed is necessary to achieve success. Organizations that skimp on planning for their EA end up spending a lot of money on a mountain of models and data that they then have no idea how to use.

In this chapter, we will focus on the architect's input to the planning process and prepare the architect both for providing input to EA planning and for reviewing EA plans. We will use the Six Step process, introduced in Chapter 1.3, as the basis for discussion. Other comprehensive approaches, such as the Architecture Development Methodology (ADM) [www.opengroup.org], cover similar topics. Figure 2.2-1 shows the Six Step process from the planning perspective. Steps 1, 2, and 3 and part of step 4 need to be performed to determine the scope of the overall architecture work. This part of planning needs to be done prior to developing or issuing a statement of work (SOW) for architecture model, product, or artifact development. Planning for the rest of step 4 and steps 5 and 6 needs to be part of planning for an architecture project. Because EAs evolve over time, the work identified in the scoping process may be addressed in more than one project. The approach to breaking up the EA work into projects and the approach to planning in general are driven by enterprise culture.

We will first address scoping the overall EA work and then address planning for EA projects.

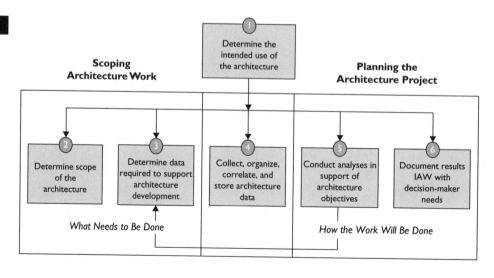

FIGURE 2.2-1

The Six Step Process from a Planning Perspective

Scoping the Architecture Work

The first few steps of the Six Step process identify what needs to be done in terms of the scope and deliverables of the EA as illustrated in Figure 2.2-2. The goal of the exercise is to establish traceability from the purpose of the architecture, in terms of the stakeholders (that is, the users of the architecture) and their issues, to the selected architecture artifacts and the data that they contain. This traceability ensures that the architecture contains the data needed to support the stakeholders' decision making. The information developed in these first few steps also includes information needed for the summary or executive overview document for the EA. This document is the Summary and Overview Information (All Viewpoints view AV-1). We will review each step in detail in the following subsections, provide an example, and summarize success factors.

Purpose

Step 1 focuses on identifying the reasons that the architecture is being developed, as summarized in Figure 2.2-3. Identifying the purpose of the architecture involves both framing the high-level problem that the architecture is being built to answer as well as identifying all the users of the architecture and their specific issues and questions. Identifying the high-level problem serves to align the architecture with strategic

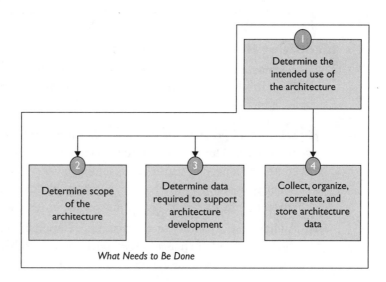

FIGURE 2.2-2

Scoping the Architecture Work

FIGURE 2.2-3

Determining the
Intended Use of
the Architecture

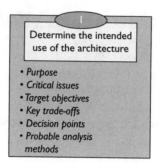

FIGURE 2.2-3

Determining the
Intended Use of
the Architecture

business or mission needs, whereas identifying the stakeholders and their specific
questions ensures that the data needed to address specific decisions is included in the
architecture with the right level of detail.

Knowing the purpose of the architecture helps the architect develop completion
criteria for the various modeling efforts. For example, a common problem is how
far to decompose an activity model. A typical question that is asked is, "We've
decomposed the activity model down five levels. Are we done?" The answer depends
on the intended use of the information, based on the specific needs of stakeholders.
Suppose the architecture purpose is to develop an understanding of the current
operations of an organization's headquarters offices for purposes of impact analysis
for proposed changes. Then the activity model needs to decompose organizational
activities down to the level where the activities performed by the headquarters offices
can be separated from the activities performed by other organizational entities.

Identifying the High-Level Purpose

The development of an architecture is usually driven by some important business
need. Often, this business need can be tied to strategic goals and objectives.
Examples of high-level purposes include the following:

- **Selection of projects for funding**   When multiple competing projects
  are requesting funding, determination of importance, "fit," priority, and
  continued longevity within an existing framework can be accomplished by
  building an architecture that encompasses the competing projects in the
  context of the operations or business of the enterprise.

- **Adding new capability to an existing operation or system**   New capabilities
  cause a ricochet of change across touch points of other operations and
  systems as well as a burden on shared infrastructures. An architecture

provides an analysis tool to determine the impact of the planned new capability and a determination of further actions required to ensure that the change is absorbed gracefully and in a planned manner.

- **Mission/business process reengineering**   Any reengineering effort involves the discovery of the current or as-is situation, setting a target direction and developing a roadmap. Along the way, impact analysis determines how the target direction affects related items. Typically, two architectures are built: an as-is and a target architecture. A transition plan involves transformation of architecture elements from the as-is to the target state.

- **Joint or mission interoperability**   Joint operations involve coordinating activities from multiple organizations with different processes, skills, training, operational structures, and organizational cultures. Mission interoperability requires "threading" activities from these multiple enterprises. Having architectures that depict the operational activities for each of these enterprises is useful to support the definition of mission "threads."

- **Impact analysis for proposed changes**   Any change tends to be disruptive. Being able to anticipate that disruption and deal with it is a way to ensure that changes are successfully dealt with. Some changes are forced upon an enterprise, such as budget cuts. Others are conscious directions and strategies, such as business transformation or mergers and acquisitions. Defining an architecture for the enterprise provides a list of items that are candidates for change. Analysis of a specific type of change involves examining the perturbation (or lack thereof) that will be caused to each of the architecture elements.

- **Transition planning**   Transition planning is the activity of planning for transition of an enterprise from the current (as-is) state to the target (to-be) state. Typically, two architectures are built: an as-is and target architecture. A transition plan involves transformation of architecture elements from the as-is to the target state. The transition plan indicates which architecture elements will be deprecated, which will be carried forward, and which will be transformed or modified to be consistent with the target state.

- **Modernization**   Modernization, at least in the traditional sense, is primarily a technology transformation activity. An enterprise's legacy technology is replaced by new technology with the expectation that savings will result from operations and new opportunities for additional capabilities and services are created. As a side effect of modernization, force structures, locations and facilities, and business processes may have to be modified. Modernization is a transformational activity that must follow the same path as transition planning. This allows for an orchestrated move from the current state to the target state considering all risks and factors involved.

■ **Reorganization**   Reorganization is often a traumatic restructuring of the anatomy of an organization. Just as an anatomical change involves relocating and resizing organs, reorganization has a ripple effect on a number of items, such as facilities, roles and skills, activities, responsibilities, and objectives. An architecture provides a mechanism to perform the potential impact of reorganization before any actions are attempted.

■ **Integration of legacy systems**   Legacy systems are information systems implemented in a technology that is either obsolete or becoming obsolete but continue to exist because the business value they provide cannot be substituted easily or conveniently with newer systems built on more contemporary technologies. Integration of legacy systems involves orchestrating a set of system functions, some belonging to the legacy system and others belonging to newer systems. This orchestration also touches platform interactions, data exchanges, connectivity issues, as well as timing and execution-related parameters. An architecture description that depicts the legacy and new systems in a common way allows for the depiction of these issues and provides a means to achieving successful orchestration.

For example, in the case study in Part V of this book, the architecture is needed to help direct transition planning to keep changes and investment aligned with strategic goals.

The high-level problem may also involve at least one of the following: specific strategic objectives, key trade-offs, critical issues, critical decision points, or specific analyses. An example strategic objective for a program might be improved capability, such as increasing the overall efficiency of a mission process by a certain percentage or improving the quality of the process output. An example of a strategic objective for the Federal Aviation Authority (FAA) is to increase air traffic three times. The Next Generation Air Traffic System (NGATS) architecture is being built both to guide transition and decide the appropriate measure for air traffic. An example of a key trade-off is the trade-off between centralized data and management and distributed, replicated data and the synchronization management issues that it entails. This trade-off is frequently a key issue within the intelligence community. It involves both operational issues involving which approach best supports operations as well as technology issues involving the current technology support for data replication and synchronization. An example of a critical issue is air defense command and control in the context of a joint task force. Because any of the Military Services may staff the air defense position in a joint task force, the solution must allow flexibility for the different Services' approaches to this process.

Each problem may involve specific analyses of architecture information or of which architecture information is critical input. For example, answering questions about process improvement may involve activity-based costing analysis that will require both architecture information (an activity model) and financial/cost information. Support for selection of projects for funding may involve business case analysis. Trade-offs may require performance modeling or simulation.

Identifying Stakeholders and Their Issues

Although there is usually a single high-level purpose for building an architecture, there are usually multiple users of the architecture, whom we will call *stakeholders* in the rest of this discussion. Each of these stakeholders has specific purposes for the architecture: decisions they need the architecture to support and specific issues and questions that they want the architecture to address. Not only are there multiple stakeholders with multiple purposes, but often these purposes conflict with each other. It is important to identify all the stakeholders and to address conflicts between purposes as well as prioritization issues related to which purpose is more important to address in the face of resource constraints in developing the architecture.

Determining the full set of stakeholders and their architecture purposes may require some detective work. Stakeholders involve all architecture users as well as the architecture owners or the organizations sponsoring the architecture work. Frequently, in government or large organizations, success in achieving the owning organization's goals may include satisfying the needs of outside architecture user groups. One way of identifying internal stakeholders is to consider the levels of stakeholders identified by the Zachman Framework introduced in Chapter 1.2. Figure 2.2-4 (Department of Defense, 2009, p. 61) summarizes these levels of stakeholders.

There are often important external stakeholders. In the government, it is important to consider the various levels of decision makers who may be using the architecture. For example, in DoD, the owning organization may need the architecture to address a Military Service–specific program objective, but the Joint Requirements Oversight Council (JROC), which approves program funding, needs the architecture to determine how the proposed solution supports DoD-wide goals and objectives to improve capability. Example architecture users include the JROC,

FIGURE 2.2-4

Levels of
Stakeholders
from the
Perspective of
the Zachman
Framework

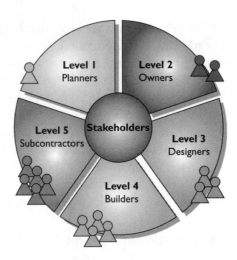

Military Service–specific investment/budget decision makers, battle integration laboratories, and Service training organizations. Architecture users also include the groups that will perform the analysis of the architecture information. Figure 2.2-5 illustrates the various levels of stakeholders who may be involved with a DoD architecture.

The high-level stakeholders, such as Government Accountability Office (GAO) and the Office of Management and Budget (OMB), identified in Figure 2.2-5, also

FIGURE 2.2-5

Levels of
Stakeholders for
DoD Within the
Government

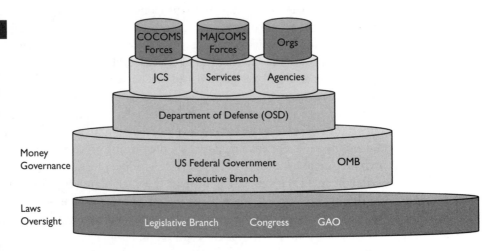

need to be considered for non-DoD federal departments, because the financial governance and legislative oversight is the same for all federal departments and agencies. OMB has very specific requirements regarding the architecture information it needs before it will approve funding for projects. For both government and commercial organizations, external partners may also be stakeholders. For example, working out details of "just-in-time" delivery of parts or supplies will involve joint analysis and agreements with the manufacturers and their suppliers. Government organizations may need to work with commercial organizations or international partners. For example, the FAA needs to coordinate with the corresponding agencies in many countries and with international aviation organizations. The Treasury Department needs to coordinate procedures with commercial banks and the Federal Reserve System. Additional discussion of stakeholders can be found in Chapter 2.4.

Scope

While step 1 of the Six Step process identifies the purposes of the architecture, step 2 sets the architecture's scope. The scope determines what is considered internal to the architecture and what is external. Frequently, an architecture may be focused on a specific aspect of a larger enterprise. Step 2 determines how to decide whether specific information should be included in the architecture. Note that the term "scope" is used differently in the Six Step process and in the Summary and Overview Information view (AV-1). This chapter focuses only on the Six Step process' usage of the term.

Typically, the scope is established by answering a number of questions related to the context of the architecture, which are listed in Figure 2.2-6 and discussed in the following bullets.

- *What's the span of the enterprise?* There needs to be a clear understanding of what level of enterprise architecture will be developed. Setting an architecture's operational bounds starts with a clear statement of any overarching enterprise and the aspect of that enterprise that is to be the subject of the architecture. For example, within a multinational corporation, an architecture might be a segment-level architecture for European operations. Within the U.S. DoD, a solution-level architecture might be specific to a single Military Service. Or a solution-level architecture may be part of the DoD business enterprise architecture but be restricted to the Army-specific aspect of that architecture.

FIGURE 2.2-6

Determining the
Scope of the
Architecture

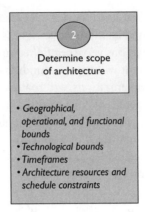

- What are the operational bounds? What missions, enterprise core functions, support business functions, or organizations are included? For example, within the DoD, the architecture may be restricted to a specific warfare mission, to a specific support service, or to missions other than war. Within a given mission, the architecture may be restricted to specific operational processes or to specific organizations. For example, an architecture might be limited to a specific combat service support process as carried out by a specific Army organization. For a corporation, the architecture might be limited to corporate financial operations or to a specific operation required by state law for all offices within that state.

- Are there geographic bounds? What geo-regions of the world, countries of the world, parts of the United States, or types of facilities and installations will be covered by the architecture effort? For example, the architecture may be focused on operations that are specific to the continental United States (CONUS) or it may involve worldwide operations. Some architectures may be specific to a particular country or geographic area, such as the Middle East, Africa, Southeast Asia, or Bosnia, or the architecture may be restricted to in-theater operations. An architecture may have more generic geographic limits, such as land, sea, littoral region, air, or space.

- What timeframes does the architecture address? The timeframe for an architecture is the range of dates for which the architecture applies. A current, objective, or as-is architecture documents the current state of the architecture and can be used to support decisions related to sustainment. Sometimes these architectures are called as-planned architectures if they include information on the changes that are planned and funded within the current budget cycle. Target or to-be architectures address the anticipated architecture of the enterprise at some future point in time. To-be architectures need to have a specific implementation date attached that indicates when the architecture should be implemented. An enterprise typically has multiple to-be architectures that contain varying levels of information and detail. For example, the long-term target or vision architecture is typically used to support strategic decision making for the longer term, while the to-be architecture for the next budget cycle documents the proposed improvements to the current architecture for which funding is being sought. This near-term to-be architecture should be implemented within the fiscal years covered by that next budget cycle. There may be multiple intermediate to-be architectures that represent expected stages in the transition process from as-is to vision architecture. The vision architecture may focus on only high-level concepts, whereas the to-be architecture for the next budget cycle needs to be very detailed and concrete. The budget cycle to-be architectures should move the enterprise in the direction of the vision architecture.

■ *Are there constraints on the technology to be considered?* The scope should identify any assumptions and constraints on the technology aspects of the architecture. As-is architectures may be limited in the extent of the information technology considered. The architecture may focus on applications only, or it may include infrastructure aspects of the technology, such as platforms and communications. Sometimes an as-is architecture may simply consist of a technology inventory. To-be architectures may be limited in terms of specific technology assumptions and constraints. Near-term to-be architectures may be limited in the technology considered by the need to remain interoperable with a specified set of external legacy systems or standards. Enterprise policy may limit technology for some parts of the enterprise, such as business operations, to available commercial off-the-shelf (COTS) technology. Other parts of an enterprise may expect the use of innovative technology to meet operational capabilities. For example, the Internal Revenue Service (IRS) needs to restrict its operational information technology (IT) to COTS technologies that have the proven capability to handle large amounts of data and transactions, whereas the intelligence community usually has requirements that "push the envelope" and necessitate innovation in terms of integration of COTS or development of new algorithms and solutions.

■ *Are there specific schedule and resource constraints?* If the material identified by the first four steps of the Six Step process is being developed in a single architecture effort, under a single funding allocation, then the schedule and resource constraints of that effort will usually result in scope limitations for that architecture. The architecture effort may be limited in the overall amount of time within which product development can take place. For example, the effort may be limited by fiscal-year boundaries or by a specific number of weeks or months. Within that period of time, there may be specific milestones that need to be met. For example, architecture guidance for key system development projects may be needed by specific dates or other types of architecture information may be needed in time for an annual investment review. In addition, the level of effort or personnel resources available to meet the milestones and schedules may be limited. If the resources are limited and there are significant schedule and milestone constraints, other aspects of the architecture scope, such as operational and geographic bounds and timeframes, may need to be revisited. Operational bounds may need to be further restricted in order to produce meaningful and useful results. For example, the operational bounds of the architecture might be further restricted to the operations supported by the system or systems for which architecture guidance is needed.

Identifying Needed Data

Step 3 focuses on identifying the types of data needed to address the architecture purposes and stakeholder questions, within the bounds of the architecture scope and without explicit consideration of which products will be used to document the information. Figure 2.2-7 summarizes the focus of this step. To identify the types of data needed and their relationships, each purpose or stakeholder question should be examined to see what types of data are needed to address the problem or answer the question and how these types of data are related. The concepts and relationships introduced in Chapter 1.3 provide a basic set of data types and relationships that can be used. Sometimes the questions may be too high-level or complex to analyze directly. In this case, each high-level question must be decomposed into a set of simpler questions whose answers provide the architecture information needed to address the original question. Further, not all the types of data required for a purpose or problem are architectural in nature. For example, questions involving cost may need substantial financial input, and most financial information is not usually captured in an enterprise architecture.

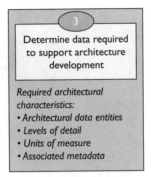

A specific example of a question involving cost is determining the return on investment (ROI) for a proposed project. ROI analysis is frequently used in answering questions having to do with selecting projects for funding. The type of data needed to calculate ROI includes the cost of current operations, cost of the change process, and cost of the reengineered operations. The architecture inputs to this calculation are the details of current operations (as-is activities), the phasing of changes (systems and system availability timelines), and the details of the reengineered operations (to-be activities). The architecture would not usually include the salary data that is used to calculate operational costs. However, the architecture could include information on the staff size and skills (roles and skills of performers in organizations) needed for current or reengineered operations. The architecture could also include summary information on operations and maintenance costs for the automated support for operations. The architecture could also include the performance measures used to evaluate the efficiency of the business process, the values of those measures for the current process, and the goals for the values of those measures for the reengineered process.

In the preceding paragraph, some of the types of data needed to answer questions about ROI have been identified: as-is and to-be activities, the systems and system availability timeline, as-is and to-be roles and skills required by organizations, and performance measures that relate to the activities. Some of these types of data and their relationships were introduced in Chapter 1.3. Where can we look to find a more comprehensive list of architecture data types and relationships to help us determine what types and relationships we need? The DoDAF has provided some data models that include the key types of architecture data and their relationships. Figure 2.2-8 is the DoDAF conceptual data model and includes the key architectural data types. The relationship lines in Figure 2.2-8 are numbered and explained in the

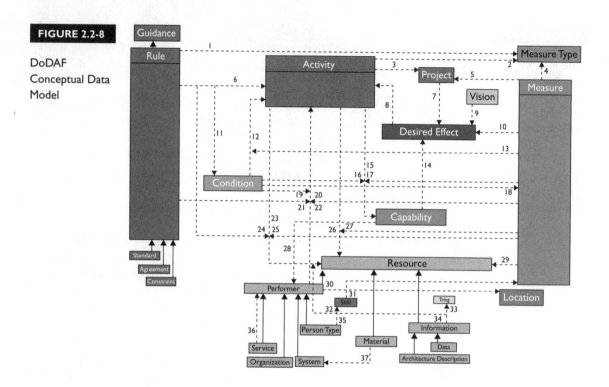

FIGURE 2.2-8

DoDAF
Conceptual Data
Model

text of the DoDAF (Department of Defense, 2009). The DoDAF also provides more detailed data models for specific key subject areas, including performers, resource flows, information and data, activities, capabilities, services, projects, goals, rules, measures, locations, training, skills, and education. Although these data models are not reproduced here, they are available in the DoDAF (Department of Defense, 2009) and can be used to help identify relevant types of architectural data.

Work is presently under way within the DoD to ensure uniform representation for the same semantic content within architecture modeling through a standard called Architecture Modeling Primitives. The Architecture Modeling Primitives, hereafter referred to as Primitives, will be a standard set of modeling elements and associated symbols mapped to the DoDAF meta-model (DM2) concepts and applied to modeling techniques. The DM2 consists of the Conceptual Data Model in Figure 2.2-8 above, the DoDAF Logical Data Model, and the DoDAF Physical Exchange Specification (PES). Using the Primitives to support the collection of architecture content in concert with the PES (Department of Defense, 2009) will aid in generating common understanding and communication among architects and tools in regard to architectural views. As the Primitives concepts are applied to more modeling techniques, they will be updated in the on-line *DoDAF Journal* (www.cio-nil .defense.gov/sites/dodaf20/journal_exp3.html) and details provided in subsequent releases of DoDAF (Department of Defense, 2009).

Alternatively, the cells of the Zachman Framework can be used to help identify the classes of architectural data that may be relevant to stakeholders and their questions, but the Zachman Framework does not detail the relationships.

Performance measures are one type of data that should not be overlooked. Many architectures have as a purpose the improvement of some business process or business outcome. OMB guidance requires performance measures to be associated with mission outcomes. Some guidance on performance measures can be found in the Federal Enterprise Architecture (FEA) Performance Reference Model (PRM) (Federal Enterprise Architecture Program Office, Office of Management and Budget, 2007). The PRM has a standard taxonomy for classifying types of performance measures and advice for creating a "line of sight" from improvements in IT performance to business outcome performance. DoD is developing its own version of this reference model for use with DoD architectures. Performance measures can be associated with (that is, related to) capabilities, business processes, or systems and services. Note that the performance measures included in the architecture are not the management performance measures applied to an architecture development project.

It is very important to determine the data needed before jumping into the architecture effort. By determining what is needed, and more appropriately, what is *not* needed, the architecture team can focus on collecting needed data and developing useful models.

Table 2.2-1 has examples of typical questions from stakeholders of solution-level business process improvement projects and some of the types of architecture data and relationships needed to answer the questions.

Determine What Models to Use: How to Organize and Correlate Data

From the perspective of scoping the work, we will limit our consideration of step 4 activities to determining how to organize and correlate the types of data identified in step 3. Architects typically organize and correlate data through the use of modeling techniques. Use of these modeling techniques ensures that the data in the structured knowledge base (see Figure 1.3-3 in Chapter 1.3) or architecture repository is consistent and complete. In planning, the architect selects models that cover the

TABLE 2.2-1   Example Solution-Level Architecture Stakeholder Questions

Question	Needed Data and Relationships
What degree of change will the new system(s) bring to the processes currently being followed?	Current (as-is) business processes (activities), systems, and the relationships between the activities and systems
	Target (to-be) business processes (activities), systems, and the relationships between the activities and systems
What is the latest time by which the new system users must be made ready?	Date when each new system becomes available for use
	Date when the existing system is removed from service
What is the quality of the incoming data for the new systems?	Data needed as input to the new systems (system resource flows)
	Measures used for the quality of data
	Expected values for the measures for the input data expected when the new systems become available
What volumes of data will need to be handled by the new system configuration?	Data needed as input to the new system configuration (system resource flows)
	Average and worst case volumes of data expected in from external systems at the time when the new systems become available
Will there be any media/infrastructure incompatibility between the old and the new system configuration?	Existing systems and their interfaces
	Existing system and communications infrastructure
	Standards for the existing systems and interfaces
	To-be systems and their interfaces
	To-be systems and communications infrastructure
	Standards for the to-be systems and interfaces
Will the data for the new system configuration be available in a timely manner?	Data needed as input to the new system configuration (system resource flows)
Are there any cross-system data dependencies between the new and legacy systems in the new system configuration?	To-be system configuration—systems and interfaces
	System data exchanges (resource flows) among the to-be systems
What are the expected improvements in the business process?	Current (as-is) business processes (activities)
	Performance measures for the business processes
	Values for the as-is business processes' performance measures
	Target (to-be) business processes (activities)
	Goal values for the to-be business processes' performance measures

| TABLE 2.2-1 | Example Solution-Level Architecture Stakeholder Questions (*Continued*) |

Question	Needed Data and Relationships
What are the expected impacts of the business process changes on organizational needs in terms of personnel numbers and skills?	Current (as-is) business processes (activities)
	As-is organizational structure with the roles and skills needed in each organization
	Relationship between the as-is activities and the organizations that perform them, including the number of personnel in which roles with what skills who do the performing
	Target (to-be) business processes (activities)
	To-be organizational structure with the roles and skills needed in each organization
	Relationship between the to-be activities and the organizations that perform them, including the number of personnel in which roles with what skills who do the performing

needed types of data identified in step 3. These models are usually selected from an integrated set of models and modeling techniques based on a corporate methodology or a standard such as the DoDAF. The DoDAF doesn't require that the models described in it (see Part III) are used to develop the architecture, it just requires that the needed data (from step 3) be represented in those standard formats for sharing among DoD architects. In this way, DoD architects don't have to learn everyone else's methodologies and models in order to understand their architectures. Figure 2.2-9 summarizes all the activities to be accomplished in step 4. The activities covered in this section are limited to organizing and correlating the architecture data.

| FIGURE 2.2-9 |

Organize and
Correlate
Architecture Data

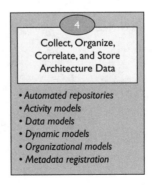

Planning activities in step 4 complete the traceability from architecture purpose and stakeholder questions both to the architecture data needed to answer the questions and to the models needed to capture that data and ensure it is consistent and complete. This traceability ensures a useful architecture with integrated models and data. Figure 2.2-10 illustrates the importance of establishing this traceability to the development of a useful architecture.

Many people jump straight to step 4 when planning an architecture and end up wasting time and effort. They spend resources on false starts and in building views that are not useful because they are not related to stakeholder (that is, decision-maker) needs. Any time spent in performing steps 1 through 3 is more than made up for by the improved and more complete decisions made in step 4. These better decisions, in turn, ensure useful architecture results.

For purposes of this text, we will use the DoDAF-described models, presented in Part III of this book, as our integrated set of models to choose from. The process of selecting models is not a simple step. The architect must select the appropriate viewpoints, the views and models, and the options and tailoring needed for each view or model. Each of these steps is discussed in the following subsections.

FIGURE 2.2-10

Traceability to Stakeholder Needs Ensures Useful Architectures

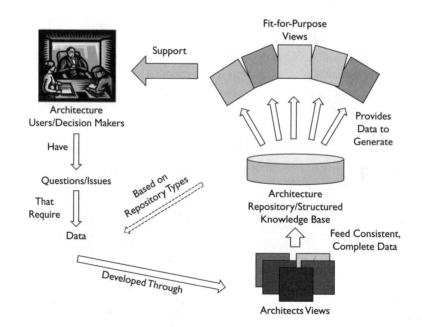

Selecting Viewpoints

The DoDAF organizes its models, also called views, into a set of eight viewpoints, defined in Figure 2.2-11. This figure also identifies the changes to these viewpoints in Version 2.0 of the DoDAF. Although the All View (AV) products are always included in an architecture, the inclusion of other viewpoints is determined by the types of data identified in step 3. As an architecture evolves and matures, additional viewpoints may be added. It is not necessary to build all the views at the same time.

As an enterprise initiates its architecture efforts, the viewpoints included may be limited, depending on the immediate needs of the enterprise as reflected by stakeholder questions and issues. For example, an enterprise's immediate need may be a better understanding of its current operations. Newly formed organizations, such as the Department of Homeland Security (DHS), may need to start with the Operational Viewpoint. An older enterprise's immediate need might be to gain control over its technology inventory in order to manage software licensing problems. Such enterprises may need to start with the Systems Viewpoint, although

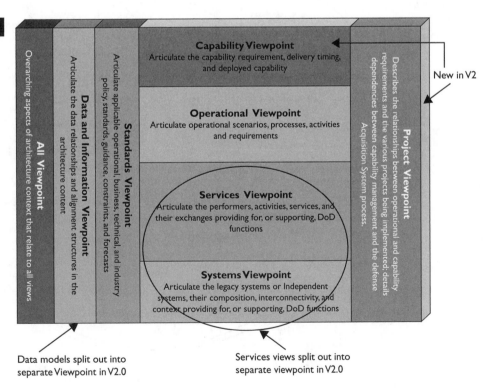

FIGURE 2.2-11

DoDAF Version 2.0 Viewpoints

the Systems Viewpoint's view links to Operational Viewpoint views must remain to be determined (TBD) in the initial architecture. Other enterprises may decide to focus early architecture efforts on interoperability issues. These enterprises might start with a Standards Viewpoint. In this case, the Standards Viewpoint's view links to Systems Viewpoint products must remain TBD until the Systems Viewpoint is developed. Any of these enterprises may include a Capability Viewpoint or Project Viewpoint to provide a basis for focusing new projects on strategic needs.

Figure 2.2-12 shows some of the relationships among the viewpoints and provides a foundation for understanding how the views integrate across the viewpoints. The Systems and Service Viewpoints map to the Operational Viewpoint by showing how IT supports operations. The Standards Viewpoint maps to the Systems and Services

FIGURE 2.2-12

Relationships Among the DoDAF Viewpoints

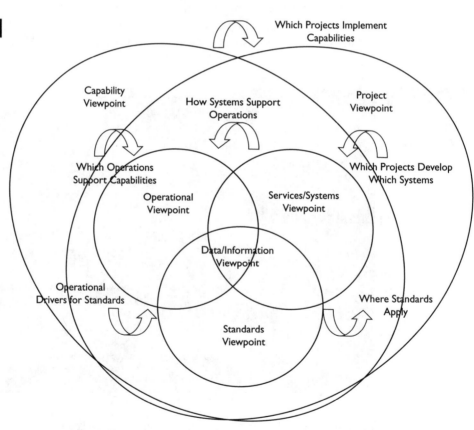

Viewpoints by showing where the standards apply or should apply. The Operational Viewpoint maps to the Standards Viewpoint by providing operational needs for interoperability standards. This last relationship is not currently supported directly in the DoDAF views but can easily be added by tailoring products. The Capability Viewpoint maps to the Project Viewpoint through the projects that implement the capabilities. The Capability Viewpoint maps to the Operational Viewpoint in terms of the operational activities that implement the capabilities. The Project Viewpoint maps to the Systems and Services Viewpoints in terms of the projects that develop the systems or services. The Data and Information Viewpoint is shown in the middle because enterprise data can be important to understanding any of the other viewpoints.

Selecting Views

In general, you want to select views or models to address the types of architecture data identified in step 3. However, because there are a large number of potential views to pick from, the FEAC has some general guidance on where to start. For each of the levels of architecture (enterprise, segment, and solution), we have identified a set of *core* views that we recommend for that level. The core views for a given level of architecture are the basic set of views that we recommend architectures at that level include. The core set for solution-level architectures is a proven set that most solution architectures contain. The core sets for enterprise- and segment-level architectures are new, because the DoDAF has only recently been expanded to include Capability and Project Viewpoints. Each of these sets of core views is presented in the following subsections together with its rationale.

The core set of views for solution-level architectures is listed in Table 2.2-2. The label in parentheses is the shorthand name for the view in the DoDAF. The set of letters preceding the V is an acronym for one of the DoDAF viewpoints and the number is an arbitrary number assigned to the view or model within the viewpoint. The core set for the solution-level architectures includes different options depending on which of the Systems or Services Viewpoints is included. (If the as-is portion of a solution architecture uses the Systems Viewpoint and the to-be portion of the solution architecture uses the Services Viewpoint, then both sets of views will be included in the overall architecture.) The integration of these core views is well defined, as illustrated in Figure 2.2-13, which shows only the Systems Viewpoint core view (instead of both the Systems and Services Viewpoint core views). The Capability to Operational Activities Mapping is not included in the figure because it is optional and should be included in the solution-level core set only when

TABLE 2.2-2	**Solution-Level Architecture Goal:** Provide traceability from performers to the operational activities they perform and to the IT that supports those activities. The resources or information exchanged is a key part of this traceability.
Core Views for Solution-Level Architectures	

View/Model	Rationale
High-Level Operational Concept Description (OV-1)	Provides a graphical view of the problem and solution from the Operational Viewpoint, including key performers, activities, and communications
Operational Resource Flow Description (OV-2)	Identifies the key performers and their resource or information products and needs with a mapping to the activities performed by each performer
Operational Resource Flow Matrix (OV-3)	Details the resources or information exchanged by the performers, together with the key attributes of the exchanges
Operational Activity Model (OV-5a,b)	Details the operational activities and their inputs and outputs
System Interface Description/ Services Context Description (SV-1)/(SvcV-1)	Describes the systems and their interfaces (when the System Viewpoint is used) or the layout of specific service implementations (with service-level agreements [SLAs]) across platforms and interfaces (when the Services Viewpoint is used)
Services Functionality Description (SvcV-4)	Describes the abstract services, their standard interfaces, and their producer/consumer relationships (when the Services Viewpoint is used)
Standards Profile (StdV-1)	Identifies the standards that apply to the systems or services
Capability to Operational Activity Mapping (CV-6)	Links the solution-level activities to the enterprise or segment capabilities they implement (for use only for those solution-level architectures that have either overarching segment- or enterprise-level architectures with capabilities identified)

the solution-level architecture has an overarching enterprise of segment-level architecture that includes capabilities.

The views that are not designated "core" for the solution-level architecture are called "supporting" in the FEAC's terminology. The supporting views are included in the architecture as required by the purpose of the architecture. For example, Table 2.2-3 provides a list of the views that are "supporting" for solution-level

FIGURE 2.2-13 Integration for the Solution-Level Architecture Core Views

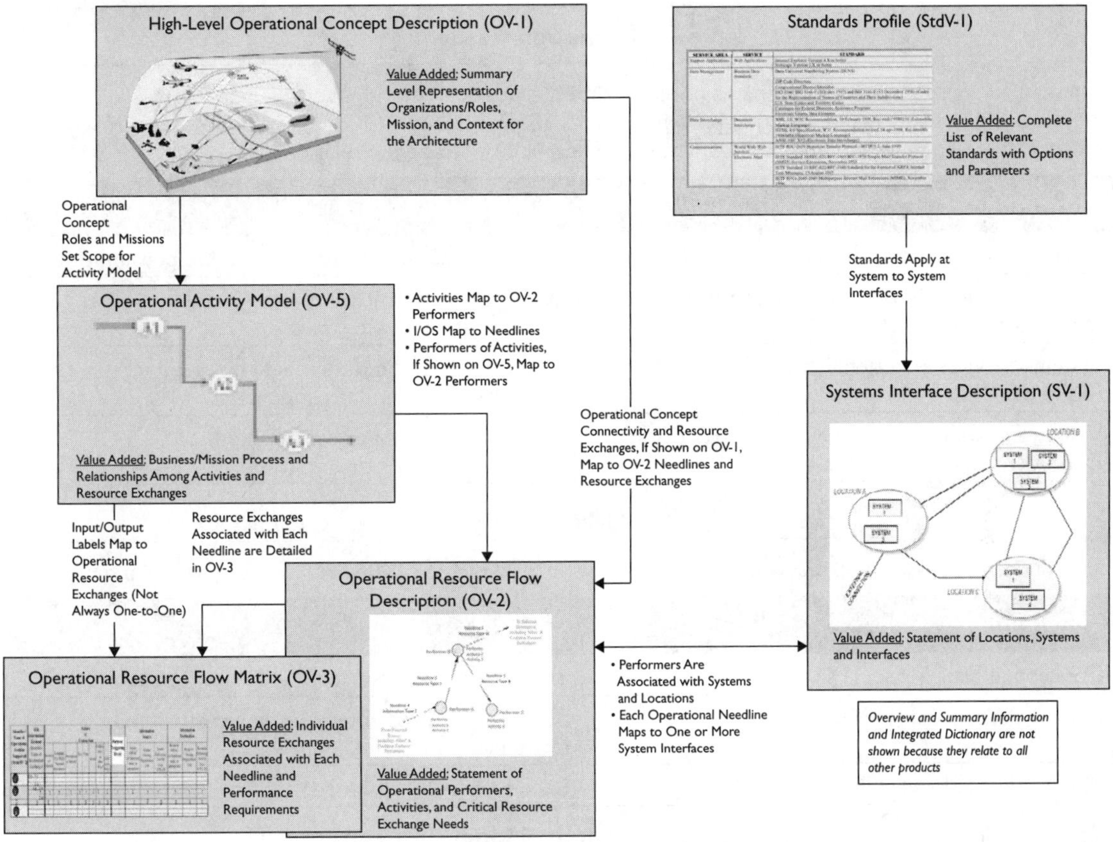

architectures. Because the DoDAF view numbers are strictly arbitrary, this list is organized into categories that may help in selecting views. (More detail on these views can be found in Part III of this book.) Note, however, that some Capability and Project Viewpoint views listed below may not be appropriate for a solution-level architecture. For example, the Project Timelines view (PV-2) is designed to compare and relate project timelines over multiple projects. It is not appropriate to use PV-2 for one project. The timeline for a specific project by itself is of interest only to the immediate project management and sponsor. The Project Timelines view is to support coordination and management of multiple projects.

TABLE 2.2-3   Supporting Views for Solution-Level Architecture, by Category

New Information Category	
These views include information that is not found in other views. These products include information on organizational structures, roles, and responsibilities; details of communications networks that support system interfaces; system functions and their data flows; and capabilities and their relationships.	
View/Model	**Contents**
Organizational Relationships Chart (OV-4)	Organizational structures, roles, and responsibilities
Systems/Services Resource Flow Description (SV-2/SvcV-2)	Details of communications networks that support system or services interfaces
Systems/Services Functionality Description (SV-4/SvcV-4)	System functions and their data flows/services functions, SLAs, and dependencies
Vision, Capability Taxonomy, and Capability Dependencies (CV-1, CV-2, CV-4)	Capabilities and their relationships

Data Model Category	
(Also now a viewpoint.) Views focus on representations of shared, structured enterprise concepts and data.	
View/Model	**Contents**
Conceptual Data Model (DIV-1)	Shared enterprise concepts and their relationships
Logical Data Model (DIV-2)	Shared, structured enterprise data entities and relationships
Physical Data Model (DIV-3)	Implementation of shared, structured enterprise data

Sequence and Timing Model Category	
Views are models that capture dynamic aspects of the enterprise and support executable architectures. The *a* options are rules models, the *b* options are state transition models, and the *c* options are scenario-based models. Each type of model is the same, regardless of viewpoint, although the focus of the model will be different, depending on viewpoint.	
View/Model	**Contents**
Operational Rules Model (OV-6a), Systems Rules Model (SV-10a), Services Rules Model (SvcV-10a)	Rules constrain some aspect of the enterprise
Operational State Transition Description (OV-6b), Systems State Transition Description (SV-10b), Services State Transition Description (SvcV-10b)	State or status flow for objects (that is, data or other elements of the architecture)
Operational Event/Trace Description (OV-6c), Systems Event/Trace Description (SV-10c), Services Event/Trace Description (SvcV-10c)	Scenarios that show sequences of events, messages, and actions

| TABLE 2.2-3 | Supporting Views for Solution-Level Architecture, by Category (*Continued*) |

Transition Planning Category

Views contain information about transition strategy and plans. These views contain information on project timelines and relationships, how capabilities are supported over time, when new or upgraded automated systems will become operational, the performance improvements expected based on these system changes, and the status of new technology and standards needed for the new systems and upgrades.

View/Model	Contents
Systems/Services Measures Matrix (SV-7/SvcV-7)	Performance measures and time-phased performance goals
Systems/Services Evolution Description (SV-8/SvcV-8)	Timeline for system/service availability
Systems/Services Technology & Skills Forecast (SV-9/SvcV-9)	Forecasts of systems/services technology in selected areas together with the skill sets needed for the new technology
Standards Forecast (StdV-2)	Forecasts of standards changes
Capability Phasing (CV-3)	Dates when new capabilities become available and which projects provide the capability over time (not recommended for solution-level architectures)
Project Timelines (PV-2)	Project start and stop dates and dependencies (not recommended for solution-level architectures)

Matrix Views Category

Views share the same matrix style format and link together information found in other views, sometimes with additional new information.

View/Model	Contents
Systems-Systems Matrix/Services-Services Matrix (SV-3/SvcV-3)	Interfaces between systems or services (summarizing information on System Interface Description or Services Context Description)
Operational Activity to Systems Function/Service Traceability Matrix (SV-5/SvcV-5)	Maps systems functions or services to the operational activities they support
Systems/Services Resource Flow Matrix (SV-6/SvcV-6)	Identifies system/service resource exchanges and their attributes
Capability to Organizational Development Mapping (CV-5)	Maps (by phase) capabilities to the organizations that use them
Capability to Services Mapping (CV-7)	Maps capabilities to the services that support them
Project Portfolio Relationships (PV-1)	Maps projects to the organizations that manage them
Project to Capability Mapping (PV-3)	Maps projects to the capabilities that the project's products support

The core set of views for enterprise-level architectures is listed in Table 2.2-4. These views are from the Capability and Project Viewpoints and support the type of basic information that is needed for enterprise-level decision processes such as Portfolio Management and Investment Management. Figure 2.2-14 illustrates the integration of the core views for enterprise-level architectures.

A segment-level architecture may be used to manage a subset of capabilities from an enterprise-level architecture as well as coordinate the set of solution architectures that will provide those capabilities. Thus, segment-level architectures

TABLE 2.2-4 Core Views for Enterprise-Level Architectures	**Enterprise-Level Architecture Goal:** Provide traceability from the enterprise strategic vision, goals, and objectives to the capabilities needed to achieve those objectives and traceability from the capabilities both to the projects (and their managing organizations) that implement those capabilities and to the organizations that use the capabilities. Phasing and timelines are a key part of this traceability.

View/Model	Rationale
Vision (CV-1)	Identifies the needed capabilities (i.e., products and services) and maps them to the enterprise strategic vision, goals, and objectives
Capability Phasing (CV-3)	Allows tracking of changing capability configurations, by name, over time
Capability Dependencies (CV-4)	Identifies capability dependencies as well as the capability specialization hierarchy
Capability to Organizational Development Mapping (CV-5)	Establishes the relationships among the capabilities, the organizations that use the capabilities, and the capability configurations with the delivery dates from the projects
Project Portfolio Relationships (PV-1)	Links the projects to the organizations responsible for them
Project Timelines (PV-2)	Provides project delivery timelines and their cross-project dependencies
Project to Capability Mapping (PV-3)	Provides a direct linkage between capabilities and the projects that provide systems/services that implement those capabilities
Organizational Relationships Chart (OV-4)	Identifies the organizations that appear in the Project Portfolio Relationships and the Capabilities to Organizational Development Mapping and the management and collaboration relationships among those organizations

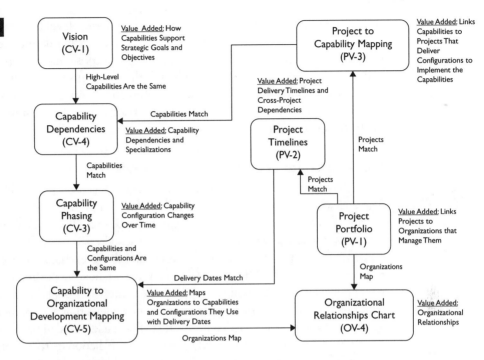

FIGURE 2.2-14

Integration for Enterprise-Level Architecture Core Views

may have the characteristics of both enterprise-level architectures and solution-level architectures. If the segment-level architecture is to be used for Investment Management or Portfolio Management for the capabilities included in the segment, then the core views for the segment should include the same views identified as core for an enterprise-level architecture. In the case of a segment-level architecture, those core views will be restricted to the subset of capabilities, projects, and organizations that fall within the scope of the segment. If the segment-level architecture is to be used to coordinate a set of solution-level architectures, then the core views for the segment should include the same views identified as core for a solution-level architecture. However, in the case of a segment-level architecture, these views will be focused on providing business context, documenting the support of the systems to the high-level business processes, and documenting the business process and system interfaces necessary to ensure the necessary interoperability across all the systems in all the solution architectures within the scope of the segment.

In addition to views, Reference Models (RMs) may also be included or associated with architectures. Enterprise-level and segment-level architectures may use the various types of RMs to provide consistency and continuity of vocabulary and content across all the related segment- and solution-level architectures. For example, a Business Reference Model can be used to further define the business areas and missions included in the scope of the enterprise. Each related segment- and solution-level architecture can identify the relevant sets of business areas and missions. Enterprise- and segment-level architectures can use a Technical Reference Model to define the superset of standards that will constrain the standards included in all the related solution-level architectures.

General Guidance on Selecting Views

For each needed viewpoint, build the core views for the appropriate level of architecture. These views cover the information commonly needed in that level of architecture and provide the commonality needed for comparisons across different DoD architectures. If there is any needed data from step 3 that is not addressed by the core views, select supporting views (for the appropriate level of architecture) that cover that data. Some regulations, such as DoD directives, may require particular supporting views. If there is additional needed data that cannot easily be addressed by supporting views, even with tailoring, you may need to add fit-for-purpose views that are not included in the set of views and models included in this text. These additional views may range from reports based on information already captured in the dictionary to complex models for executable architectures. You may choose to include some additional fit-for-purpose views—such as dashboards, pie charts, bar charts, or fusion diagrams—that draw on the data developed by more formal models and present that data in a form that supports the specific needs of decision-makers. That is, the views and models used by architects may not be the best format for presenting data to decision makers.

Added fit-for-purpose views should be documented in the Overview and Summary Information (AV-1). A discussion of the semantics of the graphic notation should be included or a reference should be added to readily available texts that discuss the new view. The data to be included in the new views will need to be identified and the relationships to the existing views will need to be defined.

To select views, you need to know the information addressed by or covered in the view. These three aspects are the view template, which provides the format for the view's graphic component; the information required by the dictionary entries for the view; and the view options. This information is covered in Part III.

Planning Examples

Here are some examples of the results of applying the preceding planning process to architectures at each architecture level. These examples are based on the case study in Part V of this book.

Enterprise-Level Architecture Planning Example

Here is an example of the documentation resulting from planning for an enterprise-level architecture.

Purpose: Provide guidance on what additional capabilities or business services will be necessary to achieve RMN Airport's strategic goals of becoming a viable alternative to LAX. The initial phase of the architecture will document the current baseline and starting point for any transition plan.

Stakeholders: Port Authority (especially the Planning Committee); RMN management.

The members of the appropriate county Port Authority Planning Committee have the following questions:

- What business services do we currently offer?
- Do these business services have any dependencies or relationships?
- How are these business services grouped into segments for management purposes?
- How do the current business services relate to the RMN strategic vision and goals? That is, how important will the current business services be to achieving our strategic goals?
- What projects, programs, or contracts do we have that provide these business services and what organizations oversee these projects or contracts?
- What organizations use the business services?
- When does the current funding for the existing projects or contracts expire? That is, for how long have the funds for these projects or contracts been committed?
- What are the current performance measures and values?

Scope:

- Enterprise-level architecture for RMN Airport
- Covers all missions and organizations within RMN
- Geographical bounds: RMN Airport grounds, airspace, and associated business offices
- Technology constraints: N/A (enterprise level)
- Timeframe: as-is

Required Data and Selected Views: Table 2.2-5 identifies the data needed to answer these questions and the views (with selected options/tailoring) used to capture the data. There is no "stakeholder" column in this table because all the stakeholders have the same questions in this example.

TABLE 2.2-5 Mapping of Enterprise-Level Questions to Required Data and Views

Question	Required Data	Views
What business services does RMN currently offer?	Existing business services/capabilities	Capability Taxonomy (CV-2)
Do these business services have any dependencies or relationships?	Relationships among the business services	Capability Dependencies (CV-4)
How are these business services grouped into segments for management purposes?	Management relationships among the business services	Capability Dependencies (CV-4) tailored to highlight segment groupings
How do the current business services relate to the RMN strategic vision and goals?	Strategic vision, goals, and desired effects Relationships to current business services	Vision (CV-1) tailored to show to-be strategic vision and goals but just as-is business services/capabilities
What project/programs or contracts do we have that provide these business services?	Existing project/programs or contracts Relationship of projects/programs/contracts to business services	Project to Capability Mapping (PV-3)
What RMN organizations oversee these projects or contracts?	Organizational chart of RMN	Organizational Relationships Chart (OV-4)
	Relationships of organizations to projects/programs/contracts they own	Project Portfolio Relationships (PV-1)
What organizations use the business services?	Organizations, including both internal and external organizations that use the business services	Organizational Relationships Chart (OV-4) tailored to include all performers, including external performers
	Relationships of organizations to the business services they use	Project to Capability Mapping (PV-3)
When does the current funding for the existing projects/contracts expire? That is, for how long have the funds for these projects/contracts been committed?	End points (based on current funding commitments) of projects/programs or end dates on contracts	Capability Phasing (CV-3) tailored to show only existing projects/programs/ contracts, i.e., showing as-is phase only
What are the current performance measures and values?	Performance measures for current business services/capabilities with the current goal values for these measures	Capability Taxonomy (CV-2) with performance measures and goals for the lowest level capabilities

Segment-Level Architecture Planning Example

Here is an example of the documentation resulting from planning for a segment-level architecture.

Purpose: Passenger Management is a segment of the RNM enterprise architecture. This segment-level architecture provides the basis for transitioning RMN passenger services over the next five years to meet RMN strategic goals. This involves the addition of new capabilities that affect passenger services.

Stakeholders: The Port Authority; RMN management; RMN employees, and unions; the local county and cities; Western state commuter airlines and cargo carriers/delivery services; the Transportation Security Administration (TSA); the Federal Aviation Authority (FAA); and current and potential vendors for customer-related services

Here is an example subset of the stakeholders' questions.

The Port Authority and RMN management have the following questions:

- What additional passenger management business services will we need to offer within the next five years?
- What are the performance measures and their five-year goal values for all the Passenger Management services (both existing business services and new business services)?
- What existing Passenger Management business services will have to be expanded?
- What are the dependencies and other relationships among the Passenger Management business services (both existing and new)?
- What existing projects and contracts will be affected by the expansion of existing Passenger Management business services?
- What new projects will be needed for the new Passenger Management business services?
- What are the major business processes that support Passenger Management business services?
- How many personnel will RMN need to execute the Passenger Management business processes? What skills will these personnel need?
- What are the major systems that will be needed to support passenger-related business services in five years?
- Which of these systems will be new and which are existing systems?
- Will any of the existing Passenger Management systems need to be upgraded?
- What are the major interfaces among these passenger management systems with other RMN segments and with external systems?

- What infrastructure will these systems use?
- What are the standards that all the systems (new and existing) will need to support five years from now?

The members of the Port Authority have the following questions.

- What Passenger Management business services will we offer in five years?
- Will these business services have any dependencies or relationships?
- How do the Passenger Management business services relate to the RMN strategic vision and goals?
- What projects, programs, or contracts should we have to provide these passenger management business services?
- What organizations should oversee these projects or contracts?
- What organizations will use the passenger management business services?
- When do new projects, programs, or contracts need to start to ensure there are no gaps in passenger management services over the next five years? Do any existing projects or programs need to be extended or upgraded?
- What are the performance measures and values for Passenger Management business services?

RMN management, TSA, local county and cities, and airlines have the following questions:

- How many passengers can the future business processes handle per hour and per day?

Scope:

- Segment Level Architecture for RMN Airport
- Covers all missions and organizations related to passenger business services at RMN airport
- Geographical bounds: RMN Airport grounds and associated business offices
- Technology constraints: COTS; compatibility with systems in other segments
- Timeframe: To-Be (present + 5 years)
- What data and selected views are required?

Table 2.2-6 identifies the data needed to answer some of these questions and the views (with selected options/tailoring) used to capture the data. The table does not include all the questions.

TABLE 2.2-6 Mapping of Segment-Level Questions to Required Data and Views

Question	Stakeholder	Required Data	Views
What are the performance measures and their five-year goal values for all the Passenger Management services (both for existing business services and new business services)?	Port Authority, RMN management	Business services with performance measures and goals	Capability Taxonomy (CV-2) with performance measures and tailored to include performance goals for a five-year period
What are the major business processes that support Passenger Management business services?	Port Authority, RMN management	Business processes	Activity Model (OV-5)
		Business services	Capability Taxonomy (CV-2) restricted to scope of the segment
		Mapping of business services to business processes	Capability to Operational Activity Mapping (CV-6)
What are the major systems that will be needed to support passenger-related business services in five years?	Port Authority, RMN management	Systems and interfaces (high-level)	System Interface Description (SV-1) with highest-level perspective
		Mapping of systems to business services	Capability to Services Mapping (CV-7) tailored to show systems instead of services
What are the major interfaces among these Passenger Management systems, with other RMN segments, and with external systems?	Port Authority, RMN management	System interfaces	System Interface Description (SV-1) with high-level perspective, including external interfaces, tailored to show which externals are to other RMN segments and which are to outside externals
What infrastructure will these systems use?	Port Authority	Systems and interfaces	System Interface Description (SV-1)
		Communications systems and networks	Systems Resource Flow Description (SV-2)
		Standards	Standards Profile (StdV-2) with a map to where the standards apply

(continued)

TABLE 2.2-6   Mapping of Segment-Level Questions to Required Data and Views *(Continued)*

Question	Stakeholder	Required Data	Views
What projects, programs, or contracts should we have to provide these Passenger Management business services?	Port Authority	Business services	Capability Taxonomy (CV-2)
		Mapping of projects to business services	Project to Capability Mapping (PV-3)
What organizations should oversee these projects or contracts?	Port Authority	Mapping of projects to organizations that own them	Project Portfolio Mapping (PV-1)
What organizations will use the Passenger Management business services?	Port Authority	Organizations	Organizational Relationships Chart (OV-4), including all involved organizations both internal and external to RMN
		Business Services	Capability Taxonomy (CV-2)
		Mapping from organizations to the business services they will use	Capability to Organizational Development Mapping (CV-5) (may be tailored to remove references to systems)
How many passengers can the future business processes handle per hour and per day?	RMN management, TSA, local county and cities, airlines	Resource exchanges	Operational Resource Flow Matrix (OV-3) with a throughput column
		Business processes with performance measures and goals	Activity Model (OV-5) tailored with performance measures and goals

Solution-Level Architecture Planning Example

Here is an example of the documentation resulting from planning for a solution-level architecture.

Purpose: One of the Passenger Management segment business services that will need to be upgraded for RMN Airport is passenger identification. This architecture will define upgraded passenger identification business processes and provide guidance on the acquisition of the required set of applications and common database to support these upgraded business processes.

Stakeholders: Port Authority; RMN management; the Department of Homeland Security (DHS); RMN employees (IT group); passenger airlines; FAA

Port Authority, RMN management, and DHS have the following issues:

- Will the new business processes and applications meet government regulations and requirements? That is, what types of passenger identification data is required?
- Who needs what data and who should provide the data?
- How do the new processes improve confidence in passenger identification? (Measures include speed, availability, and consistency of data.)

RMN management has the following issues:

- When will the upgraded processes and their supporting applications be ready for use?
- What performance, in terms of passengers per hour, should be expected from the new processes?

RMN management and DHS have the following issues:

- How many personnel will be needed for the new business processes?
- Will the personnel need additional skills?
- When will any additional personnel be needed?
- Will new facilities be required? If so, when will they become available for use?

RMN IT employees and management have the following issues:

- What are the upgraded business processes?
- How do the new applications support the business processes?
- How do the new applications, services, and databases integrate with other RNM IT?
- What infrastructure will be required?
- What standards will the new applications, systems, services, and databases use?

DHS, Airlines, and FAA have the following issues:

- What are the upgraded business processes?
- How do we use the new business processes and applications to get the data we need?

Scope:

- Solution-level architecture for the Passenger Management segment of the RMN Airport enterprise
- Covers passenger identification business services for RMN
- Geographical bounds: RMN Airport grounds and associated business offices
- Technology constraints: Overall compatibility with RMN enterprise IT standards; federal (DHS/FAA) data standards; and COTS components and infrastructure
- Timeframe: to-be (for ten years + timeframe—that is, it includes international passenger travel)

Required data and selected views:

Table 2.2-7 identifies the data needed to answer some of these questions and the views (with selected options and tailoring) used to capture the data. The table does not include all the questions.

TABLE 2.2-7   Mapping of Solution-Level Questions to Required Data and Views

Question	Stakeholders	Required Data	Views
What types of passenger identification data are required?	All	Data model	Logical Data Model (DIV-2) modeling information exchanges and activity input/output (I/O)
		Information exchanges	Operational Resource Exchange Matrix (OV-3) with basic columns
		I/Os from activities	Activity Model (OV-5)
		Government regulations and standards	Standards Profile (StdV-1) tailored to include regulations
Who needs what data and who should provide the data?	All	Performers	Operational Resource Flow Description (OV-2)
		Relationships of performers to activities	
		Information exchanges	Operational Resource Flow Matrix (OV-3)
		I/Os from activities	Activity Model (OV-5)

TABLE 2.2-7	Mapping of Solution-Level Questions to Required Data and Views (*Continued*)		
Question	**Stakeholders**	**Required Data**	**Views**
How do the new processes improve confidence in passenger identification? (Measures include speed, availability, and consistency of data.)	Port Authority; RMN mgmt; DHS	Business processes	Activity Model (OV-5) tailored to include performance measures and goals
When will the upgraded processes and their supporting applications be ready for use?	RMN mgmt	Timeline for application and process availability	Systems/Services Evolution Description (SV-8/SvcV-8) tailored to include process definition and training completion dates
What performance, in terms of passengers per hour, should be expected from the new processes?	RMN mgmt	Business processes	Activity Model (OV-5) tailored to include performance measures and goals
		Information exchanges	Operational Resource Flow Matrix (OV-3) with periodicity column (average and worst-case numbers)
How many personnel will be needed for the new business processes?	RMN mgmt; DHS	Performers	Operational Resource Flow Description (OV-2)
		Organizations and number of personnel who are performers per organization	Organizational Relationships Chart (OV-4) tailored to include the number of personnel per performer group
		Relationship between performers and organizations	Map between organizations and performers

Success Factors in Scoping the Architecture Work

The most critical success factor in scoping architecture work is getting agreement on the purpose of the architecture. Without this agreement, the various stakeholders may have false expectations and various groups of architecture developers may work at cross-purposes. Without a clear purpose, the architecture work may be poorly defined and produce results that are not useful to any of the stakeholders. Part of getting agreement on the purpose of the architecture is finding all the architecture stakeholders (that is, the users of the architecture) and identifying their issues, questions, and architecture data needs.

If there is a large group of stakeholders with a diversity of different issues, then it is important to prioritize the sets of stakeholders and issues. It is also critical to focus the architecture development efforts and generate timely and useful results. Each release of the architecture can focus on an additional set of stakeholders until all are getting the information they need.

The proof of a properly scoped (and executed) architecture effort is that the architecture data is actually used in decision-making processes.

Planning the Architecture Project

Planning for the last few steps of the Six Step process focuses on the architecture development project or program and how the work will be done, as illustrated in Figure 2.2-15. The scope of the work identified in the initial steps of the Six Step process is necessary to develop the SOW for a project and may take one or more fiscal years or budget funding cycles to accomplish. It is important to plan the architecture project, prioritizing the development of views and data into multiple builds as necessary.

FIGURE 2.2-15

How the Work Will Be Done

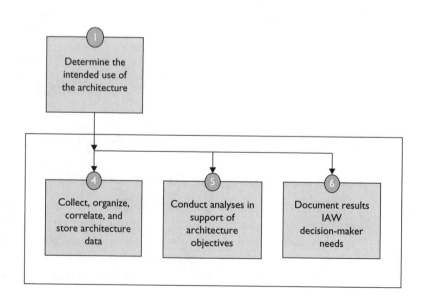

Some of the decisions made in planning the details of the architecture project may cause the initial decisions on the views and models (that is, the deliverables) to be revisited. The methodologies, techniques, and tools selected for the management and technical approaches used in a project may impact or constrain the data and models to be developed. For example, a decision to use a service-oriented architecture (SOA) approach for system/software development means that steps 3 and 4 will need to be reviewed to ensure that the views, models, and data that are focused on services have been included. The selected tools may limit the models that can be used and constrain the options and tailoring that can be supported. Some tools have specific forms of model tailoring built in, so if you use that tool, you must use that form of the model. Other tools may have limitations on the models and tailoring they can support, so if that tool is selected, compromises may have to be made with respect to the original set of models or tailoring selected in step 4.

In this section, we focus on setting up an EA program office or organization and on developing the elements of the architecture project plan. We cover the key topics briefly in this chapter, whereas details are addressed in Chapter 2.3.

The Project Plan

Rather than use a specific outline for the project plan, sometimes also called a project or program management plan, we review the key topics that any plan needs to cover:

- What is to be done: SOW, work breakdown structure (WBS), deliverables, and reviews
- Who is involved: stakeholders, project member roles
- How the work will be done: management and technical processes; methods; techniques; and tools; computer resources and facilities
- When will the work be done: project schedule and milestones

Each of these key topics is discussed in the following subsections.

What Is to Be Done

A key element of the project plan is a discussion of the work that is to be accomplished. Typically, a project starts with the development of an SOW or the receipt of an SOW from a customer who may be internal or external to the development group. The SOW spells out the work to be done in terms of deliverables (both management and technical), high-level schedule, and reviews. The following bullets provide a list of elements for an EA project SOW. Chapter 2.3 contains a discussion of the contents of each of the suggested SOW sections.

- Title
- Project background
- Project description and scope
- Architecture vision
- Management approach
- Change procedures
- Responsibilities and deliverables
- Acceptance criteria and procedures
- (High-level) project schedule
- Support

A usual response to an SOW is the development of a WBS, which outlines the tasks necessary to manage and create the deliverables in the SOW and identifies dependencies among these tasks. These tasks include both technical and management tasks that may be influenced by the specific methodology or process that will be used to perform the work. The WBS is input into the detailed work plans and schedules. For many types of system and software projects, generic WBSs are available that can be used as starting places for specific project WBSs in these areas. Typically, these generic WBS can be found in textbooks or are part of corporate or enterprise management standards. Unfortunately, EA is such a new discipline that few if any such generic WBSs have been developed. Some corporations or EA development shops may have such WBSs for use in house, but they have not yet appeared in textbooks. A generic EA project WBS is something that an EA development group may want to develop after experience with several EA projects or several iterations of builds for an evolving EA.

The technical deliverables listed in the SOW and addressed by tasks in the WBS include the views and related data identified in steps 3 and 4 of the Six Step process, as well as any necessary management reports, technical briefings, and management processes, such as configuration management. Because many architecture frameworks, such as DoDAF, provide only generic guidance, the description of the EA views needs to include any required options and tailoring as determined in step 4 of the Six Step process. The views need to include any selected fit-for-purpose views, with explicit descriptions of the desired format of these views. Technical deliverables may also include the results of analysis. This analysis may include analyses needed to develop the architecture as well as additional types of analysis where the developed architecture data is just one of the sources of input. Many types of analysis needed to support decision makers require both architecture and financial data. Examples of such analyses include ROI, business case analysis, and activity-based costing. Other types of additional technical analysis include performance or sensitivity analysis based on simulations.

The reviews of the technical deliverables also need careful identification and description. Because there is insufficient experience with EA development in both government and industry, there are no standard reviews for EA views and data during development as there are for systems and software. Each development organization must evolve through trial and error its own reasonable set of reviews. However, there are at least some known pitfalls that should be avoided. A common mistake is to try a review of "final" operational views and data prior to the development of systems or services views and data. However, EA views, such as the DoDAF views, form an integrated set. Development of systems or services views will uncover data that will cause changes in operational views and data. Placing the operational views under configuration management (CM) too early (that is, accepting a set of operational views and corresponding data as "final" through a review process prior to the development of system or services views) may significantly slow down the development process, because development of the systems or services views will predictably result in a fair number of needed changes. Review of draft views and data by viewpoint may be appropriate, but premature CM of single viewpoints should be avoided. Chapter 2.3 addresses more about EA lifecycle issues.

Who Is Responsible

The project plan must identify all the participants in the development process and their roles and responsibilities. The organizational structure of the development team needs to be spelled out and the skills required by the various team roles identified. Because EA development is a collaborative process involving both members of the enterprise and the development team, the business or mission personnel and IT personnel of the enterprise in question have roles to play as well as the members of the EA development team. The "owners" of the EA need to provide overall enterprise vision and direction. Although the EA development team can help facilitate the development of an enterprise strategy, ultimately it is the executives and business or mission leaders who must buy into and own the vision and strategy. Otherwise, the EA effort is wasted. Executives, business leaders, and subject matter experts (SMEs) must also participate in the review and validation of the architecture. This review and validation can be part of the development process and also part of the governance process discussed in Chapter 2.6.

An enterprise engaged in developing and using an EA should have an organization that is charged with the development, maintenance, and evolution of the EA. In government, this organization is usually called the EA Program Office and is usually headed by a Chief Architect. Whatever the name of this organization, best practice says that this organization needs to report directly to the enterprise's Chief Information Officer (CIO) or equivalent. If the EA program office is removed in terms of the organizational structure from the CIO's office, this is an indication that the EA program does not have an appropriate level of buy-in or support from the enterprise's high-level management. Note that the EA Program Office should report to the CIO rather than the Chief Technology Officer (CTO) because the EA needs the active participation of the mission or business management; the EA program cannot be treated as simply an IT matter if it is to succeed.

Best practice (Federal Chief Information Officer Council, 2001) also says that an EA executive steering committee needs to be established to review and formally accept the EA. The steering committee includes representatives of senior management and business unit executives. A technical review committee is established to assist the steering committee with reviewing IT aspects of the EA. The steering committee may approve the appointment of the Chief Architect.

The EA program office needs adequate staff and resources to be credible, even if most of the development or update work is outsourced to an outside contractor. The EA program office may have dedicated staff or may depend on staff brought in from other organizations. Integrated product teams (IPTs) composed of SMEs and development team members can be used to help jump start as-is portions of architectures, to brainstorm to-be portions of architectures, and to perform short-term architecture validation activities. However, IPTs are not effective for long-term activities as the SMEs have other jobs and cannot usually devote large amounts of their time on the architecture tasks.

The roles and skills needed by the EA Program Office include management, technical and business expertise, development specialists, reviewers and validators, tool support, and liaison with external enterprise organizations.

The Chief Architect's job requires a number of skills, as illustrated in Figure 2.2-16. The Chief Architect is usually the manager of the EA project, so he or she needs managerial skills and the ability to handle both in-house development and contract issues. The Chief Architect needs a good understanding of

FIGURE 2.2-16

Chief Architect
Skills

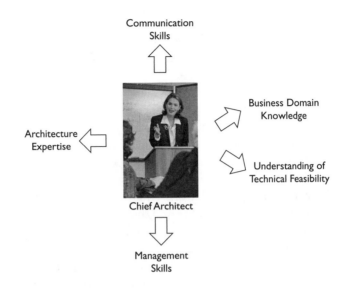

Chief Architect Skills

the enterprise business and missions as well as sufficient understanding of technical issues to know what is appropriate and feasible from a technical point of view with respect to the enterprise's domain. The Chief Architect needs a good understanding of architecture frameworks, views, methodologies, and tools, as well as the uses to which EA data will be used within the enterprise. The Chief Architect needs good communications skills in order to interface with executive management, business management, and IT management. Because all these skills and knowledge are rarely found in a single individual, a Chief Architect will typically have deputies to provide expertise in areas where he or she is not as strong.

The development specialists have expertise in the various modeling techniques and views needed for the viewpoints involved in the architecture. These viewpoints include capability or strategic, project or acquisition, operational, data, systems or services, and standards. In addition, the development specialists may include "architect's assistants" who manage the input of architecture data into complex architecture development tools. The architect's assistants allow the other development specialists to focus on modeling issues and free them from having to deal with the details of the tools.

Architecture reviewers, who check the views and data for consistency, completeness, adherence to enterprise standards, and other quality issues, may include both members of the development team, business and technical managers, and SMEs. Architecture validators determine whether the views and data appropriately reflect the current enterprise status (for as-is views) or the desired enterprise state (for to-be views). Validators need to include managers and SMEs. Care must be taken in selecting validators because various SME groups within the enterprise may have conflicting options. Representatives from the various groups need to be included. If there are conflicting options, the EA should expose the issues and support the resolution of these issues.

The development team will need access to IT specialists for installation, customization, and maintenance of the architecture development and analysis tools and their integration, as well as for general computing and communications support. Complex architecture development tools frequently have customization features that allow the tool to be adjusted to support specific view tailoring. This customization needs to be set up initially for the tailoring selected in step 4 of the Six Step process and specified in any enterprise EA standards. It will need adjustment as the EA project progresses and the tailoring is refined. In addition, the various tools used in the EA development project, including development, repository, analysis, management, and presentation tools, frequently need additional custom software to support their integration (as discussed in Chapter 2.3). These IT specialists may be dedicated members of the development team for large EA projects or they may be available from some centralized support organization.

The EA project team will need the support of additional personnel to handle tasks associated with the CM process. These personnel act as the secretariat for the EA Change Control Board (CCB), which handles such tasks as setting up CCB meetings and agendas and publishing reports on CCB activities. These personnel may be directly associated with the EA project team or may be organized in other ways, depending on corporate culture. The EA project team will need the support of quality assurance (QA) personnel. Again, these personnel may be directly associated with the EA project team or with a separate QA organization. Best practice directs that the head of QA reports to someone other than the Chief Architect.

Finally, the EA project team will need to maintain a liaison with other organizations or groups within the enterprise with which the team needs to maintain close coordination. While the EA provides information to groups such as Strategic Planning and Investment Management, decisions or changes made by these groups directly impact the EA. Although one of the Chief Architect's roles is to be the primary liaison with executive and management groups within the enterprise, he or she may want to appoint team members as special liaisons to critical external groups.

How the Work Will Be Done: Managerial and Technical Approaches

In laying out how the work will be done in a systems or software project, you would use a standard lifecycle to identify the phases involved in the scope of the project and plot your WBS tasks against the technical phases and the cross-phase categories.

Ideally, you want to develop a filled-in version of the chart in Figure 2.2-17 to fully understand the order in which tasks will accomplished and views and data developed, which techniques and tools will be used, and what reviews will be accomplished.

The challenge with an EA project is that no EA lifecycle standards are available. This means no accepted standard definitions for the phases, no standards for where to start or what to review, when to review, or what the entry and exit criteria should be. This also means that an EA project will need to make its own decisions in terms of how the work will be done, with its selected methodology being its basic guidance. Frameworks vary widely in the amount of methodology or process guidance they provide. Although the TOGAF provides a lifecycle methodology, the DoDAF provides only minimal process guidance directed at individual views. The DoDAF leaves the development organization free to select its own process or methodology. Chapter 2.3 discusses EA lifecycle issues in more detail and provides a promising example lifecycle.

At a minimum, the project plan should outline both the management approach and the technical approach. The management approach includes tasks that need to be executed continuously across all of the technical tasks. These tasks include

FIGURE 2.2-17

Basic Lifecycle Chart

	Phase I	Phase II	Phase III	Phase IV	Phase V	Phase VI
Tasks						
Views						
Methods						
Tools						
Reviews						
Management						
Tasks	Products		Methods		Tools	
Configuration Management						
Tasks	Products		Methods		Tools	
Quality Assurance						
Tasks	Products		Methods		Tools	

estimating, scheduling, tracking, reporting, configuration management, and quality assurance. The project plan needs to discuss specific methods, techniques, and tools that will be used for each of these management tasks. For example, the project plan needs to include a description of the CM processes and tools or, at the least, a pointer to a configuration management plan. Similarly, the QA processes and tools can be described or the project plan can point to a QA plan. An additional management task is risk management. This topic is discussed in Chapter 2.3.

The technical approach includes a discussion of the process or methodology and tools that will be used to develop, manage, and maintain the EA views and data. The process or methodology will include the order in which to develop views and data and the specific modeling techniques and tools used to develop them. An enterprise may develop its own EA development methodology or use a "name brand" process such as that provided by TOGAF. Part of the process needs to include or be coordinated with the following:

- Architecture validation strategy
- Architecture evolution strategy
- Architecture maintenance strategy
- Architecture dissemination strategy
- Transition planning

These topics are discussed in more detail in the following chapters. The technical process description should also include the process for EA view and data reviews and a tentative schedule for these reviews with respect to other development tasks and events.

When Will the Work Be Done

An important part of planning is the development of project schedules and a key part of developing schedules is level-of-effort (LOE) estimating for the various tasks that need to be done. Schedules for EA development are complicated by the fact that EA data is used to support decision making in major enterprise processes and decisions made during these processes may in turn affect the EA. Estimating LOE is based primarily on experience, but EA is still a new field in which most enterprises have limited experience.

Scheduling Milestones

Typical internal milestones include task completion dates, view draft delivery dates, and review dates. Scheduling must also deal with dependencies among EA development tasks. An example dependency for as-is portions of architectures includes the need to complete at least some portion of document review and SME interviews prior to beginning view development. These are typical scheduling problems, so approaches for dealing with them don't vary from those usually employed in most system or software projects.

One of the complicating issues of scheduling EA development or evolution activities is that there are many external process milestones that may constrain the EA development schedule. Examples of these external processes include the following:

- Budgeting process
- Investment review process
- System development lifecycle (SDLC) process
- System of systems (SoS) integration testing process

Each of these external processes may require types of EA data to support decision making at key milestones. Budgeting and investment review processes usually have yearly cycles and require EA data to support decisions about which systems to select, continue funding, or retire. Systems under development may require sufficient EA data to provide compliance criteria and guidance at key lifecycle milestones. Planning for SoS integration testing requires EA data, such as system internal and external interfaces. Enterprise executives may decide that the EA development or evolution schedule needs to be adjusted so that the required data is available to meet key milestone dates for any of these processes. For SDLC and SoS integration testing processes, the milestone dates are usually those associated with critical systems.

In turn, decisions made during the preceding processes may affect the EA. Budgeting and investment review decisions may impact the planned timing of systems, business process, or capability evolution and architecture transition. Budgeting and investment review decisions, as well as EA decisions driven by system development needs, may also affect the speed of technology insertion and the introduction of standards. The results of the SoS integration testing process may warrant changes to key interfaces. All of these interactions complicate the scheduling of EA development, maintenance, and evolution.

Schedules also, as always, need to take into account management reserve (that is, schedule time held in reserve to respond to unplanned events or risks) based on risk analysis and planning, as discussed in Chapter 2.3.

LOE Estimating Issues

LOE estimates per EA development task or possibly per EA view are necessary to support the development of reliable schedules. Because experience is a large factor in LOE estimating, planners must review organizational experience with EA development with respect to the following:

- The EA development process or methodology being used, including the models or views being developed
- The level of detail required in the architecture under development, including the phase of the architecture (that is, as-is or to-be) under development
- The development tools being used

If the process, model set, or development tools are new to the development organization, additional time will be required for appropriate training and the learning curve. Additional time will also be necessary to get new tools in place and integrated.

Unfortunately, there are no generic industry guidelines for LOE estimates for EA development. Government projects typically do not keep records that are detailed enough to provide meaningful guidance. Commercial firms that do keep detailed records usually consider their experience data a competitive advantage and treat it as proprietary. Few reports with detailed data are published. If the development organization has no experience with EA development or most of the personnel on the development team are not experienced with EA, then the best way to generate some initial LOE estimates is through a pilot effort. Pilot efforts are best focused on a small subset or "sliver" of the full EA that concerns a limited but well-defined mission performed by a small, well-defined, and cooperative set of operators who have a specific architecture issue. A successful pilot project can result in two beneficial outcomes: an example of an early success in the use of EA and estimates on the minimum LOE for the involved architecture tasks.

Summary of Project Planning

Organizations planning for EA development projects should follow their standard planning procedures with attention to the following differences:

- There is no standard EA lifecycle or standard set of reviews.
- The EA lifecycle or development process must interact or interface with other key enterprise processes.
- There is less organizational experience with EA processes and models and views.
- Fewer experienced personnel are available for EA development.
- Federal requirements for EA have been steadily increasing.

The increasing federal requirements, which apply to all federal agencies, are principally driven by OMB's increasing use of EA data to help with federal-level budgeting efforts. Because DoD deals with OMB only at the level of the Office of the Secretary of the Defense (OSD), most DoD services, agencies, and commands, unlike the other federal departments and agencies, don't have to deal with OMB requirements directly. However, as OSD has to provide more data to OMB, there will be more requirements for the DoD services, agencies, and commands to provide additional data.

Standard planning should result in the following characteristics:

- A clear assignment of responsibilities
- A clear identification of deliverables
- A clear description of the processes, both managerial and technical, to be used
- A detailed schedule with identification of task dependencies

Success Factors for Planning

The following factors affect successful execution of an architecture effort:

- **Clear and common objectives/purpose** The objectives for embarking on an often-expensive architecture development must be clear to both the sponsors and the architecture team itself.

- **Clear definition of stakeholders and expectations** At the outset and during the course of an architecture development, stakeholders must be clearly defined and involved in the communications process.

- **Clear and demonstrated architecting skills** Training and competence in the mechanics of modeling as well as familiarity with the vocabulary, ontology, and semantic concepts used in your EA development methodology and framework are essential.

- **A clear work plan and risk mitigation strategy** A step-by-step WBS along with a clear SOW, clearly identified deliverables, and an identification and mitigation strategy for anticipated risks is essential.

- **Clear analysis and recommendations (and follow-ups)** In architecture projects that include findings and conclusions based on analysis, documenting findings clearly and communicating the impact of issues are essential. A follow-up plan to track actions based on findings and recommendations enhances the success of the architectural effort further.

- **Clear communications** Architectures tell a story. The development of the architecture fleshes out parts of the story. The effort is akin to plotting a cast of characters, determining events and actions and sweeping a timeline forward. Any architecture effort that tells the story in a manner that is clear to an audience garners instant support.

- **Crisp execution** Ultimately, the success of architecture development efforts hinges on the crispness of the execution in terms of quality of effort and timeliness.

Summary of Six Step Process Advice

Here is a summary of advice based on the Six Step process.

- Know why you are developing the architecture. Identify the full set of architecture users—the stakeholders—and the ways in which they plan to use the architecture.

- Expect to tailor the models and views to capture the data critical to your stakeholders.

- Select a process to develop your architecture. Make sure it includes views that communicate architecture data to stakeholders and plans to share these views and supporting data with the decision makers.

■ Choose appropriate automated tools. These are needed for productivity and to support consistency of the data across the models and views, especially in the face of updates and changes.

■ Provide training for new processes and tools.

■ Be prepared to add to or modify the set of views or models as you gain experience with the architecture domain.

■ Do not develop views or models for which you can't find a customer (that is, a user). For some views, the architecture team may be the principal user.

■ Do not develop more detail than your architecture users need.

Questions

1. Why is it important to establish traceability from stakeholder issues to architecture data and views?

2. In your enterprise, who are the users of EA (that is, the stakeholders) and how do they use EA information to support decision making?

3. This chapter provides suggestions for core sets of views to be included in each of the three levels of architecture. How are additional views selected?

4. The example enterprise-level architecture for RMN Airport doesn't include local governments and citizens as stakeholders (that is, users of the architecture), yet these stakeholders will want information about increased noise and traffic and expansion of airport grounds and facilities to analyze the impact on their communities. Formulate some of their questions and issues and redo the analysis in the enterprise-level architecture example to identify any additional data and views that need to be included for these stakeholders.

5. What approach will you take to establish LOE for architecture tasks? Does your organization have existing experience on which to draw or a corporate methodology for determining LOE?

6. Why are acceptance criteria important to include in an SOW?

7. Why is it important for the Chief Architect to understand both business operations and appropriate technology?

8. How is your organization approaching the EA lifecycle? Have you developed your own EA lifecycle or are you using one from another source?

9. How is your organization integrating Reference Models with enterprise-level and segment-level architectures?

10. The solution-level example in this chapter handles only a subset of the stakeholder questions. Complete the traceability table and identify the complete set of data and views needed for the solution-level architecture. Do you see any additional questions that need to be added to the analysis? Do you see any additional data or views that can be added to the existing part of the traceability table?

11. Here are the purpose, scope, and stakeholder questions for a solution-level architecture. Develop the matrix to trace the questions to the data types needed to answer the questions and to the views (with options and tailoring) to develop and document the required data. Refer to the section "Determine What Models to Use: How to Organize and Correlate Data," for more information on views and models.

   ■ *Purpose:* Define the operational processes and IT necessary to support data sharing for a newly formed cross-agency community of interest (COI) for management of security incidents.

   ■ *Scope:*

      i. Architecture: Cross-agency solution-level architecture

      ii. Function: Airspace security incident management

      iii. Geography: CONUS, but coordination needed with international agencies

      iv. Timeframe: To-be 2015

      v. Technology constraints: COTS integration; must integrate with existing agency systems

   ■ *Issues and questions:*

      i. What is the overall operational concept?

      ii. Who are the potential members of the COI in terms of:

         a. Organization—their owning agency and reporting hierarchy

         b. Their data-sharing needs—what information they can provide and what data they need; what data they need but currently don't have access to

         c. What are the COI's shared vocabulary concepts?

         d. What are the current relevant operational processes of the COI?

e. What are the relevant legacy systems, interfaces, and standards?

f. What are nominal scenarios for key incident types?

g. What is the common information model for supporting information sharing?

h. What are the COI standards for interoperability, security, and privacy in data sharing?

i. What is the data quality, timeliness, and media (video, audio, telephonic, and Internet) attributes necessary for shared data?

j. What are the rules (based on policy) that define data creation, update, and access authorizations based on incident type?

Reference List

Department of Defense. (2009). *Department of Defense Architecture Framework Version 2.0.* www.cio-nil.defense.gov/sites/dodaf20.

Federal Chief Information Officer Council. (2001). *A Practical Guide to Federal Enterprise Architecture, version 1.0.* www.enterprise-architecture.infor/images/Documents/Federal%20Enterprise%20Architecture%20Guide%20v1a.pdf.

Federal Enterprise Architecture Program Office, Office of Management and Budget. (2007). *Federal Enterprise Architecture Consolidated Reference Model Document Version 2.3.* www.whitehouse.gov/sites/default/files/omb/assets/fea_docs/FEA_CRM_v23_Final_Oct_2007_Revised.pdf.

2.3

Implementing the Enterprise Architecture

I n this chapter, we address details of issues regarding EA development and implementation that were first identified in Chapter 2.2. The topics covered include the statement of work (SOW) and work breakdown structure (WBS) for an EA project, the EA implementation steps as identified by the selected EA development methodology and EA lifecycle, data strategies, and risk management. Corporate culture and the sociological aspects of the enterprise involved, as discussed in Chapter 2.1, heavily influence an enterprise's approach to each of these issues.

Statement of Work (SOW)

All projects, whether internal or contracted, are based on some understanding of the work that the project is to undertake. This understanding is usually documented in a written SOW. Architects need to have a good understanding of the elements of an SOW for an EA project because they may be required to develop or to respond to SOWs. The following subsections cover a generic SOW for an EA development project and highlight issues that are specific to EA projects.

The following bullet list provides an outline for an EA development project SOW. This outline is similar to that provided by The Open Group. Each of the items in the outline is discussed in a separate subsection. Key information included in the SOW is provided by the first few steps of the Six Step process discussed in Chapter 2.2, and the relationships of items in the outline are related back to the Six Step process.

- Title
- Project background
- Project description and scope
- Architecture vision
- Management approach
- Change procedures
- Responsibilities and deliverables
- Acceptance criteria and procedures
- (High-level) project schedule
- Support

Title

The title for the SOW usually includes the EA name in some form. For example, the SOW for one of the example architectures in Chapter 2.2 might be: Statement of Work for RMN Airport Passenger Management Segment Architecture.

Project Background

The SOW should include a discussion of the sponsoring organization and the context necessary for understanding its reasons for needing an EA. For example, a SOW for any of the RMN Airport architectures would contain a brief discussion of the sponsoring organizations: the Port Authority and RMN Airport Management. The SOW would also reference the strategic planning decisions that are driving the expansion of RMN. For many DoD or government architecture projects, the SOW would contain references to legislation, regulations, directives, doctrine, or specific tasking that are driving the need for change or for the development of the architecture.

Project Description and Scope

The SOW should include a discussion of the purpose of the EA and the EA scope as identified in steps 1 and 2 of the Six Step process. The entire list of stakeholder questions need not be included, but the stakeholders (that is, the users of the architecture) must be identified as well as all the scope boundaries from step 2. This section of the SOW should identify the level of architecture that is being developed (enterprise, segment, or solution).

Architecture Vision

This section might be better called "strategic vision." The SOW should include the drivers for the architecture from step 1 of the Six Step process, especially any strategic visions and plans, strategies, goals, or objectives that the EA is to support. Especially for solution architectures, it is always important to link the architecture back to the high-level business and mission requirements that are driving the need for the architecture.

Management Approach

The SOW should spell out the project management reporting that is required from the SOW's executors. This section should outline the types of estimating, scheduling, tracking, and reporting that will be expected. Configuration or version management, quality assurance, and risk management tasks and reporting should also be identified.

Change Procedures

During the course of the project, the details of the SOW may change. This is especially true of EA projects where the specific views, required data, and options or tailoring tend to evolve as the understanding of the architectural domain matures during EA development. Because the SOW is the written basis for the project, it needs to be updated to reflect these and other types of changes. If it is not updated, the different parties involved may develop divergent expectations on what the outcomes of the project should be. This type of misunderstanding can be quite serious, especially in a contractual situation or when management personnel turn over during the duration of the project.

This section of the SOW should outline the procedures for updating the SOW, including the identification of how changes are proposed and who has the authority to approve proposed changes. A committee or board may need to approve proposed changes. Note that this section specifically addresses the change procedures for the SOW itself, not any configuration management procedures for the EA views and data.

Responsibilities and Deliverables

The SOW must clearly outline what products, artifacts, data, and other outcomes need to be generated by the project and who is responsible for which outcomes. In a contractual situation, the SOW includes identification of the responsibilities of the issuers of the SOW as well as the responsibilities of the executors of the SOW. The responsibilities of the issuers of the SOW may include providing timely access to documents and subject matter experts (SMEs) for as-is portions of an EA and access to critical business and technical SME groups for to-be portions of an EA. These responsibilities need to be spelled out in the SOW to make clear the impacts of delays in gaining access to needed data and experts on the outcomes of the project. The responsibilities of the executors of the SOW include both the management and technical deliverables.

The management deliverables include required status reports and briefings with the contents based on the work identified in the Management Approach section of the SOW. The technical deliverables include the EA views and data that are identified in step 4 of the Six Step process and possibly the standard views and data identified in step 6. The SOW must spell out the options (such as the types of models) and tailoring needed for the EA views and data, identified in step 4 of the Six Step process. These options and tailoring choices can be updated with changes via the procedures in the Change Procedures section of the SOW. The electronic format for these EA deliverables should also be specified. The issuers of the SOW don't want the EA views only in a hard copy format, as the data is not useful except in an electronic format. It is important that the issuers and executors of the SOW agree on what electronic format is to be delivered. This format may be driven by a standard or by the tools that the issuer of the SOW plans to use. These types of formats are discussed further in Chapter 5.1. The electronic format may also be driven by a requirement to deliver portions of the architecture to a government repository. As an alternative to including the view options and tailoring in the SOW, the SOW can include a process for agreeing on and documenting the selected options and tailoring as part of the EA development process.

Failure to agree on view options and tailoring or on an acceptable electronic delivery format can cause serious problems, especially in contractual situations. Failure to agree on view options and tailoring can result in the delivery of architecture views and data that doesn't address the specific data needs of the stakeholders or that can't support required analysis. Failure to agree on an electronic delivery format early in the project can result in a large amount of unexpected work for the executors of the SOW at the end of the project, when the developers need to translate their views and data into an electronic format that is radically different from that provided by the tools they used.

Other items related to the technical deliverables that need to be specified in the SOW include required reviews and additional analysis tasks. Because there is no standard lifecycle for EAs, there are no standard reviews with well-known entry and exit criteria. The issuers of the SOW must identify and describe any technical view and data reviews that they want. The descriptions of any required reviews need to include when, with respect to the architecture development process, the reviews should take place and what the entry and exit criteria are. A common problem with EA projects is the request for review of operational or business views prior to the development of technical views. Because EAs have integrated views, based on a common set of data, such a review is unrealistic. Development of technical views affects the business or mission views because they are related. A better approach is to ask for a review to validate or draft business or mission views to the extent possible prior to the development of technical views.

Analysis tasks associated with EA development include types of analysis necessary to develop the architecture as well as types of analysis that use data from a completed portion of the architecture (that is, as-is or to-be data for a specific date). Types of analysis that might be included as part of architecture development are trade-off analyses and capability gap analysis. Types of analysis that use data from a completed portion of the architecture include return on investment (ROI) analysis, business case analysis, and performance analysis.

An SOW can also spell out requirements for technical briefings and additional products, such as notes resulting from interviews of SMEs.

Acceptance Criteria and Procedures

The SOW needs to specify how the technical EA deliverables will be judged acceptable. Acceptance criteria and procedures are critical in contractual situations and are different from organizational acceptance of the EA. That is, there is a difference between contractual acceptance and organizational acceptance of the EA as part of the governance process. The governance acceptance process is discussed in Chapter 2.6. Contractual acceptance criteria need to be considered carefully and spelled out explicitly in the SOW.

Acceptance criteria can include such items as compliance or conformance with a standard and consistency and completeness of views. However, notice that requiring conformance with a standard may not be sufficient to ensure useful views. For example, the DoDAF provides guidance and as long as the EA data is defined in accordance with the DoDAF metamodel (DM2) concepts, associations, and attributes, the EA is in conformance with DoDAF. However, conformance with the DoDAF doesn't mean that the data is sufficient to address stakeholder issues or support key decision making. Acceptance criteria can also be based on the ability of the EA data to support key decisions.

In addition to specifying acceptance criteria, the SOW should contain acceptance procedures. Who gets to apply the criteria to the deliverables and what is the process by which the criteria are applied? Procedures may involve review of the deliverables by a board.

High-Level Project Schedule

An SOW should include a high-level project schedule containing the major milestones for deliverables from the SOW issuer's point of view. It will be up to the executors of the SOW to develop detailed project development schedules in response to the schedule contained in the SOW. The high-level schedule should not require the delivery of final views and data from one viewpoint of the EA prior to the development of views and data from the other viewpoints. The EA views and data form an integrated set, and development of additional viewpoints, views, and data will impact the existing views and data.

Support/Automated Environment and Tools

The SOW should identify any tools or facilities that the issuer of the SOW will provide to the executor of the SOW, as well as any tool interfaces, such as an interface to the issuer's CM system or repository, to which the issuer expects the executor of the SOW to deliver data or deliverables. Any restrictions or conditions on the use of tools and facilities should be specified.

Work Breakdown Structure (WBS)

A WBS is a structured, hierarchical decomposition of the set of tasks needed to perform the work described in the SOW. The WBS is focused on the work needed to develop the deliverables specified in the SOW. The WBS is developed in response to an SOW and is a basic part of planning for a project.

Although some generic WBSs are available in texts for systems and software projects, EA is still too new a discipline for such generic WBSs to have appeared. Each EA development organization has to develop its own. Experienced EA development organizations may develop their own standard EA development WBS that projects can use as a starting point. A WBS often reflects the corporate culture of the development group and is influenced by the processes or methodologies selected for both the managerial and technical approaches. These processes identify tasks that need to be done, the order in which tasks should be done, and the dependencies or interactions among the tasks. Specific task dependencies that need to be addressed in an EA WBS include the relationships between the views to be developed and the dependencies on outside resources such as documentation and SMEs required for some of the tasks.

Implementation Steps

This section covers some of the basic elements needed for EA development. Included are discussions of EA development methodologies, EA lifecycle, tool support for processes, and the relationship of EA to the system lifecycle.

Architecture Development Methodology/Process

What is an EA development methodology or process? It provides an ordered set of technical tasks for developing the views and data and usually the models and techniques to choose from for the views, as well as the relationships among the views. (This is what Chapter 5.1 calls the *process lifecycle*.) The architecture development methodology may include a repository approach and a validation approach. The development methodology that a development group chooses to use may differ depending on the level of architecture being developed. The development methodology may also differ depending on the domain of the architecture. For example, a solution architecture development process for command-and-control domain architecture might differ from one for a logistics or data-centered domain architecture. Not only might different views be involved but the development order of those views would differ. The command-and-control domain development process might focus on process, event response, and performance whereas the development process for the data-centered domain might focus on operational data prior to considering process and deem performance to be much less critical.

EA Lifecycle

As discussed in Chapter 2.2, the EA discipline is too new to have established any lifecycle standards. Each development organization has had to develop its own lifecycle. Currently, various government agencies, contractors, and commercial corporations have developed EA lifecycles that tend to differ from one another quite a bit. Many focus on the early part of the EA lifecycle and don't yet handle maintenance in detail. Unfortunately, maintenance of the EA is the most difficult area to deal with because EA interacts with most of the other enterprise processes and lifecycles. Any EA lifecycle has to address a large set of challenges:

- Does the EA lifecycle handle problem-oriented, incremental architecture development?
- How does the EA lifecycle fit with the concept of federated architectures and Reference Models?
- How does the EA lifecycle coordinate with other related enterprise lifecycles and processes such as:
  - Strategic Planning
  - Investment Management (capital planning and investment control)
  - System engineering and the system development lifecycle (SDLC)

In this section, we will cover one of the most promising emerging EA lifecycles, review industry lessons learned about the interactions among development methodologies or processes and tools, discuss the additional processes needed in conjunction with EA development and the issues that arise with the integration of tools, and address the relationships of EA to the SDLC. The Open Group Architecture Framework (TOGAF) Architecture Development Methodology (ADM), which supplies an architecture development methodology and implies an EA lifecycle, is discussed in Chapter 1.2.

OMB Lifecycle

The Office of Management and Budget (OMB) and Government Accountability Office (GAO) have started to develop EA lifecycles so that these agencies can use them in further development of EA guidance and assessment tools for U.S. government agencies. The GAO lifecycle is still very primitive (Develop, Use, Maintain), but the OMB lifecycle is starting to evolve into a usable outline. Figure 2.3-1 shows the OMB lifecycle [Office of Management and Budget. (2009). Improving agency performance using information and information technology (Enterprise Architecture Assessment Framework v3.1, pg. 4)]. This lifecycle focuses more on how to use the EA to transition the enterprise than on the details of EA development, which is why OMB calls it an "Information and IT-enabled Performance Improvement Lifecycle." This is a useful approach because it emphasizes the role of all three levels of architecture in enterprise evolution and transition and does not address the EA as an end in itself. The enterprise transition process is based on current OMB guidance. However, more detail will be needed in the areas of EA development and maintenance to provide best-practice guidance for EA development

FIGURE 2.3-1

Office of
Management
and Budget EA
Lifecycle

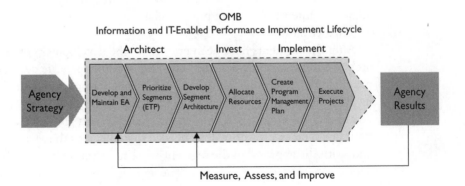

organizations and to enable comparison of EA development status in standardized terms. This development guidance will have to address development for each of the three levels of architecture. TOGAF implies some elements of an EA lifecycle in its methodology.

The OMB lifecycle shows EA as being driven by the enterprise strategy and yielding enterprise results, which, after assessment and analysis, provide additional feedback for another cycle of EA development aimed at further improvements.

The lifecycle starts with the "Develop and Maintain EA" phase. The architecture addressed at this phase is the enterprise-level architecture. It addresses the Capability Viewpoint at least and includes both as-is architectures and one or more to-be architectures. The to-be architectures usually include a vision or long-term target architecture as well as multiple intermediate transition stage architectures. OMB guidance suggests that the enterprise-level architecture include the identification of segments for which segment-level architectures will need to be developed. Segments could be captured in the Capability Taxonomy (CV-2) or Capability Dependencies (CV-4) if they were tailored to identify which capabilities belonged to which segment. This phase ends with the approval of the enterprise-level architecture by the Enterprise Architecture Executive Steering Council (EAESC) or other appropriate governance group as discussed in Chapter 2.6.

Once the enterprise-level architecture has been completed, the lifecycle moves to the next phase: "Prioritize Segments." In this phase, the enterprise decides how to prioritize and schedule the segments identified in the enterprise-level architecture and develops an enterprise transition plan (ETP). This process involves careful coordination with the enterprise strategic planning and identification of which capabilities, products, or services are most important to the enterprise. The development of the ETP may also result in the development of additional enterprise-level architectures that reflect the agreed-upon intermediate steps in the transition toward the long-term vision. This phase ends with the approval of the ETP and any additional intermediate enterprise-level architectures by the EAESC or appropriate governance authority.

After the segments have been prioritized, the development of segment-level architectures can begin. The segment-level architectures are developed in the priority order determined in the previous phase. Part of developing the segment-level architecture is identification of the solution-level architectures needed to describe all the component parts of the segment. This also includes determining what programs or projects will be needed to implement the segment. This phase ends with the approval of the segment-level architecture by the EAESC or appropriate governance authority. The various systems that are associated with each solution-level architecture can be identified in a tailored, high-level System Interface Description (SV-1) in the segment-level architecture.

Once a segment-level architecture has been developed and approved, then the next phase of the lifecycle ("Allocate Resources") can begin. Resources need to be allocated for all the programs and projects identified for the segment. The process used for this phase of the lifecycle usually involves the Investment Review Board (IRB) (or equivalent) approving budgets for these programs and projects based on information provided by the enterprise architecture and included in business case analysis and ROI-type documents (per program). Note that during this phase, the exact set of projects and solution-level architectures included in the segment may change based on IRB decisions. The segment-level architectures may need to be updated as a result of these decisions.

After a program or project has been approved, the next phase of the lifecycle ("Create Program Management Plan") can begin. The program or project management plan (PMP) needs to be developed. This plan includes tasking and the technical approach (that is, the development process or methodology and tools) for the necessary solution-level architecture(s). This phase ends with the approval of the PMP. The approval authority for the PMP varies by enterprise, based on culture, but frequently rests with the head of the organization that owns the program or project in question.

Once the PMP is in place, the final phase of the lifecycle ("Execute Projects") can begin. The program and projects develop solution-level architectures that align with the segment-level architecture for their segment. These solution-level architectures must be reviewed and approved by the appropriate governance authority. The programs and projects then perform the necessary system and infrastructure development, testing, and installation. Various elements of the enterprise execute reorganizations, initiate new or updated processes using new systems, and complete personnel actions (such as hiring) and skills training that will enable the new capabilities, product production, or service provision.

After the enterprise has been transitioned, the new processes and capabilities are measured and assessed while the programs and projects continue to maintain the new systems and infrastructure. Further requirements for improvement that impact existing segments can be fed back into the "Develop Segment Architecture" phase. In the appropriate segment-level architecture, these requirements can be allocated to the appropriate program or project or a new program or project can be identified. The segment-level architecture can be updated and the improvements implemented throughout the rest of the phases of the lifecycle. Alternatively, if the identified improvements impact the existing segment priorities, they can be fed back to the

"Prioritize Segments" phase. The existing priorities can be reexamined and the enterprise-level architecture, the enterprise transition plan, and segment priorities and schedules can be updated to reflect these additional enterprise requirements. New segments may be identified in this process. Then work on existing segments, programs, or projects can be readjusted and the additional requirements implemented throughout the rest of the lifecycle.

Figure 2.3-2 summarizes the OMB lifecycle in the format of the generic EA lifecycle chart (the Basic Lifecycle Chart) introduced in Chapter 2.2. The figure shows the basic architectures and products per phase, along with the major reviews.

Of the previously discussed EA lifecycle challenges, the OMB EA lifecycle addresses at least two. It embeds the concept of federated architecture through segment development. The OMB EA lifecycle defines how it fits in with Investment Management and the SDLC. It shows input from enterprise Strategic Planning but doesn't address the full feedback issues involved in changing enterprise strategies. However, it is not clear how the OMB EA lifecycle is adaptable to incremental architecture development as it clearly takes a full top-down approach.

The lifecycle diagram in Figure 2.3-1 is simplified and doesn't show the number of different segment, program, and project activities that can be going on simultaneously within an enterprise. However, it provides a good idea of how the different levels of

FIGURE 2.3-2	Phase / Details	Develop and Maintain EA	Prioritize Segments	Develop Segment Architecture	Allocate Resources	Develop PMP	Execute Projects
Lifecycle Chart for the OMB EA Lifecycle	Tasks						
	Views/Products	Enterprise-Level Architecture (with Segments Identified)	Enterprise Transition Plan	Segment-Level Architecture (with Programs/Projects Identified)	Business Case Analysis	Program Management Plan	Solution-Level Architecture
	Methods						
	Tools						
	Reviews	Enterprise-Level Architecture Acceptance by EAESC	ETP Acceptance by EAESC	Solution-Level Architecture Acceptance by EAESC	Approval of Programs by IRB	Approval of PMP	Acceptance of Solution-Level Architecture

Lifecycle Chart for the OMB EA Lifecycle

architecture need to be involved to support an enterprise transition. Obviously, the OMB EA lifecycle must evolve to show additional feedback loops and phasing details. However, it provides a good start on a standard for the government, because OMB expects government departments and agencies to report status based on this lifecycle and its successors.

Processes and Tools

Automated tools are necessary for developing architectures because of the amount of data involved and the amount of data correlation and consistency checking that is needed to support an integrated architecture. Such tools are necessary to support productivity, especially during maintenance and updates. The EA development community can learn some valuable lessons about automated tool support from the software and system development communities and their experiences with computer-aided software environment (CASE) and computer-aided design (CAD) tools. These lessons involve the integration of tools and development processes and tool and process training.

The first lesson learned is that if different methods or techniques are used on different architecture views or in different architecture levels, these different methods or techniques need to be integrated. That is, the data generated by the method or technique for one view must provide appropriate input for the next method or technique for the next view in the development process and for any method or technique that will be used to develop a view that shares data with the first view. Failure to have integrated methods and techniques will result in an inconsistent and unintegrated architecture.

The second lesson learned is that tools and development processes interact and must be integrated. Tools must be selected to support your development process. It may be tempting to try to use an inexpensive tool or one for which your organization already has a license, but if the tool and your process are a forced fit, experience shows use of the tool will be a serious mistake and cause far more development problems and delays than it is worth. Forced fits include trying to use a tool that supports one specific method or technique to support a different method or technique and trying to use a tool that enforces a specific set of policies in an organization that has a different set of policies. Even a process-appropriate tool will usually have some features that may cause you to alter your process to achieve a smooth fit. Note that this lesson implies that if separate tools are used for different views or levels of architecture, then these tools must be integrated. Tool integration issues are discussed in the subsection "Integration of Tools."

The third lesson learned is that training is necessary both for new development tools and for new development processes and methods. The learning curve for both of these items is steep and needs to be accommodated in project schedules. The best way to compensate for these new techniques and tools is training. Best practice includes having experts readily available, especially during the early days of use for new tools and techniques. Projects always encounter issues that aren't addressed in training, so prompt, experienced help can prevent serious delays or missteps that have serious impacts later on. Program or project guides for the specific options and tailoring required for architecture views are also helpful.

Additional Processes

In addition to an architecture development process, the architecture group needs processes to support additional analysis, project management, and the automation environment. Further processes may be required to provide direct support to the enterprise decision-making processes that require EA-based input and result in EA-impacting output. All these processes may require additional automated tools.

As discussed in Chapter 2.2, analysis may be required during architecture development to select the best approaches or after architecture development to provide input to decision-making processes. Some of these processes use only EA data, whereas others require a combination of architecture with financial or other types of data. Examples of these types of analysis include activity-based costing analysis, business case development, ROI analysis, and performance analysis based on executable architectures or simulations. In many cases, specialized tools are used to support this analysis.

An architecture development effort also requires basic management and other cross-phase or "umbrella" processes such as configuration management and quality assurance. Management processes include estimating, scheduling, planning, tracking, and reporting. Most organizations have tools to support all these processes. Some sophisticated organizations may have management tools that integrate with the development tools to support tracking of progress against assigned tasks. Risk management is an additional area that can fit under the general management category, or it can be considered an additional process area. Risk management is discussed later in this chapter.

Configuration management (CM) is a tricky issue with architecture tools that manage integrated sets of architecture data. Architecture development organizations must modify their software or systems CM policies and processes to deal with this issue of repository data and to mesh with the policies of their evolving EA governance structures. Architecture development tools frequently support some form of version control, but additional processes and tools are necessary to support full CM, which includes configuration identification, change control, configuration status accounting, and configuration auditing. Aligning the policies implicit in development tools' version control implementations with the organizational policies for full CM may also pose a challenge and cause serious problems with some development tools.

If quality assurance is defined in the currently accepted way as "process police," then the high-level processes and concepts used for software and systems development should be easily adaptable to EA. However, these processes may place additional requirements on architecture development tools or require additional tools.

Architecture development organizations shouldn't forget the processes needed to support the architecture development tools and automated environment. The more complex architecture development tools require specialized "care and feeding." These tools frequently allow for customization to support required tailoring both for views and for the development process. This customization needs frequent updating as the tailoring evolves and tool upgrades are released. All the development organization's tools, as well as its infrastructure, need to be kept up to date with both technology improvements and security enhancements. In addition, if the organization has developed special code to support the integration of any of the tools, this integration code will need to be updated as the infrastructure changes and as new tool releases arrive.

Integration of Tools

One of the persistent challenges that architecture development organizations face is getting their automated tools to integrate properly. This issue causes development teams lots of problems. Solutions can be expensive and a lack of solutions can severely impede project productivity and product quality. There are two general types of problems: integration of the various architecture development tools with each other and integration of architecture development tools with the other tools in the project's environment. Occasionally, architecture development tools need to integrate with other tools from outside the architecture development organization. The types of tool integration are illustrated in Figure 2.3-3.

Architecture development organizations quickly learn that, regardless of the methodology and modeling techniques they select, no single tool exists that will completely meet their needs. Some architecture development tools support only

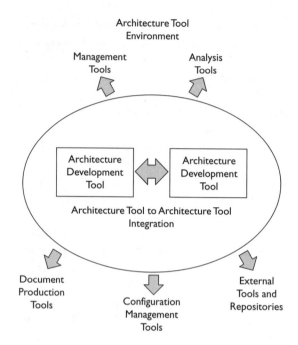

FIGURE 2.3-3

Types of Tool
Integration

a limited number of the techniques the project wants to use. Other tools support most of the techniques, but specialty tools are available that do a better job on specific types of models. As a result, most architecture development organizations are faced with the continuing challenge of integrating multiple architecture development tools. This is not a new problem; software development projects have long faced similar issues in trying to integrate tools to support the entire software lifecycle. However, because architecture views or models are integrated, all the tool interfaces must be two-way, which further complicates matters.

The expensive solution is to build custom interfaces between the tools. This is not always possible if the tools have proprietary databases and data formats that they use to store the architecture model data. Various solutions have been attempted, some excellent in theory, but none of these solutions has thus far worked well in practice. One approach is standardization of the architecture data coupled with a standard import/export format. DoD's initial attempt at these standards was based on the Core Architecture Data Model (CADM) that was developed as a standard data model for all architecture data. However, implementation efforts were hindered by the size of the data model and difficulty in mapping the data to the views in the early versions of the DoDAF. DoD is currently suggesting the Physical Exchange Specification (PES), a set of eXtensible Markup Language (XML) Schema Definition (XSD) files (one for each DoDAF Described Model) as an architecture development tool exchange format. The definitions of the architecture data in the PES are provided in the DoDAF Conceptual Data Model (CDM) and a Logical Data Model (LDM) (Department of Defense, 2009). Together, the CDM, LDM, and PES form the DoDAF metamodel (DM2).

Another approach to the development tool integration problem is based on the notion of a central architecture data repository that provides a standard import/export interface. In this approach, the repository is an independent tool, not an internal part of a tool that directly supports model or view development. Model development tools must support the import/export standard in order to integrate with the repository. These tools can take repository data as input and output data to the repository. Basically, the development tools use the repository for sharing data. However, the repository approach has additional advantages. Tools can be simpler if they don't require an internal repository. The repository can support an ad hoc reporting capability, metadata to support metrics, and version control. A repository can also support sharing of architecture data across an enterprise and the reuse of architecture data and artifacts in related architectures. This sharing of architecture data across the enterprise is the reason that DoD is so interested in a repository approach and why it is a leader in the effort to establish repository standards. The repository approach has been advocated for a long time, but it has proven difficult to implement. Repository tools are commercially available, but they typically require customization, so they are expensive for small organizations and projects. In addition, there has been limited success both in getting tools to support the repository interface standards and in developing effective standards. Figure 2.3-4 shows the different approaches to tool

FIGURE 2.3-4

Two Different
Approaches to
Tool Integration

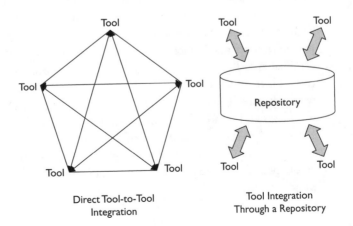

Direct Tool-to-Tool
Integration

Tool Integration
Through a Repository

integration and how the repository approach makes the number of interfaces much smaller.

Not only do the architecture development tools need to be integrated, but they also need to be integrated with analysis tools, management tools, and document and presentation tools. That is, the architecture development tools need to be able to provide input to analysis tools and, potentially, to management tracking tools and CM tools. In addition, the architecture development tools (or repository) have to be able to provide text and graphics to document and presentation tools. Failure to provide usable input for documents and presentation tools is a critical problem because documents and presentations are two of the ways of making architecture data accessible to stakeholders. Sometimes problems with graphics can be subtle. Some tools provide exportable graphics, but although these graphics are suitable for wall charts for the architects' use, the graphics are not readable when inserted into documents and presentations. Extracting readable subsets of the larger graphics can be difficult and time consuming. Usually, the interfaces from architecture development tools to other tools are one-way, so integration is easier than it is between architecture development tools.

Sometimes, architecture development tools in a development organization will have to be integrated with tools from other organizations. For example, architecture development tools may have to be integrated with requirements tools when solution-level architectures are being developed. In other cases, the architecture development tools from organizations building segment- or solution-level architectures may need to be integrated with repositories owned by organizations responsible for the enterprise-level architecture. In DoD, segment- and solution-level architectures need to be able to post architecture data to DoD enterprise-level repositories such as the DoD Architecture Registry System (DARS). The nature of these interfaces is dependent on enterprise processes and requirements.

No matter what the nature of the tool integration challenges that a development organization is faced with, the best way to test this integration, especially if the integration approach depends on COTS product support for integration, is to establish a test configuration in a laboratory environment prior to attempting to use the tools in an actual development project. This is a lesson learned from problems with software development environments. Often, COTS product support for various interfaces and standards has unforeseen limitations that severely impact the ability of the tool to integrate as expected. In general, best practice is to test the integration capabilities of the tool with the rest of the architecture development environment before purchasing the product, if at all possible. Tools that won't integrate are of very limited value.

Care must be taken to control the costs of integrating tools. Although tools can be made to integrate by using custom code or by maintaining customized repositories, the continuing costs of such an approach are frequently more than an organization or enterprise is prepared to pay. While such a customized environment may be ideal in terms of architecture development and maintenance ease, usually less expensive approaches need to be investigated. These alternative approaches may require changes in the architecture development methodology or process.

Relationship of EA to the System Development Lifecycle

The focus of EA is on coordinating the enterprise's entire set of system development/ maintenance projects. The goal of enterprise engineering is to keep the system projects coordinated and aligned with global business needs and strategic goals. In this sense, the enterprise- and segment-level architectures allocate business needs or capabilities to projects, where the outputs of several projects may be needed to support a particular capability, business-provided service, or product line. The architecture is used to ensure that all the enterprise's systems integrate and interoperate in the expected way. To this end, the architecture provides a way of ensuring that the way in which the systems produced by disparate projects are expected to fit together and the way in which these systems support the business or mission are both well understood. The architecture provides a mechanism for global identification and management of critical interfaces both of business processes and systems. The enterprise- and segment-level architectures also help ensure the correct sequencing of projects and the delivery of their systems. These architectures provide visibility into the dependencies among the various projects and their systems.

Solution-level architectures provide the most direct guidance to system development projects. Because solution-level architectures should be aligned and consistent with their higher-level segment and enterprise architectures, this means that solution-level architectures should reflect the relevant guidance from these higher-level architectures. Most organizations enforce their architectures by adding an architecture-compliance stage to each of the standard SDLC reviews (such as the system requirements, preliminary design, and critical design reviews). Usually, the project is checked for compliance with the segment- or solution-level architecture during its approval process with the enterprise IRB or an equivalent board. At each standard SDLC review, the system requirements, design, or implementation is rechecked for compliance with its solution-level architecture. This rechecking is critical, because either the architecture guidance may have changed (for example, changes may have been made in the enterprise standards set) or the system design or implementation may have strayed, due to local (rather than global) needs, from the enterprise standards or from the segment-level cross-system interface specifications.

When compliance issues are discovered, a negotiation process is needed to decide whether the project must make changes to return to compliance, the architecture will change to accommodate the project approach, or the project will proceed under a waiver from architecture compliance. The nature of this decision-making process is part of EA governance and varies based on enterprise processes and culture.

Data Strategies

Because data is so important in architectures, architecture programs need to develop a set of data-related strategies to complement and support the view/model development process. These data-related strategies include data management, data validation, and data dissemination.

Data Management Strategy

The data management strategy needs to encompass all the various project data stores that contain architecture data. These data stores may include development tool-specific data stores, a development tool–independent architecture repository (of the kind discussed previously in this chapter), and other external data stores that supply or receive architecture data from the project. The data management strategy must address the methods, processes, and procedures that will be used to coordinate the data (or at least the portion related to the architecture project) in all these data stores. It needs to address data integrity and consistency issues so that if data appears in more than one data store or multiple times within a single data store, the data is the same. If multiple data stores are used and their data contents overlap, data synchronization issues need to be addressed as well. When and how will the common data in multiple data stores be synchronized and, if the data stores are geographically dispersed, how will synchronization be handled in the face of interrupted communications or unreliable communications? The data management strategy strives to ensure that the various data stores function as a virtual architecture repository even if a physical one does not exist.

The project data strategy also has to address CM issues. Once architecture data and views are reviewed, accepted, and placed under CM, how will the CM of the collection of integrated architecture data be handled? Development tools often provide version management (that is, management of data associated with specific versions of views or models), but full CM requires not only version management but also change management and configuration status accounting. If multiple development tools are used, how will versioning be coordinated across all the tools? If a CM tool is used in addition to development tools, how will the potentially different approaches to versioning be integrated and managed? CM issues need to be resolved in a way that is consistent with the EA governance and corporate culture. For example, change management issues are decided by a Configuration Control Board (CCB) or an equivalent body, but the membership of the CCB or the identity of the change authority varies by organization, as do the CM procedures. The data strategy has to ensure that the architecture data is managed in a way consistent with the enterprise CM policies and procedures.

The data management strategy must also address security and access control issues. Who is authorized to access or update what types of architecture data and under what conditions? Availability is an additional security issue, especially if the various members of the architecture project or the architecture users are geographically scattered.

Finally, if the development team is geographically dispersed, the data management strategy must deal with the issues of distributed data creation and management. This affects all of the previously discussed areas.

Data Validation Strategy

The architecture views and models assist in ensuring that the architecture is consistent, but is the data correct? That is, the data can be consistent but incorrect. SMEs are the ultimate source of information on the correctness of the architecture data. However, for SMEs to review and validate the architecture data, the data has to be provided to the SMEs in a form they can understand. In some cases, the SMEs can understand the standard architecture views, especially if a skilled facilitator helps to walk them through it. In other cases, fit-for-purpose views must be developed to present the data to SMEs for validation.

The project should have a data validation plan that complements the architecture development process. This validation plan should include validation criteria. The validation approach needs to be in place early so that its requirements for fit-for-purpose views can be included in the architecture planning cycle.

Data Dissemination Strategy

The whole point of EA is to support decision-making processes, so dissemination of architecture views and data to decision makers is critical to success. The architecture program needs a plan to allow stakeholders (that is, the architecture users) access to the architecture data. In many cases, the architecture data is disseminated to stakeholders in traditional ways—through hard copy (or soft copy) versions of reports, analyses, or fit-for-purpose views. In some cases, the reports focus on the architecture itself. In other cases, the reports reflect architecture findings or the results of analyses to which the architecture data contributed. In some cases, these reports are standard products of the architecture development and maintenance process. In others, they may be special-purpose reports created to meet a one-time stakeholder need.

Popular approaches for architecture data dissemination that use today's technologies include web portals and collaborative spaces to support decision makers. However, care must be taken to ensure that the stakeholders see the data in a form they can understand. Many architecture development tools have the capability to produce views in PDF format so they can be viewed from the Web. Other tools provide reader applications so that potential users can view the tool output and navigate the architecture without needing a license for the development tool. Access to the detailed architecture data may be appropriate for architecture-savvy users, but most stakeholders will not be able to navigate an architecture by themselves. Decision makers are most frequently interested in the bottom line and not the details, so the role of the dissemination strategy is to see that each type of stakeholder gets access to the architecture data he or she needs and understands.

Risk Management

A frequently avoided but important part of project management, risk management is the act or practice of planning for the potential of future adverse impacts on the project. In the architectural community, architectural risk management is the process that normally occurs concurrently with architecture development. Through analysis, this process identifies flaws in the architecture that may have significant impact on the execution of the improved process, system, or service.

There are specific steps associated with risk management programs that are discussed briefly in this section and in more depth in the on-line *DoDAF Journal* (www.cio-nil.defense.gov/sites/dodaf20/journal_exp3.html). These include the following:

- Risk management planning
- Risk identification
- Risk assessment

- Risk quantification
- Risk response planning
- Risk monitoring and control

As risk management is discussed in this section, keep in mind that it is seldom possible, except in the most extraordinary situations, to eliminate risk completely. In fact, it is more usually the case that elimination of all risk is too costly and burdensome for most projects.

Instead, a good risk management program identifies ways to reduce some risks, manage others, and establish responsibilities for ensuring that identified risk does not get out of control. Thus, addressing risk generally involves one of three approaches: acceptance, mitigation, or transfer.

1. *Risk acceptance* means that the risk is understood, and the process owner/developer is willing to proceed with the original plan despite the risk. In this case, risk is continually assessed to ensure that the level or intensity of risk does not change in a way that would materially affect the desired process change or development.

2. *Risk mitigation* involves developing ways to reduce risk by making change in the target process and/or development plans. Once the risk is clearly understood through analysis, then specific steps are undertaken to reduce or eliminate the risk. That may involve changes in the architecture, the transition plans that define the steps necessary to execute change, or a plan to monitor change continually as it occurs to ensure that execution follows exactly the desired solution description. Like acceptance, risk mitigation requires firm, consistent oversight and continual review.

3. *Risk transfer* is the identification of specific risks through analysis and the assignment of those risks to others outside the process. Risk transfer often is identified in architecture development as a break or gap—a lack of useful data, or validated data that comes from an external source. The solution to the problem is to identify the risk to the external source and ensure that any data used follows the established conventions of the architecture and the process change. In this case, risk is periodically assessed from the perspective of data review.

Risk Management Planning

A risk management plan is critical to the success of any EA effort. The plan defines the project, stakeholders, expected or desired results, the objectives of the project, the organizational structure of the team and supporting elements, and roles and responsibilities of all participants, including those of the executive sponsor or process owner. The plan, when complete, also discusses the level of risk acceptance that can be accommodated during the effort, steps to be taken to mitigate risk, and potential transfer actions that will reduce risk.

Risk Identification

Identification of potential risks early in the project can prevent later failure. Risks include those resulting from the execution of actions described in the architecture, potential effects to others resulting from the proposed change, or even internal risks, such as the ability of the team to influence change or identification of key personnel whose support is required for change. Risk identification must include information of potential managers of risk internally, as well as possible people and organizations that can assume elements of risk identified during planning.

Risk Assessment

This step evaluates identified risks in terms of the probability that risk will exist in the project and the impact that a risk poses to the success of the program or project. Many project risk assessments utilize a simple x-y axis matrix to determine the extent and importance of risk.

Defining both probability and impact in levels ranging from low to high provides a means to determine what action may be required. A combination of probability and impact (which together define severity) determines whether the risk can be ignored or requires close monitoring, either within the project or by an outside group that accepts the risk.

Risk Quantification

Risk quantification takes the initial assessment matrices and analyzes potential effects. In architecture planning, one of the most common concerns is the "domino effect" (that is, the effect that actions taken have on other activities) and how to reduce the turbulence and undesired consequences that may result from change in one area that provides data or actions to another.

Risk Response Planning

This step takes the results of assessment and quantification and determines what actions to take in resolving or mitigating risk. Actions may vary from simple periodic monitoring on a specific timetable to transfer of the risk to another organization where the risk might be more tolerable.

Risk Monitoring and Control

Although it is possible to eliminate risk, that objective is generally cost- or time-prohibitive, and the more acceptable stance is acceptance with monitoring until the severity either becomes acceptable (considered to be within project control) or unacceptable (severity is such that the project must terminate or make major changes to accommodate the risk).

Questions

1. How does your organization address the tool integration problem? How many architecture development tools do you use on a single project and how are they integrated?
2. How many other tools (management, document production, and analysis) do your architecture development tools need to integrate with on architecture projects? How is this integration achieved?
3. This chapter identified three particular EA lifecycle challenges: problem-oriented, incremental architecture development; federated architectures and Reference Models; and integration with other enterprise lifecycles and processes (including Strategic Planning, Capital Planning and Investment Control, and SDLC). How does your EA lifecycle address these three challenges?
4. How does your EA lifecycle map or compare to the OMB EA lifecycle?
5. See whether you can find some SOWs for EA development projects. Compare the content of each SOW to the suggested SOW outline in this chapter. How are they similar and how are they different?
6. How does your organization deal with risk management? Do you have a methodology for risk assessment for EA projects?

7. What is your organization's approach to data dissemination for EAs? What group of stakeholders (that is, architecture users) is the most difficult to communicate with?

8. What is your organization's approach to EA data validation? How are the personnel who perform EA data validation integrated with the rest of the EA project team?

9. Does your organization have a standardized WBS for EA projects? If so, how do the tasks align with your EA lifecycle?

Reference List

Department of Defense. (2009). *Department of Defense Architecture Framework Version 2.0.* www.cio-nil.defense.gov/sites/dodaf20.

Federal Chief Information Officer Council. (2001). *A Practical Guide to Federal Enterprise Architecture Version 1.0.* www.enterprise-architecture.infor/images/Documents/Federal%20Enterprise%20Architecture%20Guide%20v1a.pdf.

Office of Management and Budget. (2009). *Improving agency performance using information and information technology (Enterprise Architecture Assessment Framework Version 3.1).* www.whitehouse.gov/omb/e-gov/eaaf.

2.4

Disseminating the Enterprise Architecture

D uring the planning phase of the enterprise architecture program, one of the key steps is the development of an EA marketing strategy and communications plan. The purpose of the marketing strategy and communications plan early in the EA development process is to accomplish the following:

- Keep senior executives and business units continually informed
- Disseminate EA information to management teams to secure continued support with subject matter experts and analysts and to act as the target audience

The CIO's staff, in cooperation with the Chief Architect and support staff, defines a marketing and communications plan consisting of (a) constituencies, (b) level of detail, (c) means of communication, (d) participant feedback, (e) schedule for marketing efforts, and (f) method of evaluating progress and buy-in.

One of the recommended means for marketing the EA is a primer to inform business executives and stakeholders of the EA strategy and plan. The primer can be used to express the vision of the enterprise's senior management and the role of EA in realizing that vision.

An EA marketing and communications plan may break the dissemination strategy into multiple phases. Each of these phases needs different types of dissemination. Table 2.4-1 shows one potential sample.

TABLE 2.4-1   Sample EA Marketing and Communications Plan

Phase	Purpose	Potential Dissemination Tools
Pre-Inception	Raising general awareness among decision makers on the benefits of EA in general and to the enterprise in particular	Bring in EA evangelists and luminaries to raise awareness and excite top management
Inception	Brief sponsors on the EA program plan, architecture development phases, expected deliverables, and required support	Presentation slides Project plan Deliverable mockups Resourcing plan
In-Process	Disseminate models to elicit feedback from SMEs Presentations of the in-process EA models and analysis at Program Management Reviews (PMRs) Pre-briefings to validate the direction of the EA program	Presentation slides EA project website EA project wiki Tool-generated websites

TABLE 2.4-1	Sample EA Marketing and Communications Plan *(Continued)*	
Phase	**Purpose**	**Potential Dissemination Tools**
Validation and Finalization	Pre-brief sponsors on the EA models, analysis, findings, and recommendations to determine any needed course changes and wording of critical findings and recommendations	EA program problem statement and summary EA analysis reports EA deliverable models Navigable websites of the EA Presentation slides EA project website EA project social network EA project wikis EA reports EA documentation Help documentation Training materials
Post-Release	Provide ongoing support for all stakeholders in using, navigating, downloading, and exploiting the EA for business use and as a communications tool for orientation and support for planning and decision-making efforts	EA deliverable models Navigable websites of the EA Presentation slides EA project website EA project social network EA project wikis EA reports EA documentation Help documentation Training materials

Identifying the Audience for Architecture Dissemination

During the planning phase of the architecture, stakeholders are identified who play various roles in the sponsorship, initiation, development, management, and use of the architecture. The sample dissemination plan presented in Table 2.4-1 describes some of the dissemination activities that are undertaken at each phase.

In general, stakeholders fall into the following categories.

Architecture Sponsors

These are senior management people who have understood the need for architecture, underwritten the cost of development, and are interested in solving the set of problems that drove that initial need. Unfortunately, in many enterprises, the unspoken need to undertake the development of enterprise architecture is to comply with regulatory mandates or the demands of a higher power—an oversight office such as the Office of Management and Budget in the U.S. federal government. Sponsors generally include the Chief Information Officer, executive management, and executive teams charged with effecting enterprise transformation.

Architecture Team Members

Members of the architecture team, as facilitators of transformation, are the "evangelists," or proponents, of the architecture they have built. Dissemination of the enterprise architecture in the development stages also allows team members to share information using collaborative techniques. The architecture team comprises of the Chief Architect, modelers, and business analysts. The extended architecture team includes the subject matter experts who provided the data for the architecture development.

Architecture Stakeholders

Other stakeholders are business, systems, IT infrastructure, and operations staff who are affected by the analysis, findings, and recommendations generated by the architecture effort. Sometimes members of this audience may be hostile to the EA effort because of threats to current ways of doing business.

Executive Management

The enterprise architecture represents the anatomy and physiology of an enterprise. Executive management has a stake in understanding the implications that analysts arrive at, by analyzing the EA. They are responsible for being at the helm of transformations and are therefore a very interested audience—especially when the enterprise is looking at transformation as a survival technique.

Business Partners, Suppliers, Customers, and Agents

The enterprise architecture exposes the operational, systems, services, and data "plumbing" of the enterprise. This is of interest to business partners who need to interface with the enterprise at each of these plumbing levels. Operational interface involves handshakes between business processes. Interfaces between systems and services involve orchestration of services among enterprises as well as contracts that durably preserve the interface structure. Data interfaces among partner enterprises have to rely on semantic data standards, as well as messaging and format standards. The architecture is an explicit representation of these factors and is therefore very useful for planning interfaces at all levels.

Reusers

Dissemination of architecture models in a manner that can be used by receivers for facilitating their own tasks is essential to the adoption of the EA as a valuable enterprise asset. For example, planners of a new initiative may want to describe the context of their planned initiative in terms of locations served, organizations involved, key business processes to be automated, key capabilities to be acquired, and key systems to interface with for data supply. All of this information may be available inside the architecture. By downloading and tailoring the data that comes from the EA, the team planning the initiative can produce an early concept of operations that has taken a small effort but is rooted in enterprise reality.

Communities of Interest/Communities of Practice

In recent years, with awakening interest in collaborative workspaces, wikis, and social networking, the importance of forming communities of interest and communities of practice—people with shared motivation, working collaboratively on interleaved tasks with similar interests and skills—is becoming increasingly important. On the architecture construction side, COIs and COPs can present natural viewpoints and views to be modeled by the architecture. Communities of interest (COIs) and communities of practice (COPs) are also natural targets for architecture dissemination. By also employing facilitated wikis and managed social networking interfaces, architecture content can be dramatically improved by members of the COI or COP who are familiar with the subject matter and can provide corrections and improvements readily.

Fit-for-Purpose Displays

It is important to remember that architecture stakeholders may not necessarily want to see information in the way that the architect modeled the architecture data. Dissemination often involves building composite models that may be different from the original supplying models. If there is one thing this book has stressed, it is the importance of building integrated architectures where all the models consistently share the same common architecture elements. Building an integrated architecture unifies the data consistently and allows the building of new composite models from the same data without compromising accuracy and faithfulness of semantics and structure to the originally modeled elements. These displays, built to suit the viewpoint of the audience rather than to conform to some modeling methodology that the audience does not understand, are called fit-for-purpose displays.

Preparing for Dissemination

The task of disseminating an architecture must be approached in the same way, a development organization approaches the release of a software development, for instance. Architectures must be configuration managed and versioned. Configuration management involves the following:

1. A *controlled baseline* must be maintained for the released version and read-only access must be provided to all users to prevent corruption of the EA. A formal configuration management must be maintained that identifies a specific release of the EA that will be disseminated. A controlled baseline is a formally identified release of enterprise architecture with a date and an identifier.

2. A formal process must be maintained for *validation of the enterprise architecture information* before considering dissemination. The accuracy and validity of the disseminated enterprise architecture information are essential for continued credibility and trust in the reliability of the enterprise architecture information. If the latency of validation is a hindrance to the use of EA information, markings must be made that indicate the reliability status of the information as well as when a validated product will be available.

3. The *formal approval process* must have a designated signoff for release of EA information that is comprised of business and IT management at the level of the Chief Information Officer and the Chief Architect. Upon verification and validation of the architecture, the enterprise's management chain of command, as defined by the governance structures explicitly at the inception of the effort, should approve the overall architecture. These may be the Chief Information Officer, the Enterprise Architecture Executive Steering Committee, the Chief Architect, or other designated approvers.

4. A *formal release process* must be maintained for items that must be disseminated. The EA documents extensive information about the enterprise. Careful consideration must be given to the distribution of that information. Although it is possible that an EA may not have any confidential information, the aggregation of the information may comprise a security risk. In the wrong hands, the compilation of enterprise information in the EA could render the enterprise vulnerable by providing sufficient information for infiltration and disruption. Some of the information (or an aggregation of that information) may need to be controlled and accessed on a "need-to-know" basis (examples of such information include network models, critical performance factors, and system interfaces).

5. *Means for incorporation* of EA information into people's everyday duties must be provided to the following personnel:

   a. Executive and managerial staff should be able to incorporate EA information into communications, briefings, and directives.

   b. Application architects should be able to use the disseminated architecture information developed by the EA team to analyze the models that were provided by the team against their own knowledge of business processes, systems, technology standards, etc. and identifying opportunities for improvements.

   c. Enterprise architects should be able to use the information to apply what-if analysis against the baseline.

6. *Plan for and maintain information security procedures.* The architecture core team must consider what classes of EA users will need what information: contractors, management, and enterprise staff typically focus on particular areas of the enterprise and thus may need only particular subsets of the EA. An EA that includes a comprehensive view of the details of the enterprise's systems and infrastructure could be organized in levels of detail and distributed in a tiered format corresponding to security clearances and the need to know.

Communicating the Contents of an Enterprise Architecture

An architecture description is an integrated collection of blueprints stored as electronic documents or as information in an architecture repository. This information may be disseminated to three different types of targets:

■ Enterprise architecture data and models are disseminated to another receiving enterprise repository or registry.

■ The enterprise architecture is disseminated between automated computer systems applications. Examples of target automated computer systems applications are architecture modeling tools.

■ Enterprise architecture data and models are disseminated to such people as stakeholders, sponsors of architecture efforts, users of architecture information, and enterprise architects starting a modeling assignment, for example.

We make distinctions among these three types of dissemination because each has different needs for semantic and structural data standards for the exchange that must be met in order for exchange to succeed.

Dissemination to Another Receiving Enterprise Repository or Registry

This form of dissemination requires agreed-upon protocols for information semantics as well as information formats. Consider a few examples:

■ The Federal Enterprise Architecture (FEA) Reference Models (RMs) are disseminated by the Office of Management and Budget (OMB) through the use of eXtensible Markup Language (XML). The tags for the FEA Reference Models are standardized and the semantics are published so that an organization receiving the information can decode the contents. The use of FEA dissemination is to enable agencies to comply with the federal mandate for mapping their agency enterprise architectures as well as their planned investments and initiatives to the FEA Reference Models.

■ The DoD Architecture Framework recommends that enterprises implementing their architectures register the Architecture Overview and

Summary (AV-1) model with the Defense Architecture Registry System (DARS). The DARS specifies an XML format for submissions of architecture summaries. These are kept in DARS and made available as a ready resource for interested stakeholders and modelers.

■ The DoD Architecture Framework uses two types of vocabularies through the DoDAF Metamodel (DM2) to standardize the meaning of architecture terms so that a receiver of architecture information can decode the information sent by a disseminating organization. The DM2 uses IDEAS as a foundation vocabulary to establish a set of base semantic building blocks in much the same way that the 26 letters of the English language serve as base building blocks to construct meaningful words. The IDEAS foundation vocabulary is then used to describe the DM2 architecture vocabulary. DM2 describes abstract common architectural concepts such as Performer, Activity, Project, Information, and so on as well as more concrete concepts such as Organization, Organization Type, Person Role, and System as types of performers, for instance.

Dissemination Between Automated Computer Systems Applications

This form of dissemination requires agreed-upon protocols for information semantics as well as information formats. In addition, such dissemination also requires automated services at either end: one to push information out and the other to pull the information in. Examples of dissemination between automated computer systems applications include the following:

■ The most common form of dissemination between automated computer systems is the dissemination of architectures from one modeling tool or repository to another. These are supported either by bilateral agreements between pairs of senders and receivers or by a common standard that is used by all tools.

■ The DoD Architecture Framework contains a Physical Exchange Specification (PES) that is used to specify the format for exchanges of architectural information between architecture development tools.

■ An example of an older format for exchange of information between automated tools is Common Data Interchange Format (CDIF). Another one for exchange of IDEF0 activity models is the IDEF0 Description Language (IDL).

Dissemination to People

Architecture information is disseminated to such people as stakeholders and sponsors of architecture efforts, users of architecture information, and enterprise architects starting a modeling assignment, for example. This kind of dissemination is more complex as it involves cultural, semantic, and clarity issues among others. The following are examples of some of the issues:

- How is the information presented? Will the target audience find it easily comprehensible based on past experience, knowledge, and familiarity?
- How dense is the information representation? Is the display making good use of white space?
- How actionable is the information disseminated? We define actionable information as that information that can be readily used to build value-added presentations and perform analysis without requiring retyping or manipulation of the disseminated data.
- What kinds of information patterns provide the most leverage? Some layouts tend to be a natural fit for representing types of data. For example, comparisons of numeric data can use commonly understood pie and bar chart graphics. Likewise, taxonomical representations lend themselves to the upside-down tree diagramming pattern.

The following sections clarify some of these issues and point out techniques that can be used to address them.

Architecture Presentation Techniques

Information is the lifeblood of enterprise architecture, but it can be overwhelming to decision makers when presented in a raw format. Likewise, the structured methodology of modeling enterprise architecture information is both necessary and useful for creating architectural descriptions that can be shared between organizations. However, many of the "traditional" architecture products are unwieldy because of their format and are useful only to trained architects. Many organizations develop a mandated architecture but make it expensive shelf-ware instead of using it to communicate important, accurate, and relevant information to the stakeholders who need it. Architects must be able to communicate architectural information in a meaningful way to process owners and other stakeholders; otherwise, the discipline of enterprise architecture will soon meet an untimely demise.

The results of architectural-related data collection need to be presentable to nontechnical senior executives and managers at all levels. Many managers are skilled decision makers, but have not had technical training in architectural description development. Because architectural description development efforts are designed to provide input to the decision-making process, graphical representation of data needed is a logical extension of the overall process.

Effective presentation of business information is necessary for architects to tell the story of the architectural data with stakeholders. Because the purpose of the architecture discipline is to collect and store all relevant information about an enterprise, or some specific part of the enterprise, it can reasonably be assumed that the majority of information needed by an organization's decision makers is contained somewhere in the architectural data. Many of the existing architecture methods are valuable for organizing architectural information, but less valuable for communicating that information to stakeholders. Presentation views are always dependent on the quality of the architectural information that is collected through the rigor of architecture methods. As Figure 2.4-1 illustrates, presentation techniques draw from the architectural information store and display the data to stakeholders in a variety of meaningful ways.

FIGURE 2.4-1

Architecture Data Collection Versus Presentation

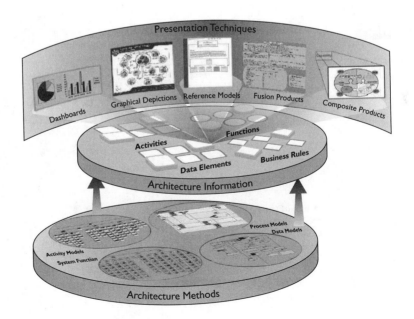

The presentation techniques and best practices described here, and documented more fully in the DoDAF (Department of Defense, 2009), were developed based on the idea that business information, captured both internally and externally to an organization's architecture in support of common user requirements, can be displayed in a way that enhances clarity and understanding and facilitates decision making. That often means complex technical information has to be "translated" into a form for presentation that is useful to management. An "Information Bridge," as shown in Figure 2.4-2, is the link between the architect and management. The bridge provides the means to recast technical information in graphical or textual terms consistent with the culture of the organization.

The DoDAF defines a set of models for visualizing, understanding, and assimilating the broad scope and complexities of an architectural description through graphic, tabular, or textual means (Department of Defense, 2009).

Choosing an Appropriate Presentation Technique

In any given business process, decisions must be made at multiple levels of the organization. Whether one is a senior-level executive, a process owner, or a system developer, he or she will need to make judgment calls based on the available data. Each level of decision making, in turn, has both a unique purpose and understanding

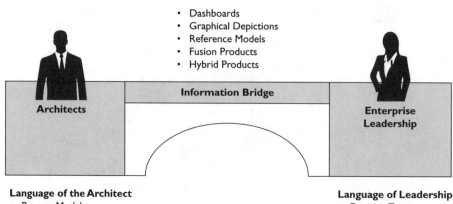

FIGURE 2.4-2

Dissemination as an "Information Bridge"

- Dashboards
- Graphical Depictions
- Reference Models
- Fusion Products
- Hybrid Products

Information Bridge

Architects

Enterprise Leadership

Language of the Architect
- Process Models
- Data Models
- Object Class Models
- Capability Models
- Project Models
- Portfolio Models
- Systems Models

Language of Leadership
- Decision Trees
- Spreadsheets
- Pie Charts
- Relationship Charts
- Mind Maps
- Management Briefings

FIGURE 2.4-3

Zachman
Framework
Perspectives of an
Enterprise

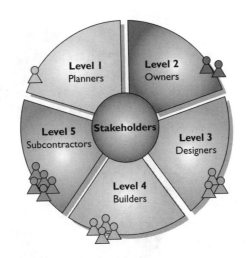

of architectural description, making it important to tailor the data to maximize its effectiveness. The presenter, with the help of an experienced architect, must determine the audience of a presentation before choosing the type of presentation technique to use. Figure 2.4-3, based on the rows of the Zachman Framework, summarizes the multiple levels of decision makers within a typical organization who make up an audience.

Each level has differing requirements for presentation of data. Level 1 planners may find a graphical wall chart more useful in making decisions, whereas a Level 4 builder will most likely require a more technical presentation, one relating more directly to the architectural description. Level 5 subcontractors are the workers who will perform the work required, and generally require varying levels of technical data and other information to accomplish their task.

Narrowing down the type of presentation required is done by asking the following question: What information does the decision maker need to make a data-supported decision? For each decision level, there is a data set that can be manipulated using a presentation technique. After analyzing the audience and type of information, the presenter should consider the various types of techniques discussed in this section.

Figure 2.4-4 is a simplified representation of the presentation development process.

It is imperative to realize that when choosing how to present data sets, there is no limit on what views to use. There are countless ways to display information to decision makers, and it is up to the presentation developer to determine the most effective way to accomplish this task.

This section describes a base of view development techniques to start from, each created to serve its own unique purpose. Details are provided on five different presentation techniques that have proven to be useful in engaging various audiences.

Presentation/
Dissemination
Development
Cycle

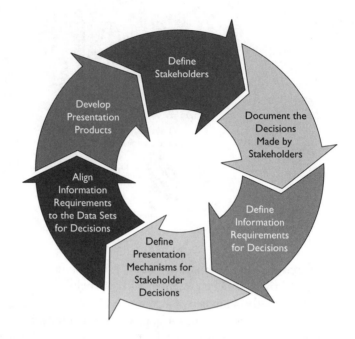

Fit-for-Purpose View Display Formats

We discussed earlier the need for fit-for-purpose views of the architecture that may not necessarily coincide with the original architecture models built by the architect, but may be composites of information from more than one mode that fits more closely with an audience's need for a communication mechanism that makes sense to them.

Fit-for-purpose views can be created utilizing the architecture data from an integrated architecture to provide forms of graphical presentation other than those used to build architecture models such as the Activity Model, Logical and Physical Data Models, and Business Process Models. Fit-for-purpose views use presentation techniques that are more common to briefings and decision analysis. The following are the five techniques commonly used:

- **Composite Views**   Display multiple pieces of architectural data in formats that are relevant to a specific decision maker
- **Dashboards**   Integrate abstracted architectural information for a given business context
- **Fusion Views**   Display multiple pieces of architectural data and incorporate disparate pieces of information that are not captured within the architectural description

- **Graphics**   Visually represent manipulated data.
- **Reference Models**   Capture the elements of the architectural data and translate those elements into text

Fit-for-purpose views provide wide flexibility for the architect and process owner to create architectural views easily understood and useful to management for decision-making purposes.

Standardized View Display Formats

Part III of this book discusses a collection of standardized models that are recognized and understood by a large community of architects. These models have been used for more than a decade and stand upon tried, well-proven, and heavily adopted modeling methodologies such as Structured Analysis and Design, Integrated Definition (IDEF) Language, Unified Modeling Language, System Modeling Language, and Business Process Modeling Notation (BPMN). The representation of models for each of these methodologies is generally standardized by the methodology. For example, IDEF0 uses the activity node tree, context diagram, and decomposition diagrams to represent activity models in a standard graphical way.

Standard model layouts generally fall into the following categories described in Table 2.4-2.

TABLE 2.4-2 Standard Model Layouts	Category	Description
	Tabular	Models that present data arranged in rows and columns, which includes structured text as a special case. Corresponds to the TOGAF 9 Matrix artifacts.
	Structural	Diagrams describing the structural aspects of architecture. Corresponds to the TOGAF 9 Diagram artifacts.
	Behavioral	Diagrams describing the behavioral aspects of architecture. Corresponds to the TOGAF 9 Diagram artifacts.
	Mapping	Matrix (or similar) mappings between two different types of information. Corresponds to the TOGAF 9 Matrix artifacts.
	Ontology	Models that extend the underlying modeling (metamodel) ontology for a particular architecture.
	Pictorial	Free-form pictures. No constraints are generally applicable to the symbols, the layout of the symbols, or graphics connecting the symbols.
	Timeline	Diagrams describing the schedule and programmatic aspects of an architecture.

Part III in this book and DoDAF (Department of Defense, 2009) describe in more detail these standardized models for representing various views of the architecture to various audiences.

Delivery of Dissemination

In this section, we talk about the various ways in which architecture information can be disseminated.

Web Delivery

By far the most convenient and popular delivery of repository content is through the World Wide Web with a web server at one end and a simple web browser application at the other. This method of publishing a website is supported by many architecture tools in the marketplace. They generate a collection of hypertext markup language (HTML) files that are linked through cross-file references. A home or index page is provided, generally with a navigation structure that has links to the various models that comprise the integrated architecture. Navigation can be accomplished from elements of one model (or view) to elements of other views. The web output is also combined with interpretive text that describes architecture elements.

The generation of HTML web pages with embedded graphics and text representing the models that are disseminated results in snapshots of the architecture. If the contents of the architecture repository were to be updated, they are not automatically reflected in the website until a new website is generated and published. For architectures that are released relatively infrequently, this is still a good solution.

More sophisticated web delivery systems use scripts to generate the web pages automatically on the fly from active repository content. Any changes to repository data are instantly reflected in the web pages. These systems tend to be repository-side applications rather than features of the architecting tool because the scripts need knowledge of the repository schema.

Architecture Website/Web Portal

The static web generation of architecture models for an integrated architecture, as we discussed earlier, is easily accomplished by commercial architecture tools. But often, more than just the models are required to be disseminated. In an architecture community of practice, other items such as Reference Models, policy and guidance, templates, and other information need to be disseminated. An architecture website or an architecture portal is often built to service a community of architecture team members as a minimum and for an extended community of stakeholders when architecture efforts begin to mature and a large number of models and related information have been generated and need to be disseminated.

Architecture websites must follow all the rules of good website design:

- Clear "floor plan"
- Consistent layout of topics and navigation paths
- Appropriate use of fonts, color, and emphasis
- Design unity with complementary websites
- Consistent look and feel
- Comprehensive search capabilities
- Facilities for zooming and panning large graphical images
- Appropriate density of information

Architecture websites and portals can also be built with capabilities for wikis and social networking and provide a collaboration workspace for some tasks such as the following:

- Refining vocabulary and terminology
- Refining taxonomies and classification schemes
- Critiquing and improving architecture models
- Suggesting improvements to the architecture program
- Validating models

Discovery Services

In contemporary computing, discovery services are an important part of net-centric operations. In net-centric operations, information and software services are dispersed over a network. A using or invoking application uses "discovery services" to find appropriate data and services that it can use to accomplish its purpose. Discovery services require that the owner of the information or service "advertise" these services in a transparent manner to the discovery services. The advertising of data and services is done in much the same way as libraries advertise their holdings using index cards. The index cards that "expose" information and services are formatted in a consistent manner per some predefined metadata standards. One such standard is the Defense Discovery Metadata Specification (DDMS).

Architecture repositories can expose their information and services to the world outside (or at least the entitled and authorized world outside) using metadata specifications. Consuming applications are responsible for searching, discovering, and retrieving the data from the repository or invoking the service that is provided by the repository.

Export/Import Files

Traditional forms of dissemination of architecture data have relied on import/export capabilities within architecture tools and architecture repositories. These capabilities produce electronic files of architecture data. The files can be formatted in many ways. We present a few examples:

- **Tab, comma-separated, or some form of delimited data file**   These are the most popular because the format is both general and transparent and allows ready use of the disseminated information.

- **eXtensible Markup Language (XML) files**   These are popular because the data is self-identifying. XML tags inside the file specify the nature of the data that is enclosed between tags. The format also allows for parsing as well as schema constraint enforcement, which is important when tools and repositories also allow imports using the same file format.

- **Standardized Architecture Data Exchange Specification**   This is a standard established by bodies such as Object Management Group (OMG) or Organization for the Advancement of Structured Information Standards (OASIS) or by large-volume buyers of tools and repositories with an interest in establishing data exchange standards such as the DoD or financial services firms.

- **Binary files**   These are proprietary format files that can be understood only by the applications they are meant for. They cannot be used in any other context.

- **Microsoft Office**   MS Office has become a de facto standard in many organizations for word processing, spreadsheet, and presentation software. Disseminating architecture data in these formats provides analysts with easy-to-understand, ready-to-use architecture data for their own value-added tasks. Disseminating images using PowerPoint enables audiences to build briefings quickly from readily available, previously constructed models.

- **Acrobat PDF**   Dissemination of architecture data that must not be altered is accomplished by generating Adobe Acrobat PDF files.

Repository Services

Repository web services are a way to provide dissemination for external applications or web users. Repository web services must be published and registered on a service broker such as a Universal Description, Discovery, and Integration (UDDI) Registry. Repository services can run unattended and provide 24/7 service.

Operating repository services imposes a supplier's burden on the architecture repository and the architecture team. This burden is expressed as a commitment to a service-level agreement (SLA) to make repository services available as advertised.

Offering repository services is generally undertaken after an architecture effort has reached a maturity stage that warrants continuous availability of dissemination as a web service. Chapter 2.6 introduces the concepts of governance and describes the stages of maturity for architecture management.

Questions

1. What are the steps you would take to market the adoption of EA in your enterprise? Who are the key decision makers? Influencers? Stakeholders? Potential SMEs?

2. What are some of the steps you would use to raise the awareness of EA in your organization?

3. What are the different methods for disseminating the architecture models and information about the architecture development project? Discuss the pros and cons of each method. What method is most applicable to your own organization and why?

4. Build a simple EA marketing and communications plan for your own enterprise. Assume that your enterprise is at the pre-inception stage in Table 2-4.1. What are the risks inherent to the plan? How do you plan to address, mitigate, or eliminate these risks?

5. Identify the stakeholders for enterprise architecture in your enterprise. Describe their roles briefly and their interest in the architecture. Describe the various architecture viewpoints that are useful for each type of stakeholder. Use any of the frameworks discussed in this book to define these viewpoints.

6. What is a fit-for-purpose display? Describe some examples of customized displays you could use from an IDEF0 activity model that shows the flow of resources among activities as well as a description of the performers of the activity. Hint: Think of Responsibility Assignment Matrix (RACI) from the acronym Responsible, Accountable, Consulted and Informed.

7. Starting with any subset of the DODAF models described in this book, what kinds of fit-for-purpose displays would be useful to your organization? How would you construct them from the standard models built during the course of the architecture project?

8. What are the issues in managing the configuration of released architectures? How will you address configuration management of your own architectures? What is your strategy for approaching change control? How will you control changes and keep track of the changes for historical purposes?

9. What are the ways in which you plan to communicate the models you have built using architecture tools? How will you ensure that the intended audience does not need the specialized architecture development tools that you have used to build the models?

10. Discuss the issues that arise when architecture work has to be exported from one repository to another. What are the issues related to methodology mismatch? To metamodel mismatch between the sending and receiving repository systems? What are issues related to nonstandard uses of architecture terminology? How do you plan to address your own enterprise's submissions of architecture data and pictures to another collaborating enterprise? To a reporting enterprise?

11. Discuss the applicability of the presentation/dissemination development cycle presented in this chapter to your own enterprise. How would you streamline and standardize this process for your enterprise?

12. Provide some examples of the types of fit-for-purpose views discussed in this chapter. Which type of view is useful for which type of audiences?

13. What are some examples of formats for standardized views? What is the usefulness of having standardized views? Discuss the correspondence between standardized views and standard types of models that are prescribed by methodologies such as UML, IDEF1X, or BPMN. What are the pros and cons of using standard models prescribed by methodologies versus defining models that are tailored for a specific audience?

14. What are the different methods of disseminating architecture data? How would you plan a distributed dissemination scheme for multiple departments in your enterprise when they do not have access to the same repository?

15. What are some of the pros and cons of providing architecture discovery services so that people interested in your architectures can search, discover, and help themselves? What are some of the security issues? Authorization issues? Entitlement issues? What types of policies would you recommend for such a service-based dissemination strategy?

Reference List

Department of Defense. (2009). *Department of Defense Architecture Framework Version 2.0, Volume 2*.

EATrain2 Consortium (with the support of the Lifelong Learning Program of the European Union). (2009). *EA training 2.0–D5.1 dissemination plan. Innovative enterprise architecture education and training based on Web 2.0 technologies*.

Federal CIO Council. (2003). *Practical guide to Federal Enterprise Architecture*.

2.5

Maintaining the Enterprise Architecture

T here is a common aphorism among project managers that "all projects are under budget and on schedule on the first day." Without maintenance, enterprise architecture descriptions (model representations) are valid exactly once, if even that: at the time they were built. Architecture models are snapshots of reality.

The EA is, by definition, a set of models that collectively describe the enterprise and its future. Its value to business operations is more than just IT investment decision management. The EA is the primary tool to reduce the response time for impact assessment, trade-off analysis, strategic plan redirection, and tactical reaction. Consequently, the EA must remain current and reflect the reality of the organization's enterprise. In turn, the EA needs regular upkeep and maintenance—a process as important as its original development.

Rate and Degree of Change of Architecture Elements

Determining the frequency with which different elements of the enterprise need to be examined for change and then reflecting the changes into the enterprise architecture is complex. The frequency of change depends on a number of factors.

Variation by Architecture Object Type

The rate of change of architecture elements within an enterprise architecture is not uniform for all the various types of architecture elements. Enterprise locations tend to be long-lived. So are the mission and vision of the enterprise. Objectives change over the years, as do strategies. Given a constant mission, the products and services of an enterprise may not change. They may reflect different characteristics and employ different technology for manufacture and delivery, but the utility as well as the target market for these may not change much.

Table 2.5-1 presents a few examples to illustrate why the frequency of change of architecture object types varies from one type to another.

TABLE 2.5-1	Frequency of Change for Architecture Object Types

Architecture Object	Frequency of Change
Mission	For federal agencies, mission is based on chartering legislation. Enterprises such as the Securities and Exchange Commission, Nuclear Regulatory Commission, Offices of the Inspector General, Office of the Chief Financial Officer, and Office of the Chief Information Officer in the federal government all trace their origins to founding legislation. Without drastic changes in legislation, the mission of these types of enterprise rarely changes. On the other hand, for established commercial enterprises such as IBM and AT&T with enduring markets and customers, the overall mission also rarely changes. Likewise, for conglomerates that are bound by a financial mission of returning a profit and meeting revenue objectives, the mission rarely changes.
Objectives	Objectives change from time to time but are relatively stable for the time frame that they have been set up for. Though sometimes commercial enterprises have been accused of changing their objectives to coincide with their actual performances!
Capability	The master capability list for an enterprise is generally a function of its mission, its business areas, and lines of business. To be able to support delivery of products durably, enterprises have to establish supply chain capabilities, manufacturing capabilities, testing and integration capabilities, sales and marketing capabilities, as well as delivery and fulfillment and customer support capabilities. If the area of business and the lines of business are fairly stable, the master capability list is also fairly stable. Subcapabilities that start moving closer to a systems or services implementation may vary as the canvas of options for solutions expands due to new technologies, new techniques, or new suppliers of outsourced services, for example.
Performers/ Operational/ Business Nodes	Organizations structures do tend to change periodically, but functional organizational structures rarely change if the enterprise is engaged in providing the same products and services. External performers may change as the enterprise deals with a changing external context. New players may be introduced as business strategy changes from insourcing to outsourcing, for example.
Locations/Facilities/System Nodes	Specific physical locations and facilities do change. Functional or notional locations, however, tend to remain stable. External locations may change as partners change the places where they do business.
Activities	Activities are steps within a business process. In a continuously improving business process regime, these should and will change. Activities when modeled as decompositions tend to change at lower levels or leaf levels because of specific changes in the way the upper-level activity is realized. Mechanisms change when new systems or automated techniques are applied to a previously manual activity (for example). Controls change when policy, directives, and constraints change.

Variation by Enterprise Nature

The nature of the enterprise also determines the rate of change of architecture elements. Smaller, growing enterprises that use disruptive innovation to change the world order need to use change as a strategic weapon. Such enterprises are constantly growing by acquisitions and mergers, metamorphizing in terms of market position, market offerings, and organizational structures. As a consequence, their enterprise architecture must and will change frequently. Enterprise architecture patterns are a powerful form of knowledge that allows upstarts to analyze, emulate, or disrupt their competitors. By understanding the pattern, they can devise counter-patterns or borrow the best practices that are manifested in the patterns. For example, if an enterprise such as Wal-Mart relies on its supply chain strength, especially for suppliers from China, a counter-pattern may be a strategy based on distributed suppliers of one-of-a-kind merchandise or a supply chain based on local manufacture.

Variations Introduced by Nonlinear Events

Huge shifts may occur in both business and government enterprises. For example, two very large airlines may merge, or the United States Air Force Air Mobility Command is formed in the early 1990s after the end of the Cold War by merging functions from Strategic Air Command, Tactical Airlift Command, and Military Airlift Command. Such tectonic shifts can render previous architecture work completely inaccurate but still useful in understanding and absorbing the new transformation into a new version of the EA that is more accurate.

A Change Response Model for Reference Models

At a larger granularity than the architecture element types, the *Federal Enterprise Architecture Reference Model Maintenance Process* (Federal Enterprise Architecture Program Management Office, 2005) describes the natural relative rate of change of each of the FEA Reference Models (see Figure 2.5-1).

In Figure 2.5-1, the message is that the Business Reference Model tends to be stable and long-lived (at least for federal agencies) as the charter of these enterprises is based on founding legislation and their highest-level organizational structure and duties are spelled out in federal law. The Data Reference Model (DRM) tends to be stable because the types of information are usually the same if the area of business and line of business remain the same. The Services Reference Model (SRM), on the

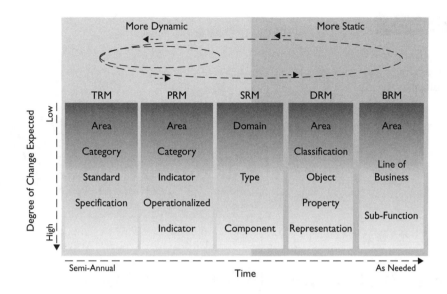

Degree of
Change of Various
FEA Reference
Models

other hand, may be less static as new services become available that improve the way processes are implemented. The Performance Reference Model (PRM) changes as new performance measurement types need to be introduced as a result of initiatives such as Balanced Score Card (BSC) and other complex measurements of enterprise performance that are trying to set more holistic metrics for goals.

Figure 2.5-1 also shows, within each reference model, what aspect of that Reference Model changes more rapidly than others.

The Practical Guide to Federal Enterprise Architecture (Federal CIO Council, 2003) describes how an architecture description must change, showing a decreasing emphasis on maintaining or extending elements of the baseline architecture but focusing on growing the target architecture. Figure 2-5.2 shows this decreasing emphasis on the baseline architecture as the implementation of the transformation process is rolled out according to the sequencing plan and as the target architecture starts becoming the new baseline. As a historical artifact, this guide was written at a time when federal agencies were undergoing very large modernization attempts (often after previous failed attempts). As an enterprise perpetuated the elements of the baseline architecture, it was assumed that the target architecture would be starved of resources and would never come to be.

The sequencing plan stays constant throughout the transition timeframe unless there is a need to resequence activities due to unforeseen circumstances or a stretching out of the timelines.

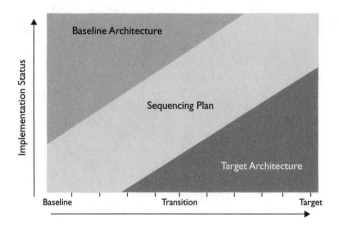

FIGURE 2.5-2

Enterprise
Architecture
Transition

Who Is Responsible for Maintenance?

Maintaining the EA should be accomplished within the enforcement structure and configuration control mechanisms of the organization. Chapter 2.6 deals with governance issues.

EA maintenance is generally the responsibility of the CIO, Chief Architect, and the Enterprise Architecture Program Office, often through a delegation chain of architecture team members. Using a system of oversight processes and independent verification, the architecture core team periodically assesses and aligns the EA to the ever-changing business practices, funding profiles, and technology insertion.

The EA should remain aligned to the organization's modernization projects and vice versa. The management controls to accomplish EA maintenance are the same ones established to initiate the program and to develop the EA.

Planning the Cost of Maintenance

EA maintenance must be planned and budgeted for. Because EA projects themselves compete for resources against enterprise initiatives, a clear business case must be made for both the initial EA development and the follow on maintenance funding required to keep the architecture data up to date and useful. Enterprise architecture itself is and should be treated as a capital asset that depreciates without maintenance. Maintenance is used to retain asset value.

Out-of-date architecture data can have an extremely detrimental impact on planning. The assumptions implicit in the architecture also forms the basis of assumptions for roadmaps. The Architecture Overview and Summary (described in Chapter 3.2) must explicitly specify assumptions, constraints, and the validity for the architecture timeframe.

The Business Case for EA Maintenance

If the EA is not kept current, it will quickly become "shelf-ware," yet another well-intentioned but unusable plan for improving the enterprise. Perhaps even more damaging, if the EA fails to embody the agency's most current strategy, it may limit the organization's ability to meet its goals and achieve its mission. The EA necessitates a specific organizational and process structure that will ensure the currency of EA content over time. The EA should reflect the impact of ongoing changes in business function and technology on the enterprise and, in turn, support capital planning and investment management in keeping up with those changes. Consequently, each component of the EA baseline architecture, target architecture, sequencing plan, and all the products that constitute them need to be maintained and kept accurate and current.

Periodic Architecture Reassessment

For it to be useful and relevant, the architecture as a living document must be periodically reviewed against the reality of the enterprise to determine if it still accurately represents the state of the enterprise.

The Need for Periodic Reassessment

Periodically, it is necessary to revisit the vision that carried the organization to this point and to reenergize the agency to realize that vision. Continually, typically in conjunction with capital planning and investment control (CPIC), the EA should be reviewed to ensure the following:

■ The current or baseline architecture accurately reflects the current status of the IT infrastructure.

■ The target architecture accurately reflects the business vision of the enterprise and appropriate technology advances that have occurred since the last release.

■ The sequencing plan reflects the prevailing priorities of the enterprise and resources that will realistically be available.

The assessment should generate an update to the EA and corresponding changes in dependent projects. The baseline should continue to reflect actions taken to implement the sequencing plan and actions otherwise taken to upgrade the legacy environment as the organization modernizes. The EA assessment and update should be managed and scheduled to in turn update the agency's strategic plan and process for selecting system investments.

Models Must Reflect Reality—Always

An agency is a business entity that remains responsive to business drivers (including new legislation and executive directives), emerging technologies, and opportunities for improvement. The EA reflects the evolution of the agency and should continuously reflect the current state (baseline architecture), the desired state (target architecture), and the long- and short-term strategies for managing the change (the sequencing plan). Figure 2.5-2 illustrates the type of continuous changes that should be illustrated by the EA. Recognizing that the baseline architecture, the sequencing plan, and the target architecture are all moving forward (today's target architecture will become tomorrow's baseline and the sequencing plan will no longer reflect transformations that have already been accomplished and a new version of the target architecture is formulated based on new or evolving enterprise needs and contexts), the EA maintenance must, at all times ensure updates of all three components shown in Figure 2-5.2.

Leverage Solution Architectures to Grow the EA

Figure 2.5-3 shows that enterprises can adopt one of the following three strategies for enterprise architecting:

- ■ Drive the development of solution architectures in a top-down manner by first defining the enterprise architecture. This is not usually feasible for enterprises that have been operational for many years. More often, enterprise architecture is a conversion of the implicit aspects of a working enterprise to an explicit representation that can add planning and transformational activities.

- ■ Drive the development of the enterprise architecture in a bottom-up manner by aggregating elements from all the various solution architectures. This is an acknowledgment that the enterprise is actually the sum total of its solutions. This approach grandfathers any architectural disconnects and mismatches

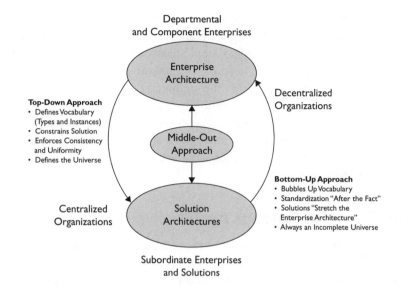

FIGURE 2.5-3

The Iterative
Dependence
Between EA
and Solution
Architectures

that exist in reality across solutions and generates an as-is enterprise architecture that is representative of the current state of the enterprise. At the same time, portions of the enterprise may not currently have any solution architectures defined. This approach ignores such missing solutions in representing the enterprise.

■ A blending of top-down and bottom-up using a middle-out approach. In this approach, the top-down architecture is built at the same time as the solution architectures are baselined. The gap between the current state and the target state is used to drive transformational activities.

In the second (bottom-up) and third strategy (middle-out) approach, discovery of unmodeled representations from modeling solution architectures is flowed back to the enterprise architecture (in a more abstract manner consistent with the level of modeling of the EA) to "grow" the EA.

Ensure That Business Direction and Processes Reflect Operations

A critical responsibility for the EA program is to monitor the changes in business operations that affect the organization, the business processes, and the strategic direction of the business. The business artifacts of the baseline architecture may reflect changes in business processes that were initiated by process improvement, organizational change, or mandate. Business unit management and their subject matter experts (SMEs) should report changes in their organizations and initiatives to the Chief Architect and architecture core team. Correspondingly, the Chief Architect ensures that the architecture core team is gaining sufficient insight into the evolution of the operations. Plans and expectations may change as priorities shift over time; these changes may need to be reflected in modifications to the target architecture. Priority shifts and the realities of budget constraints may need to be reflected in the sequencing plan. Thus, EA maintenance is both reactive and proactive.

Ensure That the Current Architecture Reflects System Evolution

Despite the best operational management and systems maintenance planning, the current architecture and infrastructure may need unanticipated changes. As each new system is deployed and each legacy system reaches a maintenance milestone (for example, the renewal of maintenance contracts), the baseline for the current architecture changes. In addition, system patches should be introduced frequently or system design changes implemented to respond to high-priority requests. These changes should be reflected in the current architecture artifacts.

Evaluate Legacy System Maintenance Requirements Against the Sequencing Plan

As the current architecture evolves to reflect the reality of the legacy systems, new information may emerge that will change the maintenance plans and subsequent organizational and systems transition. For example, system vendors may unexpectedly cease supporting critical components of the agency's infrastructure. Alternative actions should be weighed and decisions made regarding replacing the components, paying for additional specialized contractor support, or changing the strategy for phasing in other components in the target architecture. The total cost of ownership of the system versus alternative systems, as well as outsourcing, may need to be considered. All of these considerations, alternatives, and decisions may dramatically alter the sequencing plan.

Maintain the Sequencing Plan as an Integrated Program Plan

The development of the sequencing plan is linked to the acquisition and enterprise engineering processes. The architect works in partnership with managers who understand the evolving business objectives, as well as the individual program management offices that oversee the acquisition and development of new IT systems. The sequencing plan should be maintained, reviewed, validated, and approved to reflect continually the organization's mission and vision, just as any product in the architecture package and plan should be. The sequencing plan delineates the IT management scheme for systems insertion in support of the organization's long-term business strategies.

Continue to Consider Proposals for EA Modifications

Although the enforcement process helps to ensure that the EA guidance is followed, it is unreasonable to assume that new business priorities and technologies, funding issues, or project challenges will not require modification to the plans, baselines, and products incorporated in the EA. Emerging technologies continue to necessitate changes to the enterprise. Many of the considerations for changes to the EA are the same considerations that needed to be addressed during its development. Also, the architectural principles need to be continuously addressed.

Proposals for modifying the architecture should address the following questions, among others:

- How does the proposed modification support the organization in exploiting IT to increase the effectiveness of IT's organizational components?
- How does the modification impact information sharing and interoperability among organizational components?
- What are the security implications? For example, will the modifications need certification of enhanced systems?
- Does the proposed modification use proven technologies and conforming commercial off-the-shelf (COTS) products to satisfy requirements and deliver IT services? Are these technologies and related standards in the industry mainstream, thereby reducing the risk of premature obsolescence?
- Does the acceptance of this proposal position other standards or products for obsolescence? If so, identify them.

- What is the impact on the organization and suborganizations if the proposal is not accepted? What is the result of the cost/benefit analysis?
- What external organizations or systems will be affected? What action will they have to take?
- What is the estimated overall programmatic cost of the proposed changes, including changes to the EA and/or redirection of dependent projects?
- What alternatives have been considered and why were they not recommended?
- What testing should be completed, and by whom, for implementations that will result from acceptance of the proposal?
- What is the recommendation of the Enterprise Change Control Board?

Proposals requesting modifications to the EA need to address these issues explicitly. The proposal should be presented to and reviewed by the Technology Review Committee (TRC) (for review by architectural team and SMEs) and passed to the Enterprise Architecture Executive Steering Council (EAESC) with a recommendation. In cases where the EAESC cannot reach a consensus, a working group may be formed to investigate and propose recommended actions.

TOGAF 9 ADM Phase H: Architecture Change Management

In TOGAF 9, Phase H (Architecture Change Management) of the Architecture Development Methodology (ADM) addresses the issues of maintaining an architecture once it has been developed. TOGAF 9 identifies three types of architecture changes: (1) simplification of an architecture; (2) incremental evolution of an architecture; and (3) redevelopment of an architecture. Each of these can be handled incrementally or through a subset of the phases of the ADM, or may require an entire iteration through the ADM (for example, re-architecting).

The following are the objectives of performing architecture change management for TOGAF:

- Ensure that baseline architectures are fit to purpose.
- Assess the performance of the architecture and make recommendations for change.

■ Assess changes to the framework and principles.

■ Establish an architecture change management process for the new EA baseline.

■ Maximize business value from the architecture.

■ Operate the governance framework.

The steps recommended for architecture change management for TOGAF are described in Table 2.5-2.

TABLE 2.5-2   TOGAF 9 Steps for Architecture Change Management

	Step	Description
1	Establish Value Realization Process	Establish a process that ensures that business projects realize value from the EA. This step also involves formulating direct and indirect metrics to correlate the outcomes of the project in terms of the EA context.
2	Deploy Monitoring Tools	Deploy tools for monitoring various aspects such as technology changes; business changes; enterprise architecture capability maturity; deployment of tracking tools such as asset management programs; quality of service.
3	Manage Risks	Assess enterprise architecture risks and develop plans to deal with those risks.
4	Provide Analysis for Architecture Change Management	Conduct various types of analysis on the architecture effort as well as the scope and content of the architecture to determine whether changes are to be made.
5	Develop Change Requirements to Meet Performance Targets	Determine changes needed to the architecture to meet the performance targets that are driven by business requirements.
6	Manage Governance Process	Conduct proceedings of the Architecture Board.
7	Activate the Process to Implement Change	Initiate the activities needed to produce architecture change, such as an architecture change request or an investment request for a project to implement the change request. Ensure that all change requests and architecture change implementation projects are registered in the Architecture Repository.

Questions

1. Do all the architecture elements modeled in the enterprise architecture change at the same rate with time? Are there types of architecture elements that change more rapidly than others? Why?

2. How does the maintainability of business functions compare to the maintainability of activities used in business processes? Remember that business functions tend to be very stable if the mission of an enterprise has not changed.

3. What is the effect of the nature of an enterprise on the rate of change of architecture representations? Discuss what types of changes may occur in a hypothetical startup enterprise that result in the need to change the EA.

4. If you were to build an enterprise architecture repository maintenance plan for your own enterprise with the granularity of quarterly time periods (with three monthly maintenance periods), what types of architecture elements would be maintained at what frequency on the schedule? Why?

5. In your own enterprise, who is responsible for maintaining the enterprise architecture? How frequently is it maintained? Are there any policies related to maintenance frequency, schedule, responsibility, and oversight? How does your enterprise plan for the cost of maintenance?

6. What are the symptoms of poorly maintained enterprise architecture? How are these symptoms manifested in the enterprise? What is the effect of poorly maintained enterprise architecture on the planning aspects of the enterprise? On the operational aspects? The system's aspects?

Reference List

Federal CIO Council. (2003). *Practical guide to Federal Enterprise Architecture.*

Federal Enterprise Architecture Program Management Office. (2005). *Federal Enterprise Architecture Reference Model maintenance process: a proposal from the Federal CIO Council Architecture and Infrastructure Committee and E-GOV.*

2.6

Governing
the Enterprise
Architecture

I n this chapter, we talk about the governance of enterprise architecture. When we think of governance related to enterprise architecture, we can think of two types:

- Governance over the enterprise architecting itself. This type ensures that the architecture meets the enterprise needs for architectural representation, support for policy formulation, and so on.
- Governance that the enterprise architecture provides for other enterprise processes such as capital planning, investment reviews, promotion of standards for development, and infrastructure, and building of forward-looking plans such as technology roadmaps or transformation roadmaps.

In this chapter, our primary concern is the governance of the enterprise architecture, not how enterprise architecture assists in the governance of other enterprise processes. The interaction of EA and the enterprise business processes is discussed in Part IV for the federal government and the Department of Defense and for commercial enterprises.

The purpose of EA control and oversight is to ensure that the EA development, implementation, and maintenance practices are being followed, and to remedy any situations or circumstances where they are not and action is warranted. Control and oversight are continuous, ongoing functions performed throughout the EA lifecycle process. Effective control and oversight is a key to ensuring EA program success. Through it, information is gathered for accountable decision makers to alert them as to whether effective EA development, implementation, and maintenance activities are being performed and whether EA program goals are being met on schedule and within budgets.

Though specific organizations adopt specific governance strategies, the following are some of the considerations that generally apply to all governance strategies:

- **Assessment of maturity of an enterprise's EA implementation**   This involves assessing where a particular enterprise's EA efforts lie when benchmarked with other enterprises. The Government Accounting Office (GAO) has developed a framework called the Enterprise Architecture Maturity Management Framework (EAMMF). The Office of Management and Budget (OMB) has also developed an EA assessment framework for federal agencies that grades agencies on their degree of implementation and adoption of EA into their business processes.

■ **Assessing the effectiveness of EA through metrics**   In enterprises, metrics such as return on assets, return on investment, and others are frequently used to assess the cost/benefit equation for initiatives. In enterprise architecture, such metrics are an emerging field used to determine the value of architecture as a capitalized or expensed asset or as a knowledge base that somehow supports enterprise prioritization, planning, and transformational efforts but may not necessarily be quantifiable in benefit.

■ **Managing access to the EA itself and dealing with security and authorization-related matters**   The EA is especially a vulnerable target for competition and for disgruntled internal personnel. At the same time, widespread access to the EA is desired for promoting enterprise coherence as well as the consistency and transparency of architecture elements in order for diverse groups to collaborate effectively. This tension between the need for transparency and communication and the need for security and access control must be carefully managed.

■ **Enforcement of EA standards**   An enterprise architecture program must itself adopt standards for modeling methodologies, artifacts, repository metamodel structures, and repository and architecture tool exchange standards. Such standards are necessary in order for the EA to be both a long-lived asset as well as one that can interact with architectures, tools, and methodologies used by partner enterprises and subenterprises.

■ **Configuration management of the EA**   We have already discussed the issues and concerns related to configuration management of the enterprise architecture, such as releasing increments in an evolutionary manner and controlling updates and changes by authorized stewards in Chapter 2.5. The enterprise architecture, to act as a durable resource, must continue to be kept up to date. Different aspects of the enterprise architecture change at different rates. For example, the business architecture's Business Reference Model (BRM) and business functions may not change unless the mission and the lines of business of the enterprise changes. The technology architecture may change more frequently as advances in products make previous versions obsolete.

■ **EA policy and procedures**   Lastly, we discuss the enterprise architecture policy that must be undertaken by the enterprise. Policy is often perceived as burdensome by operational staff. EA policy must complement existing policies and not add an undue burden. The value of EA is often to the management of an enterprise, but implementers of solutions or subcontractors may perceive EA as an obstacle.

To explain these concepts further, we will use a generalized governance framework using a model from the Infosys white paper *Enterprise Architecture: A Governance Framework* (Infosys, 2005).

Governance Framework

Figure 2.6-1 describes the various components of a governance framework. Each must be addressed to achieve EA governance. The annotations of terms such as "Doctrine," "Organization," and "Leadership" beside the circles represents an overlay of the familiar military tenets of DOTMLPF: doctrine, organization, training, materiel, leadership, personnel, and facility.

Leadership

Leadership provides the drive needed to propel architecting efforts forward and to achieve widespread acceptance. Because of the potential perception that EA is not essential to day-to-day operations, functional managers tend to focus more on putting out the fire of the day. However, EA is a key part of planning and prioritization for upper management. Without strong leadership, the interest of the enterprise's holistic view is often sacrificed for immediate (and sometimes noncritical) needs. Leadership in the form of executive management and sponsorship, in addition to

FIGURE 2.6-1

Governance
Components

full support from the CIO, is essential for a successful CIO strategy. To achieve buy-in from leadership, the Chief Architect and the CIO have to "sell" the benefits of enterprise architecture and demonstrate early results and payoffs from the EA program. Governance involves displaying explicit roles for executive management and sponsorship within the EA effort and at different stages of the EA lifecycle.

Investment

The EA program often requires a significant investment by an organization in architecture. John Zachman asserts that the resulting architecture be perceived as an asset that keeps on giving—to every meaningful activity of the enterprise. However, because of the inevitable change in the information that is represented in the architecture, over time, architecture becomes a perishable asset that needs to be constantly refreshed. An enterprise making the initial investment in the development of EA must also be ready to invest in the maintenance and evolution of the EA as well. This readiness is exhibited in planned investments for EA in a phased and multiyear manner. Governance involves displaying commitment to a phased and funded investment strategy for the EA lifecycle.

Organization

Organization is required to implement a set of formal structures to oversee EA implementation and use. In most organizations, this is achieved through the appointment of formal bodies that take the form of councils, review boards, working groups, and integrated project teams. A formal organizational structure consists of a charter, criteria for membership, roles and responsibilities, a calendar for working meetings, and a framework for decision making. The formal organization structure also describes accountability for the various roles concerned and forms the basis for collecting metrics needed for control.

Governance involves detailing an organization chart that lays out specific organizations, their roles, and their responsibilities with respect to the EA lifecycle.

In the *Practical Guide for the Federal Enterprise Architecture* (Federal CIO Council, 2001), the suggested organization structure, at a minimum, for successful EA development, maintenance, and use within a federal agency is comprised of the following:

- The Enterprise Architecture Executive Steering Council (EAESC)
- The Chief Information Officer (CIO)
- The Chief Architect

Principles and Policies

Principles are guiding tenets that are enduring and establish the fundamental backbone of the EA program in an enterprise. Principles should be a few in number and general enough that they are not specific to a situation or timeframe. Policies are guiding principles that are enforceable and measurable in terms of compliance. Explicit guidance is essential for requiring compliance. Principles and policies must therefore be explicitly published and communicated to stakeholders. Governance involves publishing explicit principles and policies for the various steps of the EA lifecycle.

Processes

Processes that are well thought out and documented are essential to the development, maintenance, use, and evolution of the enterprise architecture. Processes must be simple and streamlined, yet comprehensive. Any issues and defects that arise from improper execution of the steps must be analyzed to determine how improvements can be made to the overall process. The process must not be burdensome to the stakeholders. Process definition includes the sequence of detailed steps for various aspects of the EA lifecycle: from setup of an EA program office; to the development of models, roadmaps, and plans; to the maintenance of the EA information; to use in business processes of the enterprise; and to the actual assessment of maturity metrics and effectiveness metrics for the EA program. Governance involves documented and communicated business processes, with steps and major phases, identification of roles and responsibilities of the various players, and controls for monitoring and governing the activity.

One of the processes that are essential to document and communicate is the process for controlling the EA lifecycle. The enterprise architecture program, like any major program, establishes expectations of results, deliverables, and outcomes at the beginning of the program. As the program continues, course corrections may need to be made and expectations reset based on actual experience rather than the initial hopes and assumptions that were built into the planning. Independent program reviews by a quality assurance function or by verification and validation (V&V) agents are used to identify deviations from expectations. These deviations may be related to program management, such as omission of work tasks, delays in the completion of work tasks, or additional costs to complete work tasks; or they may be related to management functions, such as not following change control procedures, not adhering to the selected EA framework, or not engaging subject matter experts (SMEs) and domain owners within business and technical areas.

Tools and Methods

The lifecycle of architecture requires the use of automated tools such as the ones used to build models, as well as repositories to manage the architecture information for data quality, consistency, accuracy, and timeliness and to support analysis and reporting. The development of models must follow some consistent and standard methodology. By applying standard methodologies, the models that are built are consistent across modeling efforts and also can be easily understood by personnel who are trained in those methodologies. Examples of standard methodologies are Unified Modeling Language (UML), Integrated Definition Language (IDEF), Structured Analysis and Design (SADT), Business Process Modeling Notation (BPMN), and Business Process Execution Language (BPEL). Most commercial architecture development tools provide support for standard methodologies. Chapter 5.1 has a more extensive discussion of tools, methodologies, and repositories. It is important to govern the selection of tools, methodologies, and repositories to ensure that the EA effort is not isolated simply to the group developing the architecture but that the results are applicable to a broader audience. Governance involves establishing clear criteria for standards and for selection of tools, methods, and a repository for the EA lifecycle.

Measurements

In the words of the Government Accountability Office, "The ability to effectively manage any activity (e.g., architecture development, maintenance, and use) depends upon having meaningful measures of that activity in relation to some standard. Such measurement permits managers to assess progress toward the desired end and to take corrective action to address unacceptable deviations" (2003, pg 5).

Measurement is essential for control. Measurements provide a way to determine whether desired results are forthcoming. They provide a basis for analysis and for devising a course of action that will produce more favorable outcomes.

Measurement can be performed informally through reports (oral and written and ad hoc) and formal and informal reviews. Measurements can also be gathered through periodic or surprise audits.

EA Maturity Assessment

From the components of governance, we could construct a simple but serviceable EA maturity framework by assigning a level or degree of maturity that each

TABLE 2.6-1	Leadership	Investment	Organization	Principles and Policy	Processes	Tools and Methods	Measurements
Inception: Starting Out							
Developed but Not Repeatable							
Repeatable but Not Managed							
Managed but Not Optimized							
Optimized and Improving							

Sample Maturity Assessment Matrix

component has achieved and assign some type of scoring to determine a maturity index. Table 2.6-1 shows an example.

This simple exercise is an illustration of more sophisticated EA maturity assessment models.

Maturity assessment of enterprise architecture management has been approached from various perspectives. Traditional methods have been based on the maturity of process and governance mechanisms. Of particular interest is the General Accountability Office's EAMMF. Though a little dated and revised since its inception, the EAMMF is useful to illustrate the concepts of EA management maturity.

GAO EA Management Maturity Assessment Framework (EAMMF)

The GAO established in 2002 an initial framework for assessing the maturity of enterprise architecture at federal agencies. Version 1.0 of the EAMMF was based on the process guidance and architecting steps provided by the *Practical Guide to Federal Enterprise Architecture* (Federal CIO Council, 2001). In 2003, the GAO quickly followed up with version 1.1 of the EA Management Maturity Framework. Version 1.1 (Government Accountability Office, 2003) of the EAMMF also follows the practice guidance advocated by the FEA *Practical Guide* and outlines, in increasing order of maturity, five stages of the EAMMF lifecycle.

The EAMMF is a framework that is laid out as a matrix. The columns of the matrix represent the stages of maturity for EA development as described in the FEA *Practical Guide*. The rows of the EAMMF are key attributes associated with the maturity stages that are critical to the successful performance of any management function.

The Five Stages of Maturity

Each of the five stages of maturity is shown in Figure 2.6-2 and described in the following subsections.

Stage 1: Creating EA Awareness

At stage 1, either an organization does not have plans to develop and use an architecture or it has plans that do not demonstrate an awareness of the value of having and using an architecture. Although stage 1 agencies may have initiated some EA activity, these agencies' efforts are ad hoc and unstructured, lack institutional leadership and direction, and do not provide the management foundation necessary for successful EA development as defined in stage 2.

Stage 2: Building the EA Management Foundation

An organization at stage 2 recognizes that the EA is a corporate asset by vesting accountability for it in an executive body that represents the entire enterprise. At this stage, an organization assigns EA management roles and responsibilities and establishes plans for developing EA products and for measuring program progress and product quality; it also commits the resources necessary for developing an architecture—people, processes, and tools.

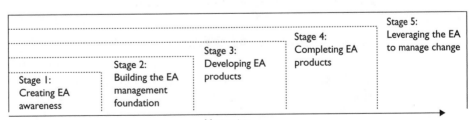

FIGURE 2.6-2

Five Stages of Enterprise Architecture Maturity

Specifically, a stage 2 organization has designated a chief architect and established and staffed a program office responsible for EA development and maintenance. Further, it has established a committee or group that has responsibility for EA governance (that is, directing, overseeing, and approving architecture development and maintenance). This committee or group is often called a steering committee, and its membership includes both business and IT representatives (that is, the committee has enterprisewide representation).

At stage 2, the organization either has plans for developing or has started developing at least some EA products, and it has developed an enterprisewide awareness of the value of EA and its intended use in managing its IT investments. The organization has also selected a framework and a methodology that will be the basis for developing the EA products and has chosen a tool for automating these activities.

Stage 3: Developing the EA

An organization at stage 3 focuses on developing architecture products according to the selected framework, methodology, tool, and established management plans. Roles and responsibilities assigned in the previous stage are in place, and resources are being applied to develop actual EA products. Here, the scope of the architecture has been defined to encompass the entire enterprise, whether organization-based or function-based.

Although the products may not be complete, they are intended to describe the organization in business, performance, information/data, service/application, and technology terms (including security explicitly in each) as provided for in the framework, methodology, tool, and management plans. Further, the products are to describe the current (as-is) and future (to-be) states and the plan for transitioning from the current to the future state (the sequencing plan). As the products are developed and evolve, they are subject to configuration management. Further, through the established EA management foundation, the organization is tracking and measuring its progress against plans, identifying and addressing variances as appropriate, and then reporting on its progress.

Stage 4: Completing the EA

An organization at stage 4 has completed its EA products, meaning that the products have been approved by the EA steering committee (established in stage 2) or an investment review board and by the CIO. The completed products collectively describe the enterprise in terms of business, performance, information/data, service/

application, and technology for both its current and future operating states, and the products include a sequencing plan for transitioning from the current to the future state. Further, an independent agent has assessed the quality (that is, completeness and accuracy) of the EA products.

Additionally, evolution of the approved products is governed by a written EA maintenance policy approved by the head of the organization.

Stage 5: Leveraging the EA to Manage Change

An organization at stage 5 has secured senior leadership approval of the EA products and a written institutional policy stating that IT investments must comply with the architecture unless granted an explicit compliance waiver. Further, decision makers are using the architecture to identify and address ongoing and proposed IT investments that are conflicting, overlapping, not strategically linked, or redundant. Thus, stage 5 entities are able to avoid unwarranted overlap across investments and ensure maximum systems interoperability, which in turn ensures the selection and funding of IT investments with manageable risks and returns. Also at stage 5, the organization tracks and measures EA benefits or return on investment, and adjustments are continuously made to both the EA management process and the EA products.

The Critical Attributes

The rows of the EAMMF that represent the critical attributes associated with the five stages are

- Attribute 1: demonstrates commitment
- Attribute 2: providing capability to meet commitment
- Attribute 3: demonstrates satisfaction of commitment
- Attribute 4: verifies satisfaction of commitment

Attribute 1: Demonstrates Commitment

Because the EA is a corporate asset for systematically managing institutional change, the support and sponsorship of the head of the enterprise are essential to the success of the architecture effort. An approved enterprise policy statement provides such support and sponsorship, promoting institutional buy-in and encouraging resource commitment from participating components. Equally important in demonstrating commitment is vesting ownership of the architecture with an executive body that collectively owns the enterprise.

Attribute 2: Provides Capability to Meet Commitment

The success of the EA effort depends largely on the organization's capacity to develop, maintain, and implement the EA. Consistent with any large IT project, these capabilities include providing adequate resources (that is, people, processes, and technology); defining clear roles and responsibilities; and defining and implementing organizational structures and process management controls that promote accountability and effective project execution.

Attribute 3: Demonstrates Satisfaction of Commitment

Demonstrating satisfaction of the organization's commitment to develop, maintain, and implement an EA is evidenced by the production of artifacts (for example, the plans and products). Such artifacts demonstrate "follow-through"—actual EA production.

Satisfaction of commitment is further demonstrated by senior leadership approval of EA Page 11 GAO-03-584G Enterprise Architecture Management documents and artifacts (Government Accountability Office, 2003); this approval communicates institutional endorsement and ownership of the architecture and the change that it is intended to drive.

Attribute 4: Verifies Satisfaction of Commitment

This attribute focuses on measuring and disclosing the extent to which efforts to develop, maintain, and implement the EA have fulfilled stated goals or commitments. Measuring such performance allows for tracking progress that has been made toward stated goals, allows appropriate actions to be taken when performance deviates significantly from goals, and creates incentives to influence both institutional and individual behaviors.

The assessment framework in its entirety is therefore the grid formed by combining the critical attributes and the maturity stages, as shown in Figure 2.6-3.

At each association of the critical attribute and a maturity stage (except for maturity stage 1), the EAMMF describes core elements that measure the maturity. Figure 2.6-4 shows all the core elements at the intersection of the maturity stages and the critical attributes.

FIGURE 2.6-3

Critical Attributes
Versus EA
Maturity Stages

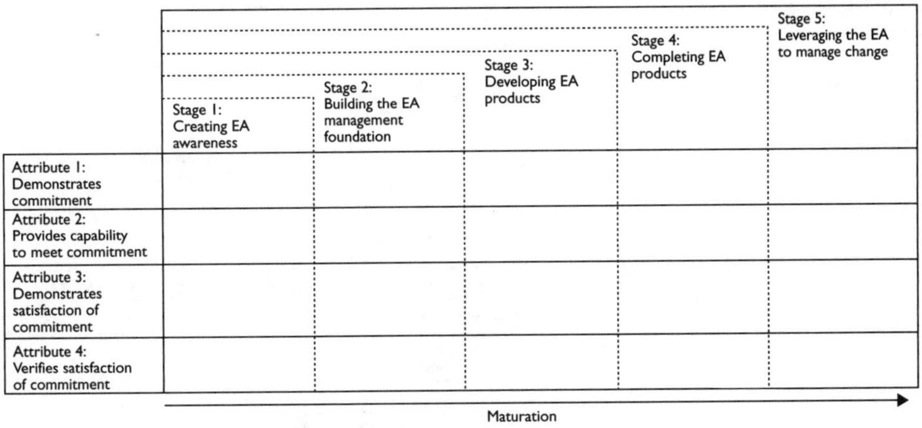

	Stage 1: Creating EA awareness	Stage 2: Building the EA management foundation	Stage 3: Developing EA products	Stage 4: Completing EA products	Stage 5: Leveraging the EA to manage change
Attribute 1: Demonstrates commitment					
Attribute 2: Provides capability to meet commitment					
Attribute 3: Demonstrates satisfaction of commitment					
Attribute 4: Verifies satisfaction of commitment					

Maturation →

Other Maturity Assessment Models

There have been other EA maturity assessment models since the GAO EAMMF. Some of these are detailed in this section as well as in the references.

The Ross, Weill, and Robertson Model in Enterprise Architecture as Strategy

In their book *Enterprise Architecture as Strategy*, Jeanne W. Ross, Peter Weill, and David C. Robertson (2006) describe their model as consisting of four stages of architecture maturity:

- **Stage 1: Existence of business silos**   In this stage, companies focus their IT investments on delivering solutions for local business problems and opportunities. The role of IT during the business silo stage is to automate specific business processes.

- **Stage 2: Standardized technology**   At this stage, companies shift some of their IT investments from local applications to shared infrastructure. Companies then establish technology standards intended to decrease the number of platforms they manage. Fewer platforms mean lower cost.

- **Stage 3: Optimized core**   In this stage, companies move from a local view of data to an enterprise view. Transaction data is extracted from individual systems and made accessible to all appropriate processes. Companies are

FIGURE 2.6-4

Full EA Maturity Assessment Framework

	Stage 1: Creating EA awareness	Stage 2: Building the EA management foundation	Stage 3: Developing EA products	Stage 4: Completing EA products	Stage 5: Leveraging the EA to manage change
Attribute 1: Demonstrates commitment		Adequate resources exist. Committee or group representing the enterprise is responsible for directing, overseeing, or approving EA.	Written and approved organization policy exists for EA development.	Written and approved organization policy exists for EA maintenance.	Written and approved organization policy exists for IT investment compliance with EA.
Attribute 2: Provides capability to meet commitment		Program office responsible for EA development and maintenance exists. Chief architect exists. EA is being developed using a framework, methodology, and automated tool.	EA products are under configuration management.	EA products and management processes undergo independent verification and validation.	Process exists to formally manage EA change. EA is integral component of IT investment management process.
Attribute 3: Demonstrates satisfaction of commitment		EA plans call for describing both the "as-is" and the "to-be" environments of the enterprise, as well as a sequencing plan for transitioning from the "as-is" to the "to-be." EA plans call for describing both the "as-is" and the "to-be" environments in terms of business, performance, information/data, application/service, and technology. EA plans call for business, performance, information/data, application/service, and technology descriptions to address security.	EA products describe or will describe both the "as-is" and the "to-be" environments of the enterprise, as well as a sequencing plan for transitioning from the "as-is" to the "to-be." Both the "as-is" and the "to-be" environments are described or will be described in terms of business, performance, information/data, application/service, and technology. Business, performance, information/data, application/service, and technology descriptions address or will address security.	EA products describe both the "as-is" and the "to-be" environments of the enterprise, as well as a sequencing plan for transitioning from the "as-is" to the "to-be." Both the "as-is" and the "to-be" environments are described in terms of business, performance, information/data, application/service, and technology. Business, performance, information/data, application/service, and technology descriptions address security. Organization CIO has approved current version of EA. Committee or group representing the enterprise or the investment review board has approved current version of EA.	EA products are periodically updated. IT investments comply with EA. Organization head has approved current version of EA.
Attribute 4: Verifies satisfaction of commitment		EA plans call for developing metrics for measuring EA progress, quality, compliance, and return on investment.	Progress against EA plans is measured and reported.	Quality of EA products is measured and reported.	Return on EA investment is measured and reported. Compliance with EA is measured and reported.

Maturation →

also developing interfaces to critical corporate data and if appropriate, standardizing business processes and IT applications.

- **Stage 4: Business modularity**   This stage allows the company to take advantage of customized or reusable modules. The modules provide large-grain patterns of reuse that allow the company to quickly replicate and proliferate them in order to expand the business.

A more detailed discussion of the maturity stages and examples are in Ross, Weill, and Robertson (2006).

OMB EA Assessment Framework

The OMB Enterprise Architecture Assessment Framework (EAAF) version 3.1 (Office of Management and Budget, 2009) identifies the measurement areas and criteria by which agencies are expected to use the EA to drive performance improvements that result in the following outcomes:

- Closing agency performance gaps identified via strategic planning and performance management activities coordinated among agencies
- Saving money and avoiding cost through collaboration and reuse, productivity enhancements, and elimination of redundancy
- Strengthening the quality of agency investment portfolios by improving security, interoperability, reliability, availability, solution development and service delivery time, and overall end-user performance
- Improving the quality, availability, and sharing of data and information governmentwide
- Increasing the transparency of government operations by increasing the capacity for citizen participation and cross-governmental collaboration

The scope of EAAF version 3.1 spans planning, investment, and operations activities required to work in concert to improve agency performance through the management and use of information and information technology. EAAF version 3.1 features the use of key performance indicators (KPIs) to measure the effectiveness of EA relative to the following three EA capabilities areas:

- Completion
- Use
- Results

It also moves agency EA submission to a template-based model aimed at improving reporting and assessment via an automated process and delivery mechanism. Artifacts are posted on the MAX collaboration environment.

EAAF version 3.1 also changes the assessment and reporting process. Instead of relying on a single annual assessment, version 3.1 moves to posting relevant artifacts for the completion, use, and results capability areas in order to better align the use of EA with agency planning, investment management, budget formulation, and decision-making processes relevant to the annual budget cycle.

The EAAF supports the policy implementation assessment and enforcement for achieving the EA and related requirements set forth in OMB Circulars A-130 and A-11. The latest EAAF is closely aligned with the methodologies, reporting templates, and tools such as the Federal Transition Framework (FTF), the Federal Segment Architecture Methodology (FSAM), and Visualization to Understand Expenditures in Information Technology (VUE-IT).

Gartner EA Maturity Assessment Framework

The Gartner Group also uses for its clients an EA assessment framework (Architecture Program Maturity Assessment, or APMA) that uses surveys to measure various components of the EA program (Burke and James, 2008). Gartner uses the results of these surveys to make recommendations regarding future direction.

The following components are surveyed to assess maturity:

- **Architecture scope and authority**   The framework measures the span and influence of the architecture through the breadth of key stakeholders of the enterprise. A common understanding and approach to the business strategy across the enterprise must drive a mature architecture program. To succeed, the program must support business change across multiple programs, business units, and even companies. Success in this dimension requires optimizing end-to-end processes, implementing a common infrastructure, and creating appropriate governance structures.

- **Stakeholder involvement**   The involvement and support of key stakeholders—including enterprise senior executives and IT managers, along with key members of the enterprise's lines of business and the wider architecture community—are critical to program maturity. Key to fostering this support is clear and accessible communication of the EA, tailored to the needs of different stakeholder groups.

- **Architecture definition process**   This process should be well defined, clearly articulated, and pragmatically executed, using regular iterations to expand the EA's scope progressively and to improve and update its individual elements. This process should also involve appropriate stakeholders and be integrated with related processes such as business planning and IT portfolio management.

- **Business context** A common approach to the business strategy across the enterprise must drive a mature architecture program. To succeed, the program must support business change across multiple programs, business units, and even companies. Mature EA programs are explicitly linked to the business strategy and can demonstrate that they deliver business value.

- **Architecture content** This component measures the adequacy of content within the EA to meet the needs of key stakeholders. Expression of the EA should address three basic viewpoints—business, information, and technology—and how these viewpoints combine to create solutions. It should also address three levels—conceptual, logical, and implementation—moving from high-level to detailed expressions of the architecture.

- **Future state realization** Enterprise architecture must be actionable. An actionable architecture favorably alters the future state of the enterprise. The most mature architecture programs are actionable, defining, planning, and initiating the projects that will be executed to achieve the defined future state.

- **Architecture team resources** To be successful, an enterprise architecture team must have skilled and talented resources. Because the talents and skills that a successful enterprise architect must possess are in short supply, a focus on recruiting talented individuals and providing the necessary professional development and training is key. It is also important for architects in complex and sophisticated environments to have tools to help them understand the range of information assets, relate these assets to each other and to the business strategy, and communicate this information to stakeholders.

- **Architecture impact** Without defined program goals, EA programs will struggle to provide ongoing justification of the value of EA and the impact of the EA program on the business. To improve EA program effectiveness, sophisticated metrics—including measures of financial efficiency and business effectiveness—should be used to measure the program's impact on the business. Each of these scores with a five-point maximum for any dimension are totaled and compared against similar enterprises. Gartner maintains a database of scores of various enterprises that can be used as a benchmark.

Security and Access and Privacy Issues

Another key aspect of governance is to address the need for security controls on the enterprise architecture. Arguably, the aggregation of many elements of information creates an asset that is of greater value as a whole than the sum of its parts. Governance involves developing, publishing, enforcement, and measurement of compliance with security policies for the enterprise architecture. Security measures are easier to enforce when the enterprise architecture resides in a central repository or system of repositories. They are harder to enforce when the architecture development is scattered over a number of tools. Security is enforced either at the database level through mechanisms embedded inside the repository database or through common authorization and entitlement services that are invoked by all repository applications and tools.

The following are the basic steps in implementing IT security (Arizona Department of Administration, 2008):

1. **Identification**   The process of distinguishing a specific individual against others

2. **Authentication**   The process of identifying the individual

3. **Authorization and Access Control**   The means of establishing and enforcing user rights and privileges

   a. **Object-Level Security**   Security measures are defined for each architecture element or collection of architecture elements in the architecture repository. An access control list associates specific groups, roles, or even individuals to specific architecture elements. A degree of access (for example, Read-Only, Change, Delete, and so on) is associated with the object for that group, role, or individual.

   b. **Permission-Based Security**   Actions that can be performed are set up as permissions. An access control list associates specific groups, roles, or even individuals to specific permissions.

4. **Administration**   The process of establishing, managing, and maintaining security functions and activities

5. **Audit**   The process of monitoring the identification, authentication, authorization, and access control and administration to determine whether proper security measures have been taken

In addition, the following are some of the considerations that guide the formulation of specific policies for security:

■ Balancing the need for widespread dissemination and transparency of EA information against vulnerabilities and threats

■ Promoting cross-business domain integration, federation, and aggregation of architecture elements while securing information against misuse

■ Compliance with regulatory directives such as the Federal Information Security Act (FISMA) and the Privacy Act to drive policy that governs security classification, requirements for encryption, and handling of person identification information (PII).

EA Standards Compliance

Another aspect of EA governance is the need to formulate policy to enforce compliance with standards. EA standards are simply a subset of a larger group of standards that must be adopted by enterprises for interoperability and leveraging market forces.

The following are some of the areas that may require a standards policy:

■ Architecture framework
■ Repository/metamodel
■ Standards
■ Tool import/export standards
■ Architecture data exchange standards
■ Architecture data translation/mediation standards
■ Controlled vocabularies and ontology standards
■ Use of standard taxonomies
■ Metadata specifications for architecture elements
■ Integrated architecture development
■ Federated architecture development

In these sections, we have presented the governance aspects of enterprise architecture primarily as seen by government enterprises such as State and Federal government. In the following discussion we cover how the TOGAF describes governance in terms of relevance to the private sector as well.

Architecture Governance in TOGAF (TOGAF 9)

TOGAF 9 defines architecture governance as "the practice by which enterprise architectures are managed and controlled." Governance ensures that business is conducted properly. TOGAF draws upon the definition from the basic principles of corporate governance: "Corporate governance involves a set of relationships between a company's management, its board, its shareholders, and other stakeholders. Corporate governance also provides the structure through which the objectives of the company are set, and the means of attaining those objectives and monitoring performance are determined. Good corporate governance should provide proper incentives for the board and management to pursue objectives that are in the interests of the company and its shareholders and should facilitate effective monitoring." (Organization for Economic Co-operation and Development (OECD), 2004, pg 11).

Architecture governance includes the following:

- Installing and managing controls on the creation and monitoring of components and activities, ensuring introduction, implementation, and evolution of architectures
- Ensuring compliance with internal and external standards and regulatory obligations
- Supporting management of that compliance
- Ensuring accountability to external and internal stakeholders

Architecture governance in TOGAF lies at the lowest level of a governance hierarchy that includes the following (listed from broadest to narrowest in scope):

1. Corporate governance
2. Technology governance
3. IT governance
4. Architecture governance

This is in keeping with the TOGAF's focus on architecting solutions that are driven by the IT organization rather than a pure business-driven architecture that is IT solution agnostic.

Organizational Structure for Architecture Governance

TOGAF depicts a typical organization structure for an architecture organization that supports architecture governance, as shown in Figure 2.6-5.

In the figure, the Chief Information Officer/Chief Technology Officer is ultimately responsible for governance through all stages of IT solution delivery (Development, Implementation, and Deployment). At each of the individual solution phases, different groups of people are responsible for governance as shown in the figure. Enterprise architects and domain architects are responsible for developing the architecture aspects of the solution that ensure that the solution is compliant with enterprise standards and fits correctly into the context of the larger enterprise. Using home construction parlance, the architects are responsible for ensuring that the design confirms to "building codes, zoning regulations, and other regulations."

The Program Management Office entrusted with delivering the solution is responsible for the governance of construction practices, use of predefined implementation patterns, that ensure a quality solution implementation. The Program Office is also responsible for ensuring that the implementation follows the architecture guidance from the development phase.

The service management organization that is responsible for releasing and deploying the solution and overseeing maintenance and customer support activities is responsible for governance of solution changes and continued conformance with the implementation patterns and the architecture guidance from the previous phases.

All three phases draw upon the resources from the TOGAF Enterprise Continuum (see Section 4.3).

Key Architecture Governance Processes

Governance processes are required to identify, manage, audit, and disseminate all information related to architecture management, contracts, and implementation. These governance processes will be used to ensure that all architecture artifacts and contracts, principles, and operational-level agreements are monitored on an ongoing basis with clear auditability of all decisions made. The key architecture governance processes described by TOGAF 9 are described in the following subsections.

Policy Management and Take-On

All architecture amendments, contracts, and supporting information must come under governance through a formal process in order to register, validate, ratify, manage, and publish new or updated content. These processes ensure the orderly

FIGURE 2.6-5

Organizational
Structure for
Supporting
Governance

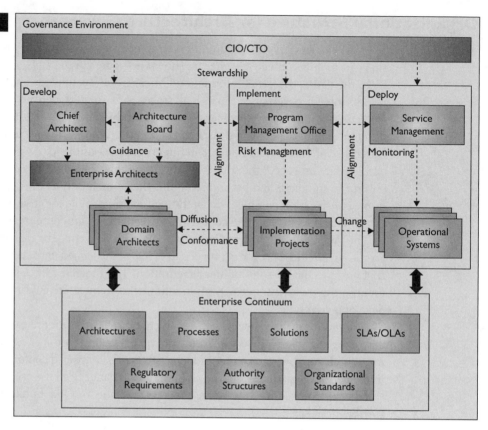

integration with existing governance content such that all relevant parties, documents, contracts, and supporting information are managed and audited.

Compliance

Compliance assessments against service-level agreements (SLAs), operational-level agreements (OLAs), standards, and regulatory requirements are implemented on an ongoing basis to ensure stability, conformance, and performance monitoring. These assessments are reviewed and either accepted or rejected depending on the criteria defined within the governance framework.

Dispensation

A compliance assessment can be rejected if the subject area (design, operational, service level, or technology) is not compliant. In such circumstances, interim conformance can be achieved in one of two ways:

- The subject area can be adjusted or realigned in order to meet the compliance requirements.
- The subject area can request a dispensation.

Dispensations are granted for a given time period during which a set of identified service and operational criteria must be enforced. Dispensations are not granted indefinitely, but are used as a mechanism to ensure that service levels and operational levels are met while providing a level of flexibility in their implementation and timing. The time-bound nature of dispensations ensures that they are a major trigger in the compliance cycle.

Monitoring and Reporting

Performance management is required to ensure that both the operational and service elements are managed against an agreed-upon set of criteria. This will include monitoring against service and operational-level agreements, feedback for adjustment, and reporting.

Business Control

Business control relates to the processes invoked to ensure compliance with the organization's business policies.

Environment Management

This process identifies all the services required to ensure that the repository-based environment underpinning the governance framework is effective and efficient. This includes the physical and logical repository management, access, communication, training, and accreditation of all users.

All architecture artifacts, service agreements, contracts, and supporting information must come under governance through a formal process in order to register, validate, ratify, manage, and publish new or updated content. These processes ensure orderly integration with existing governance content such that all relevant parties, documents, contracts, and supporting information are managed and audited.

The governance environment will have a number of administrative processes defined in order to facilitate a managed service and process environment. These processes include user management, internal SLAs (defined in order to control the environment's own processes), and management information reporting.

Questions

1. What is the difference in the frequency of change among different types of architecture elements in the enterprise? How do you account for these differences when developing a plan to maintain your enterprise architecture?

2. True or false: The business functions of the mission change only when the mission changes. Explain your answer. Is this also true for the business processes of the enterprise? Is this also true for the types of technology infrastructure that support the business processes?

3. How does the nature of the enterprise affect the rate at which the architecture must evolve? How does the architecture for a small startup enterprise vary from that of a long-term business with a stable collection of mature products that has been serving the same marketplace for decades?

4. Discuss the rate of change of the five Federal Enterprise Architecture Reference Models.

5. Who are the various people and roles responsible for the maintenance of an enterprise architecture?

6. How can solution architecture development be used to evolve the enterprise architecture?

7. How would you go about planning and budgeting for enterprise architecture maintenance within your own enterprise? How would you justify the investment in maintaining the EA?

Reference List

Arizona Department of Administration, McDowell, John, Chief Technology Planner. (2008). *An information technology security architecture for the State of Arizona,* final draft. State of Arizona.

Aziz, Sohel, Obitz, Thomas, Modi, Reva, & Sarkar, Santonu. Infosys. (2005). *Enterprise architecture: a governance framework*. White paper presented at InfoSys Knowledge Sharing Series Web Seminar, August 3rd and September 6th, 2005. http://www.infosys.webex.com.

Burke, Brian, & James, Greta. (2008). *The maturity of your enterprise architecture*. http://gitl.gartner.com/ea/survey.aspx?modelid=fc3bf454-b994-422b-817

Federal CIO Council. (2001). *Practical guide to Federal Enterprise Architecture*.

Government Accountability Office. (2003). *GAO executive guide: a framework for assessing and improving enterprise architecture management Version 1.1*. GAO-03-584G. GAOr.

Office of Management and Budget. (2009). *Enterprise Architecture Assessment Framework 3.1*. http://www.whitehouse.gov/omb/e-gov/eaaf.

Organisation for Economic Co-operation and Development (OECD). (2004). *OECD principles of corporate governance*. www.oecd.org/dataoecd/32/18/31557724.pdf

Ross, Jeanne W., Weill, Peter, & Robertson, David C. (2006). *Enterprise architecture as strategy: creating a foundation for business execution*. Harvard Business School Press.

2.7

Using the EA

A n enterprise architecture is a tool to support decision making, and in this chapter, we examine some of the decision-making contexts in which an EA can be used. Because most decision making affects some type of enterprise transformation, explicit or otherwise, we begin by reviewing the various dimensions of enterprise change. We then present approaches and examples of using EA in selected areas, including investment management and capital planning, organizational change, transition planning, and security.

Dimensions of Enterprise Transformation

There are two common models that capture dimensions of enterprise change. One we have seen before: the Zachman Framework (introduced in Chapter 1.2). The Zachman Framework is widely used in commercial enterprises and in non-DoD federal agencies. The other model is the DoD Doctrine, Organization, Training, Materiel, Leadership, Personnel, and Facilities (DOTMLPF) breakout.

We review both of these models in turn.

Zachman Framework Dimensions of Change

The Zachman Framework provides the dimensions of enterprise change in its six columns:

- What: data
- How: process
- Where: location
- Who: role
- When: time
- Why: motivation

Usually, the data ("what") that an enterprise uses remains fairly stable. Major changes in the types of data collected and stored are driven by strategic changes ("why"), that is, by major changes in the business direction of the enterprise. Although small changes in the amount of detail included in the data used by the enterprise or changes in the relationships among the data types may be common, major changes or additions to the types of data captured and used by the enterprise usually signal a change in the type of business the enterprise is involved in.

Changes in process ("how") can be driven both by business process reengineering and by technology change. Business process reengineering frequently calls for changes in the supporting systems and infrastructure, whereas technology change can impact the business processes by automating additional portions of the process or increasing the performance of the process in terms of time or number of personnel involved.

Changes in location ("where") can impact the business process because these changes may change the need to exchange information or resources among sites or performers and thus impact process performance. Changes in location may also impact organizations ("who") because changes in the location of personnel may enable or disrupt the organizational structure.

As previously discussed, a variety of other types of changes can affect the time it takes to perform business processes or the timing of process cycles. The need to improve performance or shorten cycle time may require changes in the business process, technology, or location.

A change in business strategy can impact all the other areas of change.

DoD Dimensions of Enterprise Change

DOTMLPF is the way DoD likes to categorize the dimensions of change. This model is not radically different from the Zachman Framework model in terms of coverage, but is better aligned with DoD decision making. DoD requires that all the areas of DOTMLPF be considered before making major decisions:

- *Doctrine* provides motivation for DoD activities. Doctrine prescribes process ("how") and performers ("who") and impacts location ("where") and timing ("when").
- *Organization* overlaps the Zachman "who" dimension.
- *Training* emphasizes an aspect of the Zachman "who" dimension that is not highlighted by the Zachman Framework. DoD needs to ensure that personnel are properly trained before they assume their assigned roles.
- *Materiel* includes parts of the Zachman "what," "how," and "where" dimensions. DoD makes a clear distinction between solutions that require materiel (nonpersonnel resources, including data) and those that just require changes in process (doctrine). Data is included in this category because it usually requires a materiel solution to manage and deliver data. (Even a manual data management process requires paper and filing cabinets.)

When changes in materiel requirements are identified, physical resources need to be acquired, and the acquisition of materiel involves major DoD decision-making processes, including Planning, Programming, Budgeting, and Execution (PPBE); portfolio management; and the Defense Acquisition System (DAS). Materiel also involves locations because managing physical resources and delivering them where they are needed (which entails logistics and the supply chain) is a major issue for DoD. DoD is required to consider nonmaterial solutions before materiel solutions.

■ *Leadership* emphasizes another aspect of the Zachman "who" dimension that is not highlighted by the Zachman Framework. Can solutions to problems be achieved with a change to the military units and leadership structures involved?

■ *Personnel* is yet another aspect of the Zachman "who" dimension. Can solutions to problems be achieved with different types of roles, or do solutions require a different set of skills? How many personnel are needed and what skill sets are involved?

■ *Facilities* is one aspect of the Zachman "where" dimension and covers fixed sites and buildings. It may also cover mobile facilities within mobile platforms such as ships or mobile command posts.

Changes to Multiple Dimensions

As previously discussed, changes in one change dimension may affect other change dimensions. Many decisions made in enterprises involve more than one change dimension. For example, a decision to reengineer business processes involves potential changes to business processes, technology, organization, roles and skills, and business cycles. In addition, process reengineering may also involve changes in location.

One of the lessons learned from software and systems engineering experience is that projects that propose to make changes in multiple aspects of the system concurrently are high risk. For example, a project that needs to move software to a new platform while upgrading the software functionality is best designed to first move the existing software to the new platform and then, in a second project phase, upgrade the software. This experience implies that if an enterprise decision affects multiple dimensions, then implementation of those changes is best scheduled in ways that impact one dimension of change at a time. In the preceding example of business process reengineering, one application of this advice would be to implement the included changes in this order:

1. Move personnel and involved IT (as necessary) to the new locations.
2. Make the organizational changes.
3. Implement the new IT (but do not start using it yet).
4. Train the personnel in new skills.
5. Implement the new process using the new IT.

What's the contribution of EA to all of this? First, an analysis comparing the as-is to the to-be (end-state) architectures will clearly identify all the dimensions of change involved. Then intermediate to-be architectures can be developed to show each step of the transition and highlight any issues or extra work required to achieve smooth operations at each stage of the transition. Note that the changes reflected in some of the intermediate architectures may be subtle. For example, the intermediate architecture for the "train the personnel in the new skills" phase needs to show how the time needed to train personnel may affect normal business operations. This can be done by tailoring the Organizational Relationships Chart (OV-4) to include the number of personnel, by skill set, and the training needed for each skill set in each organization. Performance measures and goals need to be included in the architecture (associated with the major business processes, for example) that show the impact on productivity while personnel are in training.

Using EA in Capital Planning and Investment Control (CPIC)

One of the original drivers for the development of EA in federal agencies was the need to justify IT investments in terms of expected business outcome improvements. The Clinger-Cohen Act (Clinger-Cohen Act, 1996), discussed in more detail in Chapter 4.1, was passed to enforce this relationship. Thus, it is not surprising that EA is widely used to support Capital Planning and Investment Control (CPIC) and that there is extensive guidance for using EA in this enterprise management process. CPIC includes Portfolio Management, is driven by Strategic Planning, and is linked to transition planning, as discussed later in this chapter. CPIC usually impacts the "how" and "when" dimensions of change for an enterprise. That is, the investments involved tend to focus on changing business processes and their technology support, and this frequently includes changes in performance and business cycles. However, capital investments may also affect any of the "what," "where," and "who" dimensions as well. For example, if the enterprise is being expanded with the addition of new business processes, business services, or products, then new data types or major modifications to current data types may also be involved. If the enterprise uses CPIC to manage all its capital investments, then the acquisition, construction, or modification of facilities may also be included, especially since most modern facilities include built-in IT infrastructure. Changes to the business processes and locations may indirectly include changes to the organization, although changes in organization do not usually require additional funding.

This section covers relevant guidance from the Office of Management and Budget (OMB) on the investment management process and from the Government Accountability Office (GAO) on IT investment management process maturity. This guidance includes the use of EA in the investment management process. This guidance applies directly to all U.S. federal agencies and also provides some common-sense direction for commercial organizations, as much of the guidance is based on industry best practice.

EA in the Investment Management Process

This section reviews the investment management process requirements presented in OMB Circular A-130: Management of Federal Information Resources (OMB, 1996). OMB requires federal agencies to establish and maintain a CPIC process and use it to link the resources being invested in (that is, information and information technology) to the results achieved in meeting agency mission needs. The CPIC process must be based on the agency's EA and driven by its associated transition plan for transforming the as-is state into the to-be or target state. The CPIC process must have three phases:

- Selection
- Control
- Evaluation

An agency's CPIC process must be iterative. These CPIC process requirements are summarized in Figure 2.7-1 (GAO, 2004).

OMB expects agencies to develop two plans to support the CPIC process. One is a strategic plan, the Information Resources Management (IRM) Strategic Plan; the other is an operational (that is, yearly) plan, the Information Technology

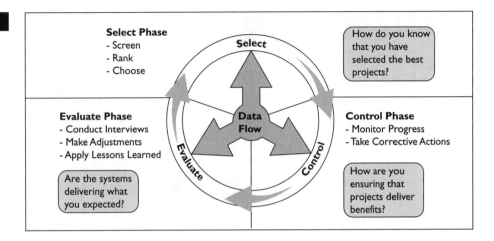

(IT) Capital Plan. The IRM Strategic Plan covers all the information resources managed by the agency. This plan describes how the agency IRM activities help to accomplish the agency missions as described in the agency Strategic Plan, which is required by another OMB Circular A-11: Preparation, Submission, and Execution of the Budget (OMB, 2010). The goal of the IRM Strategic Plan is to ensure that the agency IRM decisions are integrated with the other agency decisions as outlined in the agency Strategic Plan.

The IT Capital Plan is an implementation plan for the budget (fiscal) year. It supports the goals and missions of the IRM Strategic Plan and reflects the agency's EA. That is, the IT Capital Plan addresses only IT systems or infrastructure already identified through the agency's EA development and acceptance processes. So, all IT systems and infrastructure proposed in the IT Capital Plan should be identifiable in the near-term to-be agency EA (in the Systems Viewpoint or Services Viewpoint). Obviously, there may be changes from the EA based on budgetary restrictions and very recent technology changes. However, these deviations from the agency EA must be reconciled with the EA through the EA governance processes. Otherwise, the EA and the actual agency IT configuration may diverge. The IT Capital Plan contains the following:

- IT capital asset plans for major information systems or projects
- The agency IT investment portfolio
- The criteria used to select the investment into the portfolio

TABLE 2.7-1

How the IT
Capital Plan
Reflects the EA

IT Capital Plan Item	EA Viewpoint/View
System	Visible in Systems Viewpoint: System Interface Description (SV-1)
Service	Visible in Services Viewpoint: Services Context Description (SvcV-1), or Service Functionality Description (SvcV-4)
IT Infrastructure	Visible in Systems Viewpoint: Systems Resource Flow Description (SV-2) or Services Viewpoint: Services Resource Flow Description (SvcV-2)
Project	Visible in Project Viewpoint: Project Portfolio Relationships (PV-1) or Project to Capability Mapping (PV-3)
Relationship of Project to Systems, Services, or Infrastructure	Documented in All Viewpoint: Integrated Dictionary (AV-2)
Alignment of Projects to Agency Missions	Visible in Project Viewpoint: Project to Capability Mapping (PV-3)

- The process for controlling and managing the investments
- The process for evaluating investments using actual accomplishments versus planned performance
- A summary of the security plan

The IT Capital Plan thus reflects the agency's EA in the ways described in Table 2.7-1.

Each phase of the CPIC process is examined in more detail in the following subsections. The role of EA in the decision-making process of each phase is highlighted.

Example of Results of a Poor CPIC Process

Here is an example of what can happen when an agency has a poor CPIC process. Agency X invested in a project to update an existing headquarters system. The nominal justification for the project was to lower system maintenance costs by making the system easier to maintain. Part of the system update would make it client-server in design and thus make the system more easily distributable. However, the project transition plan revealed that the actual project strategy was to lower headquarters operations and maintenance (O&M) costs by transferring most of them to the regional offices. That is, the transition plan showed regional system data and server functionality being transferred down to the regional sites. The regional sites would become responsible for the regional data and its processing instead of all data and processing being centrally located at headquarters. However, there was no agency-level decision to make the regional sites responsible for the database administration and systems administration that would go along with this transfer. There were no plans for the regional sites to have personnel with skills for these new activities and no budget for either the new activities or the IT infrastructure to support them at the regional level. The project focused on local optimization (that is, the lowering of headquarters O&M costs) while impacting global enterprise optimization and costs in an unexamined, unapproved, and potentially negative way. After the project started to run late and over budget, a review team pointed out these problems with the project strategy. The project was cancelled but the money had already been spent and the agency never obtained any benefit from the project.

CPIC Selection Phase

In the CPIC selection phase, the agency identifies and analyzes each proposed project's risks and returns. The agency selects—that is, commits funds to—those projects that will best support the mission needs. Each proposed project or investment requires the analyses identified in Table 2.7-2, which also shows the EA input to each analysis type. In addition to needing the analyses shown in Table 2.7-2, each investment must answer the "three pesky questions" from Clinger-Cohen:

- Does the investment support core mission functions appropriate to the federal government?
- Are there any effective alternatives to the investment that exist in the private sector or from another government source?
- Do the work processes need to be simplified or redesigned to reduce costs, improve effectiveness, and maximize use of commercial off-the-shelf (COTS) solutions?

If any of the answers to these questions is yes, then alternatives to the investment need to be investigated. The EA provides information that helps answer these questions, such as the agency business (that is, work) processes; performance measures and goals for capabilities, business services, and business processes; and the systems that support the business processes.

Additional agency requirements for the CPIC selection phase include:

- Maintain a portfolio of major information systems (to prevent redundancy and to identify opportunities for sharing resources).

TABLE 2.7-2	Required Analysis	EA Input
Select Phase Investment Analyses	Return on Investment	Input to cost analysis in terms of systems/services, configurations, and required standards (tailored Systems or Services Viewpoint views) Input to return analysis in terms of business outcome improvement (performance measures and goals) associated with capability, business services, or products (Capability Viewpoint)
	Lifecycle Cost/Benefit Analysis (per System)	Input to cost analysis in terms of system/service configuration and required standards (tailored Systems or Services Viewpoint views) Input to benefits analysis (per system) in terms of system support to operations and line-of-sight performance measures from business outcome goals to business processes and systems (Capability Viewpoint, tailored Operational Viewpoint, and tailored Systems/Services Viewpoint)
	Risk Analysis	Input may vary with the analysis process used but includes support for technology risk analysis (Systems or Services Viewpoint and Standards Viewpoint), single-point-of-failure analysis (Systems or Services Viewpoint and Operational Viewpoint), and resource adequacy analysis (Operational Viewpoint)
	Consistency with Federal, Agency, and Bureau EAs	Input is the entire EA
	Redundancy Analysis	Input in the form of system/service to operational activity mapping to identify potential sources of IT capability redundancy (Systems or Services Viewpoints)
	Security and Privacy Analyses	Input is entire EA (views will require tailoring)

■ Ensure that the selected process or system maximizes usefulness of information, minimizes the burden on the public, and preserves security and privacy.

■ Ensure that the process or system facilitates accessibility.

■ Establish oversight mechanisms to evaluate and ensure continuing security, interoperability, and availability of systems and data.

Note that some of the analyses in Table 2.7-2 support the preceding requirements.

CPIC Control Phase

In the CPIC control phase, the agency ensures that as projects develop and investment expenditures continue, the project continues to meet mission requirements at the expected levels of cost and risk. The OMB requires the enterprise to use a performance-based management approach to controlling projects. Such an approach includes establishing performance measures for projects so that progress toward milestones and desired capabilities can be measured and that timeliness and quality of products and overall project costs can be assessed and controlled. In this way, actual project performance is measured and compared to expected (that is, planned) results. In addition, the agency must establish oversight mechanisms for periodic review of IT systems against changing mission needs, including future system performance goals and interoperability and maintenance requirements. Together, the performance-based management processes and oversight mechanisms ensure that major information systems proceed toward system development lifecycle milestones and continue to deliver intended benefits, meet user needs, and offer security protections.

Note that EA development projects need to be managed using the same type of performance-based management and oversight mechanisms so that EA milestones are reached. The EA is developed and maintained on schedule and transition milestones specified in the EA are met.

For the control phase, the relevant to-be phase of the EA includes information about the following:

- Future system performance goals (Services Viewpoint or tailored Systems Viewpoint views)
- Interoperability requirements (Systems or Services Viewpoint views)
- Technology change requirements (Systems or Services Technology Forecasts [SV-9 or SvcV-9] and Standards Forecast [StdV-2])

The EA also provides input into the following analyses needed to meet the OMB requirements previously listed:

- Capability
- System performance
- Benefits
- Security

CPIC Evaluation Phase

The CPIC evaluation phase starts after the IT system has been delivered and is in use. In the CPIC evaluation phase, the agency compares the actual project and information system results to the expected or planned results. During evaluation, the project's impact on mission performance is assessed and needed changes or modifications in the project are identified. In addition, the investment management processes are revised based on any lessons learned from the project results.

OMB requires an agency to conduct post-implementation reviews (PIRs) of information systems to validate estimated benefits and costs. The agency needs to ensure a positive return on investments. So, during each system PIR, the agency needs to decide whether continuation, modification, or termination of the system is necessary. Part of a PIR involves reassessing the investment's business case and compliance against the EA, including technical compliance. Another result of the PIRs is a set of lessons learned that can be used to update the capital planning process.

The most current version of the as-is EA should be used during the PIRs to evaluate EA compliance of existing information systems. This EA also supports the update of the investment's business case analysis, cost analysis, and return on investment. The system decisions made as a result of the PIR, concerning system modification or termination, should be used to update the EA.

EA in Investment Management Maturity

The GAO Information Technology Investment Management (ITIM) Framework provides more detailed guidance on the role of EA in investment management and on investment process evolution. The ITIM Framework is designed to assess the maturity of an agency's investment management process and to guide process improvement. The ITIM Framework should be used with other relevant GAO guidance, such as the GAO EA Maturity Model Framework (EAMMF) (GAO, 2003).

The ITIM has five stages, as summarized in Figure 2.7-2 (GAO, 2004):

- Stage 1: creating investment awareness
- Stage 2: building the investment foundation
- State 3: developing a complete investment portfolio
- Stage 4: improving the investment process
- Stage 5: leveraging IT for strategic outcomes

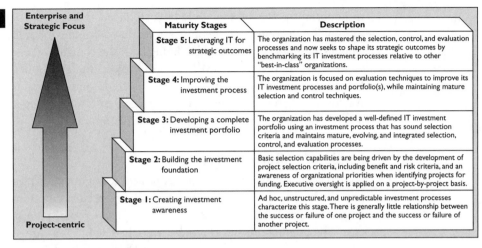

FIGURE 2.7-2

ITIM Provides a
Maturity Model

The agency EA plays an important role in each stage except stage 1. The ITIM introduces the important concept of "reselection" for IT projects and information systems that further refines financial management guidance from the OMB. Each stage is reviewed in more detail in the subsections that follow.

Stage 1: Creating Investment Awareness

An agency at stage 1 maturity is selecting investments in an unstructured, ad hoc manner. Project outcomes are unpredictable and successes are not repeatable. Most agencies at stage 1 maturity have some type of project selection process in place as part of their annual budgeting activity. However, this selection process is frequently rudimentary, poorly documented, and inconsistently applied. During stage 1, the agency is creating awareness of the investment process.

Stage 2: Building the Investment Foundation

During stage 2 maturity, the agency develops critical processes that lay the foundation for a sound IT investment process. These processes include basic selection capabilities, including selection criteria—benefit criteria, risk criteria, and organizational priorities—and basic project control capabilities. Other foundation elements include an IT investment board and identified business needs and opportunities. These critical processes should utilize input from the agency EA.

An important process that should be introduced at stage 2 is the concept of reselection. Reselection is an ongoing process that continues for as long as a project is receiving funding. (This should be during both the control and evaluation phases, as described previously, from OMB A-130.) Projects in development that are not meeting goals and objectives should be "deselected," and projects in O&M should receive continuing reviews (that is, PIRs). Stage 2 calls for a policy-driven, structured method for reselecting ongoing projects for further funding.

Example of Failure to Reselect

A national agency personnel and payroll project (Songini, 2005) was approved to move the health services personnel, payroll, and related functions from legacy, stovepiped systems to a COTS integrated enterprise resource planning (ERP) package. The original transition project was scheduled to last three years at a cost of $10.7 million. However, after ten years and $180 million (the cost of a 600-bed hospital), the work on the project was finally stopped. The pilot site had problems, and the first four installations continued to have numerous problems. Some employees were not being paid, and others were paid the wrong amount. The overall benefits of the project were questionable because of the manual labor involved in fixing errors and continuously updating the system. (COTS ERP packages usually need to be "customized" to fit the specific enterprise where they are to be installed.)

This project is also an example of what can happen when projects are undertaken without a sound as-is EA in place. Without the as-is EA, an accurate assessment of the costs and risks of using the COTS ERP package could not be made. The enterprise did not understand the true complexities of the legacy business processes and systems. This complexity was discovered piecemeal as errors and problems occurred with the new system. The project discovered over 2,500 variations in payment "arrangements" across the entire health care system. This level of complexity was not understood when the customization for the COTS package was first estimated, so the project cost estimate was unrealistic.

Stage 3: Developing a Complete Investment Portfolio

At stage 3, the agency moves from project-centric processes to a portfolio approach and builds on its project-centric management processes. The potential investments are evaluated based on how well they support the agency's mission, strategies, and strategic goals. The investment processes themselves are evaluated through the results of PIRs.

The portfolio management processes rely on information from the EA, and these links between the EA and the investment portfolio processes are explicitly defined and documented. The portfolio selection criteria are based on information from the EA.

Stage 4: Improving the Investment Process

At stage 4, the focus is on improving the investment processes based on lessons learned. The agency uses evaluation techniques to improve its IT investment processes and its IT portfolio. Many of these lessons learned are outcomes from PIRs. The agency is able to identify and deselect obsolete, high-risk, or low-value IT investments. One of the criteria used to evaluate investments is alignment with the most current version of the EA. The agency also conducts IT succession activities as it removes deselected investments from its portfolio, retains currently beneficial investments, and adds new investments.

Stage 5: Levering IT for Strategic Outcomes

At stage 5, the agency shapes its strategic outcomes by accomplishing the following:

- Using its EA as a critical frame of reference to ensure alignment of investments with the target (to-be) architecture
- Learning from other organizations
- Continuously improving the manner in which it uses IT to support and improve business outcomes
- Focusing on flexibility and becoming a more agile enterprise that relies on its architecture for its vision of the future and its investment process as a means of implementing that future

The agency looks for breakthrough information technologies that enable it to change and improve its business performance. In terms of architecture, this means that the agency does forecasting and tracking of relevant technologies.

Summary of the Role of EA in ITIM

By establishing the agency's EA, including the as-is environment, the to-be environment, and the transition plan, decision makers have an explicit and meaningful structural framework for making IT decisions. The EA and sequencing plan (that is, the transition plan) can be useful guides in managing the succession of information systems and in evaluating which investments should be phased out and which should be retained. The IT investment process should specify how it coordinates with other agency plans, processes, and documents, including the strategic plan, budget, and EA, at a minimum. In particular, the EA should be reflected in the selection criteria for investments. Policies and procedures for identifying, classifying, and organizing business needs and IT projects typically specify that each IT system is within the agency's EA and established security standards. Further, selected investments that are not consistent with the EA should either be assimilated into the EA or be provided with a waiver. There should be a documented process for reconciling differences between the IT investment portfolio and the organization's EA.

Using EA in Reorganization

There are two types of situations that involve organizational transformation. One is reorganization without other types of changes. The other is reorganization as part of business process reengineering that may involve changes in location as well as changes in organization and business process. We will look at both cases.

"Pure" Reorganization

Many enterprises routinely reorganize without including change in other dimensions. A typical problem with this "pure" reorganization in enterprises without an EA is that some required performers, activities, or processes are overlooked in the reorganization. Personnel are confused when they can't find a home for their processes or activities on the new organization chart and do not know to whom they report. Other confusion results if the performers of one activity can no longer locate the performers of the next activity in the process and don't know whom to hand their outputs to. Enterprises with an EA can use the business processes and activities (from the Activity Model OV-5) as a checklist to ensure that responsibilities for all current processes and activities are accounted for in the new organization. The performers from the Operational Resource Flow Description (OV-2) can be mapped to the new organizations to ensure that all groups of performers are also accounted for. Checking the relationships among the Activity Model, the Operational Resource Flow Description, and the updated Organizational Relationships Chart (OV-4) ensures that the relationships between organizations and performers and between performers and activities remain consistent after the reorganization. These relationships are illustrated in Figure 2.7-3. In addition, the critical working groups in the as-is Organizational Relationships Chart

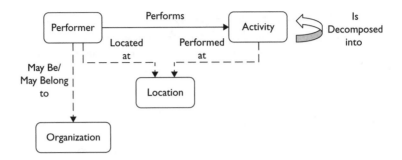

FIGURE 2.7-3

Relationships
Among
Organizations,
Performers, and
Activities

can be reviewed for relevance in the new organization. The working groups that are still needed can be reconstituted in the new organization and their membership redefined in terms of the new organizations.

Organizational Transformation in Conjunction with Other Transformations

Organization transformation is a frequent side effect of business process reengineering. Business processes can be reengineered to add new capabilities, business services, or enterprise products or to improve performance of existing processes. The new business processes need to be analyzed to identify the performers in terms of skill sets and numbers needed to perform each activity. Then the groups of performers need to be allocated to new or existing organizations. The EA views and data provide a way to ensure that the relationships among the performers, activities, and organizations remain consistent in light of changed or additional business processes.

Organization transformation is also frequently associated with location transformation. As agencies move to new locations or alter their offices or workspaces, the resulting rearrangement of personnel may result in a need for reorganization. Performer groups, who used to perform the same activities in different locations and under the control of different organizations, may become co-located and merged into the same organization to simplify the management structure. Similarly, groups of performers who were co-located and under control of the same organization may end up physically separated and reorganized into separate organizations to keep management local. Again, the EA views and data provide a way to ensure that the relationships among the performers, activities, and organizations remain consistent in light of changed or additional business processes. The models support analysis to ensure that new organizational structures minimize redundancy and keep the management structure as flat as is reasonable.

Transition Planning

Many government definitions of enterprise architecture require the architecture to include an as-is architecture, one or more to-be or target architectures, and a transition plan. However, architecture developers usually think of an enterprise architecture in terms of one phase of that architecture (that is, the as-is or to-be phase). Certainly, the different phase architectures are used to develop the transition plan, although some would say that the transition plan should be developed in conjunction with a to-be architecture in order to ensure that the to-be architecture is indeed reachable from the current architecture. Part of this relationship between the to-be architecture and the transition plan is related to the actual timeframe of the to-be architecture or architectures involved.

Certainly, if the to-be architecture in question is a near-term architecture—that is, an architecture for the next budget cycle or next few budget cycles—and is based on relatively small changes to the as-is architecture, the transition plan can be developed after the to-be architecture. However, care must be taken to ensure that changes are not made to too many dimensions of change at once.

If there are multiple to-be architectures—for example, a long-term or vision architecture—and multiple intermediate to-be architectures, as are often found in segment-level architectures, then coordination of the transition plan and the various to-be architectures is more critical. The intermediate to-be architectures can be thought of as documenting specific key stages in the more detailed transition plan. For example, consider a segment-level architecture that will be used to guide the consolidation of a common business function from multiple suborganizations into a centralized, stand-alone organization. The as-is architecture is needed as a starting point for planning the consolidation process, whereas the target or vision to-be architecture documents the end goal of the consolidation process and may include additional new capabilities or business services. The intermediate to-be architectures document the expected stages in the consolidation process, while the transition plans document the details of transforming the enterprise from one stage to the next.

In this transformation, care must be taken not to affect too many dimensions of change during each step. The first phase or stage of the example transformation might focus primarily on changing location. All the people, processes, and needed resources for the common business function can be co-located. This change in location may require remodeling of existing facilities, acquisition of new facilities, or both. It may also require some reorganization so that some of the existing management organizations that oversee the common business function are merged. The first intermediate to-be architecture documents the expected architecture at the end of the co-location process.

The second phase or stage of the transformation might focus primarily on consolidating and standardizing the business process for the common business function. This involves process change and related changes to data, IT, roles, and, potentially, skills. This phase also involves further consolidation of organizations or reorganization. This part of the transformation is more challenging, as it involves changes in more dimensions. This phase might therefore take longer or even be broken down into subphases. The second intermediate to-be architecture documents the expected architecture at the end of the business process consolidation. This to-be architecture must evolve as the details of business process consolidation—for example, systems or automated services consolidation or replacement—become clearer. The initial to-be architecture for this phase may be more high-level or conceptual. The architecture will become more concrete and detailed as the decisions identified in the transition plan are made.

The final phase of the transformation might address the more visionary aspects of the enterprise strategic planning that initiated the transformation. This phase may call for additional management or organizational changes to provide increased oversight of this now common business process as well as increased automation of the process, making the business function more easily accessible to distributed facilities of the enterprise. The long term target or vision to-be architecture documents the expected state of the enterprise on the completion of this final phase of transformation. Again, the vision architecture will evolve over time and become more detailed and concrete. Note that the whole transformation process needs close coordination with the enterprise's strategic planning function. The phased or staged transformation process can be outlined in an expanded High-Level Operational Concept Graphic (OV-1), as illustrated in Figures 2.7-4 through 2.7-7.

As-Is Architecture Concept

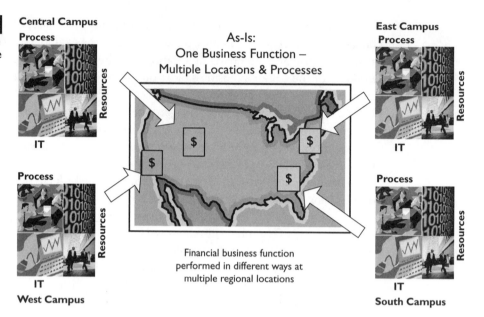

Central Campus

Process

Resources

IT

Process

Resources

IT

West Campus

As-Is:
One Business Function –
Multiple Locations & Processes

Financial business function
performed in different ways at
multiple regional locations

East Campus

Process

Resources

IT

Process

Resources

IT

South Campus

To-Be Architecture for Co-location Concept

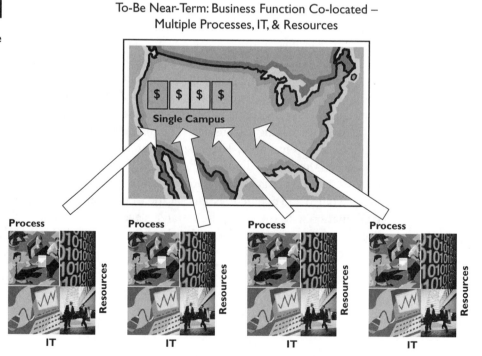

To-Be Near-Term: Business Function Co-located –
Multiple Processes, IT, & Resources

Single Campus

Process

Resources

IT

Process

Resources

IT

Process

Resources

IT

Process

Resources

IT

FIGURE 2.7-6

To-Be Architecture
for Process
Consolidation
Concept

To-Be Midterm: Business Function Co-located with Standard Processes, IT, and Unified Resources

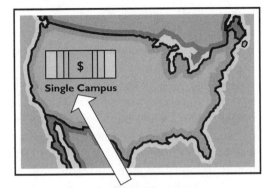

Single Campus

Standard
Process

Benefits:
• Standardized Processes
• Lower O&M Costs

Unified Resources

Standard IT

FIGURE 2.7-7

Vision
Architecture
Concept

To-Be Vision: Business Function Accessible from Mobile Devices

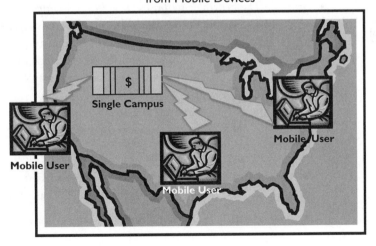

Single Campus

Mobile User

Mobile User

Mobile User

Security

Enterprise architecture is a good tool for addressing chronic problems with security. In the past, security architectures addressed only IT issues and were not integrated with the rest of the technical architecture. However, security needs to be traceable to and driven by business needs. The enterprise needs a holistic approach to security with all aspects—physical, procedural, and technical—well integrated. The holistic approach is especially important because many times IT security measures are bypassed using "social engineering" techniques that attack weaknesses in physical or procedural security as well as weaknesses in personnel training and awareness. The major issue with integrating security into enterprise architecture is how to include security information with the architecture data and views. The standard views (discussed in the third section of this book) do not directly address security issues, so tailoring will be required. In this section, we look at some of the guidance provided on security issues and outline an approach to including security in enterprise architecture.

There are general sources of security guidance that enterprises can use. Most governments have guidance for both national security and non-national security information systems. In the United States, the National Institute of Standards and Technology (NIST) provides this guidance in the form of standards (Federal Information Processing Standards [FIPS]) and guidance (special publications in the 800 series). These standards and guidance are focused on information systems. A risk management framework is also included in the NIST materials. OMB's Federal Enterprise Architecture Program Management Office and the Federal CIO Council also provide *The Federal Enterprise Architecture Security and Privacy Profile (SPP)*, which provides a methodology for addressing information security and privacy from a business-driven, enterprise perspective (Federal Enterprise Architecture Program Management Office, 2006). On the more generic and commercial side, there are texts, such as John Sherwood, Andrew Clark, and David Lynas's *Enterprise Security Architecture* (2005).

Some of the NIST guidance (NIST, 2009) identifies the following "security objectives" that can be associated with the information processed by non-national security information systems:

- **Confidentiality** Protection from unauthorized or unintended disclosure.
- **Integrity** Protection from unauthorized modification.
- **Availability** Protection from denial of authorized access.

However, at least two of these security objectives, integrity and availability, can also be applied to noninformation business assets such as personnel and physical resources. For example, personnel need to be protected from injury on the job ("integrity") and they or their skills need to be available to the enterprise ("availability") if business processes are to proceed as necessary. This latter requirement is why continuity of operations planning, including backup plans for key personnel, is usually included under security. This approach of extending security objectives to noninformation assets is one way to start to extend some of the available guidance to look at security from the enterprise business perspective.

A basic approach to dealing with including security in an architecture is to follow the advice of the Six Step process, discussed in Chapter 2.2, by identifying appropriate security-focused stakeholders and including their issues and questions in the planning of the architecture. This approach is consistent with the SPP methodology. Here are some example security-related issues that might be included:

- What mission/business assets need to be protected and in what way? This question requires identification of all business asset types, including information, information systems, and other resources, and association of security objectives, such as the NIST security objectives discussed previously, with each of the asset types.

- What logical and physical data elements represent the protected assets? It is important to ensure that the protections (that is, security objectives) associated with physical assets are consistent with the protections associated with the information (both logical and physical) about that type of asset. For example, if some kinds of assets, such as unexcavated archeological sites, should be confidential, then the location of these sites (that is, information about these sites) should have the confidentiality security objective as well.

- How important to the enterprise are these protections? That is, what are the criticality and priority of these protections? A risk analysis will be needed to determine criticality and priority.

- What approaches (prevention, detection, response) should be taken to ensure the protections for each asset? Again, choices here need to be based on risk analysis.

- Who is responsible for the protection of assets? The question here is really about identifying the steward for each type of asset. Who has the business authority to grant access and other permissions for the asset? The steward is not, in general, a security group, whose role is to arrange for technical access based on approval (that is, authorization) from the asset steward.

- Who (in terms of roles) is allowed access to the protected assets?
- What mission or business events or cycles involve protected assets?
- What mission or business processes or activities access protected assets?
- What systems or system functions support the access of business activities to protected assets?
- What types of security services support the security approaches? This is a business-level question rather than a technical question. It is not an implementation question. For example, access control is a type of security service that can be used to support a prevention approach to enforce confidentiality, but access control can be implemented in a variety of ways, including ways that don't involve technology. Access control can mean a guard at a door or fence with a gate as well as some form of automated controls governing access to data or applications on a computer. Once the types of security services needed are identified, then concern can pass to how these services can be implemented.
- How should implementation of these services be allocated to physical, procedural, and technical means?
- What system events and cycles involve protected data?
- What types of system mechanisms or functions are used to support the security services? For example, there are a variety of different mechanisms used to implement identification and authentication (I&A) services. I&A can use something you know (that is, a password), something you have (that is, a secure ID), something you are (biometric), or some combination of these other mechanisms.
- What system components implement the selected mechanisms?
- How do all the security-related system pieces fit together? The answer to this question needs to address both static and dynamic relationships.
- Are all the business assets currently adequately protected and will they be adequately protected in the future? Judging adequacy here also requires a risk analysis.

Inclusion of security-related stakeholders and issues will require additional views or models to be included in an architecture and will certainly require additional tailoring of these views. For example, asking about stewardship for assets will require the Organizational Relationships Chart (OV-4) to be tailored to include information about the stewardship roles and responsibilities of each organization. The requirement to identify asset stewards may also cause more organizations to be included in the Organizational Relationships Chart. That is, organizations that might otherwise be considered outside the scope of a solution-level architecture might need to be included if these organizations are stewards for the protected assets included in the architecture (that is, those assets being created, accessed, or modified by the business processes included in the scope of the architecture). For an enterprise-level architecture, inclusion of security issues might cause the inclusion of views or models to identify all the high-level business asset types, their security objectives, and some additional security attributes that should be consistent across the enterprise, such as overall criticality and priority of the security attributes for these asset types. Segment- and solution-level architectures can then add detail to the business assets within their scope and further refine their security objectives and attributes within the context of the specific segment or solution. Enterprise-level architectures might also need to include some views that set standards for security services and mechanisms that need to be uniform across the enterprise.

The architects also face the problem of what to do with the risk analysis. Some results of the risk analysis can be included in tailored versions of the standard views, such as criticality and priority, but there is no view or model included that captures the risk analysis itself. The risk analysis can be considered as outside the scope of architecture, or a fit-for-purpose view can be defined to capture the key elements of the risk analysis.

Questions

1. Who are the architecture users in your organization? What decisions are made with input from an architecture? What level of architecture (enterprise, segment, or solution) is this input from?

2. Does your organization have an investment management process? If so, do a quick assessment to see how it rates on the GAO's ITIM scale.

3. Does your organization have all three types of investment management phases (selection, control, and evaluation)? What EA information is used in the reviews in each phase?

4. Does your organization maintain a portfolio of IT investments? How is this portfolio coordinated with any architecture? What documented criteria are used to select or remove investments from the portfolio?

5. How does your organization manage organizational change? That is, what is the process for revising or developing new organizational structures? Is EA information used in this process? What EA data is or would be useful in this process?

6. Does your organization use a business process reengineering methodology when business processes need to be upgraded or changed? If so, does this methodology address reorganization? What EA information is used by the methodology and how are the multiple domains of change coordinated?

7. Have you participated in any transition planning activities for your own organization or for any customers? If so, how many domains of change were involved? How many intermediate stages were used to help phase the transition? What types of architecture data were used in transition planning? Would the existence of a documented architecture have helped with the planning process?

8. Develop a set of High-Level Operational Concept Graphics (OV-1), similar to those presented in this chapter, to describe the phases in any transition that you know about.

9. Consider the example security-related questions presented in this chapter. Can you use them to select and tailor some architecture views to support security following the planning process introduced in Chapter 2.2? Remember that you will need to scope the architecture first. (Details on the views can be found in Part III of this book.)

Reference List

Clinger-Cohen Act (Information Technology Management Reforms Act) of 1996. (1996). www.cio.gov/Documents/it_management_reform_act_feb_1996.html.

Department of Defense. (2009). *Department of Defense Architecture Framework Version 2.0.* www.cio-nil.defense.gov/sites/dodaf20.

Federal Enterprise Architecture Program Management Office. (2006). *The Federal Enterprise Architecture Security and Privacy Profile Version 2.0.* www.cio.gov/documents/Security_and_Privacy_Profile_v2.pdf.

Government Accountability Office. (2003). *Information technology: a framework for assessing and improving enterprise architecture management Version 1.1.* (GAO-03-584G). www.gao.gov.

Government Accountability Office. (2004). *Information technology investment management: a framework for assessing and improving process maturity Version 1.1.* (GAO-04-0394G). www.gao.gov.

National Institute of Standards and Technology (NIST). (2009). *Recommended security controls for federal information systems,* rev. 3, SP 800-53. csrc.nist.gov/publications/nistpubs/800-53-rev3/sp800-53-rev3-final_updated-errata_05-01-2010.pdf.

Office of Management and Budget. (1996). OMB *Circular A-130: management of federal information resources.* www.whitehouse.gov/search/site/Circular%20A-130?filters=im_og_gid:10275.

Office of Management and Budget. (2010). OMB *Circular A-11: preparation, submission, and execution of the budget.* www.whitehouse.gov/search/site/Circular%20A-11?filters=im_og_gid:10275.

Sherwood, John, Clark, Andrew, & Lynas, David. (2005). *Enterprise security architecture.* CMPBooks.

Songini, Marc. (2005). *Irish agency halts work on two SAP application projects.* Computerworld, October 17. www.computerworld.com/s/article/105468/Irish_agency_halts_work_on_two_SAP_applications.

Part III

Viewpoints and Models

3.1

Introduction to Viewpoints and Models

I f you have ever been lost in a strange town without a map or a Global Positioning System (GPS), you know the importance of a map and a plan. As you drive from one unfamiliar-looking intersection to another, you vow that the next time, things will be different—you will arm yourself with a map or GPS!

If you have ever tried to build additions to an older house without the original plans, you know all about the surprises you encounter along the way. You know that you probably should have surveyed that old construction, made pictures, and taken measurements before starting on your remodeling project. As you are starting to demolish what looks like an internal wall, you find to your horror that it is also a load-bearing wall.

If you have ever tried to assemble a complex piece of mechanical equipment without reading the user manual first, you know the importance of clear pictures, schematics, checklists, and directions. You are sitting there with a half-finished assembly only to find out that your first step was wrong and you are now 30 steps into the assembly with no hope of fixing the problem without dismantling all the work you have completed. You made a promise that henceforth, reading the manual would be the first thing you do before touching screwdriver, wrench, or power drill.

When you joined that first job in a large enterprise, it took you awhile to get oriented to the facilities, the people, the organization structures, and the implicit culture and obtain clear knowledge of your responsibilities. As you walked, lost in the maze of cubicles, greeting the CEO as another face in the corridor and insulting the Vice President of Marketing at a meeting in a minor argument that escalated into a full battle, you vowed that someday, you'll have it all together.

The truth of the matter is that all of us as human beings are using models to help us fathom the unknown. For the vast majority of us who are not adventurous, we are always looking for familiar patterns among the largely unknown to guide us toward a course of actions that we hope are non-risky and non-disastrous. We have become used to reading the language of everyday models. And everyday models tend to be represented in the form of pictures.

Models

Pictorial representations (models) are tools for helping readers orient themselves and understand the larger context. Pictures are invaluable in architecture work. But is a specific picture universally clear across a wide audience with different backgrounds, knowledge, and experiences? For example, will the picture of a bar code on a product provide any significance to a Bushmen tribe in deepest Africa, removed from commerce? It becomes immediately clear that there are specific audiences for specific picture content—and that the meaning of objects inside a picture is also subjective.

The language of engineering and architecture is the language of models. A model is often a formal pictorial representation (though models are not restricted to pictures) that has specific meaning to a specific audience inside the symbols and the connections between the symbols.

Examples of Models

In the home, we are surrounded by models of various aspects of the house, some we think of as traditional blueprints, and some that are not:

- A floor plan was used by the architect to design the layout of the various rooms. The rooms on the floor plan are connected by corridors and doorways that allow people to go from one room into another. The floor plan also contains locations of openings such as windows. It provides a ready assessment of the layout—you can easily tell whether noise in the family room can disturb people sleeping in the bedrooms, for example. The floor plan also partitions the layout of a large building into multiple floor plan sections that lay out multiple floors. The plan is used by the electrical contractor; the heating, ventilation, and air conditioning (HVAC) contractor; and other trades to determine and design the layout of electrical sockets, plumbing fixtures, built-in cabinets, and appliances and the routing of electrical wiring, plumbing pipes, sewage pipes, and heating and cooling ducting.

- The electrical wiring diagram, usually overlaid on the floor plan, shows the location of electrical sockets, junction boxes, switches, circuit protection panel, and locations of lamps, electrical appliances, ceiling fans, and other items. The electrical wiring diagram is used by the electrical contractor to estimate capacity for wires, safety factors, as well as compliance with building codes before actual electrical work can commence.

- The plumbing diagram, also usually overlaid on the floor plan, shows the location of the plumbing fixtures such as faucets, toilets, cisterns, tanks, showers, tubs, sinks, water heaters, water filters, water softeners, and the runs of plumbing that connect them. The plumbing diagram shows the hot and cold water flow paths. The plumbing diagram is used by the plumbing contractor to estimate pipe capacities; separation of hot and cold water circuits; and requirements for water softening, overflow protection, pressure regulation, and more.

- The HVAC contractor also uses a diagram that overlays the duct work on the floor plan. He or she is interested in ensuring straight runs to prevent air flow from being hampered, as well as ensuring that height clearances are maintained once the ducts are installed to avoid ceilings that are too low for a comfortable living space.

- The realty listing for a specific property in an automated listing service is also another type of standard model, although we may not think of it as such. By standardizing the format in which information about a house is listed, it becomes easy for potential buyers to compare houses—number of bedrooms, full baths, square footage, year built, type of construction, special features, or land area, to cite a few example criteria. The realty listing model is used by a real estate agent to list a property and by the owner to make a full disclosure related to the property.

- The mortgage application form for a loan application for a house is yet another nontraditional form of a standard model. By standardizing the questions and information about the property and the applicant loan, providers can make consistent decisions on loan awards. The mortgage application model is used by a borrower to make full disclosure of the property and his or her capacity to repay the loan; it is also used by the lender to assess the creditworthiness of the borrower and the collateral potential of the property being purchased.

Models Versus Pictures

Architecture models (sometimes called blueprints, from the old engineering drawings made on ammonia paper) are formal representations, not simply randomly drawn pictures. They follow a discipline and act as a graphical language for communicating ideas, specifications, designs, constraints, and relationships in a structured manner. The following are some of the differences between a randomly drawn or constructed picture and an architecture model:

- *Models show symbols that are universally understood within a profession.* The symbols showing a window or a door opening are understood by architects as well as electrical, HVAC, and plumbing contractors. Commonality is achieved by sustained practice over a long period of time, the availability of standards that are promulgated by standards bodies, or generally accepted methodologies that prescribe commonality.

- *Models relate symbols with meaningful lines.* The line that denotes a connection between two plumbing fixtures is clearly meaningful to a plumber as is the electrical diagram that shows a wire between two electrical points. Model elements have relationships based on some defined semantics—that is, they are not haphazard assemblies of architecture elements but follow constraints described by a methodology or accepted set of practices. These semantics may be driven by the laws of nature, existential relationships, human creations, or abstractions. Architecture models are therefore pictorial or other representations that have structure and meaning to specific audiences.

- *Models are consistent from blueprint to blueprint.* Blueprints are drawn using the same symbol set and line set repeatedly. In other words, they are drawn using the same methodology. There is a common grammar that is used by a type of blueprint. The grammar defines the types of permissible symbols and the types of relationships that are permissible between them. For example, a toilet cannot be mounted on a ceiling.

- *Models, though generally pictorial in nature, also have a lot of text annotation next to the symbols that elaborate some aspect of the symbol.* Text next to a toilet fixture may indicate the cistern and toilet water capacity in keeping with building codes designed to conserve water in certain areas.

- *Models are specifically geared toward specific audiences.* Though the floor plan is used as a general orientation mechanism and is geared to a broader audience than the architect who drew them up, the electrical wiring diagram is geared toward the electrical contractor, the plumbing diagram is geared toward the plumbing contractor, and the HVAC diagram is geared toward the HVAC contractor. Blueprints are therefore designed to inform a specific audience with a specific viewpoint and interest in the design.

- *Models are used as commonly understood representations of design across stakeholders.* The city or county inspector uses the same blueprint that is used by the architect. The Fire Department trying to fight a fire in a building will use the floor plan if available to understand the layout of the building. Every hotel is required to display a floor plan showing an evacuation route for every floor inside the door of each hotel room. A hotel guest simply has to consult the floor plan to make a quick exit when the fire alarm goes off.

Viewpoints and Interests

We have presented a wide range of models all purporting to represent some aspect of the house, though none of the models is a replacement for the other. Each of these models supports the interests of some party but they all relate to the same residential property. Some of these parties have no interest in some of the types of models. For example, the mortgage lender, satisfied that the property meets code is not interested in the HVAC diagrams or the electrical blueprints. Each of these different stakeholders has a different viewpoint and interests that stem from that viewpoint.

Viewpoints may contain overlapping information. For example, the number of rooms on the floor plan must exactly coincide with the number of rooms stated in the realty listing. As we have discussed, time and time again, the importance of an integrated architecture is that all the models share common architecture elements and represent them consistently with the same names, properties, and definitions.

Viewpoints make objects invisible. The average homeowner is unaware of the pressure regulator that the county requires on his plumbing because his viewpoint is not that of a plumber. A traveler walking through the concourses of RMN Airport is oblivious of the equipment stacked against the wall inside the rooms he passes by—the door is locked and only authorized personnel are allowed inside. On the other hand, an airline employee with the right badge has full visibility of that same equipment because he or she is authorized to enter the room that contains the equipment.

Viewpoints are driven by self-interest. People have little time and patience for matters that do not concern them. Presenting elaborate wall chart–like models designed for one viewpoint may be totally counterproductive for an audience with a different viewpoint, as process, network, and data modelers have found out the hard way. How many architects have been disappointed that upper management showed little interest in the detailed flow charts that depicted workflows in great detail between four suborganizations but asked only two questions: "Which are the top 10 percent of activities that when reviewed and improved can reduce the overall time by at least 40 percent? And what is the impact of changing those activities?"

Understanding the viewpoints of the various audiences for a proposed architecture effort is one of the first activities to be undertaken and documented in the AV-1

Architecture Overview and Summary/Business Problem Statement model, as we will see in later parts of this book. An architecture effort frequently must satisfy more than one viewpoint. Investors are generally interested in the return on investment. Financial and operational management is interested in returns on assets and metrics that measure all the important health indicators for an enterprise (such as the balanced scorecard [BSC] measures). Engineering management is often interested in the various development and maintenance projects undertaken by the enterprise. They are also interested in getting clear, concise, yet comprehensive business requirements for driving the projects to a successful completion where solutions address business problems.

IEEE 1471 Definitions of Viewpoints and Views (IEEE 1471)

Arguably, one of the earliest bodies to standardize the concepts and terminology of architecture in a domain of systems engineering is the Institution of Electrical and Electronics Engineers (IEEE). IEEE is an internationally recognized standards body that has brought a number of standards to the world in the area of electrical engineering, computing, and communications. The topic of systems engineering becomes especially important when systems become increasingly complex and the number of stakeholders begins to multiply and IEEE recognized the increasing complexity of electrical, electronics, computing, and communication systems as the technology evolved and provided increasing capabilities to enterprises for building very large systems, families of systems, and systems of systems.

The Institute of Electrical and Electronics Engineers (IEEE) offers these definitions related to viewpoints and views:

- **Architectural description (AD)**   A collection of products to document an architecture.
- **Architecture**   The fundamental organization of a system embodied in its components, their relationships to each other, and to the environment, and the principles guiding its design and evolution.
- **System**   A collection of components organized to accomplish a specific function or set of functions. The term *system* encompasses individual applications; systems in the traditional sense; subsystems; and systems of systems, product lines, product families, whole enterprises, and other aggregations of interest.
- **System stakeholder**   An individual, team, or organization (or classes thereof) with interests in, or concerns relative to, a system.

- **View**   A representation of a whole system from the perspective of a related set of concerns.
- **Viewpoint**   A specification of the conventions for constructing and using a view. It is a pattern or template from which to develop individual views by establishing the purposes and audience for a view and the techniques for its creation and analysis.

TOGAF Definitions of Viewpoints and Views (TOGAF 9-2009)

The Open Group Architecture Framework also attempts to standardize architecting vocabulary. Many of these definitions are borrowed from the IEEE definitions and are not inconsistent with those definitions.

A *view* is a representation of a whole system from the perspective of a related set of concerns. *Concerns* are the key interests that are crucially important to the stakeholders in the system and determine the acceptability of the system. Concerns may pertain to any aspect of the system's functioning, development, or operation, including considerations such as performance, reliability, security, distribution, and evolvability.

In capturing or representing the design of a system architecture, the architect typically creates one or more architecture models, possibly using different tools. A view comprises selected parts of one or more models, chosen so as to demonstrate to a particular stakeholder or group of stakeholders that their concerns are being adequately addressed in the design of the system architecture.

- A *viewpoint* defines the perspective from which a view is taken. More specifically, a viewpoint defines how to construct and use a view (by means of an appropriate schema or template); the information that should appear in the view; the modeling techniques for expressing and analyzing the information; and a rationale for these choices (for example, the viewpoint may describe the purpose and intended audience of the view).
- A view is what you see. A viewpoint, in contrast, is where you are looking from—the vantage point or perspective that determines what you see.
- Viewpoints are generic and can be stored in libraries for reuse. A view is always specific to the architecture for which it was created.
- Every view has an associated viewpoint that describes it, at least implicitly. ISO/IEC 42010: 2007 encourages architects to define viewpoints explicitly. Making this distinction between the content and schema of a view may seem at first to impose unnecessary overhead, but it provides a mechanism for reusing viewpoints across different architectures.

Architecture views are representations of the overall architecture in terms meaningful to stakeholders. They enable the architecture to be communicated to and understood by the stakeholders so they can verify that the system will address their concerns.

DoDAF 2 Definition of Viewpoints and Views

Visualizing architectural data is accomplished through models (for example, the products described in previous versions of DoDAF). Models (which can be documents, spreadsheets, dashboards, or other graphical representations) serve as a template for organizing and displaying data in a more easily understood format. When data is collected and presented in this way, the result is called a *view*. Organized collections of views (often representing processes, systems, services, standards, and so on) are referred to as *viewpoints*, and with appropriate definitions, they are collectively called the *architectural description*.

Integrated Architecture Development

In the past, enterprises wound up building different models independently to satisfy individual viewpoints. Because the models were constructed independently, it was hard to match up elements of one model against elements of other models. In the Defense Department, the acquisition of a large asset such as an airplane involves many models, many documents, and many viewpoints—from the U.S. Air Force as the acquirer, to the acquisition community overseeing the orderly purchase of the asset, to the logistics community that delivers and maintains the asset, to the airframe manufacturer who is responsible for prototyping, designing, testing, manufacturing, and certifying the airplane for operations. Many of these models share information about the same asset. To coin an uncommon scenario, it would help if the general briefing the U.S. Air Force on the range, speed, and aerobatic characteristics of the proposed airplane were in sync with the specification document that went into the request for bids.

An integrated architecture is one where all the models that represent different facets of the architecture share and represent common architecture elements consistently. One of the goals of an enterprise architecture team is to deliver an integrated architecture. When teams are composed of team members who are organizationally and geographically separated, development of integrated architecture becomes difficult. As team members develop portions of the architectures independently, they will need to "merge" the portions and resolve inconsistencies that they encounter. A centralized repository is therefore essential for an integrated architecture development effort.

One of the unifying models of an integrated architecture is the AV-2 Integrated Data Dictionary model. In past modeling efforts, every modeling team tended to present individual glossaries explaining the architecture elements and relationships in their particular model. One way of enforcing that individual models are not dissonant or divergent is to enforce the need for a universal glossary that documents all the elements of all the models in a single place.

Throughout Part III of the book, we present some of the integrating aspects across different types of models—for example, the OV-3 Operational Resource Flow Matrix that depicts resource flows between performer pairs depending on the activities they are performing must tally with the activities that are presented in an OV-5 Activity Model. The performers that are depicted inside the OV-2 Operational Node Connectivity Model must be the same performers whose organizational structure is represented by the OV-4 Organization Relationships Chart.

Federated Architecture

Enterprises do not exist in isolation. They collaborate with other enterprises in many ways. In supply chain relationships, they manage inbound goods and outbound goods with collaborating enterprises—their suppliers and their customers. In outsourced or offshored business processing, they collaborate with providers of services, often in other countries around the globe. The various uniformed military services such as the Air Force, the Army, the Marine Corps, and the Navy collaborate in warfighting efforts in a joint force structure, united in their efforts to wage and win wars. Federal agencies collaborate to accomplish their mission. Fees for security transactions collected by the Securities and Exchange Commission are transmitted to the U.S. Treasury. The Federal Emergency and Management Agency collaborates with the Air National Guard and the Coast Guard in some search and rescue missions.

One method of explicitly interlocking business processes between collaborating enterprises who do not come under the same command structure and hence must collaborate using agreements, negotiations, rules of engagement, or memoranda is to specify how the architectures of the participating enterprises will provide for the information exchanges, the business process handoffs, and the role definitions and responsibilities required for accomplishing the mission.

A federated architecture is a collection of disparate architectures that connects activities across different collaborating enterprises through process handoffs and resource flows. The enterprises are collaborating based on common motivations and purpose. Federation is sometimes represented by following a "mission thread" —

a sequence of related activities from the start of a mission to the end of a mission regardless of the performing enterprise.

Another example of a method of representing federation is to replace specific activity performance roles in a Business Process Modeling Notation (BPMN) OV-5b Activity Model with the enterprises and their major activities and developing the mission threads.

Successful federated architecture development requires the following:

- **A sound governance structure** A sound governance structure applies accountability to the development and maintenance of architecture toward set objectives, facilitating the ability to federate. It places responsibility on processes such as configuration management and quality assurance.
- **Enterprise architecture services** Enterprise architecture services allow for the visibility, accessibility, and understandability of architecture information in a consistent and efficient manner across multiple enterprises. Every federating enterprise must provide visibility of its architecture elements through enterprise architecture services.
- **Federation Architecture Registry (FAR)** FAR is a "virtual" or linked architecture registry that is set up to provide visibility of elements from multiple architectures that form the federation, potentially from multiple collaborating organizations. A FAR provides for registration and linking of architecture metadata to enable the creation of navigable and searchable federated enterprise architectures. It enforces the policies and governance that surround the usage of architecture, thus reinforcing robust interfaces and data relationships. Sharing architecture and using information and services that exist improve the agility of architecture development.
- **Vocabulary crosswalks and mediation** When a federation is comprised of enterprises with dramatically different business terminology, there is a need for explicit vocabulary publishing as well as crosswalks between terms in different vocabularies that have similar meaning. Vocabulary issues are becoming increasingly important as enterprises are developing architecture descriptions using combinations of structured and unstructured data representations.

Frameworks and Viewpoints

In Part 1, we have covered various enterprise architecture frameworks. To recap, a framework is an organizing method for architecting consistently across multiple architecture development efforts. By using a common vocabulary, methodology, and conceptual model for architecting, it becomes very easy to compare two architectures, aggregate two architectures, or federate many architectures.

It is hardly surprising that a number of these frameworks have implicitly or explicitly standardized the viewpoints that they support. We will examine a few frameworks and the viewpoints that they promote and support.

Zachman Framework

The original Zachman Framework (Zachman, 1987), as we have explained in Chapter 1.2, is a two-dimensional taxonomical framework where architecture elements are categorized by the previously discussed viewpoints in one dimension and the six interrogatives (what, how, where, who, when, and why) as the other dimension. Table 3.1-1 describes the viewpoints.

John Zachman asserts that row discipline is essential to maintain the consistency of viewpoints. A model that strides across viewpoints is likely to be confusing and

TABLE 3.1-1   Zachman Framework Viewpoints

Viewpoint	Interest
Planner	Primarily an investor in the enterprise, the planner is interested in the strategic aspects of the enterprise, such as enterprise transformation, competition, market growth, revenue growth, new lines of business, globalization, and other sweeping changes that help the enterprise, survive, adapt and thrive.
Owner	Primarily an operator of an enterprise, the owner is interested in managing and governing a running enterprise—keeping costs in line with revenues and ensuring that the enterprise operates in a compliant, efficient, and effective manner. The owner is also interested in operational improvements and technology upgrades that keep the enterprise competitive within its current operating parameters.
Designer	Primarily an architect of business processes, automated solutions, and technology infrastructure, the designer is concerned with planning and meeting the needs for solutions to operational, systems, and technology problems.
Builder	Primarily a designer of solutions that are architected by the designer, the builder is concerned with developing designs that reflect the trade-offs while satisfying the requirements under the parameters of the architecture.
Subcontractor	The subcontractor is primarily concerned with the detailed representations of the solution and its implementation, the constraints of cost and schedule, and the compliance requirements of the implemented solution.

even inaccurate. A model to be consistent with the Zachman Framework may encompass one or more dimensions represented by the interrogatives but must be contained within one of the rows. Earlier in this chapter, we illustrated the fact that viewpoints can either make an architecture element visible or invisible in our example of an airline passenger walking through the concourse of RMN Airport but unable to see the equipment behind the locked and secured doors. Zachman's assertion is therefore very simple: you can build a consistent model only when all of the model's elements are visible to the audience. When you cross viewpoints, you run the risk of introducing architecture elements that may not be recognized by the other viewpoint.

DoD Architecture Framework

A detailed discussion of the DODAF 2.0 can be found in Department of Defense (2009). Table 3.1-2 describes the architecture's viewpoints.

TABLE 3.1-2   DoDAF 2.0 Framework Viewpoints

Viewpoint	Interest
Capability	The DoD uses a capability-based acquisition process. Because the primary expense in the DoD is the procurement of very large weapons systems and military platforms, being able to perform capability-based acquisition is a very fundamental enterprise need. Another interest is to ensure that capabilities acquired are traceable to the military operations they support or that military operations are transformed to take advantage of new capabilities.
Project	The acquisition of capabilities is performed through many projects and programs. The interest is in coordinating these acquisitions to ensure that they are orchestrated in their delivery of capabilities as well as to identify responsibilities for capability development. The Project Viewpoint is not as concerned with the work breakdown structure (WBS) of each individual project as much as the portfolio of projects that together deliver desired enterprise capabilities.
Operational	The primary interest is to ensure successful military operation. Each operation is planned in uncertain warfighting conditions with a combination of forces from the uniformed military services. Coordination of activities, command-and-control relationships, and timely exchange of information and resources are all required to ensure the success of a military operation.

(continued)

TABLE 3.1-2   DoDAF 2.0 Framework Viewpoints (*Continued*)

Viewpoint	Interest
Systems	The primary interest is to plan and architect large, complex systems that are required for a globally projected force structure. Interoperability of systems is a primary driver, as is the need to resolve platform, information exchange, connectivity, and platform migration issues. The Systems Viewpoint, though complementary with the Operational Viewpoint in terms of showing how systems support individual activities, covers a family of operations that the system supports. Systems planning is based on total automated infrastructure to support a family of operations that comprise the mission of the enterprise.
Services	With the move to a service-oriented solution delivery approach and the transformation of military forces to net-centric operations and warfare, the DoD is interested in planning, architecting, designing, and implementing service solutions to replace legacy systems. Planning a service strategy that is based on distributed ownership, distributed development, loose coupling, and interoperability uncertainties, especially for critical business solutions, requires serious architecting. The family of services supporting an enterprise forms a service-oriented architecture (SOA) for the enterprise with a taxonomy component and several orchestrations for several purposes.
Data and Information	The interest in data and information is driven by the need to deal with widespread, authorized, and entitled dissemination of data outside of operational and systems boundaries and the need to decrease the latency of data availability to increase the effectiveness of information-powered operations. The collection of data and information models represents information independently of operational and systems boundaries and is an invaluable resource for integration, interoperability, and communications purposes. We consider the structural and semantic aspects of data and information in this viewpoint.
Standards	The interest of people with the Standards Viewpoint is to deal with the perennial problems of interoperability in all dimensions: interoperability of operating platforms, interoperability of communications equipment, interoperability of allied and coalition forces, interoperability in austere and foreign environments, and so on.
All View	Based on past experience with nonintegrated architecture developments, the interest in an All View Viewpoint is to produce an architecture summary that serves to advertise the existence of a specific architecture, its scope, the purpose for which it was built, the models that were developed, the applicable timeframes, and the results of any analysis performed, such as findings and recommendations. In addition, the All View Viewpoint also promotes the development of an integrated dictionary that ensures that an architecture development delivers an integrated architecture.

Federal Enterprise Architecture Framework (FEAF)

Table 3.1-3 describes FEAF's viewpoints. A more detailed discussion of the Federal Enterprise Architecture Framework can be found in Federal CIO Council (1997).

Federal Enterprise Architecture (FEA)

Though not strictly an architecture framework, the FEA is one of the tools used by the Office of Management and Budget (OMB) under the authority of the Clinger-Cohen Act to enforce management and governance. Table 3.1-4 describes FEA's viewpoints.

More information on the Federal Enterprise Architecture can be found in OMB (2007).

TABLE 3.1-3 FEAF Viewpoints

Viewpoint	Interest
Business	The Business Viewpoint represents the strategic and operational aspects of the enterprise. This viewpoint is supported by models that support this interest, such as strategic plans, ends and means models, financial models, projects or initiatives models, planning models, roadmap models, process models, flow charts, activity decompositions, event trace models, and state transition models of an operational or business nature.
Applications	The Applications Viewpoint represents the interests of people concerned with the systems and automated information system aspects of the enterprise. Systems functionality descriptions, systems connectivity models, systems performance models, and systems behavioral models are examples of the types of models that are useful to support the Applications Viewpoint stakeholders.
Data	The Data Viewpoint represents the interests of people concerned with the data and information management functions of the enterprise. High-level conceptual data models, logical data models, physical database schemas, vocabulary, taxonomy and ontology models, message models, and information exchange models are all examples of models that are understood by Data Viewpoint stakeholders.
Technology	The Technology Viewpoint represents the interests of people concerned with the technology infrastructure. Network and connectivity models, technology standards profiles, models of the various platforms, and services supporting the application architecture are all examples of the models that support this viewpoint.
Transformation	The Transformation Viewpoint represents the interests of the architect and the stakeholders who are the prime movers of the transformation. Technology roadmaps, application migration roadmaps, project rollouts, and schedules are examples of the models that support this viewpoint.

TABLE 3.1-4   FEA Viewpoints

Viewpoint	Interest
Performance	The viewpoint and the terminology for expressing performance are represented in the FEA Performance Reference Model (PRM). This viewpoint represents the interests of governance in specifying performance targets and measuring actual achievements. The measures of performance are specified in the PRM. The aspects of the EA that report mappings to the PRM are of interest to stakeholders with this viewpoint. Because the FEA is a product of the Office of Management and Budget, measurements for financial and governance performance are an essential viewpoint. Some of the models that support this viewpoint are Exhibit 300 for business case justifications of initiatives, A-11 and mappings to the FEA to establish correspondence for aggregation, and rollups across agencies.
Business	The Business Viewpoint is reflected in the FEA Business Reference Model, the primary focus of which is on business areas, lines of business, business functions, and the model in which services are delivered.
Service	The Service Viewpoint is reflected in the FEA Service/Component Reference Model, the primary focus of which is business services (automated and nonautomated) that are required to support the lines of business and business functions.
Data	The Data Viewpoint is reflected in the FEA Data Reference Model, the primary focus of which is representing structured, semistructured, and unstructured data, as well as the modeling of data storage and data exchange.
Technology	The Technology Viewpoint is reflected in the FEA Technical Reference Model. The interest in the Technology Viewpoint is to provide a standard classification scheme for technology profiles that allows disparate organizations to compare technology standards and determine an interoperability strategy or a migration strategy that is based on harmonizing technology standard differences.

The Open Group Architecture Framework (TOGAF)

The Open Group Architecture Framework also introduces various viewpoints of interest to various types of stakeholders. The viewpoints described by TOGAF roughly correspond to the viewpoints in some of the other frameworks described earlier. Table 3.1-5 describes the TOGAF viewpoints associated with the appropriate stakeholder interests.

TABLE 3.1-5	TOGAF Viewpoints
Viewpoint	**Interest**
Business Architecture	The primary audience is users, planners, and business management. Their interests include the following detailed aspects of the business: Business Function View, Business Services View, Business Process View, Business Information View, Business Locations View, Business Logistics View, People View (Organization Chart), Workflow View, Usability View, Business Strategy and Goals View, Business Objectives View, Business Rules View, Business Events View, and Business Performance View.
Data Architecture	The primary audience is database designers and administrators and systems engineers. Their interests include the following detailed views of data and information: Data Entity View, Data Flow View (Organization Data View), and Logical Data View.
Applications Architecture	The primary audience is systems and software engineers. Their interest includes the following detailed views of applications architecture: Software Engineering View, Applications Interoperability View, and Software Distribution View.
Technology Architecture	The primary audience is acquirers, operators, administrators, and managers. Their interests include the following detailed view of technology architecture: Networked Computing/Hardware View, Communications Engineering View, Processing View, Cost View, and Standards View.
Systems Engineering View	This view spans the interests of all people involved in the development of solutions and incorporates the aspects of the Data, Applications, and Technology architectures.
Enterprise Security View	This view represents a holistic interest in security aspects of the business, data, application, and technology architectures.
Enterprise Manageability View	This view represents a holistic interest in management, control, and governance across the business, application, data, and technology architectures.
Enterprise Quality of Service View	This view is another crosscutting interest in performance, quality, repeatability, and other quality-related measurement processes.
Enterprise Mobility View	This view is recognition of the importance of providing mobility for business, data, applications, and technology in today's distributed, globalized world.

Office of Management and Budget

Although OMB is not an architecture framework, its statutory responsibilities as the office of primary responsibility for implementation of the Clinger-Cohen Act's mandates are assisted by models that support the viewpoints described in Table 3.1-6.

TABLE 3.1-6	OMB Viewpoints
Viewpoint	**Interest**
Capital Investments	Managing the capital investment process for information technology to ensure that there is a strong business justification of investments and that the payback for investments is very clear.
EA Maturity Assessment	Ensuring that enterprise architecture development is performed to the extent required by law and to assess the maturity and effectiveness of investments in enterprise architecture development itself.
Security and Privacy Compliance	Ensuring that the provisions of federal laws related to information security and privacy are enforced and reflected in the architecture, design, and implementation of IT systems that support the mission of federal agencies.
Data Exchange and Data Transparency	Ensuring that data that is collected and managed by the federal government is available to the public based on determination of eligibility, entitlement, and authorization concerns. The interest is also in promoting the use of metadata standards used for "tagging" data assets to allow for searching and discovery. The viewpoint is also concerned with the promotion of data exchange standards at the semantic level to take advantage of the semantic web, such as the National Information Exchange Model (NIEM).
Transformational Processes	Promoting the provision of transformational laws such as the E-Government Act to provide access of services to citizens through the Web and the promotion of the reuse of line-of-business solutions between agencies based on common needs and common drivers.

Methodologies

Earlier in this chapter, we discussed models as blueprints—their structured representations of information using standard symbols, the standard relationships between the information elements, and a disciplined method for constructing them.

Methodologies in architecture are prescriptive procedures for developing architecture representations that are recognizable and comprehensible by a community of architects trained in that methodology. It is outside the scope of this book to discuss the various methodologies that are available. Methodologies tend to become religions unto themselves, with dedicated followers who declare that a particular methodology is the best. Each methodology was developed at a specific time to meet the specific needs of that moment. As time went on, needs have changed and some methodologies are less relevant to contemporary needs today than they were when they were first formulated.

Integrated Definition Language (IDEF)

The Integrated Computer-Aided Manufacturing Definition Language (IDEF) was a product of the Integrated Computer-Aided Manufacturing program funded by the U.S. Air Force. Later renamed the Integration Definition Language, IDEF is still used extensively, the premier versions currently being the IDEF 1X Data Modeling technique and the IDEF0 Activity Modeling techniques (National Institute of Standards and Technology, 1994).

IDEF0 is a function modeling technique that builds on the Structured Analysis and Design Technique (SADT) and incorporates modeling of resource flows as inputs and outputs of activities as well as the progressive refinement of decomposing activities.

IDEF1X is based on the entity relationship modeling technique and is used to represent shared data representations that separate entity concepts and establish relationships between them as well as provide property attribution for the entity concepts.

Unified Modeling Language (UML)

The Unified Modeling Language (UML) was adopted as a modeling language standard by the Object Management Group in 1997 and refined continuously. The current specification is UML Version 2.3 (OMG, 2010). UML is a visual language for specifying, constructing, and documenting the artifacts of systems using pictures with symbols and links representing language constructs. The language can be used with all processes, throughout the development lifecycle, and across different implementation technologies. UML is based on object-oriented analysis and design techniques (OOA/D) and is a foundational language for higher-level systems modeling and simulation languages and for construction of higher-order vocabularies based on stereotyping UML classes. In fact, many higher level architectural languages such as System Modeling Language (SysML) and the Universal Profile for MODAF and DODAF used to define an architecture exchange mechanism for defense architectures are based on the foundations of UML.

Universal Profile for DoDAF and MoDAF

The Universal Profile for DoDAF and the Ministry of Defense Architecture Framework (MODAF) is an evolving standard promoted by the Department of Defense and undergoing the standards process at the Object Management Group. UPDM specifies a collection of stereotypes for UML classes that represent the object classes for architecture and systems engineering as specified as concepts within the DoDAF and MoDAF.

Activity-Based Methodology (ABM)

The Activity-Based Methodology (ABM) (Huei, Nicholson, & Mercer, 2005) was developed by the MITRE Corporation to establish a common means to express integrated architecture information consistent with the intent of DoDAF. The ABM takes a data-centric approach for architecture element and product generation rather than the product-centric approach inherent in the DoDAF 2.0. The ABM was developed specifically to provide a tool-independent method for architecture description that focused on the flow of "activities" within the architecture.

Although the ABM effort focused on the creation of an architecture description process, subsequent development of the Architecture Specification Method (ASM) was focused on providing a tool- and methodology-independent, semantically complete model of the concepts used in understanding and describing DoD architectures. DoDAF 2.0 incorporates the lessons learned from ABM and ASM, using a data-centric approach to architecture representation rather than a picture-centric one and focusing on the semantics of the data and the relationships between data items.

Architecture Development Method (ADM)

The Open Group Architecture Framework, based originally on the Department of Defense's Technology Architecture for Information Management (TAFIM), has become an enterprise architecture framework in its own right. The framework is based on a process modeling concept, the Architecture Development Method (ADM), and includes definition of a business architecture, an applications architecture, a technology architecture, and a transition plan from the as-is state to the to-be state.

DoDAF Six Step Architecting Process

The DoD Architecture Framework, though offering implementing organizations freedom of choice, promotes a very general six-step architecting process that is explained in Chapter 2.2. The Six Step process defines the following steps:

1. Determine the intended use of the architecture.
2. Determine the scope of the architecture.
3. Determine what data is required to support architecture development.

4. Collect, organize, correlate, and store architecture data.

5. Conduct analyses in support of architecture objectives.

6. Document results in accordance with the decision maker's needs.

Business Process Modeling Notation (BPMN)

The BPMN 1.0 specification was released to the public in May 2004. The primary goal of the BPMN effort was to provide a notation that is readily understandable by all business users, from the business analysts who create the initial drafts of the processes, to the technical developers responsible for implementing the technology that will perform those processes, and, finally, to the business people who will manage and monitor those processes. BPMN will also be supported with an internal model that will enable the generation of executable BPEL4WS. Thus, BPMN creates a standardized bridge for the gap between the business process design and process implementation.

BPMN defines a Business Process Diagram (BPD), which is based on a flow-charting technique tailored for creating graphical models of business process operations. A Business Process Model (BPM), then, is a network of graphical objects, which are activities (that is, work) and the flow controls that define their order of performance (White, 2006).

Model Representations

In this section, we will discuss specific models that are used in architecture work to represent different views of the architecture to different audiences with different backgrounds and interest in the architecture.

In the government world, the DoDAF is arguably one of the more comprehensive frameworks in terms of the number of different viewpoints represented, though it is not comprehensive in coverage of all the viewpoints possible within an enterprise. The DoDAF also describes standard types of models (views) that it promotes but does not prescribe for the enterprise. Each of these models is categorized by the viewpoint it serves.

The Treasury Enterprise Framework, which has been superseded by the FEAF and the FEA as guidance, was another specification that supported a rich set of model types.

In the commercial world, TOGAF 9 also provides a large number of artifact types (model types) that can be used to represent aspects of different viewpoints.

The TOGAF 9 model types leverage evolutions in enterprise architecture and architecting from both the federal and DoD arenas to provide support for a rich modeling effort.

All of the aforementioned frameworks provide a rich set of model types that essentially represent similar types of aspects for similar types of stakeholder audiences. The models representing structured data assets are all based on an entity relationship or an object-based paradigm. Semantic data models representing unstructured data assets are based on ontology representations such as semantic networks. Process models are generally centered on activities, performers, inputs, outputs, activity orchestration, information, and resource flows and metrics to measure effectiveness for all of these frameworks.

For consistency and simplicity in this book, we will use the DoDAF to illustrate the types of models that can be built to support enterprise architecture. Many of the architecture frameworks and viewpoints mentioned in this chapter have equivalent types of models that are similar in representation and purpose to the DODAF models. The merit in using the DoDAF as an illustration for modeling is that the terminology of architecture objects is consistent across models and is therefore more conducive to building integrated architectures.

DoDAF Viewpoints and Model Types

The Department of Defense Architecture Framework (Department of Defense, 2009) and its predecessor frameworks from the US Department of Defense are arguably some of the earliest integrated architecture frameworks that represent an architecture description in terms of a collection of multiple models that share common architecture elements but cater to different viewpoints for different stakeholders. Table 3.1-7 depicts the eight viewpoints and the several types of models that cater to those viewpoints.

Core Model Set

The DoDAF provides a grand buffet of more than 50 model types that can be used to represent different aspects of the enterprise. Not all the models are useful for all audiences, nor is there any recommendation that an enterprise build all the models. And as with any grand buffet, indigestion is a very probable event!

Figure 3.1-1 describes a unified way of looking at the various viewpoints and how they present different facets of the enterprise architecture. The figure is meant to be

TABLE 3.1-7		DODAF Viewpoints and Models	

Viewpoint	Short Name	Model Name	Model Description
All Viewpoint	AV-1	Overview and Summary Information	The description of a project's visions, goals, objectives, plans, activities, events, conditions, measures, effects (outcomes), and produced objects.
	AV-2	Integrated Dictionary	An architectural data repository with definitions of all terms used throughout the architectural data and presentations.
Capability Viewpoint	CV-1	Vision	The overall vision for transformational endeavors, which provides a strategic context for the capabilities described and a high-level scope.
	CV-2	Capability Taxonomy	A hierarchy of capabilities which specifies all the capabilities that are referenced throughout one or more Architectural Descriptions.
	CV-3	Capability Phasing	The planned achievement of capability at different points in time or during specific periods of time. The CV-3 shows the capability phasing in terms of the activities, conditions, desired effects, rules complied with, resource consumption and production, and measures, without regard to the performer and location solutions.
	CV-4	Capability Dependencies	The dependencies between planned capabilities and the definition of logical groupings of capabilities.
	CV-5	Capability to Organizational Development Mapping	The fulfillment of capability requirements. The CV-5 shows the planned capability deployment and interconnection for a particular Capability Phase. It also defines the planned solution for the phase in terms of performers and locations and their associated concepts.
	CV-6	Capability to Operational Activities Mapping	A mapping between the capabilities required and the operational activities that those capabilities support.
	CV-7	Capability to Services Mapping	A mapping between the capabilities and the services that these capabilities enable.

(continued)

TABLE 3.1-7   DODAF Viewpoints and Models *(Continued)*

Viewpoint	Short Name	Model Name	Model Description
Data and Information Viewpoint	DIV-1	Conceptual Data Model	The required high-level data concepts and their relationships.
	DIV-2	Logical Data Model	The documentation of the data requirements and structural business process (activity) rules. In DoDAF V1.5, this was the OV-7.
	DIV-3	Physical Data Model	The physical implementation format of the Logical Data Model entities, e.g., message formats, file structures, physical schema. In DoDAF V1.5, this was the SV-11.
Operational Viewpoint	OV-1	High-Level Operational Concept Graphic	The high-level graphical/textual description of the operational concept.
	OV-2	Operational Resource Flow Description	A description of the resource flows exchanged between operational activities.
	OV-3	Operational Resource Flow Matrix	A description of the resources exchanged and the relevant attributes of the exchanges.
	OV-4	Organizational Relationships Chart	The organizational context, role, or other relationships among organizations.
	OV-5a	Operational Activity Decomposition Tree	The capabilities and activities (operational activities) organized in a hierarchical structure.
	OV-5b	Operational Activity Model	The context of capabilities and activities (operational activities) and their relationships among activities, inputs, and outputs. Additional data can show cost, performers, or other pertinent information.
	OV-6a	Operational Rules Model	One of three models used to describe activity (operational activity). It identifies business rules that constrain operations.
	OV-6b	State Transition Description	One of three models used to describe operational activity (activity). It identifies business process (activity) responses to events (usually, very short activities).

TABLE 3.1-7 DODAF Viewpoints and Models (*Continued*)

Viewpoint	Short Name	Model Name	Model Description
	OV-6c	Event-Trace Description	One of three models used to describe activity (operational activity). It traces actions in a scenario or sequence of events.
Project Viewpoint	PV-1	Project Portfolio Relationships	It describes the dependency relationships among the organizations, projects, and organizational structures needed to manage a portfolio of projects.
	PV-2	Project Timelines	A timeline perspective on programs or projects, with the key milestones and interdependencies.
	PV-3	Project to Capability Mapping	A mapping of programs and projects to capabilities to show how the specific projects and program elements help to achieve a capability.
Service Viewpoint	SvcV-1	Services Context Description	The identification of services, service items, and their interconnections.
	SvcV-2	Services Resource Flow Description	A description of resource flows exchanged between services.
	SvcV-3a	Systems-Services Matrix	The relationships among or between systems and services in a given architectural description.
	SvcV-3b	Services-Services Matrix	The relationships among services in a given architectural description. It can be designed to show relationships of interest (e.g., service-type interfaces, planned versus existing interfaces).
	SvcV-4	Services Functionality Description	The functions performed by services and the service data flows among service functions (activities).
	SvcV-5	Operational Activity to Services Traceability Matrix	A mapping of services (activities) back to operational activities (activities).
	SvcV-6	Services Resource Flow Matrix	It provides details of service resource flow elements being exchanged between services and the attributes of that exchange.
	SvcV-7	Services Measures Matrix	The measures (metrics) of Services Model elements for the appropriate timeframe(s).

(*continued*)

TABLE 3.1-7	DODAF Viewpoints and Models (Continued)

Viewpoint	Short Name	Model Name	Model Description
	SvcV-8	Services Evolution Description	The planned incremental steps toward migrating a suite of services to a more efficient suite or toward developing current services for a future implementation.
	SvcV-9	Services Technology & Skills Forecast	The emerging technologies, software/hardware products, and skills that are expected to be available in a given set of timeframes and that will affect future service development.
	SvcV-10a	Services Rules Model	One of three models used to describe service functionality. It identifies constraints that are imposed on systems' functionality due to some aspect of system design or implementation.
	SvcV-10b	Services State Transition Description	One of three models used to describe service functionality. It identifies responses of services to events.
	SvcV-10c	Services Event-Trace Description	One of three models used to describe service functionality. It identifies service-specific refinements of critical sequences of events described in the Operational Viewpoint.
Standards Viewpoint	StdV-1	Standards Profile	The listing of standards that apply to solution elements.
	StdV-2	Standards Forecast	The description of emerging standards and their potential impact on current solution elements within a set of timeframes.
System Viewpoint	SV-1	Systems Interface Description	The identification of systems, system items, and their interconnections.
	SV-2	Systems Resource Flow Description	A description of resource flows exchanged between systems.
	SV-3	Systems-Systems Matrix	The relationships among systems in a given architectural description. It can be designed to show relationships of interest (e.g., system-type interfaces, planned versus existing interfaces).
	SV-4	Systems Functionality	The functions (activities) performed by systems and the system data flows among system functions (activities).

TABLE 3.1-7   DODAF Viewpoints and Models (*Continued*)

Viewpoint	Short Name	Model Name	Model Description
	SV-5a	Operational Activity to Systems Function Traceability Matrix	A mapping of system functions (activities) back to operational activities (activities).
	SV-5b	Operational Activity to Systems Traceability Matrix	A mapping of systems back to capabilities or operational activities (activities).
	SV-6	Systems Resource Flow Matrix	The details of system resource flow elements being exchanged between systems and the attributes of that exchange.
	SV-7	Systems Measures Matrix	The measures (metrics) of Systems Model elements for the appropriate timeframe(s).
	SV-8	Systems Evolution Description	The planned incremental steps toward migrating a suite of systems to a more efficient suite, or toward developing a current system for a future implementation.
	SV-9	Systems Technology & Skills Forecast	The emerging technologies, software/hardware products, and skills that are expected to be available in a given set of timeframes and that will affect future system development.
	SV-10a	Systems Rules Model	One of three models used to describe system functionality. It identifies constraints that are imposed on systems functionality due to some aspect of systems design or implementation.
	SV-10b	Systems State Transition Description	One of three models used to describe system functionality. It identifies responses of systems to events.
	SV-10c	Systems Event-Trace Description	One of three models used to describe system functionality. It identifies system-specific refinements of critical sequences of events described in the Operational Viewpoint.

a simplified conceptual illustration, not an exhaustive list of all the various elements of the architecture.

In practice, however, we define a "core set" of models that are advisable to build a fairly comprehensive "starter" integrated architecture (see Table 3.1-8). We have described an integrated architecture as one whose many models share common

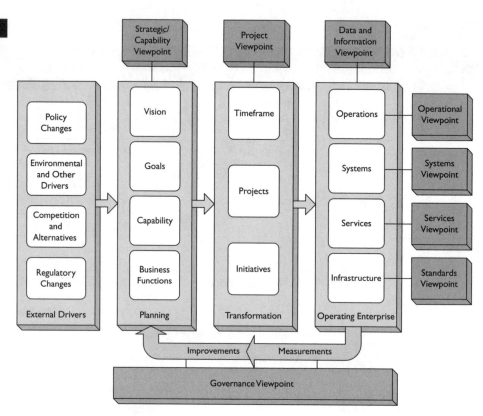

FIGURE 3.1-1

Unified View
of Viewpoints
That Supports
Integrated
Architectures

architecture elements. The set of models together provide the common architecture elements that are required for most architectures.

Table 3.1-9 displays the suggested core set of models for almost any integrated architecture that has to align the operational viewpoint to the Systems and Services viewpoints and align the Systems and Services viewpoint to the Technology Infrastructure Viewpoint.

Specific types of architectures, such as enterprise, segment, and solution, require more architecture elements than the core set defined in Table 3.1-9. In addition, the architect is also encouraged to develop a fit-for-purpose view that assembles architecture elements in a manner that is tailored to a specific audience.

Table 3.1-10 shows the suggested DoDAF-described models for the various types of architecting scale.

TABLE 3.1-8	Examples of Architecture Primitives

Architecture Element	Description
Operational Activities	In a process-driven enterprise, these are business activities, functions, and processes that are performed to fulfill the mission of the enterprise. Activities may create added value; support the creation of added value; provide monitoring, control, direction, resourcing, and enablement; or document and create audit trails. In an operation-driven enterprise, operational activities are tasks that are performed by military personnel or civilian personnel in the conduct of a military or civilian operation.
Operational Locations	These are physical and notional locations that are the place where operational activities are conducted.
System/Service Functions	These are usually named, automated collections of functions that perform or aid the performance of activities in support of the mission of the enterprise. Services may represent packaged business services such as outsourced payroll processing or software services such as in an SOA. Depending on the level of abstraction of the architecture, specific operations may also be exposed for a service.
System/Service Locations	These are physical or notional locations where systems or services are housed. In a service-oriented environment that represents outsourced business services, location has importance because of the constraints it imposes on the services. In a system-oriented environment, locations identify the places where processing platforms are located and represent both a risk and a constraint.
Operational Performers	These are human and organizational performers of operational activities. Organizations may be real organizations with a charter, place of business, and an office symbol, or they may be notional and be represented by the type of functions they perform. Humans are generally represented by the roles they play in the architecture context.
Systems/Services	Systems and services are automated performers of business functions.
Information/Resource	Information is represented at various levels—as business terms in a conceptual model, as logical data entities in a logical data model, or specific message formats or storage schemas in a physical data model. Generalization of information as a physical resource creates analogous structures—conceptual models containing business terms, logical resource models that break down terms into bills of materials, and physical resource models that represent warehouse storage, for example.
Platforms/Standards	These are the various agreements for technical and nontechnical specifications that enable an enterprise to interoperate and collaborate both internally and with external partners.

TABLE 3.1-9 Core Model Suggestion

Short Name	Model	Purpose
AV-1	Architecture Overview and Summary	This model provides a ready reference "index card" for an architecture, indicating its name, version, date of creation, scope, purpose, viewpoint, involved stakeholders, assumptions, constraints, findings, and recommendations.
AV-2	Integrated Architecture Dictionary	AV-2 provides a ready reference for the terminology and resolves consistency issues between model elements.
OV-1	Operational Concept Graphic	This model offers a pictorial (free-form) representation of the concept of operations of the subject matter of the architecture description. It generally provides a quick overview for high-level decision makers and gives context for the rest of the models. The OV-1 exposes key players, key activities, key events, and key locations that are used in the other models.
OV-2	Operational Resource Flow Description	OV-2 provides a graphical picture of all players that are involved within the scope of an architecture (internal and external) and their needs for exchanging resources, including information and data. The OV-2 exposes key players; optionally, their activities; and needlines—that is, needs for resource exchange—and, optionally, specific contents that flow between the needlines.
OV-3	Operational Resource Flow Matrix	This offers more elaboration of the OV-2 by specifying actual resources that flow between the players in an architecture.
OV-5	Activity Model	This model provides a clear representation of the various activities involved, their orchestration, and the flow of resources between them and their performers. It exposes activities, performers, resource and information flows, and guidance and constraints on activities.
SV-1	Systems Interface Description	SV-1 provides a pictorial view of the various systems involved in the architecture and their need to exchange information. The SV-1 exposes systems and interfaces and optionally the systems' locations and the details of the resource and information that flows through the interfaces.
SvcV-1	Services Interface Description	In a service-oriented architecture, services perform automated or delegated functions. SvcV-1 exposes services, operations, service providers, and the invocation relationships with the payload that is passed between invoking and invoked service.
StdV-1	Standards Profile	This model provides a summary of all applicable standards that govern the architecture elements used within the scope of the architecture. StdV-1 exposes standards service areas, services, and standards.

Supporting Model Set

In addition to the core model set, other models from the DoDAF and other framework models are useful in supporting the architectural representations of an integrated architecture. Some of these models, such as the SvcV-3, are used to summarize large, complex service interface description diagrams using a simple matrix. Other models,

TABLE 3.1-10   Suggestions for Models for Architecting Scales

Architecting Scale	Core Model Set	Notes
Enterprise Architectures	CV-1	Because it identifies the capabilities and ties them to strategic goals and objectives.
	CV-3	Because it allows tracking of changing capability configurations (only by name) over time.
	CV-4	Because it captures the capability dependencies as well as the taxonomy.
	CV-5	Because it has relationships between capabilities, organizations that perform those capabilities, and the capability configurations (at least by name) with delivery dates from the projects.
	CV-6	Because it maps the capabilities to the functions depicted in the OV-5a.
	PV-1	Because it links projects to the organizations responsible for them.
	PV-2	Because it provides project timelines and their dependencies.
	OV-4	Because it identifies organizations that appear in CV-5 and PV-1.
	OV-5a (Business Reference Model style) to establish a functional context	Enterprises are comprised of many operations, systems, services, and standards. The EA represents a functional view of the enterprise, not an operational view. The capabilities, systems, services, and technology investments form portfolios that need to be constantly balanced and rebalanced based on threats, opportunities, and weaknesses. One of the key drivers is the need to generate roadmaps to assist planning for the future and to effect transformations and enterprise interventions.

(continued)

TABLE 3.1-10	Suggestions for Models for Architecting Scales (*Continued*)	
Architecting Scale	**Core Model Set**	**Notes**
Segment Architectures	The segment is a smaller subset of the enterprise focused on a large-grain business function or line-of-business or product line. The core views for a segment must be chosen with the same considerations as for the enterprise architecture. The segment architectures may also have an interest in representing cross-functional "mission threads" based on activity handoffs or information exchanges.	Segments are also similar to enterprises except in scope. They tend to perform a narrow band of functions that are used by other segments in a larger enterprise context.
Solution Architectures	OV -1	Provides a graphical view of the problem and solution from the operational viewpoint, including key performers, activities, and communications.
	OV-2	Identifies the key performers and their resource or information products and needs with a mapping to the activities performed by each performer.
	OV-3	Details the resources and information exchanged by the performers, together with the key attributes of the exchanges.
	OV-5a,5b	Details the operational activities and their inputs and outputs.
	SV-1/SvcV-1	Describes the systems and their interfaces (when the Systems Viewpoint is used) or the layout of specific service implementations (with service-level agreements) across platforms and interfaces (when the Services Viewpoint is used).
	SvcV-4	Describes the abstract services, their standard interfaces, and their producer/consumer relationships (when the Services Viewpoint is used).
	StdV-1	Identifies the standards that apply to the systems or services.

TABLE 3.1-10   Suggestions for Models for Architecting Scales (*Continued*)

Architecting Scale	Core Model Set	Notes
-	CV-6	Links the solution-level activities to the enterprise or segment capabilities they implement (for use only for those solution-level architectures that have either overarching segment- or enterprise-level architectures with capabilities identified). Solutions are specific to a particular operation or family of operations. Determining the relevance of the solution to the operation and the solution to the infrastructure is a key architectural analysis need.
"Fit for Purpose" Architectures	Views are chosen based on needs.	These are architectures built to represent the larger context for a specific problem, issue or need or some targeted project activity. Speed of development and rapidity of analysis are often key drivers.

such as the SvcV-7, are used to specify the service-level agreements that represent the expected performance parameters from a business or a software service for acceptable delivery of that service. Models such as the OV-4 Organization Relationships Chart are always useful in describing the roles and positions of the internal and external players within the scope of an architecture as well as the existence of formal reporting and collaboration relationships.

Supporting models are chosen based on the questions that the architecture effort has to answer or to provide the information that the architecture-related decisions need. In Chapter 2.2, which covered the planning phase of the architecture, we have discussed the importance of documenting the questions that the architecture will answer and the types of products that will help answer those questions.

The funding for architecture projects tends to be limited and the choice of which models to build must be driven by a recognition of resource constraints coupled with a clear understanding of the information requirement priorities.

Overarching Context of the Example Models

In earlier discussions, we had alluded to the different scales of architecting—enterprise, segment, or solution. Each level of architecting provides the context for the next level, as shown in Figure 3.1-2.

The example models will be drawn from each of these scales of architecting. We will specifically choose the levels described in Table 3.1-11.

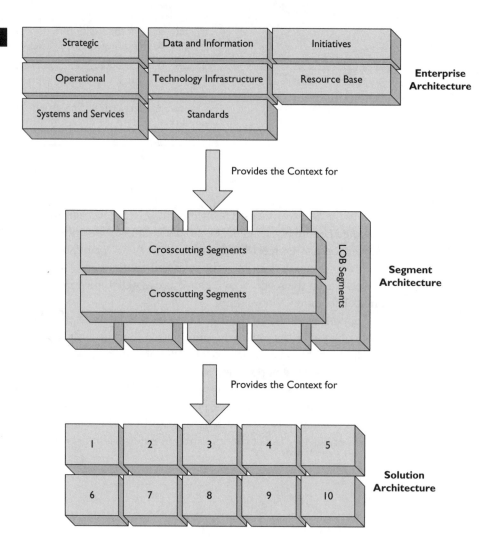

FIGURE 3.1-2

Context
Definition
Hierarchy

TABLE 3.1-11	Examples and Levels of Architecting

Level	Description
Enterprise	This level encompasses all RMN operations as explained in the OV-5a BRM for RMN Airport.
Segment	The Terminal Operations Division is responsible for all terminal operations functions as shown in the BRM.
Solution	Passenger identification is a solution area under the Terminal Operations Division that requires a service/system solution.

Modeling Section Summary

Using the DoD Architecture Framework's abundant definition of DoDAF-described models (views), we have presented a number of examples that illustrate how architecture representations can be built using a technique that is standardized across the enterprise. It is important to realize that the DODAF model set presented here is not comprehensive in depicting all possible models or all possible viewpoints. For example, the OMB's management and budget viewpoint requires the building of artifacts such as the A-11, Exhibit 300, which may be deemed to be models in their own right. DoDAF allows modelers to define their own model types, which are tailored or constructed to suit a specific audience or analyst group's needs. The problem with fit-for-purpose types of models that are cobbled together for a specific audience is that they are not general enough to translate well to other audiences.

It is important to use established modeling techniques such as those supported by a specific popular, well-understood, and widely published methodology such as SADT, UML, or IDEF to build models that are shareable and familiar to other architects—especially those involved in a collaborative architecture development exercise.

Questions

1. What is a model? What is the difference between a randomly constructed picture and a model? Provide some examples of models from your own enterprise. Who is the audience for these example models? What are the rules of construction and the elements of these models?

2. What is a viewpoint?

3. What is a view?

4. Describe the relationship between viewpoints and views.

5. Compare and contrast the IEEE definition of views and viewpoints against the DoDAF definition of views and viewpoints.

6. What is an integrated architecture? Which DoDAF model promotes the integration of other models through the use of common architecture elements?

7. What is a federated architecture? What is the difference between a federated architecture and an integrated architecture? Where are some of the applications of federated architecture within your own enterprise? Discuss how federation can be accomplished (1) through relating processes across federating enterprises (process-based federation); (2) through common vocabularies that establish the same terminology and information artifacts across federating enterprises (data- and information-based federation); and (3) through roles that are commonly understood and act as liaisons between the federating enterprises (role-based federation).

8. What viewpoints are expressed in the Zachman Framework? What is the difference in interest between the planner and the builder?

9. How might organizational conflict result when stakeholders from two different viewpoints are unable to agree on priorities, strategy, or approach?

10. Discuss the relationship between viewpoints and organizational culture. In your own enterprise, are there dominant viewpoints?

11. Who is the audience for the Capability Viewpoint in the DoDAF? And for the Project Viewpoint?

12. What is the difference in viewpoints between the Federal Enterprise Architecture represented as a set of taxonomy models and the FEAF, which is represented as a set of architectures?

13. Compare and contrast the viewpoints expressed in the DoDAF against the viewpoints that are expressed in the TOGAF.

14. What is a methodology? Why is it important to agree upon a methodology for development of architectures? Who are the stakeholders who need to be involved in the selection of methodologies? What are some of the criteria you would use for selecting one or more methodologies for architecting your enterprise?

15. Compare and contrast the DoDAF Six Step Architecting Process against the TOGAF ADM. Which process is more applicable to your own enterprise? Why?

16. What are the advantages for an enterprise to standardize the types of models it builds? What are some of the disadvantages?

17. What are architecture primitives (from the context of this chapter)?

18. What are core products of an integrated architecture set? What architectural dimensions (columns) of the Zachman Framework are exposed by the core products?

Reference List

Department of Defense. (2009). *DoD Architecture Framework Version 2.0, Volumes 1 and 2*. United States Department of Defense.

Federal CIO Council Architecture Working Group. (1999). *Federal Enterprise Architecture Framework Version 1.1, September 1999*. Federal Chief Information Officer's Council.

Huei Wan Ang, Nicholson, Dave, & Mercer, Brad. (2005). *Improving the practice of DoD architecting with the Architecture Specification Model. The MITRE Corporation*. http://www.mitre.org/work/tech_papers/tech_papers_05/05_0423/05_0423.pdf.

International Organization for Standardization (ISO)/International Electrotechnical Commission (IEC). (2007). *Recommended practice for architecture description of software-intensive systems*. International Standards Organization.

International Organization for Standardization (ISO)/International Electrotechnical Commission (IEC). (2007). *Systems and software engineering—recommended practice for architectural description of software-intensive systems*. International Standards Organization.

National Institute of Standards and Technology (NIST). (1994). *FIPS 183 IDEF0 "Integration Definition for Functional Modeling (IDEF0)" and FIPS 184 IDEF1X "Integration Definition for Data Modeling (IDEF1X)"*. National Institute of Standards and Technology.

Object Management Group. (2010). *Documents Associated with Unified Modeling Language Version 2.3*. http://www.omg.org/spec/UML/2.3/.

Object Management Group. (2010). *Universal Profile for MODAF and DoDAF (UPDM) Version 1.1*. http://www.omg.org/spec/UPDM/1.1/Beta2/index.htm.

Office of Management and Budget. (2007). *Federal Enterprise Architecture Combined Reference Model Version 2.3.* http://www.whitehouse.gov/sites/default/files/omb/assets/fea_docs/FEA_CRM_v23_Final_Oct_2007_Revised.pdf.

Office of Management and Budget (OMB). (2007). *FEA Consolidated Reference Model Document Version 2.3.* (Executive Office of the President of the United States.) http://www.whitehouse.gov/sites/default/files/omb/assets/fea_docs/FEA_CRM_v23_Final_Oct_2007_Revised.pdf.

The Open Group. (2009). *The Open Group Architecture Framework (TOGAF) 9.0.* The Open Group.

Sowa, J.F & Zachman, John A. (1992). *Extending and Formalizing the Framework for Information Systems Architecture.* J. F. Sowa and J. A. Zachman. IBM Systems Journal, vol. 31, no. 3, 1992.

White, Stephen A. (2006). *Introduction to BPMN.* IBM Corporation. http://www.omg.org/bpmn/Documents/Introduction_to_BPMN.pdf.

Zachman, John A. (1987). *A Framework for Information Systems Architecture.* IBM Systems Journal, vol. 26, no. 3, 1987.

3.2

All Viewpoint

T he All Viewpoint refers to the totality of the different viewpoints that are used to present different types of models to different users. The All Viewpoint is the one that unifies all the architecture elements as one collection. The viewpoint is necessary for an audience that has an interest in the architecture data as well as the architecture project as a whole. The All Viewpoint is therefore essential to the repository that must hold all the architecture data from all the viewpoints as well as to the architecture development team that has to develop an integrated architecture that must provide many models to support many viewpoints.

Architecture Overview and Summary

The Architecture Overview and Summary (AV-1) model (see Figure 3.2-1) is the representation of all the information that relates to an architecture development effort, including its ultimate configuration management, versioning, and release. The AV-1 is the very first model constructed during an architecture development effort. It establishes the purpose for building the architecture as well as the scope of the architecture coverage in terms of key performers, locations, activities, information exchanges, resource flows, events, external players, and external exchanges. It also describes the viewpoints that are modeled and details the specific models that will be built as well as the assumptions and constraints that bound the architecture effort. The model serves simultaneously as an advertising document, an informative abstract, and a mea culpa for the architect. It also describes the types of planned analysis after the architecture is developed, and at the end of the architecture effort, it is also used for recording analysis results, findings, and recommendations for future actions.

The Integrated Architecture Dictionary (AV-2) is an authoritative and integrated dictionary for all architecture elements used in all models that support all viewpoints (see Figure 3.2-2). As an authoritative reference, the AV-2 definitions for architecture element terms are often drawn from policy and guidance documents. In previous nonintegrated architecture modeling efforts, each model was accompanied by its own dictionary or model glossary that defined the terms used inside that specific model. The integrated dictionary forces disparate elements from multiple models to be resolved by the modeling teams and presents consistent and distinct architecture elements. The AV-2 may also contain taxonomies (classification schemes) for

FIGURE 3.2-1

Integrated Models
for All Viewpoint
(1) Integrated
Dictionary

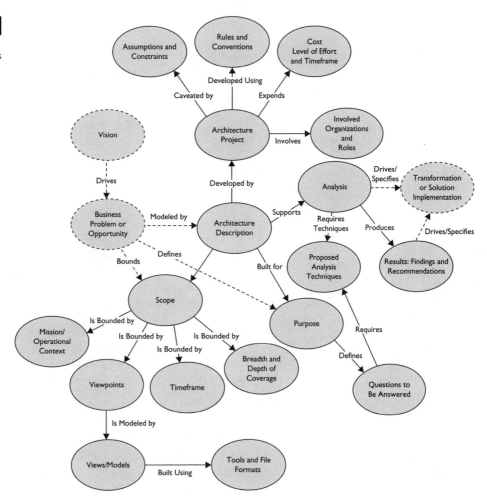

architecture elements to provide abstraction hierarchies that allow integration of detailed models with abstract models. Semantic relationships are often also described.

The AV-2 Integrated Dictionary is usually generated in a tabular format with a long list of architecture elements, their expanded acronyms, their descriptions, authoritative sources that are the origins of the definitions, and a cross-reference of

Integrated
Model for AV-2
Integrated
Dictionary

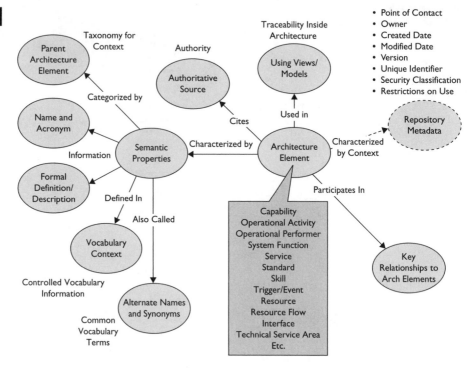

usage of architecture elements in the various models of the architecture description.
Many architecture tools automatically generate the AV-2 as a byproduct of
architecture development, but the ultimate burden of ensuring an integrated
architecture—consistent use of architecture elements across models—still falls
on the architect. This is also true for architecture repositories that generate AV-2
automatically for a specific architecture.

The AV-2 is a valuable tool for the architecture integrator—the person or persons
responsible for delivering an integrated architecture. When the same architecture
element is named differently in different models, integration does not occur; analysis
will be faulty as the intersection of common elements across models will not occur
and any searching and querying method returns incomplete information. It is
recommended that the AV-2 be continuously generated throughout the architecture

development and efforts expended to ensure that the architecture elements are rationalized constantly—especially if multiple people are developing different models at different locations and bringing them together for integration.

In TOGAF 9, additional models are recommended to support the Preliminary Phase and the Architecture Vision phases of the Architecture Development Method where the All Viewpoint models are developed. These additional models are the following:

- ■ **Architecture Vision** The Architecture Vision is created early in the project lifecycle and provides a high-level, aspirational view of the end architecture product. The purpose of the vision is for stakeholders to agree at the outset what the desired outcome should be for the architecture, so that architects can then focus on the critical areas to validate feasibility. Providing an Architecture Vision also supports stakeholder communication by providing an executive summary version of the full architecture definition.

- ■ **Principles Catalog** This model lists the guiding principles for architecture development.

- ■ **Stakeholder Map Matrix** This matrix depicts the stakeholders and their roles in the architecture.

In the TOGAF, the Architecture Repository stores the Integrated Architecture Dictionary (AV-2). In addition, the Architecture Requirements Specification is an important document that acts as a companion to the Architecture Definition Document (AV-1). The Architecture Roadmap lists individual increments of change and lays them out on a timeline to show progression from the baseline architecture to the target architecture. The Architecture Roadmap forms a key component of transition architectures and is incrementally developed throughout phases B, C, D, E, and F within the Architecture Development Method (ADM). Another important model that supports the All Viewpoint is the Request for Architecture Work (for TOGAF) or a statement of work (for federal agencies) that describes the tasks that are to be performed during the architecture development. The Statement of Architecture Work defines the scope and approach that will be used to complete an architecture project. The Statement of Architecture Work is typically the document against which successful execution of the architecture project will be measured and may form the basis for a contractual agreement between the supplier and consumer of architecture services (The Open Group, 2009).

AV-1 Architecture Overview and Summary

The AV-1 can be short and provide the minimum metadata related to an architecture development. It can also be a long and comprehensive description of the context of the architecture with a detailed description of the problem that is being addressed by the architecture development. Many enterprises standardize the format of the AV-1 to enable uniform registration of multiple architectures using similar attributes. An integrated architecture repository that is used to generate the text-based AV-1 automatically will also enforce this discipline. Table 3.2-1 describes AV-1 at a glance.

Table 3.2-2 shows a short form template for the AV-1.

TABLE 3.2-1   AV-1 Architecture Overview and Summary—Model at a Glance

Model Short Name	AV-1
Name	Architecture Overview and Summary
Other Names	Business Problem Statement (federal) Architecture Definition Document (TOGAF)
Viewpoint	All Views
Model Intent	Summarize the purpose, scope and viewpoints of the architecture; present results of analysis, findings, and recommendations for actions based on analysis; describe the architecture's project-related details, such as duration, involved personnel, and level of effort.
Model Audience	Sponsors of the architecture effort; all people with an interest in getting a broad and brief view of the overall architecting effort.
Formal Modeling Methodology	None. An enterprisewide standard template will help standardize recording of the AV-1 and facilitate the loading of repositories with homogeneous data structures. The AV-1 is usually a text-based document that is unstructured and descriptive. A structured version of the AV-1 can be used to store architecture descriptions inside a registry to support discovery of architectures. This method is employed by the Defense Architecture Registry System (DARS) to collect and publish architecture descriptions of various architectures developed throughout the DoD.
Integration of Model with Other Views	The AV-1 describes elements of scope that are shared by all other architecture viewpoints and models. The span of performers, activities, capabilities, services, systems, locations, and other architecture elements must match the contents.

| TABLE 3.2-2 | AV-1 Sample Architecture Overview and Summary Template |

Architectural Description Identification

Name of the architecture

Name of the architect

Name of the organization developing the architectural description

List of assumptions and constraints

Approval authority

Architecture completion date

Description of the level of effort required

Scope

Viewpoints addressed by the architecture representation

Models (views) developed

Timeframe addressed by the architecture, such as by specific years or by designations such as "current," "target," or "transitional"

Organizational entities that fall within the scope of the architectural description

Purpose and Perspective

The need that drives the development of the architectural description

The types of analyses that will be applied to the architecture

Who is expected to perform the analysis

What decisions are expected to be made based on each form of analysis

Who is expected to make those decisions

What actions are expected to result

The perspective from which the architectural description is developed

Context

Mission addressed by the architecture

Doctrine

Relevant goals and vision statements

Concepts of operation

Scenarios

Information assurance context (e.g., types of system or service data to be protected, such as classified or sensitive but unclassified, and expected information threat environment)

(continued)

| TABLE 3.2-2 | AV-1 Sample Architecture Overview and Summary Template (*Continued*) |

	Other threats and environmental conditions
	Geographical areas addressed, where applicable
	Authoritative sources for the standards, rules, criteria, and conventions that are used in the architecture
	Any linkages to parallel architecture efforts
Status	
	Status of the architecture at the time of publication or development of the AV-1 (which might precede the architectural development itself). Status refers to creation, validation and assurance activities.
Tools and File Formats Used	
	Tool suite used to develop the architectural description
	Filenames and formats for the architectural models if appropriate
Assumptions and Constraints	
	Assumptions
	Constraints
Architecture Development Schedule	
	Start date
	Development milestones
	Date completed
Findings	
	Findings and recommendations that have been developed based on the architectural effort. Examples of findings include identification of shortfalls, recommended system implementations, and opportunities for technology insertion.
Costs	
	Architecture budget
	Cost projections, or actual costs that have been incurred in developing the architecture and/or undertaking the analysis. This might include integration costs, equipment costs, and other costs.

Richard M. Nixon Airport Enterprise Architecture (RMN-EA) Architecture Overview and Summary (AV-1)

The example in this section describes a comprehensive AV-1 for the Richard M. Nixon (RMN) Airport enterprise architecture. This AV-1 is intended to be a foundational document for a multiyear enterprise transformation and the primary purpose is to establish a lasting and living directional document for enterprise architecture development. In Chapter 5.2 we present the environment and challenges of transforming Richard M. Nixon airport as a case study supporting the AV-1.

Executive Summary

The Richard M. Nixon Airport enterprise architecture development is a project that delivers a baseline enterprise architecture version 0.5 in a six-month timeframe and a first release six months later. The purpose of the RMN-EA is to support planning efforts for RMN's ambitious transformation roadmap to provide a viable alternative to the crowded Los Angeles International Airport (LAX).

RMN is a public-private enterprise that is transforming itself ultimately from a small general aviation airport to a major destination and en-route point for local, national, and international air traffic with facilities for cargo and passenger processing.

RMN's transformation efforts, documented using Department of Defense (2009), are designed to attract commercial and government air carriers to use the airport as a vital point on their air routes into and out of LAX. RMN's vision is to be a passenger-friendly airport with speedy transportation to points in Los Angeles and offer convenient and rapid passenger processing facilities through security screening, customs and immigration, boarding and deplaning, and baggage drop-off and pickup.

RMN's transformation roadmap is predicated on availability of capital in the form of offerings on the securities/capital markets as well as working capital generated from operating revenues. Operating revenues result from flying operations as well as terminal and land operations such as parking, building leases, and so on. The enterprise architecture will be used as a way to calibrate the impact of deviations in plan in capital availability and revenue generation and modify the roadmap for capability development accordingly.

The enterprise architecture will be used to assess portfolios in terms of relevance to the business and prioritize initiatives.

RMN anticipates that the enterprise architecture program can recover more than ten times the investment in the Architecture Program Office through savings resulting from smart planning and agile redirection of roadmaps.

Architecture Identification

In this section we formally identify the architecture effort with a name, and additional metadata including versioning, status, and release information. This section is also useful to catalog this architecting effort along with others inside the RMN Architecture Repository. The identification information in this section is used to create an architecture "index card" for searching and retrieval purposes inside the repository.

Formal Name: Richard M. Nixon International Airport—Enterprise Architecture
Abbreviated Name: RMN-EA
Version: 0.5
Applicability: Timeframe: 2011–2015
Release Status: Draft
Certified By: Not currently certified

Architecture Purpose

Richard M. Nixon Municipal Airport (RMN) in Los Caballeros, California, is a small commuter airport approximately 40 miles southeast of Los Angeles International Airport. The airport, named after a former president of the United States, is a tribute to a fallen god yet still a reputed son of California and Los Angeles.

With the tremendous pressure of increasing traffic at LAX, RMN is looking at opportunistically drawing the traffic from LAX and the other Los Angeles area airport, Orange County. At this point, RMN is a sleepy, small airport servicing hobby pilots and small commuter aircraft. Harvesting the promise of the opportunity is a challenge in risk taking, planning, prioritization, and implementation—the kinds of things that enterprise architecture promises to facilitate.

LAX is not only a destination airport for passengers bound for Los Angeles, it is also a gateway airport into the United States and is used to process passengers for customs and immigration on flights that are arriving from foreign lands. LAX is also a hub airport for passengers transiting to other destinations. As a result, at any given moment, a passenger at LAX may be arriving at Los Angeles, departing Los Angeles, transiting from an inbound flight to an outbound flight, or coming into the United States as a U.S. citizen, immigrant, visitor, or student.

Processing people coming into and departing out of any airport from the United States on a flight bound to a foreign destination involves the United States Immigration and Customer Enforcement (ICE) organization. Furthermore, for passengers carrying dairy and farm products, the U.S. Department of Agriculture is also involved through the Agriculture Public Health Inspection Service (APHIS). Passengers must comply with the United States laws relating to immigration and the transport of goods into and out of the country. Laws such as the International Trafficking in Arms Regulations from the U.S. Department of Commerce ban the transport of materiel sensitive to the interests of the United States. The Drug Enforcement Agency is entrusted with the control and prevention of drug traffic into and out of the United States.

With the increased security posture in the United States after 9/11 and the use of airliners loaded with fuel as bombs by foreign terrorist organizations, passenger safety and national security interests have intersected and airports are at the front line of defense. Airport security, which formerly was a matter for contracted security personnel and local and state law enforcement officials, now involves the Department of Homeland Security through the presences of screening personnel employed with the Transportation Safety Administration (TSA). TSA applies mandated screening procedures under the authority of the laws of the United States. TSA also provides for federal sky marshals who travel on randomly selected air routes to assist in counterterrorism and apprehension activities on board an aircraft.

Civil aviation in the United States is federally regulated because of the safety issues, coordination, and collaboration challenges as well as the use of shared resources such as the airspace over the United States. The Federal Aviation Administration (FAA)—a federal agency—is responsible for managing traffic inside U.S. domestic airspace. The FAA has a presence in the control tower of every airport. FAA traffic management facilities are provided to controllers to assist them in coordinating landings, takeoffs, and holding patterns and guiding air traffic from sector to sector.

Any expansion of the physical land around the existing airspace requires dealing with local and state authorities for permissions. Many local communities have noise-related ordnances and require noise abatement procedures. Bringing wide-body jets into RMN must include plans to lengthen and broaden existing runways. At the same time, to provide nonstop operations and provide multiple runways in different directions to take advantages of prevailing and changing wind conditions. The path of this potential new runway intersects with a neighboring bedroom community of high-dollar single-family residential housing.

Passenger Processing Capabilities

To be an attractive alternative to LAX, RMN will have to provide significantly greater capabilities for passenger management, comfort, convenience, and safety:

- Passenger management includes processing passengers from the point of check-in to the point of boarding their aircraft, or from debarking to finally collecting their baggage and being on their way to their destination. Passengers may also use RMN to connect to other flights as well. Passenger management includes completion of customs and immigration requirements, safety screening procedures, guided access through airport public areas, and requirements for identification as well as authorization to travel at all times.

- Passenger comfort involves providing environmental conditions for temperature control and management of passenger areas; adequate seating and resting facilities, amenities such as clean restrooms; areas in which baby diapers can be changed; potable water sources such as coolers in hallways; fatigue-resistant flooring; and movement areas such as elevators, escalators, and corridors.

- Passenger convenience is the provision of facilities inside the airport itself that are adequate for passenger's travel and work-related needs. These can range from providing in-airport services for wireless Internet and electronic mail connections, electricity ports for passengers to recharge their electronics equipment, facsimile and printing services for business documents, and help desks with maps and local tourist areas and personnel to assist passengers to rapid transit to downtown Los Angeles and other points through partnerships with local authorities and rapid transit organizations. Providing facilities for passenger baggage storage, in-airport post offices, and other conveniences are intended to make RMN an inviting departure, destination, and transit hub for airlines.

- Passenger safety has become a very important concern in the post 9/11 world. Ever since a group of terrorists hijacked an airliner and used it as a guided missile to destroy key buildings, the fear of plane hijacking and terrorism has rippled through U.S. airports. The increased alert posture of airports has also affected RMN. From the entrance ramps of the highway that provides access to the airport to an array of equipment used for baggage and passenger screening, RMN is deeply committed to providing passenger safety. RMN is also concerned with privacy and antidiscrimination laws that prevent profiling of passengers. Law enforcement capabilities are provided by a detachment of local law enforcement assigned to RMN airport. Airport authorities, screeners, and other personnel involved in passenger screening and detection of explosives and lethal weapons in hand-carried and -checked baggage refer any incidents to these local law enforcement authorities.

■ Another important part of passenger safety is the need for well-established personnel support, processes and services for evacuation, fire protection, medical care and triage services, ambulance services, sick bays, and other equipment needed to respond immediately and decisively to emergencies. Each of these services reach back to the broader system of hospitals, firefighting forces, and other state, local, and county resources. RMN has established the principle of a minimum presence in first response given that its financial capabilities to keep a standing army of first responders are very limited. But RMN has also stipulated that escalation of first response will be the preferred approach to handling emergencies. RMN has routinely run drills and exercises to test the principle, although no major event has occurred in the history of its existence. Given the planned escalation of the size, capacity, and scope of the airport, it is anticipated that some of the assumptions related to escalation may need to be revisited.

Cargo Processing Capabilities

In addition to needing the ability to manage passengers, RMN also requires capabilities to manage cargo operations. These include capabilities for cargo handling, tracking, inspection for customs purposes, and warehousing and storage, as well as constraints on the handling of hazardous materials and potentially dangerous cargo. Thus RMN must allocate space and facilities for cargo operations in addition to the passenger terminal operations. Although some of the capabilities needed to support cargo processing are the primary responsibilities of the carriers—such as a package express company or the cargo operations arm of an airline—the airport management and facilities need to be able to support cargo operations to be able to sustain them at RMN safely, efficiently, and effectively. The following are some details regarding the required cargo processing capabilities:

■ Cargo handling capabilities require acquiring and operating equipment such as forklifts, pallets, containerized handling equipment, roll-on and roll-off containers, materials handling equipment, and so on.

■ Cargo tracking capabilities require automated identification technologies such as radio frequency ID (RFID) tagging and bar codes as well as a system of tracking that allows these identifiers to be captured at various points of the cargo processing cycle.

- Cargo inspection requires that various cargo items be checked in accordance with the laws of the United States. These laws are enforced by various federal agencies. The Department of Agriculture and APHIS enforce laws that control importation of plant and animal products. The Department of Commerce enforces laws related to the International Arms Trade (ITARS). The Department of Customs and Border Protection enforces laws related to the assessment, charging, and collection of customs duty.

- Cargo storage and management require space and segregated areas within the airport. For example, a bonded warehouse is required for customs-cleared cargo. A quarantine area is required when cargo suspected of containing harmful plant or animal material needs to be sequestered before being destroyed. Cargo storage also requires security and fire protection forces.

- Hazardous material (HAZMAT) cargo must be clearly identified as such and its storage managed to prevent potential chemical, biological, radiation, or nuclear explosion events (CBRNE).

Revenue Generation Capabilities

Although passengers and cargo movement are the primary focus of the enterprise, there are many other stakeholders to satisfy. Passengers, although they generate revenue through financial transactions performed at the airport, are not the primary sources of revenue to the airport:

- Concessions are contracted vendors who occupy the airport terminal premises and operate businesses that cater to passengers' needs. Concessions pay fees to be able to set up and use the terminal facilities for retail storefronts and restaurants. These fees are fixed and form a very stable and predictable part of the airport's revenue streams. Concessions are negotiated once every two years (unless there are closings and bankruptcies in between) and are based on contractual agreements that bind the concessionaire to pay fixed fees in return for accommodation, water, sewage, electricity, and natural gas connections. The Small Business Administration requires that a certain number of concessions be awarded to small minority and woman-owned businesses in a bid to increase the participation of such enterprises in the state's economy. RMN in principle has agreed that promoting small minority and woman-owned businesses is a priority but not to a point where the revenues of RMN are compromised by risk. RMN has agreed to cap the involvement of small business in a protected mode to 10 percent of its concession revenues or 10 percent of the retail space available for concessions, whichever is more.

■ Airlines pay landing fees to the airport each time a plane lands at the airport. Landing fees are recovered from passengers as part of the cost of a ticket. These fees are charged on a schedule that makes them slightly higher during peak periods; discounts are offered for landings that occur during off-peak periods. RMN in principle wants to have a smooth flow of traffic through all times of the day, but recognizes that there will be morning and evening peaks as business passenger traffic finds those times more convenient.

■ The airport also stands to receive subsidies from the State of California as part of a state initiative to reduce congestion at LAX and incentivize smaller airports to offload the peak traffic over the skies of Los Angeles. These subsidies are offered on a sliding scale with a large amount being available initially to jump start operations and tapering off over a 15-year period, with the assumption that the airport's natural growth of revenues would be able to sustain operations without the state subsidies. However, the confidence level in actually ever receiving these subsidies is not very high given the large shortfalls in the state budget and the tendency of lawmakers to legislate away subsidies when the involved constituency is not loud, vociferous, or influential. RMN has been lobbying lawmakers and representatives from the region to influence legislative directions. Given the uncertainty of state funding and all the various restrictive clauses that constrain the airport's degrees of freedom, RMN, in principle, is intent on avoiding government subsidies that are tied to the whims of legislators and the availability of public monies.

■ The airport has been looking at land use for potential revenue generation. More than 200 acres have been zoned for parking and can produce significant revenues once a steady stream of loyal passengers begin using RMN as their preferred airport to LAX, Burbank, or Orange County. At this time, no parking ramps have been built, but there are plans to float bonds to acquire funds for parking ramps and state-of-the-art facilities such as electronic annunciators and indicators for vacant spaces, display systems to help direct traffic, pay system facilities to allow passengers to pay at the airport terminal itself, and people movement systems to move passengers rapidly from the terminal to parking areas.

- The airport also charges airlines with leases for occupation of space inside the terminal and outside. Airlines maintain office space for administrative operations that are not directly related to flying operations (back-office operations) and front desk space for greeting, receiving, and checking in passengers. Airlines also maintain check-in baggage areas outside the terminal by the passenger entrances. All airport-owned space that is used by airlines is charged out completely. Leases are renegotiated every two years. The principle of fairness is used to charge all airlines the same normalized rate. There are different rates for different types of spaces. The airport will not undertake customized building of offices, cubicles, and partitions of the space and it is up to the airline to customize its own areas at their own expense. The airport does mandate standards, look-and-feel guidance, and uniformity of how spaces are built out. These mandates are nonnegotiable and built in to the airlines leases as terms and conditions.

Stakeholders

RMN is also more than an airport facility in human terms. It also has its own internal permanent community of airport employees, concession employees, baggage transfer operators, custodians, parking lot attendants, parking shuttle drivers, airport management, airport security, fire protection personnel, aircrew, airline employees, flight kitchen attendants, and many other workers. Note the following details regarding this community:

- As a community sponsor, RMN must provide mechanisms and facilities that are used by these stakeholders, such as parking facilities, restrooms, recreation and exercise facilities, and storage lockers.
- RMN, as an employer of more than 50 employees, also comes under federal regulations and labor laws related to the forming of unions, assembly, and peaceful protest, as well as statutory limits on work time and overtime and regulations regarding employment conditions, occupational safety, and health issues. RMN is committed to compliance with all regulations related to labor that are required under federal, state, and local law.
- In addition to dealing with the organization and management aspects of such a diverse workforce, RMN is also concerned with identification of valid

employees through the issuing of photo badges with biometric employee information, implementation of access controls on secured facilities, and the tracking of employees' movement in sensitive areas of the airport. Processes are in place to provide badging, control authorized access, and monitor movement of employees where security issues are likely to cause disruption or threaten the airport's normal operations. Also in place are processes for terminated or retiring employees to ensure that all identification materials are recovered before these personnel exit the airport premises permanently as employees.

■ RMN, though committed to laws related to organized labor, has not had a labor union in its history. But as it expands, there has been a groundswell by various labor groups to canvas each other and try to form a labor union. Political parties and national labor unions have also been active in trying to activate the groundswell and push for the formation of a local chapter of national trade unions.

■ The State of California and the municipality and county that surround RMN are also stakeholders. The federal government is interested in a strategic alternative to LAX that is very close and is viable in the event of LAX closing due to unforeseen events. The State of California is interested in RMN as a facilitator for commerce as well as a port of embarkation for people, goods, and cargo that increases the tempo and magnitude of economic activity within the region. RMN is also a taxpaying entity that provides tax revenues for local, county, state, and federal government. The airport raises money through bonds that are guaranteed by state and local government.

Geographical Considerations

The layout of the current runways limits operations in only one direction when the wind is right. RMN would greatly benefit from a cross-runway system for taking advantage of changes in wind direction and saving valuable fuel through correct alignment with prevailing winds.

The construction of an additional runway system has not been studied, but its undertaking is a significant financial and civil engineering operational exercise in budgeting, raising monies, and planning and execution. In addition, integrating the new runway requires coordination with air traffic management, the FAA, and other federal agencies. The science and engineering are well understood and can be undertaken with little risk, but the financial risk of raising funds and paying for the effort and the trade-off against the increased revenues and capability improvements need to be analyzed.

One of the runways is shorter than the 4,500 feet needed by wide-body airliners and some of the larger cargo aircraft. This has resulted in a number of airlines continuing to fly LAX for their wider-body aircraft. Increasing the runway length cannot be undertaken without an additional runway to absorb the load while the lengthening operations are in process. While the runway is being lengthened, operations are severely limited and the presence of construction equipment so close to other operating runways requires close supervision and that extra procedures are put in place for safety purposes. The financing for lengthening the runways may have to be performed in a different manner than the financing for new runways, as it may come under operational improvements.

Information and Technology Infrastructure

RMN is slowly transforming itself from a small, sleepy, rural airport to a modern port of call for passenger airlines and cargo. The use of information technology is being slowly phased in for various aspects of the operation:

- Terminals are being equipped with wireless hubs to enable passengers to connect to the Internet. Wireless access points, electric charging points, and desks and stations for laptops and notebooks are being provided in the terminal area for passengers.
- The surveillance capabilities are being integrated into the digital infrastructure to be able to store the large amounts of surveillance data picked up by terminal and cargo area cameras and index and recall them when required for forensic and operational analysis needs.
- Airport back office operations are being integrated from a set of stovepiped systems to loosely coupled, service-oriented systems that are at once flexible and agile and can support a variety of orchestrated functions.
- The airport IT infrastructure is being looked upon as a backbone platform to run the various federal agency system components such as those required by the Customs and Border Protection, the Department of Agriculture, APHIS terminals, and the Department of Homeland Security and TSA systems for flight manifests, no-fly lists, name searches, and other security measures. This infrastructure will also run the FAA's system of weather and other sensing equipment, along with automation and information requirements for the air

traffic management operations, including tower operations, radio equipment for communications between aircraft and ground controllers, and terminal radios for gate personnel.

■ As a backbone, the airport will provide an enterprise service bus and an Internet transport layer, as well as connectivity, data exchange services, and a network of networks. The IT data centers for RMN have been allocated and located at various strategic locations inside the airport perimeter along with alternate sites for continuity of operations (COOP).

■ One of the principles of RMN's enterprise is to outsource all non–mission-related services to the maximum extent possible. As a result of this principle, RMN has determined to outsource payroll processing to a commercial payroll services provider; security services to a local security services provider; benefits processing to a commercial provider of health care, dental care, and disability benefits and another provider of life and disability insurance services. RMN has also contracted with a local hospital to set up, manage, and operate the sick bays and ambulance services and to stand by to provide triage in the event of emergencies, terrorist incidents, accidents, and other unforeseen disastrous events.

■ The outsourcing decisions will continue to be made on a case-by-case basis and RMN needs a framework to make such outsourcing decisions for business services. The framework must factor in the cost/benefit equation, the division of responsibilities between the service provider and RMN, and the level of service required and guaranteed, as well as the evaluation of risks involved. The IT group, with its expertise in building models, has been tapped to assist in the development of a framework for the evaluation of service outsourcing.

■ A big change for RMN on its journey from a small, rural airport to a vibrant aviation hub for passengers and cargo is the transformation from people-oriented operations to process-oriented operations. In the past, a combination of training and hiring the right people was sufficient for the right decisions to be made and for smooth operations on a lightweight scale. Today, the magnitude and speed of operations (commonly called operations tempo) have introduced new needs for documented, enforced, and monitored processes that supplement the traditional human resource–based approach of hiring the right people; training, assessing, and educating them in the elements of the job to be performed; and rewarding or punishing employees for good or bad performance. The transformation from people-oriented, relatively autonomous decision making to a process-centric, command-and-control decision-making process is a big change that is expected to produce a lot of pushback. With the potential for the formation of strong labor unions, egged on by national trade unions looking to establish a beachhead, there is a need to understand and manage cultural issues. The IT staff has been tapped for the process modeling efforts to be able to model, represent, and promulgate process flows for the new ways of doing business. However, there is still a need for operations managers to address issues of process implementation and culture transformation.

■ As part of the U.S. federal government initiatives, the FAA has also tapped the CIO of RNM to assist in contributing to the evolving National Information Exchange Model (NIEM) that is harmonizing data specifications across multiple agencies. Because the airport information systems need to feed or consume information from so many federal agencies, it is essential that the planning and evolution of these systems benefit from and contribute to the NIEM efforts.

■ RNM has paid a Washington-based think tank for studies related to unmanned aerial vehicle (UAV) operations in the 2015–2020 timeframe to examine the implications of package express companies and cargo carriers moving to UAV operations. The report has indicated that several changes need to be made at all levels of command and control, tower operations, safety measures, facilities, locations, runways, and parking spaces. The hope is that the enterprise architecture effort can represent the state of the airport in 2015 with UAV operations to support the analysis required to plan, budget, acquire, undertake, and achieve UAV operations with a three-year advance notice if required.

Management and Governance

It is clear that any transition from the current state of operations of Richard M. Nixon Airport to the future requires significant planning skills based on hard information and the documentation of assumptions, constraints, and risks. It also requires generating funds based on clearly articulated plans, benefits, and financial analysis. The undertaking of stovepipe initiatives is not an option because of the cross-coupling of issues and the effect of changes on operational, systems, and technology elements in support of one initiative often have significant detrimental side effects on other aspects of the operation.

The types of problems and challenges as well as opportunities that have emerged are all complex and hard to understand without having some way of modeling and asking trade-off related questions. At the same time, modeling the enterprise requires that all items of the enterprise be visible and relatable in some manner, somehow.

The management of Richard M. Nixon Airport has heard that enterprise architecture is the body of knowledge that can help it represent the enterprise to support the types of decisions that it needs to make. Thus management has consulted the FEAC Institute for expertise on how to go about modeling various aspects of the enterprise architecture, knowing that the managers will not be able to model every aspect of the enterprise, nor will they be able to detail every aspect of the enterprise where all the implementation risk and details are also exposed.

In short, FEAC advised the management of Richard M. Nixon Airport that the following steps are required:

1. Build a high-level set of models (enterprise architecture) that represent the current state of RMN. These models represent the current state of the mission and the goals and objectives, the lines of business, services and products, capabilities/and business functions, locations, organizations and roles, systems and services, technology elements, and standards. These models provide classification schemes (taxonomies) and relationships that relate the various model elements. For example, the mission drives the types of products and services; the need to provide those products and services drives the need for capabilities or business functions; and each function needs a set of resources such as performers, locations, systems, services, and technology elements (ways and means).

2. Collect candidate problems and issues as well as areas of opportunities. Analyze these in the light of the elements of the high-level models previously built. This analysis will yield insight into what problems and issues can be solved (or not), what is the magnitude of the effort and complexity in solving those problems, and what are the costs and benefits in solving those problems. The analysis will also address which opportunities can be harvested immediately or for the short term, which opportunities cannot readily be harvested without significant risk or delay, and which opportunities are not worth pursuing. Opportunity analysis must of course be supplemented by strategic analysis, which includes looking at alternatives and competition.

3. Formulate a portfolio of business initiatives that are in line with the ability to raise funding, that fit within the resource constraints and risk tolerance of the enterprise, and that can be undertaken to produce results that are within the window of the problem requirement or opportunity timeframes. Remember that the business initiatives may address one or more problem areas or opportunity areas and may not have a 1:1 correspondence with problems or opportunities. The portfolio is an important concept in assessing the effectiveness of investments in the initiatives. Managing initiatives as a portfolio provides a holistic view of where to put the enterprise dollars—and in what proportion in terms of importance to the mission and goals (short term and long term) of the enterprise.

4. Formulate a portfolio of solutions that form the basis for projects. These projects are budgeted and planned through the initiatives. Once again, an initiative may define one or more projects. Managing the implementation of these initiatives is a conventional operational exercise that enterprises have learned and performed over many projects. Implementation initiatives have been managed through combinations of agile techniques of spiral development, project management controls such as Earned Value Management, and close tracking and monitoring, as well as the establishment of personal incentives to project teams through motivational management.

The FEAC Institute also pointed out that the enterprise architecture can support many of the business and decision-making processes of the enterprise. Each of these processes supports some aspect of enterprise transformation:

- **Strategic transformation**   A fundamental change in the business areas, lines of business, and offered products and services as a result of reinvention or as a reaction to competitive pressures.

- **Operational transformation**   A change in the ways in which business is currently done with the objective of effecting improvements, controlling costs, improving transparency or visibility of operations, motivating internal stakeholders, or satisfying pressures from external stakeholders or some other operational objective. Transformations can also relate to dealing with the complexities of increasing the scale of operations or speeding up the operations tempo to provide faster, better services.

- **Services transformation**   A change in the way that the capabilities of the enterprise are achieved and a shift away from or into using internal operations versus retaining external service providers. The benefits of services transformation is that the enterprise can leverage specialized, advanced services at lower cost than it can implementing smaller-scale, rudimentary operations in-house. Also, by taking a discrete service view of operations rather than using embedded functions, RMN can capitalize on the opportunities offered by outsourcing or creating internal profit centers that provide packaged business services.

- **Systems transformation**   A change in the way that systems (IT or otherwise) are architected to leverage architectural improvements in separation of concerns, loose coupling, modularity, scalability, and survivability. RMN also wants to view systems themselves, forming a larger family of systems (FoS) or a system of systems (SoS).

- **Technology transformation**   A change in technologies that provides a refresh of current technology to bring benefits of contemporary technology to all stakeholders. Examples of contemporary technology that is useful to stakeholders include the availability of wireless Internet services, small self-serve applications that provide data or perform atomic functions, ubiquitous voice and data transmission capabilities, and other such items that users are beginning to take for granted. Because of the diversity of technologies, RMN wants to establish a well-ordered and widespread categorization scheme for technology areas and technology services. This taxonomy scheme must be consistent with the external partners of RMN, such as the FAA, to ensure interoperability of specific items of technology.

The Way Forward

The strategic planning activities conducted by a strategic planning team to define the strategic vision and phased roadmap resulted in the "Richard M. Nixon International Airport 2011–2015 and Beyond" vision document. Put simply, the strategic vision is "Upgrade Richard M. Nixon Airport to become a viable alternative for LAX to local, national, and international passengers as an en-route point or as a destination within a 15-year timeframe."

Figure 3.2-3 shows the ambitious, phased implementation of the vision as foreseen by the strategic planning team. RMN management is convinced that without the enterprise planning support that comes from the EA team, the vision will simply remain a vision.

The Chief Architect and CIO of RMN, working with the executive management team, have taken on the responsibility of converting strategy into planning and planning into execution. Based on internal strategy meetings and discussions, they explored the following approaches for transforming the strategic plan into a budget, a program, and an initiative roadmap and then moving forward to the aggressive implementation schedule.

In Figure 3.2-3, one of the approaches was based on applying best practices in the U.S. federal government to build architectural representations to assist in the transformation of the strategic plan to a planning roadmap. This approach is applied at each of the major phases of the RMN transformation roadmap into the year 2025:

- The (implicit) enterprise architecture represented by the collection of viewpoints (Business/Process, Data/Information, Systems/Applications, and Technology and Standards) is based on the FEAF and represents the elements of transformation.

- An initial representation of a portfolio of candidate programs and initiatives is developed by looking at the various dimensions of transformation as evidenced by the enterprise architecture.

- A business justification model is used to allocate funding and resources and refine the initial portfolio into a set of projects.

- The DoDAF Project Viewpoint is used to construct models of the Project Portfolio, which is then tied to capability developments that produce desired effects.

- The changes caused in the enterprise as a result of achieving the desired effects are applied to the enterprise architecture.

Another approach that the Chief Architect and CIO examined was based on the DoDAF approach used by the Department of Defense. The difference between the earlier approach, based on defining an end state of the enterprise and developing capabilities to reach the end state, and the DoD Planning process is that the latter is based on capability-based acquisition rather than solution acquisition at the planning stage. By deferring the actual design of the solution to a later step, the architect can take advantage of advances in solution building, materials, technology, and more.

In this approach, strategic goals and objectives are transformed into statements of capability needs. For example, a strategic objective to provide a facility for international flights may require the following capabilities:

- Runway capabilities for landing wide-body aircraft
- Capabilities for 300 or more passengers coming in on a flight
- Multilingual information desk capabilities for passenger assistance

FIGURE 3.2-3 Vision for the Evolution of RMN

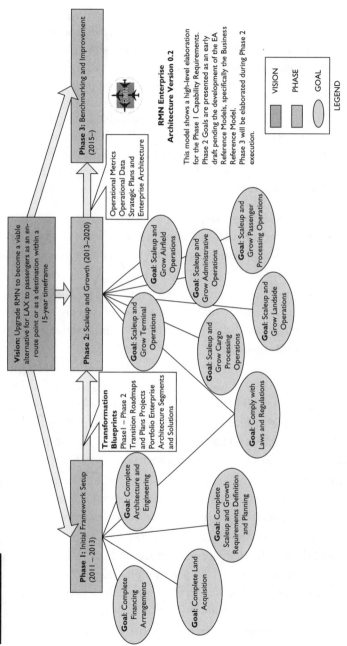

Vision: Upgrade RMN to become a viable alternative for LAX to passengers as an en-route point or as a destination within a 15-year timeframe

Phase 1: Initial Framework Setup (2011 – 2013)

Goal: Complete Financing Arrangements

Goal: Complete Land Acquisition

Goal: Complete Scaleup and Growth Requirements Definition and Planning

Goal: Complete Architecture and Engineering

Transformation Blueprints
Phase I – Phase 2 Transition Roadmaps and Plans Projects Portfolio Enterprise Architecture Segments and Solutions

Phase 2: Scaleup and Growth (2013–2020)

Goal: Comply with Laws and Regulations

Goal: Scaleup and Grow Terminal Operations

Goal: Scaleup and Grow Cargo Processing Operations

Goal: Scaleup and Grow Airfield Operations

Goal: Scaleup and Grow Administrative Operations

Goal: Scaleup and Grow Landside Operations

Goal: Scaleup and Grow Passenger Processing Operations

Operational Metrics
Operational Data
Strategic Plans and
Enterprise Architecture

Phase 3: Benchmarking and Improvement (2015–)

RMN Enterprise Architecture Version 0.2

This model shows a high-level elaboration for the Phase 1 Capability Requirements. Phase 2 Goals are presented as an early draft pending the development of the EA Reference Models, specifically the Business Reference Model.
Phase 3 will be elaborated during Phase 2 execution.

VISION

PHASE

GOAL

LEGEND

The DoDAF Capability and Project Views are used to represent the need and the implementation plan respectively as portfolios that have internal dependencies and must be orchestrated in a synchronized manner to deliver the strategic goal.

Rather than making an early decision on the approach, the Chief Architect and CIO have left it to the EA team to determine the actual modeling and representation approach.

Because of the need for a common context across all stakeholders of RMN, the RMN Board, through the Chair of the RMN Airport Authority, has commissioned an EA team to build an enterprise-level architecture of the as-is airport operations. In kicking off the efforts, the Chair instructed the CIO who was made responsible for execution and oversight to see to the following:

- The enterprise architecture must cover the breadth of the operations fully and reflect the complex nature and interconnections of various operational architecture elements. The enterprise architecture must reference the mission and current vision of RMN.

- The EA will be used to set up a common understanding of RMN's operations as well as to provide a context for analyzing the roles of systems, systems functionality, technology, and other standards and to understand the span and influence of specific initiatives.

- The EA will provide the basis for a transformation vision that will be part of the strategic plan for RMN as well as a stated driver for initiatives. The transformation vision for RMN is driven by competitive pressures, regulatory environment, opportunities afforded by market forces, technology drivers, and changes in demographics and air travel in the future. Transformations may occur in one or more of the following dimensions:

  - **Transformation of business processes**   These are transformations that change the types of activities performed; their performers; their locations; the inputs and outputs that they produce, consume, or transform; and the sequencing of business processes.

  - **Transformation of technology infrastructure**   These are transformations that result in infusion of new technologies, replacement of obsolete equipment and technologies, and exploitations of innovations in the aviation and airport management industry worldwide.

  - **Transformation of human resource infrastructure**   This involves changing the skill mix of the types of human resources, selective automation and replacement of manual operations with automated ones, and retraining of human resources to face new business challenges and take advantage of new business opportunities.

■ **Transformation of processing locations**   These involve changes in the locations where business activities occur, splitting up or co-locating activities for more effective and efficient processing, or performing location consolidations for locations that have mushroomed from piecemeal changes in processes such as the grafting of Homeland Security procedures after 9/11.

■ **Transformation of motivation**   These involve finding new ways to motivate organizations supporting, running, and managing the airport, such as promotion of commercial enterprises through outsourcing, new incentive schemes, and other methods to use motivation techniques to achieve increased effectiveness and efficiencies.

■ To manage the EA efforts and ensure that they stay within bounds, the RMN Chair has instructed the CIO to guide the EA team on partitioning (segmenting) the enterprise architecture along lines of business, product lines, or functional lines. The segments will provide a "smaller unit" of enterprise architecting than the entire RMN enterprise. Rather than think of segments as organized by current organizational boundaries, the RMN Chair has instructed that segments must represent logical line-of-business boundaries for products and services.

■ After the completion of the as-is EA representation effort, the RMN Chair and the Board will commission a to-be version of the EA where various current state items will be replaced by future state items. These include business processes, systems, personnel roles, organizational structures, and methods of information exchanges between RMN's partners and stakeholders. At the completion of the representation of the to-be architecture for RMN, the enterprise architect will also be required to provide a transition roadmap that arranges the various initiatives in chronological order for sequenced implementation. The roadmap will incorporate dependencies between initiatives.

■ At the same time, the RMN Chair and Board will also commission the elaboration of line-of-business and crosscutting segments through a segment architecture set of projects. These will be decided on a case-by-case basis based on planned initiatives that require the information from a more detailed segment architecture rather than the more abstract EA.

■ All initiatives will use the EA as a knowledge base to show how they will accomplish the vision, and also describe which elements of the enterprise architecture they touch. Initiatives are also required to describe those elements of the as-is state of the enterprise that will not be transformed, changed, or replaced (that is, invariants) in the transformation effort.

■ The enterprise architecture will also be used as a pattern to benchmark the span and depth of the RMN enterprise against comparable airports as well as larger airports that represent a vision of where RMN is headed. Benchmarking is done by comparing common architectural elements as well as by comparing patterns of elements as used by RMN against similar patterns elsewhere.

Questions Architecture Will Answer

The purpose of an architecture effort is to gather and represent data about the problem that will answer the questions that the business wants answered. The answers to the questions will also provide the insight for formulating strategic, operational, systems and technology solutions to the problems the enterprise is trying to resolve or the transformations that the enterprise has undertaken. Some of the questions that the RMN Enterprise Architecture effort must answer, once the data is gathered and the models built, are:

■ What are the various core mission segments and crosscutting support segments for RMN?

■ Who are the major stakeholders that the airport has to deal with?

■ What are the various types of systems that are used to automate the RMN operations?

■ What are the various environmental factors, such as national, state, and local legislation, that constrain the operations of RMN?

Proposed Analysis That Architecture Will Support

The enterprise architecture is intended to form a context into which more detail can be filled in. As a result, the approach to defining the EA relies heavily on taxonomy (classification) models to reflect the various dimensions of the enterprise:

■ Motivation

■ Capability segments

■ Locations

■ Stakeholders/performers

■ Information

■ Event types

The initial analysis focuses on determining whether the taxonomical architecture elements reflect the breadth of the RMN enterprise. This analysis is based on validating whether all elements of the enterprise are reflected appropriately under the various taxonomies for the dimensions described. This analysis ensures that the EA taxonomies provide the foundational bedrock for more detailed work that has more immediate use for transformational initiatives.

Nature of Decision Support Required

The decisions that need to be made within the architectural timeframe are primarily planning and prioritization decisions for investments related to initiatives as well as a recognition of gaps in the current operations of RMN Airport that need to be addressed for RMN to transform itself in line with the strategic goals and objectives.

Nature of Solution to Be Provided

In this phase, the focus is on laying out the anatomy of the RMN enterprise to be able then to overlay the systems and solutions and processes on a firm foundation to assist in planning and moving forward. Two other concurrent architecting efforts are directed at developing segment architecture for a segment of the enterprise and a solution architecture for a specific subarea within the selected segment.

Architecture Development

This section describes the key players, timeframes and intended scope of the architecture development effort.

Developing organizations include the following:

- RMN Enterprise Architecture Project Office
- Development contractor support
- Office of the RMN Chief Architect

The development time period is as follows:

- Six months after kickoff for release of draft 0.5
- One year after kickoff for release of Version 1.00 of the RMN-EA

Development Conventions, Methodologies, Standards, and Practices

The RMN architecture team will approach the architecture development by partitioning it into three types of architecture, each layer of which will provide context for the succeeding layers. Each succeeding layer will refine and detail the abstractions of a previous layer. The refinement may be a transformation rather than a direct 1:1 correspondence between the items of the two layers. This is consistent with the OMB Practice Guidance (OMB, 2007) promoted by the federal government of the United States.

The process framework used to develop the architecture will be chosen from either the DoDAF Six-Step Architecture Development Process (Department of Defense, 2009) or the TOGAF Architecture Development Methodology (The Open Group, 2009).

Architecture Key Drivers and Goals

Table 3.2-3 describes the key drivers that make the development of the enterprise architecture an imperative.

TABLE 3.2-3   Key Drivers for Architecture Development

Driver	Description
Complexity	Without the EA, RMN planners have no way of placing their plans in a common context and analyzing the impact of change on each other's plans. The sheer scale and complexity of the RMN enterprise is overwhelming. The enterprise architecture organizes this complexity using a gradual "unfolding" scheme for placing every aspect of the enterprise in context to every vested stakeholder.
Urgency	Without the EA, RMN's ambitious transformation schedule is at great risk of delivering too little too late. The EA provides a governance mechanism that will allow RMN to make course corrections or anticipate and plan for problems on a very large scale, long before they become obstacles.
Decision Support	The EA provides information for decision support at the planning stage itself. By making better early decisions, it is anticipated that failure probabilities are reduced. At the same time, making decisions earlier in a phased roadmap prevents wasted activity and redirection at the implementation stage.
Managing Resource Constraints	Although RMN managers have been very good at managing individual programs and initiatives, without an EA, making portfolio prioritization and resource allocation decisions is difficult, if not impossible. RMN's ambitious growth and transformation plan is predicated on the availability of capital as well as increasing revenues. If these are not to be, the roadmap may have to reflect resource shortfalls and address slower growth or reduced scope.

Architecture Scope

The enterprise architecture project team broke down the complex, large EA representation effort into smaller modeling tasks that would individually develop facets of the enterprise architecture but ensure that an individual element of architecture in each facet corresponds to the same element within another facet and the architecture as a whole is free of inconsistencies and disconnects (that is, the EA would be an integrated architecture). The EA team also internally decided on a few key principles that will be managed to control scope creep and keep the level of abstraction high and consistent.

Core Models

The architecture policy established by the CIO working with the Chief Architect, and the EA team requires the development of the following "core" models for representing the RMN enterprise architecture.

For capability-based projection and enterprise management needs, the following models are required:

- CV-1, because it identifies the capabilities and ties them to strategic goals and objectives
- CV-3, because it allows tracking of changing capability configurations (only by name) over time
- CV-4, because it captures the capability dependencies as well as the taxonomy
- CV-5, because it has relationships between capabilities, organizations that perform those capabilities, and the capability configurations (at least by name) with delivery dates from the projects

For portfolio-based views of projects and initiatives, the EA requires the following models:

- PV-1, because it links projects to the organizations responsible for them
- PV-2, because it provides project timelines and their dependencies

For clear delineation of authority and responsibility through formal organization structures, the following model is required:

- OV-4, because it identifies organizations that appear in CV-5 and PV-1

The policy also allows the RMN EA team to build additional models that are "fit for purpose," with the caveat that these models, if sufficiently diverse and nonstandard, may hinder communications. The policy encouraged the definition of standardized "templates" even for customized fit-for-purpose models to promote sharing, aggregation, and comparison types of analysis.

As part of this integrated architecture, the team planned to build the following model representations:

- Capability Viewpoint
- A Goals model that describes the vision and goals of RMN as an enterprise and relates them to a set of capabilities that are required to fulfill the goals (CV-1)
- A Capability Hierarchy model that decomposes the higher-level capabilities described within the Goals model into a capability hierarchy (CV-2)
- A cross-reference between the capabilities described within the Business Reference Model (BRM) and the capabilities inside the Goals and Capability Hierarchy models (CV-6)

Enterprise Business Taxonomies

The enterprise architecture will make use of hierarchical (taxonomical) model representations to describe the breadth and depth of various dimensions of the enterprise and cross-reference models that relate elements from the hierarchical models:

- A *Business Reference Model* (BRM) will describe the various areas of operations of RMN and progressively represent products and services in each of these areas of business. The BRM will also list under each product and service the sub-functions that are required to produce them. Each function will further be elaborated with a top-level process that represents a currently identified cohesive set of activities for which policy guidance, execution instruction, rules, and procedures have been established (OV-5a). The BRM will also be used to define enterprise architecture segments of the RMN enterprise: either as vertical line-of-business (LOB) segments or as crosscutting segments that are used by and affect every vertical segment. A separate set of EA projects will deal with modeling the segment architectures.

- A *Performance Reference Model* (PRM) will describe the various performance measures that are currently used to manage specific areas of business and lines of businesses (SvcV-7).

- A *Service Reference Model* that describes the various types of automated services available will be displayed as a taxonomy. These services are required to support and automate the business functions and processes described inside the BRM (SvcV4).

- A *Technology (Standards) Reference Model* will describe the taxonomy of standards (not vendor products) that is currently in effect at RMN and is assisting RMN in procuring and integrating elements of technology (StdV-1).

- An *Organization Relationships Model* will describe the various stakeholders that are part of the RMN internal enterprise and the extended enterprise, such as federal, state, and local agencies and communities (OV-4).

In addition, in much the same way as a town planning exercise has to address key landmarks, highways, water supply and sewage lines, and land drainage issues, planning at the RMN enterprise level also requires the articulation of a number of portfolios such as Systems Portfolio, System Function/Services Portfolio, system processing facilities, platforms and processing assets, and communication networks that form the "town planning" parts of the RMN enterprise.

Key Information Exchanges

RMN also wants to represent an understanding of the information highways that are needed or that exist to connect various stakeholders and pipe the information they need for decision-making and performance of mission activities. These highways have two flavors:

- A logical map of the various information exchanges that flow between RMN and its external stakeholders (OV-2). The level of the modeling is to sketch out the needs for information exchange and not to enumerate all the specific information exchanges. The result of such models is a clear understanding of the topology of information exchanges in the manner of information pipelines required to connect the various stakeholders.

- Systems/Services Connectivity Description, a high-level physical information connectivity model that depicts the mechanisms that support connectivity between RMN and its stakeholders (SV-2/SvcV-2). The level of the model is to record key logical information transfer networks but not to detail the various links and network connections that are required at the physical connection level. This model requires an information pipeline between systems and services and establishes the minimum connectivity topology requirements for systems and services to be able to exchange information with each other.

Information Models

Exchanging information is not sufficient. It is important that the receiving party (stakeholder or system/service) understands the meaning of the information it received. The use of conceptual data models that are shared at the enterprise level establishes the context for data at lower levels. Shared data models enable shared understanding of semantics. The RMN EA team decided to build the following models:

■ A high-level Conceptual Data Model that establishes the various types of information to be managed by RMN. The model is used to establish a categorization scheme for information and will represent a type of Data Reference Model (DIV-1). The decision of building more detailed logical data models was left as a segment architecture effort that was outside the scope of the larger RMN enterprise architecture.

■ A Semantic Model for representing the key business concepts and relationships. The RMN EA team was also interested in exploring the use of semantic representation schemes for the business terms and definitions. Their belief was that a lot of the airport terminology was fairly commonplace within the aviation industry and was amenable to being recorded and managed as a readily available body of knowledge that could be used for powering web search applications, referencing document storage, and other opportunities where English-like searching and concept-based retrieval of information were essential. This effort would be part of RMN's decision to participate in Semantic Web (Web 2.0) to provide information to the public in an intuitive and simple way.

Enterprise Architecture Stakeholders

Table 3.2-4 describes the RMN EA stakeholders.

TABLE 3.2-4	Architecture	Audience	Stakeholders
Stakeholders for the Chosen Architecture Scope	Enterprise	All stakeholders, both internal and external	RMN Board; RMN executive management; RMN investors; RMN customers, RMN partners; regulatory authorities; state, local, and federal partners.
	Segment	Business owners	Responsible divisions and departments, their management and staff. External partners in business processes who either provide process support or need to exchange information with RMN.
	Solution	Users and developers	Program managers, planners, solution developers, contractors, and subcontractors.

Assumptions and Constraints

The following assumptions were made by the architecture team. The findings and recommendations that will be generated at the end of the architecture effort are subject to these assumptions:

Assumptions

A fundamental assumption is the durability of planning structures. The enterprise architecture development scope is bracketed by the strategic plan, strategic goals, and objectives. If these change, the enterprise architecture scope must also change. The elements of the strategic plan form the basis for the strategic elements of the EA, such as the capability needs and the BRM.

The operating plan describes current operations in terms of line items, capital requirements, revenues, and projected costs and profits. The scope of the operations usually must lie within the parameters of revenues and costs. The assumption is that RMN is at a point where the fidelity of the operations plan to actual numbers is good—in short, the years of operation of RMN have lent stability to operations plans. The elements of the operations plan form the basis for the operational viewpoints of the RMN enterprise architecture.

The EA is constrained by regulatory assumptions. For this version of the EA, the following regulatory bodies or authority will be considered for regulatory impact:

- The Federal Aviation Administration for flight safety and air traffic management
- The Department of Homeland Security and the Transportation Safety Administration for passenger, baggage, and cargo–related constraints as well as requirements for airport terminal safety
- County and city regulations for local ordinances related to noise pollution, traffic, and other items
- The Environmental Protection Agency for hazardous cargo, pollution, and disposals
- The Occupational Health and Safety Administration (OSHA) for occupational safety and health of airport staff and contract personnel
- Sarbanes-Oxley for fiscal and operational transparency of RMN operations

Constraints

For the first version of the EA, access to stakeholders and subject-matter experts is limited because of unavailable time or access and insufficient resources to canvass and arrange interviews and set up post-processing of interview results.

RMN is an ongoing operation where execution of activities takes precedence to EA and planning-related activities that are perceived as peripheral and counterproductive. Until the EA can produce results that command attention, this will remain a culture issue. For the first version of the EA, the culture of treating EA and planner interactions as a low-priority item compared to the operational challenges of the day will remain a barrier.

Architecture-Specific Stakeholders

The following key players are stakeholders who have an interest in the architecting effort and the outcome of the architecture effort in terms of plans, roadmaps, proposed transformations, and courses of action that are driven by the results of the architecture project:

Sponsor

The primary sponsor of the enterprise architecture effort is the RMN Board authorizing the CEO and Airport Administrator to proceed with the architecting initiative.

The CEO, in turn, has delegated the task of actually developing, presenting, and using the EA to the Chief Information Officer. The CIO has appointed the Chief Architect and has entrusted him with the task of developing, maintaining, and extending the enterprise architecture. The CIO has also charged the Chief Architect with the task of developing a governance plan that will allow the architecture to be used as an ongoing tool in planning initiatives and systems solutions.

Participating Organizations

The organizations participating are the various divisional chiefs responsible for segments of the business operations as well as the headquarters staff organization responsible for generating strategic, operational, and financial plans. These chiefs and staff organizations will reach back into their organizations for specific subject-matter expertise.

Validating Organizations

The division chiefs and staff organizations will also be responsible for validating the representations of the enterprise architecture. They will comment on the appropriateness and accuracy of findings and the analyses and will assist in developing the ingredients of the evolving enterprise transformation plan. They will ultimately be the offices of primary responsibility (OPR) for the action items and initiatives described in the RMN transformation plan.

Architecture Governance

The RMN CIO working with the Chief Architect will develop an architecture governance plan. The plan will be responsible for describing the following:

- **Policy** Policies that incorporate the enterprise architecture. Examples of such policies are the purchase of IT equipment and platforms in accordance with the Technical Reference Model and the standards documented by the EA; and the use by software solutions of the shared data models that are generated by the enterprise architecture to improve data quality, consistency, and interoperability.

- **Organization** Organizational structures in support of reviews and assessments of initiatives and assessments being made in alignment with EA principles. These are temporary bodies made up of people from functional organizations, development organizations, and the architecture program office. The purpose of these bodies is to review proposed developments and initiatives to ensure alignment with the EA principles and EA context as well as compliance with architecture-related policies.

■ **Process**   Development, communication, and enforcement of architecture-related processes. The articulation of standard processes, roles, and expected inputs and outputs, as well as specific guidance, is a step forward in the architecture maturity cycle.

Architecture Maintenance

The RMN EA development team will put an EA maintenance plan in place. Different aspects of the architecture change at different rates. For example, the core business and mission do not change as often as the technology aspects of the architecture. RMN will continue to host air operations, terminal operations, etc. New technology infusion, on the other hand is constantly occurring as better methods, automation and techniques supplant older ones. The Federal CIO Council (2005) cites that, for the FEA Reference Models, an "aging" phenomenon occurs in which the Technical Reference Model and Performance Reference Model evolve more frequently than the Service, Data, and Business Reference Models. This phenomenon must be accommodated into the RMN EA maintenance plan.

The architecture maintenance strategy describes the following:

■ Principles for approaching the modeling of various elements of the architecture. An example of such principles is the use of notional performers rather than actual performers by defining roles rather than organizations or specific people. Another example is the use of a notional location such as the Fuel Storage Facility instead of Building 1600. Notional architecture elements are more stable but may be more difficult to recognize by stakeholders who are looking for the occurrence of their real world data inside the models.

■ Maps showing the durability of the architecture information. Unfortunately, this is a trade-off between long-lived generalities and very useful but short-lived specificity.

■ A maintenance approach spelling out the maintenance process, roles, activities, inputs, outputs, and constraints.

■ A configuration management strategy for the architecture as well as release frequency, release identification, management of defects and issues, and ultimate improvement of the architecture.

Mapping of Models to EA Goals and Drivers

To ensure that the enterprise architecture effort is aligned with the original drivers, a matrix tracing the drivers to elements of the enterprise architecture will be presented.

Enterprise Architecture Development Approach

The Chief Architect, working with the CIO's staff, evaluated the following architecture frameworks to determine which of them most suit the specific needs of RMN. The initial assumption that the evaluators started with was that the RMN architecture team would have to build architectures at multiple levels of abstraction to deal with the scale, complexity, and volume of the architecture representations. They adopted the tried-and-trusted partitioning approach of breaking the architecture representations into the following classes:

- A single RMN enterprise architecture.
- Many segment architectures representing models of the various business segments identified in the EA.
- As many solution architectures as are required to provide support for business processes with a combination of manual and automated operations. Solution architectures could either be contained within and supporting a single segment or span and support multiple segments.

Table 3.2-5 shows the architecture framework assessments of RMN Chief Architect and the CIO staff.

Development Methods and Techniques

The choice of development methodology for the architectures will primarily be driven by the following principles:

- Taxonomy structures are homogeneous tree-style classification models. They will be built using taxonomy tools. However, the architecture elements they represent will be managed inside the repository.
- The architecture team will be building more than one architecture, as described in Section 3.2 (the EA, segment architectures, and solution architectures will be required, for example). Each architecture will be elaborated using multiple viewpoints and models (views) that will serve different constituencies and interests.

TABLE 3.2-5	Assessments of Architecture Frameworks for Use by RMN	
Framework	**Assessment**	**Recommendation**
Federal Enterprise Architecture Framework	With its focus on the business, technology, application, and data dimensions of the enterprise, it was considered more IT-centric. But RMN determined that by generalizing the application to automated systems such as baggage handling systems (BHS) as well as information processing systems, the FEAF could be adapted to the RMN need. The transformation focus of the FEAF was important to RMN, as were the various transformation processes. The breakdown of a large enterprise into segments was very appropriate for RMN as well. The FEAF does not provide specific guidance on types of models that can be built or the means to integrate these models.	The FEAF's focus on enterprise transformation is right in line with RMN's intention of transforming itself strategically and operationally from a minor airport to a major alternative to LAX in a 15-year timeframe. The FEAF's IT focus may need to be broadened to accommodate non-IT systems planning and transformation initiatives. Use the FEAF as a general framework for expressing the EA as a support for enterprise transformation.
DoD Architecture Framework	The viewpoints of the DoDAF are readily applicable to RMN. The viewpoints represent the strategic, initiative development, operational, systems, services, standards, and technology infrastructure interests of RMN and are useful in representing models that are of immediate use to transformation agents. The DoDAF generalizes the architecting approach beyond IT and is therefore more generally applicable. The DoDAF stresses the need for integrated architecture development that ensures consistent model development across groups and provides the potential to aggregate and compare architecture across the various business segments.	The models of the DoDAF have gained currency within a broad audience and provide the mechanism needed to develop an integrated architecture model set. Several tools are available for producing DoDAF-described models. A large body of trained and available contractors is capable of providing modeling support. Use the DoDAF as the primary modeling guidance. Because the DoDAF is nonprescriptive for the selection of modeling techniques, but is very insistent that the output of these techniques be integrated, RMN should focus on selecting a set of complementary techniques that will result in integrated architectures.

TABLE 3.2-5	Assessments of Architecture Frameworks for Use by RMN (*Continued*)	
Framework	**Assessment**	**Recommendation**
The Open Group Architecture Framework	The Architecture Development Method (ADM) is an excellent process framework for developing architectures. TOGAF does not specify methodologies or specific types of models and viewpoints, although it does specify the types of artifacts that are deemed deliverables at each stage gate of the ADM process. TOGAF also embraces the viewpoints of the FEAF—Business, Application, Data, and Technology—and is therefore more IT-centric than the DoDAF, which was aimed at acquisition of large and complex IT and non-IT systems, systems of systems, and families of systems.	TOGAF was deemed to be too IT-centric, but the use of the ADM as a process methodology was inviting because the DoDAF does not provide a more prescriptive process than the general Six Step architecting method. The use of ADM should be evaluated as a candidate for use as a process framework. ADM may have to be tailored to be simplified based on determination of core steps that need to be retained while preserving the integrity of the framework.

- Architecture must be integrated—all models that provide views of that architecture must consistently share architecture elements.

- Multiple architectures must also share consistent architecture elements when they reference the same item to enable federation across architectures. When external architectures are modeled, "crosswalks" may be established between similar architecture elements that come from diverse sources and must be maintained in the source formats.

- All methodology choices must be amenable to the preceding principles. No single methodology was found to cover all the viewpoints and all the models that are anticipated for use at RMN. Because of this unavailability of a single integrating methodology, multiple but noncompeting methodologies will be used for building the various models and views of the architecture that are required.

Tools, Repository, Security, and Data Management

The first task that will be undertaken after kickoff by the RMN enterprise architecture development team is the selection of tools, formats in which the models will be built and delivered, the choice of repository, and an environment for architecture data management that encompasses the needs for secure access, ubiquity, convenience, and availability.

Related Architecture Developments and Dependencies

The RMN enterprise architecture is intended to provide a backbone structure for overlaying segment architectures for individual business segments. The focus of the RMN EA is therefore to represent the breadth of the enterprise as a context-establishing mechanism. This breadth is represented using taxonomies for various enterprise dimensions. The RMN EA provides context for the following:

- Segment architectures for core mission (vertical) segments and supporting (horizontal) segments. Each of these is individually developed for each segment.
- Each segment architecture provides the context for one or many solution architectures. A solution is specific to a business segment (segment solution) or may serve more than one business segment (crosscutting solution).

The RMN enterprise architecture must also work with other architectures yet to be identified. The following are some examples of such architectures:

- Federal Aviation Administration's NextGen architecture
- State of California architectures
- San Miguel County architectures
- Department of Homeland Security architectures
- Department of Agriculture architectures
- Department of Justice architectures
- Commercial airline architectures

Architecture Release Schedule

The RMN EA Team will deliver the enterprise architecture models, analysis, and findings in increments to support a phased transformation plan that will move RMN to the vision it has set for itself. The release schedule for these increments is:

- Version 0.5 of the RMN enterprise architecture is scheduled to be delivered in a time period of six months after initial kickoff.
- Version 1.0 will be released in a time period of 12 months after initial kickoff. The 12-month period runs concurrently with the development of Version 0.5.
- Subsequent releases of the architecture will be delivered annually. Major releases of the architecture will coincide with major phase gates for RMN's transformation plan. The specific details of these dates are yet to be decided.

Findings and Recommendations

These are to be added after completion of Version 0.5 of the RMN enterprise architecture.

Appendices

The appendices to the Architecture Overview and summary will contain the explanation for the terms used for the architecture project itself and references to related architecture developments. The description of the actual architecture elements that form the content of the models for the EA are depicted in the Integrated Architecture Dictionary (AV-2).

AV-2 Integrated Data Dictionary

Before the advent of the DoD Architecture Framework, architecture projects delivered several models that were accompanied by their own glossary/dictionary. Each of these dictionaries or glossaries defined the architecture elements specific to the model they were documenting. The DoDAF, in an attempt to force the integration of these models (standardizing references to common elements), recommended the development of a single Integrated Dictionary (AV-2). The AV-2 forces architects to resolve conflicts and definitional issues across models, and provide a single consistent dictionary for the architecture as a whole.

Table 3.2-6 summarizes an AV-2 data dictionary.

TABLE 3.2-6	Model Information at a Glance	
Integrated Architecture Dictionary (AV-2) Model at a Glance	**Model Short Name**	AV-2
	Name	Integrated Data Dictionary
	Other Names	Integrated Model Glossary, Glossary
	Viewpoint	All Views
	Model Intent	Provide authoritative (sourced definitions) for architecture elements. Resolve inconsistencies between disparate definitions and names across different models of an integrated architecture.
	Model Audience	Everyone
	Formal Modeling Methodology	None
	Integration of Model with Other Views	AV-2 must define every term in every model that represents an architecture element. In addition, AV-2 must expand acronyms and abbreviated terms for all architecture elements.

Table 3.2-7 shows a sample AV-2 integrated architecture dictionary for the solution architecture developed for passenger identification. The example can be tailored by adding more information in additional columns, such as authoritative sources or references for the information (recommended) as well as alternative terms for the same architecture element (synonyms).

TABLE 3.2-7   Passenger Identification Solution Architecture AV-2 Example

Name	Type	Acronym	Description	Used in
Passenger Management System	System	PMS	Manages all aspects of passengers, including identifying passengers, entitling them for services, and managing interactions with them.	SV-1, SV-2, SV-3, SV-4, SV-5, SV-6, SV-8, SV-9
Airline Reservation and Ticketing System	System	ARTS	Manages bookings, ticketing, generation of boarding passes, and baggage tags.	SV-1, SV-2, SV-3, SV-4, SV-5, SV-6, SV-8, SV-9
Comprehensive Screening System	System	CSS	Manages all aspects of passenger hand luggage and personal screening.	SV-1, SV-2, SV-3, SV-4, SV-5, SV-6, SV-8, SV-9
Law Enforcement and Training System	System	LETS	Provides law enforcement support and is also used to train law enforcement officers.	SV-1, SV-2, SV-3, SV-4, SV-5, SV-6, SV-8, SV-9
Airline Reservation and Ticketing System (Mobile)	System	ARTS (Mobile)	Mobile version of ARTS to provide mobile access to passenger information.	SV-1, SV-2, SV-3, SV-4, SV-5, SV-6, SV-8, SV-9
Airline Reservation and Ticketing System (Kiosk)	System	ARTS (Kiosk)	Kiosk version of ARTS to provide boarding gate processing facilities.	SV-1, SV-2, SV-3, SV-4, SV-5, SV-6, SV-8, SV-9
Airport Baggage Tracking System–Commercial	System	ABTS (Commercial)	Airport-wide system to track all baggage at any place in the airport. Deployed at commercial baggage drop-off franchisees.	SV-1, SV-2, SV-3, SV-4, SV-5, SV-6, SV-8, SV-9
Customs and Border Protection System	System	CBPS	An external system fielded by the Customs and Border Protection Agency to provide customs processing of passengers from international flights.	SV-1, SV-2, SV-3, SV-4, SV-5, SV-6, SV-8, SV-9

Questions

1. For which types of stakeholders does the All Viewpoint provide benefits?
2. What are the challenges you foresee in developing an AV-1 for your own project in the following areas?
   a. Identifying and stating the problem that needs to be solved by using the architecture development as a representational and clarifying exercise.
   b. Identifying the stakeholders who are involved and must sponsor, support, collaborate on, and be the audience for the architecture development.
   c. Identifying the types of questions the architecture must answer as well as the types of analysis that must be performed and also the data that the analyses require.
   d. Identifying and specifying a scope and restricting yourself to it in order to prevent project or program "creep."
3. True or false: Provide clarifying statements to support your answer.
   a. The AV-1 is the very first model (or artifact) that is built in order to establish the scope, purpose, viewpoints, and models that will be covered by the architecture effort.
   b. The AV-1 is the very last model to be completed because at the end of an architecture development, the architecture team records its findings and recommendations also inside the AV-1.
4. What is the advantage of an integrated architecture dictionary (a single one for an entire architecture development effort) versus having a separate model glossary for each model that is built? What are the pros and cons?
5. What are the dimensions of scope that are described inside an AV-1? (Hint: Scope must define the breadth and depth of the architecture modeling domain, numbers, and types of models built and many others.)
6. For your own enterprise, who would be the various stakeholders in the enterprise architecture? What are the types of models you would build to provide value to them?
7. What is the purpose of including architecture development timeframes, costs, levels of effort involved, and development organizations inside the AV-1?
8. What are the pros and cons of using the AV-1 as an "index card" to contain information about your architecture in some larger architecture library or registry?

The Defense Architecture Registry System (DARS) is one such registry. What would you recommend as a method or mechanism to transmit, store, and manage the AV-1 in such a registry? How would someone use discovery techniques to browse such a registry?

9. What are the types of architecture elements documented in the AV-2 dictionary?

10. What is the purpose of the Integrated Architecture Dictionary?

11. What are some of the challenges in integrating AV-2 dictionaries across different enterprises? Discuss some of the problems with structural integration, such as data formats as well as semantic integration and differences in vocabularies and meanings.

Reference List

Department of Defense. (2009). *DoD Architecture Framework 2.0, Volumes I and II*. United States Department of Defense.

Federal CIO Council. (2005). *FEA Reference Model maintenance process*. A Joint Proposal of the Architecture and Infrastructure Committee and Federal Enterprise Architecture Program Management Office, June 2005.

Office of Management and Budget. (2007). FEA Practice Guidance, Federal Enterprise Architecture Program, Management Office, OMB, November 2007.

The Open Group. (2009). TOGAF Architecture Development Methodology (ADM). *The Open Group Architecture Framework (TOGAF), Version 9, Enterprise Edition*. The Open Group.

3.3

Strategic/Capability Viewpoint

The Strategic/Capability Viewpoint is useful primarily to enterprise planners who have a longer window of planning than simply dealing with tactical battles and support of current operations. For example, in the federal government, this planning window must extend to at least five years and the strategic plan must be revised at least once in three years. The Strategic/Capability Viewpoint provides the context for laying out projects and initiatives that are consistent with the goals and objectives of the enterprise.

The U.S. federal government and the Department of Defense have taken slightly different approaches to the Strategic/Capability Viewpoint. The federal government's planning cycle is based on programs and initiatives that are related to goals and objectives and the mission of a specific agency. The planning cycle for the DoD, on the other hand, is driven by capability needs for readiness to face and overcome threats to the nation. In a constantly changing world, the planning cycle is focused on the acquisition and development of capabilities as well as the closing of capability gaps that are distilled from lessons learnt during actual conduct of war and military exercises.

Government Performance Results Act (GPRA)

The Government Performance Results Act of 1993 (Office of Management and Budget, 1993) was enacted in response to the following findings by Congress and the General Accountability Office (GAO):

■ Waste and inefficiency in federal programs undermine the confidence of the American people in the government and reduces the federal government's ability to address adequately vital public needs.

■ Federal managers are seriously disadvantaged in their efforts to improve program efficiency and effectiveness, because of insufficient articulation of program goals and inadequate information on program performance.

■ Congressional policy making, spending decisions, and program oversight are seriously handicapped by insufficient attention to program performance and results.

The GPRA demands the following:

- The head of each agency is to submit to the Director of the Office of Management and Budget and to the Congress a strategic plan for program activities. Such plan shall contain the following:
  - A comprehensive mission statement covering the major functions and operations of the agency
  - General goals and objectives, including outcome-related goals and objectives, for the major functions and operations of the agency
  - A description of how the goals and objectives are to be achieved, including a description of the operational processes, skills, and technology and the human, capital, information, and other resources required to meet those goals and objectives
  - A description of how the performance goals included in the plan required by section 1115(a) of title 31 will be related to the general goals and objectives in the strategic plan
  - An identification of those key factors external to the agency and beyond its control that could significantly affect the achievement of the general goals and objectives
  - A description of the program evaluations used in establishing or revising general goals and objectives, with a schedule for future program evaluations
- The strategic plan is to cover a period of not less than five years forward from the fiscal year in which it is submitted, and will be updated and revised at least every three years.
- The GPRA also requires a performance plan: "The Director of the Office of Management and Budget shall require each agency to prepare an annual performance plan covering each program activity set forth in the budget of such agency. Such plan shall:
  - Establish performance goals to define the level of performance to be achieved by a program activity
  - Express such goals in an objective, quantifiable, and measurable form unless authorized to be in an alternative form
  - Briefly describe the operational processes, skills, and technology, and the human, capital, information, or other resources required to meet the performance goals

■ Establish performance indicators to be used in measuring or assessing the relevant outputs, service levels, and outcomes of each program activity

■ Provide a basis for comparing actual program results with the established performance goals

■ Describe the means to be used to verify and validate measured values

As we see, through the GPRA mandate, governance requires the ability to relate the mission of the enterprise to its goals and objectives. Each of these goals and objectives must relate to the major functions and operations of the enterprise. The achievement of goals and objectives must be tied to the use of operations, skills, and resources of the enterprise, and investments in programs and initiatives must also be traceable to the goals and objectives that they support.

The FEA Performance Reference Model describes the cause-and-effect relationship between inputs, tangible outputs, and strategic outcomes. Inputs to the agency are typically resources such as money, people, skills, and technology. These enable the processes of the agency. The processes and activities of the agency deliver outputs (such as funds, grants, research programs) and performance results. The outputs and performance results impact the outcomes, such as mission, business, and customer results. Figure 3.3-1 depicts this "line of sight"—a term of art commonly used within EA to refer to how the inputs to an enterprise can be traced to the outcomes they influence. Line of sight provides direct traceability from the resources consumed by an organization to the activities that consume them to produce results that conform to goals set by the organization, which in turn produce strategic outcomes.

The Strategic Viewpoint deals with the interests of planners. In the federal government, the following are the architecture elements of interest for the Strategic Viewpoint:

■ Mission

■ Goals and Objectives and Measures

■ Initiatives, Programs, and Investments

■ Linkages to the External Environment

■ Relationships between these elements

Balanced Scorecard

The balanced scorecard is a strategic planning and management system that is used extensively in business and industry, government, and nonprofit organizations worldwide to align business activities to the vision and strategy of the organization,

Government Performance Results Act (GPRA) **383**

FIGURE 3.3-1

Line of Sight

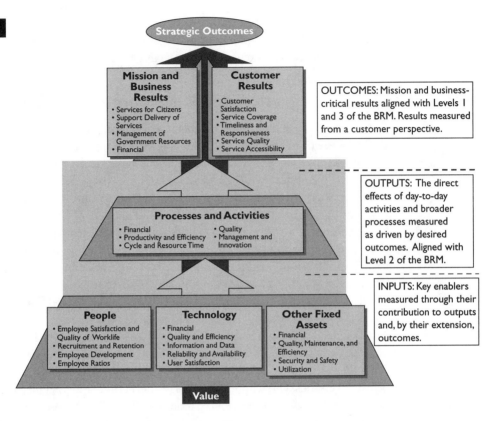

Strategic Outcomes

Mission and Business Results
• Services for Citizens
• Support Delivery of Services
• Management of Government Resources
• Financial

Customer Results
• Customer Satisfaction
• Service Coverage
• Timeliness and Responsiveness
• Service Quality
• Service Accessibility

OUTCOMES: Mission and business-critical results aligned with Levels 1 and 3 of the BRM. Results measured from a customer perspective.

Processes and Activities
• Financial
• Productivity and Efficiency
• Cycle and Resource Time
• Quality
• Management and Innovation

OUTPUTS: The direct effects of day-to-day activities and broader processes measured as driven by desired outcomes. Aligned with Level 2 of the BRM.

People
• Employee Satisfaction and Quality of Worklife
• Recruitment and Retention
• Employee Development
• Employee Ratios

Technology
• Financial
• Quality and Efficiency
• Information and Data
• Reliability and Availability
• User Satisfaction

Other Fixed Assets
• Financial
• Quality, Maintenance, and Efficiency
• Security and Safety
• Utilization

INPUTS: Key enablers measured through their contribution to outputs and, by their extension, outcomes.

Value

improve internal and external communications, and monitor organization performance against strategic goals. It was originated by Dr. Robert Kaplan (of the Harvard Business School) and Dr. David Norton as a performance measurement framework that added strategic nonfinancial performance measures to traditional financial metrics to give managers and executives a more "balanced" view of organizational performance. Although the phrase "balanced scorecard" was coined in the early 1990s, the roots of the this type of approach are deep, and include the pioneering work of General Electric on performance measurement reporting in the 1950s and the work of French process engineers (who created the Tableau de Bord—literally, a "dashboard" of performance measures) in the early part of the 20th century.

The balanced scorecard has evolved from its early use as a simple performance measurement framework to a full strategic planning and management system. The "new" balanced scorecard transforms an organization's strategic plan from an attractive but passive document into the "marching orders" for the organization on a daily basis. It provides a framework that not only provides performance measurements, but helps planners identify what should be done and measured. It enables executives to execute their strategies.

Joint Capabilities Integration and Development System (JCIDS)

Identification of capabilities is a fundamental step in planning for requirements in the Department of Defense. The Joint Capabilities Integration and Development System (JCIDS) probably had its beginning in the Quadrennial Defense Review Report for 2001 after the 9/11 attacks on U.S. soil where Secretary of Defense Donald Rumsfeld asserts "The new defense strategy is built around the concept of shifting to a 'capabilities-based' approach to defense." That concept reflects the fact that the United States cannot know with confidence what nation, combination of nations, or non-state actor will pose threats to vital U.S. interests or those of U.S. allies and friends decades from now. It is possible, however, to anticipate the capabilities that an adversary might employ to coerce its neighbors, deter the United States from acting in defense of its allies and friends, or directly attack the United States or its deployed forces (Defense Strategy Quadrennial Defense Review Report). A capabilities-based model—one that focuses more on how an adversary might fight than who the adversary might be and where a war might occur—broadens the strategic perspective. It requires identifying capabilities that U.S. military forces will need to deter and defeat adversaries who will rely on surprise, deception, and asymmetric warfare to achieve their objectives. Moving to a capabilities-based force also requires the United States to focus on emerging opportunities that certain capabilities, including advanced remote sensing, long-range precision strike, transformed maneuver and expeditionary forces and systems, to overcome anti-access and area denial threats, can confer on the U.S. military over time.

JCIDS was a departure from requirements-based planning to capabilities-based planning. [DoD 2009, pg 67] defines capability as, "The ability to achieve a Desired Effect under specified [performance] standards and conditions through combinations of ways and means [activities and resources] to perform a set of activities".

A capability is a way to couch an enduring requirement without defining the solution. Requiring a capability to fly through the atmosphere does not predicate a specific type of flying vehicle. In general, a capability can be satisfied by many solutions, each of which has different costs and complexities and entails different types of trade-offs. A specific capability may require the availability of another capability before it can be realized. For example, being able to get on a bicycle, get off a bicycle, and stay on a bicycle is essential before embarking on a bicycle journey toward a destination.

A capability configuration is a set of related capabilities that must all be planned together to ensure that critical dependencies are not missed. For example, an aircraft engineer must plan the airframe, the engine, the landing gear, and a host of other subsystems together at the same time. Typically, complex, large-scale capabilities are delivered in increments and in pieces by multiple project teams working often in multiple locations under multiple enterprises. Unless there is a carefully planned strategy to manage the capability configuration and the orchestration of capability development projects, the odds of successfully delivering a complex integrated capability are very low.

In this section, we will present some examples of the models that support the capability viewpoint:

- **CV-1 Vision** The CV-1 is a key model that provides "line of sight" traceability of capability needs back to the vision and goals of the enterprise. By examining capability mappings to the goals, an enterprise can prioritize during the capability-based acquisition process of capability needs submitted by multiple contenders for funding and resourcing. The CV-1 is similar in scope and intent to models in the federal government and commercial industry that require that transformation initiatives be mapped back to strategic goals and objectives in the strategic plan, and to key ingredients of the strategy that support the vision.

- **CV-2 Capability Taxonomy** The CV-2 is used to decompose a complex capability need into smaller, simpler capability needs that can then be mapped to a capability development timeline. The decomposition is arranged as a tree, and the leaf nodes of the tree may be associated with specific measures of performance or effectiveness for the leaf-level capability. We can also view the CV-2 as an elaboration of a capability configuration—the decomposition of a whole part that establishes all the smaller grain capabilities required to achieve a larger grain capability.

- **CV-3 Capability Phasing** The CV-3 takes the capability configuration concept to its logical conclusion: if all the component capabilities of the CV2 were to be developed in disparate projects, how do we orchestrate the delivery of capabilities from each of these projects to be able to assemble the larger-grain capability in an orderly manner? The CV-3 maps capability developments to time phases and projects to describe what capability will be available in what timeframe.

- **CV-4 Capability Dependency**   The CV-4 explicitly represents dependencies of a specific capability on another capability. Knowledge of capability dependencies is essential to orchestrate capability developments in such a manner that a predecessor capability is developed first before the enterprise attempts to develop a successor capability that depends on it.

- **CV-5 Capability to Organizational Development Mapping**   The CV-5 traces capability developments to developing organizations. The model is used by the capability planner to determine points of contact and control for various capability developments as well as to orchestrate the deployment of the capabilities in collaboration with the developing organizations.

- **CV-6 Capability to Operational Activities Mapping**   In acquiring capabilities, it is important to represent the mission or business activity that will use and benefit from that capability. The CV-6 establishes mappings between a capability configuration and the set of operational activities (business processes) that will harness the capability.

- **CV-7 Capability to Services Mapping**   The solutions for problems may lie in the procurement of outsourced business services or in automation—use of automated software services. The Service Viewpoint models (SvcV) address the modeling of the service-based models. The CV-7 provides traceability of service-based solutions back to the original capabilities that were planned. The CV-7 also supports capability audits that trace capabilities down to the solutions that provide the capability.

TOGAF 9 Support for Capability and Strategy

Before embarking upon a detailed architecture definition, it is valuable to understand the baseline and target capability level of the enterprise. A capability assessment is usually performed. The following are questions that are to be answered during the capability assessment activity:

- What is the capability level of the enterprise as a whole? Where does the enterprise wish to increase or optimize capability? What are the architectural focus areas that will support the desired development of the enterprise?

- What is the capability or maturity level of the IT function within the enterprise? What are the likely implications of conducting the architecture project in terms or design governance, operational governance, skills, and organization structure? What is an appropriate style, level of formality, and amount of detail for the architecture project to fit with the culture and capability of the IT organization?

■ What is the capability and maturity of the architecture function within the enterprise? What architectural assets are currently in existence? Are they maintained and accurate? What standards and Reference Models need to be considered? Are there likely to be opportunities to create reusable assets during the architecture project?

■ Where capability gaps exist, to what extent is the business ready to transform in order to reach the target capability? What are the risks to transformation, cultural barriers, and other considerations to be addressed beyond the basic capability gap?

The outputs of the capability assessment include the following types of products:

■ A *business capability assessment,* including identification of baseline capabilities, capability gaps, and future capability needs from a business perspective

■ An *IT capability assessment* from the IT perspective

■ An *architecture maturity assessment* that determines the level of maturity of the architecture development effort and identifies gaps in scope (depth and breadth) and coverage as well as in its use and dissemination

■ A *business transformation capability assessment* that determines the capabilities needed as well as the readiness of the enterprise in undertaking transformations.

Capability Viewpoint Integrated Models

All the Capability Viewpoint models (see Figure 3.3-2) share the capability architecture element. Many of the models provide "gateway" relationships to other viewpoints to ensure that these viewpoints integrate with the Capability Viewpoint. The following are examples of such gateway relationships:

■ CV-5 relates the Capability Viewpoint to the Project Viewpoint by relating the developers of capabilities to the projects that deliver those capabilities.

■ CV-6 relates the Capability Viewpoint to the Operational Viewpoint to ensure that capabilities that are being acquired by the enterprise support some named enterprise activity specifically.

Integrated
Model Set for
the Capability
Viewpoint

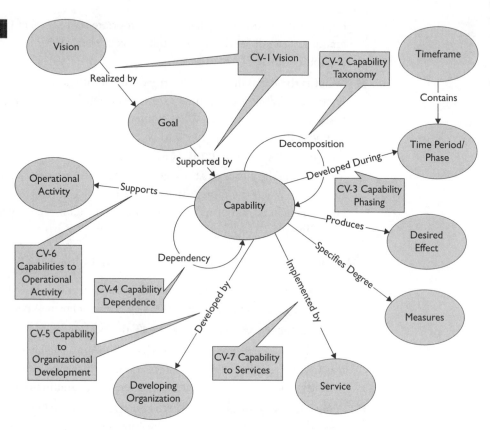

- CV-7 relates the Capability Viewpoint to the Services Viewpoint to ensure that business or software services are traceable to the capability they implement.
- CV-1 implies a relationship to a Strategic Viewpoint if one exists that deals with the vision, goals, strategies, and objectives of the enterprise and is of interest to the strategic planner.

CV-1 Vision

The primary purpose of the Capability and Vision Model (CV-1) is to provide a context for defining which capabilities are important to the enterprise. This context can be described by using ways, means, and ends to show how activities relate to capabilities relate to goals and vision.

The Vision and goals define the ends and capabilities provide the means to achieve those ends. The operational activities described in the Operational Viewpoint represent the ways or the "hows". The CV-1 therefore links the activities to the capabilities (ways to means) and the capabilities to the goals and vision (means to the ends).

Model Information at a Glance	
Model Short Name	CV-1
Name	Vision
Other Names	Strategic Vision Architecture Vision (TOGAF) Capability Assessment (TOGAF)
Viewpoint	Capability
Model Intent	Record the strategic drivers for enterprise capabilities and document the relationships between these drivers and the capability.
Model Audience	Planners at the enterprise level that must deal with prioritization of capability development with resource and schedule constraints.
Formal Modeling Methodology	None. Contains elements from standard strategic planning with relationships to capability.
Integration of Model with Other Views	Capabilities in CV-1 must be consistent with capabilities in all other CV models.

Example 1: RMN Enterprise CV-1

The RMN CV-1 depicts a phased strategy to achieve within a 15-year timeframe the RMN vision of becoming a viable alternative to Los Angeles International for passengers using it as an en-route point or as a destination (see Figure 3.3-3).

FIGURE 3.3-3 RMN Enterprise Vision CV-1

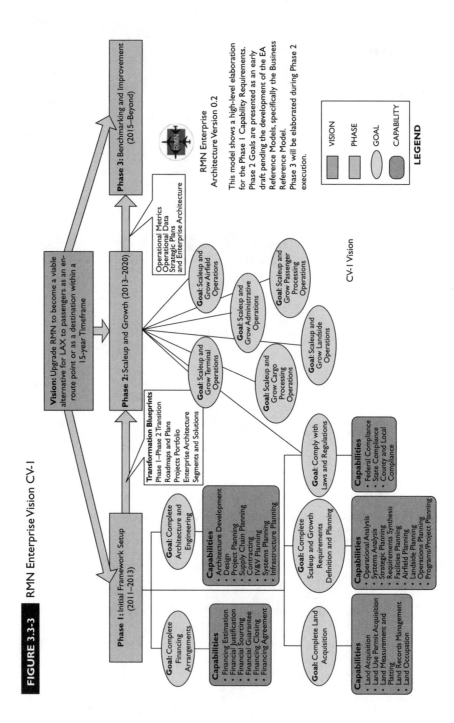

CV-2 Capability Taxonomy

Model Information at a Glance	
Model Short Name	CV-2
Name	Capability Taxonomy
Other Names	Capability Hierarchy, Master Capability List, Joint Capability Area (DoD) Function Decomposition Diagram (TOGAF 9) Capability Assessment (TOGAF 9)
Viewpoint	Capability
Model Intent	Depict a decomposition hierarchy for capabilities that represent how a higher-level capability can be built using combinations of lower-level capabilities. Level denotes granularity and scope.
Model Audience	Planners at the enterprise level interested in decomposing abstract capabilities progressively into concrete capabilities that can form the basis for projects to develop those capabilities.
Formal Modeling Methodology	None. Hierarchical decomposition.
Integration of Model with Other Views	Capabilities in CV-2 must be consistent with capabilities in all other CV models.

Example 1: RMN Terminal Operations CV-2

Figure 3.3-4 shows the decomposition of capabilities that are required to sustain terminal operations at RMN Airport. The CV-2 depicted here is to support the segment architecture for terminal operations.

Example 2: Passenger Processing CV-2

Figure 3.3-5 shows the CV-2 associated with the solution architecture for passenger identification. In this model, we have selected a single aspect: passenger identification from the architecture segment: terminal operations from the enterprise: Richard M. Nixon Airport.

FIGURE 3.3-4   RMN Terminal Operations CV-2 Capability Taxonomy

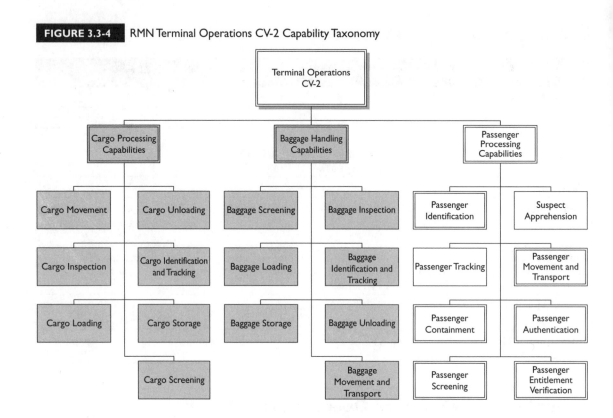

Example 3: Passenger Identification CV-2

Verify Passenger Identity
Read Identity Document
Read RFID Passport
Read Machine-Readable Passport
Read Magnetic ARC
Read DHS Trusted Traveler Card
Read Foreign Passport
Read REAL State Drivers License
Read REAL State-Issued Identity

Verify Passenger Identity
Validate Identity
Validate State Identity
Validate U.S. Citizen Identity
Validate Foreign Citizen Identity
Validate Canadian Citizen Identity
Validate U.S. Permanent Resident Identity
Provide Issue/Confirmation
Provide Clandestine Confirmation
Provide Audible Confirmation
Provide Visual Confirmation

FIGURE 3.3-5 Passenger Processing CV-2 Capability Taxonomy

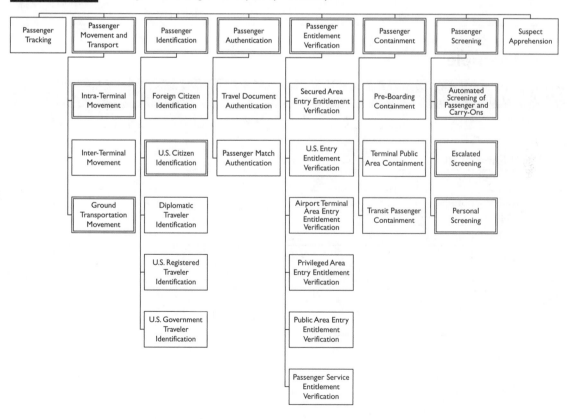

CV-3 Capability Phasing

Model Information at a Glance	
Model Short Name	CV-3
Name	Capability Phasing Project Context Diagram (TOGAF 9)
Other Names	Capability Roadmap
Viewpoint	Capability
Model Intent	Depict a roadmap showing the phased development of capabilities.
Model Audience	Planners at the enterprise level interested in ensuring orderly development of capabilities based on identified dependencies (CV-4).
Formal Modeling Methodology	None. A diagram or a tabular format can be used to represent this model.
Integration of Model with Other Views	Capabilities in CV-3 must be consistent with capabilities in all other CV models. Timeframes and phases must be consistent with architecture timeframe and phases as well as the timeframes described in the Project Viewpoint models and the Systems, Services, and Standards viewpoint models.

CV-3 Example

	2010	2011				2012	
Capability	4Q	1Q	2Q	3Q	4Q	1Q	2Q
Verify Passenger Identity							
Read Identity Document	XXX	XXX					
Read RFID Passport	XXX						
Read Machine-Readable Passport	XXX						
Read Magnetic ARC		XXX					
Read DHS Trusted Traveler Card		XXX					
Read Foreign Passport		XXX					
Read REAL State Drivers License	XXX						

Capability	2010	2011					2012	
	4Q	1Q	2Q	3Q	4Q	1Q	1Q	2Q
Read REAL State-Issued Identity		XXX						
Validate Identity		XXX	XXX	XXX	XXX			
Validate State Identity			XXX					
Validate U.S. Citizen Identity			XXX					
Validate Foreign Citizen Identity				XXX	XXX			
Validate Canadian Citizen Identity				XXX				
Validate U.S. Permanent Resident Identity			XXX					
Provide Issue/Confirmation		XXX	XXX	XXX	XXX			
Provide Clandestine Confirmation				XXX				
Provide Audible Confirmation				XXX				
Provide Visual Confirmation				XXX				

CV-4 Capability Dependencies

Model Information at a Glance	
Model Short Name	CV-4
Name	Capability Dependencies Business Footprint Diagram (TOGAF 9)
Other Names	
Viewpoint	Capability
Model Intent	Depict explicitly the development dependencies between capabilities to reflect the fact that one capability may need the completed development of another.
Model Audience	Planners at the enterprise level interested in ensuring orderly development of capabilities based on identified dependencies and project schedules (PV Models).
Formal Modeling Methodology	None. Either a diagram or a tabular format may be used to represent the model.
Integration of Model with Other Views	Capabilities in CV-3 must be consistent with capabilities in all other CV models. Timeframes and phases must be consistent with architecture timeframe and phases.

CV-4 Example

Primary Capability	Dependent Capability	Read Identity Document							Validate Identity					Provide Issue / Confirmation		
		Read RFID Passport	Read Machine-Readable Passport	Read Magnetic ARC	Read DHS Trusted Traveler Card	Read Foreign Passport	Read REAL State Drivers License	Read REAL State-Issued Identity	Validate State Identity	Validate U.S. Citizen Identity	Validate Foreign Citizen Identity	Validate Canadian Citizen Identity	Validate U.S. Permanent Resident Identity	Provide Clandestine Confirmation	Provide Audible Confirmation	Provide Visual Confirmation
Verify Passenger Identity																
Read Identity Document																
Read RFID Passport										X						
Read Machine-Readable Passport	X				X					X						
Read Magnetic ARC					X		X	X					X			
Read DHS Trusted Traveler Card										X						
Read Foreign Passport											X	X				
Read REAL State Drivers License									X							
Read REAL State-Issued Identity									X							
Validate Identity																
Validate State Identity							X	X						X	X	X
Validate U.S. Citizen Identity		X	X											X	X	X
Validate Foreign Citizen Identity				X										X	X	X

Primary Capability	Dependent Capability	Read Identity Document							Validate Identity					Provide Issue / Confirmation		
		Read RFID Passport	Read Machine-Readable Passport	Read Magnetic ARC	Read DHS Trusted Traveler Card	Read Foreign Passport	Read REAL State Drivers License	Read REAL State-Issued Identity	Validate State Identity	Validate U.S. Citizen Identity	Validate Foreign Citizen Identity	Validate Canadian Citizen Identity	Validate U.S. Permanent Resident Identity	Provide Clandestine Confirmation	Provide Audible Confirmation	Provide Visual Confirmation
Validate Canadian Citizen Identity						X								X	X	X
Validate U.S. Permanent Resident Identity					X									X	X	X
Provide Issue/Confirmation																
Provide Clandestine Confirmation																
Provide Audible Confirmation																
Provide Visual Confirmation																

CV-5 Capability to Organizational Development Mapping

Model Information at a Glance	
Model Short Name	CV-5
Name	Capability to Organizational Development Mapping
Other Names	Business Footprint Diagram (TOGAF 9) Business Interaction Matrix (TOGAF 9)

(continued)

Model Information at a Glance	
Viewpoint	Capability
Model Intent	Show the relationships between capabilities and the organizations responsible for their development. This helps fix responsibilities and determine coordination activities and players to ensure that capability development proceeds in an orderly manner.
Model Audience	Planners at the enterprise level, interested in ensuring orderly development of capabilities based on identified development organizations.
Formal Modeling Methodology	None. A simple matrix can be used to represent this type of model.
Integration of Model with Other Views	Capabilities in CV-5 must be consistent with capabilities in all other CV models. Organizations may or may not correspond to Operational Viewpoint (OV) performers because OV performers represent a "treating patients view of a hospital" while an organization in CV is "building the hospital."

Example

Primary Capability	Responsible Organization	Department of State	State Governments	Canadian Government	Department of Homeland Security	Interpol	RMN IT Services (Integrator)
Verify Passenger Identity							
Read Identity Document							
Read RFID Passport		X					
Read Machine-Readable Passport		X					
Read Magnetic ARC		X					
Read DHS Trusted Traveler Card					X		
Read Foreign Passport						X	
Read REAL State Drivers License			X				

Primary Capability	Responsible Organization	Department of State	State Governments	Canadian Government	Department of Homeland Security	Interpol	RMN IT Services (Integrator)
Read REAL State-Issued Identity			X				
Validate Identity							X
Validate State Identity			X				
Validate U.S. Citizen Identity		X					
Validate Foreign Citizen Identity						X	
Validate Canadian Citizen Identity				X			
Validate U.S. Permanent Resident Identity		X					
Provide Issue/Confirmation							X
Provide Clandestine Confirmation							X
Provide Audible Confirmation							X
Provide Visual Confirmation							X

CV-6 Capability to Operational Activities Mapping

Model Information at a Glance	
Model Short Name	CV-6
Name	Capability to Operational Activities Mapping
Other Names	Business Footprint Diagram (TOGAF 9) Value Chain Diagram (TOGAF 9)
Viewpoint	Capability

(continued)

Model Information at a Glance	
Model Intent	Depict the relationship between capabilities and the activities they enable. The activity may be viewed as a meaningful "application" for the capability. An activity is a unit of mission accomplishment. By relating capabilities to activities, we are able to assess the value of a capability not in isolation, but within a mission context.
Model Audience	Portfolio managers at the enterprise level assessing the relative value of each capability within a capability portfolio.
Formal Modeling Methodology	None. A simple matrix can be used to represent this type of model.
Integration of Model with Other Views	Capabilities in CV-6 must be consistent with capabilities in all other CV models. Activities must be consistent with the operational activities in the Operational Viewpoint.

Example: Passenger Identification CV-6

Capability	Operational Activity	Check in Passenger	Screen Passenger	Board Passenger	Receive Passenger	Conduct Immigration Inspection	Conduct Customs Inspection	Store Passenger Baggage	Process Duty-Free Purchase	Deliver Baggage
Verify Passenger Identity										
Read Identity Document	X	X	X	X	X	X	X	X	X	
Read RFID Passport	X	X	X	X	X	X	X	X	X	
Read Machine-Readable Passport	X	X	X	X	X	X	X	X	X	
Read Magnetic ARC	X	X	X	X	X	X	X	X	X	
Read DHS Trusted Traveler Card	X	X	X	X	X	X	X	X	X	
Read Foreign Passport	X	X	X	X	X	X	X	X	X	
Read REAL State Drivers License	X	X	X	X	X	X	X	X	X	
Read REAL State-Issued Identity	X	X	X	X	X	X	X	X	X	

Capability	Operational Activity	Check in Passenger	Screen Passenger	Board Passenger	Receive Passenger	Conduct Immigration Inspection	Conduct Customs Inspection	Store Passenger Baggage	Process Duty-Free Purchase	Deliver Baggage
Validate Identity		X	X	X	X	X	X	X	X	X
Validate State Identity		X	X	X	X	X	X	X	X	X
Validate U.S. Citizen Identity		X	X	X	X	X	X	X	X	X
Validate Foreign Citizen Identity		X	X	X	X	X	X	X	X	X
Validate Canadian Citizen Identity		X	X	X	X	X	X	X	X	X
Validate U.S. Permanent Resident Identity		X	X	X	X	X	X	X	X	X
Provide Issue/Confirmation		X	X	X	X	X	X	X	X	X
Provide Clandestine Confirmation		X	X	X	X	X	X	X	X	X
Provide Audible Confirmation		X	X	X	X	X	X	X	X	X
Provide Visual Confirmation		X	X	X	X	X	X	X	X	X

CV-7 Capability to Services Mapping

Model Information at a Glance	
Model Short Name	CV-7
Name	Capability to Services Mapping
Other Names	Goal/Objective/Service Diagram (TOGAF 9) Business Footprint Diagram (TOGAF 9)
Viewpoint	Capability
Model Intent	Depict the relationship between a capability as a requirement and a service as a solution.

(continued)

Model Information at a Glance	
Model Audience	Service developers can trace the services they are developing back to the enterprise operational capability. Planners can follow a capability down to its implementation as a business or software service.
Formal Modeling Methodology	None. A simple matrix can be used to represent this type of model.
Integration of Model with Other Views	Capabilities in CV-7 must be consistent with those in all other CV models. Services must be consistent with those represented inside the Service View models.

Example: Passenger Identification CV-7

Capability	Services	Read Identity Document	Validate Identity Document	Alert Airport Security (TBD)	Alert First Responders (TBD)
Verify Passenger Identity					
Read Identity Document		X			
Read RFID Passport		X			
Read Machine-Readable Passport		X			
Read Magnetic ARC		X			
Read DHS Trusted Traveler Card		X			
Read Foreign Passport		X			
Read REAL State Drivers License		X			
Read REAL State-Issued Identity		X			
Validate Identity			X		
Validate State Identity			X		

Capability	Services	Read Identity Document	Validate Identity Document	Alert Airport Security (TBD)	Alert First Responders (TBD)
Validate U.S. Citizen Identity			X		
Validate Foreign Citizen Identity			X		
Validate Canadian Citizen Identity			X		
Validate U.S. Permanent Resident Identity			X		
Provide Issue/Confirmation			X		
Provide Clandestine Confirmation			X	X	X
Provide Audible Confirmation			X		
Provide Visual Confirmation			X		

Questions

1. Who is the audience for the Strategic/Capability Viewpoint? In your own enterprise, who performs the planning function that requires this viewpoint?

2. Discuss the pros and cons of capability-based acquisition versus requirements-based acquisition.

3. What is the difference between the federal government approach and the Defense Department's approach to capabilities? Discuss whether the nature of the DoD enterprise (readiness-based) is fundamentally different from that of the federal government (legislation- and strategic plan–based) or is fundamentally different from that of commercial enterprise (profit-based). Do these fundamental drivers affect how capabilities are viewed, measured, and assessed for effectiveness?

4. One of the important concepts in tracing an enterprise's expended resources to strategic outcomes is called "line of sight." What is "line of sight"? Why is it important? How does an enterprise architecture support "line of sight"?

5. What is the balanced scorecard? Discuss the pros and cons of using a balanced scorecard approach to drive the enterprise's motivation. What would be the dimensions of your own enterprise's balanced scorecard? What should they be?

6. What is JCIDS? How does the DoD use JCIDS to normalize planning for capabilities across the military services? What was the predecessor for JCIDS?

7. Discuss how your own enterprise (if DoD-related) is involved in the JCIDS process (or not). Discuss the pros and cons of using a capability-based approach to managing a portfolio of requirements for the enterprise.

8. What is a capability configuration? Why is it important to manage a capability configuration in terms of investments and schedule? What types of CV models will help you manage a capability configuration? Explain why.

9. What is the CV-1? How would you use it in your own enterprise? Who would or should be using the CV-1 to communicate the enterprise vision?

10. What is the CV-2? A capability name is usually a compound phrase of a verb and a noun. Discuss the pros and cons of developing capability decomposition (CV-2) around the verb phrase and the noun phrase, respectively.

11. How does the CV-3 help orchestrate multiple capability developments? What is the impact of not developing a CV-3 to assist in a major acquisition of a new, multimillion-dollar airframe development?

12. How can you use the CV-3 (Capability Phasing) and CV-4 (Capability Dependency) together to identify and resolve issues with orchestrating capability developments?

13. What are the pros and cons of not developing a CV-5 (Capability to Organizational Development Mapping)?

14. What are the pros and cons of not developing a CV-6 (Capabilities to Operational Activity Mapping)?

15. What are the pros and cons of developing services around capabilities rather than around specific stated business needs of a specific consumer (requirements)? How will the CV-7 help in analyzing redundant services across the enterprise?

Reference List

Defense Acquisition University. (2010. Continuously Updated.) ACQuipedia. An encyclopedia of Acquisition terms for the Defense Acquisition Community. https://acc.dau.mil/CommunityBrowser.aspx?id=28947.

Department of Defense. (2009). *DoD Architecture Framework 2.0, Volume II: Architectural Data and Models—Architect's Guide*. Department of Defense.

Office of Management and Budget. (1993). Government Performance Results Act (GPRA). http://www.whitehouse.gov/omb/mgmt-gpra/gplaw2m#h1.

The Open Group. (2009). *The Open Group Architecture Framework Version 9*. The Open Group.

Quadrennial Defense Review Report. (2001). Department of Defense.

3.4

Project Viewpoint

As the traditional saying states, "Rome was not built in a day!" Complex capability developments or complex and prolonged transformation efforts (GAO, 2006) are seldom accomplished through single projects. For the planner who is developing a portfolio of such projects or initiatives (Pennypacker, 2009), the task of orchestrating the deliverables of each project to be in synchronization with the needs of another is tricky and challenging. The Project Viewpoint provides the portfolio planner with a set of models that allows him or her to orchestrate the combined planning of multiple projects. The operative words here are "multiple projects," because of the various dependencies among projects that affect their delivered capabilities and the need to plan carefully the deliverables while keeping the dependencies we have seen earlier in the CV-3 Capability Phasing and CV-4 Capability Dependency models.

In the federal government arena, projects or initiatives are used to transform government or to improve the current state of the enterprise while remaining consistent with strategic goals and objectives. A family or portfolio of projects is used to deliver a collection of related initiatives that support an enterprise transformation or phase of enterprise transformation.

In the DoD arena, projects are collections of tasks that deliver capabilities within the framework of a larger initiative called a *program*. A family of dependent and related capabilities is called a capability configuration. A capability configuration, to be useful, must deliver all of the component capabilities in a consistent and orchestrated manner. A program typically is responsible for the acquisition of large-scale, complex weapons systems or automated information systems as well as sustainment and maintenance of the system once it is acquired and deployed. Programs tend to run for multiple years and are funded in increments based on various metrics that determine the health of the program and the viability of the capabilities that are produced. In the words of the Government Accountability Office (GAO, 2005, pg 3) "U.S. weapons are among the best in the world, but the programs to acquire them often take significantly longer and cost more money than promised and often deliver fewer quantities and other capabilities than planned. It is not unusual for estimates of time and money to be off by 20 to 50 percent. When costs and schedules increase, quantities are cut, and the value for the warfighter—as well as the value of the investment dollar—is reduced."

In the commercial world, every initiative is deemed as an investment—and measured in terms of payback or return. A collection of initiatives is therefore seen as a portfolio of investments. A project or family of projects is related to a single or multiple investments. The principles and model types described in the DoDAF Project Viewpoint (PV) are applicable, adaptable, and customizable to the commercial domain as well with a change in terminology and a shift in focus. In the TOGAF 9, the formulation of opportunities and solutions is performed in Phase E of the Architecture Development Method (ADM). It is during this phase that a Project Context Diagram, similar to the PV-1 described in this chapter, is developed.

As we saw earlier, in the Capability Viewpoint we have the ability to model capability dependencies, capability taxonomies, and relationships of capabilities to development organizations, solution services, and the operational activities they enable. The Project Viewpoint must be consistent with and recognize capability dependencies. Multiproject orchestration must be consistent with capability dependencies and projects must deliver independent upstream capabilities earlier than dependent downstream capabilities.

Earlier we had introduced the notion of a capability configuration as a collection of interdependent capabilities that must be planned together. Because each of these capabilities may be developed by a different project, it is important that the Project Portfolio responsible for developing the entire capability configuration be orchestrated to reflect capability dependencies and the orderly development of capabilities in a manner that is consistent with those dependencies.

The concept is applicable to non-DoD enterprises such as the federal government as well. A transformation may be viewed as a collection of initiatives. Each of these initiatives has dependencies with other initiatives. Portfolios of projects that are responsible for delivering the collection of initiatives needed to reflect and factor in the dependencies.

The *Project Portfolio Relationships* (PV-1) model is used to depict the relationships between projects, subprojects, and responsible development organizations.

The *Project Timelines* (PV-2) model acts like an aggregated Gantt chart for a family of projects and allows a very quick view of the various timelines of the component projects within a Project Portfolio that supports the development of a capability configuration.

The *Project-Capability Mappings* (PV-3) model provides a view of the relationship of a project to the capabilities it delivers and supports analysis of capability dependencies against project orchestration.

Figure 3.4-1 shows the full integrated model set for Project Viewpoint.

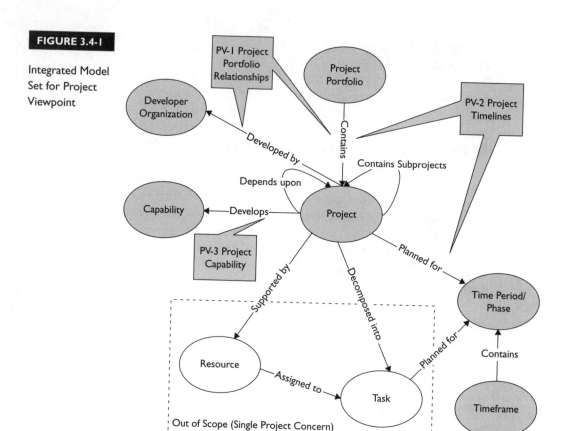

FIGURE 3.4-1

Integrated Model
Set for Project
Viewpoint

Project Viewpoint Integrated Models

Although not explicitly represented by a DoDAF-described model type, the Project Portfolio is a composition structure that describes the families of projects that form the enterprise project portfolio.

All the Project Viewpoint models must consistently reference the same project list.

The PV-2 references a timeframe, phases, and milestones. It is important that the planning window represented by these timeframes, phases, and milestones be consistent throughout the architecture and align with timeframes, phases, and milestones in other roadmap type models such as the CV-3, SV-7, SvcV-7, SvcV-8, SvcV-9, SV-8, SV-9, and StdV-2, for example. These timeframes and phases will also likely be described by the AV-1 as the applicable timeframe overall for the architecture.

PV-1 Project Portfolio Relationships

Traditional project management tools do a great job of supporting single projects—managing work breakdown structures, cost, schedule, resources, and tasks. However, in enterprise architecting, several projects must be managed and coordinated. In effect, a portfolio of projects must be managed and dependencies of each project on each other clearly represented. Some commercial project management tools (Microsoft, 2011) address the portfolio representation challenge using a Master Project approach that provides active links to several smaller subprojects. The PV-1 provides a modeling technique for representing multiple projects that comprise a single portfolio.

Model Information at a Glance	
Model Short Name	PV-1
Name	Project Portfolio Relationships
Other Names	Project Portfolio Project Context Diagram (TOGAF 9)
Viewpoint	Project
Model Intent	To manage a family of projects as a portfolio while keeping track of which organization is responsible for which project. The hierarchical nature of the PV-1 allows an enterprise to represent its projects as a well-formed hierarchy of portfolios and assign organizational responsibilities to each level of the hierarchy. In complex, multi-organization, multirole, multiproject situations, the PV-1 is an invaluable representation tool.
Model Audience	Planners managing definition of projects and assignment of responsibility to project owners. High-level decision makers interested in project outcomes and desirous of identifying responsibility.
Formal Modeling Methodology	None.
Integration of Model with Other Views	Projects in PV-1 must be consistent with projects in all other Project Viewpoint models. Organizations in PV-1 must be consistent with OV-4.

Example: Passenger Identification PV-1

Project	Description	Sponsor	Start	End
PMS Upgrade for PAXIS	Upgrade the Passenger Management System (PMS) to incorporate the centralized and standardized passenger identification services from Passenger Identification System (PAXIS).	Airlines operating at RMN	3Q2011	2Q2012
ARTS Upgrade for PAXIS	Upgrade the Airline Reservation and Tracking System to incorporate the centralized and standardized passenger identification services from PAXIS.	Airlines operating at RMN	2Q2011	2Q2012
CSS Upgrade for PAXIS	Upgrade the Common Screening System to incorporate the centralized and standardized passenger identification services from PAXIS.	Transportation Security Administration	3Q2011	2Q2012
LETS Upgrade for PAXIS	Upgrade the Passenger Management System to incorporate the centralized and standardized passenger identification services from PAXIS.	RMN Airport Authority	3Q2011	2Q2012
ARTS (Mobile) Upgrade for PAXIS	Upgrade the Airline Reservation and Tracking System to incorporate the centralized and standardized passenger identification services from PAXIS.	Airlines operating at RMN	2Q2011	4Q2011
ARTS (Kiosk) Upgrade for PAXIS	Upgrade the Airline Reservation and Tracking System to incorporate the centralized and standardized passenger identification services from PAXIS.	Airlines operating at RMN	2Q2011	4Q2011
ABTS (Commercial) Upgrade for PAXIS	Upgrade the Passenger Management System to incorporate the centralized and standardized passenger identification services from PAXIS.	RMN Airport Authority	3Q2011	3Q2012

Project	Description	Sponsor	Start	End
CBPS Upgrade for PAXIS	Upgrade the Passenger Management System to incorporate the centralized and standardized passenger identification services from PAXIS.	Customs and Border Protection	2Q2011	2Q2012
ICES Upgrade for PAXIS	Upgrade the Passenger Management System to incorporate the centralized and standardized passenger identification services from PAXIS.	Immigration and Customs Enforcement	2Q2011	2Q2012
ABTS (RMN) Upgrade for PAXIS	Upgrade the Passenger Management System to incorporate the centralized and standardized passenger identification services from PAXIS.	RMN Airport Authority	2Q2011	2Q2012
E-POSS	Upgrade the Passenger Management System to incorporate the centralized and standardized passenger identification services from PAXIS.	Baggage storage services franchisee	2Q2011	4Q2011
Smart Devices	Upgrade the Passenger Management System to incorporate the centralized and standardized passenger identification services from PAXIS.	Department of State Credit Card Issuers Department of Homeland Security Immigration and Customs Enforcement Foreign governments Department of Defense	1Q2009	4Q2010
PAXIS Development	Upgrade the Passenger Management System to incorporate the centralized and standardized passenger identification services from PAXIS.	RMN Airport Authority	1Q 2011	3Q2011

PV-2 Project Timelines

Just as the PV-1 shown earlier is a model that represents the composition of a project portfolio in terms of constituent projects, the PV-2 Project Timelines model represents a time-based schedule that depicts how these projects must be orchestrated in order for one project to provide timely deliverables to another.

Model Information at a Glance	
Model Short Name	PV-2
Name	Project Timelines
Other Names	Application Migration Diagram (TOGAF 9)
Viewpoint	Project
Model Intent	The PV-2 is intended as a timeline chart for a collection of projects. Project management tools provide Gantt charts for a project in terms of tasks and schedule. The PV-2 serves a project portfolio with a similar representation for entire projects from a portfolio on a phased timeline. Some of the uses of the PV-2 are project management and control (including delivery time scales), project dependency risk identification, management of dependencies, and Project Portfolio management.
Model Audience	Project Portfolio managers. Executive management looking at the portfolio of projects and their respective schedules on a dashboard-like display.
Formal Modeling Methodology	None.
Integration of Model with other Views	Projects in PV-2 must be consistent with those in all other Project Viewpoint models. The timeframes and phases must be consistent with the architecture timeframe and also roadmap-type models such as SV-7, SV-8, SV-9, and TV-2.

Example: Passenger Identification PV-2

Project	Description	Start	End
PMS Upgrade for PAXIS	Upgrade the Passenger Management System to incorporate the centralized and standardized passenger identification services from PAXIS.	3Q2011	2Q2012
ARTS Upgrade for PAXIS	Upgrade the Airline Reservation and Tracking System to incorporate the centralized and standardized passenger identification services from PAXIS.	2Q2011	2Q2012

Project	Description	Start	End
CSS Upgrade for PAXIS	Upgrade the Common Screening System to incorporate the centralized and standardized passenger identification services from PAXIS.	3Q2011	2Q2012
LETS Upgrade for PAXIS	Upgrade the Passenger Management System to incorporate the centralized and standardized passenger identification services from PAXIS.	3Q2011	2Q2012
ARTS (Mobile) Upgrade for PAXIS	Upgrade the Airline Reservation and Tracking System to incorporate the centralized and standardized passenger identification services from PAXIS.	2Q2011	4Q2011
ARTS (Kiosk) Upgrade for PAXIS	Upgrade the Airline Reservation and Tracking System to incorporate the centralized and standardized passenger identification services from PAXIS.	2Q2011	4Q2011
ABTS (Commercial) Upgrade for PAXIS	Upgrade the Passenger Management System to incorporate the centralized and standardized passenger identification services from PAXIS.	3Q2011	3Q2012
CBPS Upgrade for PAXIS	Upgrade the Passenger Management System to incorporate the centralized and standardized passenger identification services from PAXIS.	2Q2011	2Q2012
ICES Upgrade for PAXIS	Upgrade the Passenger Management System to incorporate the centralized and standardized passenger identification services from PAXIS.	2Q2011	2Q2012
ABTS (RMN) Upgrade for PAXIS	Upgrade the Passenger Management System to incorporate the centralized and standardized passenger identification services from PAXIS.	2Q2011	2Q2012
E-POSS	Upgrade the Passenger Management System to incorporate the centralized and standardized passenger identification services from PAXIS.	2Q2011	4Q2011
SmartDevices	Upgrade the Passenger Management System to incorporate the centralized and standardized passenger identification services from PAXIS.	1Q2009	4Q2010
PAXIS Development	Upgrade the Passenger Management System to incorporate the centralized and standardized passenger identification services from PAXIS.	1Q 2011	3Q2011

PV-3 Project to Capability Mapping

In a project portfolio of multiple projects whose primary purpose is to deliver a capability or set of capabilities, the PV-3 Project to Capability model maps each individual project to the capabilities that it delivers in the form of an intersection table. The model is very useful for detecting redundant capabilities delivered by more than one project or the total absence of an essential identified capability in the entire collection of projects, for example.

Model Information at a Glance	
Model Short Name	PV-3
Name	Project to Capability Mapping Project Context Diagram (TOGAF 9)
Other Names	
Viewpoint	Project
Model Intent	The PV-3 can be used to identify capability redundancies and shortfalls, highlight phasing issues, expose organizational or system interoperability problems, and support program decisions, such as when to phase out a legacy system.
Model Audience	Portfolio managers and planners.
Formal Modeling Methodology	None. The model can be represented using a tabular format.
Integration of Model with Other Views	Projects in PV-3 must be consistent with projects in all other Project Viewpoint models. Capabilities in PV-3 must be consistent with capabilities in the Capability Viewpoint models.

Example: Passenger Identification CV-3
Project to Capability Mapping

Project	Capability	Read Identity Document							Validate Identity					Provide Issue/ Confirmation		
		Read RFID Passport	Read Machine-Readable Passport	Read Magnetic ARC	Read DHS Trusted Traveler Card	Read Foreign Passport	Read REAL State Drivers License	Read REAL State-Issued Identity	Validate State identity	Validate U.S. Citizen Identity	Validate Foreign Citizen Identity	Validate Canadian Citizen Identity	Validate U.S. Permanent Resident Identity	Provide Clandestine Confirmation	Provide Audible Confirmation	Provide Visual Confirmation
PMS Upgrade for PAXIS																
ARTS Upgrade for PAXIS																
CSS Upgrade for PAXIS																
LETS Upgrade for PAXIS							X	X	X							
ARTS (Mobile) Upgrade for PAXIS																
ARTS (Kiosk) Upgrade for PAXIS																
ABTS (Commercial) Upgrade for PAXIS																
CBPS Upgrade for PAXIS					X						X	X				
ICES Upgrade for PAXIS		X	X	X		X				X			X			
ABTS (RMN) Upgrade for PAXIS																
E-POSS																
Smart Devices																
PAXIS Development		X	X	X	X	X	X	X	X	X	X	X	X	X	X	X

Questions

1. Discuss the challenges of managing a family of projects versus managing a single project. Will the project management tools that help manage single projects also help you manage multiple projects? How will they handle the determination of dependencies of tasks across projects?

2. What are the Capability Viewpoint models that can help you manage a family of products? How would you use the CV-3 Capability Phasing and CV-4 Capability Dependency to help you analyze the Project Portfolio?

3. Does your enterprise distinguish among programs, projects, and initiatives? Explain what these terms mean in the context of the federal government, the DoD, and commercial enterprises.

4. Where (if anywhere) are the financial aspects of a project, program, or initiative reflected inside the PV models depicted in this chapter?

5. What are the pros and cons of not developing a PV-3 Project to Capability Mapping?

6. Who is the audience for the Project Viewpoint?

7. Discuss the analysis aspects related to the costs, paybacks, and benefits of the following:

    a. A new system being developed viewed as a capital investment

    b. A project viewed as a budgeted expense that represents a sunken investment

    c. An initiative that is opportunistic and represents a gamble on the payoff

Reference List

GAO. (2005). *Best practices: better support of weapon system program managers needed to improve outcomes.* GAO-06-110. November 2005. United States Government Accountability Office. http://www.gao.gov/new.items/d06110.pdf.

GAO. (2006). Defense Acquisitions. *Major weapons systems continue to experience cost and schedule problems under DoD's revised policy.* GAO -06-368. United States Government Accountability Office. http://www.gao.gov/new.items/d06368.pdf.

Microsoft. (2011). *Plans within plans: master projects and subprojects.* Website. Support/ Project/Project 2007 Help and How-to/Managing multiple projects. http:// office.microsoft.com/en-us/project-help/plans-within-plans-master-projects- and-subprojects-HA001226035.aspx#BM#2.

Pennypacker. (2009). *Project portfolio management.* A View from the Management Trenches. The Enterprise Portfolio Management Council. Pennypacker, James and San Retna, Editors. Wiley. ISBN 978-0-470-50536-6.

3.5

Operational
Viewpoint

T he Operational Viewpoint serves the interest of an audience interested in the business processes, activities, and tasks that are performed by an enterprise or a segment or that provide the context for a business solution.

In military operations, the Operational Viewpoint models and represents the Concept of Operations (CONOPS). The military mission drives the military operation. The Operational Viewpoint represents how military tasks are orchestrated by multiple performers to achieve the desired effect or end result of the mission. A military operation also has to consider threats, battlefield conditions, and other contextual information that materially affects an operation.

In civilian government and commercial operations, the Operational Viewpoint represents the business processes and their decompositions into specific activities and steps as well as the orchestration of activities required to achieve the purpose of the process. An Operational Viewpoint involves both human and automated processes that fulfill and support the mission of the enterprise.

An operational viewpoint that represents as-is architecture elements may represent current processes with current automated and nonautomated performers that enable specific activities within the process. An Operational Viewpoint that represents to-be or target architecture elements should avoid depicting solutions and focus on defining the future state only in operational terms. Deferring the decision to design the solution but focusing on identifying and representing the business problem provides what the programming community calls "late binding"—offering a wider canvas for implementation as newer technologies and solution techniques become available.

Frequently, there is much debate among the architects and stakeholders on the distinctions between a business function that represents *what* is required in terms of the mission needs as activity and the business process that depicts *how* the function is accomplished today. In the RMN Airport example, passenger identification is a function that must be accomplished to entitle passengers to access and to services; the process that checks badges, alien registration cards, passports, and other passenger identification documents is specific to today's needs and potentially to future needs. But the primary difference is that functions are enduring while the mission is enduring, but processes can change with reorganizations, technology modernization, improved business processes, or efficiency speedups.

Aspects of the Operational Viewpoint

The models that will be described in this section represent various aspects of the Operational Viewpoint.

Concept of Operations

The OV-1 Operational Concept Graphic is a simple free-form graphical representation of the operation, depicting key players, key locations, key activities, key outcomes and results, and linkages among all of these. Aimed at the high-level decision maker who has little time but great capacity to absorb and understand well-drawn pictures in briefings, the OV-1 is essential for the architect to tell his or her operational story.

Process or Activity Aspect

The OV-5 Operational Activity Model represents the activities that support an operation or process. Depending on the type of actual modeling methodology used, such models can depict the following:

- Refinement of a larger-grain activity into smaller-grain activities using decomposition
- Sequencing of predecessor and successor activities to indicate temporal dependencies
- Resource flows (including information flows) from one activity to another.
- Constraints, rules, and guidance used to control and guide activities
- Measures associated with activity performance and resource expenditure

The Activity Model is one of the first ones to build in an integrated architecture because all dynamics in an architecture come from activities and tasks. The model defines the span of an operational lifecycle and hence serves to set the scope for the rest of the architecture. Omitting an activity also results in omitting the performers of that activity, the locations where the activity is performed, and the resource flows going in and out of the activity. Setting architecture scope frequently involves controlling the scope of the Activity Model.

Some of the modeling techniques used to model activities are: IDEF0 (1993), Business Process Modeling Notation (2011).

Resource and Information Flows

The OV-2 Operational Resource Flow description model is used to depict flow of resources between activities. Because activities are associated with performers, the OV-2 also depicts the resource flows between performers associated with the activities they are performing. Activities are also performed at business locations.

The OV-2 can therefore also depict resource flows between two locations that are hosting cooperating activities. In its simplest form, the graphical OV-2 model depicts performers as oval symbols and lines connecting pairs of performers whenever there is a need for resource flows between them (needlines). The needlines are abstract since the OV-2 depicts an abstract logistics network of resource and information flows between performers. Annotating the activities performed next to the performers provides context for the needlines. The OV-3 Resource Flow matrix is a detailed representation of all resource flows between performer pairs in the context of the activities they are performing. The OV-2 and OV-3 models therefore primarily support the interests of an audience that is interested in (1) who the players are in the Operational Viewpoint and (2) what are the needs for information and resource exchange between the players. In an OV-2, players can also be marked to indicate that they represent an external enterprise or other player who is external to the scope of the architecture. The OV2 is a valuable model for providing a very quick pictorial view of the key players in an architecture and the linkages that carry resources between them.

Organizational Relationships

In large, complex organizations, people have roles that are clearly defined in terms of authority and responsibility. An organization chart formally depicts the roles and responsibilities and reporting relationships. At the same time, in collaborative operations involving people from multiple enterprises, formal memorandum of understanding and formal rules of engagement or contracts must be put in place to ensure that collaboration will occur. The OV-4 Organization Relationships chart is a recording of all of these mechanisms for ensuring collaboration. In many operations, teams may be temporarily constituted for a specific purpose and be disbanded once the purpose is accomplished. In many governance and administrative operations, standing teams are put in place to function as oversight, steering, or coordination bodies. Each of these need to be represented in the OV-4 along with members' actual permanent roles in addition to their temporary assigned duties in the context of the Operational Viewpoint.

Operational Behaviors

All of the other operational models described in the preceding subsections depict static configurations of architecture elements for performing some role in the Operational Viewpoint. The OV6a Rules Model, OV6b State Transition Description

Model, and the OV6c Event-Trace Model all model the dynamic behavior of the operation. The OV6a Rules Model describes the constraints that are imposed upon the behavior of an activity. For example, decision points represent branching in the sequence of activity performance based on a test; rules may also constrain the relationship between a performer and an activity—for example, which type of performer is authorized to perform a specific activity. The OV6b models the dynamics of the state transition of either an object or an activity based on the occurrence of a triggering event or state-changing activity.

TOGAF 9 Support for the Operational Viewpoint

The Business Architecture (developed in Phase B of the ADM) in TOGAF represents the Operational Viewpoint. TOGAF recommends the construction of various types of models to represent various facets of the business architecture using a rich set of model types:

- The *Organization/Actor Catalog* is a list of organizations and the roles they play in the business operations.
- The *Driver/Goal/Objective Catalog* compiles a list of the motivations and business drivers.
- The *Role Catalog* is used to list a set of operational roles that represent mechanisms of a business process activity.
- The *Service/Function Catalog* is used to represent a set of business functions or business services that are required to fulfill the mission of the enterprise.
- The *Location Catalog* is used to list the locations of interest to the enterprise.
- The *Process/Event/Control/Product Catalog* lists the processes, events, and related controls and outputs of the business activities of the enterprise.
- The *Business Interaction Matrix* represents the interaction between business players.
- The *Actor/Role Matrix* represents the allocation of roles to various actors in the context of a business process.
- The *Business Footprint Diagram* traces the Systems View to the Operational View to the Strategic View.

- The *Functional Decomposition Diagram* systematically decomposes business functions into whole-part components.
- The *Product Lifecycle Diagram* is used by product manufacturing or producing enterprises to describe the various stages over the life of a product until it is withdrawn or no longer offered.
- The *Business Use Case Diagram* represents interactions among players, activities, information flows in a business scenario context.
- The *Organization Decomposition Diagram* depicts organizational relationships and whole-part composition relationships among organizations, boards, councils, committees, and working groups.
- The *Process Flow Diagram* depicts the flow of data and control between the activities that participate in a business process.
- The *Event Diagram* traces the sequence of events, the occurrence of activities, the mapping of performers to activities, and the messages and interaction between the performers in the context of the performed activity.

Operational Viewpoint Integrated Models

The Operational Viewpoint describes a set of tightly coupled models that must share many common elements, such as activities, resource and information flows, rules and constraints, performers, and more (see Figure 3.5-1). The following are a few examples of the need for consistency among models in an integrated architecture:

- If the OV-1 depicts performers and activities, they must be consistent with performers and activities in OV-2, OV-3, OV-5, OV-6a, and OV-6c.
- Resource flows if depicted in the OV-2 must be consistent with OV-3 and OV-6c.
- Activities, performers, and resource flows in OV-5 must be consistent with OV-2, OV-3, and OV-6c.
- Triggering events in OV-3 must be consistent with events in OV-6c.

FIGURE 3.5-1 Integrated Models for the Operational Viewpoint

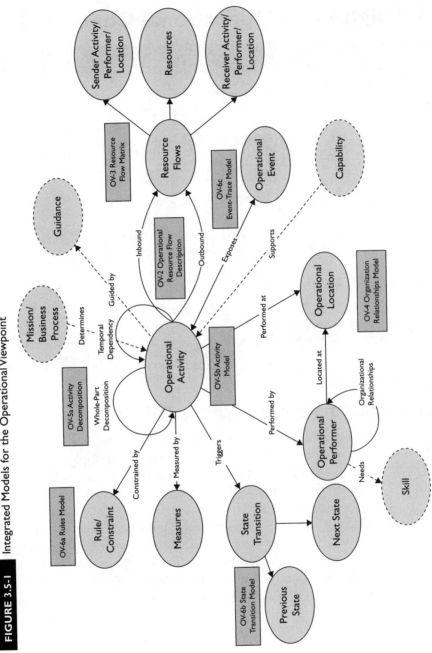

OV-1 High-Level Operational Concept Graphic

Model Information at a Glance	
Model Short Name	OV-1
Name	High-Level Operational Concept Graphic
Other Names	Graphical CONOPS Business Concept Graphic Solution Concept Diagram (TOGAF 9) Value Chain Diagram (TOGAF 9)
Viewpoint	Operational
Model Intent	The OV-1 provides a graphical depiction of what the architecture is about and an idea of the players and operations involved. An OV-1 can be used to orient and focus detailed discussions. Its main use is to aid human communication, and it is intended for presentation to high-level decision makers.
Model Audience	High-level decision makers. Anyone who needs a quick briefing on an architecture.
Formal Modeling Methodology	None. This model uses free-form graphics and is primarily intended for communication and not structure.
Integration of Model with Other Views	The OV-1 abstracts the performers in OV-2, OV-3, OV-5, and OV-6c as well as activities in OV-5 and OV-3. It may also abstract locations in OV-2, SV-1, and SvcV-1; systems in SV-1; and services in SvcV-1. It may also depict desired effects associated with the capabilities in the Capability Viewpoint.

Example: Passenger Identification OV-1

The graphic drawn as an unstructured picture simply depicts that a common form of identification will be used for the passenger at multiple locations (see Figure 3.5-2). This is a significant improvement from the current situation, where each location is performing its own passenger identification—with mixed results!

Because of the free form of expression, the architect has the freedom to choose the focus of the OV-1. In geographic military operations, for example, the backdrop of the OV-1 may be the terrain inside the theater. In phased activities, the OV-1 may have a lifecycle "arrow" depicting the phases and their sequence with markings for specific activities and players. Because of the creative freedom it offers, the OV-1 is therefore really a picture, not a model.

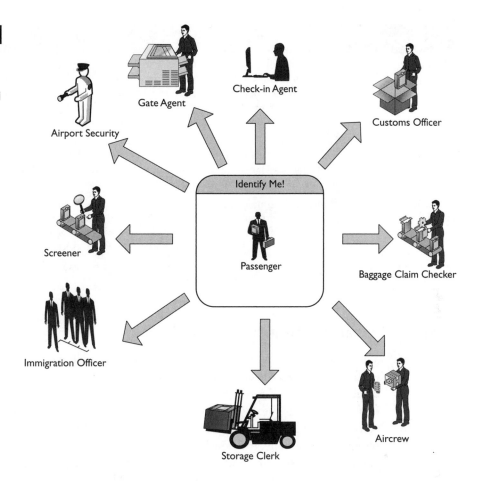

FIGURE 3.5-2

Passenger
Identification
OV-1 Operational
Concept Graphic

OV-2 Operational Resource Flow Description

Model Information at a Glance	
Model Short Name	OV-2
Name	Operational Resource Flow Description
Other Names	Operational Node Connectivity Description (Old) Business Node Connectivity Description Business Interaction Matrix (TOGAF 9)
Viewpoint	Operational

(*continued*)

Model Information at a Glance	
Model Intent	A specific application of the OV-2 is to describe a logical pattern of resource (information, funding, personnel, or materiel) flows. The purpose of an OV-2 model is to describe a logical pattern of resource flows. The logical pattern need not correspond to specific organizations, systems, or locations, allowing resource flows to be established without prescribing the way that they are handled or prescribing solutions.
Model Audience	Any planner with an interest in analyzing resource flows, such as logistics planners (materiel flows), communications network planners (information flows), and staffing and deployment planners (personnel flows).
Formal Modeling Methodology	None. At its simplest, OV-2 can be represented as a straightforward matrix of performers, with each intersection representing a resource flow. OV-2 can also be depicted graphically with performers at the end points of a pair describing a resource flow and annotations to depict activities and locations related to the performers.
Integration of Model with Other Views	OV-2 performers must be consistent with OV-3 senders and receivers, OV-5 performers, and OV-6c performers.

Example: Passenger Identification OV-2

The OV-2 is a structured graphic model depicting needlines—needs for resource exchange between the end points, typically performers, activities, and location combinations (see Figure 3.5-3). The OV-2 is simply a topological map of resource flows. The OV-2 is really an abstract graph where the vertices represent performers, activities, and locations and the edges represent needlines or needs to exchange resources. Optionally, the flow lines can be annotated with specific resources that are flowing between the end points—information elements, materiel, personnel, or funds. It is one of the simplest models to build and provides a quick overview of key players and key operational needline interfaces. It can also be more compactly depicted as a matrix, with the two axes both representing performers and the intersecting cells representing whether there is a needline requirement between the performers in the x- and y-axis for that cell.

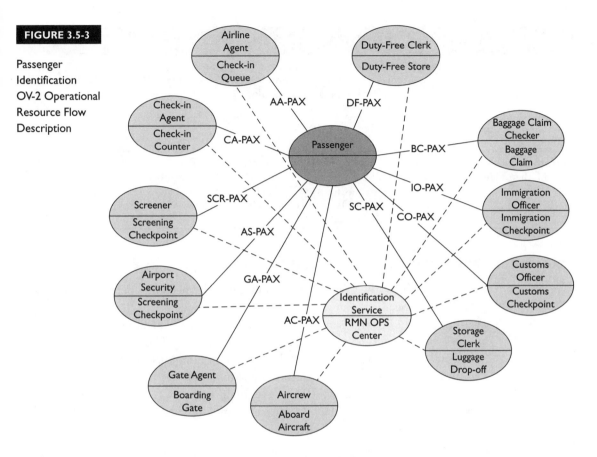

FIGURE 3.5-3

Passenger
Identification
OV-2 Operational
Resource Flow
Description

OV-3 Operational Resource Flow Matrix

Model Information at a Glance	
Model Short Name	OV-3
Name	Operational Resource Flow Matrix
Other Names	Operational Information Exchange Matrix (Old) Business Information Exchange Matrix Data Entity/Business Function Matrix (TOGAF 9) Business Interaction Matrix (TOGAF 9) (Business) Service/Information Diagram (TOGAF 9)
Viewpoint	Operational
Model Intent	Depicts resource flows (including information exchanges) between operational activities in different locations/organizations/performers. The OV-3 depicts key attributes of the resource flows and represents a logistics network for resource flow.

(continued)

Model Information at a Glance	
Model Audience	People interested in flow of resources outside the boundaries of their organizations or locations to other organizations or locations based on the activities that need to be performed at both places. These flows have to be set up with explicit agreements and rules of engagement.
Formal Modeling Methodology	None.
Integration of Model with Other Views	Performers, locations, and activities in OV-3 must be consistent with performers, activities, and locations in OV-2 and OV-5. Resource flows in OV-3 must be consistent with needlines in OV-2 and input/output flows in activity models (OV-5b). Resource flows in OV-3 must be consistent with messages exchanged between lifelines in OV-6c.

Example: Passenger Identification OV-3

Table 3.5-1 shows the OV-3 as an elaboration of the needlines depicted inside the OV-2. Each specific resource flow for each specific needline in the OV-2 is detailed with a description of the sender, receiver, sending activity, and receiving activity as well as the resource and resource type that is exchanged. The OV-3 may also show attributes of the resource flow (not shown in the example) such as throughput, measurement units, and so on. In the case of information flows, attributes such as personal identity information (PII) or security classification are important to define operationally in the OV-3 before jumping in and implementing systems exchanges that could compromise these attributes.

TABLE 3.5-1 Passenger Identification OV-3 Resource Flow Matrix (Fragment)

Needline - From OV-2	ID	Sender	Sender Activity	Receiver	Receiver Activity	Resource	Resource Type
AA-PAX	1	Passenger	Enter Passenger Queue	Airline Agent	Check Entitlement	Boarding Pass	Information
	2	Passenger	Enter Passenger Queue	Airline Agent	Check Identity	Identity Document	Information
	3	Airline Agent	Record Entitlement	Passenger	Enter Queue	Stamped Boarding Pass	Information
DF-PAX	4	Passenger	Pay for Purchase	Duty-Free Clerk	Check Entitlement	Boarding Pass	Information

TABLE 3.5-1		Passenger Identification OV-3 Resource Flow Matrix (Fragment) (*Continued*)					
Needline - From OV-2	**ID**	**Sender**	**Sender Activity**	**Receiver**	**Receiver Activity**	**Resource**	**Resource Type**
	5	Passenger	Pay for Purchase	Duty-Free Clerk	Check Identity	Identity Document	Information
	6	Passenger	Pay for Purchase	Duty-Free Clerk	Validate Payment	Payment Artifact	Information
	7	Passenger	Pay for Purchase	Duty-Free Clerk	Record Payment	Payment	Funds
	8	Duty-Free Clerk	Acknowledge Payment	Passenger	Receive Acknowledgment	Receipt Artifact	
	9	Duty-Free Clerk	Dispatch Merchandise	Passenger	Pick Up Merchandise	Merchandise	Materiel

OV-4 Organizational Relationships Chart

Model Information at a Glance	
Model Short Name	OV-4
Name	Organizational Relationships Chart Organization/Actor Catalog (TOGAF 9) Role Catalog (TOGAF 9) Actor/Role Matrix (TOGAF 9) Organization Decomposition Diagram (TOGAF 9)
Other Names	Org Chart
Viewpoint	Operational
Model Intent	Depict formal and informal organizational relationships to determine whether architectural linkages such as resource flows, are supported by organizational relationships.
Model Audience	All people interested in how the stakeholders or players in an architecture are related. Most enterprises control and publish their formal organizational charts, and joint military operations are accompanied (and coordinated) by formal organizational relationship structures.
Formal Modeling Methodology	None. Organizational charts are typically tree-structured, matrix-oriented, or combinations of tree structures with nondirect relationships between organizations.
Integration of Model with Other Views	OV-4 provides the context for all organizational performers in an integrated architecture and must be consistent with performers depicted in other Operational Viewpoint models such as OV-1, OV-2, OV-3, OV-5, OV-6a (authorization rules), and OV-6c (lifelines).

Example 1: RMN Terminal Operations Division Organization Relationships Chart

The RMN Terminal Operations Division (TOD) chart depicts the formal reporting relationships that are useful to understand in the context of the Terminal Operations Segment Architecture (see Figure 3.5-4). Not shown on this organization relationships charts are organizations external to the TOD. These will be added as the OV-2 gets fleshed out.

The example OV-4 is very simple. In reality, the OV-4 encompasses all types of organizational relationships and is not restricted to just the formal reporting structures. In fact, the OV-4 is a very useful model to clarify relationships between standing organizations (permanent structures) and temporary organizations constructed for a particular purpose such as task forces, working groups, committees, and oversight and review boards. Frequently, members of the permanent organizations are also assigned roles in these temporary structures and must be represented in the OV-4 to gain a fuller insight into their interactions.

Example 2: Passenger Identification OV-4

In the OV-4 shown in Figure 3.5-5, we have depicted in great detail the roles and organizations that surround the passenger in the context of passenger identification.

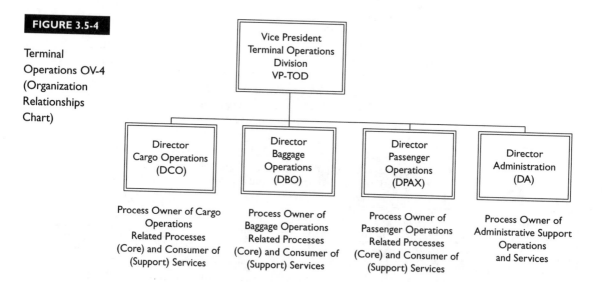

FIGURE 3.5-4

Terminal Operations OV-4 (Organization Relationships Chart)

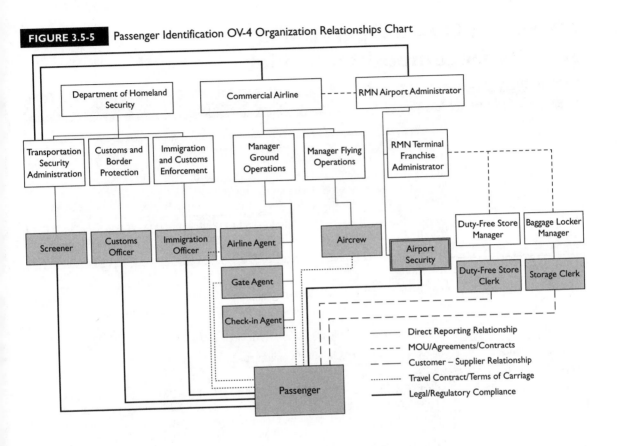

FIGURE 3.5-5 Passenger Identification OV-4 Organization Relationships Chart

We notice that these relationships are governed by many considerations: contracts and agreements, formal reporting authority, customer-supplier relationships, and legal and regulatory forces to comply. This model is more realistic of a real-world situation. In Part II of this book, we discussed the importance of culture and the distorting effect of personal influence over organizational or formal structures. The OV-4 may also be overlaid with relationships that are based on real-world aberrations as well to illustrate that these relationships do influence the behavior of the architecture.

OV-5a and OV-5b Operational Activity Decomposition/Model

Model Information at a Glance	
Model Short Name	OV-5a,OV-5b
Name	Operational Activity Decomposition (OV-5a) Operational Activity Model (OV-5b) Process/Event/Control/Product Catalog (TOGAF 9) Functional Decomposition Diagram (TOGAF 9) Process Flow Diagram (TOGAF 9)
Other Names	Activity Model (IDEF0, UML), Function Decomposition (SADT), Process Model, Workflow Model (IDEF3), Swimlane Model (BPMN), Activity-Based Costing Model (ABM)
Viewpoint	Operational
Model Intent	The OV-5a and the OV-5b describe the operations that are normally conducted in the course of achieving a mission or a business goal. It describes operational activities (or tasks), input/output flows between activities, and to/from activities that are external (outside the scope of the architectural description).
Model Audience	Process engineers, process improvement specialists, operational analysts.
Formal Modeling Methodology	There are several activity, workflow and process modeling methodologies that are applicable: IDEF0, UML activity models, BPMN, and ABM are all good techniques for representing activity models. Appleton (1993) and NIST (2003) describe the IDEF0 Method, also a federal government standard. OMG (2011) describes the BPMN method. Fowler (1996) and OMG (2005) describes the UML method. Ring (2005) describes executable architectures—activity models that can be simulated. Sharp (2001) describes workflow modeling techniques.
Integration of Model with Other Views	The OV-5a and OV-5b activities must be consistent with all operational activities used in all the models, such as OV-1, OV-2, OV-3, OV-6a (Process-Based Rules), OV-6b (Agents for State Transition), and OV-6c.

Example 1: Functional Decomposition of Richard M. Nixon Airport's Enterprise Business Functions

Although we have described the difference between business functions and process activities, we will use the OV-5a Node Tree Model to depict the decomposition of business functions at RMN (see Figure 3.5-6).

The example depicts the functional decomposition of RMN's business functions as a hierarchy (OV-5a). Core mission functions of operating an airport are distinguished from supporting functions that are required to ensure that core mission functions

FIGURE 3.5-6 RMN Enterprise Business Reference Model OV-5a

Core Mission Operations
Mission Support Operations

RMN International Operations – As-Is Business Reference Model

Airport Operations
Airport Security
Motor Vehicle Operations
Fire Safety Operations
Airport Operating Permits

Airfield Operations
Airfield Permits
Air Carrier Operating Permit
Single-Use Operating Certificate
Nonexclusive License Agreement
Motor Vehicle Permit Monthly
Motor Vehicle Operating Permit
Fuel Delivery Permit
Offsite In-Flight Catering Permit
Airfield Surface Movement Operations
Airfield Bus Operations
Service Vehicle Operations
Aircraft Movement Area Operations

Architecture and Civil Engineering
Permits
Civil Engineering Projects

Facilities and Equipment Management
Facility Maintenance
Equipment Maintenance

Terminal Operations
Passenger Information Services
Visitor Information and Services Unit
LAX Ambassador Program
Terminal Cargo Operations
Terminal Passenger Operations
Passenger Check-in
Passenger Screening
Passenger Seating
Public Address Operations
Wireless Hot Spot Operations
Restroom Operations
Left Luggage Operations

Gate/Ramp Operations
TBIT Ramp Safety
Planeside Loading/Unloading Operations
Mobile Ramp Operations
Gate Operations

Baggage Handling Operations
TBIT/T3 Baggage Handling System
Lost Baggage Services
Oversize Baggage Handling
HAZMAT/Special Baggage Handling
Baggage Tracking
Baggage Screening

TBIT Refurbishment
Secure Inline Baggage Screening Services
Northside Inline Project
Southside Inline Project
Terminal Solicitation Management Services
GM Solicitation Program

Landside Operations
Parking Services
Parking Garage Services
Public Parking Services
Airport Employee Parking Services
Airport Vehicles Parking Services
Vendors and Delivery Parking Services
Cargo Delivery and Pickup Parking Services
Delivery Mode
Overflow Parking Lots
Short-Term Parking Areas
Long-Term Parking
Valet Parking
LAX ShuttleLAX
FlyAway
Ground Transportation Permit Program
Vendor Delivery Parking Permit
LAX Employee Parking Program
Ground Transportation Services
Airport Terminal ShuttleTrain
Terminal Services
Taxi and Limousine Services
Rental Car Services

Administration
Franchisory Oversight
Financial Administration
Facility Administration
Policy and Procedures

Human Resource Management
Benefits Administration
Payroll Recruitment and Outprocessing
Union Liaison
Performance Management
Ombudsman/Mediation/Arbitration

Aircraft Operations
Noise Abatement
Engine Test Operations
Maintenance Operations
Refueling Operations
Loading/Unloading Operations
Flight Kitchen/Catering Operations
Deicing Operations
Disinfection Operations

IT Operations
Data Center Operations
Network Operations
Infrastructure Operations
Chief Information Officer
Systems Program Offices

Financial Operations
Financial Planning
Accounts Management
Contracts and Leases
Budget Planning and Execution
Investment Management

Security Operations
Airport Security
Landspace Security
Aircraft Movement Area Security
Terminal Building Security
Inline Screening Area Security
Law Enforcement

can be accomplished. A Business Reference Model such as this one is very useful for representing the span of an enterprise's functions and can be augmented to display top-level business processes under those functions.

Example 2: Passenger Identification OV-5a

The example OV-5a has been shown as activity decompositions from a variety of contexts. Each of these contexts represents some viewpoint. Figure 3.5-7 shows the decompositions from the viewpoints of the immigration officer, the duty-free store clerk, the customs officer, and the storage clerk, for example. Because each of these roles (viewpoints) can see only their own activities, we wind up with a "clump" of decompositions that must later be orchestrated by a threading model as shown in the OV-5b, described in the following subsection.

FIGURE 3.5-7   Passenger Identification OV-5a Activity Decomposition/Node Tree

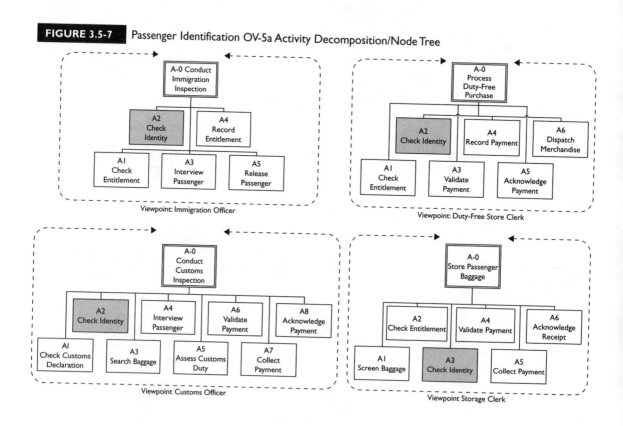

Example 3: Passenger Identification OV-5b

In this model, we represent each of the viewpoints shown in the OV-5a as a swim lane (see Figure 3.5-8). The activities inside the swim lane represent those that are visible to the respective performer. The lines are used to trace the control flow or handoffs of activities. The diagram also shows the information flows as an annotation. The OV-5b information flows must be consistent with the OV-3 in the same architecture, which also shows information flows between the performers. Notice that the OV-3 can be easily derived from an annotated BPMN activity model that shows data flows.

FIGURE 3.5-8 Passenger Identification OV-5b Activity Model

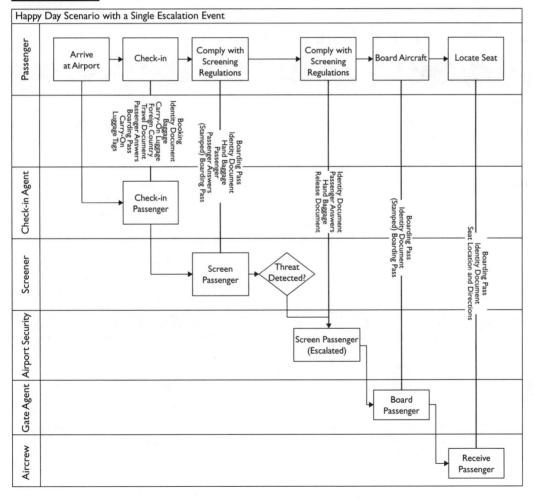

We talk about "Happy Day scenarios" as activity sequences that do not have exceptions and which thus flow smoothly. In real life, we need to take into account all outcomes of the decision boxes in an activity model and handle the processing of those decisions appropriately.

The popular and widely used IDEF0 technique is excellent for progressive refinement and exposition of activities as well as their inputs, controls, outputs, and mechanisms (ICOMS) but is not so good at representing orchestration of many activities by many performers in one diagram such as the swim-lane or BPMN method does. Some modeling techniques are good at representing the handoff of one activity to another (control flow), whereas others are better at depicting input/output flows. Each modeling technique has its strengths and weaknesses, but discussion of activity modeling is outside the scope of this book.

OV-6a Operational Rules Model

Model Information at a Glance	
Model Short Name	OV-6a
Name	Operational Rules Model
Other Names	Rules Model; Decision Tree; Decision Table
Viewpoint	Operational
Model Intent	An OV-6a specifies operational or business rules that are constraints on the way that business is done in the enterprise. At the mission level, the OV-6a may be based on business rules contained in doctrine, guidance, rules of engagement, and so on. At lower levels, OV-6a describes the rules under which activities or other elements of the architecture behave under specified conditions. Rules are frequently required for executable models.
Model Audience	Process modelers, doctrine- and policy-making organizations, data modelers, and performance and execution analysts. OV-6a, because of its granularity, is best applied to specific solution architectures rather than enterprise or segment architectures.
Formal Modeling Methodology	Decision Tree, First-Order Predicate Logic, Structured English, or other mathematical languages for expressing constraints. Rules are declarative (not procedural) and should be atomic, distinct, independent constructs. Ross (2003) describes a rules development methodology.
Integration of Model with Other Views	The rules must be associated with other elements of the architecture. That is, the rules apply to activities, state transitions, or other elements of the architecture. The terms used in business rules must be consistent with similar terms used in other models of the same integrated architecture. This varies from rule to rule. For example, authorization rules must be consistent with performers defined in other models. Actions in If Then Else rules (action assertion rules) must be consistent with operational activities; data elements used in formulae (derivation rules) must be consistent with data attributes in Data and Information Viewpoint models.

Example: Passenger Identification Rules Model OV-6a (Fragment)

The example shown in Table 3.5-2 contains the form of rules found in source documents. These would need to be translated into some formal rules notation to become useful for behavior modeling. For example, the TSA guidance listing the types of acceptable passenger identification documents would be translated into at least 16 separate formal rules (because rules need to be atomic).

TABLE 3.5-2   Passenger Identification OV-6a Operational Rules Model (Fragment)

Rule Group	Rule Statement	Source
Passenger Identification Document	Effective June 21, 2008, adult passengers (18 and over) are required to show a U.S. federal or state-issued photo ID that contains the following: name, date of birth, gender, expiration date, and a tamper-resistant feature in order to be allowed to go through the checkpoint and onto their flight.	TSA Guidance: ID Requirements for Airport Checkpoints: http://www.tsa.gov/travelers/airtravel/acceptable_documents.shtm
Passenger Identification Document	Acceptable identification documents include: U.S. passport DHS "trusted traveler" card U.S. passport card NEXUS SENTRI FAST U.S. military ID (active duty or retired military and their dependents and DOD civilians) Permanent resident card Border crossing card DHS designated enhanced drivers license Drivers licenses or other state photo identity cards issued by Department of Motor Vehicles or equivalent bureau that meets REAL ID benchmarks An airline- or airport-issued ID (under a TSA-approved security plan) Foreign government–issued passport Canadian provincial drivers license or Indian and Northern Affairs Canada (INAC) card Transportation Worker Identification Credential (TWIC)	TSA Guidance: ID Requirements for Airport Checkpoints: http://www.tsa.gov/travelers/airtravel/acceptable_documents.shtm
Passenger Identification Document	Non-U.S./Canadian citizens are not required to carry their passports if they have documents issued by the U.S. government, such as permanent resident cards. Those who do not should be carrying their passports while visiting the United States.	TSA Guidance: ID Requirements for Airport Checkpoints: http://www.tsa.gov/travelers/airtravel/acceptable_documents.shtm

It is important to cite the authority for rules. In the Rules Model, rules are generally tied to activities and performers, although they can be associated with measurement, assessment, formulae for transforming values, and so on. A tailored form of the OV-6a can be used to associate rules with architecture elements. The DoDAF (Department of Defense, 2009) categorizes rules into the following major categories:

- **Structure assertion rules**   These rules constrain structural or existential relationships. Examples of such rules are definitions of the customer, transaction, and so on. Structure assertion rules are used to build the logical data model for database implementation and often reflect data relationships.

- **Action assertion rules**   These rules constrain operational behaviors. They are frequently represented by decision boxes that apply to branching of an activity sequence based on the evaluation of conditions.

- **Derivation rules**   These are rules that determine how computations are performed to derive data from other data. Examples of these are equations, formulas, or lookup functions.

OV-6b State Transition Description

Model Information at a Glance	
Model Short Name	OV-6b
Name	State Transition Description
Other Names	Object State Transition Network (OSTN) Finite State Model
Viewpoint	Operational
Model Intent	The OV-6b is a graphical method of describing how an object class or object (frequently a data entity) responds to various events (i.e., results of activities) by changing state or status. This model describes dynamic behavior.
Model Audience	The OV-6b—like the other behavioral models, OVB-6a and OV-6c—is best applied to solution architecture descriptions and is not as applicable at the enterprise or segment architecting level. Solution architects and people interested in simulation and ensuring that behaviors are bounded in well-understood states are the audience for OV-6b.
Formal Modeling Methodology	UML State Chart, Harel Chart, Finite State Model
Integration of Model with Other Views	Activities and events in OV-6b must be consistent with activities and events in other Operational Viewpoint models.

Example: Passenger Identification OV-6b

The state transition diagram represents the state of a passenger through his or her movement through the terminal (see Figure 3.5-9). A passenger is assumed to have a prior booking. The completion of the check-in activity transforms the passenger from a booked passenger state to a checked-in passenger state. Once the passenger enters the security screening area, he or she becomes subject to the screening process. If the screening process proceeds without any exceptions—that is, no triggering of any monitors or any selection of the passenger for additional screening—the passenger is cleared. If the additional screening fails to uncover some threat, the passenger is cleared. Cleared passengers go on to board their aircraft with the agent scanning their boarding pass at the gate. If additional screening uncovers some confirmed threat, the passenger is detained.

The example serves to illustrate the technique in a deceptively simple and readable manner in a very contained scenario. In reality, state charts can get complicated, with decision boxes, nested states, and concurrent transitions that have to meet at the same point. Not every object or class has a state that may be of interest or worth recording to an analyst. This technique is best used when the understanding of state and state transitions is important to understanding how business is done.

FIGURE 3.5-9

Passenger
Identification
OV-6b State
Transition
Description

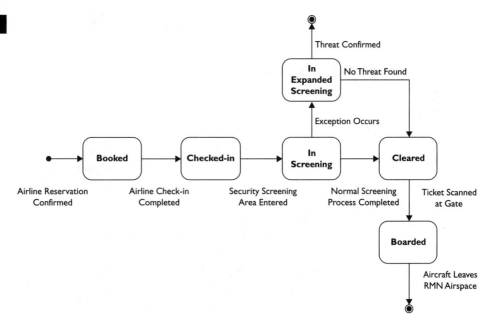

OV-6c Event-Trace Description

Model Information at a Glance	
Model Short Name	OV-6c
Name	Event-Trace Description Event Diagram (TOGAF)
Other Names	Sequence Diagram (UML)
Viewpoint	Operational
Model Intent	The OV-6c enables the tracing of actions in a scenario or critical sequence of events. OV-6c can be used by itself or in conjunction with the OV-6b (State Transition Description) to describe the dynamic behavior of business activities or a mission/operational thread. An operational thread is defined as a set of operational activities, with sequence and timing attributes of the activities, and includes the resources needed to perform the activities.
Model Audience	Process designers, process modelers, and simulation analysts who are interested in tracing the timing aspects and sequence of events as well as the actions, performers, and the exchange of resources.
Formal Modeling Methodology	None. BPMN with annotation for resource flows or payloads (in addition to the natural control flows inherent in the basic diagram) can be useful.
Integration of Model with Other Views	OV-6c must be consistent with performers in OV-2, with resource flows from OV-3 and with activities in OV-5. It may be associated with rules from OV-6a (Authorization Rules).

Example: Passenger Identification OV-6c

Each OV-6c should have associated text that describes the scenario it is based on. The scenario in the Passenger Identification Event-Trace Description is based on a passenger moving through the airport to catch a flight (see Figure 3.5-10). This scenario is familiar to all who have experience with air travel and may need only a short description for such audiences. However, for readers who are not familiar with air travel or with U.S. airport practices, the scenario might require a much more detailed description. For example, the first step is for the passenger to check in with the airline desk agent and present baggage to be checked and carried on, identity documents, and booking information. In this case, the passenger is bound for foreign travel and has the necessary documents. The check-in agent confirms the passenger's identity, reviews the travel documents, and confirms the passenger's destination. The passenger then receives his or her baggage tags and boarding pass and can proceed to the security screening area.

FIGURE 3.5-10 Passenger Identification OV-6c Event-Trace Description

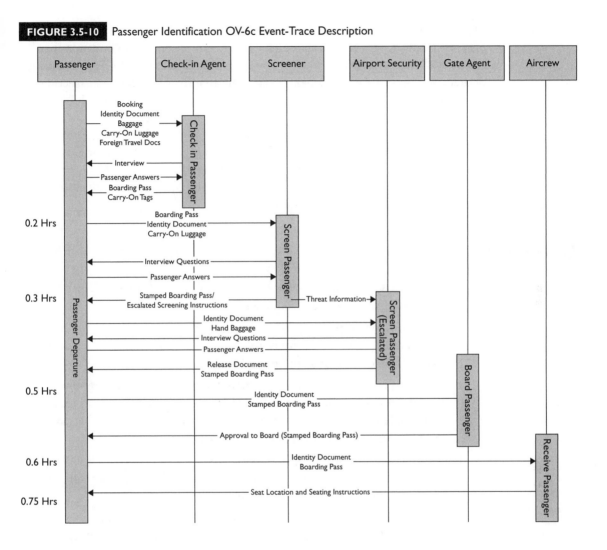

Like its counterparts in behavioral modeling, such as the OV-6a and OV-6b, the Event-Trace Model is very useful for elaborating specific scenarios and tracing the behavior of an operational situation.

Sometimes with a few changes, one type of model can be transformed into another. For example, if we were to turn an OV-6c on its side, it looks like a swim-lane diagram—the lifelines in the OV-6c are transformed into swim-lane roles. However, the swim-lane diagram misses the timing and event sequence that characterizes the

OV-6c, which is a specific scenario or sequence of events, whereas the swim-lane diagram usually depicts generic activities. The OV-3 also contains information that can be used to construct the OV-5b in a swim-lane fashion or the OV-6c as a sequence diagram or event-trace–style model. This requires that the OV-3 contain triggering events that start or trigger the resource flow represented by a row of the OV-3 (Resource Exchange Matrix).

The advantage of an integrated architecture is that all models consistently model the same baseline or planned reality. The importance of integrating your models can never be understated. As we have learned, using the AV-2 to hold our evolving architecture models guarantees that we must reconcile conflicts in architecture elements across models and modeling efforts.

Questions

1. How is the Operational Viewpoint different from the Strategic/Capability Viewpoint? Who are the stakeholders for each of these?

2. The DoDAF views the Operational Viewpoint from the perspective of military operations. Compare and contrast this perspective with the needs of federal agencies and commercial enterprises for business processes.

3. In systems engineering, there is a renewed interest in the use of repeatable patterns to shorten the design cycle. Are there operational patterns that are reusable also? Discuss operational patterns in the context of a reusing enterprise such as a fast food franchise.

4. Can you identify reusable operational patterns (a collection of activity types, role types, location types, resource types, and such that form a logical unit of mission or operation) in your own enterprise?

5. What is the purpose of the OV-1 Operational Concept Graphic? Is the OV-1 a model or a picture, using our definitions given in Chapter 3.1? Why?

6. What are the pros and cons of using a highly tailored OV-1 for a specific audience? Are there communication risks in doing so?

7. What are some of the techniques you would use in your OV-1s to involve architecture stakeholders in your enterprise?

8. How would you indicate the difference between internal and external performers in your OV-2 Resource Flow Description? What other operational model will provide validation of the ability to satisfy a needline relationship?

Hint: Reporting relationships or formal rules of engagement need to be established.

9. What is the relationship between the OV-2 Resource Flow Description and the OV-3 Resource Exchange Matrix?

10. To comply with Privacy Act requirements for protecting personal information, what attributes would you add to the OV-3 to indicate that certain resource flows will need appropriate handling for compliance? For determining the need for protecting classified information in some of the resource exchanges in the OV-3, how would you tailor the OV-3 with additional columns?

11. What types of organizational relationships are represented in the OV-4? Is the OV-4 restricted to the formal organization chart of an enterprise? If not, why not?

12. Does the OV-4 represent only permanent organizations such as business units, departments, and divisions, or does it also represent temporary working groups, task forces, and councils comprised of people drawn from permanent organizations for a specific charter or purpose?

13. What is the OV-5a? Why do you think there are two types of models, OV5a and OV5b, for representing configurations of operational activities? When is each type of model useful?

14. What is a swim-lane activity model? What advantages does a swim-lane model offer over an IDEF0 representation? What are its disadvantages?

15. What is the OV6a Operational Rules Model? Why is it useful in architecting? How (that is, through what mechanisms) are rules implemented in enterprises?

16. How would you organize the many rules in your enterprise?

17. What is the OV6b State Transition Model? How are the states of a process or object represented within an information system?

18. Discuss the applicability of state models to business needs such as providing In Process Visibility (IPV). In Process Visibility is providing explicit indication of the stage of processing of an object such as in the states of a package shipped using a package express company (picked up from customer, transported to shipping point, shipped, transported to distribution point, delivered to recipient). IPV is a method for providing transparency of processing to stakeholders and informing them of the progress of activities.

19. Discuss and build a state model for the states of a package during its transmission from a web retailer to your home using a popular package express carrier.

Reference List

Appleton, Dan. (1993). *Corporate information management: process improvement methodology for DoD functional managers*, 2nd Edition. Appleton Associates.

Department of Defense. (2009). *DoD Architecture Framework 2.0, Volumes I and II*. Department of Defense.

Fowler, Martin, Scott, Kendall. (1996). *UML distilled: applying the standard object modeling language*. Addison-Wesley.

National Institute of Standards and Technology Computer Systems Laboratory. (1993). *FIPS Publication 183: The IDEF0 standard*. National Institute of Standards and Technology.

National Institute of Standards and Technology Computer Systems Laboratory. (1993). *FIPS Publication 184: Data modeling using IDEF1X*. National Institute of Standards and Technology.

Object Management Group. (2011). *Business process modeling notation (BPMN) Version 2.0*. http://www.omg.org/spec/BPMN/2.0/

Object Management Group. (2005). *Unified modeling language (UML) Version 2.0*. Object Management Group. http://www.uml.org/#UML2.0

Ring, Steven J., Lamar, Dr. Bruce, Heim, Jacob, & Goyette, Elaine. (2005). *The future of C2: integrated architecture-based portfolio investment strategies*. Presented at the Tenth International Command and Control Research and Technology Symposium.

Ross, Ron. (2003). *Principles of the business rule approach*. Addison-Wesley.

Sharp, Alec, & McDermott, Patrick. (2001). *Workflow modeling: tools for process improvement and application development*. Artech House.

3.6

Systems Viewpoint

T he Systems Viewpoint (SV) serves the interests of people involved with the planning, design, implementation, deployment, and maintenance of automated systems, particularly automated information systems. The viewpoint can embrace a single system and its context, a family of systems (FoS), or a system of systems (SoS).

Systems engineering of complex systems requires architecture models that can deal with the complexity. A complex system (MITRE Corporation, 2004) can be characterized as one whose development and maintenance is complex, one whose behavior is complex, or usually both.

Often, the term *enterprisewide* is used to characterize a complex system. This term can signify a global business enterprise as well as collections of systems that interact across their individual boundaries to achieve some common goal.

Some salient features of complex systems (as described within MITRE Corporation, 2004, and elsewhere in the literature) include the following:

- Complex systems, usually enterprisewide systems, that are constructed by integrating multiple separate systems.
- Participants must merge their individual goals and behavior to meet the goals of the enterprise to which they belong.
- Many participants have existing systems, cultures, or practices in place that may conflict with those of other participants and are not easy to change.
- The requirements for the system are not precisely known at the start and dynamically change with time.
- Interaction among the system's components and within its environment can produce behavior that is not always predictable or explainable by observation.

The models presented in the Systems Viewpoint other than the SV-10a, 10b, and 10c are static models of systems. The SV-10a, 10b, and 10c provide modeling techniques for the behavior of the system.

With the recent interest in and promises of cloud computing and service-oriented solutions, there is belief that all systems architecting will be replaced with service-based modeling methods—that the need for a Systems Viewpoint will shortly and quickly be replaced by a Services Viewpoint. But the preponderance of systems in today's solution environment guarantees that the Systems Viewpoint is here to stay for a long time to come. Attempts at migration of current infrastructures to new target architecture will require representation of legacy systems mixed in with services, while the encapsulation of legacy functions into services will have to be modeled.

Aspects of the Systems Viewpoint

The Systems Viewpoint enables analysis of systems from many aspects. Each of the SV models has a different purpose for the system analyst. The following subsections discuss some of these aspects.

System Resource Flows/Information Exchanges

The counterpart to the Operational Viewpoint model OV-2 is the SV-1 Systems Resource Flow Model. The SV-1 replaces the operational performers and locations in the OV-2 with systems performers and systems hosting locations, and replaces the operational needlines that indicated needs for exchange of information and flow of resources with interfaces that also require the exchange of information and resource flows between systems performers. If every operational performer were to be supported by a single system, the layout of the SV-1 would perfectly match the layout of the OV-2. But in reality, multiple systems support a single performer, and nonautomated activities in the operational realm do not have a system counterpart in the systems realm. The SV3 Systems to Systems Matrix is a compact model that represents some aspects of interaction between pairs of systems. The SV3 may also be used as a compact model for representing the many interfaces in a large and complex SV-1.

Other systems resource flow models, such as the SV-6 Systems Resource Flow Matrix, focus on the details of the information exchanges and resource flows between specific systems in the context of specific system functions being performed by the systems.

Systems Functionality

Just as the operational activity was the prime ingredient for changing operational behavior, the system function is the prime ingredient that describes system behavior. The SV-4 Systems Functionality description models the system functions that have been implemented or are planned for a system as a well-ordered taxonomy. The SV-4 is useful to compare system functions across multiple systems, looking for duplication and overlaps. The SV-4 also models the input/output behavior of system functions in terms of the information and resources they consume, transform, or produce. The SV-4 can be used to examine the orchestration of information exchanges and resource flows between multiple systems.

Systems Connectivity

The interfaces that demonstrate the need for information exchange and resource flows between systems inside the SV-1 need to be implemented physically using communication paths that connect the systems together and provide a means for transmitting and receiving information and resources. In the IT sense, these are represented by paths through communication links, communication equipment, and computer networks. In the more general sense, these represent logistic chains that channel resources between systems such as concourses in airports, baggage conveyor belts, and so on. The SV-2 Systems Resource Flow Description models the physical paths that are traveled by information and resources between systems. Because the physical path may have several intermediate links that intended exclusively to route communications and resource transfer, the SV-1 may not have an exact correspondence with the SV-2, even though the end points for the path must coincide. The SV-2 is a depiction of the physical transfer path for information and resources that is depicted in the interfaces in the SV-1.

Systems Traceability to Operational Usefulness

Too often, systems are built with many features that were required at the time by business or military operations, but as time moved on, some of them became much less useful or may represent obsolete functions. The SV-5 Systems/System Function to Operational Activity Traceability Matrix maps systems and system functions to the operational activities they support. This is a useful model for analyzing the impact of change of either the operational activity or the system function on each other. For systems planned for the future, this matrix also provides an explicit plan indicating which operational activities will be enabled, facilitated, or automated by a system function.

Systems Performance Specification

Another useful model is the SV-7 Systems Measures Model used to specify the measurements for acceptance of a system or to identify specifications that drive the acquisition of system capabilities. The specification of performance measures early in a system specification allows the making of trade-offs during the design process and also establishes minimum acceptance criteria for various components as well as the system itself.

Systems Evolution

For planners, one of the important models to build is a roadmap of systems evolution. The SV-8 Systems Evolution Model offers the representation in two formats: evolution of features and functions for systems in planned release increments, and migration of multiple systems into one or more target systems. The SV-8 is a useful model for planning modernization initiatives as well as for allocating feature evolution to system increments—incremental development releases of a system that provide increasing functionality over time to users of the system.

Systems Operating Platforms

For technology infrastructure staff, it is important to map systems to the operating platforms that they need to run on. The SV-9 Systems Technology Forecast Model provides the capability of expressing a platform migration strategy for specific systems. A portfolio of SV-9 models can then be used at the enterprise level to determine mismatches in migration strategy or missed migrations, for example.

Systems Behavioral Models

For detailed modeling of systems behavior, the SV-10a Rules Model, SV-10b State Transition Description, and the SV-10c Event-Trace Description are available as counterparts of the OV-6a, OV-6b, and OV-6c operational behavioral models. These are useful for providing detailed representation of orchestration sequences of system functions, information and resource exchanges, and triggering events (the SV-10c Event Trace), or for detailed representation of algorithmic behavior used to implement system functions (the SV-10a Rules Model) or for detailed representation of the state transitions of a system or system function in the face of triggering events and activities.

Systems Viewpoint Integrated Models

For brevity, a partial subset of the Systems Viewpoint is shown in Figure 3.6-1 to illustrate the concepts of integrated models in the context of the Systems Viewpoint (omitted are the SV-9, SV-10a, SV-10b, and SV-10c).

The Systems Viewpoint also represents a tight coupling of models for consistency. Models share many common elements, such as systems, systems functions, system locations, data flows, and so on.

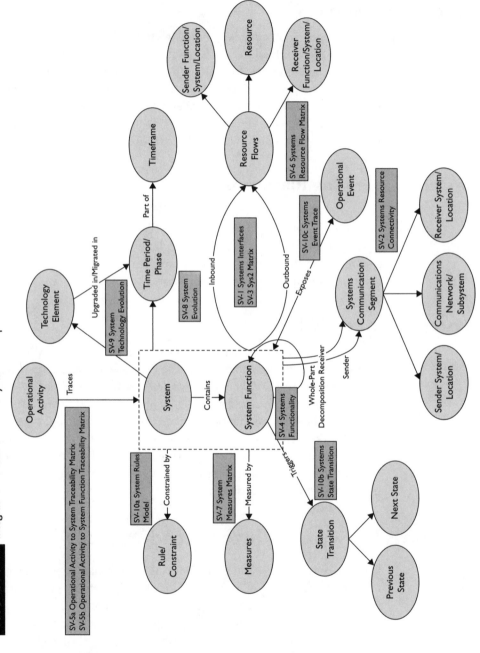

FIGURE 3.6-1 Integrated Model Set for the Systems Viewpoint

The following are some examples of the needs for consistent use of architecture elements between Systems Viewpoint models:

■ SV-1 systems must be consistent with SV-2 systems. SV-1 interfaces must be consistent with SV-4 data flows and SV-6 data exchanges between the same end-point systems.

■ SV-4 system functions must be consistent with SV-5 system functions.

In addition to the integration needs of models within the Systems Viewpoints the models need to be able to integrate with other viewpoints within the models, as in the following examples:

■ SV-5 maps the system functions and systems to operational activities defined inside the Operational Viewpoint.

■ SV-9 must be consistent in the evolution of system technology to the elements defined in the Standards Profile (StdV-1) and the Standards Forecast (StdV-2).

SV-1 Systems Interface Description

Model Information at a Glance	
Model Short Name	SV-1
Name	Systems Interface Description
Other Names	None
Viewpoint	Systems
Model Intent	A system resource flow is a simplified representation of a pathway or network pattern, usually depicted graphically as a connector (that is, a line with possible amplifying information). The SV-1 depicts all system resource flows between systems that are of interest.
Model Audience	Capability configuration planners who must consider all aspects of performers, systems, locations, and resource flows to implement a capability requirement.
Formal Modeling Methodology	None. SV-1 is built as a network graph with the vertices representing combinations of systems, locations, performers, activities, and the edges representing resource flows.
Integration of Model with Other Views	The systems in SV-1 must be consistent with systems in all other SV models. The resource flows in SV-1 must be consistent with SV-4 resource flows and SV-6 resource flows.

Example: Passenger Identification SV-1

The SV-1 is the systems counterpart of the OV-2 Operational Resource Flow Model. The human and organizational performers who represent the end points of the needlines in the OV-2 are replaced by systems representing their automation counterparts in the SV-1. The needlines of the SV-2 are transformed into the interfaces between the systems of the SV-1. Figure 3.6-2 shows the SV-1 Systems Interface Description for passenger identification at RMN Airport.

In the general case, if every operational performer had only one system representing it and every needline had only one systems interface counterpart, the

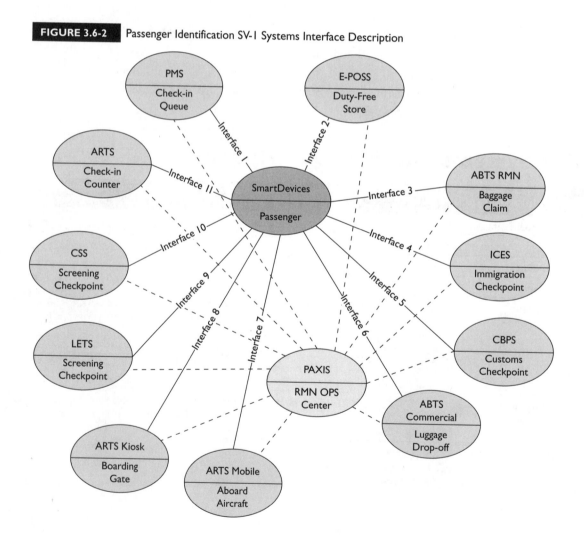

FIGURE 3.6-2 Passenger Identification SV-1 Systems Interface Description

SV-1 would be topologically the same as the OV-2. But in reality, many human and organizational activities may or may not have automated counterparts, and some systems' only purpose may be to relay the interface and thus may not play a vital part in the operations. In the example we presented, the OV-2 and SV-1 are very similar.

SV-2 Systems Resource Flow Description

Model Information at a Glance	
Model Short Name	SV-2
Name	Systems Resource Flow Description
Other Names	Systems Connectivity Description (Old)
Viewpoint	Systems
Model Intent	An SV-2 specifies the system resource flows between systems and may also list the protocol stacks used in connections. An SV-2 DoDAF-described model is used to give a precise specification of a connection between systems. This may be an existing connection or a specification for a connection that is to be made. An SV-2 comprises systems, their ports, and the resource flows between those ports. The architect may choose to create a diagram for each resource flow for all systems or to show all the resource flows on one diagram if possible
Model Audience	Resource flow planners and communications and networks analysts (connectivity analysts). Because of the complexity of the resource flow paths, an SV-2 is more applicable to solution architecture than for enterprise or segment architecture, although major "resource" highways may still be representable at these scales of architecting.
Formal Modeling Methodology	None. An SV-2 is represented as a network diagram with the vertices representing end points for resource flows and a sequence of links that make up connectivity paths between vertices.
Integration of Model with Other Views	Systems represented in an SV-2 must be consistent with systems objects in other SV models. Locations represented at each vertex of an SV-2 must be consistent with locations in other SV models such as SV-1.

Example: Passenger Identification SV-2

The SV-2 represents the physical connectivity and actual resource flow (communication) paths that achieve the interfacing represented inside the SV-1 (see Figure 3.6-3). The SV-1 provides a graphical view of these paths and allows the analyst also to annotate communication and transmission standards and protocols and bandwidth and capacity constraints and readily determine such issues as bottlenecks and capacity constraints or mismatched protocols.

| FIGURE 3.6-3 | Passenger Identification SV-2 Systems Resource Flow Description |

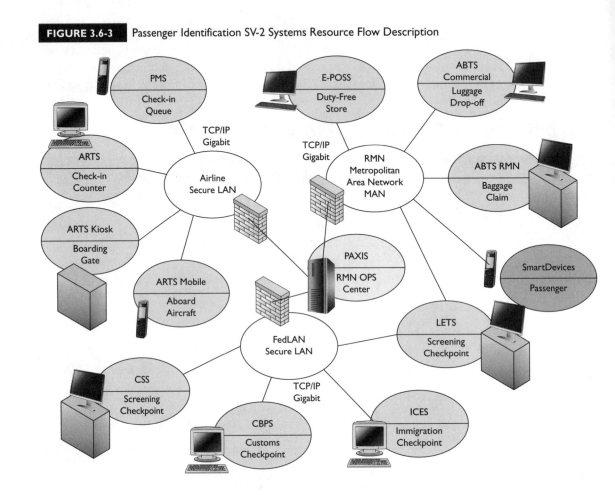

SV-3 System-to-System Matrix

Model Information at a Glance	
Model Short Name	SV-3
Name	Systems—Systems Matrix
Other Names	S2 Matrix, SXS Matrix
Viewpoint	Systems

Model Information at a Glance	
Model Intent	An SV-3 enables a quick overview of all the system resource interactions specified in one or more SV-1 Systems Interface Description models. The SV-3 provides a tabular summary of the system interactions specified in the SV-1 Systems Interface Description Model for the architectural description. The matrix format supports a rapid assessment of potential commonalities and redundancies (or, if fault tolerance is desired, the lack of redundancies). The SV-3 can be organized in a number of ways to emphasize the association of groups of system pairs in context with the architecture's purpose.
Model Audience	Executive-level planners who must digest the aggregation of many SV-1s for high-level analysis. The matrix simplifies the aggregation of many SV-1s and large SV-1s. The intersection cells of the matrix can be tailored to a specific interest for the planner or analyst.
Formal Modeling Methodology	None. SV-3 uses a simple tabular matrix format.
Integration of Model with Other Views	Systems in SV-3 must be consistent with system objects in other SV models.

Example: Passenger Identification SV-3

		Receiving System											
Sending System	Acronym	ARTS	ARTS (Kiosk)	ARTS (Mobile)	ABTS (Commercial)	ABTS (RMN)	CSS	CBPS	E-POSS	ICES	LETS	PAXIS	PMS	Smart Devices
Airline Reservation and Ticketing System	ARTS		C	C	C									C
Airline Reservation and Ticketing System (Kiosk)	ARTS (Kiosk)	C		C	C									C
Airline Reservation and Ticketing System (Mobile)	ARTS (Mobile)	C	C		C									C
Airport Baggage Tracking System—Commercial	ABTS (Commercial)	C	C	C		C								C

C = current interface; P = planned interface.

(continued)

Sending System	Acronym	ARTS	ARTS (Kiosk)	ARTS (Mobile)	ABTS (Commercial)	ABTS (RMN)	CSS	CBPS	E-POSS	ICES	LETS	PAXIS	PMS	Smart Devices
Airport Baggage Tracking System—RMN	ABTS (RMN)	C	C	C	C									C
Comprehensive Screening System	CSS										C			C
Customs and Border Protection System	CBPS										C			C
Enhanced Point-of-Sale System	E-POSS													C
Immigration and Customs Enforcement System	ICES										C			C
Law Enforcement and Training System	LETS						C	P		P				C
Passenger Identification System	PAXIS	P	P	P	P	P	P	P	P	P	P		P	C
Passenger Management System	PMS													C
Smart Devices	Smart Devices	C	C	C	C	C	C	C	C	C	C	C		

C = current interface; P = planned interface

SV-4 Systems Functionality Description

Model Information at a Glance	
Model Short Name	SV-4
Name	Systems Functionality Description
Other Names	System Function List Master System Function List

Model Information at a Glance	
Viewpoint	Systems
Model Intent	The SV-4 addresses human and system functionality. The SV-4 is the Systems Viewpoint model counterpart to the OV-5b Activity Model of the Operational Viewpoint and has the same tree decomposition structure as the OV-5a. Like the OV-5b, it can also be used to define the resource flows (for example, information exchanges) between system functions.
Model Audience	Solution architects, portfolio managers, solution planners
Formal Modeling Methodology	Dataflow diagrams (SADT), system function decomposition tree (SADT). 1. The taxonomic functional hierarchy shows a decomposition of functions depicted in a tree structure and is typically used where tasks are concurrent but dependent, such as a production line. 2. The data flow diagram shows functions connected by data flow arrows and data stores.
Integration of Model with Other Views	The system functions in SV-4 must be consistent with system functions in other SV models, such as the SV-5b, SV-6, SV-7, SV-8, SV-10b, and SV-10c. (The SV-5 model maps system functions in SV-4 to the operational activities in OV-5 and represents a solution to requirement mapping.)

Example: Passenger Identification SV-4

The example SV-4 (see Table 3.6-1) shows a hierarchy of system functions. The SV-4 also allows for a data and resource flow representation that depicts the output of a system function shown as an input of another system. This model represents inputs from human resource and data sources (external resource providers) as well as outputs that go into a storage mechanism for resources/information (sinks).

TABLE 3.6-1 Passenger Management System SV-4 Systems Functionality Description

System	System Acronym	System Function	System Function Description
Passenger Management System	PMS	Verify Passenger Identity	Verify the passenger's identity based on the identity document supplied by the passenger against information located from trusted sources.
		Display Passenger Name Record (PNR)	Display previously stored passenger information using the airline standard PNR format.
		Search Flight	Search for the flight number by destination, time, date, airline, and gate.

(continued)

TABLE 3.6-1		Passenger Management System SV-4 Systems Functionality Description (*Continued*)	
System	**System Acronym**	**System Function**	**System Function Description**
		Search Gate	Search for gate by destination, airline, date, time, and flight number.
		Display Passenger Special Request	Display any special requests for the passenger, such as wheelchair, unaccompanied minor, special meals, etc.
		Display Travel Award Information	Display the award level in the frequent flyer program for entitlement to enhanced services.
		Display Club Entitlement Information	Display entitlement to airline-operated clubs and lounges.
		Request Wheelchair Service	Request wheelchair services from the common pool of wheelchair services operated by RMN.
		Request Special Service	Request special service for hearing impaired, visually impaired, diabetic, or other passengers.
		Print Meal Voucher	Print a meal voucher to compensate for airline-caused delays.
		Print Hotel Voucher	Print a hotel voucher to compensate for airline-caused delays.
		Entitle Delayed Passenger for Hotel	Mark the passenger PNR for delayed flight entitlement to hotel accommodation.
		Entitle Delayed Passenger for Meals	Mark the passenger PNR for delayed flight entitlement to refreshments.

SV-5a and b Operational Activity to Systems-to-System Functions Traceability Matrix

Model Information at a Glance	
Model Short Name	SV-5a, SV-5b
Name	Operational Activity to Systems Traceability Matrix (SV-5a) Operational Activity to Systems Functions Traceability Matrix (SV-5b)
Other Names	None
Viewpoint	Systems
Model Intent	The SV-5a addresses the linkage between system functions described in SV-4 Systems Functionality Description and operational activities specified in OV-5a Operational Activity Decomposition Tree or OV-5b Operational Activity Model. The SV-5a depicts the mapping of system functions and, optionally, the capabilities and performers that provide them to operational activities. The SV-5a identifies the transformation of an operational need into a purposeful action performed by a system or solution.
Model Audience	Portfolio planners, solution architects, process analysts. SV-5a is more useful for segment and enterprise architecting because of the lesser degree of granularity; SV-5b is useful for solutions architecting.
Formal Modeling Methodology	None. SV-5a and SV-5b vary in degree of detail but are both represented as tabular matrices.
Integration of Model with Other Views	Systems in SV-5a and SV-5b must be consistent with systems in other SV models such as SV-1, SV-2, SV-3, SV-4, SV-6, SV-7, SV-8, SV-9, and SV-10c. System functions in SV-5a must be consistent with system functions in other SV models such as SV-4, SV-7, SV-8, SV-10b, and SV-10c.

Example: Passenger Identification SV-5a

The example SV-5a (see Table 3.6-2) shows the relationships between systems and operational activities. This correspondence is very useful to determine which system functions are useful for which operational activities and which system functions are not useful in a specific operational context. The SV-5a provides a valuable model for portfolio analysis of system functions across the spectrum of operational activities.

TABLE 3.6-2 Passenger Identification SV-5a Operational Activity—Systems Traceability Matrix

	Passenger Management System	Comprehensive Screening System	Law Enforcement and Training System	Airline Reservation and Ticketing System	Airline Reservation and Ticketing System (Mobile)	Airline Reservation and Ticketing System (Kiosk)	Airport Baggage Tracking System (Commercial)	Customs and Border Protection System	Immigration and Customs Enforcement System	Airport Baggage Tracking System - RMN	Enhanced Point of Sale System	Smart Devices	Passenger Identification System
Check-In Passenger	X		X									X	X
Screen Passenger		X	X									X	X
Board Passenger					X							X	
Receive Passenger				X								X	X
Conduct Immigration Inspection									X			X	X
Conduct Customs Inspection								X				X	X
Store Passenger Baggage							X					X	X
Process Duty-Free Purchase											X	X	X
Deliver Baggage										X		X	X

Example: Passenger Identification SV-5b

The SV-5b (see Table 3.6-3) is a more detailed model of the relationships between systems and operational activities and provides the mapping between specific system functions and operational activities. This extends the usefulness of the SV-5a to provide more fine-grain analysis of system function redundancy and system function applicability to the operational context.

TABLE 3.6-3 Passenger Identification SV-5b Operational Activity to System Function Traceability Matrix (Extract)

	PMS													ARTS						
	Verify Passenger Identity	Display Passenger Name Record (PNR)	Search Flight	Search Gate	Display Passenger Special Request	Display Travel Award Information	Display Club Entitlement Information	Request Wheelchair Service	Request Special Service	Print Meal Voucher	Print Hotel Voucher	Entitle Delayed Passenger for Hotel	Entitle Delayed Passenger for Meals	Verify Booking	Print Boarding Pass	Print Ticket	Print Ticket Receipt	Display Passenger Name Record (PNR)	Check No Fly List	Transmit PNR to SFPD	Verify Passenger Identity
Check-In Passenger																					
- Check Booking		X	X	X	X	X	X							X				X			
- Check Identity	X																				X
- Check-In Baggage																					
- Validate Carry-On Size						X															
- Validate Foreign Country Entry Authorization																					
- Interview Passenger																					
- Entitle Passenger								X		X	X				X	X	X				

SV-6 Systems Resource Flow Matrix

Model Information at a Glance	
Model Short Name	SV-6
Name	Systems Resource Flow Matrix
Other Names	Systems Data Exchange Matrix (Old)
Viewpoint	Systems
Model Intent	The SV-6 specifies the characteristics of resource flow exchanges between systems. The SV-6 is the physical equivalent of the logical OV-3 table and provides detailed information on the system connections that implement the resource flow exchanges specified in OV-3. Nonautomated resource flow exchanges, such as verbal orders, are also captured. System resource flow exchanges express the relationship across the three basic architectural data elements of an SV (systems, system functions, and system resource flows) and focus on the specific aspects of the system resource flow and the system resource content.
Model Audience	Resource flow analysts interested in capacity, throughput analysis, design of systems resource flow networks, and analysis of flows that cross enterprise boundaries to touch external systems.
Formal Modeling Methodology	None. Represented as a tabular matrix.
Integration of Model with Other Views	Producer and consumer systems in SV-6 must be consistent with systems in other SV models. Resource flows in SV-6 must be consistent with resource flows in SV-1, SV-4 (the Resource Flow Model version), and SV-10c.

Example: Passenger Identification SV-6

The example in Table 3.6-4 depicts the flow of resources between systems (and optional locations). The resource type exchanged in the example is data. Attributes of the resource exchange may also be recorded. In the example, we present data standards that govern the data being exchanged as well as a format and a size for communications personnel to use in assessing the burden on the communications network.

| TABLE 3.6-4 | | Passenger Identification SV-6 System Resource Flow Matrix | | | | | | |

Sender		Receiver		Resource		Transaction		
System	Location	System	Location	Name	Type	Format	Standard	Size (Bytes)
ARTS Kiosk	Boarding Gate Kiosk	ARTS	Airline Data Center	Passenger Boarding Pass Record	Data	Encrypted Binary	ICAO Universal Boarding Pass Standard	356
ARTS Kiosk	Boarding Gate Kiosk	ARTS	Airline Data Center	Passenger Booking Record	Data	Encrypted Binary	Airline PNR Standard	512
ARTS Kiosk	Boarding Gate Kiosk	ARTS	Airline Data Center	Passenger Identity Submission Record	Data	Encrypted Binary	NIEM Identity Data Standard	1,024
ARTS Mobile	On-Board Aircraft	ARTS	Airline Data Center	Passenger Identity Submission Record	Data	Encrypted Binary	NIEM Identity Data Standard	1,024
ARTS Mobile	On-Board Aircraft	ARTS	Airline Data Center	Passenger Boarding Pass Record	Data	Encrypted Binary	ICAO Universal Boarding Pass Standard	356

SV-7 Systems Measures Matrix

Model Information at a Glance	
Model Short Name	SV-7
Name	Systems Measures Matrix
Other Names	Systems Performance Parameters Matrix (Old)
Viewpoint	Systems

(*continued*)

Model Information at a Glance	
Model Intent	The SV-7 depicts the measures (metrics) of resources. The Systems Measures Matrix expands on the information presented in an SV-1 by depicting the characteristics of the architecture elements, such as systems, systems functions, locations, and resource flows.
Model Audience	Systems and solution specifiers for specifying target performance objectives; planners.
Formal Modeling Methodology	None. The SV-7 is laid out as a tabular grid with progressively growing timeframes generally specifying increasing targets for performance measures.
Integration of Model with Other Views	Systems in SV-7 must be consistent with those in SV-1. Interfaces or resource flows in SV-1 must be consistent with performance measures for resource flows in SV-7.

Example: Passenger Identification SV-7

The example in Table 3.6-5 shows an SV-7 performance measure specification for some system functions that are in scope for the passenger identification solution architecture.

TABLE 3.6-5 Passenger Identification SV-7 Systems Measures Matrix

	Architecture Element	Type	Measure	Demo Baseline	Initial Operational Capability Objective	Final Operational Capability Target
1	Check No Fly List	System Function	Response Time on Positive Determination	<20 Sec	<10 Sec	Near Realtime
			Response Time on Negative Determination	<30 Sec	<20 Sec	Near Realtime
2	Detect Chemicals and Hazardous Materials	System Function	Sensitivity	100 ppm	50 ppm	20 ppm
3	Detect Concealed Weapons	System Function	Ferrous Weapon Detection Accuracy	80%	90%	100%

| TABLE 3.6-5 | Passenger Identification SV-7 Systems Measures Matrix *(Continued)* |

	Architecture Element	Type	Measure	Demo Baseline	Initial Operational Capability Objective	Final Operational Capability Target
			Plastic Weapon Detection Accuracy	60%	80%	100%
4	Detect Explosives	System Function	Sensitivity	5ppm	3ppm	1ppm
5	Detect Inflammable Material	System Function	Sensitivity	10ppm	8ppm	5ppm
6	Detect Metal Objects	System Function	Detection Accuracy	80%	90%	100%
7	Detect Sharp Objects	System Function	Lethal Weapon Detection Accuracy	80%	90%	100%
			Nonlethal Sharps	70%	80%	80%
8	Display Bag Dimensions	System Function	Dimensional Accuracy	85%	90%	99%
9	Generate Coded Locker Key	System Function	Key Generation Time	20 Sec	10 Sec	Near Realtime
10	Print Baggage Storage Bar Code Label	System Function	Printing Barcode Time	20 Sec	10 Sec	Near Realtime
11	Print Baggage Storage Ticket	System Function	Printing Time	20 Sec	10 Sec	Near Realtime
12	Print Boarding Pass	System Function	Printing Time	30 Sec	20 Sec	10 Sec
13	Register Active Baggage	System Function	Transaction End to End Time	10 Sec	8 Sec	5 Sec
14	Transmit ARC Information	System Function	Transmission Time	10 Sec	5 Sec	Near Realtime

(continued)

TABLE 3.6-5	Passenger Identification SV-7 Systems Measures Matrix (*Continued*)

	Architecture Element	Type	Measure	Demo Baseline	Initial Operational Capability Objective	Final Operational Capability Target
15	Transmit Credit Card Information	System Function	Transmission Time	10 Sec	5 Sec	Near Realtime
16	Transmit DHS Entry Card Information	System Function	Transmission Time	10 Sec	5 Sec	Near Realtime
17	Transmit Drivers License Information	System Function	Transmission Time	10 Sec	5 Sec	Near Realtime
18	Transmit Passport Information	System Function	Transmission Time	10 Sec	5 Sec	Near Realtime
19	Transmit Passenger Name Record to Police Department	System Function	Transmission Time	10 Sec	10 Sec	10 Sec
20	Verify Boarding Pass	System Function	Verification Time	<30 Sec	<20 Sec	<10 Sec
21	Verify Passenger Identity	System Function	Positive Identification	<30 Sec	<20 Sec	<10 Sec
			Negative Identification	<1 Min	<30 Sec	<20 Sec
22	Weigh and Display Bag Weight	System Function	Weight Accuracy	95%	98%	100%
			Weight Result Display Time	10 Sec	10 Sec	Near Realtime

SV-8 Systems Evolution Description

Model Information at a Glance	
Model Short Name	SV-8
Name	Systems Evolution Description
Other Names	None.
Viewpoint	Systems
Model Intent	The SV-8, when linked together with other evolution models (such as CV-3 Capability Phasing and StdV-2 Standards Forecast), provides a rich definition of how the enterprise and its capabilities are expected to evolve over time. In this manner, the model can be used to support an architecture evolution project plan or transition plan. An SV-8 can either describe historical (legacy), current, and future system capabilities against a timeline. Two styles of SV-8 are defined: one is focused on how capabilities of systems are merged over a timeframe and how new systems emerge from merging or splitting system functions from legacy configurations; the other is focused on displaying, for a single system, the evolution of system capabilities over a planning timeframe.
Model Audience	Planners; systems program managers; portfolio managers.
Formal Modeling Methodology	None. A tabular or a graphical method can be used to display the evolution of a systems migration strategy for multiple systems or a single system's evolving capabilities over time.
Integration of Model with Other Views	Systems in SV-8 must be consistent with all other SV models depicting systems such as SV-1, SV-2, SV-3, SV-4, SV-5, SV-6, SV-7, SV-9, and SV-10c. System functions depicted in SV-8 must be consistent with system functions in other SV models, such as SV-4, SV-5, and SV-10c.

Example: Passenger Identification SV-8

Although the SV-8 is generally drawn as a graphic, Table 3.6-6 shows a tabular rendering of the evolution of the various systems in terms of functions that will be added in system increments over a period of time.

TABLE 3.6-6   Passenger Identification SV-8 Systems Evolution Description

	2010		2011			2012	
System	**4Q2010**	**1Q2011**	**2Q2011**	**3Q2011**	**4Q2011**	**2Q2012**	**3Q2012**
PMS					Freq Flyer Entitlement	PAXIS Upgrade	
ARTS						PAXIS Upgrade	
CSS						PAXIS Upgrade	
LETS						PAXIS Upgrade	
ARTS-Mobile					PAXIS Upgrade		
ARTS-Kiosk					PAXIS Upgrade		
ABTS-Commercial							PAXIS Upgrade
CBPS						PAXIS Upgrade	
ICES						PAXIS Upgrade	
ABTS - RMN						PAXIS Upgrade	
E-POSS					PAXIS Upgrade		
Smart Devices	Smart Reader	Machine-Readable Passports	RFID Passports	All Magnetic Stripe Devices			
PAXIS			IOC	FOC			

SV-9 Systems Technology and Skills Forecast

Model Information at a Glance	
Model Short Name	SV-9
Name	Systems Technology and Skills Forecast
Other Names	Systems Technology Forecast (Old)
Viewpoint	Systems
Model Intent	The SV-9 maps technology forecasts against an adoption timeline for the scope of the architecture system elements. This includes, for example, mapping for each system the planned infusion of new technology. The technology depiction may be general or specific to vendor products.
Model Audience	Technology planners; systems program offices; standards personnel; investment review boards.
Formal Modeling Methodology	None.
Integration of Model with Other Views	The technology classification scheme in SV-9 must be consistent with the taxonomy of StdV-1 and StdV-2 Service Areas and Services. Any standards used in SV-9 must also be consistent with StdV-1 and StdV-2 standards. Systems represented in SV-9 must be consistent with systems in other SV models, such as SV-1, SV-2, SV-3, SV-4, SV-6, SV-7, SV-8, and SV-10c.

Example: Passenger Identification SV-9

The example in Table 3.6-7 shows the planned technology upgrades and migrations for various systems over a planning timeframe. Note that the SV-9 shows actual upgrades of technology instances (Vendor Products) rather than planned adherence to technical standards such as compliance to the FIPS 127 SQL Standard. The StdV-1 focuses more on technical profiles (Service Areas, Services and Standards), whereas the SV-9 is focused more on a planned migration of specific technologies.

TABLE 3.6-7 Passenger Identification SV-9 Systems Evolution Description

| System | 2010 | 2011 | | | | 2012 | |
	4Q2010	1Q2011	2Q2011	3Q2011	4Q2011	2Q2012	3Q2012
PMS	Windows 7 Server						
ARTS	Windows 7 Server		Oracle 11		SQL Server YYY		
CSS	Windows 7 Server						
LETS	Windows 7 Server			Oracle 11			
ARTS-Mobile	Windows 7 Server			SQL Server YYY	MySQL		
ARTS-Kiosk	Windows 7 Server				SQL Server YYY		
ABTS-Commercial	Windows 7 Server						
CBPS	Windows 7 Server			Oracle 11			
ICES	Windows 7 Server		Oracle 11				
ABTS - RMN	Windows 7 Server						
E-POSS	Windows 7 Server			SQL Server YYY			
SmartDevices	Windows Mobile	ISO XXX	ISO XXX	ISO XXX			
PAXIS	Apache Web Server		IOC	FOC			

SV-10a Systems Rules Model

The SV-10a Systems Rules Model (described in Table 3.6-8) is similar to the OV-6a Operational Rules Model in that it describes the rules that constrain systems or system functions. These rules are embedded inside the logic of the system function or they may also represent constraints that govern the operator interface and permission sets.

Types of system rules in SV-10a include the following:

- *Structure assertion* rules in the SV-10a are embedded inside the database as constraints. For example, a rule may be, "A passenger is a person who has a boarding pass," to distinguish people who have simply made a booking from those who are actually traveling.

TABLE 3.6-8   SV-10a Systems Rules Model at a Glance

Model Short Name	SV-10a
Name	Systems Rules Model
Other Names	Rules Model
Viewpoint	Systems
Model Intent	DoDAF's Systems Rules Model describes the rules that control, constrain, or otherwise guide the implementation aspects of the architecture. System rules are statements that define or constrain some aspect of the business, and may be applied to the following: ■ System and human performers ■ Resource flows ■ System functions ■ System ports ■ Data elements
Model Audience	Systems and solution architects. The SV-10a is a fine-grain model that may not be applicable to enterprise and segment architecting and must be driven by various systems scenarios.
Formal Modeling Methodology	None. The model is represented using English text or formal mathematical notation, like the OV-6a Operational Rules Model.
Integration of Model with Other Views	Any architecture elements referenced by a rule must be consistent with the corresponding model elements in SV models, such as system performers in SV-1, SV-2, SV-3, SV-4, SV-6, SV-7, SV-8, SV-9 and SV-10c or resource flows in SV-1, SV-4, SV-6, and SV-10c.

- *Action assertion* rules are embedded in the processing logic of system functions. They generally have the following format: If (condition) Then (perform actions) Else (perform alternative actions).

- *Derivation* rules, such as computations—for example, to compute the probability that a specific passenger is potentially traveling under a false identity—are also embedded into the processing logic of system functions or as lookup functions.

SV-10b Systems State Transition Model

The SV-10b Systems State Transition Description (see Table 3.6-9) is similar to the Operational State Transition Description (OV-6b) described earlier. In its simplest form, it describes the change in state of a system due to system functions or system/external events. The objective of state transition diagrams is to observe the behavior of a system in terms of desired and undesired states, detect undesirable possible cycling between states, and ensure that the states are bounded and well understood when the system is deployed.

TABLE 3.6-9   SV-10b Systems State Transition Description Model at a Glance

Model Short Name	SV-10b
Name	Systems State Transition Description
Other Names	UML State Chart, Harel State Diagram, Finite State Model
Viewpoint	Systems
Model Intent	The SV-10c depicts the state transitions of system or system function states based on triggering events or actions. The explicit sequencing of service functions in response to external and internal events is not fully expressed in an SV-4 Systems Functionality Description. The SV-10b can be used to describe the explicit sequencing of the functions. Alternatively, SV-10b can be used to reflect explicit sequencing of the actions internal to a single function or the sequencing of system functions with respect to a specific resource.
Model Audience	Systems and solution architects. Simulation analysts. The SV-10c is a fine-grain model that is not readily applicable to enterprise and segment architectures.
Formal Modeling Methodology	UML State Chart, Harel Chart, Finite State Model
Integration of Model with Other Views	Actions in SV-10b must be consistent with system functions in other SV models such as SV-4 and SV-5.

SV-10c Systems Event-Trace Description

The Systems Event-Trace Description (SV-10c) (see Table 3.6-10) is similar to the Operational Event-Trace Description (OV-6c) in that it models the sequence of message exchanges between system functions in a scenario or contained situation. It also depicts the exchange of messages in the context of timing so that the architect can observe and determine timing-related issues. The SV-10c is very useful in examining a detailed scenario in terms of sender systems and receiver systems, the functions they are performing at the time of the message exchange, the type of information that forms the subject of the interaction, and timing information associated with the exchange. The SV-10c complements the SV-6 Resource Flow Matrix by laying out the data exchanges on a timeline and representing the exact sequence with which the messages are sent and received. Although we have discussed the SV-10c as a model for representing data exchange, it can also be generalized to represent the exchange of any type of resource, such as funds, people, and material.

TABLE 3.6-10   SV-10c Systems Event-Trace Description Model at a Glance

Model Short Name	SV-10c
Name	Systems Event-Trace Description
Other Names	UML Sequence Diagram
Viewpoint	Systems
Model Intent	The SV-10c provides a time-ordered examination of the interactions between functional resources such as systems. Each event-trace diagram should have an accompanying description that defines the particular scenario or situation. The SV-10c is valuable for moving to the next level of detail from the initial solution design, to help define a sequence of functions and system data interfaces, and to ensure that each participating system or system port role has the necessary information it needs, at the right time, to perform its assigned functionality.
Model Audience	Systems and solution architects. The SV-10c is not readily applicable to enterprise or segment architecting and is best used with scenarios.
Formal Modeling Methodology	A UML Sequence Diagram is used to model object class interactions.
Integration of Model with Other Views	Systems in SV-10c must be consistent with systems in other SV models. Resource flows in SV-10c must be consistent with (but not necessarily identical in level of abstraction) with resource flows in SV-1, SV-4, and SV-6.

Questions

1. What is the audience that is served by the Systems Viewpoint?

2. Discuss how your enterprise would use the Systems Viewpoint models to move to a service-oriented architecture. Which are the Service Viewpoint counterparts for the Systems Viewpoint models?

3. Which of the Data and Information viewpoints is complementary to the Systems Viewpoint models? Why?

4. Distinguish between a system function and a service.

5. What is the SV-1 Systems Interface Description? Would you expect to find all the systems of the enterprise in your SV-1? Why, or why not?

6. What is the SV-2 Systems Resource Flow Description? Would you expect to find items such as networks, routers, modems, and firewalls depicted inside the SV-1? Inside the SV-2?

7. What is the relationship between the SV-1 and the SV-2? What common architecture elements do they share?

8. What is the SV-3? How can your enterprise tailor an SV-3 to depict interfaces that are already implemented as well as planned interfaces?

9. What is the SV-4? The example depicted shows a simple, functional decomposition, but the SV-4 can also show data flows between system functions. How would you depict these data flows in a diagram? How would you accommodate operators typing data into a system or data flowing into a database? (Hint: See the discussion of data flow diagrams in Department of Defense, 2009.)

10. How can the SV-5a and SV-5b be used to determine the composition of a systems portfolio? What are the risks in using the SV-5 to determine redundancy?

11. How can you tailor the SV-6 to also include needs to capture data security classification, personal identification information, and throughput?

12. What performance measures for systems functions are commonly used in your enterprise? What other measures are applicable to other architecture elements?

13. The Systems Evolution Description (SV-8) can be rendered in two ways: system evolution of an individual system in terms of evolution of features and functions over a timeframe, or in a migration style diagram that shows which systems are merged or split to form a new systems portfolio. Discuss the applicability of these two styles of SV-8 to your own enterprise.
14. What are the elements of forecast for technology in an SV-9? Are they technical standards or are they specific vendor products? Why?

Reference List

Department of Defense. (2009). *DoDAF 2.0, Volumes I and II*. Department of Defense.

Object Management Group. (2005). *Unified Modeling Language Version 2.0*. The Object Management Group. http://www.omg.org/spec/UML/2.0/

Object Management Group. (2008). *Universal profile for DoDAF and MODAF (UPDM)*. OMG Document c4i/2008-08-13. http://www.updm.com/index.htm.

SysML Open Source Specification Project. (2008). *System Modeling Language (SysML) Version 1.1*. OMG Document Number: formal/2008-11-01. http://www.sysml.org/.

3.7

Services Viewpoint

T

he world is changing at an ever-faster rate. Traditional methods of architecting both business functions and software functionality cannot keep up with the pace of this rapid rate of change.

In the area of business functions, vertically integrated enterprises that develop their own business functions are often outpaced by nimbler competitors who offload the functions to service providers and concentrate on managing the interfaces with these service suppliers. Enterprises are increasingly focused on their "core competencies" and offload mission support functions to business partners whose own core competency is providing that function. These offloaded business functions are deemed services, although any packaged business function that is *loosely coupled* and governed by agreement or contract between the provider and consumer may be deemed a business service. The design of a service therefore requires architecture decoupling of interrelationships so that the service can be treated as a black box whose behavior and performance can be negotiated as a level of delivery of service. It also requires clear definition of service interfaces—how the service looks to the consumer—that is independent of the internal implementation of the service. Atomic services by themselves are also stateless—their invocation processes maintain the state information needed to orchestrate successfully a collection of services needed to achieve a business objective or mission.

In the area of software development, a similar solution based on vertically integrated software relies on in-house development of software functions that are tightly tied to the software solution being developed. Such tightly integrated systems are immune to adaptability because the impact of change requires widespread change to the solution. At the same time, the enterprise cannot take advantage of market forces for a software component that can be purchased, leased, or supplied by external providers. Software services are stateless providers of functionality that are stand-alone; loosely coupled; defined with clear, published interfaces; and used as building blocks to develop software applications.

TOGAF 9 distinguishes business functions, business services, and information system services from one another using the following definitions:

- **Function**   A function is a thing that a business does. Services support functions, are functions, and have functions, but functions are not necessarily services. Services have more specific constraints than functions.

- **Business service**   A business service is a thing that a business does that has a defined, measured interface and has contracts with consumers of the service. A business service is supported by combinations of people, processes, and technology.

- **Information system service**   An information system service is a thing that a business does that has a defined, measured interface and has contracts with consumers of the service. Information system services are directly supported by applications and have associations to service-oriented architecture (SOA) service interfaces.

The Service-Oriented Framework

"Service Oriented Architecture is a paradigm for organizing and utilizing distributed capabilities that may be under the control of different ownership domains" (OASIS, 2006, pg 8). A key characteristic of SOA is modularity that facilitates or enables service reuse across processes and organizational boundaries. A service that is designated for reuse or as an enterprise service, such as authentication, must reside in an environment that is discoverable, reliable, and maintainable and can be monitored. An overarching architecture is needed to contain these services as they are developed and implemented (Federal CIO Council, 2008).

The Services Viewpoint caters to the interest of people responsible for planning, architecting, developing, implementing, and deploying service-oriented solutions. This is an evolutionary field that is arguably better defined for the sphere of the software services construction but less so for the planning and architecture realms.

The Federal CIO Council (2008) depicts the layers of an agile enterprise based on the service-oriented paradigm shown in Figure 3.7-1. The layers of the framework are as follows:

- **Service-oriented enterprise (SOE)**   The business, management, and operational processes, procedures, and policies that support a services model. In essence, this is an organizational behavior model aligned with the service model and designed to facilitate and govern its effective maturation.

- **Service-oriented architecture (SOA)**   Enhanced architecture practices that leverage robust models to capture and facilitate service architecture engineering best practices. SOA is the application of the service model from EA through segment architectures to solution architectures.

- **Service-oriented infrastructure (SOI)**   The service-enabling environment, itself delivered as a collection of robust enterprise services that enable runtime connectivity and interoperability. SOI represents the operational environment that supports the service model.

FIGURE 3.7-1

Service-Oriented
Framework
(Federal CIO
Council, 2008)

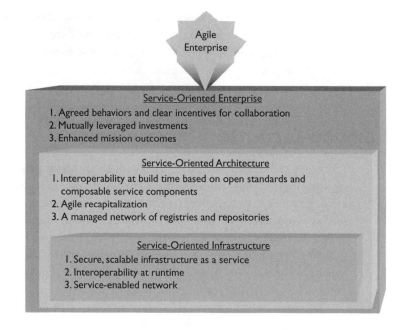

The Services Viewpoint (SvcV) allows the service planner, analyst, and architect to develop models in support of any of these three levels, enabling analysis of services from many aspects. Each of the SvcV models has a different purpose for the services analyst. The following subsections describe some of these aspects.

Service Resource Flows and Information Exchanges

The counterpart to the Operational Viewpoint model OV-2 is the SvcV-1 Services Resource Flow Model. The SvcV-1 replaces the operational performers and locations in the OV-2 with services performers and services hosting locations and replaces the operational needlines that indicated needs for exchange of information and flow of resources with interfaces that also indicate a need to exchange information and resource flows between services performers. If every operational performer were to be supported by a single service, the layout of the SvcV-1 would perfectly match the layout of the OV-2. But in reality, multiple services support a single performer and nonautomated activities in the operational realm do not have a system counterpart in the services realm. The SvcV-3 Services to Services Matrix is a compact model that represents some aspect of interaction between pairs of services. The SvcV-3 may also be used as a compact model for representing the many interfaces in a large and complex SvcV-1.

Other services resource flow models, such as the SvcV-6 Services Resource Flow Matrix, focus on the details of the information exchanges and resource flows between specific services in the context of specific service operations being performed by the services.

Services Functionality

Just as operational activity was the prime ingredient for changing operational behavior, the service operation is the prime ingredient that describes system behavior. The SvcV-4 Services Functionality Description models the service operations that have been implemented or are planned for a system as a well-ordered taxonomy. The SvcV-4 is useful to compare service functions across multiple services, looking for duplication and overlaps. The SvcV-4 also models the input/output behavior of service operations in terms of the information and resources they consume, transform, or produce. The SvcV-4 can be used to examine the orchestration of information exchanges and resource flows between multiple services.

Services Connectivity

The interfaces that demonstrate the need for information exchange and resource flows between services inside the SvcV-1 need to be implemented physically using communication paths that connect the services together and provide a means for transmitting and receiving information and resources. In the IT sense, these are represented by paths through communication links, communication equipment, and computer networks. In the more general sense, these represent logistic chains that channel resources between services, such as concourses in airports, baggage conveyor belts, and so on. The SvcV-2 Services Resource Flow Description models the physical paths that are traveled by information and resources between services. Because the physical path may have several intermediate links that exist purely to route communications and transfer resources, the SvcV-1 may not have an exact correspondence with the SvcV-2, even though the end points for the path must coincide. The SvcV-2 is a model of the physical transfer path for information and resources that is depicted in the interfaces in the SvcV-1.

Services Traceability to Operational Usefulness

Too often, services are built with many features that were required at the time by business or military operations. As time goes on, some of these features may not be very useful or may represent obsolete functions. The SvcV-5 Services/Service Operation to Operational Activity Traceability Matrix maps services and service operations to the operational activities they support. This is a useful model for analyzing the impact of change of either the operational activity or the service operation on each other. For future planned services, the SvcV-5 also provides an explicit plan of which operational activities will be enabled, facilitated, or automated by a service operation.

Services Performance Specification

Another useful model is the SvcV-7 Services Measures Model used to identify the measurements for acceptance of a system or specifications that drive the acquisition of system capabilities. The identification of performance measures early in a system specification makes trade-offs possible during the design process and also establishes minimum acceptance criteria for various components as well as for the system itself.

Services Evolution

For planners, one of the important models to build is a roadmap of services evolution. The SvcV-8 Services Evolution Model offers the representation in two formats: evolution of features and functions for services in planned release increments, and migration of multiple services into one or more target services. The SvcV-8 is a useful model for planning modernization initiatives as well as for allocating feature evolution to system increments.

Services Operating Platforms

For technology infrastructure staff, it is important to map services to the operating platforms that they need to run on. The SvcV-9 Services Technology Forecast Model provides the capability of expressing a platform migration strategy for specific services. A portfolio of SvcV-9 models can then be used at the enterprise level to determine mismatches in migration strategy or missed migrations, for example.

Services Behavioral Models

For detailed modeling of services behavior, the SvcV-10a Rules Model, SvcV-10b State Transition Model, and the SvcV-10c Event-Trace Description are available as counterparts of the OV-6a, OV-6b, and OV-6c operational behavioral models. These are useful for providing detailed representation of orchestration sequences of service operations, information and resource exchanges, and triggering events (the SvcV-10c Event Trace); for detailed representation of algorithmic behavior used to implement service operations (the SvcV-10a Rules Model); or for detailed representation of the state transitions of a system or service operation in the face of triggering events and activities.

A detailed discussion of services, service-oriented architectures, service design, the use of service patterns, and the implementation of services using the Web Services Description Language (WSDL) is beyond the scope of this book. However, it is important to understand that WSDL is the language in which the service specification is described so that a computer requiring a service can request the service from the provider of that service. WSDL specifies the service and smaller units of functionality called operations or methods within the service. WSDL also supports the specification of a service request by specifying what inputs are required and what outputs are produced by the service.

However, such topics represent a specialty in architecting and engineering, and professionals with such expertise should be part of an EA team.

Services Viewpoint Integrated Models

For brevity, a partial subset of the Services Viewpoint is shown in Figure 3.7-2 to illustrate the concepts of integrated models in the context of the Services Viewpoint (missing are the SvcV-9, SvcV-10a, SvcV-10b, and SvcV-10c). A simplistic view of the various elements that are visible to the Service Viewpoint, Figure 3.7-2 is more a picture than a formal model representing key concepts as ovals with lines representing relationships between the concepts.

The Services Viewpoint also represents a tight coupling of models for consistency. Models share many common elements, such as services, services functions, system locations, data flows, and more.

FIGURE 3.7-2 Integrated View of the Services Viewpoint

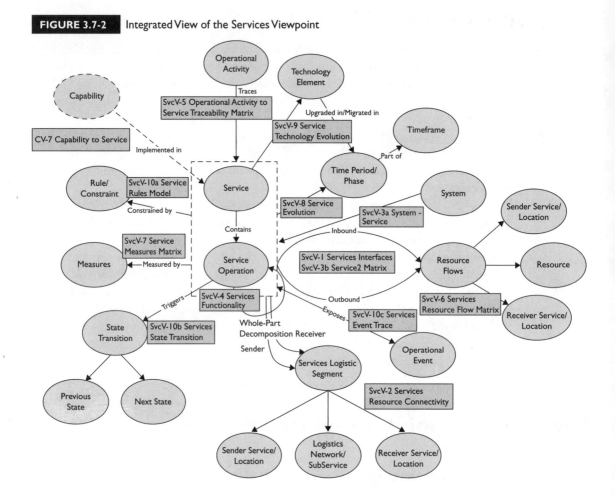

The following are some examples of the need for consistent use of architecture elements between Services Viewpoint models:

- SvcV-1 services must be consistent with SvcV-2 services. SvcV-1 interfaces must be consistent with SvcV-4 data flows and SvcV-6 data exchanges between the same end-point services.
- SvcV-4 service operations must be consistent with SvcV-5 service operations.

In addition to the integration needs of models within the Services Viewpoint, there are integration needs implicit inside the models to other viewpoints, as in the following examples:

■ SvcV-5 maps the services functions and services to operational activities defined inside the Operational Viewpoint.

■ SvcV-9 must be consistent in the evolution of system technology to the elements defined in the Standards Profile (StdV-1) and the Standards Forecast (StdV-2).

SvcV-I Services Context Description

Example: Passenger Identification SvcV-I

The SvcV-1 Services Context Description in Figure 3.7-3 shows the services at different locations. The locations also represent different types of activities that are being performed by various performers at those locations.

Model Information at a Glance	
Model Short Name	SvcV-1
Name	Services Context Description
Other Names	None.
Viewpoint	Services
Model Intent	In addition to depicting services (performers) and their structure, SvcV-1 addresses service resource flows. A service resource flow, as depicted in SvcV-1, is an indicator that resources pass between one service and the other. In the case of services, this can be expanded into further detail in the SvcV-2 Services Resource Flow Description Model. A service resource flow is a simplified representation of a pathway or network pattern, usually depicted graphically as a connector (that is, a line with possible amplifying information). The SvcV-1 depicts all resource flows between resources that are of interest.
Model Audience	SOA architects, portfolio planners, solution architects.
Formal Modeling Methodology	None.
Integration of Model with Other Views	Services in SvcV-1 must be consistent with services in all other SvcV models, such as SvcV-2, SvcV-3, SvcV-4, SvcV-6, and SvcV-10c.

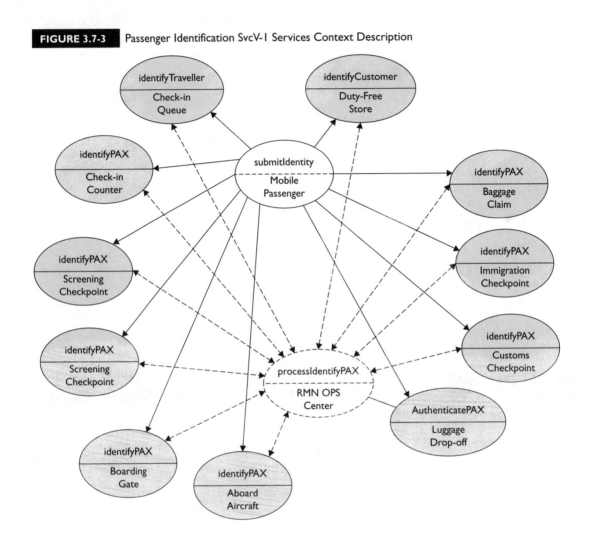

The diagram shows the as-is interfaces as solid lines. In the as-is situation, the various services are independently invoking their own passenger identification operations internally (this is not shown in the figure). The dotted lines show the proposed interface configuration where a single passenger identification service (processIdentifyPAX) is provided centrally from the RMN Operations Center and can service each of the locations from a single point. The proposed solution will eliminate differing business rules in the separate implementations of passenger identification and provides uniform updates for all stakeholders.

The solid lines indicate the as-is need for interaction between services representing independent implementations, whereas the dotted lines show the proposed configuration with a centralized service, processIdentifyPAX at the RMN Operations Center, which provides identification services to all invoking services located at the various locations.

SvcV-2 Services Resource Flow Description

Model Information at a Glance	
Model Short Name	SvcV-2
Name	Services Resource Flow Description
Other Names	None.
Viewpoint	Services
Model Intent	An SvcV-2 specifies the resource flows between services and may also list the protocol stacks used in connections. An SvcV-2 DoDAF-described model is used to give a precise specification of a connection between services. This may be an existing connection or a specification of a connection that is to be made for a future connection. For a network data service, an SvcV-2 comprises services, their ports, and the service resource flows between those ports. The SvcV-2 may also be used to describe non-IT type services such as search and rescue. The architect may choose to create a diagram for each service resource flow and the producing service or for each service resource flow and consuming service or to show all the service resource flows in one diagram, if this is possible.
Model Audience	Service designers, SOA architects, resource planners.
Formal Modeling Methodology	None.
Integration of Model with Other Views	The services in SvcV-2 must be consistent with services used in other SvcV models, such as SvcV-1, SvcV-3, SvcV-4, SvcV-6, SvcV-7, SvcV-8, SvcV-9, and SvcV-10c.

Example: Passenger Identification SvcV-2

The SvcV-2 shown in Figure 3.7-4 is for architecting the boarding gate kiosk. The kiosk allows a passenger to insert a combination of magnetically encoded identification cards and/or machine-readable passports. The kiosk invokes a common service, validateIdentityDocument, provided by the RMN data center to all consumers who wish to validate magnetic cards and machine-readable passports.

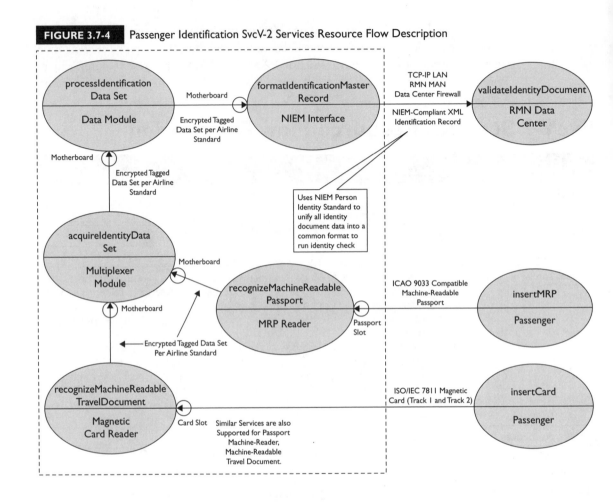

FIGURE 3.7-4   Passenger Identification SvcV-2 Services Resource Flow Description

SvcV-3 a, b Systems-Service and Services-Service Matrices

Model Information at a Glance	
Model Short Name	SvcV-3a, SvcV-3b
Name	Systems–Service Matrix (SvcV-3a) Services-Service Matrix (SvcV-3b)
Other Names	SvcV-2 Matrix
Viewpoint	Services

Model Information at a Glance	
Model Intent	An SvcV-3a enables a quick overview of all the system-to-service resource interactions specified in one or more SvcV-1 Services Context Description models. The SvcV-3a provides a tabular summary of the system and services interactions specified in the SvcV-1 Services Context Description for the architectural description. This model can be useful in support existing systems that are transitioning to provide services. The matrix format supports a rapid assessment of potential commonalities and redundancies (or, if fault-tolerance is desired, the lack of redundancies). An SvcV-3b enables a quick overview of all the services resource interactions specified in one or more SvcV-1 Services Context Description models. The SvcV-3b provides a tabular summary of the services interactions specified in the SvcV-1 Services Context Description for the architectural description.
Model Audience	Service portfolio managers, planners, SOA architects, solution architects.
Formal Modeling Methodology	None.
Integration of Model with Other Views	The services in SvcV-3 must be consistent with services used in other SvcV models, such as SvcV-1, SvcV-2, SvcV-4, SvcV-6, SvcV-7, SvcV-8, SvcV-9, and SvcV-10c.

Example: Passenger Identification SvcV-3

The SvcV-3a shown in Table 3.7-1 depicts current interfaces between systems and services as well as the planned interfaces. We notice clearly the planned transition of all systems to a single, consistent identifyPassenger service that will eliminate the inconsistencies, ambiguities, and inaccuracies that are evident in the current multiplicity of independent interfaces to independent services. We show the timeframe for the migration that is implied inside the SvcV-3a in the SvcV-8 Systems Evolution Description. The advantage of each of these models is that they elaborate some aspect of the architecture, but each model adds a different dimension for a different audience. Without integration, the models would very quickly become inconsistent.

The SvcV-3b—a variant of the SvcV-3a—expresses relationships between services in much the same way that the SvcV-3a showed the relationship between systems and services. The cell intersections can carry any information that is a characteristic of the association between system and service (or service and service), such as Planned or Current, as we have chosen to do in this example.

The SvcV-3 models provide a compact representation for interactions between systems and services and also between services themselves. The meaning of the

| TABLE 3.7-1 | Passenger Identification SvcV-3a System to Services Matrix (P = Planned Interface; C = Current Interface) |

System \ Service	identifyCustomer	identifyPassenger (to-be)	identifyPAX (Airline)	identifyPAX (Airport)	identifyPAX (Customs)	identifyPAX (Immigration)	identifyPAX (Screening)	identifyTraveler
Airline Reservation and Ticketing System	C	P	C					
Airline Reservation and Ticketing System (Kiosk)		P	C					
Airline Reservation and Ticketing System (Mobile)		P	C					
Airport Baggage Tracking System (Commercial)		P	C					
Airport Baggage Tracking System (RMN Airport)		P	C	C				
Comprehensive Screening System		P		C			C	C
Customs and Border Protection System		P			C		C	
Enhanced Point-of-Sale System	C	P						
Immigration and Customs Enforcement System		P				C	C	
Law Enforcement and Training System		P					C	C
Passenger Identification System		P						
Passenger Management System		P	C	C				C
Smart Devices		P						C

intersection cell is left to the modeler and must be described in a legend accompanying the model. The SvcV-3 model can be used to display the information in a large and complex SvcV-1 compactly into a single matrix instead of a large diagram running into several pages.

SvcV-4 Services Functionality Description

Model Information at a Glance	
Model Short Name	SvcV-4
Name	Services Functionality Description
Other Names	Service Component Reference Model (SRM)
Viewpoint	Services
Model Intent	The primary purposes of SvcV-4 are the following: ■ Develop a clear description of the necessary data flows that are input (consumed) by and output (produced) by each resource ■ Ensure that the service functional connectivity is complete (that is, that a resource's required inputs are all satisfied) ■ Ensure that the functional decomposition reaches an appropriate level of detail The SvcV-4 is the Services Viewpoint counterpart to the OV-5b Operational Activity Model of the Operational Viewpoint.
Model Audience	SOA architects for planning the service decomposition tree and for analyzing composition and orchestration issues. Service planners and portfolio managers for the system decomposition.
Formal Modeling Methodology	None. Based on the dataflow diagram methodology for systems.
Integration of Model with Other Views	The services in SvcV-4 must be consistent with services used in other SvcV models, such as SvcV-1, SvcV-2, SvcV-3, SvcV-6, SvcV-7, SvcV-8, SvcV-9, and SvcV-10c.

Example: Passenger Identification SvcV-4 (Functional Decomposition)

The SvcV-4 model shown in Figure 3.7-5 decomposes the services into component services and operations (service methods). Notice that we use verb decomposition in the name of the service to decompose a larger-grain service into smaller-grain component services (whole-part) whereas we use noun decomposition to denote a variant of a service that may have different business rules or exhibit different behavior. We could have collapsed the services that have noun variants and moved the various noun variants into the inputs for a single service and buried the logic for branching inside the algorithms of the single service. These are the kind of trade-offs that the SvcV-4 model helps analyze.

FIGURE 3.7-5

Passenger
Identification
SvcV-4 Service
Functionality
Description

1. **Read Identity Document**
   1.1 Recognize Identity Document Type
      1.1.1 Recognize Drivers License
      1.1.2 Recognize Machine-Readable Passport
      1.1.3 Recognize Machine-Readable Travel Document
   1.2 Acquire Identity Dataset
      1.2.1 Acquire Magnetic CardDataset
      1.2.2 Acquire Machine-Readable Passport Dataset
      1.2.3 Acquire Machine-Readable Travel Document Dataset
   1.3 Process Identification Dataset
      1.3.1 Process Driver License Dataset
      1.3.2 Process U.S. Passport Dataset
      1.3.3 Process Foreign Passport Dataset
      1.3.4 Process Travel Document Dataset
   1.4 Format Identification Master Record
      1.4.1 Load Identification Master Record
      1.4.2 Store Identification Master Record
2. **Validate Identity Document**
   2.1 Validate U.S. Passport Identity
   2.2 Validate Foreign Passport Identity
   2.3 Validate U.S. Drivers License Identity
   2.4 Validate Travel Document Identity
      2.4.1 Validate DHS Travel Document Identity
      2.4.2 Validate BIA Travel Document Identity
      2.4.3 Validate Canadian Travel Document Identity
3. **Alert Airport Security (TBD)**
4. **Alert First Responded (TBD)**

SvcV-5 Operational Activity to Services Traceability Matrix

Model Information at a Glance	
Model Short Name	SvcV-5
Name	Operational Activity to Services Traceability Matrix
Other Names	None.
Viewpoint	Services
Model Intent	The SvcV-5 addresses the linkage between service functions described in SvcV-4 and operational activities specified in OV-5a Operational Activity Decomposition Tree or OV-5b Operational Activity Model. The SvcV-5 depicts the mapping of service functions (and, optionally, the capabilities and performers that provide them) to operational activities and thus identifies the transformation of an operational need into a purposeful action performed by a service solution.
Model Audience	Portfolio managers to assess relevance of services to the mission as represented by operational activity mappings. Planners. SOA architects.
Formal Modeling Methodology	None.
Integration of Model with Other Views	The services in SvcV-5 must be consistent with services used in other SvcV models such as SvcV-1, SvcV-2, SvcV-3, SvcV-6, SvcV-7, SvcV-8, SvcV-9, and SvcV-10c. The activities in SV-5 must be consistent with operational activities in OV-1, OV-2, OV-3, OV-5, and OV-6c

Example: Passenger Identification SvcV-5

Although in Table 3.7-2 it appears that the intersections of services are for all operational activities (within the scope of this SvcV -5 model), the important finding is that the reuse potential for the services is extremely high because identity documents are read and validated at each point at which determining a passenger's identity through an identification document is important.

In general, the SvcV-5 model allows the service architect to establish correspondence between a service and the operational context in which it is useful. Planning a family of services is similar to a product planning exercise where the planner is determining the product features that maximize market coverage and minimize development investments.

TABLE 3.7-2 Passenger Identification SvcV-5 Operational Activity to Services Traceability Matrix

Services	Operational Activities								
	Check in Passenger	Screen Passenger	Board Passenger	Receive Passenger	Conduct Immigration Inspection	Conduct Customs Inspection	Store Passenger Baggage	Process Duty-Free Purchase	Deliver Baggage
1. Read Identity Document	X	X	X	X	X	X	X	X	X
1.1 Recognize Identity Document Type									
1.1.1 Recognize Drivers License									
1.1.2 Recognize Machine-Readable Passport									
1.1.3 Recognize Machine-Readable Travel Document									
1.2 Acquire Identity Data Set									
1.2.1 Acquire Magnetic Card Data Set									
1.2.2 Acquire Machine-Readable Passport Data Set									
1.2.3 Acquire Machine-Readable Travel Document Data Set									
1.3 Process Identification Data Set									
1.3.1 Process Drivers License Data Set									
1.3.2 Process U.S. Passport Data Set									

Operational Activity							
1.3.3 Process Foreign Passport Data Set							
1.3.4 Process Travel Document Data Set							
1.4 Format Identification Master Record							
1.4.1 Load Identification Master Record							
1.4.2 Store Identification Master Record							
2. Validate Identity Document	X	X	X	X	X	X	X
2.1 Validate U.S. Passport Identity							
2.2 Validate Foreign Passport Identity							
2.3 Validate U.S. Drivers License Identity							
2.4 Validate Travel Document Identity							
2.4.1 Validate DHS Travel Document Identity							
2.4.2 Validate BIA Travel Document Identity							
2.4.3 Validate Canadian Travel Document Identity							
3. Alert Airport Security (TBD)	X	X					
4. Alert First Responders (TBD)	X						

SvcV-6 Services Resource Flow Matrix

Model Information at a Glance	
Model Short Name	SvcV-6
Name	Services Resource Flow Matrix
Other Names	None.
Viewpoint	Services
Model Intent	Service resource flow exchanges express the relationship across the three basic architectural data elements of an SvcV (services, service functions [operations], and service resource flows) and focus on the specific aspects of the service resource flow and the service resource content. These aspects of the service resource flow exchange can be crucial to the operational mission and are critical to understanding the potential for overhead and constraints introduced by the physical aspects of the implementation, such as security policy, communications, and logistics limitations.
Model Audience	SOA architects and service planners who plan the resource flows.
Formal Modeling Methodology	None. The model is represented in a tabular format.
Integration of Model with Other Views	The services in SvcV-5 must be consistent with services used in other SvcV models, such as SvcV-1, SvcV-2, SvcV-3, SvcV-6, SvcV-7, SvcV-8, SvcV-9, and SvcV-10c. The activities in SV-5 must be consistent with operational activities in OV-1, OV-2, OV-3, OV-5, and OV-6c. Service functions must be consistent with SvcV-4, SvcV-5, SvcV-8, and SvcV-10c.

Example: Passenger Identification SvcV-6

Table 3.7-3 shows a sample resource flow matrix that corresponds to the SvcV-2 model presented earlier. The SvcV-6 tabulates the resource flows (in this case data exchanges) and also depicts, optionally, standards, formats, media types, criticality, and other attributes of the resource exchange that help the architect assess and promote interoperability between the exchanging services.

TABLE 3.7-3 Passenger Identification SvcV-6 Resource Flow Matrix

Sender Service Provider	Sender Service	Receiver Service Provider	Receiver Service	Resource	Resource Type	Standard	Format
Boarding Gate Kiosk	insertCard	Magnetic Card Reader	recognizeMachine ReadableTravel Document	Magnetic Card Travel Document	Materiel	ISO/IEC 7811 Magnetic Card (Track1 and Track 2)	Encoded Magnetic Stripe
Magnetic Card Reader	recognizeMachine ReadableTravel Document	Multiplexer Module	acquireIdentity DataSet	Encrypted and Tagged Passenger Information Dataset	Data	ICAO Airline Agreement	Encrypted Digital Data Stream
Multiplexer Module	acquireIdentity DataSet	Data Module	processIdentification DataSet	Encrypted and Tagged Passenger Information Dataset	Data	ICAO Airline Agreement	Encrypted Digital Data Stream
Data Module	processIdentification DataSet	NIEM Interface	formatIdentification MasterRecord	Encrypted and Tagged Passenger Information Data Set	Data	ICAO Airline Agreement	Encrypted Digital Data Stream
NIEM Interface	formatIdentification MasterRecord	RMN Data Center	validateIdentity Document	NIEM-Compliant Passenger Identification XML Document	Data	National Information Exchange Model Passenger Identification Standard	Encrypted Digital Data Stream

SvcV-7 Services Measures Matrix

Model Information at a Glance	
Model Short Name	SvcV-7
Name	Services Measures Matrix
Other Names	None.
Viewpoint	Services
Model Intent	The SvcV-7 depicts the measures (metrics) of resources. This model specifies qualitative and quantitative measures (metrics) of resources. It specifies all of the measures. The measures are selected by the end-user community and described by the architect. Performance parameters include all performance characteristics for which requirements can be developed and specifications defined. The complete set of performance parameters may not be known at the early stages of architectural description, so it is to be expected that this model will be updated throughout the specification, design, development, testing, and possibly even its deployment and operations lifecycle phases.
Model Audience	SOA architects for planning the performance requirements. Services planners. Service development program managers.
Formal Modeling Methodology	None.
Integration of Model with Other Views	SV-7 elements such as service and service operation must be consistent with their counterparts in other SvcV models.

Example: Passenger Identification SvcV-7

In Table 3.7-4, the SvcV-7 specifies baseline (current), threshold (acceptable), and objective (desired) performance parameters for the identifyPassenger service. In reality, a service-level agreement (SLA) is used to specify service levels for both business and software services and acts as a durable agreement between service provider and service consumer that guarantees a level of service under contractual penalties.

TABLE 3.7-4   Passenger Identification Service Measures Matrix SvcV-7

Service	Measure	Baseline	Threshold	Objective
identifyPassenger	Availability	98.00%	99.00%	99.9999 %
identifyPassenger	Response Time	2 Seconds	1.5 Seconds	1 Second
identifyPassenger	Accuracy	95%	98%	99.5%

SvcV-8 Services Evolution Description

Model Information at a Glance	
Model Short Name	SvcV-8
Name	Services Evolution Description
Other Names	None.
Viewpoint	Services
Model Intent	To depict the evolution of a portfolio of services over time, showing margining or splitting of functionality between services and rearrangement of service boundaries; to depict the evolution of a service in terms of functionality over time.
Model Audience	Service planners; SOA architects; service development program managers; portfolio managers; services roadmap developers.
Formal Modeling Methodology	None. The model can be represented graphically with a timeline backbone or as a table.
Integration of Model with other Views	The services in SvcV-8 must be consistent with services used in other SvcV models, such as SvcV-1, SvcV-2, SvcV-3, SvcV-5, SvcV-6, SvcV-7, SvcV-9, and SvcV-10c.

Example: Passenger Identification SvcV-8

Figure 3.7-6 shows the evolution of the identifyPassenger service and the migration of independent services currently used by various systems (as shown in the SvcV-3a Systems to Services Matrix) to a common identifyPassenger service that incorporates common algorithms and business rules and researches comprehensive data sources to provide a single unified, consistent service.

The SvcV-8 can be built using one of two styles:

- A migration-style diagram that shows how multiple services are migrated over time into one or more services, as shown in Figure 3.7-6

- An evolution-style diagram (not shown) that generally describes how a service or collection of services from a single provider evolves in terms of functionality over a time period

SvcV-9 Services Technology and Skills Forecast

The SvcV-9 Service Technology and Skills Forecast (described in Table 3.7-5) is similar to the SV-9 Systems Technology and Skills Forecast and depicts the planned insertion of technology into a collection of services over a period of time. It may also depict the need to acquire and insert skills for operators, developers, and maintainers of these services at the same time to ensure that skill development is orchestrated with service upgrades.

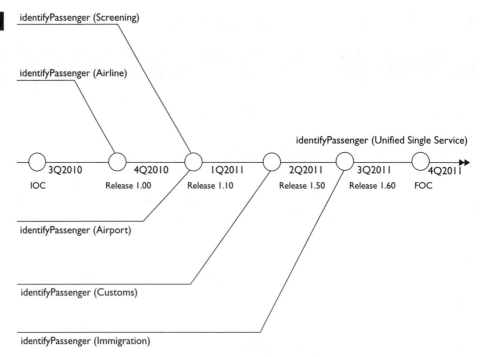

FIGURE 3.7-6

Passenger
Identification
Service Evolution
Description
SvcV-8

TABLE 3.7-5	SvcV-9 Services Technology and Skills Forecast at a Glance
Model Short Name	SvcV-9
Name	Services Technology and Skills Forecast
Other Names	None.
Viewpoint	Services
Model Intent	To model the insertion of technology (and consequent need to acquire skills) into services on a timeline. The specific types of technologies may be couched generically in terms of the service areas, services, and standards or specifically in terms of vendor products.
Model Audience	Technology roadmap planners; service development program office; SOA planners; service planners.
Formal Modeling Methodology	None.
Integration of Model with Other Views	The services in SvcV-9 must be consistent with services used in other SvcV models, such as SvcV-1, SvcV-2, SvcV-3, SvcV-5, SvcV-6, SvcV-7, SvcV-8, and SvcV-10c. The technology classification scheme must be consistent with the one used in StdV-1 and StdV-2.

SvcV-10a Services Rules Model

Model Information at a Glance	
Model Short Name	SvcV-10a
Name	Services Rules Model
Other Names	None.
Viewpoint	Services
Model Intent	The SvcV-10a describes the rules that control, constrain, or otherwise guide the implementation aspects of the architecture. Service rules are statements that define or constrain some aspect of the business and may be applied to the following: ■ Performers (services) ■ Resource flows ■ Service functions ■ System ports ■ Data elements
Model Audience	Service designers/developers; solution architects; service planners.
Formal Modeling Methodology	Rules languages, structured English, first order logic, pseudocode, algorithmic languages
Integration of Model with Other Views	Any architecture elements referenced by a rule must be consistent with the corresponding model elements in SvcV models, such as service performers in SvcV-1, SvcV-2, SvcV-3, SvcV-4, SvcV-6, SvcV-7, SvcV-8, SvcV-9 and SvcV-10c or resource flows in SvcV-1, SvcV-4, SvcV-6, and SvcV-10c.

Example: Passenger Identification SvcV-10a

Table 3.7-6 shows the Service Rules Model as applied in the passenger identification example. Service rules constrain some aspect of the service, such as behavior. They are embedded inside the logic that implements the service. For business services, service rules may be provided as a constraint specification by the business entity that is sponsoring the service. Typically, these may be rules that must flow through to service providers such as in regulatory scenarios or in compliance with requirements of policy.

TABLE 3.7-6	Passenger Identification SvcV-10a Services Rules Model

Service	Rule	Authority/Source Reference
Read Identity Document	Identity documents that are implemented in magnetic cards must comply with ISO/IEC 7811 standards.	ICAO DOC-9303
	Machine-readable passports must comply with the ICAO 9303 Part 1 standards for fonts, printing, sizing, and proportions.	RMN Identification Procedures Manual 2010
	If an identity document cannot be read automatically by a machine, a human operator must be alerted with an audible signal that must also be capable of being turned off.	RMN Identification Procedures Manual 2010
	After three unsuccessful attempts at reading a machine-readable identity document, the operator must ask for an alternative form of identification.	RMN Identification Procedures Manual 2010
	Machine attempts at reading machine-readable documents must be nondestructive.	RMN Identification Procedures Manual 2010
	If a machine accidentally alters a machine-readable document, the operator is required to provide an alternative form of identification that is acceptable to airport authorities.	RMN Identification Procedures Manual 2010

SvcV-10b Services State Transition Description

Model Information at a Glance	
Model Short Name	SvcV-10b
Name	Services State Transition Description
Other Names	UML State Chart, Harel State Diagram
Viewpoint	Services
Model Intent	The SvcV-10b is a graphical method of describing a resource's (or function's) response to various events by changing its state. The diagram basically represents the sets of events to which the resources (services) in the activities (service operations) respond (by taking an action to move to a new state) as a function of its current state. Each transition specifies an event and an action.
Model Audience	Service designers; SOA architects.
Formal Modeling Methodology	UML
Integration of Model with Other Views	The granularity of SvcV-10b generally will not match other nonscenario-based larger-grain models, but actions must be consistent with service operations in SvcV-4, SvcV-5, and SvcV-8.

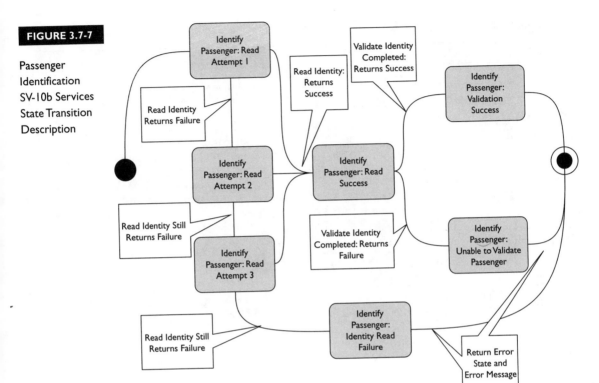

FIGURE 3.7-7

Passenger
Identification
SV-10b Services
State Transition
Description

Example: Passenger Identification SvcV-10b

Figure 3.7-7 shows the states of a service "Identify Passenger". The diagram depicts a very constrained scenario where the service reads a passenger document and attempts to validate the identity of the passenger. The service makes up to three attempts in reading the passenger document.

SvcV-10c Services Event-Trace Description

The Services Event-Trace Description (see Table 3.7-7) is similar to the Systems Event-Trace Description (SV-10c) except that the lifelines depict services (and service providers) and the exchange of messages represents interactions between the services as depicted over a timeline. The SvcV-10c allows the architect to describe detailed interactions between services to examine issues related to timing as well as responsibility. The SvcV-10c is typically used to elaborate a scenario or contained situation and is generally too fine-grained for enterprise architecture representation.

TABLE 3.7-7	SvcV-10c Services Event-Trace Description Model at a Glance
Model Short Name	SvcV-10c
Name	Services Event-Trace Description
Other Names	Sequence Diagrams, Timing Diagrams, Event Scenarios.
Viewpoint	Services
Model Intent	The SvcV-10c provides a time-ordered examination of the interactions between services functional resources. Each event-trace diagram should have an accompanying description that defines the particular scenario or situation. The SvcV-10c specifies the sequence in which resource flow elements are exchanged in the context of a resource or service port. The components of an SvcV-10c include functional resources (services) or service ports and the owning performer (provider), as well as the port that is the subject of the lifeline.
Model Audience	Service designers, SOA architects.
Formal Modeling Methodology	UML
Integration of Model with Other Views	The services in SvcV-10c must be consistent with services used in other SvcV models, such as SvcV-1, SvcV-2, SvcV-3, SvcV-5, SvcV-6, SvcV-7, SvcV-8, and SvcV-9.

Questions

1. What is a service? Distinguish between a business service and a software service.

2. What is a service-level agreement? Which of the Service Viewpoint models describes the elements of a service-level agreement?

3. How are operational performers such as service providers reflected in the Service Viewpoint? Which models represent service providers?

4. True or false:

   a. Service models can be represented from the view of the service provider or the service consumer. What is the primary difference between models depicting the provider's view from models that depict the consumer's view?

   b. A service can be provided by more than one provider.

   c. A service can be provisioned from more than one location.

   d. The SvcV-2 model can represent service brokers because they are intermediaries and are not directly involved in the providing or consumption of the service.

5. What is the usefulness of the SvcV-1?

6. Which model would you develop to forecast and plan for platform migrations for a family of services?

7. Which service model would you use to develop and refine service functionality and represent, in detail, the decomposition of services down to the level of WSDL operations?

8. Which model would you use to represent compactly the interfaces between services?

9. Which model would you use to describe the data exchange protocols between services using message templates and automated data exchanges?

10. How would you restrict the scope of detailed, fine-grain behavioral modeling such as for the SvcV-10b and SvcV-10c?

11. What is the relationship between the SvcV-6 and the SvcV-10c? Which elements are required to be consistent for the models to be part of the same integrated architecture?

12. Which model would you use to trace a service back to the operational activity that it supports?

13. Which model would you use to trace the service back to a capability that the enterprise identified as a requirement?

14. Compare and contrast the SvcV-1 Services Context Description, the SvcV-6 Services Resource Flow Matrix, and the SvcV-10c Service Event-Trace Description. All of these models depict resource flow exchanges between services. Which type of model is useful for what purpose?

Reference List

Federal CIO Council. (2008). *"Enabling the mission": A Practical Guide to Federal Service Oriented Architecture Version 1.1*. Architecture and Infrastructure Committee, Federal Chief Information Officers Council.

OASIS. (2006). *Reference Model for Service Oriented Architecture 1.0 OASIS Standard*, 12 October 2006. Organization for the Advancement of Structured Information Standards (OASIS). http://docs.oasis-open.org/soa-rm/v1.0/.

3.8

Data and Information Viewpoint

What Is the Difference Between Data and Information?

Both data and information represent knowledge. Data is the lowest or rawest form in which that knowledge is stored and managed, such as in a database, in an electronic file, or even as text on a paper document. Information results from processing data to extract meaning and provides the level of knowledge needed to drive action. Information is modeled using semantic models, whereas data is modeled using structural models. One example of the latter is the use of a Logical Data Model to elevate the meaning of the tables in a relational database schema. In fact, both data and information are two points in the continuum: Data → Information → Knowledge → Wisdom.

Modeling data in the past has been an exercise in understanding the data plumbing; a database management system is akin to a cistern holding the water whereas the messaging is like the pipes that carry water to consuming systems. Much effort has been spent in standardizing the layout of the cisterns and planning the sizes and data types of the pipes. The task of standardizing data formats and relational database schemas has been the responsibility of the database administrator. Only in recent times has the focus shifted to the content of the pipes—the meaning of the data. The data administrator has been responsible for standardizing the meaning and interpretation of the data in terms of "logical" data standards that are focused more on the meaning and less on the data representation. Today, the data administrator also needs to become the information administrator, with the skills needed to understand the science of meaning, information concepts and relationships (ontology), and classification techniques (taxonomy) as well as the fact that different groups of people often define their own set of terms and definitions (vocabularies) that are specific to their own domain while the same terms may have different meanings and interpretations in other domains.

The Data and Information Viewpoint must cater to the interests and needs of data management personnel as well as data administration personnel who are charged with developing standards for information representation. We will present

The Data and Information Viewpoint caters to all producers, consumers, and managers of the data that is generated and consumed by the operations, systems, and services.

a few terms before we launch into the detailed models that the DoDAF describes as supporting the Data and Information Viewpoint. For readers who are well versed in "traditional" data modeling techniques such as IDEF1X, information engineering entity-relationship modeling techniques, or object class modeling techniques, the concepts presented in this chapter are a departure from the familiar. Such readers will initially need to embrace a shift in worldview, from structured data management and data engineering techniques toward the recognition of the existence of information in all forms and representations that require different treatment than traditional approaches offer.

The concepts of ontology are based on the existence of information and methods to represent the existence. Arguably, traditional approaches have tried to "coerce" information into a format suitable for machine processing. The result of that coercion is to drive data schemas into a format that few people outside of the data management and application development community understand. The focus of the newer approaches to information management is to provide a form of data representation that is more easily and universally understood—especially across the World Wide Web. The Semantic Web is commonly perceived as the next leap forward in information transparency and ubiquitous use. Without the semantic models of information, traditional models are constrained to be accompanied by applications that transform the internal models of data into information.

Ontology

Ontology is an explicit formal specification of the concepts in a domain and the relations among them (World Wide Web Consortium, 2004). Implicit in this definition is the existence of a contained or restricted domain of applicability, called a *domain of discourse*, and a formal specification of the concepts and relationships among the concepts. One example of a formal specification is the Web Ontology Language (OWL), a standard sponsored by the World Wide Web Consortium (W3C).

Ontologies are very useful in compressing knowledge using abstract relationships. We will illustrate with a simplified organizing of information into an ontological framework:

- John drives a Ford sedan.
- Jill drives a Subaru sedan.
- John is a man.
- Jill is a woman.

- A sedan is a type of car.
- A Ford sedan is an instance of a sedan.
- A Subaru sedan is an instance of a sedan.

The underlying *concepts* of these statements include the following:

- Person
- Man (a type of person)
- Woman (a type of person)
- Car
- Sedan (a type of car)
- Ford (an instance of a sedan)
- Subaru (an instance of a sedan)

Also, the following relationships are stated:

- Person is the generalization of a man.
- Person is the generalization of a woman.
- A car is the generalization of sedan.
- A person drives a car.
- A Subaru sedan is an instance of a sedan.
- A Ford sedan is an instance of a sedan.

We immediately notice that relationships themselves can be grouped into generalizations, instantiations, and associations in our short example. We also notice that such items as Subaru and Ford represent specific instances (proper nouns) whereas concepts such as Car and Person are quite general and describe a class of automobiles and people. The language that is used to express this "upper level" set of things and types, and relationship types, is called a foundation ontology in much the same way that alphabets are used to construct words and words are used to make sentences.

It is beyond the scope of this book to cover the details and use of ontologies, but it is useful to know that new architecture frameworks such as DoDAF 2.0 are based more on the use of ontologies to represent knowledge of architecture elements and less on the specific modeling technique metamodels, as earlier architecture techniques tended to be. In fact, the Zachman Framework was one of the first architecture frameworks to provide a conceptual mechanism for representing meaningful architecture elements independent of the modeling technology.

Taxonomy

Taxonomy is the science of classification. A taxonomy is a specific classification of entities (in a domain of interest) based on an ordering imposed by the "is-a-type-of" (or "is-a-member-of") relationship. Taxonomy consists of a set of *taxa*, or categories. The set of taxa form a hierarchy (a "tree"). Each level—formally called a *rank*—of the hierarchy is usually given a name. The set of *taxon* names (or categories) is the classification. The levels (or ranks) establish the "is-a-type-of" relationship among the taxa.

A taxonomy of a domain can be derived from an ontology of that domain by selecting all entities of interest that stand in an "is-a-type-of" relationship to one another. A taxonomy can also be developed independently of any explicit ontology for a domain of interest and be incorporated later into an explicit ontology of the domain.

Ontologies and taxonomies can serve several purposes. For example, they can serve to formalize and standardize the vocabulary of a domain, facilitating communication and understanding among domain users and systems developers. The process of developing a domain ontology and associated taxonomies can both inform the development of other domain artifacts, such as architectures and data models, or be used to analyze existing domain artifacts constructively. A formal ontology is a prerequisite for automated (machine) reasoning and is necessary to realize the vision of the Semantic Web.

Controlled Vocabularies

A vocabulary is a collection of terms and definitions used by a community to describe real-world and abstract concepts. Because vocabularies evolve without conscious control and new terms are coined to represent existing concepts, resolution of terms and their meanings becomes increasingly difficult over time. Understanding the meaning of terms without ambiguity is essential for the architectural representations that will be built based upon that understanding. Vocabulary control (ANSI/NISO, 2005) is the process of organizing a list of terms (a) to indicate which of two or more synonymous terms is authorized for use; (b) to distinguish between *homographs* (one of two or more words that have the same spelling but different meanings and origins); and (c) to indicate hierarchical and associative relationships among terms in the context of a controlled vocabulary or subject heading list.

FEA Data Reference Model

Unlike the FEA Business Reference Model that specifies the business areas, lines of business, and business functions that are performed by the U.S. federal government, the Data Reference Model (DRM) is presented as an abstract framework from which concrete implementations may be derived (Office of Management and Budget, 2005). The DRM's abstract nature enables agencies to use multiple implementation approaches, methodologies, and technologies while remaining consistent with the foundational principles of the DRM. For example, the DRM abstract model can be implemented using different combinations of technical standards.

As shown in Figure 3.8-1, the DRM describes three areas of standardization for data across the federal government:

- Data context
- Data description
- Data sharing

Data Context

A community of interest (COI) is a group that shares common goals and missions. A COI should agree on the context of the data needed to meet its shared mission business needs. The community should be able to answer basic questions about the data assets that it manages:

- What are the data (subject areas) that the COI needs?
- What organizations are responsible for maintaining the data?

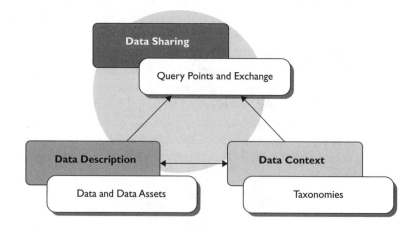

FIGURE 3.8-1

FEA Data Reference Model: Areas of Standardization

- What is the linkage to the FEA Business Reference Model (BRM)?
- What services are available to access the data?
- What databases are used to store the data?

Data context provides the basis for data governance with the COI. The data context standardization area establishes an approach to the categorization of data assets using taxonomies and other descriptive information. In general, data context answers key questions about the data required within a COI and establishes the basis for data governance. Data context also enables discovery of data and can provide linkages to the other FEA Reference Models, which are themselves taxonomies.

Data Description

A COI should agree on the meaning and structure of the data that it needs in order to use the data effectively. The data description standardization area provides a means to capture the semantic and syntactic structure of data uniformly. This enables comparison of metadata (data about data) for purposes of harmonization and supports the ability to respond to questions regarding what data descriptions (metadata) are available.

Data Sharing

Data sharing is a standardization area within the DRM. A COI should have common capabilities to enable information to be accessed and exchanged. Hence the DRM provides guidance for the types of services that should be provisioned within a COI to enable this information sharing.

DIV-1 Conceptual Data Model (Semantic Data Model)

The DIV-1 Conceptual Data Model represents the business concepts that apply to the domain and scope of the architecture. These concepts represent real-world and abstract items of information that must be managed by the enterprise. The purpose of the DIV-1 is to document and describe the information concepts in terms of model elements that the business can easily recognize. The DIV-1 caters to the data administrator's interests as well as the interests of the business analyst. The model is easily validated by subject matter experts who understand the model elements and can provide constructive feedback to improve and finalize the model.

In the unstructured data management world, the DIV-1 is also used to define the *concepts* that can be associated with unstructured data to provide context, although the representation of the unstructured data format (such as document outline structure) can be considered a physical representation (DIV-3). For example, document section names can be associated with the semantic concepts that they document. The DIV-1 can also be used as a high-level "subject area" classification for more detailed DIV-2 modeling efforts. In such a use, the DIV-1 becomes a taxonomy scheme for categorizing logical data entities.

The DIV-1 can be used to construct a business glossary. If the proliferation of terms is controlled and managed by a registration and stewardship process, the business glossary can also become an enterprise vocabulary. Constructing an enterprise vocabulary requires resolving differences of meanings across different parts of the same enterprise (a tank for a civil engineer is a container for fluids; a tank for an Army commander is an armored vehicle capable of shooting at the enemy).

DIV-2 Logical Data Model (Key-Based/ Fully Attributed Logical Data Model)

The DIV-2 Logical Data Model is the first step toward engineering the information representation for implementation as a data management schema. In the logical model, independent concepts are identified and separated. Trying to identify independent concepts often involves looking at properties of some of the business entities in the DIV-1 and determining whether they should be independent concepts in their own right or are subordinate attributes of an entity. Identifiers are assigned to each of these independent concepts to allow machine identification of instances of such concepts and to enforce relationship integrity. Indeterminate relationships (many-to-many relationships) are resolved into associative entities. The resulting model (the Key-Based Logical Data Model) has the graphical topology of the ultimate DIV-2.

Finally, attributes are added to the Key-Based Logical Data Model to create a Fully Attributed Logical Data Model.

The entity-relationship–style Logical Data Model DIV-2 tends to be more applicable to the design of data management solutions for transaction-based systems and does not in general lend itself to the complex and rich set of relationship models typically found in unstructured data sources or in complex data elements that intersect many concepts. For example, a single complex data element used in a census survey may report on the average income of an undivided American family residing in the continental United States (CONUS) for the period 2000–2010.

DIV-3 Physical Schema

The DIV-3 Physical Schema is a detailed representation of the physical data formats. To follow our earlier analogy, the DIV-3 models the data plumbing. It enforces the needs for consistency, uniformity, and compatibility of data formats to ensure successful data management of the physical data.

Because different types of technologies are used to implement data management solutions, the DIV-3 is specific to the technology of the implemented database and organization. The DIV-3 model must obey the constraints of the technology used to implement it and reflect a real-world implementation. Some examples of DIV-3 representation are Structured Query Language (SQL) Data Definition Language (DDL) statements; eXtensible Markup Language (XML) schemas; and U.S. Message Text Format (USMTF) templates.

Relationships Between the Data and Information Viewpoint Integrated Models

For simplicity, we have depicted the DIV-1 as a business dictionary with informal ontology relationships and taxonomy, DIV-2 as an entity-relationship model, and DIV-3 as a relational database management schema instance (see Figure 3.8-2). Other forms of technology representations, such as Web Ontology Language (OWL) for representing DIV-1 and XML Schema Definition Language for representing DIV-3, are also applicable.

The Data and Information Viewpoint, rather than requiring an exact match of architecture elements, requires a transformation consistency and must be able to trace back from, say, the DIV-3 Physical Data Model to the DIV-2 Logical Data Model.

FIGURE 3.8-2 Integrated Model Set for Data and Information Viewpoint

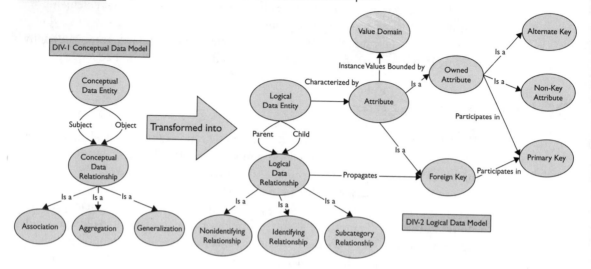

There is traceability between the DIV-1 to the DIV-2 to the DIV-3 as follows:

- The information representations in the DIV-1 are transformed into the data representations in the DIV-2. The DIV-1 information representations can range in detail from concept lists to structured lists (that is, whole-part, super-subtype) to interrelated concepts. At the DIV-1 level, any relationships are simply declared and then at the DIV-2 level they are made explicit and attributed. Similarly, attributes (or additional relationships) are added at the DIV-2 level.

- The DIV-3's performance and implementation considerations usually result in standard modifications of the DIV-2, so it traces quite directly. That is, no new semantics are introduced going from the DIV-2 to the DIV-3.

Figure 3.8-3 shows the traditional steps involved in transforming a Semantic Data Model (a DIV-1 Conceptual Model) to a key-based and fully attributed DIV-2 Logical Data Model and then to a DIV-3 Physical Data Model in a structured data management regime.

FIGURE 3.8-3

Transformation
Steps in Data
and Information
Modeling

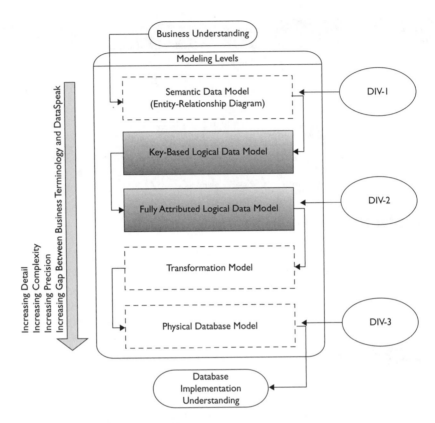

DIV-1 Conceptual Data Model

Model Information at a Glance	
Model Short Name	DIV-1
Name	Conceptual Data Model
Other Names	Business Data Model, Entity-Relationship Model, Ontology Model, Data Reference Model, Class Diagram (UML) Data Entity/Component Catalog (TOGAF 9) Class Hierarchy Diagram (TOGAF 9)
Viewpoint	Data and Information
Model Intent	The DIV-1 Conceptual Data Model addresses the information concepts at a high-level on an operational architecture. The DIV-1 is used to document the business information requirements and structural business process rules of the architecture. It describes the information that is associated with the information of the architecture. Included are information items, their attributes or characteristics, and their interrelationships. Unlike the DIV-2 and DIV-3 models, which are arranged to support automated data processing, the DIV-1 describes data in terms of the business language.

(continued)

Model Information at a Glance	
Model Audience	Business analysts, data administrators, data standards personnel, logical data modeling personnel (using the model as a higher-level context for more detailed logical data models). The DIV-1 is used to establish the business ontology and taxonomy for the enterprise as well as the vocabulary of business terms.
Formal Modeling Methodology	Ontology modeling using OWL, Resource Description Framework (RDF), entity-relationship modeling, object class modeling
Integration of Model with Other Views	The DIV-1 concepts and relationships must be consistent with their transformation into DIV-2 entities and relationships and DIV-3 technology data objects such as relational tables and columns or XML simple types and complex type definitions.

Example: Passenger Identification DIV-1

The small example shown in Figure 3.8-4 depicts a subtype hierarchy of data concepts. The names of the concepts are couched in simple business terms. The model helps us distinguish between the various types of passenger identification documents to enable more detailed analysis of the data structures that need to be constructed for both messaging and data storage downstream.

FIGURE 3.8-4   Passenger Identification DIV-1 Conceptual Data Model

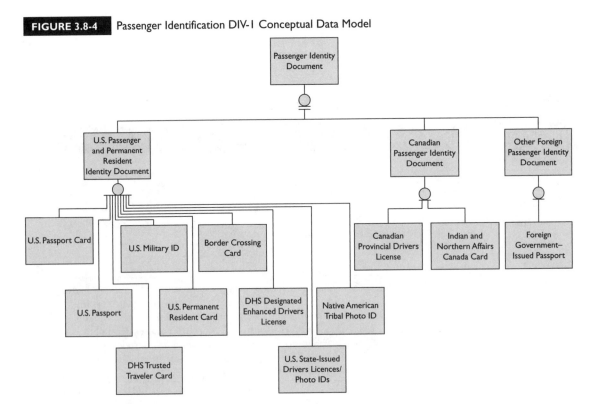

DIV-2 Logical Data Model

Model Information at a Glance	
Model Short Name	DIV-2
Name	Logical Data Model
Other Names	Key-Based Logical Data Model; Fully Attributed Logical Data Model; Class Diagram (UML); Data Entity/Component Catalog (TOGAF 9); Class Diagram (TOGAF 9)
Viewpoint	Data and Information
Model Intent	The primary purpose of the Logical Data Model is to transform business concepts into data management concepts that are compatible with principles that promote data quality, such as normalization and referential integrity. The DIV-2 provides a data representation that can be implemented in multiple messaging and storage technologies and is independent of technology. The DIV-2 also establishes a data dictionary and definitions for shared data in a data management function for the enterprise.
Model Audience	Data administrators, database administrators, application developers
Formal Modeling Methodology	IDEF1X, UML Object Class Diagram, Generalized Chen E-R Modeling, information engineering
Integration of Model with Other Views	The DIV-2 entities, attributes, and relationships must be consistent with the higher-level business ontology expressed in the DIV-1. They must also be consistent with transformed physical data objects in DIV-3 that are used to implement data management and data communication solutions.

Example: Passenger Identification DIV-2

In the model shown in Figure 3.8-5, we have started to elaborate on the conceptual model by separating out independent and dependent parts of the concepts in the DIV-1. The construction of the DIV-2 starts by examining the DIV-1 Conceptual Model and separating out candidate logical data entities. These are then examined to determine and separate the independent entities from the dependent entities. Relationships are established to reflect this dependence. These relationships are characterized by cardinality and can express a zero-to-many, one-to-many, or many-to-many set of relationships between two entities (not shown in Figure 3.8-5).

During the construction of the DIV-2, we also start establishing identifiers—unique attributes of an entity that help to identify an instance of that entity. Identifiers form the primary key for an entity. Sometimes a natural attribute of an entity can be used as a primary key by itself, but in most cases, a single attribute may not serve to identify an entity instance uniquely; a surrogate key is a made-up identifier that serves as a unique identifier in databases.

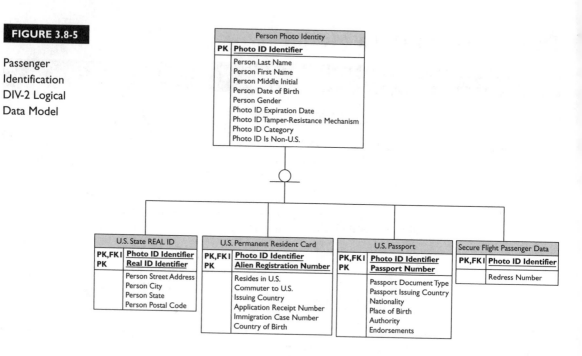

FIGURE 3.8-5

Passenger
Identification
DIV-2 Logical
Data Model

Designing a logical data model is a specialty skill. It is outside the scope of this book to discuss detailed data modeling techniques such as the IDEF1X or the UML object class modeling techniques. There are several good books on data modeling such as Tom Bruce's seminal book on the IDEF1X technique (1992) or Martin Fowler's *UML Distilled* (1997).

DIV-3 Physical Data Model

Model Information at a Glance	
Model Short Name	DIV-3
Name	Physical Data Model
Other Names	Database Schema, XML Schema Document (XSD), RBMS Schema, Message Template
Viewpoint	Data and Information
Model Intent	DIV-3 represents data and information at the systems level for use by automated application systems or services. DIV-3 transforms the abstract logical data model DIV-2 into an implementable technology model such as an RDBMS schema, an XSD, or a USMTF message template.

Model Information at a Glance	
Model Audience	Database administrators, application developers, and designers of standard message communication semantic protocols.
Formal Modeling Methodology	Technology-specific. Examples are Relational Database/SQL; XSD; COBOL file, record, and field structures; object-oriented design (OOD) object class structures; and CORBA Interface Description Language (IDL) interfaces.
Integration of Model with Other Views	The DIV-3 data objects must be consistent with the DIV-2 logical data entities and attributes, which in turn must be consistent with the DIV-1 ontological concepts.

Example: Passenger Identification Model DIV-3

Figure 3.8-6 shows an example of a physical schema for implementation in an Oracle database management system. The DIV-3 is dependent on the implementation technology because it deals with detailed specifications for data representations, including data formats, physical constraints, and grammars for representation.

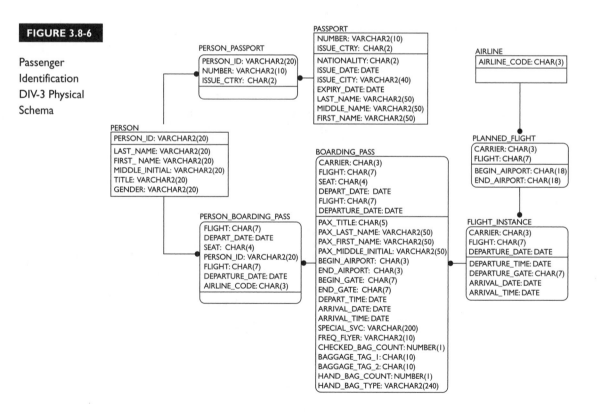

FIGURE 3.8-6

Passenger Identification DIV-3 Physical Schema

To illustrate the technology dependence of the DIV-3, the following listing presents another example of a DIV-3 using XSD:

```xml
<?xml version="1.0" encoding="UTF-8"?>
<xs:schema xmlns:xs="http://www.w3.org/2001/XMLSchema">
      <xs:simpleType name="T_MIDDLE_INITIAL">
            <xs:restriction base="xs:string">
                  <xs:enumeration value="Q"/>
            </xs:restriction>
      </xs:simpleType>
      <xs:complexType name="T_Passenger">
            <xs:sequence>
                  <xs:element ref="PNR"/>
                  <xs:element ref="LAST_NAME"/>
                  <xs:element ref="FIRST_NAME"/>
                  <xs:element ref="MIDDLE_INITIAL"/>
                  <xs:element ref="TITLE"/>
                  <xs:element ref="GENDER"/>
                  <xs:element ref="PASSPORT"
maxOccurs="unbounded"/>
                  <xs:element ref="BOARDING_PASS"
maxOccurs="unbounded"/>
            </xs:sequence>
      </xs:complexType>
      <xs:complexType name="T_PASSPORT">
            <xs:sequence>
                  <xs:element ref="ISSUE_CTRY"/>
                  <xs:element ref="ISSUE_CITY"/>
                  <xs:element ref="ISSUE_DATE"/>
                  <xs:element ref="NUMBER"/>
                  <xs:element ref="NATIONALITY"/>
            </xs:sequence>
      </xs:complexType>
      <xs:complexType name="T_HAND_BAGGAGE">
            <xs:sequence>
                  <xs:element ref="BAG_TYPE"
maxOccurs="unbounded"/>
            </xs:sequence>
            <xs:attribute ref="COUNT" use="required"/>
      </xs:complexType>
      <xs:complexType name="T_CHECKED_BAGGAGE">
            <xs:sequence>
                  <xs:element ref="BAG_TAG"
maxOccurs="unbounded"/>
            </xs:sequence>
            <xs:attribute ref="COUNT" use="required"/>
```

```
        </xs:complexType>
        <xs:complexType name="T_CHECKED_BAG">
                <xs:sequence>
                        <xs:element ref="BAG_TAG"
maxOccurs="unbounded"/>
                </xs:sequence>
                <xs:attribute ref="COUNT" use="required"/>
        </xs:complexType>
        <xs:complexType name="T_BOARDING_PASS">
                <xs:sequence>
                        <xs:element ref="BEGIN_AIPORT"/>
                        <xs:element ref="BEGIN_GATE"/>
                        <xs:element ref="END_AIRPORT"/>
                        <xs:element ref="END_GATE"/>
                        <xs:element ref="DEPART_DATE"/>
                        <xs:element ref="DEPART_TIME"/>
                        <xs:element ref="ARR_DATE"/>
                        <xs:element ref="ARR_TIME"/>
                        <xs:element ref="CARRIER"/>
                        <xs:element ref="FLIGHT"/>
                        <xs:element ref="SEAT"/>
                        <xs:element ref="SPECIAL_SVCS"/>
                        <xs:element ref="FREQ_FLYER"/>
                        <xs:element ref="CHECKED_BAGGAGE"/>
                        <xs:element ref="HAND_BAGGAGE"/>
                </xs:sequence>
                <xs:attribute ref="ID" use="required"/>
        </xs:complexType>
        <xs:attribute name="ID" type="xs:byte"/>
        <xs:attribute name="COUNT" type="xs:byte"/>
        <xs:element name="TITLE" type="xs:string"/>
        <xs:element name="SPECIAL_SVCS" type="xs:string"/>
        <xs:element name="SEAT" type="xs:string"/>
        <xs:element name="Passenger" type="T_Passenger"/>
        <xs:element name="PNR" type="xs:string"/>
        <xs:element name="PASSPORT" type="T_PASSPORT"/>
        <xs:element name="NUMBER" type="xs:string"/>
        <xs:element name="NATIONALITY" type="xs:string"/>
        <xs:element name="MIDDLE_INITIAL" type="T_MIDDLE_INITIAL"/>
        <xs:element name="LAST_NAME" type="xs:string"/>
        <xs:element name="ISSUE_DATE" type="xs:date"/>
        <xs:element name="ISSUE_CTRY" type="xs:string"/>
        <xs:element name="ISSUE_CITY" type="xs:string"/>
        <xs:element name="HAND_BAGGAGE" type="T_HAND_BAGGAGE"/>
        <xs:element name="GENDER" type="xs:string"/>
```

```
                    <xs:element name="FREQ_FLYER" type="xs:string"/>
                    <xs:element name="FLIGHT" type="xs:short"/>
                    <xs:element name="FIRST_NAME" type="xs:string"/>
                    <xs:element name="END_GATE" type="xs:string"/>
                    <xs:element name="END_AIRPORT" type="xs:string"/>
                    <xs:element name="DEPART_TIME" type="xs:string"/>
                    <xs:element name="DEPART_DATE" type="xs:date"/>
                    <xs:element name="CHECKED_BAGGAGE" type="T_CHECKED_
BAGGAGE"/>
                    <xs:element name="CHECKED_BAG" type="T_CHECKED_BAG"/>
                    <xs:element name="CARRIER" type="xs:string"/>
                    <xs:element name="BOARDING_PASS" type="T_BOARDING_PASS"/>
                    <xs:element name="BEGIN_GATE" type="xs:string"/>
                    <xs:element name="BEGIN_AIPORT" type="xs:string"/>
                    <xs:element name="BAG_TYPE" type="xs:string"/>
                    <xs:element name="BAG_TAG" type="xs:int"/>
                    <xs:element name="ARR_TIME" type="xs:string"/>
                    <xs:element name="ARR_DATE" type="xs:date"/>
          </xs:schema>
```

This example represents a physical schema built to model the data elements, simple types and complex types. Notice the difference in style between the cross-connected (network graph) RDBMS schema and the hierarchical definition of the XML Schemas (Tree Graph).

Questions

1. What is the difference between data and information? What transformations need to be made to data to convert it into information?

2. What is an ontology? Why is the understanding of ontology fundamental to communications and language? Provide an example of a language used for modeling ontologies.

3. How can ontology be used for compressing knowledge representation?

4. (Advanced.) How does ontology representation in OWL compare with the representation of object classes in UML?

5. What is a taxonomy? Why is a taxonomy useful in architecture work? How does taxonomy organize knowledge?

6. What is a vocabulary? What is a controlled vocabulary? How is the proliferation of terms controlled in a controlled vocabulary? Name a standard that governs controlled implementations for monolingual vocabularies.

7. Why did the FEA choose to use a three-pronged approach to defining a data reference model rather than list a collection of common entities, such as PERSON, ORGANIZATION, BUSINESS-UNIT, or OPERATING-DIVISION across multiple agencies and standardizing attributes and relationships? (This is what the DoD attempted to do for more than two decades.)

8. What is the difference between data context and data description in the FEA Data Reference Model?

9. How is your specific enterprise approaching the need for an enterprise data model? How are data standards developed, promulgated, and implemented?

10. What is the DIV-1 Conceptual Data Model? What are the steps you would use to construct a DIV-1 Conceptual Data Model inside your enterprise? How would you start to organize and lay out the model?

11. What is the DIV-2 Logical Data Model? How is it useful to the enterprise? What are some of the transformations that need to be made to the DIV-1 Conceptual Data Model to convert it into a DIV-2 Logical Data Model?

12. What is the cardinality of a relationship inside a DIV-2 Logical Data Model?

13. What is the primary key for a PERSON, PASSPORT, or BOARDING PASS? (Remember that two countries can issue passports with identical passport numbers.) Make any reasonable assumptions you want regarding the attributes.

14. What is the DIV-3 Physical Schema? Why is it technology-dependent?

15. If you were to specify the exact format of message templates to define interoperability between two systems, would you build a DIV-1, DIV-2, or DIV-3 model? Why?

Reference List

American National Standards Institute (ANSI)/National Information Standards Organization (NISO). (2005). *Guidelines for the construction, format and management of monolingual controlled vocabularies.* ANSI.

Bruce, Thomas A., M.D. (1992). *Designing quality databases with IDEF1X information Models*. Dorset.

Fowler, Martin. (1997). *UML Distilled: a brief guide to the standard object modeling language, 2nd edition*. Addison-Wesley.

National Institute for Standards and Technology. (1993). *Integration definition for information modeling (IDEF1X)*. NIST/U.S. Department of Commerce.

Office of Management and Budget. (2005). *Federal Enterprise Architecture Data Reference Model, Version 2.0*. Executive Office of the President of the United States.

World Wide Web Consortium. (2004). *OWL Web Ontology Language semantics and abstract syntax*. http://www.w3.org/TR/owl-semantics/.

3.9

Technology and Standards Viewpoint

T he world runs smoothly on standard. When you swipe that credit card through the card reader on the gas pump, the use of a common standard guarantees that the card reader reads the magnetic stripe and retrieves the encoded information that was stored by your bank or credit card provider. When you slide the boarding pass issued by one airline into a card reader operated and used by another airline, your flight and booking information travels smoothly to the carrier and you are authenticated and welcomed aboard the aircraft.

The Standards Viewpoint (StdV) is the minimal set of rules governing the arrangement, interaction, and interdependence of system parts or elements. Its purpose is to ensure that a system satisfies a specified set of operational requirements. The StdV provides the technical systems implementation guidelines upon which engineering specifications are based, common building blocks are established, and product lines are developed. It includes a collection of the technical standards, implementation conventions, standards options, rules, and criteria that can be organized into one or more profiles that govern systems and system or service elements in a given architectural description.

The Standards Viewpoint caters to the need of people responsible for interoperability-, integration-, and federation-related activities.

For example, operational interoperability requires common semantic vocabularies between multiple performers—in an emergency response scenario, first responders use an abbreviated (terse) form of communication that is understood by everyone who is familiar with and using that standard. An example of such a standard is that of the ten-codes formerly used by police and citizens' band (CB) radio operators.

Ten-codes (Reyes & Felsen, 2005), properly known as ten signals, are code words used to represent common phrases in voice communication, particularly by law enforcement and in CB radio transmissions. The codes, developed in 1937 and expanded in 1974 by the Association of Public-Safety Communications Officials–International (APCO), allow for brevity and standardization of message traffic. They have historically been widely used by law enforcement officers in North America, although in 2005 the U.S. federal government recommended they be discontinued in favor of everyday language. Ten-codes are not standardized across states, so any scenario that requires multistate, multipolice jurisdiction attention may be hampered by the lack of common standards.

In the words of the Department of Homeland Security, "In an attempt to reduce the volume of radio traffic and add a layer of privacy when communicating, law enforcement officers began using a coded language over the radio called '10-codes.' Law enforcement agencies began to develop their own proprietary 10-code system; as a result, 10-88 may mean 'present phone number' in one agency and 'officer needs help' in another. Because coded language is not standardized across jurisdictions, using 10-codes can result in miscommunication and confusion when multiple agencies and disciplines respond to an incident. This interoperability challenge has resulted in a push for implementing plain language across agencies for mutual aid events so that various disciplines can effectively share information. Plain language, according to NIMS [the National Incident Management System], is the use of common terms and definitions that can be understood by individuals from all responder disciplines. Established by the Secretary of Homeland Security, NIMS only requires plain language for mutual aid scenarios, though it strongly encourages the use of plain language during day-to-day operations as well" (Department of Homeland Security, 2007, pg 2).

We are all familiar with the effect of standards on interoperability. Major advances in the widespread proliferation of computer communications began to occur after the majority of vendors adopted the TCP/IP protocol. The HTTP and XML standards are other examples of communications protocols that have been behind the explosive adoption of the World Wide Web. In the area of data standards, financial institutions have established interbank funds transfer standards to enable disparate banks to conduct financial transactions automatically through messaging.

The Standards Viewpoint is therefore both (1) a plan to enhance interoperability by publishing enterprisewide guidance that requires adherence to standards for items such as business processes, military operations, systems hardware and software components, communication devices and links, and materiel that is used by processes; and (2) a recording of the disparate standards currently in use with an intent of reducing variety and fostering more uniformity and consistency in the future.

Standards Viewpoint Integrated Models

The Standards Viewpoint models (see Figure 3.9-1) tend to stand alone, more as guidance for the enterprise in the acquisition process, to promote interoperability as early as possible. However, the SV-9 Systems Technology and Skills Forecast and the SvcV9 Services Technology and Skills Forecast both must be consistent with the StdV-1 Standards Profile and the StdV-2 Standards Forecasts.

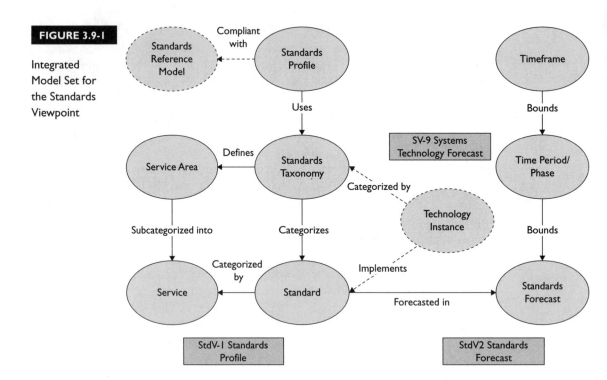

FIGURE 3.9-1

Integrated
Model Set for
the Standards
Viewpoint

StdV-1 Standards Profile

The StdV-1 uses a normative classification scheme, sometimes called the Technology Reference Model, to record the current list of technology standards that are used within an enterprise; more broadly, the StdV-1 also covers operational standards. It provides a view to the architect of the dissonance and the need to formulate strategies to reduce the dissonance if warranted or justify the need for multiple standards based on mission requirements.

The importance of using the same classification scheme for standards across cooperating and collaborating enterprises is that they can lay their StdV-1 models side by side and make comparisons that find dissonance in their standards postures. Because of the sheer magnitude of the lists of standards that are applicable to an enterprise, without a classification scheme that is commonly understood and adopted, these comparisons become tedious and fraught with the possibility of errors (even with computer-based searching and matching).

Federal agencies must use the Federal Enterprise Architecture's Technical Reference Model (TRM) as the overarching categorization scheme. Individual agencies may develop their own standards profiles that extend the FEA TRM (OMB, 2007) and may also list vendor products in addition to technology standards. The Federal Government had recognized very early that technical standards were fundamental to interoperability. The National Institute of Standards and Technology (1993) promulgates the Application Portability Profile that establishes technical standards for vendors selling solutions into the Federal Government.

DoD enterprises must use the Defense Information Technology Standards Registry (DISR, 2008) provided by the Department of Defense both for a standard classification scheme as well as a list of registered standards. In general, not all standards that are used by all DoD enterprises are available in the DISR—only those that are common to multiple enterprises.

There are other classification schemes for technology standardization. Standards bodies such as the American National Standards Institute (ANSI), the Institute of Electrical and Electronics Engineers (IEEE), the International Standards Organization (ISO), and the International Civil Aviation Organization (ICAO) have also developed standards. These bodies appoint committees and working groups that lay out these standards according to their own internal grouping schemes.

Table 3.9-1 provides a summary of the StdV-1 Standards Profile model.

Example: Passenger Identification StdV-1

In the example shown in Table 3.9-2, we have invented a classification scheme for RMN that has a progressive structure with three levels: Service Area, Service, and Subservice. Standards are then categorized by this three-level classification scheme.

Because the categorization scheme is used to group literally thousands of technologies in large enterprises, the importance of standardizing the categorization scheme itself is considered a very important exercise in architecting the enterprise.

The Department of Defense maintains a standard technology classification using the DISR. The DISR is intended to provide a common classification model for all defense enterprises to make StdV-1 submissions that can be unified and aggregated at a higher level in the DoD.

The Federal Enterprise Architecture also standardizes a technology classification scheme called the Technical Reference Model. The DISR and the TRM provide a standard list of categories under which technology standards can be grouped.

TABLE 3.9-1	StdV-1 Standards Profile Model at a Glance

Model Short Name	StdV-1
Name	Standards Profile
Other Names	Technology Reference Model (TRM), Technical Profile (old name) Technology Standards Catalog (TOGAF 9) Technology Portfolio Catalog (TOGAF 9)
Viewpoint	Services
Model Intent	The StdV-1 defines the technical, operational, and business standards, guidance, and policy applicable to the architecture being described. In addition to identifying applicable technical standards, StdV-1 also documents the policies and standards that apply to the operational or business context. StdV-1 is a model that is equally applicable to the enterprise architecture as it is to solution architectures. The StdV-1 compiles all applicable standards. At an enterprise level, this may be too large a number of standards, so a proper taxonomy or grouping scheme is required to provide a way to understand the complexity. A standards reference model is useful for performing this categorization. The DISR provides a standard service area/service/standard categorization scheme for DoD enterprises, which may have their own categorization scheme. For comparisons and understanding the dissonance in standards, especially in the presence of a large number of standards, common taxonomies are essential.
Model Audience	Standards personnel; integration and cross-functional interoperability groups.
Formal Modeling Methodology	None. The DoD DISR and the FEA Technical Reference Model are two examples of formal, well-established classification schemes for technology standards.
Integration of Model with Other Views	The StdV-1 elements must be consistent with SV-9, SvcV-9, and StdV-2 elements.

The TOGAF—which traces its origins to the original Defense Department Technology Architecture Framework for Information Management (TAFIM)— also provides for a Technical Reference Model that implementing organizations can use to categorize their technology standards. The technology architecture for an enterprise is one of the important components of TOGAF 9. The TOGAF distinguishes between technology standards such as POSIX or FIPS 127 Structured Query Language, which are modeled in the technology Standards Catalog, from the actual instances of technology, such as an Oracle Database or a Microsoft Server, which are modeled inside the Technology Portfolio Catalog.

The StdV-1 may also be tailored to cross-reference the architecture elements that use or reference a specific standard. Table 3.9-2 shows the issue date (year) of the standard as well as the status of the standard at the time the architecture was built.

TABLE 3.9-2   Passenger Identification StdV-1 Standards Profile

RMN Service Area / RMN Service	RMN Subservice	Standard				
		Number	Authority	Title	Issue Date	Status
Identification						
Machine Identification						
Magnetic Identification Cards						
		ISO 7810	ISO/IEC	Physical Characteristics of Credit Card Size Document	2003	Current
		ISO 7811-1	ISO/IEC	Part 1: Embossing	2002	Current
		ISO 7811-2	ISO/IEC	Part 2: Magnetic Stripe— Low Coercivity	2001	Current
		ISO 7811-3	ISO/IEC	Part 3: Location of Embossed Characters	1995	Withdrawn
		ISO 7811-4	ISO/IEC	Part 4: Location of Tracks 1 and 2	1995	Withdrawn
		ISO 7811-5	ISO/IEC	Part 5: Location of Track 3	2001	Withdrawn
		ISO 7811-6	ISO/IEC	Part 6: Magnetic Stripe— High Coercivity	2008	Current
		ISO 7813	ISO/IEC	Financial Transaction Cards	2006	Current
Optical Character Recognition						
Alphanumeric Character Recognition						
		ISO 1073/II	ISO/IEC	Alphanumeric character sets for optical recognition Part 2: Character Set OCR-B—shapes and dimensions of the printed image	1976	Withdrawn
		ISO 1831	ISO/IEC	Printing specifications for optical character recognition	1980	Current
		ISO 3166-2	ISO/IEC	Codes for the representation of countries and their subdivision. Part 1: country codes	2007	Current
		ISO/IEC 7810	ISO/IEC	Identification Cards: physical characteristics	2003	Current
		ISO 8601	ISO	Data Elements and Data Interchange Formats: information interchange; representation of dates and times	2001	Current

StdV-2 Standards Forecast

The StdV-2 Standards Forecast is primarily to support planners' needs for developing roadmaps for future standards adoption and implementation. The StdV-2 collects projections of standards maturity over a time period to determine which standards will become obsolete and which standards will be supplemented with newer versions within the timeframe of interest.

The StdV-1 and StdV-2 must share the same classification scheme and standards coding scheme for traceability and integration.

Table 3.9-3 provides a summary of the StdV-2 Standards Profile Model.

Example: Passenger Identification StdV-2

In the example StdV-2 in Table 3.9-4, we depict a timeline of ten years with short-term, midterm, and long-term forecasts for each standard of interest. The purpose of

TABLE 3.9-3   StdV-2 Standards Forecast Model at a Glance

Model Short Name	StdV-2
Name	Standards Profile
Other Names	Technology Reference Model (TRM), Technical Profile (old name)
Viewpoint	Services
Model Intent	The StdV-2 defines the technical, operational, and business standards, guidance, and policy applicable to the architecture being described. In addition to identifying applicable technical standards, StdV-2 also documents the policies and standards that apply to the operational or business context. StdV-2 is a model that is equally applicable to the enterprise architecture as it is to solution architectures. The model compiles all applicable standards. At an enterprise level, this may be too large a number of standards, so a proper taxonomy or grouping scheme is required to provide a way to understand the complexity. A standards reference model is useful for performing this categorization. The DISR provides a standard service area/service/standard categorization scheme for DoD. Enterprises may have their own categorization scheme. For comparisons and understanding the dissonance in standards, especially in the presence of a large number of standards, common taxonomies are essential.
Model Audience	Standards personnel; integration and cross-functional interoperability groups
Formal Modeling Methodology	None. The DoD DISR and the FEA TRM are two examples of formal, well-established classification schemes for technology standards.
Integration of Model with Other Views	The StdV-2 elements must be consistent with SV-9, SvcV-9, and StdV-2 elements.

TABLE 3.9-4	RMN Enterprise StdV-2 Standards Forecast			
RMN Service Area and RMN Service	**RMN Subservice**	**Standards Forecast**		
		Short-Term (<2 Years)	**Midterm (1-5 Years)**	**Long-Term (5–10 Years)**
Identification				
Machine Identification				
	Magnetic Card Identification	Expected to use heavily in 80 percent of identification cases. Solid, reliable, and established.	Shift to biometric techniques. Still expected to use in 40 percent of identification cases.	Eliminate all nonbiometric methods because they can be taken by force from owners.
	Bar Code Identification	Very limited use (<10 percent). Single-dimensional bar code information density not acceptable.	Expect to use two-dimensional bar codes in 5 percent of identification cases.	Eliminate all nonbiometric methods because they can be taken by force from owners.
	Smart Chip Identification	Currently being used in U.S. passports and select country passports.	Increasing use of noncontact RF detection and interrogation methods (60 percent) with photo image information.	Augmented to contain also biometric information.

the StdV-2 is to assist in developing a standards roadmap for RMN that will layout a blueprint for architects that clearly shows some of the assumptions for standards evolution and will guide them in making acquisition-, design-, and development-related decisions.

Questions

1. Why are standards important to the enterprise? Who is the audience for the Standards Viewpoint? Why?

2. Why are standards important across enterprises? Name some examples of scenarios where multiple enterprises are involved and where the lack of standards is a serious impediment to interoperability.

3. What is a Technical Reference Model? Why is a common standards classification scheme important for various parts of the enterprise to interoperate? Does a Technical Reference Model contain vendor products or simply industry, de facto, and other standards specifications?

4. What is a Standards Profile? How does your enterprise generate a Standards Profile? Does the enterprise Standards Profile match one of the Reference Models mentioned in this chapter, such as the FEA TRM or the Defense Department's DISR? Does your enterprise standardize the classification scheme and categories and standards specifications or does it categorize vendor platforms such as IBM DB2, Oracle for RDBMS, or IBM Web Server for web services? Why?

5. What is a Standards Forecast? How does your enterprise generate Standards Forecasts? For what timeframes? How do the timeframes in the StdV-2 tie in to and remain consistent with other timeframe models such as the SV-9?

6. What is the relationship between the Standards Profile (StdV-1), the Standards Forecast (StdV-2), and the Systems Technology Forecast (SV-9) and the Services Technology Forecast (SvcV-9) models?

Reference List

Department of Homeland Security. (2007). *Plain Language Guide—Making the Transition from Ten Codes to Plain Language*. Brochure. http://www.safecomprogram.gov/NR/rdonlyres/5945AFE3-ADA9-4189-83B0-4D8218D0CA2F/0/PlainLanguageGuide.pdf.

DISR. (2008). Defense Information Technology Standards Registry (DISR). Baseline Release 08-20 July 2008. ASD(NII)/DCIO/IMI&T - periodically updated with new standards. http://www.disa.mil (protected access).

National Institute of Standards and Technology (NIST). (1993). NIST APP. Application Portability Profile (APP) - Open System Environment Profile, OSE/1 Version 2.0, NIST Special Publication 500-210, June 1993.

Office of Management and Budget. (2007). *FEA Technical Reference Model section of FEA Consolidated Reference Model Version 2.3*. October 2007. http://www.whitehouse.gov/sites/default/files/omb/assets/fea_docs/FEA_CRM_v23_Final_Oct_2007_Revised.pdf.

Part IV

EA Examples

4.1

EA in Government

Enterprise architecture in the U.S. federal government owes its impact to a great deal of legislation that created specific mandates that require it. This legislation cites EA "as a key tool for performing enterprise-level strategic planning" (Treasury Enterprise Architecture Framework, CIO Officer Council, 2000, pg 8). The major legislation and guidance for EA including the following:

- The Information Technology Management Reform Act (ITMRA) of 1996 (known as the Clinger-Cohen Act)
- The Government Performance and Results Act (GPRA) of 1993
- The Federal Enterprise Architecture Framework (FEAF) of 1999

Clinger-Cohen Act of 1996

In Clinger-Cohen, Section 5125(b)(2) states, "The Chief Information Officer of an executive agency shall be responsible for developing, maintaining, and facilitating the implementation of a sound and integrated information technology architecture for the executive agency."

The act requires the following:

- The appointment of a Chief Information Officer (CIO) who ensures implementation of information policies
- An integrated framework for evolving and maintaining existing IT and acquiring new IT to achieve an agency's strategic goals
- The development and maintenance of a strategic IT plan that describes how IT activities help accomplish the agency mission
- That IT operations and decisions be integrated with agency plans, budgets, and human resources management
- That each agency establish goals, responsibilities, and methods for measuring IT contributions to program productivity, efficiency, and effectiveness
- That a current and complete inventory of the agency's major information resources be developed and maintained

The OMB Circular A–130 (1997) and its draft proposed update (2000) and OMB Memorandum 97–16 (1997) further define the roles and responsibilities of federal agencies in meeting the Clinger-Cohen mandates. The policies in these directives require each federal enterprise to develop and use an enterprise architecture as a mechanism to achieve these objectives.

The Government Performance and Results Act (GRPA)

The Government Performance and Results Act requires that each federal agency do the following:

- Develop and implement systematic performance measures for judging the effectiveness of the agency based on its outputs
- Justify IT expenditures based on how they support the accomplishment of the agency's mission, goals, and objectives
- Identify objective, quantifiable, and measurable metrics that can be used to determine whether or not the system is helping to achieve those goals
- Report the results to Congress

Federal Enterprise Architecture Framework (FEAF)

In 1999, the Federal CIO Council, which was formed in response to these mandates, developed the FEAF. The FEAF is designed to support the development of crosscutting interagency enterprise architecture segments that, in turn, support collaboration, consistency, and reuse among agencies that have common or interdependent missions.

The Influence of the Zachman Framework

As we have discussed in previous chapters, the history of enterprise architecture can arguably be traced to John Zachman's early formulation of a framework for an information systems architecture that laid the foundation for what he later renamed as the Zachman Framework. His framework has greatly impacted the government and commercial sectors.

In the commercial world, in such organizations as IBM, AT&T, NCR, Capgemini, and more, a number of frameworks were developed that aligned with the Zachman Framework. These later became incorporated or aligned with The Open Group Architecture Framework, discussed in Chapter 4.3.

In government domain, both within federal agencies and defense, Zachman's approach is evident in the different views and interrogatives comprising each of the major frameworks employed. In the latter, this led to the 1994 development of the Technical Architecture Framework for Information Management (TAFIM), which later was the foundation for a more extensive architecture approach in the C4ISR (Command, Control, Computers and Communication, Intelligence, Surveillance, and Reconnaissance) Architecture and the later iterations of the Department of Defense Architecture Framework (DoDAF), such as versions 1.0, 1.5, and 2.0, as discussed in Chapter 4.2.

The Influence of NIST

In 1999, the Federal Enterprise Architecture working group published the first version of the FEAF, which comprised models and definitions to create and document architecture descriptions for agencies of the federal government. According to the FEAF Version 1.1 document published in 1999, the developers of the FEAF drew from the National Institute of Standards and Technology (NIST) model, which was a tool to show the "interrelationship enterprise business, information, and technology environments" (The Practical Guide to Federal Enterprise Architecture, CIO Council, pg iv). The five-layered model allows for organizing, planning, and building an integrated set of information and information technology architectures. The five layers are defined separately but are interrelated and interwoven (see Figure 4.1-1).

The FEAF and NIST are consistent with Zachman in focusing on business, data, applications, and technology as interconnected architectures, as seen in the initial graphical representation of FEAF (see Figure 4.1-2).

The definitions of business, data, applications, and technology architectures in the FEAF are consistent with their description in The Open Group Architecture Framework (TOGAF). The Business (or Business Process) Architecture defines the business strategy, governance, organization, and key business processes. The Data Architecture describes the structure of an organization's logical and physical data

FIGURE 4.1-1

NIST Five-
Layered Model

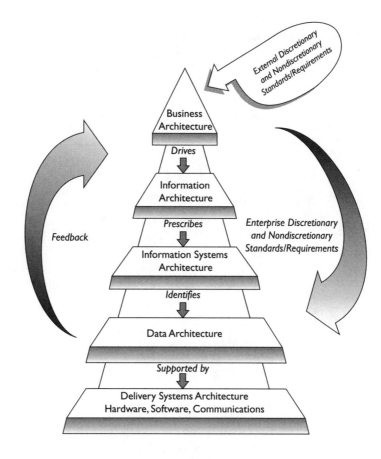

assets and data management resources. The Applications Architecture provides a
blueprint for the individual application systems to be deployed, their interactions,
and their relationships to the core business processes of the organization. Technology
Architecture describes the logical software and hardware capabilities that are required
to support the deployment of business, data, and application services. This includes
IT infrastructure, middleware, networks, communications, processing, standards,
and the like.

FIGURE 4.1-2   Federal Enterprise Architecture Framework (FEAF)

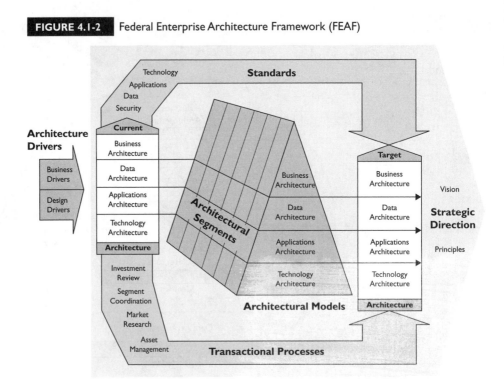

The FEAF is comprised of three related architectures: the baseline or as-is architecture, the to-be or target architecture, and the transitional architecture that provides the approach for moving from as-is to the target.

Treasury Enterprise Architecture Framework (TEAF)

At the same time as the FEAF was established, the Treasury Department developed its own version, known as the Treasury Enterprise Architecture Framework, which was published in 1999. The TEAF also contained the four architecture

FIGURE 4.1-3

Treasury
Enterprise
Architecture
Framework

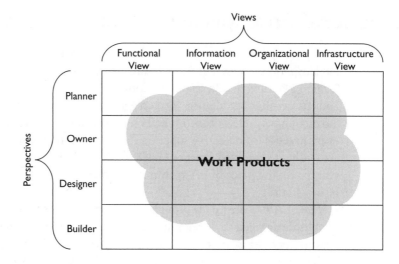

levels (business, data, application, and technology) and contained a set of views corresponding to several drawn from Zachman and referred to as the Functional, Information, Organizational, and Infrastructure views. Each of these views contained a number of products or model types that comprised the architecture. Figure 4.1-3 shows the TEAF (p 119).

In 2000, the TEAF was published with a description of the work products involved, and a correspondence was made between the TEAF and the FEAF, as shown in Figure 4.1-4.

FIGURE 4.1-4

Correspondence
Between the
TEAF and the
FEAF

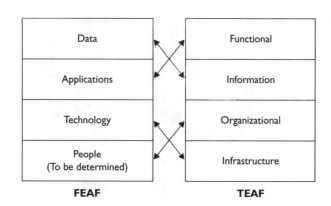

The Federal Enterprise Architecting Process

Enterprise architecture is recognized as central to a number of government modernization requirements, including and especially portfolio management and the Capital Planning and Investment Control (CPIC), which manages IT investments and ensures they are aligned with an agency's mission. The process involves three distinct phases: select, control, and ongoing evaluation. These phases ensure that every investment objective supports the business and mission needs of the agency. According to the *FEA Practice Guide* (Office of Management and Budget, 2007, year, pg 8), the place of EA within government is expressed in the diagram shown in Figure 4.1-5.

The *FEA Practice Guide* provides a lifecycle process that begins with every agency establishing a need to develop its EA and formulating a strategy that includes a definition of vision, objectives, and principles. This process can be easily compared to the Six Step Process of the DoDAF and the TOGAF Architecture Development Methodology (ADM). The *Practice Guide* utilizes the diagram shown in Figure 4.1-6 to illustrate this lifecycle.

Since the FEAF was initially published, there have been two major advances in the architecture: the development of Federal Enterprise Architecture Reference Models and Segment Architecture (FSAM).

FIGURE 4.1-5 Place of Enterprise Architecture Within Government (Office of Management and Budget, 2007)

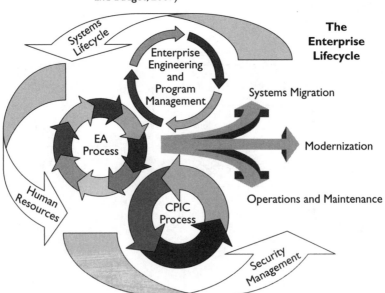

FIGURE 4.1-6 Enterprise Architecture Development Lifecycle (Office of Management and Budget, 2007, pg 9)

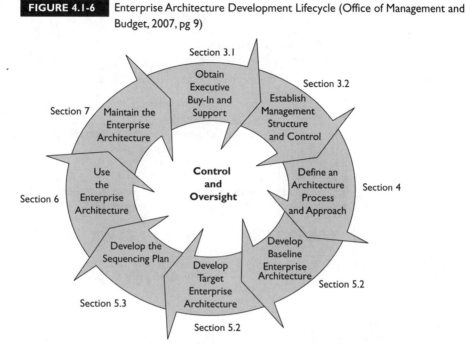

The OMB FEA Reference Models

In October 2007, the Office of Management and Budget (OMB) published a set of FEA Reference Models to provide a taxonomy and ontology to facilitate cross-agency analysis and the identification of duplicative investments, gaps, and opportunities for collaboration within and across agencies in the federal government (FEA Reference Model Mapping Quick Guide (FY10 Budget Preparation, 2008, pg 1). These Reference Models provide a common framework and vocabulary so that IT portfolios are better managed. These models (illustrated in Figure 4.1-7) are the following:

- Performance Reference Model (PRM)
- Business Reference Model (BRM)
- Service Component Reference Model (SRM)
- Technical Reference Model (TRM)
- Data Reference Model (DRM)

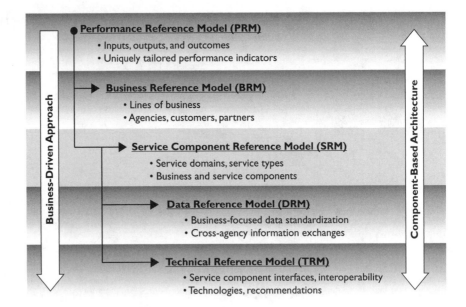

FIGURE 4.1-7

FEA Reference
Models

Performance Reference Model (PRM)

The Performance Reference Model draws from a number of industry performance methodologies, such as balanced scorecards. The PRM provides a framework for measuring performance using "output measurements" relevant to federal government goals. It is designed to enable agencies to manage their organizations better strategically by providing a method for the agency's EA to measure the success of its IT investments and their effects on strategic outcomes. It is proposed that the model accomplishes this by creating "a common language" whereby the agency EA can describe the outputs and measures employed to achieve the agency's program and business objectives. The PRM provides a linkage between internal business components and business- and customer-centric outputs. This facilitates resource-allocation decisions based on comparative determinations of which programs and organizations are more efficient and effective.

The objectives of the PRM are to produce performance information for decision support, improve alignment of inputs to outputs that provides a "line of sight" to desired results, and to identify improvement opportunities. This "line of sight" is articulated through the use of the measurement area, category, grouping, and indicator hierarchy as expressed in the diagram shown in Figure 4.1-8.

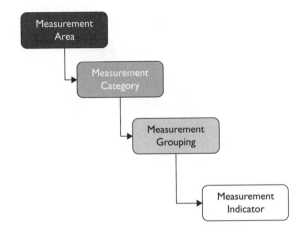

The OMB developed a PRM framework to articulate the cause-and-effect relationships among inputs, outputs, and outcomes. This provides a "line of sight" that is critical for decision makers to understand how inputs enable progress toward outputs and outcomes. The Reference Model documentation describes how the PRM captures line of sight to "reflect how value is created as inputs (such as Technology) are used to create outputs (through Processes and Activities), which in turn, impact outcomes (such as, Mission, Business and Customer Results)" (FEA Consolidated Reference Model Document Version 2.3, 2007, pg 5). Guiding the entire PRM are Strategic Outcomes, representing broad policy priorities driving the direction of government (such as to secure the homeland). This is represented in Figure 4.1-9.

The Business Reference Model (BRM)

The BRM is a framework providing a functional view of the lines of business (LoBs) in government. This includes internal operations and service to citizens who are independent of agencies and department. The BRM describes government around common business areas rather than through stovepipe, agency-specific views. It is designed to promote interagency collaboration and lays the foundation for FEA and E-Gov strategies. The BRM is structured into a tiered hierarchy representing the business functions of the federal government, as represented in Figure 4.1-10.

The BRM business areas separate government operations into high-level categories that relate to the services-for-citizens purpose of government. It addresses the

FIGURE 4.1-9

Performance
Reference Model

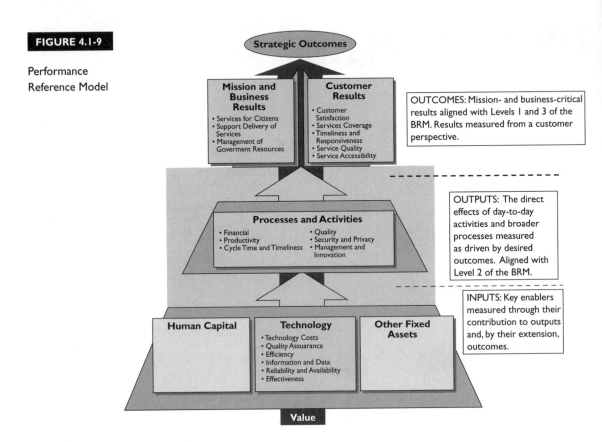

FIGURE 4.1-10

Business
Reference Model

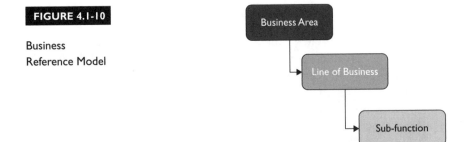

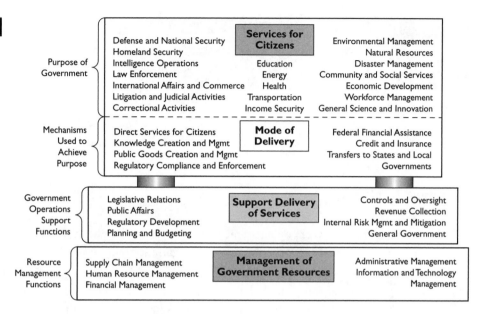

FIGURE 4.1-11

Categorization
Inside the
Business
Reference Model

mechanisms to achieve this purpose as modes of delivery, the support functions
required to conduct government operations, and the resource management functions
enabling this. The business areas break down into LoBs, where each is comprised of
sub-functions that represent the "lowest level of granularity" in the BRM. Figure 4.1-11
shows this model.

The Service Component Reference Model (SRM)

The SRM, like each of the other Reference Models, is a framework to classify service
components according to how they support business and performance objectives.
It classifies horizontal and vertical service components and their IT investments
and assets. This assists recommendations of service capabilities supporting the reuse
of business components and services across agencies. According to the SRM, IT
investments can be either service providers or consumers. The SRM is hierarchically
constructed, organized across horizontal service areas, and independent of business
functions. This enables it to leverage the reuse of applications, capabilities, components,
and business services. Figure 4.1-12 shows the structured hierarchy of the SRM (FEA
Consolidated Reference Model Document Version 2.3, pg 47).

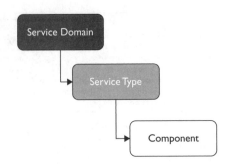

The SRM is structured around the following:

- Service domains that provide high-level views of the services and capabilities that support enterprise and organizational processes and applications
- Service types providing an additional layer of categorization in a service domain, which defines the business context of a specific component within a given domain, such as supply chain management
- Service components as a service type that provides "building blocks" to deliver component capability to the business

This structure is exemplified in Figure 4.1-13.

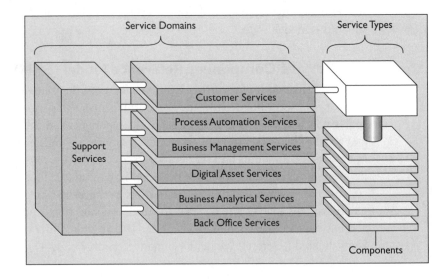

The Technical Reference Model (TRM)

The TRM is a "component-driven, technical framework categorizing the standards and technologies to support and enable the delivery of Service Components and capabilities" (FEA Consolidated Reference Model Document Version 2.3, pg 65). It provides a foundation for the reuse and standardization of technology and service components across government agencies. The alignment of agency capital investments to the TRM allows a common vocabulary that promotes interagency collaboration and interoperability. Figure 4.1-14 shows the TRM.

Data Reference Model (DRM)

The DRM is a standards-based framework enabling information sharing and reuse of data across government agencies. This is done through a standard description of common data and uniform data management practices. The DRM provides a standard

---

FIGURE 4.1-14 Technical Reference Model

Service Access and Delivery			
Access Channels	**Delivery Channels**	**Service Requirements**	**Service Transport**
Web Browser	Internet	Legislative/Compliance	Supporting Network Services
Wireless/PDA	Intranet	Authentication/Single Sign-on	Service Transport
Collaboration/Communications	Extranet	Hosting	
Other Electronic Channels	Peer to Peer (P2P)		
	Virtual Private Network (VPN)		

Service Platform and Infrastructure				
Support Platform	**Delivery Servers**	**Hardware/Infrastructure**	**Software Engineering**	**Database/Storage**
Wireless/Mobile	Web Servers	Servers/Computers	Integrated Dev Environment	Database
Platform Independent	Media Servers	Embedded Technology Devices	Software Configuration Mgmt.	Storage
Platform Dependent	Application Servers	Peripherals	Test Management	
	Portal Servers	Wide Area Network (WAN)	Modeling	
		Local Area Network (LAN)		
		Network Devices/Standards		
		Video Conferencing		

Component Framework				
Security	**Presentation/Interface**	**Business Logic**	**Data Management**	**Data Interchange**
Certificates/Digital Signature	Static Display	Platform Independent	Database Connectivity	Data Exchange
Supporting Security Services	Dynamic Server-Side Display	Platform Dependent	Reporting and Analysis	
	Content Rendering			
	Wireless/Mobile/Voice			

Service Interface and Integration		
Integration	**Interoperability**	**Interface**
Middleware	Data Format/Classification	Service Discovery
Enterprise Application Integration	Data Types/Validation	Service Description/Interface
	Data Transformation	

DRM
Standardization
Areas

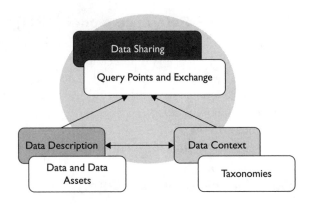

by which data can be described, categorized, and shared. This is reflected within each of the DRM's three standardization areas: data description, data context, and data sharing (see Figure 4.1-15).

The Federal Segment Architecture Methodology (FSAM)

The second major advance in FEAF development is the Federal Segment Architecture Methodology, or FSAM. In November 2007, the OMB published its FEA *Practice Guide*, which distinguished three levels relevant to EA: enterprise architecture, segment architecture, and solutions architecture. This document recognized the relationship of segments across different agencies and describes how a single agency may contain both core mission area segments and business service segments (Office of Management and Budget, 2007). The *Practice Guide* defines enterprise services as those crosscutting services that span multiple segments. Thus segments can be leveraged within an agency, across agencies, and across the entire government (see Figure 4.1-16) (FEA Practice Guide, pg 5).

The three levels of architecture identified by the *Practice Guide*—enterprise, segment, and solution—are distinguished from each other by the level of detail and the way in which they address related but different concerns (see Figure 4.1-17).

At its highest level, EA concerns all stakeholders and is presented at the most general level of detail. As EA is strategy-driven, it enables an agency to identify the alignment of its resources with mission, goals, and objectives. EA is used to drive decisions about IT investments and allows the traceability of business decisions to determine effects across the entire enterprise. As such, the primary stakeholders of EA are senior managers and executives "tasked with ensuring the agency fulfills its mission as effectively and efficiently as possible" (FEA Practice Guide, pg 5).

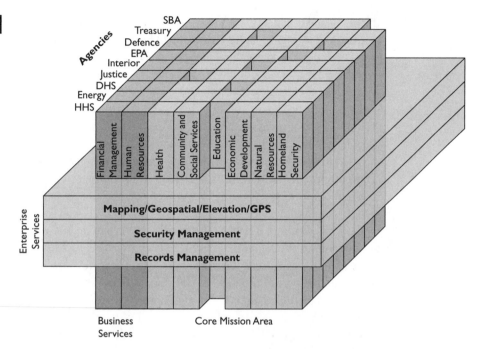

FIGURE 4.1-16

Federal Segment
Architecture
Methodology

The concept of segment architecture is used to define a roadmap for a specific core mission area, business service, or enterprise service. Segment architecture (SA) is driven by business management to deliver products to provide services to citizens and agency staff. Taken from the investment perspective, SA enables decision making for a business case or cases to support the core mission area or shared service. Consequently,

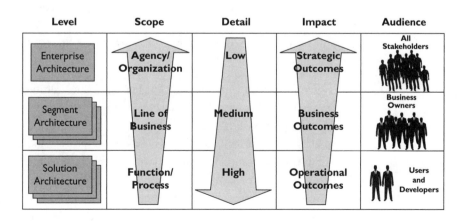

FIGURE 4.1-17

Enterprise,
Segment, and
Solution Levels
of FEA

the major stakeholders for SA are business owners and managers. The *Practice Guide* defines how segment architecture is related to EA through three principles: structure, reuse, and alignment. Segment architecture inherits the agency EA framework but may extend it to meet specific needs. It also reuses assets at the enterprise level such as data, business processes, investments, applications, and technologies. It also aligns with business strategies, mandates, standards, and performance goals at the enterprise level (Office of Management and Budget, 2007, pg 5).

Solution architecture defines IT assets such as applications or components that are used to automate and improve individual agency business functions. Hence, its scope is normally limited to a single project and is used to implement all or part of a system or business solution. The primary stakeholders for solution architecture are system users and developers.

Our concern in this book is the development of segment architecture and its relationship to the larger EA of which it is a part.

In January 2008, the Federal Segment Architecture Working Group (FSAWG) was created as part of the Federal CIO Council's Architecture and Infrastructure Committee (AIC) to develop an approach to create and use segment architectures. The FSAWG developed the FSAM, a step-by-step process that incorporates best practices from the federal EA community and provides templates to expedite architecture development and maximize architecture use.

The top level of FSAM has five process steps to "identify and validate the business need and scope of the architecture, define the performance improvement opportunities within the segment, and to define the target business, data, services, and technology architecture layers required to achieve the performance improvement opportunities" (FEA Practice Guide 2007, pg 2-7). The process steps conclude with a modernization blueprint that provides a transition-sequencing plan for using and implementing the segment architecture These top-level process steps are shown in Figure 4.1-18.

The following is an extended quote taken from the *Practice Guide* to describe these process steps:

1. *Determine participants and launch the project.* The architect leverages the guidance in this process step to engage with key stakeholders to establish the segment governance framework, validate the business owner(s) for the segment, formally appoint an executive sponsor and a core team, and establish the purpose statement to guide the architecture development. This process step also includes guidance for introducing a solid project management foundation for the segment architecture development effort with the creation of a project plan and communications strategy.

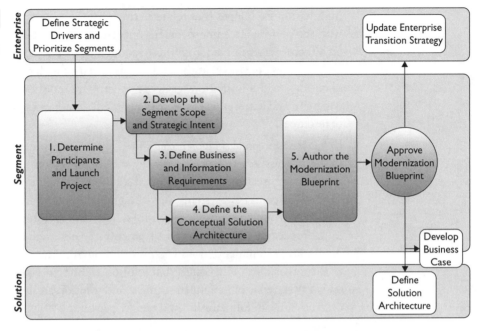

FIGURE 4.1-18

Top-Level Process
Steps for a
Modernization
Blueprint

2. *Define the segment scope and strategic intent.* The architect leverages the
   guidance in this process step to engage with key stakeholders to produce a
   segment scope and to define the strategic improvement opportunities for
   the segment. The architect then defines the segment strategic intent which
   consists of the target state vision, performance goals, and common/mission
   services and their target maturity levels. The subsequent FSAM process steps
   provide guidance for architects to align the architecture with the strategic
   intent to create a complete segment performance line-of-sight and to support
   achieving the target state vision.

3. *Define business and information requirements.* The architect leverages the
   guidance in this process step to engage with key stakeholders to analyze
   the segment business and information environments and determine the
   business and information improvement opportunities that will achieve the
   target performance architecture. Within this step, the architect begins by
   developing a broad, holistic view of the overall business and information
   requirements associated with the strategic improvement opportunities
   identified in the previous step. Information requirements include the

information exchanges that relate to the critical business processes associated with the performance improvement opportunities. The business and data architectures are derived from these requirements. The business and data architectures developed at the end of this step may include the specification of business and information services respectively, and should be sufficiently complete and actionable to result in more efficient processes and allocation of resources.

4. *Define the conceptual solution architecture.* The architect leverages the guidance in this process step to engage with key stakeholders to produce the conceptual solution architecture. The conceptual solution architecture is an integrated view of the combined systems, services, and technology architectures that support the target performance, business, and data architectures developed in the preceding process steps. This process step also includes guidance for developing recommendations for transitioning from the current (as-is) state to the target state. The conceptual solution architecture produced at the end of this step is of benefit to segment and solution architects as well as to downstream capital planning and budget personnel.

5. *Author the modernization blueprint.* The architect leverages outputs from previous process steps to engage with key stakeholders to create a segment architecture blueprint including sequencing and transition plans. The outcome of this process step is a series of validated implementation recommendations supported by holistic analysis of segment business, data, technology, systems, and service components. The modernization blueprint includes findings and recommendations as well as supporting artifacts and diagrams that illustrate the analysis performed throughout the architecture development process. For instance, artifacts such as the SWOT [Strengths, Weakness, Opportunities, and Threats] analysis and the conceptual solution architecture are key visuals in the modernization blueprint. Note that recommendations in the modernization blueprint typically span a strategic time horizon on the order of 3–5 years (Office of Management and Budget, 2007, pg 2-7).

Rapid Segment Architecture Methodology (RSAM)

What happens if there is an urgent need for segment architecture? In 2009, Mary Forbes, as Lead Architect of the Department of Health and Human Services,

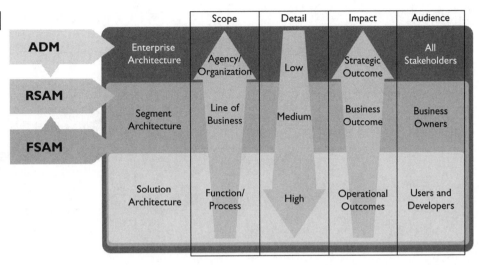

FIGURE 4.1-19

Rapid Segment Architecture Methodology

created the Rapid Segment Architecture Methodology, or RSAM. This initiative grew out of the Health and Human Services (HHS) Architecture Development Methodology (ADM),[1] which led to its being renamed as FSAM at the end of 2008. Then, in 2009, Forbes and her colleagues developed the Rapid approach to segment architecture "to quickly respond to pressing business needs with limited resources." Forbes situates the RSAM at the top of FSAM to denote a fast process that is part of a segment, as shown in Figure 4.1-19.

The intent of RSAM is to provide just enough architecture to address a pressing business need. In FSAM, the concept of segment is highly flexible, being scoped by a particular business need; a segment can be part of a larger FEA segment or may cut across multiple FEA segments. The RSAM leverages FSAM and is in no way opposed to it. This is expressed in the basic principles underlying its use:

- The RSAM must be consistent with the FSAM
- It must leverage the HHS EA repository.
- The methodology must be "just-in-time" architecture (in a matter of weeks or months, rather than quarters or years).

---

[1] This differs from the TOGAF ADM of the same name.

Mapping of RSAM
Against the FSAM

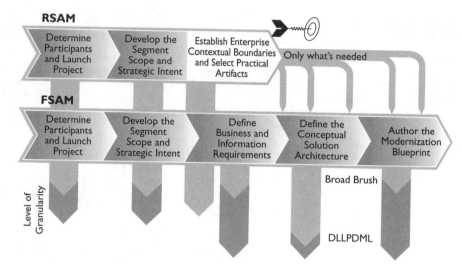

At a high level, the RSAM can be mapped against the FSAM as shown in Figure 4.1-20.

The RSAM is designed to allow enterprise architecture to be highly agile and adaptive.

The Future of EA in Government

As this book is being written, new advances are continually being discussed within the federal EA community. One current initiative is to develop a Unified Government EA Framework (UGEAF), for which a shared interest group (SIG) working group is being created. Another recent initiative is the Citizen Empowering Open Government program as a virtual, agile, and adaptive program for responding to citizen needs. The UGEAF "describes how citizens will be able to use data to create blended suites of government services to seamlessly navigate major "life events" (Tiemann, 2010, presentation to Industry Advisory Council).

These initiatives for EA would by their very nature be an ongoing process. There is a growing recognition of Gartner's description of emergent enterprise architecture, which captures the complexity of organizations and is consistent with the understanding that organizations are organic and adaptive mechanisms. EA is not a static picture, and the as-is state is really a more limited-perspective snapshot. Doing EA is always a moving target as enterprises, both governmental and nongovernmental, are continually adapting and in motion.

EA Assessment Tools

The U.S. government has two types of assessment tools related to EA. One is the EA Management Maturity Framework (EAMMF) from the Government Accountability Office (GAO). The other is the EA Assessment Framework (EAAF) from OMB. The EAMMF is designed for use by organizations to assess the management maturity of their EA processes. The EAAF is a reporting tool required for use by all federal agencies. Each of these assessment tools is reviewed briefly in the following subsections.

EAMMF

The governmental mandates such as the Clinger-Cohen Act and follow-up legislation triggered the development of mechanisms to measure the quality of agency enterprise architectures. This led the Office of Management and Budget to develop a maturity framework that involves a rating scale from red to green. This involved a tool for ranking utilized by the GAO and known by its acronym, EAMMF. This framework proffers a method for measuring progress toward the development of an acceptable EA within an agency and ways to take effective corrective action. In 2002, the first version of the EAMMF was developed, which contained three basic components: (1) hierarchical stages of management maturity; (2) categories of attributes that are vital to the successful management of projects; and (3) elements of EA management that formed the core of the Federal CIO Council's *Practical Guide to Enterprise Architecture.*

The EAMMF is composed of five stages of EA maturity,[2] each including elements contained in the previous stages. The first stage is to create EA awareness within an agency. At this stage, an organization may not have plans to develop and use an architecture or even show an awareness of its value. Some agencies may have initiated some EA activity, although these efforts are often ad hoc, unstructured, and lacking the leadership, direction, and management foundation required for successful EA development. In the second stage of maturity, the agency builds an EA management foundation. Here the organization recognizes EA as an asset and forms an executive body to establish accountability for it that represents the enterprise. At this stage, the organization begins to establish EA management roles and responsibilities and develops plans for creating EA products or models for measuring program progress and model quality. It also commits resources for developing an

[2] This section paraphrases the GAO Accountability Framework.

architecture in terms of resources, processes, and tools. This includes the designation of a Chief Architect and staffing a program office for EA development and maintenance, as well as creating an initial governance structure. The organization now has developed EA models and a general awareness of the value of EA along with its use in the management of IT investments.

In the third stage, the organization is focused on developing EA models according to a selected framework and is utilizing a methodology and an EA tool. At this point, the scope of the architecture has been defined and encompasses the entire enterprise, such that it describes the organization in business, performance, information, data, service, application, and technology. Also at this stage there is a clearly defined baseline, or as-is and to-be states, and a transitional architecture or plan for reaching the enterprise's goals. The organization is also practicing configuration management and measuring its progress.

In the fourth stage, the EA has completed its first iteration of EA products. These products have been approved by a steering committee established in the governance plan developed in stage two or by some other authority. In the fifth stage, EA is leveraged to manage change. Now the organization has secured senior approval of its EA products or models and there is a formal institutional policy established that mandates that IT investments must comply with the architecture. That is, IT investments are made in terms of EA and there is a tracking of business processes on the IT infrastructure of the enterprise.

EAAF

OMB requires federal agencies to report EA information using the EAAF. OMB uses this information in the analysis and selection of IT initiatives and investments during the federal budgeting process. The EAAF has evolved over time as OMB has increased its EA reporting requirements and the framework may evolve further in the future. The assessment criteria of EAAF Version 3.1 focus on EA completion, use, and results. These criteria are quite specific and require documented proof of achievement.

For EA completion, the criteria address the characteristics of the Target Enterprise Architecture and Enterprise Transition Plan, architecture prioritization, and scope of completion and inclusion of Internet Protocol Version 6 (IPv6). For example, the Target Enterprise Architecture and Enterprise Transition Plan should include performance goals and transition milestones so that progress can be monitored.

For EA use, the criteria address performance improvement integration; CPIC integration; FEA Reference Model and Exhibit 53 mapping, collaboration, and reuse; and EA governance, program management, change management, and deployment. Exhibit 53 is part of the budget submission process (as described in OMB Circular A-11). Exhibit 53 and Exhibit 300 from A-11 require EA information.

For EA results, the criteria address mission performance, cost savings and avoidance, and measurement of the EA program's value. OMB seeks to understand how agencies are using their EA to drive program performance improvement, manage cost, and support decision making.

Questions

1. What is the basis for governmental mandates for doing enterprise architecture?
2. What is the relationship among the NIST, TEAF, and the FEAF frameworks?
3. How is the Zachman Framework used as a reference architecture for the different governmental frameworks?
4. How does the ADM of the TOGAF compare with the FEAF Enterprise Architecture Development lifecycle?
5. What is the rationale for the formation of the OMB Federal Enterprise Architecture Reference Models?
6. Why are the OMB FEA Reference Models not an architecture framework?
7. What is meant by the concept of "line of sight" and where does the line end in the PRM?
8. How does the relationship of SRM to business functions provide for reuse of applications, application capabilities, components, and business services?
9. What would be an example of a sub-function for a line of business within the BRM?
10. What does the alignment of agency capital investments to the TRM allow for in terms of interagency collaboration and interoperability?
11. What does the Data Reference Model provide for and how does it facilitate the sharing of data across agency boundaries?
12. What is the relationship of segments in FSAM to enterprise architecture?
13. How does RSAM relate to FSAM and what is it place within it?

Reference List

CIO Council. (2007). *FEA consolidated Reference Model Version 2.3*. Federal
   Government Document.

CIO Officer Council. (2000). *Treasury Enterprise Architecture Framework, Version 1*.

Government Accountability Office. (2003). *Information technology: a framework for
   assessing and improving enterprise architecture management (V1.1)*. www.gao
   .gov/new.items/d03584g.pdf.

Government Accountability Office. (2010). *A framework for assessing and improving
   enterprise architecture management (version 2.0)*. GAO-10-846G. U.S. Federal
   Government Publication.

Office of Management and Budget. (2007). *FEA Practice Guide*. U.S. Federal
   Government Publication.

Office of Management and Budget. (2009). Improving agency performance using
   information and information technology (Enterprise Architecture Assessment
   Framework v3.1). www.whitehouse.gov/omb/e-gov/eaaf.

Office of Management and Budget. (2010). OMB Circular A-11: preparation,
   submission, and execution of the budget. http://www.whitehouse.gov/omb/
   circulars_a11_current_year_a11_toc.

U.S. Department of the Treasury Chief Information Officer Council. (2000).
   Treasury Enterprise Architecture Framework Version 1. July 2000.

Zachman, John. (1987). A framework for information systems architecture. *IBM
   Systems Journal*, Number 3, Page 27.

4.2

Enterprise Architecting in Defense

The United States Defense Department is arguably one of the largest enterprises in the world. As a complex, global, highly structured organization created by law, driven by doctrine, policy, and regulations, and managed under standard operating procedures and regulations, it also naturally lends itself to the use of explicit, documented architecture patterns and the application of architecture work universally to benefit activities and processes.

The DoD Enterprise

The Department of Defense is headed by the Secretary of Defense, a cabinet member of the Executive Branch of government on par with other cabinet departments such as the Department of State, Department of Agriculture, Department of Energy, Department of Interior, and Department of Commerce, to name a few. As a cabinet-level agency, the DoD is committed to and bound by the same enterprise architecture policy directives and requirements that the Office of Management and Budget imposes on all federal agencies—the need to support the position of a CIO, develop enterprise architecture, and use the enterprise architecture to justify initiatives and investments. At the same time, because of the nature of its business, the DoD also has a different priority for the use of architecture than the information technology (IT) focus promoted by the need of federal agencies to comply with the Clinger-Cohen IT Management Reforms Act. Spending in the DoD on Automated Information System (AIS) IT is significantly smaller than the investment in weapons systems such as aircraft carriers, battleships, fighter aircraft, and armored land vehicles. However, these weapon systems are increasingly dependent on embedded IT that supports such functions as command and control, communications, targeting, and avionics. Interoperability among all the weapons systems and their IT is a major issue for DoD as is the match among the weapons systems, military forces, and doctrine.

By law, the warfighting branches of the DoD must exist separately from the branches responsible for readiness—those that train, equip, and organize warfighting forces. Warfighting forces are organized into the unified combat commands, but are recruited, organized, trained, and equipped by the military services: the Army, Air Force, Navy, and Marine Corps. The operational responsibility for conducting military responsibilities rests with the Joint Forces whereas the acquisition of supplies, materiel, and information technology in the form of systems, services, networks, and communications rests with the individual military services.

Enterprise Challenges

Arguably the biggest challenge facing the DoD is the ability to conduct two simultaneous, major, multiyear wars in Afghanistan and Iraq while staying ready to deal with threats from other major world powers and also from terrorist threats to U.S. soil. As a result of lessons learned in battle, a number of capabilities that were not on the radar are becoming increasingly important. For example, the capability to withstand explosions from improvised explosive devices (IEDs) is critical for armored deployed vehicles in Iraq and Afghanistan. To sustain an ongoing battle, the DoD has had to retrofit armored vehicles currently on the battlefield with plates to deflect IED explosions. A warfighting enterprise such as the DoD is always faced with constantly changing threats that it must absorb and adapt to. In this regard, the DoD is not unlike a commercial enterprise that is always facing competitive threats that must be addressed, faced, and overcome. Lessons from current wars are coming fast and furiously. Each of these lessons must be converted into an action plan that addresses the issues caused by capability gaps. Architecture is a fundamental ingredient of the knowledge needed to be able to develop a course of action.

Asymmetrical warfare, such as that being waged by the enemy in Afghanistan and Iraq and by terrorists worldwide, tends to take advantage of the highly structured processes of U.S. and coalition forces and predictable patterns that emerge from architected operations. Process-modeling techniques originally developed by the Air Force—such as Observe-Orient-Decide-Act (OODA) —are effective in situations where a process has to constantly adapt to changing situations. In OODA, the next process step is constantly computed in a loop that is comprised of the following steps: Observe, Orient, Decide, and Act (see Figure 4.2-1).

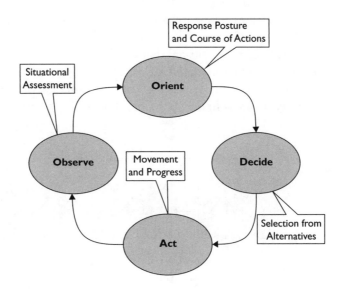

FIGURE 4.2-1

Observe-Orient-Decide-Act (OODA) Loop

Contrast OODA that is situation-driven against traditional plan-driven activity that roughly follows the pattern shown in Figure 4.2-2.

The difference with OODA is that the process is constantly adapting to a changing situation. For OODA to be successful, the length of the total loop must be shorter than the duration of situational changes; otherwise, the orientation, decision making, and actions may not be consistent with a changed situation.

Architecture provides the patterns that planners need to analyze—differences between business process patterns that supply troops in the theater with ammunition, equipment, and warfighting processes that are based on situation assessment, course of action alternatives, decisions, and action.

Interoperability has always been a challenge—aggravated by the division of responsibility between the Joint Staff and the military departments and further amplified by procurement of equipment, weapons, materiel, and capabilities in the form of programs that tend to be stovepipes themselves. This lack of interoperability is manifested in radios that don't talk to each other; multiple terminals on a desk, one for each system; or multiple communication networks, each of them supporting different systems that are all supposed to assist the same operational activity. Over the years, many of the interoperability challenges at the systems and infrastructure level have been identified, addressed, and overcome. The emergence of a few dominant standards that are globally applicable, including in the commercial marketplace, has significantly reduced technology-related interoperability issues. The ubiquity of computing, mobile applications, and information interchange has also provided impetus for DoD leveraging IT. Unfortunately, ubiquity of technology also eliminates competitive advantage, as adversaries also have access to the same technologies.

The largest leap forward that the DoD has taken is the move toward net-centric operations and warfare (NCOW). This leap forward is based on ubiquitous access to information and service assets by any warfighter or warfighting system worldwide through a Global Information Grid (GIG). This ambitious plan has many components

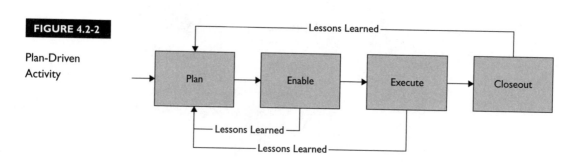

FIGURE 4.2-2

Plan-Driven
Activity

that need to be aligned before the vision can become a reality. The move to net-centricity is a logical evolution of widespread data access as demonstrated by the World Wide Web and the widespread access to web services—also demonstrated in mobile applications today and in the service-oriented architectures (SOAs) that enterprises are embracing.

Cyber attacks on the information infrastructure are increasingly a threat. The ability to access computer networks without a physical presence requires new forms of information warfare. The DoD is adapting to recognize and address cyber warfare as another form of warfare where the objective is to have the enemy destroy itself through its own information infrastructure. With increasing reliance on the U.S. infrastructure—such as the power grid, telephone network, manufacturing automation, and transportation on networks of computers and software for command and control—the magnitude of cyber threats cannot be underestimated. On the other side of the coin, the ability to wage cyber attacks is a competitive advantage in strikes against enemies.

Increasingly complex technology provides tremendous advantages. For example, a Beyond Line of Sight (BLOS) strike involves targeting an enemy that is beyond the horizon—he or she cannot even see the strike coming. Unmanned aerial, submarine, and surface vehicles provide tremendous potential for lethal weapons delivery with risks of loss of life for the United States. But incorporating this complexity into weapons systems increases the complexity of planning, the breadth of options, the impacts to be considered, and even changes in doctrine and policy and tactics, techniques, and procedures (TTPs) to accommodate a change in the style of fighting introduced by technology changes. The use of architecture to support planning the acquisition of very complex systems and then assisting the contractor in trade-offs and implementation issues is essential for the success of weapons acquisition programs.

Enterprise Initiatives

We will cover a few initiatives to provide a sense of the kinds of transformations that the Department of Defense is undergoing, driven by technology-driven opportunities such as unmanned aerial vehicles, lessons learned from ongoing wars, and strategic changes in doctrine, to cite a few drivers.

Net-Centric Warfare

Arguably, one of the most far-reaching transformational initiatives undertaken by the U.S. Department of Defense is the concept of net-centric warfare. DoD recognizes that today's weapons systems and warfighters are powered by information that makes them effective and lethal to the enemy. Net-centric warfare connects information providers to information consumers through an information grid, called the Global Information Grid. The purpose of the information grid is to deliver high-quality and timely information required by a weapons system or a warfighter through a process of search and discovery that is transparent to the information supplier and driven by warfighting needs.

NCES Overview Presentation: Net-Centric Enterprise Services (NCES) (Defense Information Services Agency, 2010) describes the DoD Net-Centric Data Strategy, issued by the DoD CIO May 9, 2003. Figure 4.2-3 shows the plan for the department's information resources.

One of the big changes with NCES is the shift from producer-centric information distribution, where a consumer of information is required to know who has the information and be able to request it from them, to consumer-centric information, where producers advertise the availability of information and the services that can be used to access that information (see Figure 4.2-4). With this approach, consumers can help themselves to the information they need to support their specific mission (with security safeguards and appropriate entitlement and access controls).

The planned move to a user-centric, net-centric operational environment has been the impetus for the Service Viewpoint in the Department of Defense Architecture Framework (DoDAF). The SvcV provides the ability to model the desired service-based environment, and together with the other viewpoints provides

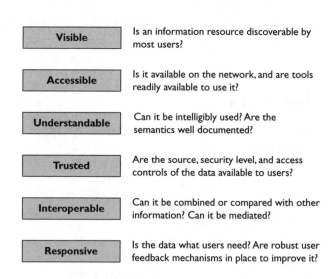

FIGURE 4.2-3

DoD Net-Centric Strategy

Visible — Is an information resource discoverable by most users?

Accessible — Is it available on the network, and are tools readily available to use it?

Understandable — Can it be intelligibly used? Are the semantics well documented?

Trusted — Are the source, security level, and access controls of the data available to users?

Interoperable — Can it be combined or compared with other information? Can it be mediated?

Responsive — Is the data what users need? Are robust user feedback mechanisms in place to improve it?

FIGURE 4.2-4   Shift from Producer-Centric to Consumer-Centric Information

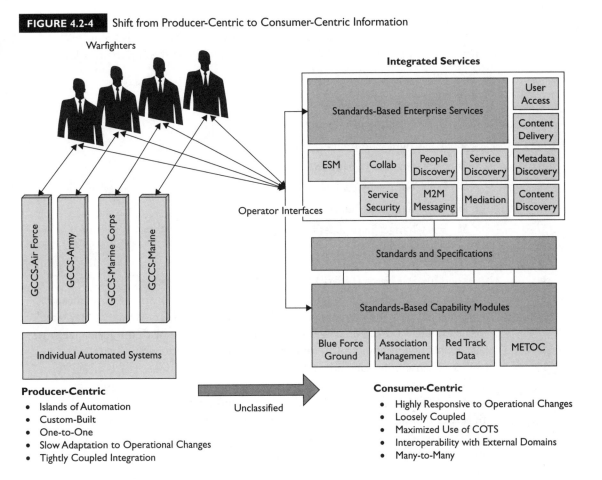

a holistic way to represent and plan for a transformation that cuts across changes in operations, guidance, warfighting strategy, procurement of information and weapons systems, and the way that information will be used in the DoD to power the warfighting mission.

Unmanned Platforms and Weapons Systems

In the area of warfighting materiel—weapons systems, platforms, and equipment—the DoD is making a fundamental shift toward unmanned vehicles—in land, air, sea surface, and subsurface conditions. The use of remotely piloted vehicles (RPVs) provides a significant combat advantage and should reduce U.S. casualties. Development of a materiel acquisition strategy based on RPV also requires changes in other aspects of the military organize, train, and equip the mission focus, DOTMLPF-P, which stand for the following:

- D = *Doctrinal* changes
- O = *Organizational* changes
- T = Changes in *training*
- M = Changes in *materiel*
- L = Changes in *leadership*
- P = Changes in *personnel*
- F = Changes in *facilities*
- P = Changes in *policy*

The U.S. Air Force (USAF) UAS Flight Plan (Headquarters, United States Air Force, 2009) describes a family of unmanned aircraft consisting of small, man-portable vehicles, including micro- and man-sized vehicles, medium "fighter-sized" vehicles, large "tanker-sized" vehicles, and special vehicles with unique capabilities, all capable of autonomous (no human in the loop) operations that include the ability to sense, infer, and adapt to changing battle conditions. The concept is to build a common set of airframes within a family of systems with interoperable, modular, "plug-and-play" payloads, with standard interfaces, that can be tailored to fit one or more USAF core functions in support of the Joint Forces' priorities.

Planning and effecting these changes involves looking at DOTMLPF-P in an integrated manner, using the DoD Architecture Framework and a model-based approach.

Asymmetrical Warfare

For most of the second half of the twentieth century, America's primary enemy was the Soviet Union and its satellite states. During the cold war, the two major powers trained, organized, and equipped with a relatively sure knowledge of each other's capabilities and recognized the need for deterrence as a way to avoid waging costly, large-scale wars. In the twenty-first century, after the collapse of the Soviet Union, the United States is arguably the last surviving superpower. The wars of today are fought against enemies with vastly inferior technology and mobilization capabilities that are nevertheless still lethal and long-lived, as the wars in Afghanistan and Iraq have proven. The ability to reflect on cold war capabilities and reposition and retool them for asymmetric warfare is an architectural exercise.

DoD Architecting Levels

The DoD Architecture Framework (Department of Defense, 2009) describes the various scopes and purposes for different levels of architecting throughout the Department of Defense (see Figure 4.2-5).

Figure 4.2-5 describes core decision-making activities on the left side. Planning at the level of the Office of the Secretary of Defense (OSD) is performed with department-level architecture. This is called the DoD Enterprise Architecture. The DoD EA supports OSD in making decisions regarding planning. Each of the component military departments (the Air Force, Army, Navy, and Marine Corps) also has its own department-level (component) architecture.

FIGURE 4.2-5 DoD Processes and Architecting Levels (Department of Defense, 2009)

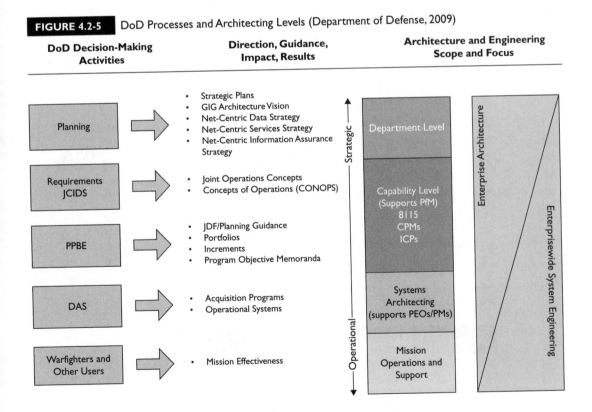

Capability-level (segment) architectures are produced to represent joint mission threads that expose capability needs and display capability use in multiservice joint operations. Capability-level architectures are used to build operational concepts that tie together multiservice tasks, systems, and services in support of a common mission.

Capabilities are also used to analyze and determine the requirements for systems and services that are needed to support joint mission threads. The Joint Capabilities Identification and Development System (JCIDS) is the DoD business process for identifying, elaborating, and prioritizing capability needs in the context of the department's warfighting needs and warfighting-support needs.

Capability-level architectures are also used to support Planning, Programming, Budgeting, and Execution (PPBE). Programs are units of allocated moneys that are intended to deliver specific stated capabilities.

The systems architecting level is used to support the acquisition of specific systems, families of systems, or system of systems. These include automated information systems (AIS) as well as weapons systems and systems comprised of people, equipment, and materiel as well. The Defense Acquisition System (DAS) is a formal, milestone-based process for acquisition and sustainment of systems. An acquisition program is a unit of acquisition that has already been allocated resources and is intended to acquire a system and all other configuration items related to a system.

Mission operations and support architectures are "fit-for-purpose" architectures used to represent, understand, and analyze a specific military operation or collection of support activities for a variety of purposes, such as improving operational efficiency, understanding bottlenecks, streamlining use of resources, and more.

In earlier chapters, we introduced the three levels of architecting as enterprise, segment, and solution. Table 4.2-1 shows the mapping of the DoD levels of architecting to these three fundamental levels.

Table 4.2-1 also shows that as we descend down the architecting levels (that is, as we move from planning to solution building), we start transitioning from enterprise architecture to system engineering.

TABLE 4.2-1 Mapping Between the Standard Architecting Levels and the DoD Levels

Level	DoD Level of Architecting
Enterprise	DoD EA, component EAs
Segment	Capability architectures
Solution	Systems architectures, mission architectures

DoD Architecture Framework

Earlier chapters covered in fair detail the DoDAF. The stated purpose of the DoDAF is as follows:

"The Department of Defense Architecture Framework (DoDAF), Version 2.0 serves as the overarching, comprehensive framework and conceptual model enabling the development of architectures to facilitate the ability of Department of Defense (DoD) managers at all levels to make key decisions more effectively through organized information sharing across the Department, Joint Capability Areas (JCAs), Mission, Component, and Program boundaries. The DoDAF serves as one of the principal pillars supporting the DoD Chief Information Officer (CIO) in his responsibilities for development and maintenance of architectures required under the Clinger-Cohen Act. It also reflects guidance from the Office of Management and Budget (OMB) Circular A-130, and other Departmental directives and instructions" (Department of Defense, 2009, pg ES-1).

The vision for utilization of DoDAF is to accomplish the following:

- Provide an overarching set of architecture concepts, guidance, best practices, and methods to enable and facilitate architecture development in support of major decision processes across all major departmental programs, military components, and capability areas that is consistent and complementary to Federal Enterprise Architecture Guidance as provided by OMB.

- Support the DoD CIO in defining and institutionalizing the Net-Centric Data Strategy (NCDS) and NCSS of the department, to include the definition, description, development, and execution of services through the introduction of service-oriented architecture (SOA) development.

- Focus on architectural data as information required for making critical decisions rather than emphasizing individual architecture products. DoDAF is to enable architects to provide visualizations of the derived information through combinations of DoDAF-described models, and fit-for-purpose views commonly used by decision makers, allowing flexibility to develop those views consistent with the culture and preferences of the organization.

- Provide methods and suggest techniques through which information architects and other developers can create architectures responsive to and supporting departmental management practices.

It is not the purpose of the DoDAF to define any of the following:

- Prescriptive models
- Prescriptive methodologies
- Prescriptive tools

DoD Business Processes Supported by the DoDAF

The Department of Defense has three principal decision-making support systems, all of which have been significantly revised over the past few years. These systems are the following:

- **Planning, Programming, Budgeting, and Execution (PPBE) process**
  The department's strategic planning, program development, and resource determination process. The PPBE process is used to craft plans and programs that satisfy the demands of the national security strategy within resource constraints.

- **Joint Capabilities Integration and Development System (JCIDS)**
  The systematic method established by the Chairman of the Joint Chiefs of Staff for identifying, assessing, and prioritizing gaps in joint warfighting capabilities and recommending potential solution approaches to resolve these gaps. CJCS Instruction 3170.01 and the *JCIDS Manual* describe the policies and procedures for the requirements process.

- **Defense Acquisition System (DAS)**
  The DAS is the management process by which the department acquires weapon systems and automated information systems. Although the system is based on centralized policies and principles, it allows for decentralized and streamlined execution of acquisition activities. This approach provides flexibility and encourages innovation while maintaining strict emphasis on discipline and accountability.

Figure 4.2-6 shows how the three systems, their oversight, and regulations provide an integrated approach to strategic planning, identification of needs for military capabilities, systems acquisition, and program and budget development:

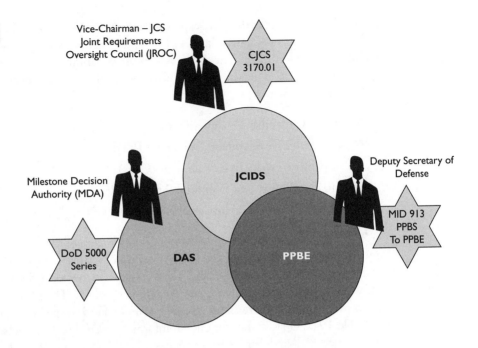

FIGURE 4.2-6

Governance and
DoD Processes

JCIDS and Capability-Based Assessment (JCIDS/CBA)

The primary objective of the JCIDS process is to ensure the capabilities required
by the joint warfighters to execute successfully the missions assigned to them are
identified together with their operational performance criteria. This is done through
an open process that provides the Joint Requirements Oversight Council (JROC)
the information it needs to make decisions on required capabilities. The requirements
process supports the acquisition process by providing validated capability needs and
associated performance criteria to be used as a basis for acquiring the right weapon
systems (Joint Staff, 2007; Defense Acquisition University, 2010).

Additionally, JCIDS provides the PPBE process with affordability advice supported
by the capabilities-based assessment (CBA) and identifies capability gaps and potential
materiel and nonmaterial solutions.

Interoperability and Supportability for Information Technology (IT) and National Security Systems (NSS)

Chairman of the Joint Chiefs of Staff Instruction (CJCSI) 6212.10E Interoperability
and Supportability for Information Technology and National Security Systems is

the guidance that links the JCIDS process and the DoDAF views for solution-level architectures. This document lays out the requirements for the views that need to be included in the key documents to support Interoperability and Supportability (I&S) certification decision making at key milestones in the JCIDS process. The following are the key documents:

- Initial Capability Document (ICD)
- Capability Development Document (CDD)
- Capability Production Document (CPD)
- Interoperability and Supportability Plan (ISP)
- Tailored Interoperability and Supportability Plan (TISP)

Table 4.2-2 lists the DoDAF views required for each of these documents. As the note in the figure points out, the DoDAF terminology used in the figure is that of DoDAF version 1.5. The TV-1 and TV-2 views from version 1.5 translate into the StdV-1 and StdV-2, respectively, in DoDAF version 2.0. The OV-7 and SV-11 views from version 1.5 translate into DIV-2 and DIV-3, respectively, in version 2.0. In Table 4.2-2, GTG stands for Global Information Grid (GIG) Technical Guidance (GTG) and IA stands for Information Assurance. One emphasis in these required views is on external interfaces because interoperability is a focus of the analysis to be supported.

Planning, Programming, Budgeting, and Execution (PPBE)

The purpose of the PPBE process is to allocate resources within the Department of Defense (Defense Acquisition University, 2010). It is important for program managers and their staffs to be aware of the nature and timing of each of the events in the PPBE process, because they may be called upon to provide critical information that could be important to program funding and success. In the PPBE process, the Secretary of Defense establishes policies, strategy, and prioritized goals for the department, which is subsequently used to guide resource allocation decisions that balance the guidance with fiscal constraints. The PPBE process consists of four distinct but overlapping phases; each described in the following subsections.

Planning

The planning phase of PPBE is a collaborative effort by the Office of the Secretary of Defense and the Joint Staff in coordination with DoD components. It begins

TABLE 4.2-2   DoDAF View Requirements for JCIDS Documents

Document	Supportability Compliance	DoD Enterprise Architecture Products (IAW DODAF) (see Note 5)																Data/Service Exposure Sheets	IA Compliance	GTG Compliance
		AV-1/AV-2	OV-1	OV-2	OV-3	OV-4	OV-5	OV-6C	OV-7	SV-1	SV-2	SV-4	SV-5	SV-6	SV-11	TV-1	TV-2			
ICD			X																		
CDD	X	3	X	X	X	X	X	X			X	X	X	X		2	2	1	X	X
CPD	X	3	X	X	X	X	X	X	1		X	X	X	X	1	2	2	1	X	X
ISP	X	3	X	X	X	X	X	X	4		X	X	X	X	4	2	2	1	X	X
TISP	X	3	X		X		X	X		X			X	X		2	2	1	X	X
ISP Annex (Svcs/Apps)	X	3	X				X				X	X	X	X		2	2	1	X	X

X: Required (PM needs to check with their Component for any additional architectural/regulatory requirements for CDDs, CPDs, ISPs/TISPs. (e.g., HQDA requires the SV-10c)).
Note 1: Required only when IT and NSS collects, processes, or uses any shared data or when IT and NSS exposes, consumes, or implements shared services.
Note 2: The TV-1 and TV-2 are built using the DISRonline and must be posted for compliance.
Note 3: The AV-1 must be uploaded onto DARS and must be registered in DARS for compliance.
Note 4: Only required for Milestone C, if applicable (see Note 1).
Note 5: The naming of the architecture views is expected to change with the release of DODAF v2.0 (e.g., StdV, SvcV, StdV, DIV). The requirements of this matrix will not change.

with a resource-informed articulation of national defense policies and military strategy known as the Guidance for the Development of the Force (GDF). The GDF is used to lead the overall planning process. This process results in fiscally constrained guidance and priorities—for military forces, modernization, readiness, and sustainability—and supports business processes and infrastructure activities for program development in a document known as the Joint Programming Guidance. The Joint Programming Guidance is the link between planning and programming, and it provides guidance to the DoD components (military departments and defense agencies) for the development of their program proposals, known as the Program Objective Memorandum (POM).

Programming

The programming phase begins with the development of a POM by each DoD component. This development seeks to construct a balanced set of programs that respond to the guidance and priorities of the Joint Programming Guidance within fiscal constraints. When completed, the POM provides a fairly detailed and comprehensive description of the proposed programs, including a time-phased allocation of resources (forces, funding, and manpower) by program projected six years into the future. In addition, the DoD component may describe important programs not fully funded (or not funded at all) in the POM and assess the risks associated with the shortfalls. The senior leadership in OSD and the Joint Staff review each POM to help integrate the DoD component POMs into an overall coherent defense program. In addition, the OSD staff and the Joint Staff can raise issues with selected portions of any POM, or any funding shortfalls in the POM, and propose alternatives with marginal adjustments to resources. Issues not resolved at lower levels are forwarded to the Secretary for decision, and the resulting decisions are documented in the Program Decision Memorandum.

Budgeting

The budgeting phase of PPBE occurs concurrently with the programming phase; each DoD component submits its proposed budget estimate simultaneously with its POM. The budget converts the programmatic view into the format of the congressional appropriation structure, along with associated budget justification documents. The budget projects resources only two years into the future, but with considerably more financial details than the POM. Upon submission, each budget estimate is reviewed by analysts from the office of the Under Secretary of Defense (Comptroller) and the Office of Management and Budget (OMB). Their review ensures that programs are funded in accordance with current financial policies and are properly and reasonably priced. The review also ensures that the budget documentation is adequate to justify the programs presented to the Congress. Typically, the analysts provide the DoD components with written questions in advance of formal hearings, where the analysts review and discuss the budget details. After the hearings, each analyst prepares a decision document (known as a Program Budget Decision, or PBD) for the programs and/or appropriations under his or her area of responsibility. The PBD proposes financial adjustments to address any issues or problems identified during the associated budget hearing. The PBDs are staffed for comment and forwarded to the Deputy Secretary of Defense for decisions. These decisions are then reflected in an updated budget submission provided to the OMB. After that, the overall DoD budget is provided as part of the President's budget request to the Congress.

Execution

The execution review occurs simultaneously with the program and budget reviews. This review provides feedback to the senior leadership concerning the effectiveness of current and prior resource allocations. Over time, metrics are being developed to support the execution review that will measure actual output versus planned performance for defense programs. To the extent that performance goals of an existing program are not being met, the execution review may lead to recommendations to adjust resources and/or restructure programs to achieve desired performance goals.

Defense Acquisition System (DAS)

The Defense Acquisition System is the management process for all DoD acquisition programs (Defense Acquisition University, 2010). DODI 5000.01, "Defense Acquisition System," provides the policies and principles that govern defense acquisition (Department of Defense, 2008a). DODI 5000.02, "Operation of the Defense Acquisition System," establishes the management framework that implements these policies and principles (Department of Defense, 2008b). Key aspects of the DAS include the following:

- The Defense Acquisition Management System is an event-based or "stage-gated" process. Acquisition programs proceed through a series of milestone reviews and other decision points that may authorize entry into a significant new program phase.

- One key principle of the Defense Acquisition System is the use of acquisition categories (ACAT), where programs of increasing dollar value and management interest are subject to increasing levels of oversight. The most expensive programs are known as Major Defense Acquisition Programs (MDAPs) or Major Automated Information System (MAIS) programs. MDAPs and MAIS programs have the most extensive statutory and regulatory reporting requirements.

- Some elements of the Defense Acquisition System apply only to weapon systems, some elements apply only to automated information systems, and some elements apply to both.

Figure 4.2-7 shows the Defense Acquisition Management System (Department of Defense, 2008a, 2008b) for materiel acquisition. The process assumes that a materiel

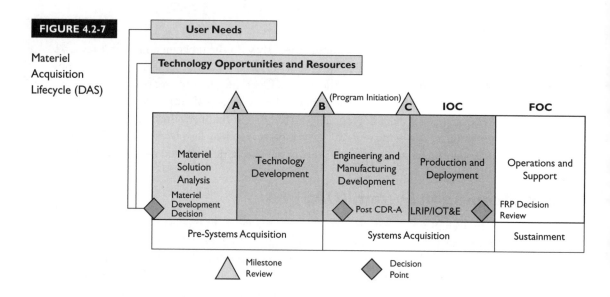

FIGURE 4.2-7

Materiel
Acquisition
Lifecycle (DAS)

solution has been determined necessary and that the user's need cannot be met by
nonmaterial DOTMLPF changes.

Systems Engineering Process (SE)

Numerous definitions of systems engineering exist. DoD has adopted the following
formal definition, derived from EIA/IS 632, "Processes for Engineering a System":
"Systems engineering is an interdisciplinary approach encompassing the entire
technical effort to evolve and verify an integrated and total life cycle balanced
set of system, people, and process solutions that satisfy customer needs. Systems
engineering is the integrating mechanism across the technical efforts related to the
development, manufacturing, verification, deployment, operations, support, disposal
of, and user training for systems and their life cycle processes. Systems engineering
develops technical information to support the program management decision-
making process" (Defense Acquisition University, 2011).

For DoD, systems engineering is the set of overarching processes that a program
team applies to develop an operationally effective and suitable system for a stated
capability need. Systems engineering processes apply across the acquisition lifecycle
(adapted to each phase) and serve as a mechanism for integrating capability needs,
design considerations, design constraints, and risk, as well as limitations imposed

by technology, budget, and schedule. The systems engineering processes should be applied during concept definition and then continuously throughout the lifecycle.

Systems engineering is a broad topic that includes hardware, software, and human systems. It is an interdisciplinary approach for a structured, disciplined, and documented technical effort to design and develop systems products and processes simultaneously for creating and integrating systems (hardware, software, and human) to satisfy the operational needs of the customer. It transforms needed operational capabilities into an integrated system design through concurrent consideration of all lifecycle needs.

As systems become larger and more complex, the design, development, and production of such systems or systems of systems (SoS) require the integration of numerous activities and processes. Systems engineering is the approach to coordinating and integrating all these acquisition lifecycle activities. It integrates diverse technical management processes to achieve an integrated systems design.

The systems engineering process is interlocked with the events in the DAS, as shown in Figure 4.2-8.

Portfolio Management (PfM)

DoDD 8115 (Assistant Secretary of Defense for Networks and Information Integration/ Department of Defense Chief Information Officer, 2005) establishes policy and assigns responsibilities for the management of DoD IT investments as portfolios that focus on improving DoD capabilities and mission outcomes.

IT investments are to be managed as portfolios to ensure that IT investments support the department's vision, mission, and goals; to ensure efficient and effective delivery of capabilities to the warfighter; and maximize return on investment to the enterprise. Each portfolio is to be managed using the GIG architecture plans, risk management techniques, capability goals and objectives, and performance measures.

Portfolios are to be nested and integrated at the enterprise, mission area, and component levels. The enterprise portfolio is divided into mission area portfolios, which are defined as warfighting, business, DoD portion of intelligence, and Enterprise Information Environment. Mission area and component portfolios may be divided into subportfolios (for example, domains) or capability areas that represent common collections of related, or highly dependent, information capabilities and services.

Portfolios are to be used as a management tool in each of the department's decision support systems, including the JCIDS, PPBE system, and DAS. Mission area leads are to provide portfolio recommendations to the appropriate officials for consideration in the department's decision-support systems.

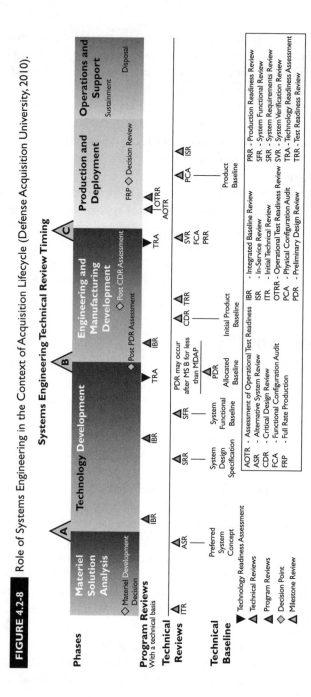

FIGURE 4.2-8 Role of Systems Engineering in the Context of Acquisition Lifecycle (Defense Acquisition University, 2010).

DoD Enterprise Architecture Examples

It is difficult to present moving targets inside a printed book. We will present a few examples of architecting within the Department of Defense realm to present a sense of the manner in which the architectures have been developed as well as to provide insight into their scopes. We will point the reader to references and other DoD resources for the latest versions of these architectures.

DoD EA

The DoD EA is an architectural description that is an enterprise asset used to assess alignment with the missions of the DoD enterprise, to strengthen customer support, to support capability PfM, and to ensure that operational goals and strategies are met. The DoD EA is shown in Figure 4.2-9.

The DoD EA is comprised of DoD architecture policy, tools, and standards; DoD-level architectural descriptions such as the DoD Information Enterprise Architecture (DoD IEA); DoD-level capability architectural descriptions; and component architectural descriptions. Its purposes are to guide investment portfolio strategies and decisions, define capability and interoperability requirements, provide access to segment architecture information, establish and enforce standards, guide security and information assurance requirements across the Department of Defense, and provide a sound basis for transitioning from the existing DoD environment to the future. The DoD EA is a federation of architectural descriptions to which solution architectural descriptions must conform. Its content includes but is not limited to rules, standards, services, and systems lifecycle information needed to optimize and maintain a process, or part of a process that a self-sufficient organization wants to create and maintain by managing its IT portfolio. The DoD EA provides a strategy that enables the organization to support its current operations while serving as the roadmap for transitioning to its target environment. Transition processes include an organization's PfM, PPBE, and EA planning processes, along with services and systems lifecycle methodologies.

The JCA portfolios describe future, required operational, warfighting, business, and defense intelligence capabilities together with the systems and services required. They provide the organizing construct for aligning and federating DoD EA content to support the department's PfM structure. The description of the future DoD operating environment and associated capability requirements represent the target architecture of the DoD EA. These are time-phased as determined by functional owners and JCA developers.

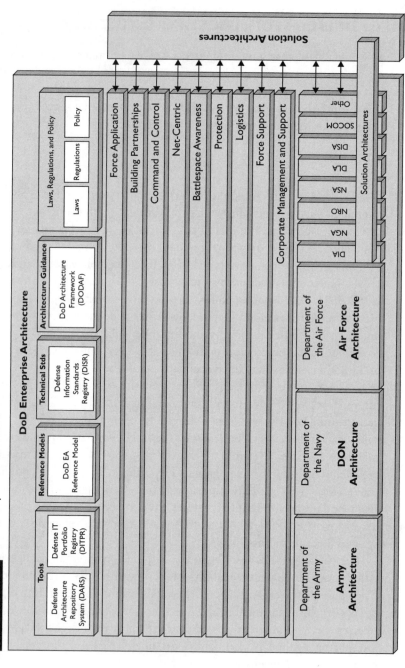

FIGURE 4.2-9 DoD Enterprise Architecture

Department of the Air Force EA

The Air Force (AF) EA is a strategic information resource that documents the capabilities of the Air Force in terms of its people, processes, and technology and relates those capabilities to the strategic vision, strategies, and plans of the Air Force. It serves as a reference for multiple decision-making processes. The EA also reflects the decisions already made and provides the basis for future decisions addressing how the AF is organized, how it performs its mission, the information it produces and consumes, and the systems and technologies it uses.

The AF EA has been implemented using a federated approach that partitions the AF EA into a hierarchy of smaller scope architectures that are developed and managed by separate AF organizations (see Figure 4.2-10). The intent is to leverage the subject matter expertise throughout the AF and to enable the development of architectures that directly support and are responsive to decision makers at all levels of the AF structure. However, all AF architectures, wherever developed, are considered part of the AF EA and must be consistent with it. The AF has established an architecture governance process to ensure that all architectures are aligned and consistent with the other constituent parts of the AF EA. The AF EA is described in *USAF Enterprise Architecture Version 3.4.5 (Draft)* (Secretary of the Air Force, Office of Warfighting Integration and CIO, 2009).

The Air Force enterprise architecture is built in accordance with the Air Force Enterprise Architecture Framework published earlier (see Figure 4.2-11).

FIGURE 4.2-10   U.S. Air Force Enterprise Architecture

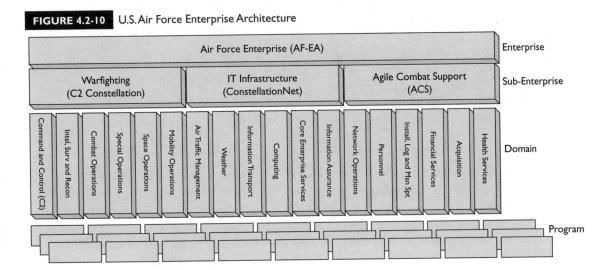

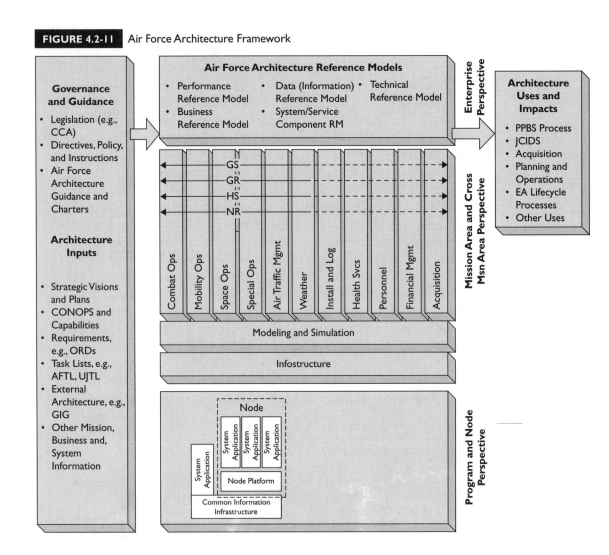

FIGURE 4.2-11 Air Force Architecture Framework

Navy EA

The Department of the Navy (DON) is too large and complex to be described within a single integrated architecture. Typical enterprise architecture efforts suffer from one of two problems: they either abstract the architecture content into simple, high-level views that do not support analysis, or they compile massive amounts of data that make comprehension difficult at best. One of the primary objectives of enterprise architectures is to describe the enterprise so that decision makers can make informed decisions within a common context. The DON EA Management View provides a comprehensive view of architecture efforts across the DON and aligns and federates them in support of DON strategic goals.

The DON Enterprise Architecture helps decision makers make informed decisions about investments in new technology and, at the same time, capitalize on vast existing technology assets. In addition, the DON EA is focused on maintaining alignment between the department's goals and objectives and its information management/information technology (IM/IT) investments.

Because both technology and business needs change over time, the DON EA must be flexible enough to respond to these changes, yet do so in a controlled manner and with minimal adverse effect.

The DON EA's success is dependent upon its relevance and value to DON decision makers and program managers. As the Chief Architect of the department, the DON Chief Information Officer is leading the effort to design and develop a single, integrated DON EA that includes Navy and Marine Corps architectures and federates with external partners' and organizations' architectures.

The DON EA will describe policy requirements, processes, information flows, solutions, data descriptions, technical infrastructure, and standards. It will support developing weapons, intelligence and business systems, and enterprise IT infrastructure and core services. Currently, DON EA compliance is incorporated into two existing processes: the Clinger-Cohen Act (CCA) confirmation process and the IM/IT investment review process. Additionally, the requirement for assessing compliance, with the DON EA as part of these processes, has been incorporated into the department's annual IT budget execution policy.

DON EA Federation Goals

Federation techniques allow disparate architectures to be meaningfully related through the DON EA and permit the acceleration of new architectures to support DON decision makers. The DON EA federation goals include the following:

- Creating an environment to support the decision makers and their staffs with access to a set of common architecture artifacts. This enables a common understanding of the DON enterprise that can be used to support DON decision making at the enterprise level.
- Developing a means to identify internal and external interfaces to the DON enterprise.

■ Improving EA information sharing of architectural content, ensuring that users, including unintended users, can find and use the right information.

■ Leveraging existing architecture and/or artifacts to swiftly adjust or expand their capabilities through architecture reuse and integration.

DON EA Federation Principles

Department of Navy EA federation is guided by the following principles:

■ Respect the diverse requirements of individual DON elements while focusing on the associations that cut across organizational boundaries, statutory roles, and responsibilities for the DON elements.

■ Focus on federating existing disparate architecture artifacts regardless of structure and format—not rebuilding architectures.

■ Maximize the reuse of existing architectures at all tiers.

■ Evolve from a product-centric approach (such as DoDAF and other work products produced by architecture developers) to a data-centric architecture approach that focuses on common semantics.

■ Support the DON's net-centricity objectives (for example, making information and services visible, accessible, and understandable) and vision.

■ Leverage existing Department of Navy taxonomies. Architecture elements represent the critical taxonomies, requiring concurrence and standardization for an integrated architecture as described by the DoDAF. They comprise the lexicon for the three views of the architecture framework: the Operational View (OV), System View (SV), and Technical Standards View (StdV). Their use is a step toward ensuring integration of systems within a system of systems and alignment of information technology functionality to mission and operational needs.

The DON Enterprise Architecture can be found at http://www.doncio.navy.mil/EATool/index.htm.

Army EA

The Army Enterprise Architecture (AEA), based on publicly available sources, is still evolving at this time. Figure 4.2-12 provides an overview. (For more detail, visit http://architecture.army.mil/AEA-Technical/architectureintro.html.)

Benefits

To be a useful tool for supporting the decisions of the widest range of Army stakeholders, the AEA is organized to accommodate a variety of viewpoints and perspectives, including the following:

- The soldier: speed of receiving capabilities
- Senior leadership: strategic assessment, process change, and synchronization
- Budgeting personnel and planners: cost efficiencies
- Policy and doctrine developers: compliance
- The operational community: responsiveness

FIGURE 4.2-12 U.S. Army Enterprise Architecture

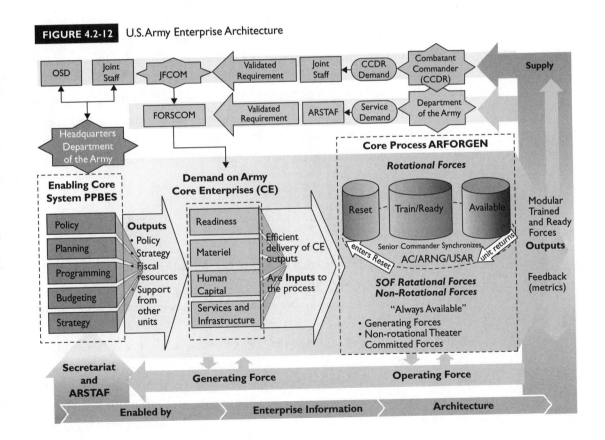

Objective

Establishing the AEA as a knowledge base of integrated information will help the Army evolve from its current network of unique, mission-centric systems to an enterprise that acts cohesively—one that operates with full knowledge about changes to, and the status of, goals, plans, processes, actions, results, relationships, and key interdependencies.

Army Enterprise Operating Model

The Army Enterprise Operating Model represents a holistic lifecycle model of how the Army operates and does business, establishing the context for understanding the purpose, contribution, and value of the AEA.

How It Works

- The Army Force Generation (ARFORGEN) process is driven and initiated by validated Joint Forces and Army requirements.
- The Army's four core enterprises (CEs) develop, field, and deliver capabilities to Army forces.
- All Army activities are facilitated and supported by the Army's PPBE system.
- Gaps in DOTMLPF are identified when capabilities are used in support of operational and institutional missions.
- Using capabilities drives the next iteration of the lifecycle model.

What Will the AEA Do?

Building on the holistic Army Enterprise Operating Model, the AEA will accomplish the following:

- Integrate an extensive knowledge base of information so that it is accessible to the right people, at the right time, in the right way.
- Enable the whole Army to better understand, manage, and fulfill support to ARFORGEN.
- Help assess second- and third-order effects and avoid unintended consequences of change.
- Capture requirements and constraints, ensuring that transformational goals and priorities are followed during acquisition, design, and implementation phases.
- Assist in managing unit activation, transformation, and sequencing of the capabilities fielded in support of ARFORGEN.

Because the Army enterprise is so diverse and complex, the AEA foundation provides that common, needed, organizing structure and support environment for Army decision support.

DoD Information Enterprise Architecture

The DoD Information Enterprise Architecture (IEA) provides a common foundation to support accelerated DoD transformation to net-centric operations and establishes priorities to address critical barriers to its realization (Department of Defense Chief Information Officer, 2009). The DoD information enterprise (IE) comprises the information, information resources, assets, and processes required to achieve an information advantage and share information across the department and with mission partners. The DoD IEA describes the integrated DoD IE and the rules for the information assets and resources that enable it (see Figure 4.2-13).

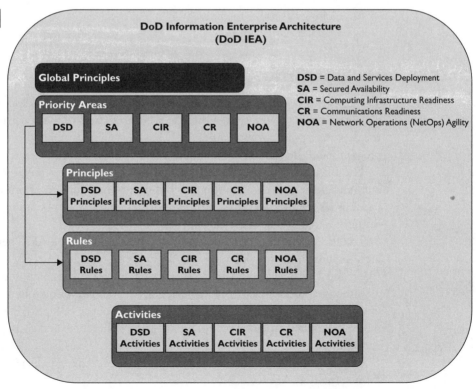

FIGURE 4.2-13

Defense Information Enterprise Architecture

DoD IEA 1.1 unifies the concepts embedded in the department's net-centric strategies into a common vision, providing relevance and context to existing policy. DoD IEA 1.1 highlights the key principles, rules, constraints, and best practices drawn from collective policy to which applicable DoD programs, regardless of component or portfolio, must adhere in order to enable agile, collaborative, net-centric operations. In today's information environment, the DoD IEA rules apply within the persistently connected Internet Protocol (IP) boundaries of the GIG. Outside of these boundaries, the principles still should be considered, but the rules of the DoD IEA must yield to the state of technology and the needs and imperatives of the department's missions.

Core principles and rules are organized around five key priorities where increased attention and investment will bring the most immediate progress toward realizing net-centric goals:

- Data and services deployment (DSD)
- Secured availability (SA)
- Computing infrastructure readiness (CIR)
- Communications readiness (CR)
- NetOps agility (NOA)

DoD Business Enterprise Architecture

The DoD Business Enterprise Architecture (BEA) architectural description provides a comprehensive description of the major business areas of the department and serves the departure point for integrating DoD business services across the departmental programs and the JCAs (see Figure 4.2-14).

The BEA is the enterprise architecture for DoD's business mission area. The architecture defines the department's business transformation priorities, the business capabilities required to support those priorities, and the combinations of systems and initiatives that enable these capabilities.

The BEA is an integrated architecture, as defined by DoDAF. There are four architecture views: the All View (AV), the Operational View (OV), Systems View (SV), and Technical Standards View (StdV). Each view is composed of sets of architecture products depicted through graphic, tabular, or textual documents. Each of the four views depicts certain architecture attributes. Some attributes integrate multiple products, thereby providing integrity, coherence, and consistency to the architecture.

The BEA is described in detail in the *BEA Architecture Product Guide* (Business Transformation Agency, 2009).

FIGURE 4.2-14 Business Enterprise Architecture

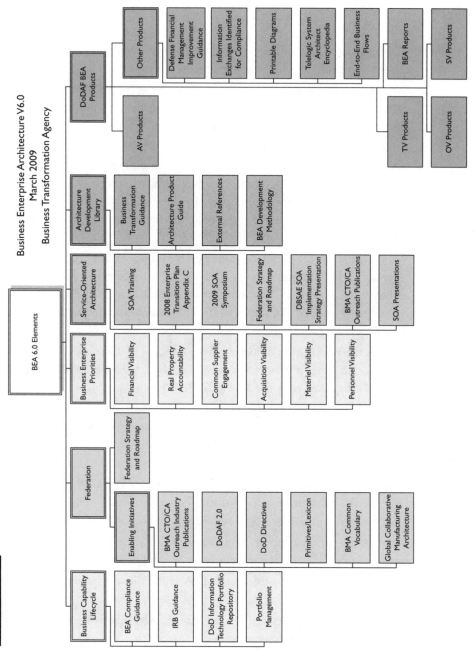

Questions

1. What are the new challenges facing the defense enterprise? How are these related to a need for enterprise architecture?

2. What is capability-based acquisition? What is the role of JCIDS? How do capability needs translate into an acquisition strategy? What are the key architectural documents that are required by JCIDS?

3. What is the Observe-Orient-Decide-Act (OODA) loop? How is it different from the planned action cycle? Under what conditions is OODA a better method for decision making than the plan-driven activity? Would you recommend OODA as a methodology for standard enterprise business processes that are repeatable and used to produce repeatable products for the enterprise? Why, or why not?

4. What is the concept of net-centric operations and warfare (NCOW)? How does the planning of net-centric operations affect the operational architecture, systems architecture, services architecture, and data architecture? Are net-centric operations different from distributed operations? Explain any differences.

5. What is the implication of moving from a producer-centric to a consumer-centric environment? Contrast or compare the DoD approach to electronic business conducted over the World Wide Web.

6. What in your opinion are the architectural implications of conducting aerial warfare from unmanned platforms and abandoning manned aerial operations? What is the effect or impact on DOTMLPF aspects?

7. How are the key DoD business processes—JCIDS, PPBE, DAS, and systems solutions—interrelated? What is requirements-based acquisition (RBA)? How is RBA different from capabilities-based acquisition? Discuss the pros and cons of requirements-based acquisition and capabilities-based acquisition.

8. What are the three levels of architecting at the DoD? Describe each of them briefly and provide examples to illustrate the differences.

9. What is the stated purpose of the DoD Architecture Framework? What are its envisioned benefits to the DoD?

10. What is systems engineering? What is the difference between systems engineering and software engineering? How are the systems engineering processes accommodated by the Defense Acquisition System?

11. What is Portfolio Management? What are the various operations performed by a Portfolio Manager?

12. Explain the DoD Enterprise Architecture depicted in Figure 4.2-8. How is the DoD EA similar to or different from the FEA Business Reference Model?

13. Discuss the differences between the DoD Enterprise Architecture and the Air Force Enterprise Architecture. How does the Air Force Enterprise Architecture Framework differ from the Air Force Enterprise Architecture?

14. Compare and contrast the Army Enterprise Architecture with the Air Force Enterprise Architecture. Make sure you define the criteria for comparison first before actually performing the comparison.

Reference List

Assistant Secretary of Defense for Networks and Information Integration ASD[NII])/ Department of Defense Chief Information Officer (DoD CIO). (2005). *Information technology portfolio management.* DODD 8115.01. Department of Defense.

Business Transformation Agency. (2009). *BEA architecture product guide.* Department of Defense. Business Transformation Agency (BTA).

Defense Acquisition University. (2011). *Defense Acquisition Guidebook (DAG).* Online guidebook requires account setup. http://akss.dau.mil/dag/welcome.asp.

Defense Information Services Agency (DISA). (2010). *NCES overview presentation: Net-centric Enterprise Services (NCES).* Defense Information Systems Agency.

Department of Defense. (2009). *Department of Defense Architecture Framework Version 2.0 Volume I: manager's guide.* ASD (NII)/DoD CIO.

Department of Defense Chief Information Officer. (2009). *Department of Defense Information Enterprise Architecture Version 1.1.* Department of Defense.

Department of Defense USD/ATL (2008b). *Operation of the Defense Acquisition System.* DODI 5000.02. December 2008. http://www.dtic.mil/whs/directives/corres/pdf/500002p.pdf.

Deputy Secretary of Defense. (2002). *Global Information Grid (GIG) overarching policy.* DODD 8100.1. Department of Defense. http://biotech.law.lsu.edu/blaw/DODd/corres/pdf/d81001_091902/d81001p.pdf.

Deputy Secretary of Defense. (2004). *Data sharing in a net-centric Department of Defense*. DODD 8320.2, 2. Department of Defense. http://www.fas.org/irp/doddir/dod/d8320_2.pdf.

Headquarters, United States Air Force. (2009). *United States Air Force unmanned aircraft systems flight plan 2009-2047 (unclassified)*. United States Air Force, Headquarters, Washington, DC.

Joint Staff. (2007). *Joint capabilities integration and development system*. CJCSI 3170.01 Series. Chairman of the Joint Chiefs of Staff. http://www.dtic.mil/cjcs_directives/cdata/unlimit/m317001.pdf.

Joint Staff. (2007). *Joint operations concepts development process (JOPSC-DP)*. CJCSI 3010.02. Chairman of the Joint Chiefs of Staff. www.dtic.mil/cjcs_directives/cdata/unlimit/3010_02.pdf.

Secretary of the Air Force. Office of Warfighting Integration and CIO (SAF/XC). (2009). *USAF Enterprise Architecture Version 3.4.5 (Draft)*. United States Air Force.

USD/ATL (2008a). *The Defense Acquisition System*. DODI 5000.01. Undersecretary of Defense, Acquisition, Testing and Logistics. January 2008. http://www.dtic.mil/whs/directives/corres/pdf/525001p.pdf.

4.3

Enterprise Architecture and the Commercial Sector

W e have discussed how both government and the defense domains have developed enterprise architecture frameworks that are built using different models or products specify reference models to ensure compatibility across government agencies and utilize methodologies. In United States government agencies, methodology was developed by the architecture working groups relevant to a lifecycle starting with project beginnings and continuing through governance and change management. In regard to the DoD, we discussed the Six Step process that provides the basis for DoDAF planning though the utilization of architectures and their containment in repositories. In the commercial world, enterprise architecture is strongly influenced by The Open Group.

In this chapter, we discuss the relevance of The Open Group Architectural Framework (TOGAF™) to the uses of EA across government and the private sector discussed in earlier sections. Our purpose is to help map the various TOGAF phases of the Architectural Development Methodology (ADM) to the products and concepts we have discussed in this book that have pertained to government, defense, and the case study example of building an EA for an airport. Much of this chapter is quoted directly from the TOGAF book Version 9. Because of the amount of quotation, the convention used here is not to use quotation marks for each citation.

TOGAF 9.0 in Relation to the Views and Models of This Guide

We have considered various concepts relevant to EA project management and planning. In the commercial EA world, The Open Group developed its own architecture framework, which initially was based on a Department of Defense IT model and has gone through several iterations to its current version, TOGAF 9. This version of the TOGAF is a comprehensive guide that provides a systems development lifecycle approach, known as the ADM, to developing an EA for organizations. The TOGAF also contains a number of metamodels and Reference Models that especially at the IT-level provide guidance.

Although discussed in more detail below these components comprise six sections that are briefly described as: the Architecture Development Methodology or ADM (commonly called "the crop cycle" as a type of system development lifecycle), the Enterprise Continuum (a repository of architecture information that includes an architecture continuum and a related solutions continuum ranging from the most common to organizational specific), an Architecture Content Framework that contains TOGAF views and associated artifacts, TOGAF Reference Models that comprise the Foundation Architecture of the Architecture Continuum (this includes a Technical Reference Model and an Information Reference Model [3IRM], which is a closer level view of the TRM, ADM (Architecture Development Methodology) Guidelines and Techniques that comprise a set of best practices and architectural petitioning analogous to segment architectures, and an Architecture Capability Framework that provides a method for assessing the readiness of an organization of EA and related governance structures.

Over the course of TOGAF's development, many of the different frameworks discussed in this book have been mapped to the TOGAF (for example, the Zachman Framework, DoDAF, MODAF, as well as many proprietary commercial frameworks such as NCR Global Information Technology Planning Method or GITP). Additional course readings will be provided to FEAC students, but it is worthwhile to consider briefly what the TOGAF involves and its relationship to the various products or models that we teach in our programs.

The TOGAF 9 is comprised of six major components, as shown in Figure 4.3-1.

The ADM is a powerful approach for planning, building, governing, and maintaining an architecture as a continuing endeavor of organizations. The ADM is continuous as it incorporates change management and procedures for determining when to modify or rebuild EA in concert with changing business and technological requirements.

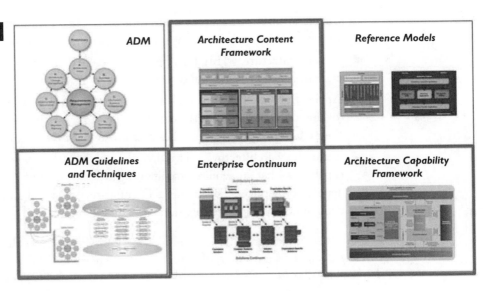

FIGURE 4.3-1

TOGAF 9
Components

ADM

Architecture Content Framework

Reference Models

ADM Guidelines and Techniques

Enterprise Continuum

Architecture Capability Framework

The Architecture Content Framework is comprised of a set of artifacts associated with different architecture views and viewpoints. This framework corresponds to the models in DoDAF and products of FEAF, which are detailed in Part III of this book. The TOGAF Reference Models are associated with the Architecture and Solutions Continuum and the Foundation Architecture. These Reference Models—including the Technical Reference Model (TRM) and the Integrated Information Infrastructure Reference Model (I3RM)—support "Boundaryless Information Flow™," which is a TOGAF trademark term referring to global interoperability in a secure, reliable, and timely manner. The ADM Guidelines and Techniques refer to a number of best practices and approaches for developing an architecture across the various phases that comprise the methodology (discussed later in this chapter). The Enterprise Continuum refers to a repository of architecture components from the most general to those that are specific to an industry or organization; this repository allows reuse of architecture and solution building blocks. Finally, the Architecture Capability Framework provides a structured definition of the organizations, skills, roles, and responsibilities to establish and operate an enterprise architecture.

The TOGAF provides the methods and tools for assisting in the acceptance, production, use, and maintenance of enterprise architecture. It is based on an iterative process model supported by best practices and a reusable set of existing architecture assets. As we have seen in previous chapters, four types of architecture are commonly accepted as subsets of an overall enterprise architecture, all of which TOGAF is designed to support:

- **Business (or business process) architecture**   This defines the business strategy, governance, organization, and key business processes.
- **Data architecture**   This describes the structure of an organization's logical and physical data assets and data management resources.
- **Applications architecture**   This kind of architecture provides a blueprint for the individual application systems to be deployed, their interactions, and their relationships to the core business processes of the organization.
- **Technology architecture**   This describes the logical software and hardware capabilities that are required to support the deployment of business, data, and application services. This includes IT infrastructure, middleware, networks, communications, processing, standards, and so on.

With these architecture types in mind, the TOGAF recognizes that there are two key elements of any enterprise architecture framework: (1) the definition of the deliverables that the architecting activity should produce and (2) a description of the method by which this should be done. Although most EA frameworks focus on a specific set of deliverables, few emphasize methods. Because TOGAF is considered a generic framework and is intended to be used in a wide variety of environments. As we discussed TOGAF does not specify any given set of deliverables. In this way TOGAF can be used on its own or with deliverables from other frameworks.

Each type of architecture framework provides for a set of different views. As we saw earlier, the Zachman Framework rows each correspond to different views, from those of the planner, business owner, and systems, from the highest business level to the most technical. We have also seen how the DoDAF initially contained a set of four views—Operational, Systems, Technical, and All—and that the most recent version, DoDAF 2.0, has extended this set of views to include Capability, Standards, Projects, and Services, as represented in Figure 4.3-2.

Likewise, TOGAF defines a set of views (see Figure 4.3-3) corresponding to the four types of architecture previously discussed and contains several of the views added to the new DoDAF.

FIGURE 4.3-2

DoDAF 2.0
Viewpoints

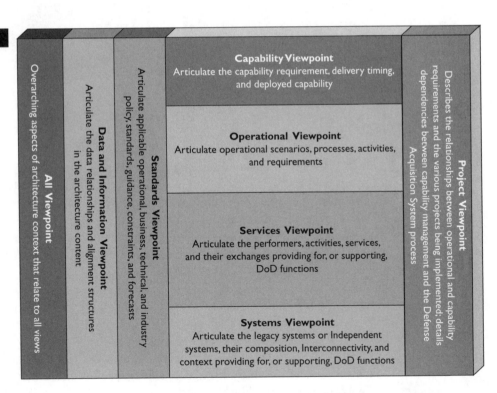

All Viewpoint
Overarching aspects of architecture context that relate to all views

Data and Information Viewpoint
Articulate the data relationships and alignment structures in the architecture content

Standards Viewpoint
Articulate applicable operational, business, technical, and industry policy, standards, guidance, constraints, and forecasts

Capability Viewpoint
Articulate the capability requirement, delivery timing, and deployed capability

Operational Viewpoint
Articulate operational scenarios, processes, activities, and requirements

Services Viewpoint
Articulate the performers, activities, services, and their exchanges providing for, or supporting, DoD functions

Systems Viewpoint
Articulate the legacy systems or Independent systems, their composition, Interconnectivity, and context providing for, or supporting, DoD functions

Project Viewpoint
Describes the relationships between operational and capability requirements and the various projects being implemented; details dependencies between capability management and the Defense Acquisition System process

FIGURE 4.3-3

TOGAF Views

To address the concerns of the following stakeholders ...			
Users, Planners, Business Management	Database Designers and Administrators, System Engineers	System and Software Engineers	Acquirers, Operators, Administrators, and Managers
.... the following views may be developed			
Business Architecture Views	Data Architecture Views	Applications Architecture Views	Technology Architecture Views
Business Function View	Data Entity View	Software Engineering View	Networked Computing/ Hardware View
Business Services View			
Business Process View			
Business Information View			
Business Locations View			Communications Engineering View
Business Logistics View	Data Flow View (Organization Data Use)	Applications Interoperability View	
People View (Organization Chart)			Processing View
Workflow View			
Usability View			
Business Strategy and Goals View	Logical Data View	Software Distribution View	Cost View
Business Objectives View			
Business Rules View			Standards View
Business Events View			
Business Performance View			
	System Engineering View		
Enterprise Security View			
Enterprise Manageability View			
Enterprise Quality of Service View			
Enterprise Mobility View			

In the TOGAF, there are three categories of content that pertain to each view. These are deliverables, artifacts, and building blocks. A deliverable is a work product that is contractually specified and in turn formally reviewed, agreed on, and signed off by the stakeholders. An artifact is a more granular architectural work product that describes architecture from a specific viewpoint, such as a network diagram, a server specification, a use-case specification, a list of architectural requirements, and a business interaction matrix. These are represented as catalogs, matrices, and diagrams—that is, the products and models discussed in our guide to models and in the DoDAF. A building block represents a potentially reusable component of business, IT, or architectural capability that can be combined with other building blocks to deliver architectures and solutions.

The TOGAF defines two types of building blocks. The first is the architecture building block (ABB), which describes required capability and shapes the specification of the second type of building block—the solution building block (SBB). The latter represents components to be used to implement the required capability. For example, a network is a building block that can be described through complementary artifacts and then put to use to realize solutions for the enterprise.

The relationship among deliverables, artifacts, and building blocks is shown in Figure 4.3-4.

The building blocks are comprised of a set of artifacts that can be mapped to the DoDAF models emphasized in this book. In the TOGAF, these are described as catalogs, matrices, and diagrams and are represented in the model shown in Figure 4.3-5, which locates artifacts by different views.

TOGAF is an architecture framework—The Open Group Architecture Framework. It enables you to design, evaluate, and build TOGAF-compliant architectures for organizations. The key to TOGAF is the ADM—a method for developing an IT enterprise architecture that meets the needs of business.

As we have described there are four types of architecture that comprise the TOGAF and that correspond to the FEAF architecture framework:

- **Business (or business process) architecture**   This defines the business strategy, governance, organization, and key business processes.

- **Information architecture**   This is in turn comprised of a data and an application architecture. The former describes the structure of an organization's logical and physical data assets and data management resources and the latter provides a blueprint for the individual application systems to be deployed,

FIGURE 4.3-4   Relationships Between Deliverables, Artifacts, and Building Blocks (TOGAF 9)

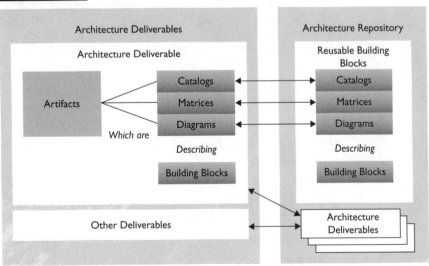

FIGURE 4.3-5 TOGAF Artifacts by View

Preliminary	Architecture Vision		
Catalogs	Matrices	Core Diagrams	
Principles Catalog	Stakeholder Map Matrix	Value Chain Diagram	Solution Concept Diagram

Business Architecture	Data Architecture	Application Architecture	Technology Architecture
Catalogs	Catalogs	Catalogs	Catalogs
Organization/Actor Catalog	Data Entry/Data Component Catalog	Application Portfolio Catalog	Technology Standards Catalog
Driver/Goal/Objective Catalog		Interface Catalog	Technology Portfolio Catalog
Role Catalog			
Service/Function Catalog	Matrices	Matrices	Matrices
Location Catalog	Data Entry/Business Function Matrix	System/Organization Matrix	System/Technology Matrix
Process/Event/Control /Product Catalog	System/Data Matrix	Role/System Matrix	
Contract/Measure Catalog		System/Function Matrix	
		Application Interaction Matrix	
Matrices			
Business Interaction Matrix	Core Diagrams	Core Diagrams	Core Diagrams
Actor/Role Matrix	Class Diagram	Application Communication Diagram	Environments and Locations Diagram
	Data Dissemination Diagram	Application and User Location Diagram	Platform Decomposition Diagram
Core Diagrams		System Use-Case Diagram	
Business Footprint Diagram			
Service/Information Diagram	Extension Diagrams	Extension Diagrams	Extension Diagrams
Functional Decomposition Diagram	Data Security Diagram	Enterprise Manageability Diagram	Processing Diagram
Product Lifecycle Diagram	Class Hierarchy Diagram	Process/System Realization Diagram	Networked Computing/ Hardware Diagram
	Data Migration Diagram	Software Engineering Diagram	Communications Engineering Diagram
Extension Diagrams	Data Lifecycle Diagram	Application Migration Diagram	
Goal/Objective/Service Diagram			
Business Use-Case Diagram		Software Distribution Diagram	
Organization Decomposition Diagram			
Process Flow Diagram	Requirements Management	Opportunities and Solutions	
Event Diagram	Catalogs	Core Diagrams	
	Requirements Catalog	Project Context Diagram	Benefits Diagram

Infrastructure Consolidation Extension   Governance Extension   Motivation Extension   Process Modeling Extension   Data Modeling Extension   Services Extension   Core Content

their interactions, and their relationships to the core business processes of the organization.

■ **Technology architecture**   This architecture describes the logical software and hardware capabilities that are required to support the deployment of business, data, and application services. This includes IT infrastructure, middleware, networks, communications, processing, standards, and so on.

The TOGAF consists of three parts:

- The **TOGAF Architecture Development Method** (ADM), which explains an approach to derive an organization-specific enterprise architecture addressing business requirements. This provides the following:
  - The TOGAF approach to developing the architecture
  - Architecture views that enable the architect to ensure that a complex set of requirements are addressed
  - Linkages to practical case studies
  - Guidelines on tools for architecture development
- **The Enterprise Continuum,** which is a "virtual repository" of all the architecture assets—models, patterns, architecture descriptions, and so on—that exist both within the enterprise and in the IT industry at large, and which the enterprise considers itself to have available for the development of architectures. At relevant places throughout the TOGAF ADM, there are reminders to consider which architecture assets from the Enterprise Continuum the architect may use. TOGAF itself provides two Reference Models for consideration for inclusion in an enterprise's own Enterprise Continuum:
  - **The TOGAF Foundation Architecture,** an architecture of generic services and functions that provides a foundation on which specific architectures and architecture building blocks (ABBs) can be built. This Foundation Architecture in turn includes the following:
    - The **TOGAF Technical Reference Model** (TRM), which provides a model and taxonomy of generic platform services.
    - The **TOGAF Standards Information Base** (SIB), which is a database of open industry standards that can be used to define the particular services and other components of an enterprise-specific architecture.
  - The **Integrated Information Infrastructure Reference Model** (III-RM), which is based on the TOGAF Foundation Architecture and is specifically aimed at helping the design of architectures that enable and support the vision of "Boundaryless Information Flow™."
- The **TOGAF Resource Base,** which is a set of resources—guidelines, templates, background information, and so on—to help the architect in the use of the ADM.

The information about the benefits and constraints of the existing implementation, together with requirements for change, are combined using the methods described in the TOGAF ADM, resulting in a target architecture or set of target architectures.

■ The **Standards Information Base** (SIB) provides a database of open industry standards that define the particular services and components required in the products purchased to implement the developed architecture. The SIB provides a simple and highly effective way to define common industry standards used within an enterprise architecture and is located at The Open Group website: www.opengroup/sib.

As mentioned the TOGAF is generic for use in a variety of environments. It can be used on its own with generic deliverables or can be replaced by other sets, such as contained in DoDAF, FEAF, Zachman, MODAF (Ministry of Defense Architecture Framework in Great Britain), NAF (NATO) and more, including various commercial proprietary frameworks.

A core concept of the TOGAF is the Enterprise Continuum. TOGAF embodies the concept of the Enterprise Continuum to reflect different levels of abstraction in an architecture development process. It provides a context for the use of multiple frameworks, models, and architecture assets in conjunction with the TOGAF ADM. By means of the Enterprise Continuum, architects can leverage all other relevant architectural resources and assets, in addition to the TOGAF Foundation Architecture, in developing an organization-specific IT architecture. In this context, the TOGAF ADM describes the process of moving from the TOGAF Foundation Architecture to an organization-specific architecture (or set of architectures), leveraging the contents of the Enterprise Continuum along the way, including the TOGAF Foundation Architecture and other relevant architecture frameworks, models, components, and building blocks.

The Enterprise Continuum has two parts: the Architectural Continuum and the Solutions Continuum, as shown in Figure 4.3-6. These two continuums comprise architectural building blocks. The arrows in the Architecture Continuum represent the bidirectional relationship that exists between the different architectures in the Architecture Continuum. The leftward direction focuses on meeting enterprise needs and business requirements, whereas the rightward direction focuses on leveraging architectural components and building blocks.

In this way the Architecture Continuum has four parts, as shown in Figure 4.3-7, which range from the most general to the organization specific, as described above.

As mentioned earlier, the Enterprise Continuum is a virtual repository of all the architecture assets that exist both within the enterprise and in the IT industry at large and which the enterprise considers itself to have available for the development

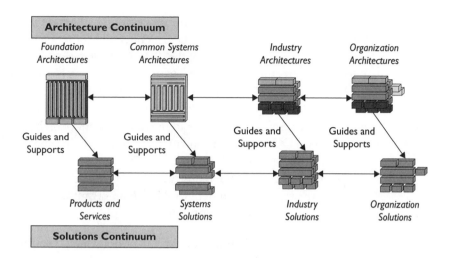

FIGURE 4.3-6

Architectural
Continuum
and Solutions
Continuum

of architectures for the enterprise. Examples of "assets within the enterprise" are the deliverables of previous architecture work, which are available for reuse. Examples of "assets in the IT industry at large" are the wide variety of industry Reference Models and architecture patterns that exist, and are continually emerging, including those that are highly generic (such as TOGAF's own TRM); those specific to certain aspects of IT (such as a web services architecture or a generic manageability architecture); those specific to certain types of information processing, such as e-commerce, supply chain management, and so on; and those specific to certain vertical industries, such as the models generated by vertical consortia, such as TMF (in the telecommunications sector), ARTS (in the retail sector), and POSC (in the petro-technical sector).

The decision as to which architecture assets a specific enterprise considers part of its own Enterprise Continuum will normally form part of the overall architecture governance function within the enterprise concerned.

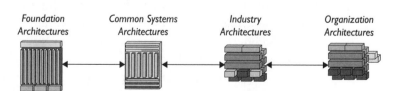

FIGURE 4.3-7

Four Parts of
the Architecture
Continuum

The TOGAF ADM describes the process of moving from the TOGAF Foundation Architecture to an enterprise-specific architecture (or set of architectures). This process leverages the elements of the TOGAF Foundation Architecture and other relevant architectural assets, components, and building blocks along the way.

At relevant places throughout the TOGAF ADM, there are reminders to consider which architecture assets from the Enterprise Continuum the architect should use, if any. In some cases—for example, in the development of technology architecture—this may be TOGAF's own Foundation Architecture. In other cases—for example, in the development of business architecture—it may be a Reference Model for e-commerce taken from the industry at large.

TOGAF provides two Reference Models an organization might consider for inclusion in its Enterprise Continuum:

- The **TOGAF Foundation Architecture**, which comprises a TRM of generic services and functions that provides a firm foundation on which more specific architectures and architectural components can be built; and a Standards Information Base (SIB), an information base of relevant specifications and standards.

- The **Integrated Information Infrastructure Reference Model** (III-RM), which is based on the TOGAF Foundation Architecture and is specifically designed to achieve architectures that enable and support the "Boundaryless Information Flow™" vision.

In developing architectures in the various domains within an overall enterprise architecture, the architect should consider the use and reuse of a wide variety of different architecture assets, and the Enterprise Continuum provides a framework (a "framework within a framework," if you like) for categorizing and communicating these different assets.

"Enterprise Continuum" is a phrase that denotes the combination of two complementary concepts: the Architecture Continuum and the Solutions Continuum. The TOGAF 9 Enterprise Edition describes the two continua as follows:

- The **Architecture Continuum** offers a consistent way to define and understand the generic rules, representations, and relationships in an information system. The Architecture Continuum represents a structuring of reusable architecture assets and is supported by the Solutions Continuum. The Architecture Continuum shows the relationships among foundational frameworks (such as TOGAF), common systems architectures (such as the III-RM), industry architectures, and enterprise architectures. The Architecture Continuum is a useful tool to discover commonality and eliminate unnecessary redundancy.

■ The **Solutions Continuum** provides a way to describe and understand the implementation of the Architecture Continuum. It defines what is available in the organizational environment as reusable solution building blocks (SBB). The solutions are the results of agreements, between customers and business partners, who implement the rules and relationships defined in the architecture space. The Solutions Continuum addresses the commonalities and differences among the products, systems, and services of implemented systems.

The Enterprise Continuum first outlines the Architecture Continuum and Solutions Continuum separately and then explains how they come together to form the Enterprise Continuum.

The Foundation Architecture is an architecture of building blocks and corresponding standards that supports all the common systems architectures and therefore the complete computing environment. It is comprised of the TOGAF Technical Reference Model and Standards Information Base. This is in turn comprised of building blocks and standards supporting the common systems architecture and the complete computing environment.

The common systems architecture is an Integrated Information Infrastructure Reference Model for information flow. It guides selection and integration of services from the Foundation Architecture and allows the building of common and reusable solutions across domains. Examples of this include network security, management architecture, network architecture, and e-mail architecture.

The next architecture in the Architectural Continuum is the industry architecture. This integrates common system components with industry-specific components. It creates common industry solutions for problems within specific industries and reflects requirements and standards specific to particular industries. In this manner, the industry architecture defines common building blocks relevant to these industries and identifies industry-specific logical and process models, application models, and testing guidelines and encourages interoperability within an industry.

The organizational Architectural Continuum guides the final deployment of components constituting solutions for a specific enterprise. This may itself involve a continuum of organizational architectures to cover an organization's requirements and result in several organizational architectures for entities in a global enterprise, such as in federated and segment architecture approaches.

FIGURE 4.3-8

Solutions
Continuum

Products and   Systems   Industry   Organization
Services   Solutions   Solutions   Solutions

The Solutions Continuum represents the implementations of the architectures at the corresponding levels of the Architecture Continuum (see Figure 4.3-8). At each level, the Solutions Continuum is a population of the architecture with reference building blocks—either purchased products or built components—that represent a solution to the enterprise's business need expressed at that level. A populated Solutions Continuum is a solutions inventory or reuse library, which can add significant value to the task of managing and implementing improvements to the IT environment.

The Architecture Development Methodology

As described in the TOGAF Enterprise Edition the Enterprise Continuum is a framework and context for the leveraging of relevant architecture assets in executing the ADM. These assets may include architecture descriptions, models, and patterns taken from a variety of sources. At relevant places throughout the ADM, there are reminders to consider which architecture assets from the Enterprise Continuum the architect should use, if any. In some cases—for example, in the development of a technology architecture—this may be the TOGAF Foundation Architecture. In other cases—such as in the development of a business architecture—it may be a Reference Model for e-commerce taken from the industry at large.

A practical use of the Enterprise Continuum takes the form of a repository that includes reference architectures, models, and patterns that have been accepted for use within the enterprise as well as actual architectural work done previously within the enterprise. The Architect would seek to reuse as much as possible from the Enterprise Continuum that is relevant to the project at hand.

The criteria for including source materials in an organization's Enterprise Continuum form part of the organization's IT governance process. Hence, the Enterprise Continuum is a framework (a "framework within a framework") for categorizing architectural source material—both the contents of the architecture working repository and the set of relevant, available Reference Models in the industry.

In executing the ADM, the architect is not only developing the end result of an organization-specific architecture but is also populating the organization's own Enterprise Continuum, with all the architectural assets identified and leveraged along the way, including, but not limited to, the resultant enterprise-specific architecture.

Architecture development is an iterative, ongoing process, and in executing the ADM repeatedly over time, the architect gradually populates more and more of the organization's Enterprise Continuum. Although the primary focus of the ADM is on the development of the enterprise-specific architecture, in this wider context the ADM can also be viewed as the process of populating the enterprise's own Enterprise Continuum with relevant reusable building blocks. Because of the circular structure of the ADM it has become known as "the crop cycle" (see Figure 4.3-9).

According to the TOGAF Practice Guide the ADM is a generic method for architecture development designed to deal with most system and organizational requirements. It will often be necessary to modify or extend the ADM to suit specific

FIGURE 4.3-9

Application
Development
Method (ADM)

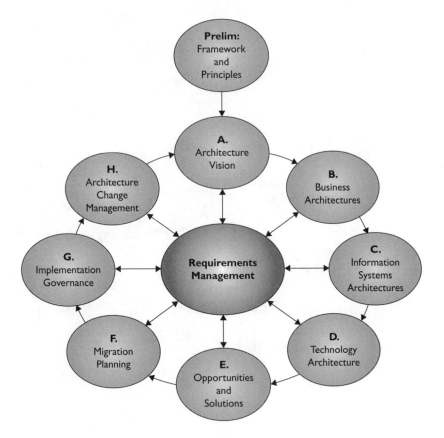

needs. One of the tasks before applying the ADM is to review its components for applicability and then tailor them as appropriate to the circumstances of the individual enterprise. This activity may well produce an enterprise-specific ADM.

MITRE developed a mapping of the ADM to DoDAF 2.0 models. The models, as discussed in previous chapters, were given an adapted meaning by us to correspond to non-DOD environments. Thus, we used the term "business" to refer to "operational," and so on. Figure 4.3-10 shows the MITRE mapping. We use this mapping in the subsequent discussion of each of the ADM phases.

FIGURE 4.3-10

Mapping of ADM
to DODAF
Models

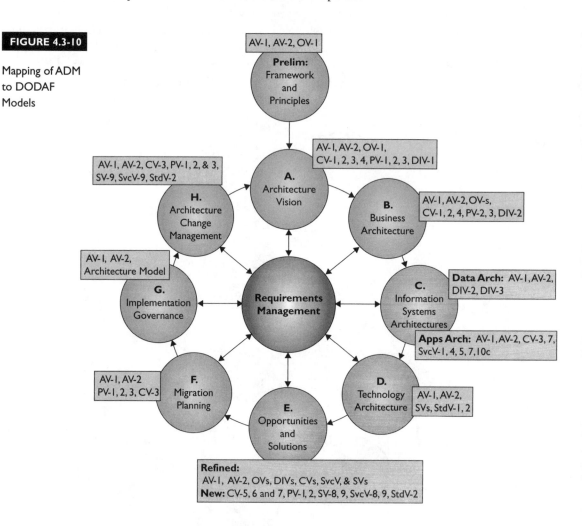

The Preliminary phase of the TOGAF defines the scope of the EA, creates its vision, identifies stakeholders, and obtains necessary approvals. This involves seven objectives:

- Confirm stakeholder commitments
- Define constraining principles
- Identify an organization's architecture footprint (who does the work, where they are located, and what their responsibilities are)
- Define the scope and assumptions
- Define the framework and methodologies
- Set up and monitor the framework's fitness for purpose (this includes a pilot or test of concept project to check validity of approach)
- Evaluation criteria for tools and repositories

TOGAF does not specify particular steps for the Preliminary phase. There are two main parts of this phase that involve the identification of principles and the establishment of governance. These concepts are discussed in other chapters of this text.

The relevant products for this phase are the architectural roadmap and the business concept graphic.

The next phase—which is the first phase, or Phase A, within the TOGAF crop cycle—is the Architecture Vision. During this phase, the project is established and an iteration of the architecture process is initiated, setting the scope, constraints, and expectations for the iteration. The phase is required to validate the business context and to create the statement of architecture work (SOW).

There are eight objectives to the Architecture Vision phase:

- Obtain management commitment
- Validate business principles, goals, and drivers
- Define the scope and prioritize architecture tasks
- Identify stakeholders, their concerns, and their objectives
- Define business requirements and constraints
- Define appropriate solutions
- Obtain formal approval to proceed
- Understand the architecture's influence on and from parallel architecture developments

This is accomplished using the following seven steps:

1. Establish the project.
2. Identify business goals and drivers.
3. Review architecture principles, including business principles.
4. Define the scope.
5. Define constraints.
6. Identify stakeholders and their concerns, business requirements, and architecture vision.
7. Document the statement of architecture work and gain approval.

This phase and each of the subsequent phases of the TOGAF have specified inputs and outputs.

Phase A: Architecture Vision

In Phase A, the inputs are as follows:

- Request for architecture work
- Business strategy, goals, and drivers
- Architecture principles, including business principles
- Enterprise Continuum—that is, existing architecture documentation (framework description, architecture descriptions, existing baseline descriptions, and so on)

The outputs for this phase are then the following:

- Approved SOW
- Refined statements of business goals and drivers
- Architecture principles, including business principles
- Architecture Vision

The Architecture Vision includes the following:

- Baseline business architecture
- Baseline data architecture
- Baseline applications architecture

- Baseline technology architecture
- Target business architecture
- Target data architecture
- Target applications architecture
- Target technology architecture

The FEAC models covered in this book are the same for the Preliminary and Architecture Vision phases: the architectural roadmap and the business concept graphic.

Phase B: The Business Architecture

The Business Architecture phase, or Phase B, is about documenting the fundamental organization of the business, embodied in its business processes and people, their relationships to each other, and the environment and the principles governing the business's evolution and design.

There are five objectives of the business architecture:

- Select architecture viewpoints to demonstrate how stakeholder concerns are addressed in the business architecture
- Select tools and techniques for viewpoints
- Describe the existing business architecture (the current baseline)
- Develop the target business architecture
- Analyze the gaps between the business and target

These are accomplished using eight steps:

1. Develop the baseline business architecture description.
2. Identify Reference Models, viewpoints, and tools.
3. Create business architecture model(s).
4. Select business architecture building blocks.
5. Conduct a formal checklist review of the architecture model and building blocks with stakeholders.
6. Review nonfunctional qualitative criteria.
7. Complete the business architecture.
8. Perform gap analysis and create the report.

This involves the following inputs:

- Request for architecture work
- Approved SOW
- Refined statements of business goals and drivers
- Architecture principles, including business principles
- Enterprise Continuum
- Architecture Vision, including the following:
  - Baseline business architecture
  - Baseline data architecture
  - Baseline applications architecture
  - Baseline technology architecture
  - Target business architecture
  - Target data architecture
  - Target applications architecture
  - Target technology architecture

The FEAC models used in this phase are the Integrated Dictionary, the Business Concept Graphic, the Business Node Connectivity Diagram, the Information Node Exchange Matrix, the Organizational Relationships Diagram, the Business Activity Model, the Business Rules Model, the Business State Transition, and the Business Event-Trace Description.

Phase C: Information Systems Architecture

This phase creates two products: the data and application architectures. The Information Systems Architecture phase is about documenting the fundamental organization of an enterprise's IT systems, embodied in the major types of information and the application systems that process them.

Data Architecture

The objective of the data architecture is to define the types and sources of data needed to support the business in a way that is understandable to stakeholders. This involves the following nine steps:

1. Develop the baseline architecture description.
2. Review and select principles, Reference Models, viewpoints, and tools.

3. Create the data architecture model(s).
4. Select data architecture building blocks.
5. Conduct a checklist review of the architecture model.
6. Review qualitative criteria.
7. Complete the data architecture.
8. Conduct checkpoint/impact analysis.
9. Perform gap analysis and create the report.

As with the other phases in the ADM, there are both inputs and outputs. The inputs to data are the following:

- Data principles
- Request for architecture work
- SOW
- Architecture Vision
- Baseline business architecture
- Target business architecture
- Baseline data architecture
- Target data architecture
- Relevant technical requirements
- Gap analysis results
- Reusable building blocks from the organization's Enterprise Continuum

These have the following outputs:

- SOW
- Baseline data architecture
- Validated data principles or new data principles
- Target data architecture
- Data architecture views corresponding to the selected viewpoints
- Data architecture report
- Gap analysis results
- Relevant technical requirements that apply to this evolution of the architecture development cycle

■ Impact analysis

■ Updated business requirements

The FEAC models for this phase are the OV7 or Logical Data Model and the SV11 or physical schema that defines the structure of the various types of system data that are utilized by the systems in the architecture.

Applications Architecture

The second part of the Information Architecture concerns applications, identifying the types of application systems necessary to process the data and support the business. This involves the following eight steps:

1. Develop the baseline applications architecture description.
2. Review and validate principles and select Reference Models, viewpoints, and tools.
3. Create data architecture model(s) for each viewpoint.
4. Identify candidate applications.
5. Conduct a checkpoint review.
6. Review the qualitative criteria.
7. Complete the applications architecture.
8. Perform gap analysis and create a report.

There are 11 inputs to this application section:

■ Application principles

■ Request for architecture work

■ SOW

■ Architecture Vision

■ Relevant technical requirements

■ Gap analysis results (from the business architecture)

■ Baseline business architecture

■ Target business architecture

■ Baseline applications architecture

■ Target applications architecture

■ Reusable building blocks from the organization's Enterprise Continuum

The outputs to this part are as follows:

- SOW
- Baseline applications architecture
- Target applications architecture
- Validated application principles or new application principles
- Application architecture views corresponding to the selected viewpoints
- Applications architecture report
- Gap analysis report
- Impact analysis
- Updated business requirements

The FEAC models for the application architecture are SV 4a (Systems Functionality Description), SV 4b (Services Functionality Description), SV 5 (Business Activity to Systems Function Traceability Matrix), SV 6 (Systems Data Exchange Matrix), SV 10a (Systems Rules Model), SV 10b (Systems State Transition Description), and SV 10c (Systems Event-Trace Description).

Phase D: Technology Architecture

The Technology Architecture phase is about documenting the fundamental organization of the IT systems embodied in the hardware, software, and communications technology. The objective of Phase D is to develop a target technology architecture that will form the basis of the subsequent implementation work.

This phase involves the following ten steps:

1. Develop the baseline technology architecture description.
2. Create the target technology architecture.
3. Create a baseline technology description in services terminology.
4. Consider different architecture Reference Models, viewpoints, and tools.
5. Create an architecture model of building blocks.
6. Select the services portfolio for each building block.
7. Confirm that the business goals and objectives are met.
8. Choose the criteria for specification selection.
9. Complete the architecture definition.
10. Conduct gap analysis.

There are up to 15 inputs to this phase:

- Technology principles (if they exist)
- Request for architecture work
- SOW
- Architecture Vision
- Baseline business architecture
- Baseline data architecture
- Baseline applications architecture
- Baseline technology architecture
- Target business architecture
- Target data architecture
- Target applications architecture
- Target technology architecture
- Relevant technical requirements
- Gap analysis results from the data and applications architectures
- Reusable building blocks

These have the following range of outputs:

- SOW (updated if necessary)
- Baseline technology architecture
- Validated technology principles or new technology principles if they were generated during this phase
- Technology architecture report summarizing the work done and the key findings
- Target technology architecture
- Technology architecture and a gap analysis report
- Viewpoints addressing key stakeholder concerns
- Views corresponding to the selected viewpoints

There are ten FEAC models for this phase:

- SV1 (Systems Interface Description)
- AV2 (Systems Communications Description)
- SV 3 (Systems-Systems Matrix)

- SV 4 (Systems Functionality Description)
- SV5 (Business Activity to Systems Function Traceability Matrix)
- SV7 (Systems Performance Parameters Matrix)
- SV10a (Systems Rules Model)
- SV10b (Systems State Transition Description)
- SV10c (Systems Event-Trace Description)
- StdV1 (Technical Standards Profile)

The next set of stages in the ADM involves implementation.

Phase E: Opportunities and Solutions

The Opportunities and Solutions phase identifies the parameters of change, the phases, and the necessary projects, using gap analysis on the business functions in the old environment and the new. The objectives of this phase are to evaluate and select implementation options (for example, whether to build, buy, or reuse), identify the strategic parameters for change and the projects to be undertaken, assess the costs and benefits of the projects, and generate an overall implementation and migration strategy and a detailed implementation plan.

There are six steps involved here:

1. Identify the key business drivers.
2. Review the gap analysis from Phase D.
3. Brainstorm technical requirements.
4. Brainstorm other requirements.
5. Assess the architecture and perform gap analysis.
6. Identify work packages or projects.

The inputs to this are, as with other phases, the following:

- Request for architecture work
- SOW
- Target business architecture
- Target data architecture
- Target applications architecture
- Target technology architecture

- Reusable architecture (solution)
- Building blocks from the organization's Enterprise Continuum
- Project information

These have the following three outputs:

- Implementation and migration strategy.
- High-level implementation plan.
- Impact analysis document; the project list section is documented during this phase.

There are three FEAC models relevant to this phase: SV8 (Systems Evolution Description), SV9 (Systems Technology and Skills Forecast), and StdV2 (Technical Standards Forecast).

Phase F: Migration Planning

This phase deals with transitions as it addresses migration planning—that is, determining how to move from the baseline to the target architecture. The objectives are to prioritize the various implementation projects and produce a prioritized list of projects. This list forms the basis of the detailed implementation and migration plan.

This phase involves the following six steps:

1. Prioritize projects.
2. Estimate the resource requirements and available resources for each project.
3. Perform a cost/benefit analysis for each project to identify the projects that will make the most impact in proportion to their costs.
4. Perform a risk assessment for each project to identify any high-risk projects.
5. Generate a proposed implementation roadmap.
6. Prepare a migration plan showing how existing systems will migrate to the new architecture.

The inputs to migration planning are as follows:

- Request for architecture work
- SOW
- Target business architecture

- Target data architecture
- Target applications architecture
- Target technology architecture
- Impact analysis and project list

The output to this process is an impact analysis, which is a detailed implementation and migration plan (including an architecture implementation contract). The SV8 (Systems Evolution Description) is the FEAC product associated with this phase.

Phase G: Implementation Governance

The Implementation Governance phase defines the architecture constraints on the implementation projects and constructs and obtains signatures on an architecture contract. The phase also includes monitoring the implementation work.

The objectives are to formulate recommendations for each implementation project, construct an architecture contract to govern the overall implementation and deployment process, perform appropriate governance functions while the system is being implemented and deployed, and ensure conformance with the defined architecture by implementation projects and other projects.

This involves three steps:

1. Formulate project recommendations.
2. Document the architecture contract.
3. Perform ongoing implementation governance.

The implementation governance inputs are as follows:

- Request for architecture work
- SOW
- Reusable solution building blocks from the organization's solution continuum
- Impact analysis and a detailed implementation and migration plan (including an architecture implementation contract)

These yield three outputs:

- Impact analysis and implementation recommendations
- Architecture contract
- The architecture-compliant implemented system

The FEAC models of this phase are those used at the beginning of the ADM cycle: the business concept graphic and the concept of operations or roadmap.

Phase H: Architecture Change Management

Change management ensures that changes to the architecture are managed in a controlled manner. The objects are to establish an architecture change management process; provide continual monitoring of changes in technology, business, and the like; and determine whether to initiate a new architecture cycle or make changes to the framework and principles.

This involves the following steps:

1. Monitor technology changes.
2. Monitor business changes.
3. Assess changes and decide if there is a need for a new iteration of the crop circle lifecycle.
4. Arrange a meeting of the architecture board.

The inputs are requests for architecture change due to technology changes and also due to business changes. The outputs are as follows:

- Architecture updates
- Changes to the architecture framework and principles
- New request for architecture work to initiate another cycle of the ADM

The FEAC models are the SV9 (Systems Technology and Skills Forecast) and the StdV2 (Technical Standards Forecast).

Requirements Management

At the center of the ADM cycle is Requirements Management (RM), which is iteratively entailed in each of the other phases. The RM process is a dynamic one addressing the identification of requirements for the enterprise, storing them and then feeding them in and out of the relevant ADM phases. The ability to deal with changes in requirements is crucial to the ADM process, because architecture by its very nature deals with uncertainty and change, bridging the divide between what stakeholders desire and what can be delivered as a practical solution.

The objectives for RM are to provide a process to manage architecture requirements throughout the phrases of the ADM cycle and identify requirements for the enterprise, store them and feed them in and out of the relevant ADM phases, which dispose of, address, and prioritize requirements.

This entails these ten steps:

1. Identify and document requirements.
2. Identify baseline requirements.
3. Monitor baseline requirements.
4. Identify changed requirements; remove, add, modify, and reassess priorities.
5. Identify changed requirement and record priorities; identify and resolve conflicts; and generate requirements impact statements.
6. Assess the impact of changed requirements on current and previous ADM phases.
7. Implement requirements arising from Phase H.
8. Update the requirements repository.
9. Implement the change in the current phase.
10. Assess and revise gap analysis for past phases.

The inputs are as follows:

- The inputs to the requirements management process are the requirements-related outputs from each ADM phase.
- The first high-level requirements are produced as part of the Architecture Vision.
- Each architecture domain then generates detailed requirements.
- Deliverables in later ADM phases contain mappings to new types of requirements (for example, conformance requirements).

These inputs result in the outputs of changed requirements and a requirements impact statement that identifies the phases of the ADM that need to be revisited to address any changes. The final version must include the full implications of the requirements (for example, costs, timescales, and business metrics).

TOGAF Iteration

We discussed how TOGAF is an iterative framework. Different phases of the TOGAF can be done in concert or concomitantly with other phases whereas others follow a particular sequence. Figure 4.3-11 shows how such iterations of parts of the cycle are represented in the approach.

The Preliminary and Architecture Vision phase entail and feed each other and represent the first iteration of work. The development of the business, information,

FIGURE 4.3-11

TOGAF Iteration

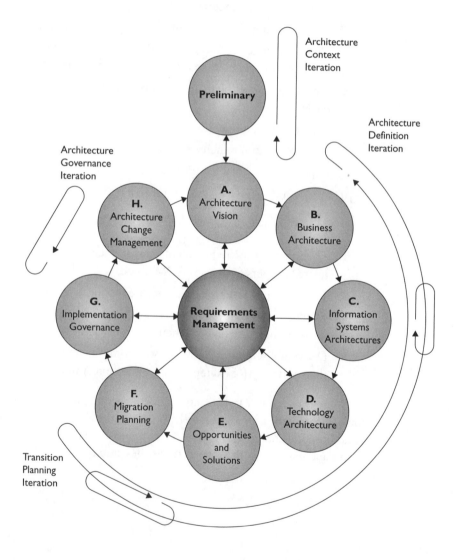

and technical architectures can be done in any order, albeit with reference to and consistency with each other. This represents another iteration and constitutes the architecture definition. The transition planning iteration incorporates the definition and revises it according to opportunities and migration planning. Finally, the governance and change in the architecture provides a governance iteration and, based on requirements, leads to change and revision of the EA.

This short account of the TOGAF is meant to supplement the reading of the TOGAF PDF book and is meant to assist FEAC students as they map their practicum efforts to this process.

Integrated Architecture

Over the years, many modeling methodologies that address some aspect of the IT acquisition cycle have come into being. Each of these methodologies is optimized for solving some part of the architecture landscape, but no one methodology has proven to be sufficiently effective for the purposes of developing an integrated architecture— one where there are touch points and semantic intersections between architecture elements in diverse models. Lacking any built-in, tool-constrained rigor, models are often built at different abstraction levels and are consequently not integratable.

To understand this issue, consider an IDEF0 Activity Model that represents information elements as inputs and outputs for a specified activity. Also consider an IDEF 1X Data Model that represents normalized entities and relationships. There is a good chance that the IDEF0 information elements are couched in terms that the business understands, whereas the IDEF1X Model has undergone transformations required for normalizing concepts and has resulted in names of entities that are not recognizable by the business.

By requiring an integrated architecture, the architect mandates that the information elements that are inputs and outputs in the Activity Model must match a business-level data model that can later be transformed stage by stage into, for example, a key-based logical model and then into a fully attributed data model, if required.

TOGAF Artifacts

In this chapter, we presented the use of FEAC models based on the DoDAF and MODAF as the artifacts used in each of the ADM phases. The TOGAF has defined a number of specific artifacts or what we refer to as models that also reference the phases that map to those we discuss in this book. These models are related to the phases in Figure 4.3-12.

FIGURE 4.3-12	Relationship of Models to Phases

Preliminary Phase	Phase B, Business Architecture	Phase C	
		Data Architecture	**Application Architecture**
• Principles catalog	• Organization/Actor catalog • Driver/Goal/Objective catalog • Role catalog • Business Service/Function catalog • Location catalog • Process/Event/Control/Product catalog	• Data Entity/Data Component catalog • Data Entity/Business Function matrix • System/Data matrix • Class diagram • Data Dissemination diagram	• Application Portfolio catalog • Interface catalog • System/Organization matrix • Role/System matrix • System/Function matrix • Application Interaction matrix • Application Communication diagram
Phase A, Architecture Vision	• Contract/Measure catalog • Business Interaction matrix • Actor/Role matrix	• Data Security diagram • Class Hierarchy diagram	• Application and User Location diagram
• Stakeholder Map matrix • Value Chain diagram • Solution Concept diagram	• Business Footprint diagram • Business Service/Information diagram • Functional Decomposition diagram • Product Lifecycle diagram • Goal/Objective/Service diagram • Use-Case diagram • Organization Decomposition diagram • Process Flow diagram • Event diagram	• Data Migration diagram • Data Lifecycle diagram	• System Use-Case diagram • Enterprise Manageability diagram • Process/System Realization diagram • Software Engineering diagram • Application Migration diagram • Software Distribution diagram
Phase D, Technology Architecture		**Phase E, Opportunities and Solutions**	**Requirements Management**
• Technology Standards catalog • Technology Portfolio catalog • System/Technology matrix • Environments and Locations diagram • Platform Decomposition diagram • Processing diagram • Networked Computing/Hardware diagram • Communications Engineering diagram		• Project Context diagram • Benefits diagram	• Requirements catalog

Questions

1. How did the TOGAF develop as a major approach in the commercial EA sector?

2. What are the components of the TOGAF 9?

3. How do the four types of architectures comprising TOGAF relate to governmental frameworks such as the FEAF?

4. What is the relationship of views to viewpoints in the TOGAF?

5. What are building blocks and what are the two major types and their relation to each other?

6. What is the relationship between artifacts in TOGAF and models in the DoDAF and FEAF frameworks?

7. What is the distinction among deliverables, building blocks, and artifacts in the TOGAF?

8. What is the Enterprise Continuum and what are the two types of continua that comprise it?

9. What are the two parts of the Foundation Architecture?

10. What are the phases of the ADM?

11. How do the models of the DoDAF map to the Architecture Content Model of the TOGAF and the artifacts relevant to the different phases of the ADM?

Reference List

Togaf Version 9—A Manual 2008. The Open Group. Van Haren Publishing; Ninth Edition.

Part V

Resources

5.1

EA Tools and Repositories

J ust like you would never think of building the Golden Gate Bridge across San Francisco Bay using hammers and chisels, embarking on an enterprise architecting project without a strategy for the right tools is a recipe for disaster. Using the right tools for the right job is essential to finishing the job on time and to a high-quality level. But how does one select the right tool? This chapter will discuss the various factors that are important in considering which tools are more appropriate than others for the specific architecture development effort.

As Sir Isaac Newton once famously remarked, "I can reach further because I stand on the shoulders of giants," the field of enterprise architecture reaches further because of all the advances in modeling methodologies, tools, repositories, and standards that evolved during the 1990s and later into the 2000s. In addition to witnessing the proliferation of modeling methods and automated software tools for creating, editing, and managing models, this period also saw the evolution of many architecture frameworks.

The fact of the matter remains that automated tools simply automate the mundane tasks associated with modeling. Choosing the right toolset—usually a set of tools—involves making early choices and decisions long before any tool purchase is contemplated.

Select Your Framework

One of the fundamental decisions that one has to make when selecting a wrench or a measuring tape is that of the system of measurements: metric or British. Everything that follows in engineering and physics is a consequence of choosing the right system of units. It is possible to translate metric measurements into British measurements and vice versa, but it is very convenient to use the right system of units from the get-go in a consistent manner through a set of equations or over the course of a design exercise.

In enterprise architecture work, it is important to decide what framework will be used. As we have learnt, enterprise architecture frameworks are common conceptual models of architectures that allow disparate organizations to roll up, aggregate, and compare their architectures. It is important to realize that frameworks also impose a vocabulary discipline that is commonly followed by all adherents. Common vocabularies for expressing architecture elements are fundamental to sharing architecture work and communicating the meaning of the architecture work. For example, using the DoD Architecture Framework (DoDAF) imposes special meaning on architecture terms such as *performer, activity, system,* and *service.* These may have a different meaning in the context of some other framework.

Just as we are able to translate metric measurements into British and vice versa, architecture tools also claim to be framework-independent and will provide capabilities to transform an architecture built using one framework into another. Unfortunately, transformation of architecture semantics from one framework to another is not a simple matter of a formula and some arithmetic computations. Semantic relationships between differing architecture terms from competing frameworks may need to resolve issues of mismatched composition, scope, scale, and detail.

The semantics of these transformations are deeply buried inside the tool, and the transformation procedures are performed automatically, sometimes opaquely. Understanding multiple frameworks as well as detailed implementation of transformation procedures may sometimes be impossible. In practice, it is important for an enterprise to pick a framework that is consistent with its architecture needs. Often this involves looking down into the various component enterprises to try to force a commonality as well as looking sideways at collaboration partners to determine what they are using so that interchange and architectural fusion can be attempted. Suffice it to say that enterprise architecture frameworks such as the Federal Enterprise Architecture Framework (FEAF), the DoD Enterprise Architecture Framework, or The Open Group Architecture Framework (TOGAF) all create sometimes differing vocabularies for architecture terms. If any architecture built using one of the frameworks needs to be transformed to use the terms of another framework, a combination of automatic translation schemes coupled with manual knowledge of the difference between the two vocabularies is required to successfully effect the transformation.

Select Your Modeling Techniques and Methodologies

In addition to selecting the framework, the enterprise architect is also advised to select the modeling technique or methodology. A technique is a collection of methods that help to generate a specific type of model repeatedly and consistently with a quality that is built into the technique. A methodology is a system of models, processes, standards, and know-how that purports to help solve a business problem or produce a software solution. The techniques of enterprise architecture modeling are arguably progressive adaptations of the techniques used by software and systems engineers over the last several decades. There is considerable debate whether techniques useful for analyzing the requirements and design trade-offs of a single solution are capable of scaling up to provide the same capability for planning and analyzing high-level requirements for a family of systems or what we have called a portfolio of systems. There is still a preponderance of diagramming tools in the industry, but a few new tools are working with data, dashboards, charts, and graphs as well as in automatic (data-driven) generation of documents, scripts, and design artifacts. The heart of such tools is their repository of data from which they compose and generate diagrams, matrices, tree views, and published documents alike.

Practice and experience has shown that diagramming approaches tend to break down rapidly in terms of communicating meaning as diagrams get large and crowded. Often, the "model gets away from the modeler" at a particular level of complexity—a level that varies from modeler to modeler. Enterprise architectures span a scope larger than the analysis of a specific business process or a specific information system or a specific product line. At the level of complexity and scale that enterprise architecture is modeled, the enterprise architect has to take recourse to data or information-based techniques rather than diagrammatic ones.

A sample of modeling technique evolution is presented in this chapter. We have not attempted to list exhaustively the many methodologies that have come and gone or are still being used. The intent is to present a sample of the types of sweeping changes that can result when methodology shifts occur.

Before the 1990s, modeling was used by software systems analysts to represent their knowledge of business processes, data flows, and human computer interactions primarily using "structured analysis" techniques. The models were frequently done using pencil and paper and blueprinting standards such as flow-charting symbols that were commonly understood.

Modeling techniques such as the family of Integrated Computer-Aided Manufacturing Definition languages—later shortened to Integrated Definition Languages or, more familiarly, IDEF (and an output of the Integrated Computer-Aided Manufacturing Project sponsored by the United States Air Force)—are based on variants of structured analysis.

For example, IDEF0 (NIST, 1993) provides a rich canvas of modeling techniques for Activity Models. Although initially used to model the transformation of raw materials as inputs that were consumed or transformed into finished product or assembly outputs, IDEF0 was rapidly used to model processes that consumed or transformed information inputs into information outputs also.

IDEF1X (NIST, 1994), as discussed in Part III of this book, provides an implementation of the entity-relationship modeling technique for representing data logically. Other variants of IDEF—such as IDEF 3 for modeling workflows (IDEF0 only models the exchange of inputs and outputs and not the change of control or handoffs)—although formalized, never gained the popularity that IDEF0 and IDEF1X enjoyed. Many of these modeling techniques have returned in the form of Business Process Modeling Notation (BPMN) (OMG, 2011) and some of the modeling needed for representing service orchestration in service-oriented architectures.

In the structured analysis approach, a few common factors are at play:

- Analysis relies on progressive decomposition (refinement) to gain a clearer understanding of a problem. For example, a high-level activity was broken down into smaller-grain activities in order to be able to identify component tasks that make up the whole.

- Analysis also relies on progressive composition or groupings to increase the abstraction level of a problem when we are awash in detail. For example, listing all the tasks performed in an organization can result in a confusing mess of tasks. Grouping these tasks into some higher-level tasks that each smaller task makes up a part of allows the analyst to switch from detail to a larger-granularity view of a problem area.

- Structured analysis generally produced diagrams (activity decomposition models, context diagrams, data flow diagrams, entity-relationship diagrams, and such) that are used by human beings to understand a problem and then produce a design that addresses the implementation of a solution.

- There was a constant need to separate process and data. The process models were used to design algorithms and sequence workflows for software applications. The data models were used to represent shared data schemas that cut across application boundaries. Hence there was a need to provide for auxiliary models that spanned the intersection of process with data, such as Create, Read, Update, and Delete (CRUD) matrices.

- The power of structured analysis was based on functional or activity modeling. Data was generally a consequence of a need for information on the part of a function or activity. Function modeling fit in very nicely with the internal paradigm of functional programming languages such as Fortran, Pascal, C, and PL/1 and was understood equally well by business subject matter experts and software analysts.

Later, in the mid-1990s, there was an explosion of techniques centered on representing a combination of data and process together using object-modeling techniques. As it generally happens in a newly exploding field, there was a plethora of variants of these techniques. Ultimately, there was a meeting of the minds and the emergence of a common modeling language for object modeling called the Unified Modeling Language (UML – OMG [2010]). In the object-modeling technique, some of the cardinal principles are assumed:

- Objects encapsulate properties and behaviors. Data and processes exist together and are encapsulated within an object class. The data and process may exist internally and be invisible to processes outside the object or they may be declared public and be visible outside the object. Processes can be invoked from inside an object or from outside. The fundamental model for object modeling is the static class model.
- Objects are polymorphic. They may present different manifestations to different audiences.
- Objects need to be orchestrated by external specifications for object interactions. Object Interaction models model the behavior of a set of objects based on their published interfaces and properties.

Object modeling was an appropriate technique for the software development regime of the late 1990s, where the constant mantra was software reuse and objects presented an obvious unit of reuse. But as a medium for communicating enterprise architecture, UML still remains a language of choice for software professionals, engineering analysts, and performers.

In the early 2000s, the pendulum swung back to functional modeling, with the popularity of service-oriented architectures and the return to modeling the service first and the data that the service needs second. Methodologies based on standards such as Business Process Modeling Notation as well as the companion Business Process Execution Language place an emphasis once again on the functions that need to be performed.

In the meantime, several adaptations had to be performed for the conventional modeling methodologies to allow them to deal with temporal concepts—an essential need for modeling of real-time phenomena and the performance of real-time systems. There has also been interest in event-driven modeling, which starts with triggering events and traces their effects on the processes and data that are involved in the event response. These are popular in the banking industry and in modeling situations that ripple from an event such as a customer action.

The fact of the matter is that trends in modeling methodologies and techniques will continue to change and evolve and preferences change over time. An enterprise architecture must live on anywhere from five to ten years or more from the time it is first completed and must not rely on outdated pictures and dated techniques for acceptance and usefulness. Models have many uses for the enterprise:

- They act as a communication medium between the enterprise architect and the intended audience. This means that any pictures or text information must be understood by the intended audience and can be clearly communicated by the architect. Too often, enterprise architects carrying large plots of highly complicated, small font, crowded pictures are unable to convey their architectural message to their audiences. They are unable to validate these unrecognizable "artifacts" by the stakeholders and are susceptible to being dismissed as irrelevant.

- Models serve to set up and illustrate key relationships between model elements. Often the lines that crisscross a diagram are not as informative as the relationships they are trying to convey. Falling back to the relationship semantics as stored inside the tool that generated the pictures is often more useful for performing impact analysis or including model elements as part of an analysis scope along with all related objects.

- They serve to provide a platform for simulation. Simulation of behaviors is a very common way to test whether designs stand up to the rigors of the wide types of inputs that are sometimes presented in the real world. Models that can be simulated are useful in validating a range of inputs and examining the outputs under various contexts and situations. Unfortunately, simulation at any level of usefulness requires building extremely detailed models, and the modeler must consider and provide probabilistic data for every branch that can be potentially taken, or exercise every branch deterministically. The cost of such detailed models becomes prohibitively high for general-purpose modeling as done for supporting enterprise architecture, for instance.

- Models serve to collect much needed analysis data in context and conveniently. In other words, often, it is easier to build an architectural picture and then take an inventory of objects inside a picture than to start out trying to list objects. Though the picture was useful in showing the modeler gaps and missing information because of its contextual nature, later, its usefulness may be overtaken by the types of analysis that can be performed on the data that underlies the picture.

Select Your Modeling Standards

The world around us is based on standards. Standards define the width of railway tracks. Standards define the standard size of automobile tires. Standards define the width of a lane on an interstate highway. Standards define the color of red that must be used for the tail lights of automobiles.

Standards help to resolve the disparate needs and designs to forge a common set of specifications that is good for the many. By the same token, choosing and adopting modeling standards are essential to orderly enterprise modeling that involves groups of people from disparate organizations building architectures that span those organizations. Modeling standards not only include choices of modeling methodology but also conventions and rules for naming architecture elements, configuration management, repeatable process standards, repeatable and consistent model governance standards, and a common blueprinting symbology that is immediately recognizable by all stakeholders who build, change, or use those models.

There are many standards that govern modeling. We present a few examples to illustrate the significance of some of these model-related standards.

Integrated Definition Language 0 (Activity Modeling)

We have already discussed the modeling standards that emerged from the Integrated Computer-Aided Manufacturing program sponsored by the United States Air Force (USAF). The name of this program's standards was later shortened to Integrated Definition Language (IDEF). IDEF was a leap forward for process improvement engineers and analysts to represent processes in a consistent and repeatable way using context and decomposition diagrams. IDEF0 also prescribed the manner in which the diagrams consistently represent inputs, controls, outputs, and mechanisms (ICOMS) for an activity. It also standardized terms such as context diagram, for-elaboration-only (FEO) diagram, notes page, activity/box, and ICOM/arrow. Adopted as a U.S. federal government standard (FIPS 183), IDEF 0 quickly became the modeling technique of choice for business process improvement analysts.

Unified Modeling Language (UML)

The Unified Modeling Language was an attempt to resolve modeling differences between three competing methodologies (although several other competing methodologies were folded into UML). The proponents of these methodologies (now known as the Three Amigos) were brought together to resolve their differences and forge a common standard for object-oriented analysis and design and later for software construction and delivery as well.

Business Process Modeling Notation (BPMN)

The need for modeling the handoffs and collaboration mechanisms between multiple performers of business activities was met by the BPMN standard. BPMN models activities in swim lanes, with each swim lane corresponding to a specific performer. Arrows that connect activities represent the flow of control from one performer/ activity pair to another.

Business Process Execution Language (BPEL)

As modeling of processes matured into accurate depictions of the workflows between business activities, the need for transforming these BPMN models into automated mechanisms such as software services has resulted in a new standard called Business Process Execution Language (BPEL). BPEL models the transformation of business processes into service-oriented solutions.

Select Your Architecture Data Exchange Standards

We live in a world of change. Old standards are cast aside and new ones emerge. This fact must be kept in mind when selecting a standard for the modeling of enterprise architecture. There are areas for which standards are slowly beginning to evolve.

Most standards are prescriptive in format because one of the primary goals is interchange, and interchange cannot occur without an engineering discipline that specifies exact formats and semantics. One example of a prescriptive standard that is emerging for exchange of models between DoDAF 2.0-compliant tools is the Physical Exchange Specification (PES) that is being promoted by the Department of Defense for vendors who want to provide DoDAF architecture modeling tools.

Selection of a modeling tool for supporting enterprise architecture development therefore requires specification of the modeling standards and interchange standards that will be adopted as a fundamental development strategy.

We use the word "model" in the general sense for any arrangement of data that is consistent with a technique, method, or prescribed format. Under this definition, models for capital planning, investment, and portfolio management are included as well as data models, process models, message and information exchange models, strategic planning models, and operations models.

Define or Select Your Modeling Lifecycle Processes

The process of modeling has been discussed in detail in previous chapters. The importance of a modeling lifecycle that has a beginning and an end, and has checkpoints or "gates" that must be passed as models mature, cannot be stressed sufficiently. Vendors of tools sometimes promote a modeling lifecycle process that leverages the built-in process management capabilities inside the tool—the tool is lifecycle-aware and provides reports of architecture elements that are in different stages of the lifecycle and carries tasks, to-do lists, and markup and annotation requests from validators as work to be performed.

Some enterprises establish a policy that governs the modeling process and enforces discipline on modelers. The policy is incrementally improved as the enterprise gains more history of its own modeling successes (or failures) and is part of a continuous quality improvement program for the enterprise architecture team.

How Do Tools Assist in EA Development?

A modeling tool will not do your thinking for you! The modeling tool has capabilities for producing professional, well-crafted model representations along with capabilities for managing model data such as exporting, importing, storing, and transforming formats or content. These capabilities eliminate tedious bookkeeping and the repeated drawing refinements that can take up an inordinate amount of the modeler's time, freeing up the modeler instead to think over the problem attack and the solution design alternatives. Tools also help with managing scale and complexity. EA representations have tremendous volumes of architecture data that are connected by a rich network of relationships:

- The data management capabilities of modeling tools are very useful in increasing the productivity of modelers. Entering data through the entry screens of tools is a very tedious process. Most tools provide bulk loading capabilities that allow the modeler to import tremendous amounts of previously created, validated, tabulated, and cleaned-up data into the tool and later manipulate the data inside the tool to build the requisite models.

- The data management capabilities of advanced tools also include a shared data repository that allows multiple project teams to share architecture model data and work on models that overlap. You'll learn more about repositories later in this chapter.

- The export capabilities of most tools are also useful to disseminate lists of architecture data that need to be validated to subject matter experts who have only general-purpose spreadsheet word processing and business graphics tools at hand.

- Most tools provide for generation of downstream products. Tools that provide automatic generation capabilities also offer "roundtrip design" capabilities. Examples of tools that generate downstream products are data modeling tools that can transform a fully attributed logical data model into a physical database schema that can be loaded into a relational database management system, for example, to create a relational database schema. Roundtrip engineering, in this case, is the capability to reflect changes made in the relational schema to the original Logical Data Model that was used to generate the schema.

- Many contemporary tools allow the modeler to publish a collection of models as an integrated website. The advantage of publishing an integrated website is that the audience needs only a web browser to interact with the models using browsing, navigation, and drilldown capabilities that are built into their browsers.

- In the federal enterprise architecture arena, a lot of activity is centered on Portfolio Management, the generation of business case justification documents, and capital planning and decision making. Tools that support EA activities in this area provide capabilities for quantitative analysis, such as dashboards depicting bar charts, pie charts, and color-coded statuses, to enable decision makers to perform rapid situation assessments and come to conclusions. These tools ease the burden of the enterprise architect and also provide enhanced decision-making capabilities. They take away the burden of data management as well as the tedious chore of converting data into actionable information.

- In the defense enterprise architecture arena, a number of tools are available that provide capabilities for compliance with mandates for architecture models that support information support plans (ISPs) and net-ready key performance parameters as part of the DoD's transformation into a net-centric enterprise.

Tools are there to assist the enterprise architect in modeling, data management, display and presentation, and searching and querying for information. The models that enterprise architects build to gain understanding for themselves are rarely the ones that are suitable for a less sophisticated audience. Tools that provide a rich range of displays, reports, and user interface conveniences will help bridge the gap from EA construction to EA dissemination.

Early versions of enterprise architectures will likely require the enterprise architecture team to act as brokers between the people who pose the business problem and the solution developers who will ultimately address the problem with a solution. As the stakeholders become familiar with the elements of the architecture and understand how the enterprise architecture is organized, they become ready to serve themselves with the information and reports they need for their decision-making, transformational, and task-specific information needs.

Methodology-Independent Tools

In our earlier discussions, we mentioned that selecting a methodology or collection of compatible methodologies was a good idea before selecting a tool. Many tools promise the capability of enabling the enterprise architect to change his or her mind midstream. Some tools may, for example, allow switch from his or her organization's proprietary Enterprise Architecture Planning (EAP) to the DoD Architecture Framework and back.

Transforming a collection of architecture models built using one methodology to another may not always be an easy or an accurate translation task. For example, transforming a fully attributed Logical Data Model built using the IDEF1X methodology into a UML static object class diagram (a roughly close equivalent) and vice versa is not feasible because of the fact that UML also models operations whereas IDEF1X does not, thus there is loss of information as a consequence of the translation.

In general, the task of translating models built using one methodology to another is similar to translating phrases from one spoken language to another distantly related or unrelated spoken language. The mode of translation is not word at a time, as the two languages may have entirely different grammars, but rather the translation of a semantic pattern in one language into an equivalent semantic pattern in another.

Test the claims of tool vendors who guarantee methodology-independent transformations. Better still, ask why you are seeking methodology-independent tools instead of selecting a stable methodology or collection of methodologies that best meets your needs and sticking with it.

Methodology-Specific Tools

Methodology-specific tools are those whose capabilities have been tuned to specific methodologies. They do not claim abilities to transform their models from one methodology to another at will. Rather, they may offer export capabilities that are compatible with other methodologies or tools.

All methodologies have a useful life. Tools that support only methodologies that are approaching the end of their usefulness may be risky choices for an enterprise architecture program that will need to exist for several years.

Process Support Tools

Process support is the capability built into some modeling tools that helps assist in a lifecycle-based approach for modeling and guide the user through the lifecycle.

Tools that support a process present a double-edged opportunity. On the one side, the process support allows the using enterprise to define a clear lifecycle for modeling that leverages built-in process support inside the tool. On the other side, the enterprise does not have the freedom to implement a process that is customized to its needs.

If you want the process orientation capabilities to be built into a process support modeling tool, you are also buying into the vendor-defined process, although most vendors provide facilities for customizing the process.

Integrated Model Development

A specific EA model is used to represent some aspect of the EA for some segment of the audience. Not all models are built to cater to all audiences. An enterprise architecture is therefore supported by a collection of models that provide elaboration on different viewpoints and for catering to different interests. An integrated architecture is one where the collections of models that form the architectural representation all share common architecture elements and there is no dissonance or discrepancy in the terms and definitions that are used across those models.

In a large architecture project, often the task of building supporting models is delegated to multiple teams. As the teams go about the task of gathering data, validating that data, and representing it in the form of structured models based on the selected framework, methodology, and techniques, there is a definite risk that one or more teams may wind up representing the same architecture element redundantly and distinctly. This redundancy can cause analysis-related issues, especially with impact analysis assessments. Eliminating a seemingly distinct architecture element that is actually identical to another one facilitates accurate impact analysis and concentrates all the relationships represented in multiple models on the same architecture element.

The risk of producing a nonintegrated architecture is high in the following situations:

- When the architecture is represented using multiple models—which is almost always the case. Enterprise architecture provides knowledge and decision-making support for different stakeholders within the enterprise. Each of these stakeholders requires a form of communication that is matched to their own paradigms.
- When the modeling effort is distributed across multiple teams. In very large architecture efforts, there is usually no choice. In federal agencies and enterprises, procurement considerations may dictate multiple contract awards and set-asides.
- When there is little or no communications between the teams.
- When modeling skill area becomes the criteria for dividing up the modeling work instead of a business domain or area of business.

When distributed modeling efforts in disparate and geographically distributed teams is coupled with the use of stand-alone tools that do not provide a mechanism for integrating the architecture data that is produced by the modeling efforts, disparities in architecture modeling such as in terminology, viewpoints, levels of abstraction, etc. become very obvious when the models are brought together for the first time to be integrated.

Problems in architecture integration can be surfaced by mandating the production and maintenance of an integrated architecture dictionary that spans all the models and serves as an authoritative source for all architecture terms and definitions.

Support for Fit-for-Purpose Views

Models that are built by enterprise architects generally conform to some standard methodology and framework and are built for exchange and communication with other architects building similar models as well as in supporting upstream and downstream transformations within a design or solution-building lifecycle.

Unfortunately, the standard model representations that work well as an architecting discipline among the architecture community may not be very useful for audiences that are not familiar with the terminology of architecture. For such audiences, displays, presentations, or data arrangements need to be devised that are specific to their purpose and viewpoint. These "fit-for-purpose" views can straddle data across multiple models to form composites that have more impact as a whole than the sum of the parts.

Without the use of tools, the burden of providing these fit-for-purpose views falls on the architect. Because tools manage the data and the display separately, they have the capacity to combine the data in different ways to produce these fit-for-purpose views.

Fit-for-purpose views may manifest themselves in the form of reports, custom-stored displays, or association matrices or taxonomy trees, to cite a few examples.

Configuration Management and Model Releases

Enterprise change is inevitable, whether it is planned or not. The useful life of an enterprise architecture can span several years. Changes can occur in organizational structures, responsibilities, portfolios of systems, projects, services, or technology infrastructures. Standards can and do evolve. New technology infusions will modify the enterprise architecture.

In a constantly changing world, the enterprise architecture is released in an evolutionary manner with a snapshot that is frozen at a point in time representing a specific release. Configuration management is the process of managing the various bits and pieces (component architecture elements) of a release and keeping track of the changes to these bits and pieces. Versioning is the mechanism used to track and manage change.

The release of an integrated enterprise architecture as a whole can be versioned. Because of legislative pressures, most organizations plan to combine the development of enterprise architecture with policy and governance strategies that mandate the use of the enterprise architecture as a compass to align business and transformation initiatives.

Individual models can also be versioned. However, within an integrated architecture, often changes in one model will ripple through other models that are using the same architecture elements and therefore versioning a subset of the models may not provide much advantage over producing a new version of the integrated architecture as a whole.

Individual architecture elements can themselves be versioned. Managing a configuration that combines versions of individual architecture elements with versions of architecture can get very complex very quickly, with few benefits other than the benefit of observing changes over a period of time or for providing audit trails for changes in architecture. The configuration management of versioned architecture elements used in versioned architecture representations can be daunting if not impossible to manage for most large scale architecture descriptions.

Tool support is essential for configuration management and release generation. Without the tool support and a degree of automated tasks, the task of keeping track of versions and the use of versioned objects becomes a prohibitive burden on the architect.

Tool-Based Document Generation

All federal enterprises require the production of documents in support of a business case for new initiatives such as the A-11 and Exhibit 300 as required by the Office of Management and Budget. The Department of Defense requires the production of Initial Capabilities Documents and Capabilities Production Documents as part of the Joint Capabilities Integration and Development System (JCIDS) processes for identifying, prioritizing, and selecting capabilities to acquire.

Both federal agencies and defense enterprises (and most commercial organizations) are required to provide architecture documents in support of their need to share common infrastructure, such as computing, communication networks, and database management systems, for example. These documents—under various headings, such as plans for certification and accreditation (C&A) or information support plans (ISPs)—are byproducts of the architecting effort.

The ability for tools to generate documents automatically that business processes require is a significant reduction of the burden on the architect. The formats for these documents change slightly, as changes in policy sometimes change data requirements for reporting.

Tool-Generated Model Dissemination

Architecture development tools are relatively expensive and entail a significant learning curve. Disseminating architectures and the component models and data to end users and intended audiences in a manner that requires them to use the architecture development tools is neither practical nor is it economical.

Architecture delivery should be made using mechanisms that are already available on the end user's desktop. Users are familiar with, and use on a daily basis, common office applications such as word processing applications, spreadsheet applications, business graphics and presentation applications, and (less commonly) desktop database tools. Users are also familiar with delivery of applications using the World Wide Web.

Many tools automatically generate a website for dissemination to end users. Delivered through a web browser, these distributions of enterprise architecture, models, and architecture data can be browsed, navigated, and drilled down for detailed analysis. This form of dissemination "frees up" the content from the original development tool and allows for widespread dissemination without the frustration and expense of requiring a software license for use of the architecture development tool by users who are only interested in using the data and not creating it.

Tool-Selection Criteria

Although tool selection is specific to an enterprise's particular needs, there are some general criteria that can assist in assessing the suitability of commercial EA tools. Several excellent tool reviews are available on the Internet that compare specific vendor products and use different types of comparison rubrics. Technology survey and research companies also offer information products that offer comparisons of enterprise architecture tools and repositories. This section will describe a sample rubric that is broadly applicable for most enterprises. We have divided the criteria into logical groupings. Because of the large number of criteria, a prioritization or weighting must be applied to each criterion. The value of the weights and the emphasis priorities vary from enterprise to enterprise.

Keep in mind that the following sample criteria are only a small subset of the types of criteria that are important in the selection of a toolset to support enterprise architecture development.

Technical Criteria

Technical criteria are factors that determine how a specific enterprise architecture toolset fits into the technology infrastructure of the currently operating enterprise and its technology roadmap for the future. Depending on the policies and culture of enterprises, these may be "make or break" factors for selecting a specific toolset. Some examples of technical criteria that may be important to enterprises are described in Table 5.1-1.

| TABLE 5.1-1 | Technical Criteria for Tool Selection |

Sample Criteria	Description
Server Platform	The toolset must run on approved server platforms. The enterprise technical profile provides a list of current and planned platforms.
Desktop Platform	The toolset must run on the enterprise standard desktop configuration for the enterprise. Many enterprises record their standard desktop configuration as a standard systems installation template and use this template to install, reinstall, and upgrade desktop software configurations.
Communications Network	The toolset must run within the confines of the network established for the enterprise. This network may include local area networks, wide area networks, routers, gateways, and firewalls. The toolset must not compromise the network.
Security Considerations	The toolset may be required to pass certification and audit requirements or obtain a certificate of net-worthiness. The toolset must not introduce security vulnerabilities.
Access Control Requirements	The toolset must not require access to sensitive, vulnerable, controlled system resources such as administrator passwords, protected directories, and such.
Integration with Directory Services and Single Sign-on Systems	The toolset must work with established directory services used by enterprises to normalize user registrations and provide single sign-on capabilities.
Distribution Media	The toolset must be distributed in read-only media that is immune to corruption by viruses and other malware. Distribution media must be consistent with enterprise policies for removable media use and restrictions on peripherals attached to a workstation or server.
Undesired Side Effects of Installation Programs	The toolset installation utility must not produce undesirable side effects such as the creation of directory structures that violate enterprise policy or creation of temporary files that are never removed. The installation utility must also provide a capability to uninstall the software when it is no longer required. This is especially true for free-trial versions of toolsets that vendors promote to expand their markets.
Compatibility With Antivirus Software	Most enterprise installations constantly run antivirus software to detect and correct security problems caused by malware. Toolsets must be qualified to operate within the constraints of such programs running on the desktop.
Sandbox Operations	Toolsets must run in an application "sandbox"—an area in computer memory that acts as a protected region—and not create the potential to crash the host system or slow down operations. Toolsets must be capable of being terminated without hanging up the host computer.

Business Criteria

Business criteria relate to the business decision to purchase toolsets from a specific vendor. Business criteria deal with the cost of acquisition, lifecycle costs for operation, vendor responsiveness, the need for training, customer support, and the purchase of maintenance for the toolset from the vendor.

Table 5.1-2 provides some examples of technical criteria that may be important to enterprises.

TABLE 5.1-2   Business Criteria for Tool Selection

Sample Criteria	Description
Vendor Viability	The real investment in an EA development is the investment in labor and the creation of a knowledge asset. The cost of a toolset is a relatively small factor, but the nuisance value of having knowledge assets locked up in a tool that was sold by a vendor that went out of business is extremely high. In the toolset vendor industry, frequent mergers and consolidations are the norm. What are the probabilities that a vendor is in merger negotiations? What is the probability of the acquiring company providing the same level of support or better?
Vendor Reputation and References	Software quality improves based on actual usage, reporting of problems, and maintenance upgrades that fix problems. Usage references and vendor reputation for quality, reliability, and timeliness of upgrades are therefore key criteria.
Cost and Licensing	The cost of the toolset is still a significant investment in dollar terms. There is the initial cost of acquisition and the inevitable maintenance costs. There is also a hidden cost to the enterprise in absorbing every new release. Vendors who provide very frequent upgrades can inflate this cost very quickly. Costing must be performed on a lifecycle basis to understand the true cost. Costs may include purchase of consulting from the vendor as a product subject matter expert (SME).
Vendor Support Availability	Availability of vendor support for installation, consulting, training, product-related assistance and help desk, and recovery of data or restoration of software.
Scalability of Vendor Support	The ability of a vendor to scale short-term support during the ramp-up stages of the EA development and stand down after the initial development moves into maintenance mode.
Training	The availability of training at the customer's location to leverage the travel-related cost of training. The types of training available including modeling, data administration and management, technical support, and advanced customizations.

(continued)

| TABLE 5.1-2 | Business Criteria for Tool Selection (*Continued*) |

Sample Criteria	Description
Latency	The amount of time that is estimated from development kickoff to a point where an EA development team is fully familiar with the use and operation of the toolset and requires minimal support and hand holding. From that point onward, team members can crosstrain each other.
Maintenance and Upgrades	What is the anticipated frequency of upgrades? Are the upgrades targeted toward bug fixes or do they also offer improvements in functionality? What has been the vendor's past history with upgrades?
Product Lifecycle Stage	In the vendor-provided software industry, the lifecycle of a software product offering is based on the economic returns to the vendor in comparison with the incremental costs expended. For example, costs are expended with each new release of a toolset. Costs are also expended when platform changes occur, such as when the customer moves from Windows XP to Windows Vista and from Windows Vista to Windows 7. Some vendors provide statements of direction that provide reassurance to customers, but others may decide to terminate all support for their products because of the unfavorable cost/return equation.

Integration Criteria

Models and architectures are not built in isolation but have to integrate into a larger context. Tools that need to manage models need import and export capabilities to allow them to consume and produce architecture data that is exchanged with other parts of the enterprise or other collaborating enterprises. The adherence to modeling standards (which establish standard terminology) and data exchange standards (that specify the format, grammar, meaning, and content scope) is essential for interoperability. Table 5.1-3 lists some examples of criteria used to assess interoperability.

Functionality Criteria

We come to the most important set of criteria: functionality. First and foremost, a toolset must successfully fulfill the tasks that it is supposed to support. Functionality criteria include ease of use; adequate support for the modeling techniques that are proposed and the various types of models that will be built; support for selected frameworks; integration of data across models; data management support and operations that are based on data, such as spell-checking and grammar checking;

TABLE 5.1-3   Integration Criteria for Tool Selection

Sample Criteria	Description
Import and Export Capability	Does the toolset provide rich capabilities for importing and exporting data to and from spreadsheets, comma-separated value (CSV) files, desktop databases, relational database management system (RDBMS) sources? Does the toolset also provide exports in some of the proprietary formats that are used by other tools?
Conformance to Industry Standards	Does the toolset conform to industry standards for data exchange from standards bodies such as American National Standards Institute (ANSI), the Object Management Group (OMG), the Institute of Electrical and Electronic Engineers (IEEE), and the International Standards Organization (ISO)?
Conformance to Modeling/ Methodology Standards	Does the toolset conform to modeling and methodology standards that have been adopted by your enterprise? How closely does it conform to the specifications? Are there customizations and extensions that must be avoided to promote sharing of architecture models?
Conformance to Industry Standard Frameworks	Does the toolset conform to your chosen architecture framework?
Architected for Interoperability	Is the toolset designed for interoperability? Many picture-drawing tools do not have a robust data management layer underneath and have problems exchanging text-based semantic information. Tools that are designed for interoperability generally have a robust database management system to manage the architecture data. All interoperability-related operations such as import, export, and transformation of data to various standards are accomplished easily because of the use of this data layer.
Ability to Interoperate with Other Tools and Repositories	What are the requirements for interoperability with partner and component enterprises? Do they use a different toolset that must be accommodated? Does the toolset under evaluation provide capabilities for sharing architecture data with these other toolsets and repositories?

support for report generation and document generation; support for collaborative spaces where users can annotate, mark up, and suggest changes to models; and more. Table 5.1-4 describes a few examples of the types of criteria that relate to functionality.

TABLE 5.1-4	Functionality Criteria for Tool Selection
Sample Criteria	**Description**
Ease of Use	Does the toolset provide ease of use through an intuitive user interface? Is the layout of the various menus, screens, and controls intuitive and in line with other comparable software interfaces? Does the toolset have a steep learning curve? Does it offer online help, context-sensitive help, and online tutorials?
Supported Modeling Types	Does the toolset support the full range of anticipated model types that will be built? For example, the DoD Architecture Framework specifies over 50 types of models for modeling DoD architectures.
Data Management	Does the toolset provide robust data management capabilities, such as searching, importing, exporting, reporting, querying, backing up, and recovering data?
Query, Search, and Report	Does the toolset provide a rich range of reports that meet the needs of the enterprise "out of the box"? Does it provide facilities for constructing custom reports? Does the toolset support an internal data dictionary that can be used to build fit-for-purpose reports from the data that is stored inside? Does the toolset provide querying and searching—specifically searching for items through raw text, keywords, and phrases without regard to their semantic typing?
Configuration Management and Release Management	Does the toolset provide capabilities for managing releases of an architecture? Does the toolset provide capabilities for storing versions of architecture data and model versions? Does the toolset provide traceability of a release to specific versions of architecture data elements?
Collaboration Space	Contemporary techniques for collaboration are based on the use of social networking and wiki technologies. Social networking involves broadcasting events of interest to many stakeholders and allowing them to vote on, comment on, and approve of the event or the circumstances around the event. Wiki technologies allow participating stakeholders to modify architecture data elements directly. Both of these techniques are very useful in improving enterprise architectures and the fidelity of architecture models as well as their validity. Does the toolset support social networking or wiki technologies? Another capability that results from collaborative workspaces is the ability to create "mashups"—combinations of existing architecture data elements that are new and innovative and are creations of the mashup author. Mashups result in interesting uses for existing information by rearranging elements to form new solutions or new formulations of a problem. Does the toolset support mashups?
Capacity, Scale, and Complexity Management	Does the toolset deal with the large volumes of architecture data that arise from an enterprise architecture development? Are there mechanisms for brokering the complexity, such as hierarchical decomposition techniques, provision of a "world view" in a corner of the screen to orient the user in large, complicated, detailed model diagrams?

TABLE 5.1-4	Functionality Criteria for Tool Selection *(Continued)*	

Sample Criteria	Description
Multi-user Support	Does the tool support concurrent use by multiple users? What are the strategies in place to prevent corruption of data in a multi-user concurrent mode of operation? What are the tool's collision-avoidance strategies? What are the measures for preventing the addition of duplicative data? What is the strategy for audit trails for changes to determine when a change was made, who made the change, and what the exact change was?
Metamodel Issues	The metamodel for a toolset is the model that describes how the data inside the tool is organized. Does the toolset publish its repository metamodel? Does the toolset provide extensibility of its internal repository data model? Does the extensibility have to be performed by the vendor or can the implementing enterprise extend the metamodel by itself?
Automated Document/ Script Generation	Does the toolset automatically generate enterprise-mandated documents such as DoD ISPs, OMB Business Cases (A-300), and other standard format artifacts that are useful outputs of architecture development? Does the toolset generate scripts for downstream solution implementation, such as the generation of SQL Data Definition Language statements from a fully attributed Logical Data Model?

What Is an EA Repository?

A repository is a shared asset base for managing architecture data that comes from multiple development projects, multiple modelers and analysts, and multiple toolsets. Repositories are used to enforce enterprise standards across these multitudes of architecture data and to promote a level of architecture data standardization that comes from a central vantage point.

Depending on the size and scale of operations of an enterprise, one or more repositories can exist within an enterprise. When there is more than one repository, the enterprise must establish governance strategies that determine which repository is an authoritative source for which types of data, synchronization processes to determine and eliminate redundant data, and concurrency management to arbitrate the sharing of data when the data may be altered by the consumer and updated back into the repository.

Repositories are storage mechanisms for architecture data. They may be built on top of a relational database management system or use a file system for physical storage.

Repository Metamodel

The organization scheme for the data storage inside a repository is called the metamodel. Although purists can argue that the concept of a metamodel is the model of a model, it has become common practice to describe the model structure that holds other models as instances of a metamodel. The metamodel describes the element types in a type of model: For example, the metamodel of RDBMS schemas expresses concepts such as RDBMS_TABLE and RDBMS_TABLE_COLUMN. The metamodel in the repository is simply another schema.

The fundamental difference between a database schema (for example, a payroll management database stored in Oracle) and a repository metamodel is that the relational schema is relatively fixed but the repository metamodel is flexible and can be changed by the repository administrator, using capabilities provided by the repository vendor. Yes, the relational schema can be changed by the database administrator and this generally requires making changes to applications that access the database. It may even necessitate the unloading and reloading of data to fit the changed schema. The architecture of repositories is based on the use of a flexible metamodel. That is, changes in the metamodel do not require software changes in the repository software or changes in the reporting mechanisms inside the repository. This is accomplished by an indirect transformation layer between the repository metamodel and the underlying data management schema. This indirect transformation layer insulates reporting, application code, and other repository mechanisms from changes.

Benefits of the Repository Metamodel

The ability to change the repository metamodel flexibly provides tremendous advantages to the enterprise architect. It enables the architect to bring in new tools and modeling methods, relate existing architecture data to other architecture data, and invent new properties that capture data of interest to the enterprise, all without changing a single line of code.

Figure 5.1-1 describes a subset of the metamodel for IDEF1X. We will develop an illustrative metamodel simply by noting the following facts about an IDEF1X model. These facts become the data requirements for developing the metamodel. The metamodel itself may be represented using IDEF1X.

- An IDEF1X model is fundamentally comprised of data entities, relationships, and attributes (E-R-A).
- Data attributes are properties of data entities and data relationships

- A data entity can be an independent entity or a dependent entity. An independent entity does not require the existence of any other entity. A dependent entity can exist only when its parent entity exists.

- A subcategory or subtype entity is a specific type of dependent entity that has all the same characteristics of its parent entity and some additional characteristics that are specific to it alone.

- A relationship is an association that associates two entities. The two entities are sometimes referred to as the parent entity and the child entity.

- A relationship can be one of three types: identifying, nonidentifying, and subcategory.

- In an identifying relationship, the existence of the child entity is predicated on the existence of the parent entity.

- In a nonidentifying relationship, the existence of the child and parent entities is independent of each other.

- A subcategory relationship associates a parent entity with its subtype child entity.

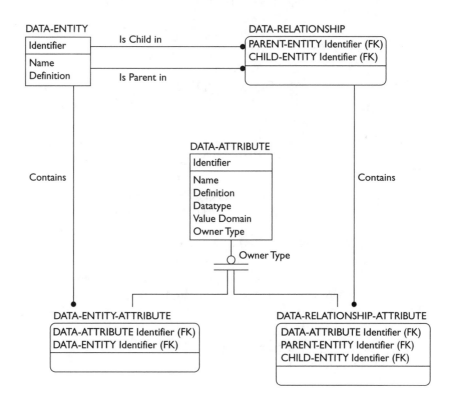

FIGURE 5.1-1

IDEF 1X
Metamodel
Subset

The following are the classic steps of data modeling to build the metamodel:

1. The candidate concepts are DATA-ENTITY, DATA-ATTRIBUTE, and DATA-RELATIONSHIP.
2. The candidate associations between the candidate concepts are as follows:
   a. DATA-ENTITY is Characterized by DATA-ATTRIBUTE.
   b. DATA-ENTITY is Child in DATA-RELATIONSHIP.
   c. DATA-ENTITY is Parent in DATA-RELATIONSHIP.
   d. DATA-RELATIONSHIP is Characterized by DATA-ATTRIBUTE.
3. We can add some minimum attribution for the concepts. These are attributes that any concept can have.
   a. DATA-ENTITY has the following attributes:
      i. NAME
      ii. DEFINITION
      iii. IDENTIFIER (for synonyms)
   b. DATA-ATTRIBUTE has the following attributes:
      i. NAME
      ii. DEFINITION
      iii. IDENTIFIER
      iv. DATATYPE
      v. MAXIMUM-LENGTH
      vi. VALUE-DOMAIN (for specifying acceptable values)
      vii. OWNER-ENTITY
   c. DATA-RELATIONSHIP has the following attributes:
      i. NAME (usually called the VERB PHRASE)
      ii. PARENT-ENTITY
      iii. CHILD-ENTITY
      iv. RELATIONSHIP-TYPE (identifying, nonidentifying, or subcategory)

As we see through this brief exercise, we are able to develop a metamodel to organize IDEF1X Data Model storage inside a repository through some simple analysis of the concepts that an IDEF1X Data Model expresses. The steps we have used are simply to illustrate the thinking behind metamodel development. In an advanced IDEF1X data modeling exercise (outside the scope of this section), there are additional constructs such as category relationships, foreign keys, owned attributes, and primary keys that need to be modeled in addition to establishing cardinalities of our associations.

The model we have developed is very powerful. It can provide an organization structure that can store any number of IDEF1X model instances. We could easily store, say, 300 IDEF1X Data Models as instances of the metamodel we have built!

By adopting the same systematic modeling strategy, we can develop metamodel fragments for UML class diagrams, UML use-case diagrams, IDEF0 Activity Models, BPMN collaboration workflow models, and more.

As we start metamodeling more and more types of models, we start to recognize that some concepts in one type of model are repeated either exactly or with a modified name in another type of model. Recognizing these overlaps of similar concepts across multiple model types is the basis for repository-based integration.

How Does a Repository Integrate Models?

Recognizing concept overlaps across metamodels of multiple model types allows a repository vendor to offer a metamodel that has collapsed redundant concepts across metamodel fragments to establish the reality that two metamodels are both using the same underlying architecture data element.

Figure 5.1-2 illustrates the simple metamodel for an Operational Resource Flow Matrix (OV-3) product used by enterprise architects to model the resource/information exchanges between two sets of performers. Because information exchanges are made based only on need, some activity that is being performed by the sender is responsible for producing information that is received by some activity being performed by the receiver. In short, adding activities to sending and receiving performers adds context to the information exchange.

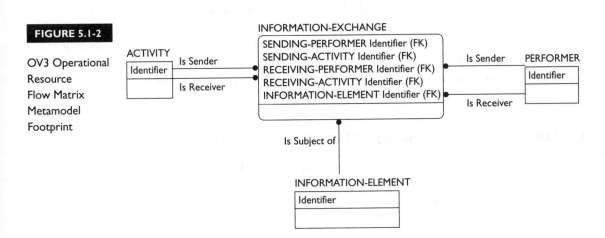

FIGURE 5.1-2

OV3 Operational Resource Flow Matrix Metamodel Footprint

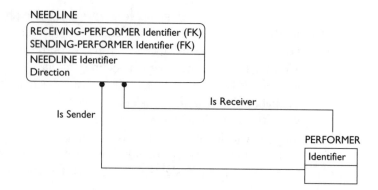

FIGURE 5.1-3

OV2 Operational
Resource Flow
Description
Metamodel
Footprint

Figure 5.1-3 illustrates the simple metamodel for an Operational Resource Flow Description (OV-2). The purpose of this diagram is to present needlines (needs for exchanges of resources/information) between two performers.

We very quickly see that in an integrated architecture, the two models must share the same semantics—that is, the resource flow diagram is simply a summarization of the resource exchange matrix without the activities or details of the resources/information elements being exchanged. This means that for an integrated architecture, the OV-3 and OV-2 must not contradict each other—the OV-3 is simply a detailed elaboration of the OV-2, but for a different audience interested in the details of the exchange. How can we integrate the two metamodel fragments for the OV-3 and the OV-2 by defining an amalgamated metamodel?

By establishing a constraining relationship that requires the performers in the OV-2 to be the same performers inside the OV-3 (see Figure 5.1-4), we integrate the two models and ensure that there is no inconsistency in the information that they provide to the analyst.

The importance of using a repository to integrate model development cannot be overstated. Repositories not only provide data management capabilities, such as normalizing architecture data elements, but also provide constraints that keep the data clean and usable.

DoDAF Core Architecture Data Model (CADM)

The CADM was the original metamodel for the precursor to the DoD Architecture Framework—the C4ISR Architecture Framework—and continued to be the recommended DoDAF metamodel up until DoDAF 1.5. With DoDAF 2.0, the CADM was replaced by the DoDAF Meta-Model (DMM, or DM2).

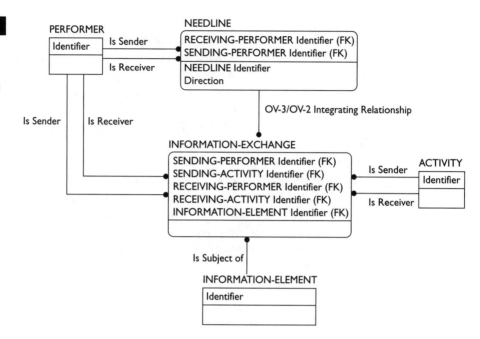

FIGURE 5.1-4

Integrated
Metamodel that
Unifies OV-2 and
OV-3 Elements

The CADM was organized using an IDEF1X Logical Data Model approach. CADM is a fully normalized, fully attributed Logical Data Model with specifications for attribute value domains that promote integration of architecture information. The CADM had its origins in the modeling of communications and data exchange networks and topology analysis techniques stemming from its purpose of supporting C4ISR architectures.

The CADM unified the metamodels of the 25+ DoDAF model types to ensure that an integrated architecture could be built.

DoDAF DM2 Repository Metamodel

The DoD Architecture Framework takes the concept of CADM repository metamodeling one step further and requires the implementation of a published and standardized DoD Architecture Framework Meta-Model (DM2). The DM2 integrates the metamodel fragments of the 50+ DoDAF-described models.

The DM2 provides a high-level view of the data normally collected, organized, and maintained in an architectural description effort. It also serves as a roadmap for the reuse of data under the federated approach to architecture development and management. Reuse of data among communities of interest provides a way for managers at any level or in any area of the department to understand what has been done by others and also what information is already available for use in their architectural descriptions and management decision-making efforts.

The DM2 has several levels, each of which is important to a particular viewer of departmental processes. A Conceptual Data Model (CDM) defines the high-level data constructs from which architectural descriptions are created in nontechnical terms so that executives and managers at all levels can understand the data basis of the architectural description (see Figure 5.1-5).

The Logical Data Model (LDM) adds technical information, such as attributes to the CDM, and, when necessary, it clarifies relationships by providing an unambiguous usage definition. A Physical Exchange Specification (PES) consists of the LDM with general data types specified and implementation attributes (for example, sources and dates) added and then generated as a set of XML Schema Definitions (XSDs).

Table 5.1-5 describes the key concepts in the DM2.

FIGURE 5.1-5

DM2 High-Level Conceptual View

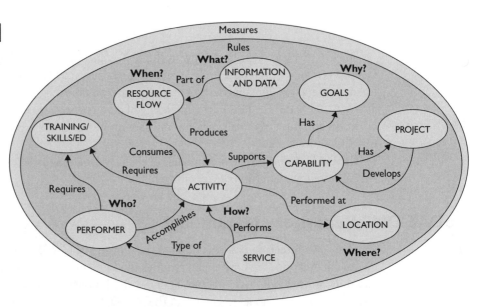

Note: Measures and rules can be applied to all other concepts.

TABLE 5.1-5   DM2 Key Concepts and Descriptions

Concept	Description
Activity	Work, not specific to a single organization, weapon system, or individual, that transforms inputs (resources) into outputs (resources) or changes their state.
Agreement	Consent among parties regarding the terms and conditions of activities that the parties participate in.
Architectural Description	Information describing an architecture such as an OV-5b Operational Activity Model.
Capability	The ability to achieve a desired effect under specified (performance) standards and conditions through combinations of ways and means (activities and resources) to perform a set of activities.
Condition	The state of an environment or situation in which a performer performs.
Constraint	The range of permissible states for an object.
Data	Representation of information in a formalized manner suitable for communication, interpretation, or processing by humans or by automatic means. Potential examples include whole models, packages, entities, attributes, classes, domain values, enumeration values, records, tables, rows, columns, and fields.
Desired Effect	The result, outcome, or consequence of an action (activity).
Guidance	An authoritative statement intended to lead or steer the execution of actions.
Information	The state of a something of interest that is materialized—in any medium or form—and communicated or received.
Location	A point or extent in space that may be referred to physically or logically.
Materiel	Equipment, apparatus, or supplies that are of interest, without distinction as to its application for administrative or combat purposes.
Measure	The magnitude of some attribute of an individual.
Measure Type	A category of measures.
Organization	A specific real-world assemblage of people and other resources organized for an ongoing purpose.
Performer	Any entity—human, automated, or any aggregation of human and automated—that performs an activity and provides a capability.
Person Type	A category of persons defined by the role or roles they share that are relevant to an architecture.
Project	A temporary endeavor undertaken to create resources or desired effects.
Resource	Data, information, performers, materiel, or personnel types that are produced or consumed.
Rule	A principle or condition that governs behavior; a prescribed guide for conduct or action.

(continued)

TABLE 5.1-5	DM2 Key Concepts and Descriptions (*Continued*)
Concept	**Description**
Service	A mechanism to enable access to a set of one or more capabilities, where the access is provided using a prescribed interface and is exercised consistent with constraints and policies as specified by the service description. The mechanism is a performer. The capabilities accessed are resources—information, data, materiel, performers, and geopolitical extents.
Skill	The ability, coming from one's knowledge, practice, aptitude, and such, to do something well.
Standard	A formal agreement documenting generally accepted specifications or criteria for products, processes, procedures, policies, systems, and/or personnel.
System	A functionally, physically, and/or behaviorally related group of regularly interacting or interdependent elements.
Vision	An end that describes the future state of the enterprise, without regard to how it is to be achieved; a mental image of what the future will or could be like.

TOGAF 9 Repository Metamodel

Figure 5.1-6 shows the Architecture Repository structure recommended by TOGAF 9. Key aspects of the structure are as follows:

- **Architecture Landscape**   The Architecture Landscape holds architectural views of the state of the enterprise at particular points in time. Due to the sheer volume and the diverse stakeholder needs throughout an entire enterprise, the Architecture Landscape is divided into three levels of granularity: Strategic Architectures, Segment Architectures, and Capability Architectures.

- **Reference Library**   The Reference Library provides a repository area to hold best-practice or template materials that can be used to construct architectures within an enterprise. Reference materials held in the Reference Library may be obtained from a variety of sources.

- **Standards Information Base**   The Standards Information Base provides a repository area to hold a set of specifications to which architectures must conform. Establishment of a Standards Information Base provides an unambiguous basis for architectural governance.

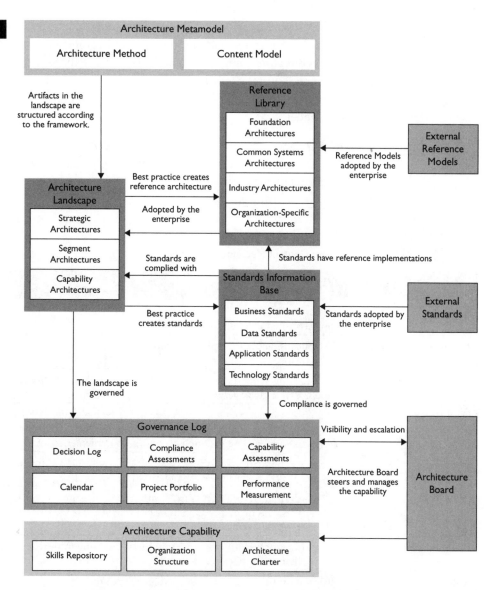

FIGURE 5.1-6

TOGAF 9
Architecture
Repository
Structure

- **Governance Log**   The Governance Log provides a repository area to hold shared information relating to the ongoing governance of projects.
- **Architecture Capability**   The Architecture Capability contains an inventory of the architecture skills available, organizational structure of the architecture team, and the charter of the architecture team.

■ **Architecture Metamodel** The Architecture Metamodel is comprised of the ADM process model as well as the architecture content metamodel. The architecture content metamodel is used to express the vocabulary of architecture terms needed to develop TOGAF views. Table 5.1-6 describes the key architecture concepts in the TOGAF 9 architecture content metamodel.

Figure 5.1-7 depicts the relationships among the core entities.

In addition to establishing the core concepts, TOGAF also provides a way ahead for extensions to tailor the repository for a specific implementation of an organization's needs, as shown in Figure 5.1-8.

TABLE 5.1-6 TOGAF 9 Core Content Metamodel Concepts

Concept	Description
Actor	A person, organization, or system that is outside the consideration of the architecture model, but interacts with it.
Application Component	An encapsulation of application functionality that is aligned to implementation structuring.
Business Service	Service that supports business capabilities through an explicitly defined interface and is explicitly governed by an organization.
Data Entity	An encapsulation of data that is recognized by a business domain expert as a discrete concept. Data entities can be tied to applications, repositories, and services and may be structured according to implementation considerations.
Function	Activity that delivers business capabilities closely aligned to an organization, but not explicitly governed by the organization.
Organization	A self-contained unit of resources with line management responsibility, goals, objectives, and measures. Organizations may include external parties and business partner organizations.
Platform Service	A technical capability required to provide enabling infrastructure that supports the delivery of applications.
Role	A position that an actor assumes to perform a task.
Technology Component	An encapsulation of technology infrastructure that represents a class of technology product or specific technology product.

FIGURE 5.1-7

Relationships
Among Core
Entities and
Relationships
in the TOGAF 9
Content
Metamodel

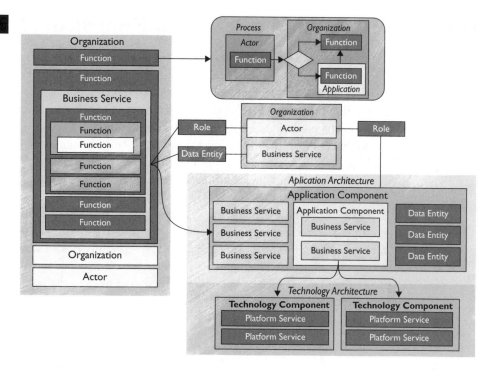

FIGURE 5.1-8 TOGAF Extensibility for the Core Metamodel

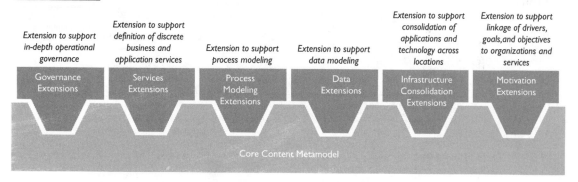

How Do EA Tools Work with a Repository?

EA tools use the repository as the authoritative store for architecture data elements. The tools themselves provide data manipulation, drawing, and composition capabilities to build models. The tools enforce methodology- and technique-related constraints to ensure that the models that are built according to an engineering discipline.

After the models are built, the tools store the models back inside the repository. As we have illustrated in the metamodel fragments in Figures 5.1-1 through 5.1-4 and the repository organization in Figure 5.1-6, the metamodel of the repository is a relatively simple data organization structure that can organize and store hundreds of models.

Figure 5.1-9 shows the repository as the hub for managing architecture data from multiple architecture tools. The repository provided value added data management functions in addition to acting as a hub. The repository can be seen as a hub for all tool-based model developments if the tools were to be viewed as the spokes. If dissimilar tools are used to build different types of models, the burden of translating the output of one tool to be compatible with the input of another frequently falls upon the repository vendor.

FIGURE 5.1-9

Repository and Tools Form a Hub-and-Spoke Relationship

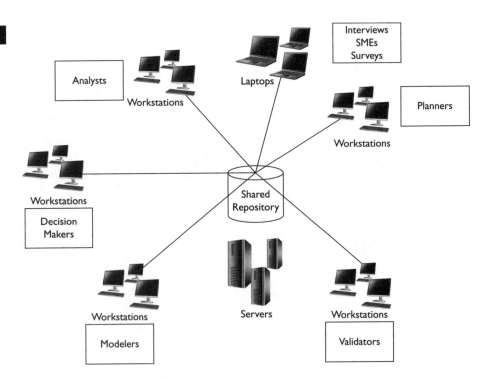

Planners can use the repository as a source of research information for scoping a planned initiative. One example of such research is to look at potentially impacted organizations, locations, systems, business functions; skill set requirements; and external stakeholders. The advantage of the repository as a research tool is that it consolidates the architecture data content of multiple developments in one place and ensures the quality of the data as well as the consistency.

Subject matter experts and analysts performing interviews can reduce the latency of the use of the raw data they are collecting by posting this collected raw data into the repository with markings to indicate the state of accuracy and completeness of the data. This allows data consumers to see the data and not wait for the interviewer's back office information processing cycle to grind its way through the data.

The following subsection discusses a few attempts at addressing the problem of transforming or translating architecture data produced by one tool to a common format or to a format accepted by another tool.

Interface Standards

One of the earliest attempts to enable exchange of architecture data from one tool to another was the establishment of common exchange standards. Early attempts included the formulation of IDEF Interface Definition Language (IDL), which allowed two process modeling tools to share IDEF0 process models. Another was Common Data Interchange Format (CDIF), which was an agreed-upon standard among multiple vendors to share architecture data. Remember that migrating data away from one tool to another is not in the first tool vendor's business interests. Many enterprises tend to standardize their tool selections to reduce the variety and the challenges of the data interchange problem. This combination of adverse commercial interest and narrow tool selections has tended to work against the establishment of interface standards. A large customer such as the U.S. Department of Defense is currently requiring that architecture tools comply with the PES of the DoDAF.

Metamodel Unification

Part of the tool data exchange problem is that the modeling methodologies used by one organization or unit is not the same as one used by another. One example is the use of IDEF1X at one location or business unit for modeling processes and the use of BPMN at another. Transforming a model built using one methodology requires translation of architecture elements in the language of that methodology to another language. In our example, a transformation of the Activity Model in IDEF1X requires determining equivalences between the IDEF0 vocabulary such as Activity, Box, Arrow, ICOM, Context Diagram, FEO Diagram, and Facing Page Notes to equivalent concepts in BPMN—which may not always exist.

Repository vendors who provide such transformation services or offer a universal repository for managing models built using multiple methodologies have to deal with unification of the inherent metamodels for these methodologies.

Standards bodies such as the Object Management Group (OMG) have been involved in developing unification models that relate multiple metamodels. Initiatives such as the Common Warehouse Model and the Information Management Metamodel are attempts in the field of data modeling to unify competing or alternative technology–based metamodels into a common "super-metamodel." OMG's approach to unification is to reduce all the component metamodels to a single modeling methodology: UML. For example, the metamodel for RDBMS that includes items such as TABLE, COLUMN, INDEX, DOMAIN, and CONSTRAINT is reduced to a UML profile. Similarly, the metamodel for XSD that includes items such as ELEMENT, COMPLEX TYPE, and SIMPLE TYPE is also reduced to a UML profile. Because UML offers comprehensive facilities for expressing aggregation/composition, subtyping/generalization, and associations, the profiles can be accurately built. The profiles are then unified through relationships.

Framework-Provided Semantics

The previous approaches are based on bottom-up resolution of a challenge that arises when tools and methodologies already exist and enterprises that have adopted dissimilar tools and methodologies needed to collaborate or exchange architecture data. Frameworks such as the DoDAF and the TOGAF specify the vocabulary or architecture elements from the inception because they believe that common vocabulary and language should be driven from the framework itself rather than allowing architects (and methodologists) to coin their own architecture vocabularies. Repositories that are built with metamodels that conform to framework-specified metamodels have a greater chance of facilitating architecture data exchanges.

Repository Selection Criteria

The repository plays a central role in model-based architecture developments. Enterprises spend a lot of effort in selecting toolsets without paying the same attention to the selection of the repository. A number of the criteria that were presented for tool selection also apply to the repository selection.

The repository is and should be viewed as an architecture asset management system. In the life of an enterprise architecture, there is potential for changing toolset selections along the way. These changes are sometimes driven by external forces, such as a vendor going out of business or being acquired by another vendor. They can also be driven by internal forces, such as changes in policy for the standard toolset of choice that are dictated by higher authority.

What lives on is the data about the enterprise—the architecture models and knowledge that has been accumulated as a result of enterprise architecture development efforts. And this data lives inside a repository. Visibility of this data and freedom from proprietary formats are fundamental criteria for repositories. Such freedom will enable an enterprise to change its toolset selection strategy without disrupting or destroying the asset that it has created at great expense and effort over the years.

Questions

1. What are the criteria you would use to select an architecture framework that is suitable for your enterprise? Using the criteria you have described, select one of the frameworks described in this book. Make a case for why that selected framework is most appropriate for your enterprise.

2. What are the criteria for selecting a modeling methodology? Should you choose more than one methodology? Using the criteria you described, make a selection of one or more methodologies that are appropriate for adoption in your enterprise. Make a case for the selected methodology (or methodologies).

3. Is there a modeling lifecycle process that is commonly used within your enterprise? Discuss the pros and cons of defining a standard model development process. How would you administer the process?

4. What are the criteria for selecting architecture development tools? Use the criteria you described to shortlist two alternatives for architecture development tools. Make a case for each set of tools.

5. What is an integrated architecture? Explain how an integrated dictionary is used to integrate multiple models. Why is an integrated architecture essential?

6. What is configuration management of architecture models? Why is configuration management useful? What are the challenges of configuration management of models in your enterprise?

7. What is an EA repository? How does a repository assist in collaborative modeling? What is the role of the repository in an architecture team–based development project?

8. What is a repository metamodel? How is it different from a database schema? How does a repository integrate models?

9. Discuss the approach you would use to recommend to an enterprise a tool and repository strategy and an implementation roadmap for supporting architecture development.

Reference List

Department of Defense. (2009). *Department of Defense Architecture Framework (DODAF) Version 2.0, Volumes I and II*. United States Department of Defense.

NIST. (1993). *Integration Definition for Information Modeling (IDEF1X)*. Draft Federal Information Processing Standards Publication (FIPS) 184. Computer Systems Laboratory, National Institute of Standards and Technology.

NIST. (1994). *Integration Definition for Function Modeling (IDEF0)*. Draft Federal Information Processing Standards Publication (FIPS) 183. December 1993. Computer Systems Laboratory, National Institute of Standards and Technology.

Object Management Group (OMG). (2010). *Documents Associated with UML Version 2.3*. Release Date May 2010. Object Management Group. http://www.omg.org/spec/UML/2.3/.

Object Management Group (OMG). (2011). *Documents Associated with Business Process Model and Notation Version 2.0*. January 2011. Object Management Group. http://www.omg.org/spec/BPMN/2.0/.

The Open Group. (2009). *The Open Group Architecture Framework 9 (TOGAF 9)*. The Open Group.

5.2

A Case Study: Richard M. Nixon International Airport, CA

T he purpose of this case study is to provide an integrated backdrop to set a collection of problems that have been modeled in various chapters of this book. An integrated backdrop is essential to demonstrate the value of integrated architectures.

The case study will also illustrate that real-life scenarios for enterprises include combinations of commercial, federal, state, and local enterprises as stakeholders and participants. In addition, it illustrates the healthy tension among conflicting needs and the constant requirement to prioritize investments consciously in the face of this tension. Sometimes we underestimate the "flooding" effect of key events that undermine and overtake all planning that had been previously performed. Examples of such events in recent memory are the attacks on the World Trade Center on September 11, 2001; Hurricane Katrina; the financial crisis on Wall Street and the demise of Bear Stearns; and more recently, the BP oil well bubbling up tens of thousands of barrels of crude oil from the floor of the Atlantic Ocean.

The common saying is that distance brings perspective. When we are deep inside the bowels of an enterprise, we are very close to our problem, but not very conscious of our surroundings. This is much like when a semitrailer truck is right behind your car on the highway, blocking your view in the rear-view mirror. Increasing the distance between the truck and your car can suddenly bring many more objects into view. If you are planning a lane change or taking an exit ramp, you have more information to guide you on the risk of that maneuver. Writing a case study is an exercise in first distancing yourself from the immediate problem, getting a broader view, and then refocusing on the problem in the context of this broader view. Often it is useful to write your own case study before embarking on a solution strategy for a specific problem, as we will find out when we write an architecture problem statement and roadmap, also known as an AV-1 Architecture Overview and Summary.

In this book, we use a collection of models to represent various aspects of an architecture. An integrated architecture is one where common architecture elements are shared across models and there is no ambiguity when the same architecture element (for example, a specific performer of an activity) appears in more than one model. Without integration, a consistent analysis cannot be performed. The purpose of modeling is to support analysis and the generation of findings that will drive a course of action.

We will use a combination of English narrative descriptions, pictures describing the case study, and a few selected sets of lists and tables to organize information related to the case study in a more compact manner than a rambling narrative would offer.

The case study illustrates how a modeling technique is used to achieve a type of representation for some aspects of the enterprise. The importance of the case study is to provide a meaningful real-world example that focuses the mind while exercising the techniques that are presented in this book.

Because of the vastness of the types of problems that are faced by the enterprise presented in the case study, the best way to approach enterprise architecture–based analysis is by (i) defining a problem, a family of problems, or a class of problems that face the enterprise, and then (ii) defining a proposed initiative, a family of initiatives, or a collection of transformation projects, and (iii) systematically building models that represent the current and future states and facilitate the formulation of the transformation strategy.

During the course of the book, each of the chapters will draw upon the example of Richard M. Nixon Airport to illustrate the techniques of enterprise architecting. As a reader, it is important to note that the specific example of the case study is not as important as the planning, analysis, modeling, representation, and solution formulation techniques, as each of these can readily be employed in any enterprise. Figure 5.2-1 shows the relatively near location of Richard M. Nixon airport to Los Angeles International and the opportunities afforded by transformation.

FIGURE 5.2-1

Richard M. Nixon
Airport Location

California

Los Angeles International
Airport (LAX)

Richard M.Nixon
Municipal Airport (RMN)

Note: The case study is completely fictitious but the facts presented are similar to real-life challenges at real-life airports.

Richard M. Nixon Municipal (RMN) Airport, in Los Caballeros, California, is a small commuter airport, approximately 40 miles southeast of Los Angeles International Airport. The airport was named after a former president of the United States as a tribute to a fallen god who is still a reputed son of California and Los Angeles.

Selecting the Scope of the Enterprise

Enterprises come in all sizes and flavors. Complex enterprises may themselves be composed of smaller, almost equally complex, enterprises. The United States federal government is a complex enterprise that is comprised of the Executive Branch enterprise, the Judiciary Branch enterprise, and the Legislative Branch enterprise, for example. Although they are supposed to complement each other through checks and balances to support the larger enterprise called the government of the United States, often they are working at cross-purposes.

The Executive Branch enterprise itself is composed of the various cabinet department agencies and other noncabinet agencies such as the Federal Election Commission or the Nuclear Regulatory Commission.

A cabinet department agency such as the Department of Health and Human Services is itself composed of a number of smaller, yet complex operating divisional enterprises such as the Centers for Disease Control, National Institutes of Health, and National Cancer Research Institute.

An enterprise such as the Centers for Disease Control is itself composed of a number of divisions, centers, branches, and departments located at various places inside the United States and worldwide.

Each of these enterprises also has dependencies or need to exchange information and resources with other enterprises. For example, the Securities and Exchange Commission feeds the collection of fees from securities filers to the Treasury Department. The Department of Homeland Security collects flight manifests from commercial airline carriers of passengers before a flight arrives at the borders of the United States.

Given the wide range of possibilities for the scope of an enterprise as well as the range of relationships and dependencies for other enterprises, choosing a case study was a careful exercise. We wanted to select an enterprise that was reasonably well understood by the average reader but also had the potential to present complex problems, formulate nontrivial solutions, and provide a canvas for debate and discussion and the posing of several alternatives. The criteria for selecting the case study also included the need to reflect multiple viewpoints—such as the strategic, operational, systems and services, and technology—while also providing focus for governance-related processes such as Capital Planning and Investment Control and transformation processes that would take the enterprise from the current state to a future target state.

Strategic Thrust

With the tremendous pressure of increasing traffic at Los Angeles International Airport (LAX), RMN is looking at opportunistically drawing the traffic from LAX and the other Los Angeles area airport, Orange County. At this point, RMN is a sleepy, small airport servicing hobby pilots and small commuter aircraft. Harvesting the promise of the opportunity is a challenge in risk taking, planning, prioritization, and implementation—the kinds of things that enterprise architecture promises to facilitate.

Planning for the Future

LAX is not only a destination airport for passengers bound for Los Angeles, it is also a gateway airport into the United States and is used to process passengers for customs and immigration on flights that are arriving from foreign lands. LAX is also a hub airport for passengers transiting to other destinations. As a result, at any given moment, a passenger at LAX may be arriving in Los Angeles, departing Los Angeles, transiting from an inbound flight to an outbound flight, or coming into the United States as a U.S. citizen, immigrant, visitor, or student.

Processing people coming into and departing from any airport from the United States on a flight bound to a foreign destination involves the United States Immigration and Customer Enforcement (ICE) organization. Furthermore, for passengers carrying dairy and farm products, the U.S. Department of Agriculture is also involved through the Agriculture Public Health Inspection Service (APHIS). Passengers must comply with the United States laws relating to immigration and the transport of goods into and out of the country. Laws such as the International Trafficking in Arms Regulations from the U.S. Department of Commerce ban the transport of materiel sensitive to the interests of the United States. The Drug Enforcement Agency is entrusted with the control and prevention of drug traffic into and out of the United States.

With the increased security posture in the United States after 9/11 and the use of airliners loaded with fuel as bombs by foreign terrorist organizations, passenger safety and national security interests have intersected and airports are at the front line of defense. Airport security, which was a matter for contracted security personnel, local and state law enforcement officials, now involves the Department of Homeland Security through the presences of screening personnel employed with the Transportation Safety Administration (TSA). TSA applies mandated screening procedures under the authority of the laws of the United States. TSA also provides for federal air marshals who travel on randomly selected air routes to assist in counterterrorism and apprehension activities on board an aircraft.

Civil aviation in the United States is federally regulated because of the safety issues, coordination and collaboration challenges, and use of shared resources such as the airspace over the United States. The Federal Aviation Administration (FAA)—a federal agency—is responsible for managing traffic inside U.S. domestic airspace. The FAA has a presence in the control tower of every airport. FAA traffic management facilities are provided to controllers to assist them in coordinating landings, takeoffs, and holding patterns and guiding air traffic from sector to sector.

Any expansion of the physical land around the existing airspace requires dealing with local and state authorities for permissions. Many local communities have noise-related ordinances and require noise abatement procedures. Bringing wide-body jets into RMN must include plans to lengthen and broaden existing runways. At the same time, to provide nonstop operations and take advantage of any wind direction, an additional runway may need to be constructed. The path of this potential new runway intersects with a neighboring bedroom community of high-dollar single-family residential housing.

Passenger Processing Capabilities

To be an attractive alternative to LAX, RMN will have to provide significantly greater capabilities for passenger management, comfort, convenience, and safety.

Passenger management includes processing passengers from the point of check-in to the point of boarding their aircraft, or from debarking to finally collecting their baggage and being on their way to their destination. Passengers may also use RMN to connect to other flights as well. Passenger management includes completion of customs and immigration requirements, safety screening procedures, guided access through airport public areas, and requirements for identification as well as authorization to travel at all times.

Passenger comfort involves providing environmental conditions for temperature control and management of passenger areas; adequate seating and resting facilities; amenities such as clean restrooms; areas in which baby diapers can be changed; and baby changing areas; potable water sources such as coolers in hallways; and fatigue-resistant flooring; and movement areas such as elevators, escalators, and corridors.

Passenger convenience is the provision of facilities inside the airport itself that are adequate for passengers' travel and work-related needs. These can include providing in-airport services for wireless Internet and electronic mail connections, electricity ports for passengers to recharge their electronics equipment, facsimile and printing services for business documents, help desks with maps, local tourist areas and personnel to assist passengers, and rapid transit to downtown Los Angeles and other points through partnerships with local authorities and rapid transit organizations. Providing facilities for passenger baggage storage, in-airport post offices, and other conveniences are intended to make RMN an inviting departure, destination, and transit hub for airlines.

Passenger safety has become a very important concern in the post-9/11 world. Ever since a group of terrorists hijacked an airliner and used it as a guided missile to destroy key buildings, the fear of plane hijacking and terrorism has rippled through U.S. airports. The increased alert posture of airports has also affected Richard M. Nixon Airport. From the entrance ramps of the highway that provides access to the airport to an array of equipment used for baggage and passenger screening, RMN is deeply committed to providing passenger safety. RMN is also concerned with privacy and antidiscrimination laws that prevent profiling of passengers. Law enforcement capabilities are provided by a detachment of local law enforcement assigned to RMN Airport. Airport authorities, screeners, and other personnel involved in passenger screening and detection of explosives and lethal weapons in hand-carried and checked baggage refer any incidents to these local law enforcement authorities.

Another important part of passenger safety is the need for well-established personnel support, processes, and services for evacuation, fire protection, medical care and triage services, ambulance services, sick bays, and other equipment needed to respond immediately and decisively to emergencies. Each of these services reaches back to the broader system of hospitals, firefighting forces, and other state, local, and county resources. RMN has established the principle of a minimum presence in first responders, given that its financial capability to keep a standing army of first responders is very limited. But RMN has also stipulated that escalation of first response will be the preferred approach to handling emergencies. RMN has routinely run drills and exercises to test the principle, although no major event has occurred in the history of its existence. Given the planned escalation of the size, capacity, and scope of the airport, it is anticipated that some of the assumptions related to escalation may need to be revisited.

Cargo Processing Capabilities

In addition to requiring the ability to manage passengers, RMN also needs capabilities to manage cargo operations. These include capabilities for cargo handling, tracking, inspection for customs purposes, and warehousing and storage, as well as constraints on the handling of hazardous materials and potentially dangerous cargo. Thus RMN must allocate space and facilities for cargo operations in addition to the passenger terminal operations. Although some of the capabilities needed to support cargo processing are the primary responsibility of the carrier—such as a package express company or the cargo operations arm of an airline—the airport management and facilities need to be able to support cargo operations in order to sustain them at RMN safely, efficiently, and effectively. The following are some details regarding the required cargo processing capabilities:

- Cargo handling capabilities require acquiring and operating equipment such as fork lifts, pallets, containerized handling equipment, roll-on and roll-off containers, materials handling equipment, and so on.

- Cargo tracking capabilities require automated identification technologies such as radio frequency ID (RFID) tagging and bar codes as well as a system of tracking that allows these identifiers to be captured at various points during the cargo processing cycle.

- Cargo inspection requires that various cargo items be checked in accordance with the laws of the United States. These laws are enforced by various federal agencies. The Department of Agriculture and APHIS enforce laws that control importation of plant and animal products. The Department of Commerce enforces laws related to the International Arms Trade (ITARS). The Department of Customs and Border Protection enforces laws related to the assessment, charging, and collection of customs duty.

- Cargo storage and management require space and segregated areas within the airport. For example, a bonded warehouse is required for customs-cleared cargo. A quarantine area is required when cargo suspected of containing harmful plant or animal material needs to be sequestered before being destroyed. Cargo storage also requires security and fire protection forces.

- Hazardous material (HAZMAT) cargo must be clearly identified as such and its storage managed to prevent potential chemical, biological, radiation, or nuclear explosion (CBRNE) events.

Revenue Generation Capabilities

Although passengers and cargo movement are the primary focus of the enterprise, there are many other stakeholders to satisfy. Passengers, although they generate revenue through financial transactions performed at the airport, are not the primary sources of revenue to the airport:

Concessions are contracted vendors who occupy the airport terminal premises and operate businesses that cater to passengers' needs. Concessions pay fees to be able to set up and use the terminal facilities for retail storefronts and restaurants. These fees are fixed and form a very stable and predictable part of the airport's revenue streams. Concessions are negotiated once every two years (unless there are closings and bankruptcies in between) and are based on contractual agreements that bind the concessionaire to pay fixed fees in return for accommodation, water, sewage, electricity, and natural gas connections. The Small Business Administration requires that a certain number of concessions be awarded to minority- and woman-owned small businesses in a bid to increase the participation of such enterprises in the state's economy. RMN in principle has agreed that promoting minority- and woman-owned small businesses is a priority but not to a point where the revenues of RMN are compromised by risk. RMN has agreed to cap the involvement of small business in a protected mode to 10 percent of its concession revenues or 10 percent of the retail space available for concessions, whichever is more.

Airlines pay landing fees to the airport each time a plane lands at the airport. These fees are recovered from passengers as part of the cost of a ticket. Landing fees are charged on a schedule that makes them slightly higher during peak periods, and discounts are offered for landings that occur during off-peak periods. RMN in principle wants to have a smooth flow of traffic through all times of the day, but recognizes that there will be morning and evening peaks as business passenger traffic finds those times more convenient.

The airport also stands to receive subsidies from the State of California as part of a state initiative to reduce congestion at LAX and incentivize smaller airports to offload the peak traffic over the skies of Los Angeles. These subsidies are offered on a sliding scale, with a large amount being available initially to jump start operations and tapering off over a 15-year period, with the assumption that the airport's natural growth of revenues would be able to sustain operations without the state subsidies. However, the confidence level in actually ever receiving these subsidies is not very high given the large shortfalls in the state budget and the tendency of lawmakers to legislate away subsidies when the involved constituency is not loud, vociferous, or influential. RMN has been lobbying lawmakers and representatives from the region to influence legislative directions. Given the uncertainty of state funding and all the various restrictive clauses that constrain the airport's degrees of freedom, RMN, in principle, is intent on avoiding government subsidies that are tied to the whims of legislators and the availability of public monies.

The airport has been looking at land use for potential revenue generation. More than 200 acres have been zoned for parking and can produce significant revenues once a steady stream of loyal passengers begin using RMN as their preferred airport to LAX, Burbank, or Orange County. At this time, no parking ramps have been built, but there are plans to float bonds to acquire funds for parking ramps and state-of-the-art facilities such as electronic annunciators and indicators for vacant spaces, display systems to help direct traffic, pay system facilities to allow passengers to pay at the airport terminal itself, and people movement systems to move passengers rapidly from the terminal to parking areas.

The airport also charges airlines with leases for occupation of space inside the terminal and outside. Airlines maintain office space for non-flying/administrative operations and front desk space for greeting, receiving, and checking in passengers. Airlines also maintain check-in baggage areas outside the terminal by the passenger entrances. All airport-owned built-up space that is used by airlines is charged for from the airport administration to the users of those spaces in the form of leases. Leases are renegotiated every two years. The principle of fairness is used to charge all airlines the same normalized rate. There are different rates for different types of spaces. The airport will not undertake custom remodeling and extensions of the space and it is up to the airline to build out its own areas at its own expense. The airport does mandate standards, look-and-feel guidance, and uniformity of how spaces are built out. These mandates are nonnegotiable and built in to the airlines leases as terms and conditions.

Stakeholders

RMN is also more than an airport facility in human terms. It also has its own internal permanent community of airport employees, concession employees, baggage transfer operators, custodians, parking lot attendants, parking shuttle drivers, airport management, airport security, fire protection personnel, aircrew, airline employees, flight kitchen attendants, and many other workers. Note the following details about this community:

■ As a community sponsor, RMN must provide mechanisms and facilities that are used by these stakeholders, such as parking facilities, restrooms, recreation and exercise facilities, and storage lockers.

- RMN, as an employer of more than 50 employees, also comes under federal regulations and labor laws related to the forming of unions, assembly, and peaceful protest, as well as statutory limits on work time and overtime and regulations regarding employment conditions, occupational safety, and health issues. RMN is committed to compliance with all regulations related to labor that are required under federal, state, and local law.

- In addition to dealing with the organization and management aspects of such a diverse workforce, RMN is also concerned with identification of valid employees through the issuing of photo badges with biometric employee information, implementation of access controls on secured facilities, and tracking of employees' movement in sensitive areas of the airport. Processes are in place to provide badging, control authorized access, and monitor movement of employees where security issues are likely to disrupt or threaten the airport's normal operations. Also in place are processes for terminated or retiring employees to ensure that all identification materials are recovered before these personnel exit the airport premises permanently.

- RMN, although committed to laws related to organized labor, has not had a labor union in its history. But as it expands, there has been a groundswell by various labor groups to canvas each other and try to form a labor union. Political parties and national labor unions have also been active in trying to activate the groundswell and push for the formation of a local chapter of national trade unions.

- The State of California and the municipality and county that surround RMN are also stakeholders. The federal government is interested in a strategic alternative to LAX that is very close and is viable in the event of LAX closing due to unforeseen events. The State of California is interested in RMN as a facilitator for commerce and as a port of embarkation for people, goods, and cargo that increases the tempo and magnitude of economic activity within the region. RMN is also a taxpaying entity that provides tax revenues for local, county, state, and federal government. The airport raises money through bonds that are guaranteed by state and local government.

Geographical Considerations

The layout of the current runways limits operations in only one direction when the wind is right. RMN would greatly benefit from a cross-runway system for taking advantage of changes in wind direction and saving valuable fuel through correct alignment with prevailing winds.

The construction of an additional runway system has not been studied, but its undertaking is a significant financial and civil engineering operational exercise in budgeting, raising monies, and planning and execution. In addition, integrating the new runway requires coordination with air traffic management, the FAA, and other federal agencies. The science and engineering are well understood and can be undertaken with little risk, but the financial risk of raising funds and paying for the effort and the trade-off against the increased revenues and capability improvements need to be analyzed.

One of the runways is shorter than the 4,500 feet needed by wide-body airliners and some of the larger cargo aircraft. This has resulted in a number of airlines continuing to fly LAX for their wider-body aircraft. Increasing the runway length cannot be undertaken without an additional runway to absorb the load while the lengthening operations are in process. While the runway is being lengthened, operations are severely limited and the presence of construction equipment so close to other operating runways requires close supervision and that extra procedures are put in place for safety purposes. The financing for lengthening the runways may have to be performed in a different manner than the financing for new runways, as it may come under operational improvements.

Information and Technology Infrastructure

RMN is slowly transforming itself from a small, sleepy, rural airport to a modern port of call for passenger airlines and cargo. The use of information technology is being slowly phased in for various aspects of the operation:

- Terminals are being equipped with wireless hubs to enable passengers to connect to the Internet. Wireless access points, electric charging points, and desks and stations for laptops and notebooks are being provided in the terminal area for passengers.

- The surveillance capabilities are being integrated into the digital infrastructure to be able to store the large amounts of surveillance data picked up by terminal and cargo area cameras and index and recall them when required for forensic and operational analysis.

- Airport back office operations are being integrated from a set of stovepipe systems to loosely coupled, service-oriented systems that are at once flexible and agile and able to support a variety of orchestrated functions.

- The airport IT infrastructure is being looked upon as a backbone platform to run the various federal agency system components, such as those required by the Customs and Border Protection, the Department of Agriculture APHIS terminals, and the Department of Homeland Security and TSA systems for flight manifests, no-fly lists, name searches, and other security measures. This infrastructure will also run the FAA's system of weather and other sensing equipment along with automation and information requirements for air traffic management operations, including tower operations, radio equipment for communications between aircraft and ground controllers, and terminal radios for gate personnel.

- As a backbone, the airport will provide an enterprise service bus and an Internet transport layer, as well as connectivity, data exchange services, and a network of networks. The IT data centers for RMN have been allocated and located at various strategic locations inside the airport perimeter along with alternate sites for continuity of operations (COOP).

- One of the principles of RMN's enterprise is to outsource all non–mission-related services to the maximum extent possible. As a result of this principle, RMN has determined to outsource payroll processing to a commercial payroll services provider, security services to a local security services provider, benefits processing to a commercial provider of health care, dental care, and disability benefits and another provider of life and disability insurance services. RMN has also contracted with a local hospital to set up, manage, and operate the sick bays, ambulance services, and to stand by to provide triage in the event of a disaster or other unforeseen emergency.

- The outsourcing decisions will continue to be made on a case-by-case basis and RMN needs a framework to make such outsourcing decisions for business services. The framework must factor in the cost/benefit equation, the division of responsibilities between the service provider and RMN, and the level of service required and guaranteed, as well as the evaluation of risks involved. The IT group, with its expertise in building models, has been tapped to assist in the development of a framework for the evaluation of service outsourcing.

- A big change for RMN on its journey from a small, rural airport to a vibrant aviation hub for passengers and cargo is the transformation from people-oriented operations to process-oriented operations. In the past, a combination of training and hiring the right people was sufficient for the right decisions to be made and for smooth operations on a lightweight scale. Today, the magnitude and speed of operations (commonly used in the military term operations tempo) have introduced new needs for documented, enforced, and monitored processes that supplement the traditional human resource–based approach of hiring the right people, training, assessing, and educating them in the elements of the job to be performed, and rewarding or punishing employees for good or bad performance. The transformation from people-oriented, relatively autonomous decision making to a process-centric, command-and-control decision-making process is a big change that is expected to produce a lot of pushback. With the potential for the formation of strong labor unions, egged on by national trade unions looking to establish a beachhead, there is a need to understand and manage cultural issues. The IT staff has been tapped for the process-modeling efforts to be able to model, represent, and promulgate process flows for the new ways of doing business. However, there is still a need for operations managers to address issues of process implementation and culture transformation.

■ As part of the U.S. federal government initiatives, the FAA has also tapped the CIO of RNM to assist in contributing to the evolving National Information Exchange Model (NIEM) that is harmonizing data specifications across multiple agencies. Because the airport information systems need to feed or consume information from so many federal agencies, it is essential that the planning and evolution of these systems benefit from and contribute to the NIEM efforts.

■ RNM has paid a Washington-based think tank for studies related to unmanned aerial vehicle (UAV) operations in the 2015–2020 timeframe to examine the implications of package express companies and cargo carriers moving to UAV operations. The report has indicated that several changes need to be made at all levels of command and control, tower operations, safety measures, facilities locations, runways, and parking spaces. The hope is that the enterprise architecture effort can represent the state of the airport in 2015 with UAV operations to support the analysis required to plan, budget, acquire, undertake, and achieve UAV operations with a three-year advance notice if required.

Management and Governance

It is clear that any transition from the current state of operations of Richard M. Nixon Airport to the future requires significant planning skills based on hard information and the documentation of assumptions, constraints, and risks. It also requires generating funds based on clearly articulated plans, benefits, and financial analysis. The undertaking of stovepipe initiatives is not an option because of the cross-coupling of issues and the effect of changes on operational, systems, and technology elements in support of one initiative often have significant detrimental side effects on other aspects of the operation.

The types of problems and challenges as well as opportunities that have emerged are all complex and hard to understand without having some way of modeling and asking trade-off–related questions. At the same time, modeling the enterprise requires that all items of the enterprise be visible and relatable in some manner, somehow.

The management of Richard M. Nixon Airport has heard that enterprise architecture is the body of knowledge that can help it represent the enterprise to support the types of decisions that it needs to make. Thus management has consulted the FEAC Institute for expertise on how to go about modeling various aspects of the enterprise architecture, knowing that the managers will not be able to model every aspect of the enterprise, nor will they be able to detail every aspect of the enterprise where all the implementation risk and details are also exposed.

FEAC's 50,000 View of the Role of the Enterprise Architecture

Figure 5.2-2 shows the recommended EA for Richard M. Nixon Airport. In short, FEAC advised the management of RMN that the following steps are required:

1. Build a high-level set of models (enterprise architecture) that represent the current state of RMN. These models represent the current state of the mission and the goals and objectives, the lines of business, the services and products, the capabilities and business functions, locations, organizations and roles, systems and services, technology elements, and standards. These models provide classification schemes (taxonomies) and relationships that relate the various model elements. For example, the mission drives the types of products and services; the need to provide those products and services drive the need for capabilities or business functions; and each function needs a set of resources, such as performers, locations, systems, services, and technology elements (ways and means).

2. Collect candidate problems and issues as well as areas of opportunities. Analyze these in the light of the elements of the high-level models previously built.

FIGURE 5.2-2

Using EA
to Assist in
Enterprise
Transformation

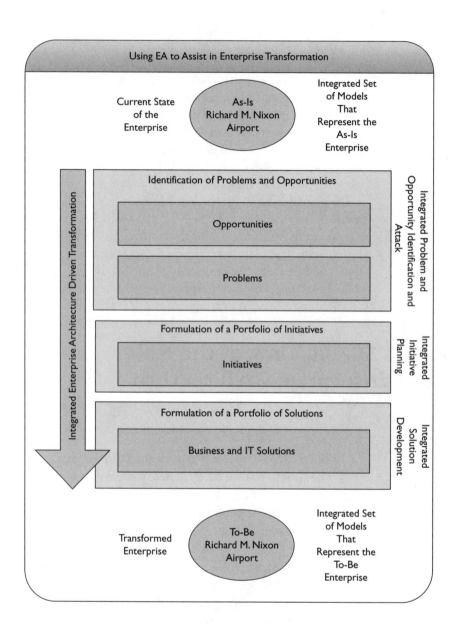

This analysis will yield insight into what problems and issues can be solved (or not), what is the magnitude of the effort and complexity in solving those problems, and what are the costs and benefits in solving those problems. The analysis will also address which opportunities can be harvested immediately or for the short term, which opportunities cannot readily be harvested without significant risk or delay, and which opportunities are not worth pursuing. Opportunity analysis must of course be supplemented by strategic analysis, which includes looking at alternatives and competition.

3. Formulate a portfolio of business initiatives that are in line with the ability to raise funding, that fit within the resource constraints and risk tolerance of the enterprise, and that can be undertaken to produce results that are within the window of the problem requirement or opportunity timeframes. Remember that the business initiatives may address one or more problem or opportunity areas and may not have a 1:1 correspondence with problems or opportunities. The portfolio is an important concept in assessing the effectiveness of investments in the initiatives. Managing initiatives as a portfolio provides a holistic view of where to put the enterprise dollars and in what proportion in terms of importance to the mission and goals (short term and long term) of the enterprise.

4. Formulate a portfolio of solutions that form the basis for projects. These projects are budgeted and planned through the initiatives. Once again, an initiative may define one or more projects. Managing the implementation of these initiatives is a conventional operational exercise that enterprises have learned and performed over many projects. Implementation initiatives have been managed through combinations of agile techniques of spiral development, project management controls such as Earned Value Management, and close tracking and monitoring, as well as the establishment of personal incentives to project teams through motivational management.

The FEAC Institute also pointed out that the enterprise architecture can support many of the business and decision-making processes of the enterprise. Each of these processes supports some aspect of enterprise transformation:

- **Strategic transformation** A fundamental change in the business areas, lines of business, and offered products and services as a result of reinvention or as a reaction to competitive pressures.

- **Operational transformation** A change in the ways in which business is currently done with the objective of effecting enhancements, controlling costs, improving transparency or visibility of operations, motivating internal stakeholders, or satisfying pressures from external stakeholders or some other operational objective.

■ **Services transformation**   A change in the way that the capabilities of the enterprise are achieved and a shift away from or into using internal operations versus retaining external service providers. The benefit of service transformation is that the enterprise can leverage specialized, advanced services at lower cost than it can implementing smaller-scale, rudimentary operations in-house.

■ **Systems transformation**   A change in the way that systems (IT and otherwise) are architected to leverage architectural improvements in separation of concerns, loose coupling, modularity, scalability, and survivability.

■ **Technology transformation**   A change in technologies that provides a refresh of current technology to bring benefits of contemporary technology to all stakeholders. Examples of contemporary technology that is useful to stakeholders include the availability of wireless Internet services, small self-serve applications that provide data or perform atomic functions, ubiquitous voice and data transmission capabilities, and other such items that users are beginning to take for granted.

Other chapters in the book use this case study and specific problems, opportunities, and initiatives and show how modeling the enterprise architecture is an essential and holistic way to address the challenges of all enterprises, including Richard M. Nixon Airport!

Glossary

ability   The quality of being able to perform.

abstraction   The technique of providing summarized or generalized descriptions of detailed and complex content. Abstraction, as in "level of abstraction," can also mean providing a focus for analysis that is concerned with a consistent and common level of detail or abstraction. Abstraction in this sense is typically used in architecture to allow a consistent level of definition and understanding to be achieved in each area of the architecture in order to support effective communication and decision making. It is especially useful when dealing with large and complex architectures, as it allows relevant issues to be identified before further detail is attempted.

access control (AC)   A security service that ensures that only those users with the correct rights can access a specific device, application, or data.

activity   (1) Work, not specific to a single organization, weapon system, or individual, that transforms inputs (resources) into outputs (resources) or changes their state. (2) A task or collection of tasks that support the functions of an organization. An example is a user entering data into an IT system or traveling to visit customers.

actor   (1) A performer that is external to and invokes the performer to be architected. (2) A person, organization, or system that has a role that initiates or interacts with activities; for example, a sales representative who travels to visit customers. Actors may be internal or external to an organization. In the automotive industry, an original equipment manufacturer would be considered an actor by an automotive dealership that interacts with its supply chain activities.

Ada   A high-level computer programming language developed by the U.S. Department of Defense (DoD) and widely used within the DoD and North Atlantic Treaty Organization (NATO) countries. It is used for real-time processing, is modular in nature, and includes object-oriented features.

address   The name of a location along with the location-finding scheme that allows a location to be found from the name. Examples include a postal address, e-mail address, URL, and data link address.

advanced technology demonstrations (ATD)   A demonstration of the maturity and potential of advanced technologies for enhanced military operational capability or cost-effectiveness. ATDs are identified, sponsored, and funded by services and agencies.

agreement   A consent among parties regarding the terms and conditions of activities that the parties participate in.

All Viewpoint (AV)   An enterprise architecture (EA) model that provides information pertinent to the entire architectural description, such as the scope and context of the architectural description. The scope includes the subject area and timeframe for the architectural description. The setting in which the architectural description exists comprises the interrelated conditions that compose the context for the architectural description. These conditions include doctrine; tactics, techniques, and procedures; relevant goals and vision statements; concepts of operations (CONOPS); scenarios; and environmental conditions.

application   A deployed and operational IT system that supports business functions and services; for example, a payroll. Applications use data and are supported by multiple technology components but are distinct from the technology components that support the application.

application architecture   A description of the major logical grouping of capabilities that manage the data objects necessary to process the data and support the business.

application component   An encapsulation of application functionality aligned to the implementation structure; for example, a purchase request processing application.

application platform   The collection of technology components of hardware and software that provide the services used to support applications.

application platform interface (API)   The interface, or set of functions, between application software and/or the application platform.

application software   Software entities that have a specific business purpose.

architectural style   The combination of distinctive features in which architecture is performed or expressed.

architecture   (1) A formal description of a system, or a detailed plan of the system at the component level, to guide its implementation (ISO/IEC, 2007). (2) The structure of components, their interrelationships, and the principles and guidelines governing their design and evolution over time.

architecture building block (ABB)   A constituent of the architecture model that describes a single aspect of the overall model.

Architecture Continuum   A part of the Enterprise Continuum. A repository of architectural elements with increasing detail and specialization. This continuum begins with foundational definitions such as Reference Models, core strategies, and basic building blocks. From there, it spans from industry architectures all the way to an organization's specific architecture.

architecture description   Architecture data elements and relationships that make up an architecture model or product. Hence, an architecture description is an architecture model or product.

Architecture Development Method (ADM)   The core of TOGAF. A step-by-step approach to develop and use an enterprise architecture.

architecture domain   The architectural area being considered. There are four architecture domains within TOGAF: business, data, application, and technology.

architecture framework (AF)   A foundational structure or set of structures that can be used for developing a broad range of different architectures. It should contain a method for designing an information system in terms of a set of building blocks, and for showing how the building blocks fit together. It should also contain a set of tools, provide a common vocabulary, and include a list of recommended standards and compliant products that can be used to implement the building blocks.

architecture governance   The practice and orientation by which enterprise architectures and other architectures are managed and controlled at an enterprisewide level. It is concerned with change processes (design governance) and operation of product systems (operational governance).

architecture landscape   The architectural representation of assets deployed within the operating enterprise at a particular point in time. The views are segmented into strategic, segment, and capability levels of abstraction to meet diverse stakeholder needs.

architecture principles   A qualitative statement of intent that should be met by the architecture. The statement should have at least a supporting rationale and a measure of importance.

architecture view   The representation of a related set of concerns. A view is what is seen from a viewpoint. An architecture view may be represented by a model to demonstrate to stakeholders their areas of interest in the architecture. A view does not have to be visual or graphical in nature.

Architecture Vision   (1) A high-level, aspirational view of the target architecture. (2) A phase in the ADM that delivers understanding and definition of the Architecture Vision. (3) A specific deliverable describing the Architecture Vision.

Architecture Working Group (AWG)   The group constituted at the federal government from across federal agencies to assist in architecture governance and practice.

artifact   An architectural work product that describes an architecture from a specific viewpoint. Examples include a network diagram, a server specification, a use-case specification, a list of architectural requirements, and a business interaction matrix. Artifacts are generally classified as catalogs (lists of things), matrices (showing relationships between things), and diagrams (pictures of things). An architectural deliverable may contain multiple artifacts, and artifacts form the content of the Architecture Repository.

as-is architecture   An architecture that represents the current state of an enterprise, operation, or solution. Also called *baseline architecture*.

availability   In the context of IT systems, the probability that system functional capabilities are ready for use by a user at any time, where all time is considered, including operations, repair, administration, and logistic time. Availability is further defined by system category for both routine and priority operations.

baseline   A specification that has been formally reviewed and agreed upon, that thereafter serves as the basis for further development or change, and that can be changed only through formal change control procedures or a type of procedure such as configuration management.

baseline architecture   The existing defined system architecture before it enters a cycle of architecture review and redesign.

batch processing   The processing of data or the accomplishment of jobs accumulated in advance in such a manner that each accumulation thus formed is processed or accomplished in the same computer run.

behavior   The manner in which an individual, group, or machine functions, operates, reacts, or responds to stimuli.

boundaryless information flow   A trademark of The Open Group for a shorthand representation of "access to integrated information to support business process improvements" representing a desired state of an enterprise's infrastructure specific to the business needs of the organization. An infrastructure that provides boundaryless information flow has open standard components that provide services in a customer's extended enterprise that combine multiple sources of information and securely deliver the information whenever and wherever it is needed, in the right context for the people or systems using that information.

building block A (potentially reusable) component of business, information technology (IT), or architectural capability that can be combined with other components to deliver architectures and solutions. Building blocks can be defined at various levels of detail, depending on what stage of architecture development has been reached. For instance, at an early stage, a building block can simply consist of a name or an outline description. Later on, a building block may be decomposed into multiple supporting building blocks and may be accompanied by a full specification. Building blocks can relate to architectures or solutions.

business architecture The business strategy, governance, organization, and key business processes information, as well as the interaction among these concepts.

business case analysis (BCA) An expanded cost/benefit analysis created with the intent of determining a best-value solution for product support. Alternatives weigh total cost against total benefits to arrive at the optimum solution.

business domain A grouping of coherent business functions and activities (in the context of a business sector) over which meaningful responsibility can be taken. Examples include finance, human resources (HR), automobile manufacturing, and retail. The term is often used to identify specific business knowledge (a business domain expert).

business function A function that delivers business capabilities closely aligned to an organization, but not necessarily explicitly governed by the organization.

business governance Discipline or practice concerned with ensuring that the business processes and policies (and their operation) deliver the business outcomes and adhere to relevant business regulation.

business process A functionally or temporally linked collection of structured activities or tasks aimed at producing specific services and products for an end user.

Business Process Model (BPM) A graphical or textual representation of business processes to enable the performing of analysis and identification of improvements.

Business Process Modeling Notation (BPMN)   A formal notation for representing business processes using graphical symbols and a constrained grammar.

Business Reference Model (BRM)   A hierarchical representation of an enterprise's areas of business, lines of business, and business functions that support the production of goods and services.

business service   (1) A thing that a business does that has a defined, measured interface and has contracts with consumers of the service. A business service is supported by combinations of people, process, and technology. (2) A service that supports business capabilities through an explicitly defined interface and is explicitly governed by an organization.

business system   Hardware, software, policy statements, processes, activities, standards, and people who together implement a business function.

C2ISR   Command, Control, Intelligence, Surveillance, and Reconnaissance.

capabilities description document (CDD)   A document that captures the information necessary to develop a proposed program(s), normally using an evolutionary acquisition (EA) strategy. The CDD outlines an affordable increment of militarily useful, logistically supportable, and technically mature capability. The CDD may define multiple increments if there is sufficient definition of the performance attributes (key performance parameters [KPPs], key system attributes [KSAs], and other attributes) to allow approval of multiple increments. The CDD supports a Milestone B decision review. The CDD format is in the Joint Capabilities Integration and Development System (JCIDS) Manual, available online.

capability   (1) The ability to achieve a desired effect under specified (performance) standards and conditions through combinations of ways and means (activities and resources) to perform a set of activities. (2) An ability that an organization, person, or system possesses. Capabilities are typically expressed in general and high-level terms and typically require a combination of organization, people, processes, and technology to achieve. Examples of capabilities include marketing, customer contact, or outbound telemarketing.

capability architecture   A highly detailed description of the architectural approach to realize a particular solution or solution aspect.

capability configuration   A combination of organizational aspects (with their competencies) and equipment that together provide a capability.

capability dependencies (CV-4)   The dependencies among planned capabilities and the definition of logical groupings of capabilities.

capability increment   (1) A capability that can be effectively developed, produced, acquired, deployed, and sustained. (2) The output from a business change initiative that delivers an increase in performance for a particular capability of the enterprise.

capability maturity model integration (CMMI)   Derived from the now-retired software capability maturity model (SW-CMM), a process improvement approach that integrates a number of disciplines into a unified model useful for process improvement. Three domain variations (CMMI constellations) of the CMMI exist: one for development organizations (CMMI-DEV), one for acquisition organizations (CMMI-ACQ), and one for service-type organizations (CMMI-SVC). All the models share a common set of core processes with additional processes added as appropriate for the domain. Although the CMMI models can provide ratings on a numerical scale (5 being the highest), DoD's preference is to use them primarily in a process improvement role, deemphasizing numerical ratings. The Software Engineering Institute (SEI) manages the three CMMI product suites.

capability phasing (CV-3)   The planned achievement of capability at different points in time or during specific periods of time. The CV-3 shows the capability phasing in terms of the activities, conditions, desired effects, rules complied with, resource consumption and production, and measures, without regard to the performer and location solutions.

capability portfolio management (CPM)   The discipline of managing capability needs as a single collection for balancing competing needs with mission requirements and priorities.

capability production document (CPD)   A document that addresses the production elements specific to a single increment of an acquisition program. The CPD defines an increment of militarily useful, logistically supportable, and technically mature capability that is ready for a production decision. The CPD must be validated and approved prior to a Milestone C decision review. The CPD format is in the Joint Capabilities Integration and Development System (JCIDS) Manual, available online.

capability taxonomy (CV-2)   A hierarchy of capabilities that specifies all the capabilities that are referenced throughout one or more architectural descriptions.

capability to operational activities mapping (CV-6)   A mapping between the capabilities required and the operational activities that those capabilities support.

capability to organizational development mapping (CV-5) A mapping that shows the planned solution for the phase in terms of performers and locations and their associated concepts. The fulfillment of capability requirements shows the planned capability deployment and interconnection for a particular Capability Phase.

capability to services mapping (CV-7) A mapping between the capabilities and the services that these capabilities enable.

Capability Viewpoint (CV) A viewpoint that captures the enterprise goals associated with the overall vision for executing a specified course of action, or the ability to achieve a desired effect under specific standards and conditions through combinations of means and ways to perform a set of tasks. It provides a strategic context for the capabilities described in an architectural description, and an accompanying high-level scope, more general than the scenario-based scope defined in an operational concept diagram. The models are high level and describe capabilities using terminology that is easily understood by decision makers and used for communicating a strategic vision regarding capability evolution.

capacity The amount a performer can hold, receive, or absorb.

Capital Planning and Investment Control (CPIC) A periodic and recurring activity performed by federal agencies to manage investments in information technology as capital assets.

catalog A structured list of architectural outputs of a similar kind, used for reference. An example is a technology standards catalog or an application portfolio.

Chief Information Officer (CIO) An executive agency official responsible for providing advice and other assistance to the head of the executive agency to ensure that IT is acquired and information resources are managed for the executive agency according to statute; developing, maintaining, and facilitating the implementation of a sound and integrated information technology architecture (ITA) for the executive agency; and promoting the effective and efficient design and operation of all major information resources management processes for the executive agency, including improvements to work processes of the executive agency. The CIO for the Department of Defense (DoD) is the Assistant Secretary of Defense for Networks and Information Integration (ASD (NII)).

Chief X Officer (CXO) The chief officer within a particular function of the business, such as the Chief Executive Officer, Chief Financial Officer, Chief Information Officer, Chief Technology Officer.

client   An application component that requests services from a server.

Clinger-Cohen Act of 1996 (CCA)   Law that recognizes the need for federal agencies to improve the way they select and manage IT resources and states, "information technology architecture, with respect to an executive agency, means an integrated framework for evolving or maintaining IT and acquiring new IT to achieve the agency's strategic goals and information resources management goals." Chief Information Officers are assigned the responsibility for "developing, maintaining, and facilitating the implementation of a sound and integrated IT architecture for the executive agency."

command and control (C2)   The exercise of authority and direction by a properly designated commander over assigned and attached forces in the accomplishment of the mission. Command and control functions are performed through an arrangement of personnel, equipment, communications, facilities, and procedures employed by a commander in planning, directing, coordinating, and controlling forces and operations in the accomplishment of the mission.

commercial off the shelf (COTS)   A commercial item (CI) sold in substantial quantities in the commercial marketplace and offered to the government under a contract or subcontract at any tier, without modification, in the same form in which it was sold in the marketplace. This definition does not include bulk cargo such as agricultural products or petroleum.

communications and stakeholder management   The management of needs of stakeholders of the enterprise architecture practice. Also the management of the execution of communication between the practice and the stakeholders and the practice and the consumers of its services.

communications network   A set of products, concepts, and services that enable the connection of computer systems for the purpose of transmitting data and other forms (such as voice and video) between the systems.

communications node   A node that is either internal to the communications network (such as routers, bridges, or repeaters) or located between the end device and the communications network to operate as a gateway.

communications system   A set of assets (transmission media, switching nodes, interfaces, and control devices) that establish linkage between users and devices.

community of interest (COI) A group of people, roles, or organizations with common motivation.

composite application An application component that is created by composing other atomic or composite applications.

Concept of Operations (CONOPS) A general idea derived or inferred from specific instances or occurrences of major planning and operating functions.

Conceptual Data Model (DIV-1/CDM) The required high-level data concepts and their relationships.

concerns The key interests that are crucially important to the stakeholders in a system and which determine the acceptability of the system. Concerns may pertain to any aspect of the system's functioning, development, or operation, including considerations such as performance, reliability, security, distribution, and evolvability.

condition The state of an environment or situation in which a performer performs.

Configuration Control Board (CCB) A collection of people constituted to provide governance and direction for configuration management of the elements of a solution.

configuration management (CM) A discipline applying technical and administrative direction and surveillance to identify and document the functional and physical characteristics of a configuration item, control changes to those characteristics, and record and report changes to processing and implementation status. Also, the management of the configuration of enterprise architecture practice (intellectual property) assets and baselines and the control of changeover of those assets.

connectivity service A service area of the external environment entity of the Technical Reference Model (TRM) that provides end-to-end connectivity for communications through three transport levels (global, regional, and local). It provides general and application-specific services to platform end devices.

constraint (1) The range of permissible states for an object. (2) An external factor that prevents an organization from pursuing particular approaches to meet its goals. For example, customer data is not harmonized within the organization, regionally or nationally, constraining the organization's ability to offer effective customer service.

continental United States (CONUS) The 48 contiguous states located on the central part of the North American continent, plus the District of Columbia; thus CONUS does not include Alaska and Hawaii.

continuity of operations (COOP) The degree or state of being continuous in the conduct of functions, tasks, or duties necessary to accomplish a military action or mission in carrying out the national military strategy. It includes the functions and duties of the Commander, as well as the supporting functions and duties performed by the staff and others acting under the authority and direction of the Commander.

contract An agreement between a service consumer and a service provider that establishes functional and nonfunctional parameters for interaction.

control A decision-making step with accompanying decision logic used to determine the execution approach for a process or to ensure that a process complies with governance criteria. For example, a signoff control on the purchase request processing procedure might check whether the total value of the request is within the signoff limits of the requester or whether it needs a higher authority to sign off on the request.

Control Objectives for Information and Related Technology (COBIT) A certification created by the Information Systems Audit and Control Association (ISACA) and the IT Governance Institute (ITGI) that provides a set of recommended best practices for the governance and management of information systems and technology.

Core Architecture Data Model (CADM) The logical data model specified by the DoD Architecture Framework (DoDAF) 1.0 and DoDAF 1.5 to describe the vocabulary of architecture elements that comprise an integrated architecture and their relationships.

cost (1) financial: The price paid to acquire, produce, accomplish, or maintain anything. (2) general: The expenditure of something, such as time or labor, necessary for the attainment of a goal.

course of action A path toward a goal.

data Representation of information in a formalized manner suitable for communication, interpretation, or processing by humans or by automatic means. Examples include whole models, packages, entities, attributes, classes, domain values, enumeration values, records, tables, rows, columns, and fields.

Data and Information Viewpoint (DIV) A viewpoint that captures the business information requirements and structural business process rules for the architectural description. It describes the information that is associated with the information exchanges in the architectural description, such as attributes, characteristics, and interrelationships.

data architecture   The structure of an organization's logical and physical data assets and data management resources.

database management system (DBMS)   An automated software mechanism that provides data management services such as storage, retrieval, and search of data from storage media.

data dependency   Resource consumed by the performer.

data dictionary   A specialized type of database containing metadata; a repository of information describing the characteristics of data used to design, monitor, document, protect, and control data in information systems and databases; an application system supporting the definition and management of database metadata.

data element   A basic unit of information having a meaning and that may have subcategories (data items) of distinct units and values.

data entity   An encapsulation of data that is recognized by a business domain expert as a thing. Logical data entities can be tied to applications, repositories, and services and may be structured according to implementation considerations.

data interchange service   A service of the platform entity of the Technical Reference Model (TRM) that provides specialized support for the interchange of data between applications on the same or different platforms.

data management service   A service of the platform entity of the Technical Reference Model (TRM) that provides support for the management, storage, access, and manipulation of data in a database.

database   A structured or organized collection of data entities that can be accessed by a computer.

Defense Acquisition System (DAS)   Management process by which DoD provides effective, affordable, and timely systems to the users.

Defense Architecture Registry System (DARS)   The DoD registry and repository of segment and solution architectures comprising the federated DoD enterprise architecture.

deliverable   An architectural work product that is contractually specified and in turn formally reviewed, agreed, and signed off by the stakeholders. Deliverables represent the output of projects and those deliverables that are in documentation form will typically be archived at the completion of a project or transitioned into an Architecture Repository as a Reference Model, standard, or snapshot of the architecture landscape at a point in time.

Department of Defense (DoD)   An agency responsible for the national defense of the United States government.

Department of Defense Architecture Framework (DoDAF)   An architecture framework that defines a common approach for DoD architecture description, development, presentation, and integration for both warfighting operations and business operations and processes. The framework is intended to ensure that architectural descriptions can be compared and related across organizational boundaries, including joint and multinational boundaries. It defines eight related views of architecture. Each view is composed of data elements that are depicted via graphical, tabular, or textual products.

Department of Defense Discovery Metadata Specification (DDMS)   A specification that describes and codifies the metadata elements needed to expose information and service assets in a net-centric operations environment.

Department of Defense Information Enterprise Architecture (DIEA)   An enterprise architecture that defines the key principles, rules, constraints, and best practices to which applicable DoD programs, regardless of component or portfolio, must adhere in order to enable agile, collaborative, net-centric operations.

Department of Health and Human Services (HHS)   An agency of the United States government responsible for protecting the health of all Americans and providing essential human services.

Department of Homeland Security (DHS)   An agency of the federal government of the United States responsible for, among other matters, counterterrorism within U.S. borders.

desired effect   The result, outcome, or consequence of an action (activity).

desired result   The wished-for result, outcome, or consequence of an action. A desired result may be either a goal or an objective.

directive   An authoritative statement intended to impel actions and the achievement of goals.

directory service   A technology component that provides locator services that find the location of a service or the location of data or translate a common name into a network-specific address. It is analogous to telephone books and may be implemented in centralized or distributed schemes.

distributed database   (1) A database that is not stored in a central location but is dispersed over a network of interconnected computers. (2) A database under the overall control of a central database management system (DBMS) but whose storage devices are not all attached to the same processor. (3) A database that is physically located in two or more distinct locations.

doctrine   The body of principles by which an enterprise seeks to guide its activities.

Doctrine, Organization, Training, Material, Leadership and Education, Personnel, and Facilities (DOTMLPF)   DOTMLPF is an acronym used by the United States Department of Defense and is defined in the Joint Capabilities Integration Development System or JCIDS Process. JCIDS considers solutions involving any combination of doctrine, organization, training, materiel, leadership and education, personnel and facilities (DOTMLPF). As military commanders define requirements in consultation with the Office of the Secretary of Defense (OSD), they are able to consider gaps in the context of strategic direction for the total US military force and influence the direction of requirements earlier in the acquisition process.

DoD Architecture Registry System (DARS)   A software mechanism maintained by the Department of Defense to register architecture descriptions and provide metadata and location information on those architectures to a broad DoD audience.

DoD Information Technology Portfolio Repository (DITPR)   The official, unclassified DoD data source for the Federal Information Security Management Act (FISMA), E- Authentication, Portfolio Management, Privacy Impact Assessments, the inventory of MC/ME/MS systems, and the registry for systems under DoDI 5000.2.

DoD Information Technology Standards and Profile Registry (DISR)   Online repository for a minimal set of primarily commercial IT standards.

DoD Intelligence Information System (DoDIIS)   The combination of Department of Defense personnel, procedures, equipment, computer programs, and supporting communications that support the timely and comprehensive preparation and presentation of intelligence and information to military commanders and national-level decision makers.

DoD Metadata Registry (DMR) and Clearinghouse The DoD Metadata Registry and Clearinghouse provides software developers access to data technologies to support DoD mission applications. Through the Metadata Registry and Clearinghouse, software developers can access registered XML data and metadata components, and database segments and reference data tables and related metadata information.

DoDAF Meta-Model (DM2) The conceptual model that represents the concepts describing architecture elements comprising a DoDAF architecture description and their relationships.

driver An external or internal condition that motivates the organization to define its goals. An example of an external driver is a change in regulation or compliance rules that, for example, require changes to the way an organization operates, such as the regulations established by the Sarbanes-Oxley Act in the United States.

EA Maturity Model Framework (EAMMF) The Government Accountability Office's framework for assessing the maturity of enterprise architecture efforts within agencies.

earned value management (EVM) A technique for project management.

effect The result, outcome, or consequence of an action.

E-Government Act of 2002 (E-Gov Act) A U.S. law that calls for the development of enterprise architecture to enhance the management and promotion of electronic government services and processes.

end An outcome worked toward, especially with forethought, deliberate planning, and organized effort.

end user The person who ultimately uses the computer application or output.

enduring task A continuing function to be performed.

enterprise (1) An umbrella term for the management systems, information systems, and computer systems within an organization. (2) The highest level (typically) of description of an organization, typically covering all missions and functions. An enterprise will often span multiple organizations.

enterprise architecture (EA) A rigorous description of the structure of an enterprise. The description comprises enterprise components, the externally visible properties of those components, and the relationships (for example, the behavior) among them. EA describes the terminology, the composition of enterprise components, and their relationships with the external environment and the guiding principles for the requirement, design, and evolution of an enterprise.

Enterprise Architecture Assessment Framework (EAAF) A framework for assessing the quality of an agency's enterprise architecture as defined by criteria from the Office of Management and Budget.

enterprise architecture certification (EA certification) A formal process of certifying the ability of an individual to practice as an architect in the discipline of enterprise architecture.

Enterprise Architecture Executive Steering Council (EAESC) The Enterprise Architecture Executive Steering Committee or EAESC is responsible for approving the initial EA, approving significant changes to the EA, and approving the EA Program Plan.

Enterprise Architecture Management Maturity Framework AMMF Framework developed by the GAO that "Outlines the steps toward achieving a stable and mature process for managing the development, maintenance, and implementation of enterprise architecture." Using the EAMMF allows managers to determine what steps are needed for improving architecture management.

Enterprise Architecture Planning (EAP) A methodology for planning the transformation roadmap of an enterprise from the current state to a desired target state as formulated by Dr. Steven Spewak.

Enterprise Continuum A categorization mechanism useful for classifying architecture and solution artifacts, both internal and external to the Architecture Repository, as they evolve from generic foundation architectures to organization-specific architectures.

Enterprise Resource Planning (ERP) A term defined by Gartner Group to extend the definition of Material Requirements Planning (later Manufacturing Resource Planning, or MRP) and computer-integrated manufacturing (CIM).

Enterprise Resource Planning System (ERP System) A complete suite of integrated applications that support the major business support functions of an organization; for example, financial (accounts payable, accounts receivable, and general ledger), human resources, payroll, stock, order processing and invoicing, purchasing, logistics, manufacturing, and so on.

entity-relationship diagram (ERD)   An abstract and conceptual representation for data that models data concepts as entities, the associations between them as relationships, and their properties as attributes. Generally, an ERD is used as a technique for representing a Logical Data Model (LDM).

environment management   The provision and management of the environment required to support the operations of the enterprise architecture practice, including facilities, equipment, tools, and information systems.

event   (1) Something that happens at an instant in the world, that is, a zero-duration process (activity). (2) An organizational state change that triggers processing events that may originate from inside or outside the organization and may be resolved inside or outside the organization.

Event-Trace Description (OV-6c)   One of three models used to describe activity (operational activity). It traces actions in a scenario or sequence of events.

eXtensible Markup Language (XML)   A mechanism for expressing self-defining data exchanges using tags.

external environment interface (EEI)   The interface that supports information transfer between the application platform and the external environment.

facility   A real property entity consisting of underlying land and one or more of the following: a building, a structure (including linear structures), a utility system, or pavement.

family of systems (FoS)   A set of systems that provide similar capabilities through different approaches to achieve similar or complementary effects. For instance, the warfighter may need the capability to track moving targets. The FoS that provides this capability could include unmanned or manned aerial vehicles with appropriate sensors, a space-based sensor platform, or a special operations capability. Each can provide the ability to track moving targets but with differing characteristics of persistence, accuracy, timeliness, and so on.

Federal Aviation Agency (FAA)   A federal agency responsible for regulation of aviation and the aviation industry.

Federal Chief Information Officers' Council (Federal CIO Council)
An organization comprising of Chief Information Officers of federal agencies.

Federal Enterprise Architecture (FEA)   The enterprise architecture for the federal government of the United States of America.

Federal Enterprise Architecture Framework (FEAF)   A framework established by the Federal CIO Council and the Architecture Working Group in collaboration with the National Institute of Standards and Technology for developing federal enterprise architectures. The FEAF is based on Dr. Spewak's Enterprise Architecture Planning (EAP) methodology.

Federal Enterprise Architecture Performance Reference Model (PRM)   One of the Reference Models of the Federal Enterprise Architecture that is focused on defining performance measures and tracing the line of sight from the inputs to a federal agency to the strategic outcomes that result from performance of the agency's mission.

Federal Enterprise Architecture Reference Models (RM)   Models that facilitate cross-agency analysis and the identification of duplicative investments, gaps, and opportunities for collaboration within and across federal agencies. Alignment with the Reference Models ensures that important elements of the FEA are described in a common and consistent way. The DoD Enterprise Architecture Reference Models are aligned with the FEA RM.

Federal Information Process Standard (FIPS)   A standard established by the National Institute of Standards and Technology in the domain of information technology.

Federal Segment Architecture Methodology (FSAM)   The Federal Segment Architecture Methodology (FSAM) is a step-by-step process for developing and using segment architectures that was developed by distilling proven best practices from across federal agencies.

federated architecture   An architecture that links and aligns disparate architectures at all levels of the federation based on an overarching organizing construct that defines common or shared standards across autonomous architectures. A federated architecture approach recognizes the uniqueness and specific purpose of disparate architectures and allows for their autonomy and local governance while enabling the enterprise to benefit from their content.

Federated Enterprise Architecture Certification Institute (FEAC)   An organization established to provide certification in the area of enterprise architecture in collaboration with an accredited state university.

federation   A union comprising a number of partially self-governing states or regions united by a central (federal) government.

financial management   The management of the financial aspects of the enterprise architecture practice; for example, budgeting and forecasting.

Formula Translator (FORTRAN)   A high-level computer language used extensively in scientific and engineering applications.

foundation architecture   An architecture of generic services and functions that provides a foundation on which more specific architectures and architectural components can be built. The TOGAF foundation architecture includes a Technical Reference Model (TRM).

framework   A structure for content or process that can be used as a tool to structure thinking, ensuring consistency and completeness (TOGAF).

function   The action for which a person or thing is specially designed, fitted, used, or intended to accomplish or execute.

function/business function   A thing that a business does. Services support functions, are functions, and have functions, but functions are not necessarily services. Services have more specific constraints than functions.

functional decomposition   A hierarchy of the functions of an enterprise or organization.

functional dependency   A constraint on or dependence of a function on one or more outside influences, conditions, functions, triggers, or events.

functional standard   A standard that sets forth rules, conditions, guidelines, and characteristics.

gap   A statement of difference between two states. A gap is used in the context of gap analysis, where the difference between the baseline and target architecture is identified.

GIG Technical Guidance (GTG)   Technical guidance for use of the Global Information Grid.

Global Earth Observation System of Systems (GEOSS)   A specific system of systems (SoS).

Global Information Grid (GIG)   An information network developed and maintained by the Department of Defense. The GIG is a globally interconnected, end-to-end set of information capabilities for collecting, processing, storing, disseminating, and managing information on demand to warfighters, policy makers, and support personnel.

goal   (1) A desired change in the state of an effect object as a result of some activity. (2) A high-level statement of intent or direction for an organization. Goals are typically used to measure the success of an organization.

governance   The discipline of monitoring, managing, and steering a business (or an information system or information technology landscape) to deliver the business outcome required.

Government Accountability Office (GAO)   Formerly the General Accounting Office. An agency of the Legislative Branch, responsible solely to the Congress, that functions to audit all negotiated government office contracts and investigate all matters relating to the receipt, disbursement, and application of public funds. The GAO determines whether public funds are expended in accordance with appropriations.

government off the shelf (GOTS)   Software and hardware products that are typically developed by the technical staff of the government agency for which they are created. GOTS products are sometimes developed by an external entity, but with funding and specification from the agency. Because agencies can directly control all aspects of GOTS products, these are generally preferred for government purposes.

guideline   An architectural document that provides guidance on the optimal ways to carry out design or implementation activities.

hardware   The physical infrastructure needed to run software; for example, servers, workstations, network equipment, and so on.

High-Level Operational Concept Graphic (OV-1)   The high-level graphical/textual description of the operational concept.

human computer interface (HCI)   Hardware and software allowing information exchange between the user and the computer.

hype cycle   A concept invented by Gartner Group to represent the phenomenon, prevalent with high-technology innovations, of extended expectations followed by disappointment.

identification and authentication (I&A)   A program initiated by the National Institute for Standards and Technology (NIST) for improving the identification and authentication of federal employees and contractors for access to federal facilities and information systems in response to Homeland Security Presidential Directive 12 (HSPD-12).

in accordance with (IAW)   Expansion of IAW.

information   Any communication or representation of facts, data, or opinions, in any medium or form, including textual, numerical, graphic, cartographic, narrative, or audio-visual forms.

information assurance (IA)   Information operations that protect and defend information and information systems by ensuring their availability, integrity, authentication, confidentiality, and nonrepudiation. This includes providing for the restoration of information systems by incorporating protection, detection, and reaction capabilities.

information domain   Grouping of information (or data entities) by a set of criteria such as security classification, ownership, location, and so on. In the context of security, information domains are defined as a set of users, their information objects, and a security policy.

Information Management Technology Reforms Act (ITMRA)   *See* Clinger-Cohen Act of 1996 (CCA).

information resources management (IRM)   Process of managing information resources to accomplish agency missions and to improve agency performance, including the reduction of information collection burdens on the public.

information security (INFOSEC)   The protection of information and information systems against unauthorized access or modification of information, whether in storage, processing, or transit, and against denial of service to authorized users. Information security includes those measures necessary to detect, document, and counter such threats. Information security is composed of computer security and communications security.

information system (IS)   The computer- (or IT-) based portion of a business system.

information system service   (1) A thing that a business does that has a defined, measured interface and has contracts with consumers of the service. Information system services are directly supported by applications and have associations to service-oriented architecture (SOA) service interfaces. (2) The automated elements of a business service. An information system service may deliver or support part or all of one or more business services.

information technology (IT)   (1) The lifecycle management of information and related technology used by an organization. (2) An umbrella term that includes all or some of the subject areas relating to the computer industry, such as business continuity, business IT interface, business process modeling and management, communication, compliance, legislation, computers, content management, hardware, information management, Internet, networking, offshoring, professional issues, programming and software, project management, security, standards, storage, and voice and data communications. Various countries and industries employ other umbrella terms to describe this same collection. (3) A department within an organization tasked with provisioning some or all of the domains described in definition (2). (4) Alternate name commonly adopted includes information services, information management, and so on.

Information Technology Infrastructure Library (ITIL)   A library that provides a set of recommended best practices for the governance/management of information systems and technology.

information technology investment management (ITIM)   A maturity model composed of five progressive stages of maturity that an agency can achieve in its IT investment management capabilities. The framework can be used both to assess the maturity of an agency's investment management processes and as a tool for organizational improvement.

initial capabilities document (ICD)   A document that summarizes a capabilities-based assessment (CBA) and recommends materiel or nonmaterial approaches or a combination of materiel and nonmaterial approaches to address specific capability gaps. It identifies required capabilities and defines capability gap(s) in terms of the joint capability area; the relevant range of military operations; desired effects; time; Doctrine, Organization, Training, Materiel, Leadership, Education, Personnel, and Facilities (DOTMLPF); and policy implications and constraints. The ICD summarizes the results of DOTMLPF and policy analysis and the DOTMLPF approaches that may deliver the required capability. The outcome of an ICD could be one or more joint DOTMLPF change recommendations (DCRs) or recommendations to pursue materiel solutions.

installation   A base, camp, post, station, yard, center, or other activity, including leased facilities, without regard to the duration of operational control. An installation may include one or more sites.

Institute of Electrical and Electronic Engineers (IEEE)   A standards body.

instruction   An imparted or acquired item of knowledge.

integrated architecture   An architecture in which architecture data elements are consistently used across all views (models) and viewpoints within the architecture.

Integrated Dictionary (AV-2)   An architectural data repository with definitions of all terms used throughout the architectural data and presentations.

integrated master schedule (IMS)   An integrated and networked multilayered schedule of program tasks required to complete the work effort captured in a related integrated master plan (IMP). The IMS should include all IMP events and accomplishments and support each accomplishment closure criteria.

integrated product team (IPT)   Team composed of representatives from appropriate functional disciplines working together to build successful programs, identify and resolve issues, and make sound and timely recommendations to facilitate decision making. There are three types of IPTs: overarching IPTs (OIPTs) that focus on strategic guidance, program assessment, and issue resolution; working-level IPTs (WIPTs) that identify and resolve program issues, determine program status, and seek opportunities for acquisition reform; and program-level IPTs (PIPTs) that focus on program execution and may include representatives from both government and industry after a contract is awarded.

Integration Definition for Function Modeling (IDEF0)   A technique for process modeling that resulted from the Integrated Computer-Aided Manufacturing program of the U.S. Air Force and is based on structured analysis and design techniques.

interaction   A relationship between architectural building blocks (that is, services or components) that embodies communication or usage.

interaction model   An architectural view, catalog, or matrix that shows a particular type of interaction; for example, a diagram showing application integration.

interface   Interconnection and interrelationships between, for example, people, systems, devices, applications, or the user and an application or device.

Internal Revenue Service (IRS)   An organization under the Department of the Treasury responsible for the collection of taxes.

International Council on Systems Engineering (INCOSE)   An international organization promoting standards and practices related to the discipline of systems engineering.

International Standards Organization (ISO)   A worldwide federation of national standards bodies from about 100 countries, one from each country. The ISO is a nongovernmental organization established to promote the development of standardization and related activities in the world with a view toward facilitating the international exchange of goods and services and toward developing cooperation in the spheres of intellectual, scientific, technological, and economic activity. ISO's work results in international agreements, which are published as international standards.

Internet Protocol Version 6 (IPv6)   A version of the Internet Communication Protocol standard.

interoperability   (1) A category of measures of the ability of two or more performers to exchange resources and to use the resources that have been exchanged. (2) The ability to share information and services. (3) The ability of two or more systems or components to exchange and use information. (4) The ability of systems to provide and receive services from other systems and to use the interchanged services to enable them to operate effectively together.

Interoperability and Supportability (I&S)   Standards developed by the Defense Systems Information Agency (DISA) to ensure that the development of systems and equipment conforms to technical and procedural standards for interface, interoperability, and compatibility.

Interoperability and Supportability Plan (ISP)   A requirement for all Acquisition Category (ACAT) programs that connect in any way to the communications and information infrastructure, including both information technology (IT) and National Security System (NSS) programs. The ISP identifies and documents information needs, infrastructure support, and IT and NSS interface requirements and dependencies, focusing on net-centric, interoperability, supportability, and sufficiency concerns. The ISP is summarized in the Acquisition Strategy and reviewed at Milestones B and C.

Investment Review Board (IRB)   A board that provides oversight of investment review processes for business systems supporting activities under their designated area of responsibility. Certification authorities for defense business systems are required to establish and charter an IRB. IRBs include representatives from combatant commands (COCOMs); the components; and the Joint Chiefs of Staff (JCS), who will participate as appropriate based on the types of business activities and system modernizations being reviewed and certified. The IRB review of business systems also functions as the Overarching Integrated Product Team (OIPT) review in support of an acquisition milestone decision review (MDR) for Acquisition Category (ACAT) IAM business systems.

Joint C4I Program Assessment Tool (JCPAT)   A tool that formally assesses systems and capabilities documents (initial capabilities documents, capability development documents, and capability production documents) for Joint Staff interoperability requirements certification and serves as the ITS/NSS Lifecycle Repository and the archives.

Joint Capabilities Integration and Development System (JCIDS)   The formal United States Department of Defense (DoD) procedure that defines acquisition requirements and evaluation criteria for future defense programs based on a capability-based acquisition (CBA) approach.

joint capability areas (JCA)   Collections of like DoD capabilities functionally grouped to support capability analysis, strategy development, investment decision making, capability portfolio management, and capabilities-based force development and operational planning.

Joint Common System Function List (JCSFL)   A common lexicon of systems/service functionality supporting joint capability. The JCSFL is provided for mapping functions to supported activities and the systems or services that host them. Chairman of the Joint Chiefs of Staff Instruction (CJCSI) 6212.01E prescribes the JCSFL for use in developing a common vocabulary for architecture development.

Joint Requirements Oversight Council (JROC)   A council that assists the Chairman of the Joint Chiefs of Staff (CJCS) in identifying and assessing the priority of joint military requirements (including existing systems and equipment) to meet the national military and defense strategies. JROC also considers alternatives to any acquisition program that has been identified to meet military capabilities by evaluating the cost, schedule, and performance criteria of the program and of the identified alternatives. The council oversees the Joint Capabilities Integration and Development System (JCIDS) and supports the Defense Acquisition Board (DAB) by validating key performance parameters (KPPs) prior to each DAB review of Major Defense Acquisition Programs (MDAPs) (including, unless otherwise directed by the Secretary of Defense [SECDEF], highly sensitive classified programs). The CJCS is the Chairman of the JROC. The functions of the JROC Chairman are delegated to the Vice Chairman of the Joint Chiefs of Staff (VCJCS). Other members of the JROC are officers in the grade of General or Admiral from the Army, Navy, Air Force, and Marine Corps. Service representatives are recommended by their military department secretary and approved by the Chairman after consultation with the SECDEF. *See* Joint Capabilities Integration and Development System (JCIDS).

key interface (KI)   A systems interface representing information exchanges that span systems that are in scope for an architecture at one end and systems that are external to the architecture at the other.

key performance indicator (KPI)   A factor that is used to quantify the performance of the business or project.

key performance parameter (KPP)   A type of measure that indicates a dimension of performance that is deemed critical for operations.

knowledge   The awareness and understanding of facts, truths, or information gained in the form of experience or learning (a posteriori) or through introspection (a priori). Knowledge is an appreciation of the possession of interconnected details which, in isolation, are of lesser value.

Knowledge Management/Decision Support (KM/DS)   A tool used by DoD components to submit documents and comments for O-6 and flag reviews, search for historical information, and track the status of documents.

level of effort (LOE)   Effort of a general or supportive nature that does not produce definite end products or results, that is, a contract for man-hours.

lifecycle   The period of time that begins when a system is conceived and ends when the system is no longer available for use.

lines of business (LOB)   A division of business areas in the FEA Business Reference Model into business service areas comprising of various types of services provided to citizens (external lines of business) and services that are comprised of support functions internal to the government (internal lines of business).

location   (1) A point or extent in space that may be referred to physically or logically. (2) A place where business activity takes place and which can be hierarchically decomposed.

logical   An implementation-independent definition of the architecture, often grouping related physical entities according to their purpose and structure. For example, the products from multiple infrastructure software vendors can all be logically grouped as Java application server platforms.

logical application component   An encapsulation of application functionality that is independent of a particular implementation; for example, the classification of all purchase request processing applications implemented in an enterprise.

logical data component   A boundary zone that encapsulates related data entities to form a logical location to be held; for example, external procurement information.

Logical Data Model (DIV-2)   The documentation of the data requirements and structural business process (activity) rules. In DoDAF Version 1.5, this was the OV-7.

logical technology component   An encapsulation of technology infrastructure that is independent of a particular product; a class of technology product; for example, supply chain management software as part of an Enterprise Resource Planning (ERP) suite or a commercial off-the-shelf (COTS) purchase request processing enterprise service.

maintainability measure   A category of measures of the amount of time a performer is able to conduct activities over some time interval.

Managing Successful Programs (MSP)   A best practice methodology for program management, developed by the UK Office of Government Commerce (OGC).

manual   A small reference book, especially one giving instructions.

materiel   Equipment, apparatus, or supplies that are of interest, without distinction as to its application for administrative or combat purposes.

matrix   A format for showing the relationship between two (or more) architectural elements in a grid format.

means   An action or system by which a result is brought about; a method to make proficient by instruction and practice in particular knowledge or skills.

measure (1) The magnitude of some attribute of an individual. (2) An indicator or factor that can be tracked, usually on an ongoing basis, to determine success or alignment with objectives and goals.

mechanism An instrument or a process, physical or mental, by which something is done or comes into being.

memorandum of agreement (MOA) (1) In contract administration, an agreement between a Program Manager (PM) and a contract administration office (CAO) establishing the scope of responsibility of the CAO with respect to the earned value management system (EVMS) criteria surveillance functions and objectives and/or other contract administration functions on a specific contract or program. (2) Any written agreement in principle as to how a program will be administered.

memorandum of understanding (MOU) De facto agreement that is generally recognized by all partners as binding even if no legal claim could be based on the rights and obligations delineated therein.

metadata (1) Information about information. (2) Data about data, of any sort in any media that describes the characteristics of an entity.

metamodel A model that describes how and with what the architecture will be described in a structured way.

metaview A metaview acts as a pattern or template of the view from which to develop individual views. A metaview establishes the purposes and audience for a view, the ways in which the view is documented (for example, for visual modeling) and the ways in which it is used (for example, for analysis).

method A defined, repeatable approach to address a particular type of problem.

methodology A defined, repeatable series of steps to address a particular type of problem, which typically centers on a defined process, but may also include definition of content.

milestone Something that happens at an instant in the world, i.e., a zero-duration process (activity).

Ministry of Defense Architecture Framework (MODAF) An integrated architecture framework, corresponding to the DoDAF, that is promulgated by the United Kingdom Ministry of Defense.

mission   The task, together with the purpose (desired effect), that clearly indicates the action (activity) to be taken and the reason (desired effect); a duty (activity) assigned to an individual (personnel type) or unit (organization).

model   (1) A template for collecting data. (2) A representation of a subject of interest. A model provides a smaller-scale, simplified, and/or abstract representation of the subject matter. A model is constructed as a "means to an end." In the context of enterprise architecture, the subject matter is a whole or part of the enterprise and the end is the ability to construct "views" that address the concerns of particular stakeholders; that is, their "viewpoints" in relation to the subject matter.

modeling   A technique for the construction of models that enables a subject to be represented in a form that allows reasoning, insight, and clarity concerning the essence of the subject matter.

multimedia service   A service of the Technical Reference Model (TRM) that provides the capability to manipulate and manage information products consisting of text, graphics, images, video, and audio.

National Institute of Standards and Technology (NIST)   The U.S. institute (formerly the National Bureau of Standards) that establishes standards for technology. It was founded in 1901 as a nonregulatory federal agency within the U.S. Department of Commerce. Its mission is to promote U.S. innovation and industrial competitiveness by advancing measurement science, standards, and technology in ways that enhance economic security and improve our quality of life.

National Security Systems (NSS)   An acquisition category that requires special treatment during acquisition and when deployed.

NATO Architecture Framework (NAF)   The architecture framework, based on the DoD Architecture Framework, that is promulgated by the North Atlantic Treaty Organization (NATO).

Naval Architecture Elements Reference Guide (NAERG)   A reference for standard terms used by the Navy and Marine Corps. The architecture elements represent the critical taxonomies requiring concurrence and standardization for an integrated architecture. They comprise the lexicon for the three views of the architecture framework: the operational (OV), system (SV), and technical standards (TV) views.

needline   An information technology requirement that is the logical expression of the need to transfer

net-centric enterprise services (NCES)   Services that enable information sharing by connecting people and systems that have information (data and services) with those who need information.

net-centric operations (NCO)   Operations based on the information technology (IT) concept of an assured, dynamic, and shared information environment that provides access to trusted information for all users, based on need, independent of time and place. NCO is an initiative of the United States Department of Defense, which has promulgated it as the blueprint for how it will conduct business operations, warfare, and enterprise management in the future.

network   An interconnected or interrelated chain, group, or system.

Next Generation Air Traffic System (NGATS)   The Next Generation Automatic Test Station (NGATS) addresses the increased issue of obsolescence in currently fielded test equipment. The NGATS reduces the fielded footprint and increases the warfighter capability while maintaining the ability to support the current force using existing test program sets.

North Atlantic Treaty Organization (NATO)   A coalition of countries established on the basis of a treaty between the countries and the United States.

not applicable (N/A)   An abbreviation frequently used in tables or grids in which information is expected to appear in a row or column but is not available or relevant.

Object Management Group (OMG)   A consortium and standards body responsible for establishing standards originally founded to formulate and manage standards for object-oriented analysis and design and promulgators of the Unified Modeling Language (UML) and other popular standards.

objective   (1) A clearly defined, decisive, and attainable end toward which every operation is directed. An objective is a specific, time-targeted, measurable, and attainable target that an enterprise seeks to meet in order to achieve its goals. (2) A time-bounded milestone for an organization used to demonstrate progress toward a goal; for example, "Increase Capacity Utilization by 30% by the end of 2009 to support the planned increase in market share."

object-oriented analysis and design (OOAD)   A software engineering modeling technique that models a system as a group of interacting objects. Objects are characterized by structure and behavior.

occupational training   Knowledge, practice, aptitude, and so on, to do something well.

Office of Management and Budget (OMB)   A cabinet-level office within the Executive Office of the President of the United States (White House) responsible for budget and governance activities over the Executive Branch of government.

Office of Management and Budget Circular A-11 Section 300 (S-300)   A document that establishes, in Part 7, policy for planning, budgeting, acquisition, and management of federal capital assets and provides instruction on budget justification and reporting requirements for major information technology (IT) investments and for major non-IT capital assets. OMB provides procedural and analytic guidelines for implementing specific aspects of these policies as appendices and supplements to this circular and in other OMB circulars.

Office of Management and Budget Circular A-130 (A-130)   A document that "Establishes policy for the management of Federal information resources" and calls for the use of enterprise architectures to support capital planning and investment control processes. The circular includes implementation principles and guidelines for creating and maintaining enterprise architectures.

Office of Management and Budget Enterprise Architecture Assessment Framework (EAAF)   An architectural framework developed by the OMB that serves as the basis for enterprise architecture maturity assessments. Compliance with the EAAF ensures that enterprise architectures are advanced and appropriately developed to improve the performance of information resource management and IT investment decision making.

Office of the Secretary of Defense (OSD)   An organization directly charged with supporting the Secretary of Defense, a cabinet officer.

open specifications   Public specifications that are maintained by an open, public consensus process to accommodate new technologies over time and that are consistent with international standards.

open system   A system that implements sufficient open specifications for interfaces, services, and supporting formats to enable properly engineered application software (a) to be ported with minimal changes across a wide range of systems; (b) to interoperate with other applications on local and remote systems; and (c) to interact with users in a style that facilitates user portability.

operating system service   A core service of the application platform entity of the Technical Reference Model (TRM) that is needed to operate and administer the application platform and provide an interface between the application software and the platform (for example, file management, input/output, and print spoolers).

operational activity   An action performed in conducting the business of an enterprise. It is a general term that does not imply a placement in a hierarchy (for example, it could be a process or a task as defined in other documents and it could be at any level of the hierarchy of the Operational Activity Model). It is used to portray operational actions, not hardware or software system functions.

Operational Activity Decomposition Tree (OV-5a)   A model that features the capabilities and activities (operational activities) organized in a hierarchal structure.

Operational Activity Model (OV-5b)   A model that provides the context of capabilities and activities (operational activities) and their relationships among activities, inputs, and outputs. Additional data can show cost, performers, or other pertinent information.

Operational Activity to Services Traceability Matrix (SvcV-5)   A mapping of services (activities) back to operational activities (activities).

Operational Activity to Systems Function Traceability Matrix (SV-5a)   A mapping of system functions (activities) back to operational activities (activities).

Operational Activity to Systems Traceability Matrix (SV-5b)   A mapping of systems back to capabilities or operational activities (activities).

operational condition   A statement of the values or states needed for the execution of actions within the processes and transactions of an enterprise.

operational governance   Governance that looks at the operational performance of systems against contracted performance levels, the definition of operational performance levels, and the implementation of systems that ensure effective operation of systems.

Operational Requirements Document (ORD)   A formatted statement containing performance and related operational parameters for the proposed concept or system. The document is prepared by the user or user's representative at each milestone, beginning with Milestone I, Concept Demonstration Approval of the Requirements Generation Process.

Operational Resource Flow Description (OV-2)   A description of the resource flows exchanged between operational activities.

Operational Resource Flow Matrix (OV-3)   A description of the resources exchanged and the relevant attributes of the exchanges.

Operational Rules Model (OV-6a)   One of three models used to describe activity (operational activity). It identifies business rules that constrain operations.

Operational Viewpoint (OV)   The model that captures the organizations, tasks, or activities performed and information that must be exchanged among them to accomplish DoD missions. It conveys the types of information exchanged, the frequency of exchange, the tasks and activities that are supported by the information exchanges, and the nature of information exchanges.

operations and maintenance (O&M)   Appropriations to fund expenses such as civilian salaries, travel, minor construction projects, operating military forces, training and education, depot maintenance, stock funds, and base operations support.

operations tempo   The rate at which military or nonmilitary operations are conducted with consequent consumption of resources, expenditure of energy, and shrinking of critical timeframes.

organization   (1) A specific real-world assemblage of people and other resources organized for an ongoing purpose. (2) A self-contained unit of resources with line management responsibility, goals, objectives, and measures. Organizations may include external parties and business partner organizations.

organization type   A type of organization.

organization unit   A self-contained unit of resources with line management responsibility, goals, objectives, and measures. Organizations may include external parties and business partner organizations.

Organizational Relationships Chart (OV-4)   A model representing the organizational context, role, or other relationships among organizations.

outcome   An end result; a consequence.

Overview and Summary Information (AV-1)   A model that describes a project's visions, goals, objectives, plans, activities, events, conditions, measures, effects (outcomes), and produced objects.

packaged services   Services that are acquired from the market from a commercial off-the-shelf (COTS) vendor rather than being constructed via code build.

patterns   A technique for putting building blocks into context; for example, a pattern might be used to describe a reusable solution to a problem. Building blocks are what you use; patterns can tell you how you use them, when, why, and what trade-offs are that you have to make in doing so.

performance management   The monitoring, control, and reporting of the enterprise architecture practice performance. Performance management is also concerned with continuous improvement.

performance measure   A category of quality measures that address how well a performer meets capability needs.

performer   Any entity—human, automated, or any aggregation of human and/or automated—that performs an activity and provides a capability.

performer role   Any entity—human, automated, or any aggregation of human and/or automated—that performs a function, activity, or role or provides a capability.

performer supporting activity   A type of activity–performer overlap between a performer and those activities that may not necessarily be carried out by the performer but which are necessary for the performance of the activity.

person type   A category of persons defined by the role or roles they share that are relevant to an architecture.

phasing/evolution/forecast   A phase is a stage in a process of change or development. Evolution is any process of formation, growth, or development. To forecast is to predict a future condition or occurrence.

physical   To be a real-world entity. Physical elements in an enterprise architecture may still be considerably abstracted from solution architecture, design, or implementation views.

physical application component   An application, application module, application service, or other deployable component of functionality. An example is a configured and deployed instance of a commercial off-the-shelf (COTS) Enterprise Resource Planning (ERP) supply chain management application.

physical data component   A boundary zone that encapsulates related data entities to form a physical location to be held. An example is a purchase order business object comprised of a purchase order header and item business object nodes.

Physical Data Model (DIV-3)   The physical implementation format of the Logical Data Model entities, such as message formats, file structures, and physical schema. In DoDAF Version 1.5, this model was the SV-11.

Physical Exchange Specification (PES)   The exchange specification for DoDAF-compliant architecture data among conformant architecture tools to allow portability of architecture data.

physical technology component   A specific technology infrastructure product or technology infrastructure product instance. Examples include a particular product version of a commercial off-the-shelf (COTS) solution or a specific brand and version of server.

plan   A set of activities that result in a goal, desired effect, outcome, or objective.

Planning, Programming, Budgeting, and Execution (PPBE)   The primary resource allocation process (RAP) of DoD. It is one of three major decision support systems for defense acquisition along with Joint Capabilities Integration and Development System (JCIDS) and the Defense Acquisition System (DAS). PPBE is a formal, systematic structure for making decisions on policy, strategy, and the development of forces and capabilities to accomplish anticipated missions. PPBE is a biennial process that in the on-year produces Guidance for Development of the Force (GDF), Joint Programming Guidance (JPG), approved Program Objectives Memoranda (POMs) for the military departments and defense agencies covering six years, and the DoD portion of the President's Budget (PB) covering two years. In the off-year, adjustments are made to the Future Years Defense Program (FYDP) to take into account fact-of-life changes, inflation, new programmatic initiatives, and the result of congressional enactment of the previously submitted PB based on guidance from the Under Secretary of Defense (Comptroller) (USD(C)) and the Director of Cost Assessment and Program Evaluation (CAPE).

platform   A combination of technology infrastructure products and components that provides the prerequisites to host application software.

platform services   A technical capability required to provide enabling infrastructure that supports the delivery of applications.

policy   A course of action, guiding principle, or procedure considered expedient, prudent, or advantageous.

port   An interface (logical or physical) provided by a system. A port is specified by the service description. The mechanism is a performer. The "capabilities" accessed are resources— information, data, materiel, performers, and geopolitical extents.

portability   (1) The ease with which a system or component can be transferred from one hardware or software environment to another. (2) A quality metric that can be used to measure the relative effort to transport the software for use in another environment or to convert software for use in another operating environment, hardware configuration, or software system environment. (3) The ease with which a system, a component, data, or a user can be transferred from one hardware or software environment to another.

portfolio   The complete set of change activities or systems that exist within the organization or part of the organization. Examples include an application portfolio and project portfolio.

Portfolio Management   The discipline of managing multiple investments as a single collection that is periodically balanced against competing needs and drivers.

post-implementation review (PIR)   A review conducted after a system has been implemented.

principle   A qualitative statement of intent that should be met by the architecture. A principle has at least a supporting rationale and a measure of importance.

process   (1) A logical, systematic sequence of activities, triggered by an event, producing a meaningful output. (2) A sequence of activities that together achieve a specified outcome, can be decomposed into subprocesses, and can show operation of a function or service (at next level of detail). Processes may also be used to link or compose organizations, functions, services, and processes.

product   Output generated by a business; the business product of the execution of a process.

profile   A set of one or more base standards and, where applicable, the identification of those classes, subsets, options, and parameters of those base standards, necessary for accomplishing a particular function.

profiling   Identifying standards and characteristics of a particular system.

program (1) A directed, funded effort that provides a new, improved, or continuing materiel, weapon, or information system or service capability in response to an approved need. (2) A coordinated set of change projects that deliver business benefit to the organization.

program element (PE) The basic building block of the 11 major programs of the Future Years Defense Program (FYDP). It is "an integrated combination of men, equipment, and facilities, which together constitute an identifiable military capability or support activity." It also identifies the mission to be undertaken and the organizational entities to perform the mission. Elements may consist of forces, manpower, materials, services, and/or associated costs, as applicable. A PE consists of seven digits ending with a letter indicating the appropriate service.

Program Executive Officer (PEO) A military or civilian official who has responsibility for directing several Major Defense Acquisition Programs (MDAPs) and for assigned major system and nonmajor system acquisition programs. A PEO normally has no other command or staff responsibilities within the component and only reports to and receives guidance and direction from the DoD Component Acquisition Executive (CAE).

Program Manager (PM) Designated individual with responsibility for and authority to accomplish program objectives for development, production, and sustainment to meet the user's operational needs. The PM is accountable for credible cost, schedule, and performance reporting to the Milestone Decision Authority (MDA).

Program Objective Memorandum (POM) A document displaying the resource allocation decisions of the military department regarding a component in response to, and in accordance with, the Guidance for Development of the Force (GDF) and Joint Programming Guidance (JPG). The POM is the final product of the programming process within DoD. The POM shows programmed needs six years hence (that, in fiscal year 2008, POM 2010–2015 was submitted).

Project (1) A temporary endeavor undertaken to create resources or desired effects. (2) A single change project that delivers business benefit to the organization.

Project Management Body of Knowledge (PMBOK) An evolutionary body of knowledge maintained by the Project Management Institute on best practices in project management.

Project Portfolio Relationships (PV-1)   A model that describes the dependency relationships among the organizations, projects, and organizational structures needed to manage a portfolio of projects.

Project Timelines (PV-2)   A model that provides a timeline perspective on programs or projects, with the key milestones and interdependencies.

Project to Capability Mapping (PV-3)   A mapping of programs and projects to capabilities to show how the specific projects and program elements help to achieve a capability.

Project Viewpoint (PV)   A model that captures how programs are grouped in organizational terms as a coherent portfolio of acquisition programs. It provides a way of describing the organizational relationships between multiple acquisition programs, each of which are responsible for delivering individual systems or capabilities.

Projects in Controlled Environments (PRINCE2)   A standard project management method (TOGAF).

quality assurance (QA)   A planned and systematic pattern of all actions necessary to provide confidence that adequate technical requirements are established, that products and services conform to established technical requirements, and that satisfactory performance is achieved.

quality management   The management of the quality aspects of the enterprise architecture practice; for example, management plans, quality criteria, and review processes.

quality of services   The ability to provide different priority to different applications, users, or data flows or to guarantee a certain level of performance to a data flow.

rate throughput   The ratio of the effective or useful output to the total input in any system.

reference architecture (RA)   An abstract architecture pattern that serves as common basis to compare actual architectures to support federation and benchmarking.

Reference Model (RM)   An abstract framework for understanding significant relationships among the entities of an environment and for the development of consistent standards or specifications supporting that environment. A Reference Model is based on a small number of unifying concepts and may be used as a basis for education and explaining standards to a nonspecialist. A Reference Model is not directly tied to any standards, technologies, or other concrete implementation details, but it does seek to provide common semantics that can be used unambiguously across and between different implementations.

reliability   A category of measures of the ability of a performer to perform its required activities under stated conditions for a specified period of time.

repository   A system that manages all of the data of an enterprise, including data and process models and other enterprise information. Hence, the data in a repository is much more extensive than that in a data dictionary, which generally defines only the data making up a database.

requirement   (1) A singular documented need of what a particular product or service should be or do. (2) A quantitative statement of a business need that must be met by a particular architecture or work package.

resource   Data, information, or performers.

resource management   The acquisition, development, and management of human resources within the enterprise architecture practice in response to demand for enterprise architecture services and financial constraints.

responsibility   Accountability for something within one's power, control, or management.

return on investment (ROI)   A measure used to evaluate the efficiency of an investment in finance and economics. The return refers to the payback from an investment.

Richard M. Nixon International Airport (RMN)   A fictitious airport used as a case study throughout this book.

risk management   The management of risks and issues that may threaten the success of the enterprise architecture practice and its ability to meet its vision, goals, objectives, and, importantly, its service provision.

roadmap   An abstracted plan for business or technology change, typically operating across multiple disciplines over multiple years. The term is normally used in such phrases as technology roadmap and architecture roadmap.

role (1) A set of similar or otherwise logically related activities, implying a set of skills or capabilities, to which a performer may be assigned. (2) The usual or expected function of an actor, or the part that somebody or something plays in a particular action or event. An actor may have a number of roles. (3) The part that an individual plays in an organization and the contribution he or she makes through the application of his or her skills, knowledge, experience, and abilities.

rule A principle or condition that governs behavior; a prescribed guide for conduct or action.

scalability The ability to use the same application software on many different classes of hardware/software platforms, from PCs to supercomputers (extending the portability concept). It is also the capability to grow to accommodate increased workloads.

schedule dependency A dependency that involves resources that an activity requires in order to proceed.

security Services that protect data, ensuring its confidentiality, availability, and integrity.

Security Attributes Group The group of information security marking attributes in which the use of the attributes *classification* and *ownerProducer* is required. This group is to be contrasted with group *SecurityAttributesOptionGroup*, in which use of those attributes is optional.

security measure A measure of the ability of a performer to manage, protect, and distribute sensitive information.

segment architecture A detailed, formal description of areas within an enterprise, used at the program- or portfolio-level to organize and align change activity.

server An application component that responds to requests from a client.

service (1) A mechanism to enable access to a set of one or more capabilities, where the access is provided using a prescribed interface and is exercised consistent with constraints and policies as specified by the service description. The mechanism is a performer. The "capabilities" accessed are resources—information, data, materiel, performers, and geopolitical extents. (2) A logical representation of a repeatable business activity that has a specified outcome. A service is self-contained, may be composed of other services, and is a "black box" to its consumers. Examples are "check customer credit," "provide weather data," and "consolidate drilling reports."

service channel   A logical or physical communication path between requisitions and services.

service description   Information necessary to interact with the service in such terms as the service inputs, outputs, and associated semantics. The service description also conveys what is accomplished when the service is invoked and the conditions for using the service.

service function   White box implementation of the activities of the service.

service level   A measurement of the performance of a system or service.

service-level agreement (SLA)   Part of a service contract where the level of service is formally defined.

service management (SM)   The management of the execution and performance of the enterprise architecture practice services. This includes managing the "pipeline" plus the current service portfolio.

service orientation   A way of thinking in terms of services and service-based development and the outcomes of services.

service-oriented architecture (SOA)   An architectural style that supports service orientation. It has the following distinctive features: It is based on the design of the services—which mirror real-world business activities—comprising the enterprise (or inter-enterprise) business processes. Service representation utilizes business descriptions to provide context (that is, business process, goal, rule, policy, service interface, and service component) and implements services using service orchestration. It places unique requirements on the infrastructure—it is recommended that implementations use open standards to realize interoperability and location transparency. Implementations are environment-specific—they are constrained or enabled by context and must be described within that context.

service policy   An agreement governing one or more services.

service port   A part of a performer that specifics a distinct interaction point through which the performer interacts with other performers. This isolates dependencies between performers to particular interaction points rather than to the performer as a whole.

service quality   A preset configuration of nonfunctional attributes that may be assigned to a service or service contract.

service registry (SR)   A registry that provides enterprisewide insight, control, and leverage of an organization's services. It captures service descriptions and makes them discoverable from a centrally managed, reliable, and searchable location.

Services Context Description (SvcV-1)   The identification of services, service items, and their interconnections.

Services Event-Trace Description (SvcV-10c)   One of three models used to describe service functionality. It identifies service-specific refinements of critical sequences of events described in the Operational Viewpoint.

Services Evolution Description (SvcV-8)   The planned incremental steps toward migrating a suite of services to a more efficient suite or toward evolving current services to a future implementation.

Services Functionality Description (SvcV-4)   The functions performed by services and the service data flows among service functions (activities).

Services Measures Matrix (SvcV-7)   The measures (metrics) of Services Model elements for the appropriate timeframe(s).

Services Resource Flow Description (SvcV-2)   A description of resource flows exchanged between services.

Services Resource Flow Matrix (SvcV-6)   A model that provides details of service resource flow elements being exchanged between services and the attributes of that exchange.

Services Rules Model (SvcV-10a)   One of three models used to describe service functionality. It identifies constraints that are imposed on systems functionality due to some aspect of system design or implementation.

Services State Transition Description (SvcV-10b)   One of three models used to describe service functionality. It identifies responses of services to events.

Services Technology and Skills Forecast (SvcV-9)   The emerging technologies, software and hardware products, and skills that are expected to be available in a given set of timeframes and that will affect future service development.

Services Viewpoint (SvcV)   A model that captures system, service, and interconnection functionality, providing for, or supporting, operational activities. DoD processes include warfighting, business, intelligence, and infrastructure functions. The SvcV functions and service resources and components may be linked to the architectural data in the Operational Viewpoint. These system functions and service resources support the operational activities and facilitate the exchange of information.

Services-Services Matrix (SvcV-3b)   The relationships among services in a given architectural description. It can be designed to show relationships of interest (such as service-type interfaces and planned versus existing interfaces).

site   Physical (geographic) location that is or was owned by, leased to, or otherwise possessed. Each site is assigned to a single installation. A site may exist in one of three forms: (1) Land only, where there are no facilities present and where the land consists of either a single land parcel or two or more contiguous land parcels. (2) Facility or facilities only, where the underlying land is neither owned nor controlled by the government. A stand-alone facility can be a site. If a facility is not a stand-alone facility, it must be assigned to a site. (3) Land and all the facilities thereon, where the land consists of either a single land parcel or two or more contiguous land parcels.

Six Step process   The architecture development process described by the DoD Architecture Framework.

skill   (1) The ability, coming from one's knowledge, practice, aptitude, and so on, to do something well. (2) The ability to perform a job-related activity that contributes to the effective performance of a task.

SoA Service   A distinct part of the functionality that is provided by a technical system on one side of an interface to a general system on the other side of the interface (derived from IEEE 1003.0). It is characterized by transparency, autonomy, loose coupling, and discovery.

Software Engineering Institute (SEI)   A federally funded research and development center (FFRDC) sponsored by the Office of Under Secretary of Defense for Acquisition, Technology, and Logistics (OUSD [AT&L]). The SEI's mission is to provide leadership in advancing the state of the practice of software engineering to improve the quality of systems that depend on software.

solution architecture   A description of a discrete and focused business operation or activity and how information system (IS) or information technology (IT) supports that operation. A solution architecture typically applies to a single project or project release, assisting in the translation of requirements into a solution vision, a high-level business and/or IT system specifications, and a portfolio of implementation tasks.

solution building block (SBB)   A candidate physical solution for an architecture building block (ABB); for example, a commercial off-the-shelf (COTS) package that is a component of the Acquirer View of the architecture.

Solutions Continuum   A part of the Enterprise Continuum. A repository of reusable solutions for future implementation efforts. It contains implementations of the corresponding definitions in the Architecture Continuum.

source   One, such as a person or document, that supplies information.

Specific, Measurable, Attainable, Realistic, and Time-bound (SMART)   An approach to ensure that targets and objectives are set in a way that can be achieved and measured.

stakeholder   An individual, team, or organization (or classes thereof) with interests in, or concerns relative to, the outcome of the architecture. Different stakeholders with different roles will have different concerns.

standard   A formal agreement documenting generally accepted specifications or criteria for products, processes, procedures, policies, systems, and/or personnel.

Standards Forecast (StdV-2)   The description of emerging standards and potential impacts on current solution elements within a set of timeframes.

Standards Information Base (SIB)   A database of standards that can be used to define the particular services and other components of an organization-specific architecture.

Standards Profile (StdV-1)   The listing of standards that apply to solution elements.

Standards Viewpoint (StdV)   The minimal set of rules governing the arrangement, interaction, and interdependence of system parts or elements. Its purpose is to ensure that a system satisfies a specified set of operational requirements. The StdV provides the technical systems implementation guidelines upon which engineering specifications are based, common building blocks are established, and product lines are developed. It includes a collection of the technical standards, implementation conventions, standards options, rules, and criteria that can be organized into profile(s) that govern systems and system or service elements in a given architectural description.

State Transition Description (OV-6b)   One of three models used to describe operational activity (activity). It identifies business process (activity) responses to events (usually, very short activities).

statement of work (SOW)   That portion of a contract that establishes and defines all nonspecification requirements for contractor's efforts, either directly or with the use of specifically cited documents

strategic architecture   A summarized formal description of the enterprise, providing an organizing framework for operational and change activity and an executive-level, long-term view for setting direction.

strategy   A long-term plan to achieve preset goals.

Structured Analysis and Design Technique (SADT)   A technique for analysis and design of software systems based on progressive refinement and decomposition techniques.

subject matter expert (SME)   A person who is familiar with the subject matter of a business, system, or architectural domain and can provide information to assist the architect in representing that domain.

supplier management   The management of suppliers of products and services to the enterprise architecture practice in concert with larger corporate procurement activities.

system   (1) A functionally, physically, and/or behaviorally related group of regularly interacting or interdependent elements. (2) A collection of components organized to accomplish a specific function or set of functions.

System and Network Management Service   A cross-category service of the application platform entity of the Technical Reference Model (TRM) that provides for the administration of the overall information system. These services include the management of information, processors, networks, configurations, accounting, and performance.

system development lifecycle (SDLC)   The set of phases that are involved in the development of a system from its concept to its retirement.

system function   A function that is performed by a system. Although commonly used to refer to the automation of activities, data transformation, or information exchanges within IT systems, the term also refers to the delivery of military capabilities.

system of systems (SoS)   System of systems is a collection of task-oriented systems that pool resources and capabilities together to obtain a more complex 'meta-system' that offers more functionality and performance than the sum of the constituent systems.

system stakeholder   An individual, team, or organization (or classes thereof) with interests in, or concerns relative to, a system.

systems engineering   The discipline of planning, analysis, design, and construction of systems.

Systems Event-Trace Description (SV-10c)   One of three models used to describe system functionality. It identifies system-specific refinements of critical sequences of events described in the Operational Viewpoint.

Systems Evolution Description (SV-8)   The planned incremental steps toward migrating a suite of systems to a more efficient suite or toward evolving a current system to a future implementation.

Systems Functionality Description (SV-4)   The functions (activities) performed by systems and the system data flows among system functions (activities).

Systems Interface Description (SV-1)   The identification of systems, system items, and their interconnections.

Systems Measures Matrix (SV-7)   The measures (metrics) of systems model elements for the appropriate timeframe(s).

Systems Resource Flow Description (SV-2)   A description of resource flows exchanged between systems.

Systems Resource Flow Matrix (SV-6)   A model that provides details of system resource flow elements being exchanged between systems and the attributes of that exchange.

Systems Rules Model (SV-10a)   One of three models used to describe system functionality. It identifies constraints that are imposed on systems functionality due to some aspect of system design or implementation.

Systems State Transition Description (SV-10b)   One of three models used to describe system functionality. It identifies responses of systems to events.

Systems Technology and Skills Forecast (SV-9)   The emerging technologies, software and hardware products, and skills that are expected to be available in a given set of timeframes and that will affect future system development.

Systems Viewpoint (SV)   A viewpoint that captures the information on supporting automated systems, interconnectivity, and other systems functionality in support of operating activities. Over time, the Department of Defense's emphasis on service-oriented environment and cloud computing may result in the elimination of the Systems Viewpoint.

Systems-Services Matrix (SvcV-3a)   The relationships among or between systems and services in a given architectural description.

Systems-Systems Matrix (SV-3)   The relationships among systems in a given architectural description. It can be designed to show relationships of interest (such as system-type interfaces and planned versus existing interfaces).

tactic   A short-term action used to accomplish a strategy.

tactics, techniques, and procedures (TTP)   The actions and methods that implement doctrine and describe how forces will be employed in operations.

Tailored Interoperability and Supportability Plan (TISP)   To tailor is to modify or exclude portions of the standard ISP format under special circumstances. *See* Interoperability and Supportability Plan (ISP).

target architecture   The description of a future state of the architecture being developed for an organization. There may be several future states developed as a roadmap to show the evolution of the architecture to a target state.

task   A action, activity, or undertaking enabling missions, activities, or functions to be performed or accomplished.

taxonomy of architecture views   The organized collection of all views pertinent to an architecture.

Technical Reference Model (TRM)   A structure that allows components of an information system to be described in a consistent manner (that is, the way in which you describe the components).

technical standards   Standards that document specific technical methodologies and practices to design and implement.

technology   The application of science to meet one or more objectives.

technology architecture   The logical software and hardware capabilities that are required to support deployment of business, data, and application services. This includes IT infrastructure, middleware, networks, communications, processing, and standards.

technology component   An encapsulation of technology infrastructure that represents a class of technology product or specific technology product.

test and evaluation (T&E)   Process by which a system or components are exercised and results analyzed to provide performance-related information. The information has many uses, including risk identification, risk mitigation, and empirical data to validate models and simulations. T&E enables an assessment of the attainment of technical performance, specifications, and system maturity to determine whether systems are operationally effective, suitable and survivable for intended use, and/ or lethal. There are three distinct types of T&E defined in statute or regulation: developmental test and evaluation (DT&E), operational test and evaluation (OT&E), and live fire test and evaluation (LFT&E).

The Open Group Architecture Framework (TOGAF)   An architecture framework sponsored, developed, and promoted by The Open Group, a consortium.

time period   The timeframe over which the potential impact is to be measured.

timeliness   The time from the occurrence of an event to the time required action occurs.

to be determined (TBD)   An acronym frequently used in planning when variables have not been set.

to-be architecture   The desired future state of an architecture. Also called *target architecture*.

transaction   Interaction between a user and a computer in which the user inputs a command to receive a specific result from the computer.

transaction sequence   Order of transactions required to accomplish the desired results.

transition architecture   A formal description of the enterprise architecture showing periods of transition and development for particular parts of the enterprise. Transition architectures are used to provide an overview of current and target capability and allow for individual work packages and projects to be grouped into managed portfolios and programs.

trigger   Something that happens at an instant in the world, that is, a zero-duration process (activity).

trustworthiness   A category of measures of the degree to which a performer avoids compromising or corrupting sensitive information or delaying its dissemination.

Unified Modeling Language (UML)   A technique for object-oriented analysis and design that integrates multiple techniques and offers a unified framework for analysis and design that is based on object-oriented principles.

Unified Profile for DoDAF and MODAF (UPDM)   A standard sponsored by the DOD and the Object Management Group for the development of a common vocabulary (metamodel) for DoDAF and MODAF using the UML as a base language.

Universal Joint Task List (UJTL)   A common language and common reference system for Joint Force Commanders, combat support agencies, operational planners, combat developers, and trainers to communicate mission requirements. UJTL is called for by the Chairman of the Joint Chiefs of Staff Manual 3500.04C (CJCSM). It is the basic language for development of a Joint Mission Essential Task List (JMETL) or Agency Mission Essential Task List (AMETL) that identifies required capabilities for mission success.

use-case   A view of organization, application, or product functionality that illustrates capabilities in context with the user of that capability.

user   (1) Any person, organization, or functional unit that uses the services of an information processing system. (2) In a conceptual schema language, any person or anything that may issue or receive commands and messages to or from the information system.

user interface service   A service of the application platform entity of the Technical Reference Model (TRM) that supports direct human-machine interaction by controlling the environment in which users interact with applications.

view   (1) A representation of a related set of information using formats or models. A view, as described in DoDAF 2.0, is a representation of data in any understandable format. Formats can include any of the presentation styles (such as dashboards, spreadsheets, diagrams, data models, and so on) that convey the meaning of data. (2) The representation of a related set of concerns. A view is what is seen from a viewpoint. An architecture view may be represented by a model to demonstrate to stakeholders their areas of interest in the architecture. A view does not have to be visual or graphical in nature.

viewpoint   (1) A model that describes data drawn from one or more perspectives and organized in a particular way useful to management decision making. More specifically, a viewpoint definition includes the information that should appear in individual views; an explanation of how to construct and use the views (by means of an appropriate schema or template); the modeling techniques for expressing and analyzing the information; and a rationale for these choices (by describing the purpose and intended audience of the view, for example). (2) A definition of the perspective from which a view is taken. It is a specification of the conventions for constructing and using a view (often by means of an appropriate schema or template). A view is what you see; a viewpoint is where you are looking from—the vantage point or perspective that determines what you see.

Vision (CV-1)   The overall vision for transformational endeavors, which provides a strategic context for the capabilities described and a high-level scope.

work breakdown structure (WBS)   An organized method to break down a project into logical subdivisions or subprojects at increasingly lower levels of detail. It is very useful in organizing a project.

work package   A set of actions identified to achieve one or more objectives for the business. A work package can be a part of a project, a complete project, or a program.

XML Schema Definition (XSD)   A standard for specifying and constraining the structure of eXtensible Markup Language (XML) documents.

INDEX

E

P